JUVENILE JUSTICE

SECOND EDITION

JUVENILE JUSTICE

SECOND EDITION

■ **ROBERT W. DROWNS**

Metropolitan State University

■ **KÄREN M. HESS**

Normandale Community College

■ WEST PUBLISHING COMPANY

MINNEAPOLIS/ST. PAUL   NEW YORK   LOS ANGELES   SAN FRANCISCO

WEST'S COMMITMENT TO THE ENVIRONMENT

In 1906, West Publishing Company began recycling materials left over from the production of books. This began a tradition of efficient and responsible use of resources. Today, up to 95% of our legal books and 70% of our college texts and school texts are printed on recycled, acid-free stock. West also recycles nearly 22 million pounds of scrap paper annually—the equivalent of 181,717 trees. Since the 1960s, West has devised ways to capture and recycle waste inks, solvents, oils, and vapors created in the printing process. We also recycle plastics of all kinds, wood, glass, corrugated cardboard, and batteries, and have eliminated the use of Styrofoam book packaging. We at West are proud of the longevity and the scope of our commitment to the environment.

Production, Prepress, Printing and Binding by West Publishing Company.

 TEXT IS PRINTED ON 10% POST CONSUMER RECYCLED PAPER

 Printed with Printwise
Environmentally Advanced Water Washable Ink

PRODUCTION CREDITS

Copyedit: Betty O'Bryant
Interior Design: Diane Beasley
Illustrations: Carto-Graphics
Indexing: Christine Hess Orthmann
Composition: Carlisle Communications

Library of Congress Cataloging-in-Publication Data

Drowns, Robert W.
    Juvenile justice / Robert Drowns, Kären M. Hess. — 2nd ed.
      p. cm.
    Includes bibliographical references and index.
    ISBN 0-314-04454-X (hard)
    1. Juvenile justice, Administration of—United States.
  2. Juvenile delinquency—United States. I. Hess, Kären M., 1939-
    II. Title.
HV9104.D76 1995
364.3'6'0973—dc20

94-44142
CIP

DEDICATION

Dedicated to those in juvenile justice responsible

for the awesome task of the "best interest" of the child,

and to the youths they serve, so they may succeed

in life.

CONTENTS IN BRIEF

SECTION I

The Evolution of the Juvenile Justice System   1

SECTION II

Our Nation's Youth: A Challenge to the Justice System   107

SECTION III

The Contemporary Juvenile Justice System   281

SECTION IV

Theory into Practice in Juvenile Justice and a Look to the Future   459

CONTENTS

SECTION I

The Evolution of the Juvenile Justice System   1

SECTION II

Our Nation's Youth: A Challenge to the Justice System   107

SECTION IV

Theory into Practice in Juvenile Justice and a Look to the Future 459

FIGURES

TABLES

CASES

Numbers following dates in citations are the pages on which cases are mentioned in this text.

Bellotti v. Baird, 443 U.S. 622, 99 S.Ct. 3035, 61 L.Ed.2d 797 (1979), 523.

Bethel School District #403 v. Fraser, 478 U.S. 675, 106 S.Ct. 3159, 92 L.Ed.2d 549 (1986), 160, 162.

Breed v. Jones, 421 U.S. 519, 533, 95 S.Ct. 1779, 1787, 44 L.Ed.2d 346 (1975), 62, 344.

City of Akron v. Akron Center for Reproductive Health, 462 U.S. 416, 103 S.Ct. 2481, 76 L.Ed.2d 687 (1983), 523.

Commonwealth v. Fisher, 213 Pa. 48, 62 A. 198, 199, 200 (1905), 40, 340.

In re Daniel, 274 Cal. App. 2d 749, 754, 79 Cal. Rptr. 247, 250 (1969), 51.

Dow v. Renfrow, 475 F. Supp. 1012 (N.D. Ind. 1979), *aff'd in part, remanded in part,* 631 F. 2d 91 (7th Cir. 1980), *reh'g en banc denied,* 635 F. 2d 582 (7th Cir. 1980), *cert. denied,* 451 U.S. 1022, 101 S.Ct. 3015, 69 L.Ed.2d 395 (1981), 523.

Ex parte Crouse, 4 Whart. 9 (Pa. 1838), 19.

In re Gault, 387 U.S. 1, 19–21, 26–28, 87 S.Ct. 1428, 1439–1440, 1442–1444, 18 L.Ed.2d 527 (1967), 49–51, 343, 368.

Haley v. Ohio, 332 U.S. 596, 68 S.Ct. 302, 92 L.Ed. 224 (1948), 48.

Harling v. United States, 295 F. 2d 161 (D.C. Cir. 1961), 99.

Hazelwood School District v. Kuhlmeier, 484 U.S. 260, 108 S.Ct. 562, 98 L.Ed.2d 592 (1988), 160–62.

H. L. v. Matheson, 450 U.S. 398, 101 S.Ct. 1164, 67 L.Ed.2d 388 (1981), 523.

Ingram v. Wright, 430 U.S. 651, 97 S.Ct. 1401, 51 L.Ed.2d 711 (1977), 194.

Jewish Child Care Association v. Elaine S. Y., 73 A.D.2d 154, 425 N.Y.S.2d 336 (1980), 523.

Kent v. U.S., 383 U.S. 541, 86 S.Ct. 1045, 16 L.Ed.2d 84 (1966), 48–49, 51, 58, 97, 356.

Martarella v. Kelley, 349 F. Supp. 575 (S.D.N.Y. 1972), 63.

McKeiver v. Pennsylvania, 403 U.S. 528, 547, 91 S.Ct. 1976, 1987, 29 L.Ed.2d 647 (1971), 62, 344.

Morales v. Turman, 364 F. Supp 166 (E. D. Tex. 1973), 63.

Nebraska v. Wedige, 205 Neb. 687, 289 N.W. 2d 538 (1980), 523.

Nelson v. Heyne, 491 F.2d 352 (7th Cir. 1974), 63.

New Jersey v. T. L. O., 469 U.S. 325, 105 S.Ct. 733, 83 L.Ed.2d 720 (1985), 160–61, 523.

ACRONYMS

ABA	American Bar Association
ACA	American Correctional Association
ACLD	Association for Children with Learning Disabilities
ACT	Assault Crisis Team
ACYF	Administration for Children, Youth and Families
AIDS	Acquired Immune Deficiency Syndrome
AMA	American Medical Association
APA	American Psychological Association
ATF	Bureau of Alcohol, Tobacco and Firearms
ATSDR	Agency for Toxic Substances and Disease Registry
BA	Balanced Approach
BA/RJ	Balanced Approach/Restorative Justice Program
BGCA	Boys and Girls Clubs of America
BJS	Bureau of Justice Statistics
CAR	children at risk
CASA	Center on Addiction and Substance Abuse
CASA	Court Appointed Special Advocate for Children
CHINS	children in need of supervision
CHIPS	children in need of protection or services
CIC	children in custody
CINS	children in need of supervision
CRASH	Community Resources Against Street Hoodlums
DARE	Drug Abuse Resistance Education
DPP	DARE Parent Program
DSO	Deinstitutionalization of Status Offenders
EBD	emotionally/behaviorally disturbed
EEG	electroencephalogram
EM	electronic monitoring
FAS	fetal alcohol syndrome
FCP	Family Crisis Program
FINS	families in need of supervision
GAO	General Accounting Office
GETUP	Graffiti Enforcement through Undercover Program
GO-CAP	Gang-Offender Comprehensive Action Plan

GRATS	Gang-Related Active Trafficker Suppression
GREAT	Gang Resistance Education and Training Program
GREAT	General Reporting, Evaluating and Tracking
HEW	Health, Education and Welfare
HIV	Human Immunodeficiency Virus
IACP	International Association of Chiefs of Police
IDP	Intensive Discipline Program
JINS	juveniles in need of supervision
JJDP Act	Juvenile Justice Delinquency Prevention Act
JPOI	Juvenile Probation Officer Initiative
LD	learning disability
LRE	Law Related Education
MBD	minimal brain dysfunction
MINS	minors in need of supervision
NAC	National Advisory Committee
NCADBIP	National Center for the Assessment of Delinquent Behavior and Its Prevention
NCCD	National Council on Crime and Delinquency
NCJA	National Criminal Justice Association
NCJFCJ	National Council of Juvenile and Family Court Judges
NCJJ	National Center for Juvenile Justice
NCMEC	National Center for Missing and Exploited Children
NCPC	National Crime Prevention Council
NCPCA	National Committee for Prevention of Child Abuse
NCS	National Crime Survey
NIC	National Institute of Corrections
NIJ	National Institute of Justice
NISMART	National Incidence Studies of Missing, Abducted, Runaway and Thrownaway Children in America
NJDA	National Juvenile Detention Association
NOSR	National Office for Social Responsibility
OIC	Opportunities Industrialization Center
OJJDP	Office of Juvenile Justice Delinquency Prevention
PAL	Police Athletic League
PDC	Probation Detention Center
PINS	persons in need of supervision
POST	Peace Officer Standards and Training
PSI	presentence investigation
RESTTA	Restitution Education, Specialized Training and Technical Assistance Program
RHY Act	Runaway and Homeless Youth Act

RICO	Racketeer Influenced and Corrupt Organizations Act
RJ	restorative justice
SAFE POLICY	School Administrators For Effective Police, Prosecution Operations, Leading to Improved Children and Youth Services
SAI	Special Alternative Incarceration
SHOCAP	Serious Habitual Offender Comprehensive Action Program
SHO/DI	Serious Habitual Offender/Directed Intervention
START	Short-Term Adolescent Residential Training
STAY	Short-Term Aid Youth
TARAD	Teens as Resources against Drugs
TC&C	Teens, Crime and the Community
TOP	Teens on Patrol
TQM	Total Quality Management
UCR	Uniform Crime Reports
VORP	Victim Offender Reconciliation Program
YOU	Youth Opportunities Unlimited
YSB	Youth Services Bureau
YSP	Youth Services Program

FOREWORD

The juvenile justice system—and there are those who would put quotation marks around "system"—has several specialized components. Each component has long been used to autonomy. Each too often has only superficial knowledge of the other components. And the components seldom work together, even though each may be managing the same problem.

The system should be more than this. Our children are entitled to more. Their lives and their parents' lives are greatly affected by the agencies' responses to their problems. Unfortunately, the responses often are unintentionally inconsistent and noncomplimentary.

For the system to improve, it must know itself. And that means that each professional within each component must know the functions and functioning of all other professionals in the system as they relate to the delinquency, misconduct and neglect of children. At the least, the classic function of each component must be recognized:

- *The police*—must protect the safety of children and the public and investigate the behavioral facts.
- *Welfare and probation services*—must investigate the social facts and provide inpatient and outpatient counseling and supervision of children and their parents.
- *Schools*—must educate children academically and, to a great extent, socially and must ensure peace within their walls.
- *Lawyers*—must stand in for their clients, advocating the views of each, whatever they may be.
- *Service providers*—must have treatments that can reunite families and prevent a recurrence of the misconduct that initiated the public's intervention.
- *The court*—must arbitrate and insist on rehabilitative and protective dispositions, and must use force and power within the confines of statutes and the Constitution to ensure due execution of these dispositions.

Each should perform its function knowledgeable of what the others are or may do and of the impact each may have on the others. There needs to be a coordination, a flow, a focus on the child and the family.

Beyond this primary interagency knowledge and respect, there must exist within families—whether the children's own or ones found for them or provided by the streets—solid values, caring and stability. Youths will reflect the values and stability of their families. Therefore, the system cannot focus only on the child. It must look at the affective family for its influence on both the causes and the rehabilitation of misconduct, whether it be delinquency, status offenses or inadequate parental care.

Each component must look at the family as it affects its own particular function but, more, it must share its investigation and consider the investigations of others, moving toward a collaborative disposition involving the family that will be the most effective for the children.

And even this is not enough. Each professional working with children must understand children, their behavioral patterns and psychological development, and their changing emotional needs as they mature, seek independence and acquire sexual appetites. They must understand that boys don't truant just because they don't like school and that they join gangs because gangs can better satisfy emotional needs that their families have not. Children are not small adults. Legally, they are infants, lacking the maturity to make important judgments, under the stress of changing bodies, and with the insistent need for independence.

The juvenile justice system must understand itself and become a system in the true sense of the word, working together toward the common goal of assisting children in trouble and protecting them and the public. The juvenile justice system must know itself. This book can be its primer.

Judge Emeritus Lindsay G. Arthur

ACKNOWLEDGEMENTS

We would personally like to acknowledge those who gave special help and encouragement so that this book could become a reality. Our sincere thanks.

Since the last edition two great contributors have passed away: William A. Drowns (1992) and Rose Totino (1994), both of whom had "the best interests of children" in all their works. They will be sadly missed.

United States Contributors:

Arizona: Betty Drowns; Mary Ann, Karen and Steve Schmidt; David Lind, Tempe Police Department.

Michigan: Ira Schwartz, formerly of the University of Michigan; the Flint Police Department.

Minnesota: Lorraine Drowns, a patient and beautiful lady; Susan and Rolf Jostad; Leonora Drowns-Kissell; Romaine Drowns; William Drowns; "Al" and Susan Campbell and all my in-laws; Thomas and JoAnn Elwell; Dr. Robert Pockrass, Dr. N. Doran Hunter, and my students at Mankato State University; a special thanks to Lindsay Arthur, retired judge, Juvenile Court, Hennepin Co., who formed instead of reformed children; Anoka Police Chief Andrew Revering and Tiffany Revering; Judy Babcock; Mary Baldwin; Paul Gasner; Rene Litecky; Dan Laurila; Kay Pranis; and Judge Michael Roith.

Texas: Dr. Lyndal Bullock, University of North Texas.

Virginia: Dr. Stanton Samenow, a friend and author of the book *Before It's Too Late.*

International Contributors:

Australia: Senior Sergeant Terry O'Connell, New South Wales Police Department.

Scotland: Jean Raeburn; Donald Stirling; Ian Fowler; Kenneth Thompson.

North Wales: Diane and Gary Lewis.

West Manchester: Veronica and Mick Aston.

Israel: Dr. Meir Hovav, Ministry of Labour and Social Affairs; Zvi Eisikovitz, University of Haifa; Lutfis Labon and Jacoub Hindiyeh, truly dedicated to brotherly love and children.

For this second edition we would like to add our gratitude to the reviewers of the first edition for their constructive suggestions: Jerald C. Burns, Alabama State University; Burt C. Hagerman, Oakland Community College; Patricia M. Harris, University of Texas, San Antonio; Frederick F. Hawley, Western Carolina University; Robert Ives, Rock Valley Community College; Peter C. Kratcoski, Kent State University; Matthew C. Leone, University of Nevada, Reno; and Clarence Augustus Martin, University of Pittsburgh.

A heartfelt thank you also to Christine Hess Orthmann for her hours of typing and indexing, to copyeditor Betty O'Bryant, and to editors Robert Jucha and Steven Yaeger, for their attention to detail and their support throughout the revision of the text. Their expertise has been of great help.

INTRODUCTION

Few social problems arouse public concern more than the problem of juveniles who exhibit antisocial behavior, whether it be minor offenses, such as smoking, or major crimes, such as murder. Any such activities evoke a demand from society for corrective action.

Theories about *why* juveniles exhibit delinquent behavior, as well as how to prevent it, abound. It is an area charged with emotion. Because of this, clear vision is imperative when considering how Americans raise, direct and guide their youths and how they attempt to make youths' activities conform with social standards, to shape the children's growth and that of the nation.

The causes of problematic youth activity present an intricate puzzle. No easy explanation fits the observed facts. Parents blame social and economic pressures along with lack of cooperation from the school and social services. The school, police, social agencies and the court blame parents and each other.

What society is willing to call juvenile violations of the law depends in part on what it thinks it can do about the behavior in question. The effectiveness of facilities in rehabilitation, social service placements, the family and youth reform depends on recognized influences in the control of behavior.

Although rehabilitation of youthful offenders is a worthy goal, society lacks a proven means to accomplish it. Society is always faced with the difficult task of weighing individual liberties against protecting its members from harm.

To focus on only one portion of the youth problem without knowledge of the system in which it is embedded can result in a distorted or misleading interpretation of the juvenile justice system. Not only must the system concern itself with youths who break the law, it is also responsible for children who are abandoned, neglected or abused—no small responsibility. These children are in dire need of protection and help. Yet, frequently, they are placed into the same facility as juvenile delinquents. Further, such children are at much greater risk of becoming delinquents than are children who have not been mistreated.

Juvenile justice is, indeed, a complex topic, and the literature on it is vast. The intent of this text is to discuss as many key issues as possible. Each section is but a small window into an extensive, complicated area of debate. An understanding of youths, their protection and control, must be based on an awareness of youth behavior and the total juvenile justice system involved.

The first section of this text describes the evolution of the juvenile justice system from its historical and philosophical roots through its evolution in the United States in the twentieth century. The second section describes our nation's youth, how they grow and develop, the influence of family and school and the major classifications of youth with whom the juvenile justice system interacts: youth who are victims, those who break the law and who victimize and those who belong to gangs. The third section takes an up-close look at our contemporary juvenile justice system and its three major components: law enforcement, the juvenile/family court and corrections. It then places the system within its larger context, the community, and examines the role of that larger community. The fourth and final section goes from the theoretical to everyday practices and programs being conducted in the juvenile justice system. It includes current approaches to prevention and treatment, as well as an examination of innovations in juvenile justice in several other countries. The text concludes with a discussion of the need for rethinking juvenile justice and how it might look and function as it moves into the twenty-first century.

Caring for children in need of protection or correction is a proper concern of society at large, as well as of the law enforcement community and others within the juvenile justice system. This concern carries with it the needs to be informed, to take into account opposing viewpoints and to keep the principles of justice and fairness in the forefront.

How to Use This Book

Juvenile Justice is more than a textbook; it is a planned learning experience. The more actively you participate in it, the better your learning will be. You will learn and remember more if you first familiarize yourself with the total scope of the subject. Read and think about the Table of Contents; it outlines the many facets of juvenile justice. Then follow these steps as you study each chapter:

1. Read the objectives at the beginning of the chapter. These are stated as "Do You Know?" questions. Assess your current knowledge of each question. Examine any preconceptions you may hold.
2. Read the chapter, underlining, highlighting or taking notes, if that is your preferred study style.
   a. Pay special attention to all information that is highlighted For example,

---

■ Juvenile justice currently consists of a "one-pot" jurisdictional approach.

   The key concepts of the chapter are presented this way.
   b. Look up unfamiliar words in the Glossary at the back of the book.
3. When you have finished reading the chapter, reread the "Do You Know?" questions at the beginning of the chapter to make sure you can give an educated response to each question. If you find yourself stumped by one, find the appropriate section in the chapter and review it.
4. Finally, read the Discussion Questions and be prepared to contribute to a class discussion of the ideas presented in the chapter.

By following these steps, you will learn more information, understand it more fully and remember it longer. It's up to you. Good learning!

ABOUT THE AUTHORS

ROBERT W. DROWNS, MS, is a retired police officer and an instructor at Metropolitan State University. In addition to conducting seminars and workshops on various aspects of juvenile justice, he is a consultant to the Office of Juvenile Justice Delinquency Prevention (OJJDP).

KÄREN M. HESS, PhD, has written extensively in the field of law enforcement and criminal justice. Dr. Hess is a frequent instructor for report writing workshops and seminars for law enforcement agencies. She is a member of the English department at Normandale Community College and president of the Institute for Professional Development. Dr. Hess belongs to the National Criminal Justice Association and the National Council of Teachers of English. She is also a member of the Bloomington Crime Prevention Association board of directors.

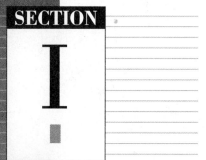

The Evolution of the Juvenile Justice System

The farther backward you can look, the farther forward you are likely to see.

Winston Churchill (1874–1965)

Our juvenile justice system is a complex, changing network that is apart from, yet a part of, the broader criminal justice system. It is apart *from* that system in that it is charged with protecting youth from harm, neglect and abuse, both emotional and physical. This protection frequently involves the criminal justice system as well as numerous public agencies and organizations. The juvenile justice system is a part *of* the criminal justice system in that it is charged with dealing with youth who break the law, and some juveniles may end up in the adult system.

A separate system for youthful offenders is, historically speaking, relatively recent. An understanding of how this system evolved is central to understanding the system as it currently exists and to understanding the challenges it faces.

It has been said that the historian is a prophet looking backward. History reveals patterns and changes in attitudes towards youths and how they are to be treated. In the treatment of juveniles, the emphasis has changed from punishment to an opposite emphasis on protection and back. As one emphasis achieves prominence, problems persist and critics clamor for change. History also reveals mistakes that can be avoided in the future as well as hopes and promises that remain unfulfilled. History *does* repeat itself in many ways.

This section looks first at the historical and philosophical roots of the juvenile justice system, which, until this century, are inseparable from the broader criminal justice system (Chapter 1). This is followed by an examination of trends within the American juvenile justice system in the twentieth century (Chapter 2). The section concludes with an in-depth look at the Uniform Juvenile Court Act passed in 1968 to provide direction for juvenile justice (Chapter 3). The three chapters of this section help students of juvenile justice understand the contemporary system and its many complexities. The present was built upon the past and will greatly influence the future.

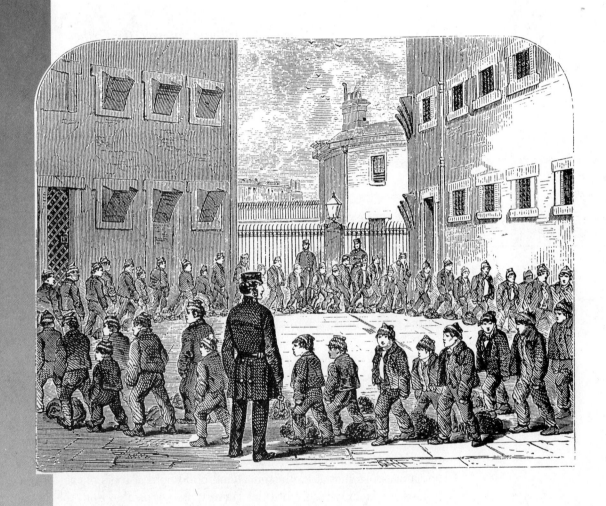

The Historical and Philosophical Roots of the Juvenile Justice System

History is a vast early warning system.
Norman Cousins

▌ Do You Know?

What principles were established by the Code of Hammurabi?
Why *parens patriae* is important in juvenile justice?
What Bridewells were and when they were established?
Who were among the key reformers of the Enlightenment and the contribution of each?
What concepts were important to the classical view of criminality? The positivist view?
When the term juvenile delinquency was first used and what it was considered to cause?
When and where the first House of Refuge was opened in the United States?
What reform schools emphasized?
Who the child savers were and what their philosophy was?
What contribution John Augustus made to the criminal justice system?
When the position of probation officer was officially recognized as an arm of the court?
When and where the first juvenile court was established?
How the first juvenile courts functioned?
How probation was to function in the juvenile court?

▌ Can You Define the Following Key Terms?

Bridewell, child savers, classical view of criminality, corporal punishment, delinquency, delinquent, determinism, *lex talionis*, medical model, *parens patriae*, poor laws, positivist view of criminality, retaliation, social contract, status offense

INTRODUCTION

Anthropologists have concluded that since the earliest time, people have banded together for companionship and protection. As societies developed, they established rules to assure their safety. Those who broke the rules were severely punished. Also since the beginning of recorded history, societies have sought to keep their young under control and to encourage the young to conform to society's expectations.

Most early societies have treated all wrongdoings and criminal offenses alike. Children and adults have been subject to the same rules and laws. They have been tried under the same legal process and, when convicted, have suffered the same penalties and punishments.

This chapter traces the development of laws and methods of enforcing those laws from ancient times to this century. Figure 1–1 provides a timeline to guide you on this historical overview and to illustrate the overlap of influences at different times in history.

SOCIAL CONTROL IN EARLY SOCIETIES

Even the most primitive tribes exercised some form of social control over the behavior of its members. In primitive societies, **retaliation** was the accepted way to deal with members of the tribe who broke the rules. Personal revenge was sometimes broadened so that the victim's entire family or tribe retaliated against the offender's family or tribe, resulting in blood feuds. However, blood feuds were sometimes avoided by establishing a system whereby the wrongdoer could pay the victim money or give the victim property.

As tribal leaders emerged, they began to help victims by imposing fines and punishments on wrongdoers. If the wrongdoer refused to pay the fine or accept the punishment, that person was declared an *outlaw*, that is, outside the law and, therefore, banished, probably to be eaten by wild animals or killed by the elements. Banishment was one of the earliest forms of social vengeance. Such social vengeance is also the forerunner of our criminal law, taking *public* action against those who do not obey the rules of the society. Eventually, tribal leaders and rulers took over the task of punishing those who broke the law. Ancient societies confined wrongdoers in dungeons and towers in castles, or even in animal cages. Children as well as adults were subject to such confinement.

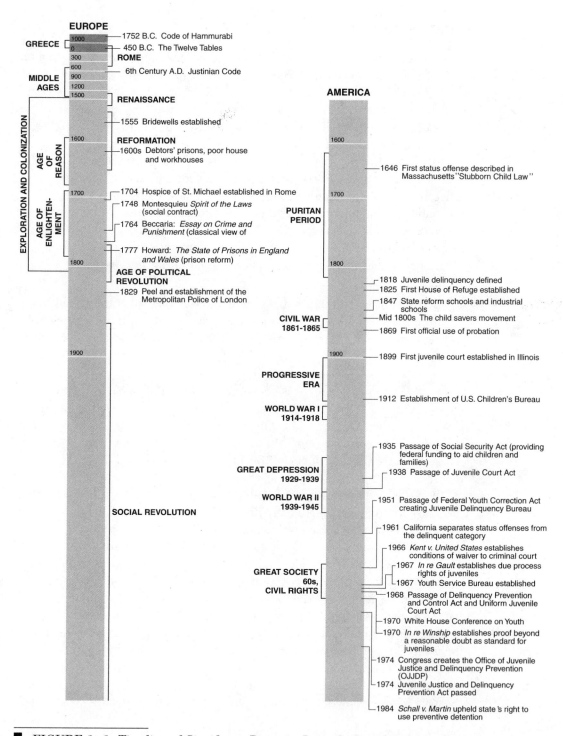

■ FIGURE 1–1 Timeline of Significant Dates in Juvenile Justice

The Code of Hammurabi

As societies developed writing skills, they began to record their laws. Around 1752 B.C. the Babylonian king Hammurabi (dates unknown, but thought to be ca. 1792–1750 B.C.) set forth rules for his kingdom establishing offenses and punishments. Hammurabi, like all kings in his day, was the supreme executive, lawmaker and judge. His famous code, issued late in his reign, had great influence throughout the Middle East.

Historians view the *Code of Hammurabi* as the first comprehensive description of a system society used to regulate behavior and at the same time take vengeance on those failing to comply with its rules. Punishments were severe and public, including forced labor, branding, whipping, mutilation, burning at the stake, crucifixion, hanging and drowning. Capital crimes included bigamy, cowardice in the face of the enemy, incest, kidnapping, adultery, theft, and false witness and malfeasance in public office (but curiously, not murder).

▪ The Code of Hammurabi's main principle was that the strong shall not injure the weak. It established a social order based on individual rights. It is the origin of the legal principle of **lex talionis,** that is, an eye for an eye.

In this society the man was the head of the family, charged with many responsibilities to his wife and children. In such patriarchial societies rebellion against the father, even by adult sons, was not tolerated. Punishment was swift and severe. For example, Item 195 of the Code of Hammurabi states: "If a son strikes his father, one shall cut off his hands" (Kocourek and Wigmore, 1951, p. 427).

Another indication of father-son conflict comes from an essay written by a young man attending a Sumerian academy (located in what is now Iraq). The youths of that time, 1750 B.C., started school at an early age and continued to young manhood. They attended school from sunrise to sunset, every day, year around. The academies exalted the values of formal education. Industriousness was encouraged by generous use of **corporal punishment** (inflicting bodily pain). The essay describes the father's admonitions to his indifferent son. The father instructs the son to attend school, stand with respect and fear before his professor, complete his assignments and avoid wandering about the public square or standing idly in the streets. In short, the son was to be about the business of getting an education. The father scolded his son for lack of industriousness, failure to support him, too great an interest in material wealth and refusal to follow his father's vocation (Kramer, 1963). Many of these admonitions sound familiar today.

Ancient Greece and Rome

Ancient Greece and Rome also established many laws that would be passed on to future generations. In addition to the death penalty, ancient Greece and Rome also used imprisonment as a primary means of punishment.

In 640 B.C. Mamertine Prison was built in Rome. This prison consisted of a vast series of dungeons under Rome's main sewer. Both ancient Greece and Rome also used strong cages and rock quarries as prisons. These prisons held not only criminals but also political dissidents and social misfits.

In Greece, the harsh, cruel Draco, ruler in 621 B.C., prescribed corporal punishment so extensively that the *Code of Draco* was rumored to be written in blood. Among the punishments were flogging, branding, drawing and quartering, stretching on the rack and mutilation. Thieves had their hands cut off and liars their tongues cut out. Rapists' genitals were removed. The minor offense of stealing cabbages was punishable by death.

Roman law began around 450 B.C. with the *Twelve Tables*. It was at this time Rome shifted from a kingdom to a republic, and the common people demanded more fairness in the administration of justice. The Twelve Tables put custom into writing and became the foundation of law throughout the Roman Empire's history, which ended near the end of the Middle Ages. Thus, the laws set forth in the Twelve Tables were in effect for nearly a thousand years.

The father in ancient Roman culture (as in the Babylonian culture) exercised unlimited authority over his family. He had the authority to administer corporal punishment and could even sell his children into slavery. One important concept from the Roman civilization that influenced the development of juvenile justice was *patria postestas*—referring to the absolute control fathers had over their children and the children's absolute responsibility to obey. This concept would eventually evolve into the concept of *parens patriae,* to be discussed shortly.

THE MIDDLE AGES

Historians generally consider the Middle Ages to encompass the period A.D. 500 to A.D. 1500. During the Middle Ages, tribal societies developed into nation states and kings consolidated their "fatherly" control through written systems of laws.

In the sixth century Emperor Justinian (A.D. 483–565), called together twelve experts to review the laws of Rome and to organize the laws into a document called the *Corpus Juris Civilis.* A key part of the *Corpus* was the *Justinian Code.* The provisions of the Justinian Code were the law throughout most of Europe until modern times. The Code, as did Roman law, greatly influenced Anglo-American law as well.

Under Justinian law, infancy ended at age seven (Griffin and Griffin, 1978, p. 6). Rabbinic law divided youths and their level of responsibilities into three classifications: (1) infant—birth to age six, (2) prepubescent—age seven to puberty and (3) adolescent—puberty to age 20 (Griffin and Griffin, 1978, p. 6).

The earliest legal document written in English contained the laws of King Aethelbert (around A.D. 600). These laws made no special allowance for an offender's age. In fact several cases throughout history document children as young as six being hanged or burned at the stake.

Early in English history, how children were viewed was greatly influenced by the Church of Rome. Church doctrine stated that under age seven, children had not yet reached the age of reason and, thus, could not be held liable for sins. English law adopted this same perspective. Under seven years of age, children were not considered legally able to have the required *intent* to commit a crime. From ages 7–14, it was presumed they did not have such intent, but if evidence proved differently, children could be found guilty of committing a crime. After age 14, individuals were considered adults.

After the fall of the Roman Empire, general disorder prevailed. Kings were in complete authority, making laws and enforcing them as best they could. The gap between the rich and the poor was tremendous, with those in power seeking control over the lowly masses. Kings sought to maintain control and to suppress threats to their rule by executing those who opposed them.

THE FEUDAL PERIOD

The Feudal Period falls near the end of the Middle Ages, covering roughly the ninth to fifteenth centuries. The period can be broadly characterized as a time when central governments broke down and control of political, social and economic life passed to feudal lords. The lord's court literally became the seat of justice for his vassals. Vassals were considered equals or peers of the lord and were granted land in return for their fidelity to the lord (LaMonte, 1949, pp. 221–223). As a result, in the twelfth century a common punishment for those breaking the law of the feudal lord was forfeiting land and property.

During the thirteenth century in England, the distinction was made between criminal and civil law. A violation of the criminal law was viewed as a crime against the state. A violation of the civil law, in contrast, was viewed as a wrong against an individual. The civil law's goal was restitution for the victim as in ancient times.

In thirteenth century England common law (law of custom and usage) gave the king of England the power of being the "father of his country." The king was perceived as guardian over the person and property of minors, who were considered wards of the state and, as such, were provided special protection (Rendleman, 1979). The Latin phrase meaning "father of the country" is **parens patriae,** a concept critical to the evolution of juvenile justice.

∎ *Parens patriae* is the right and responsibility of the government to take care of minors and others who cannot legally take care of themselves (Oran, 1983, p. 304).

Parens patriae was used to justify the state's intervention in the lives of its feudal lords and their children. The chancery courts were one means by which the king maintained control of the wealthier class, while at the same time the state could act in the best interests of its children. These courts heard issues involving guardianship, for example. The courts did *not* have jurisdiction over children who committed crimes. Such youths were handled within the criminal court system.

THE RENAISSANCE

The Middle Ages are generally conceded to have ended with the discovery of America in 1492. The next two centuries in Europe, often referred to as the Renaissance, marked the transition from medieval to modern times. The Renaissance was characterized by an emphasis on art and the humanities, as well as a more humanistic approach to criminal justice.

The first correctional institutions appeared in England in the 1500s.

■ Bridewells, the first houses of correction, confined both children and adults who were considered idle and disorderly.

London's **Bridewell Prison** was the first institution of its kind to control youthful beggars and vagrants. The underlying theme for Bridewell was work and severe punishment to provide discipline, deterrence and rehabilitation. Grunhut (1948, p. 15) describes the goals of the institution as follows: "To make them earn their keep, to reform them by compulsory work and discipline, and to deter others from vagrancy and idleness."

Because they were so successful, Parliament passed a law in 1576 calling for Bridewell-type institutions in every county. Modeled after the first prison, the

■ *London's Bridewell was similar to a debtor's prison. It confined both children and adult "vagrants."*

Bridewells combined the principles of the workhouse and the poorhouse, as well as the penal institutions' formalities. Some parents placed their children into these Bridewell-type institutions believing the emphasis on hard work would benefit the child.

During Elizabeth I's reign, the English passed **poor laws,** which established the appointment of overseers to *indenture* poor and neglected children into servitude. Such children were forced to work for wealthy families who, in turn, trained them in a trade, domestic service or farming. Such involuntary apprenticeships were served until the youths were 21 or older. These Elizabethan poor laws were the model for dealing with poor children for the next two hundred years. One consequence of the poor laws was the debtors' prison, established for those who could not pay their debts. Many died there. These debtor's prisons also confined criminals and social misfits under miserable conditions.

In England in 1563, the Statutes of Artificers inaugurated a system of *indenturing* and *apprenticeship* for children over ten years of age. While the primary aim of the legislation was to ensure an adequate labor supply, the statutes served to provide and promote an approved method of child care (Zietz, 1969, p. 6). Four hundred years later, California used this same method, applying it to reformatories and programs for early release.

Thus, in the sixteenth century, vagrants, the unemployed, the elderly and minor offenders began to be cared for in community workhouses. During this time, much of the criminal law was directed against idleness. For example, the Elizabethan Vagabonds Act of 1597 listed several classes of undesirables including idle people, rogues, sturdy beggars and vagabonds. However, such people could avoid spending time in a debtor's prison or receiving corporal punishment by enlisting in the military. From 1600 to 1776 England also sent many of its unwanted social, political and religious misfits and criminals to America as indentured servants.

In 1601 England proposed establishing large workhouses where children who could not be supported by their parents would be placed and "bred up to labor, principles of virtue implanted in them at an early age, and laziness be discouraged . . . and, settled in a way serviceable to the public's good and not bred up in all manners of vice" (Webb and Webb, 1927, p. 52). This proposal was finally implemented with the passage of the Gilbert Act of 1782. The Act decreed that all poor, aged, sick, and those too infirm to work were to be placed in *poorhouses* (almshouses). Provisions in the Act are forerunners of present-day standards established in juvenile detention centers. Under the Act, poor infants and children who could not go with their mothers were not placed in the poorhouse but with a "proper person," presumably in a family setting (de Scheveinitz, 1943, pp. 20–21).

Up to the eighteenth century public corporal punishment of some form was the most common method of "correction." Imprisonment did not begin until the eighteenth century in Europe and the nineteenth century in the United States, but the origin of locking people up can be found in the Renaissance in the form of workhouses and jails.

THE REFORM MOVEMENT

By the eighteenth century conditions in workhouses, jails and houses of correction throughout Europe had deteriorated to the extent that they could be described as human cesspools. But, because places of confinement were physically located away from the general population, the public was unaware of the deplorable conditions—"out of sight, out of mind."

Another problem existed in the laws themselves and how they were administered. According to Stojkovic and Lovell (1992, p. 38):

> [C]onditions in eighteenth-century Europe allowed the arbitrary execution of punishment and a complete lack of accountability of criminal justice officials. . . . Investigators and judges used torture to gain confessions from the accused, and secret trials ended with prison sentences and further torture on the slimmest evidence. Sentences issued by the courts depended on the power, wealth, and status of the convicted. The time was ripe for reformers to demand change.

Historians have labeled the eighteenth and nineteenth centuries as the Age of Enlightenment. One important milestone in the development of juvenile justice during this time was the founding of the London Philanthropic Society in 1817. One purpose of this society was reformation of juvenile offenders. The Society opened the first English house of refuge for children, a prototype for houses of refuge in the United States. The houses of refuge were a major shift from family-oriented discipline to institutional treatment.

Also during the eighteenth and nineteenth centuries, French, English and Italian reformers openly criticized the existing laws, the extensive use of corporal punishment and the deplorable conditions under which people were incarcerated.

■ Among the key reformers of the Enlightenment were Montesquieu, Beccaria, Howard, Peel and Lombroso.

Montesquieu

The French historian and philosopher, Charles Louis de Secondat, Baron de laBrede et de Montesquieu (1689–1755), was a founder of political science. His most influential work, *The Spirit of the Laws* (1748), advocated a system of checks and balances that found its way into the U.S. Constitution. According to Gay (1966, p. 59):

> Montesquieu thought that the British subject's sense of liberty—his feeling of safety and security—sprang from the separation of the government's powers into three parts. The king held executive power only, he said, while Parliament alone could make laws; and the judiciary functioned independent of them both.

■ Montesquieu's philosophy centered around the **social contract** whereby free, independent individuals agree to form a community and to give up a portion of their individual freedom to benefit the security of the group.

Montesquieu was a harsh critic of inhumane punishments, advocating more humane conditions and making the punishment fit the crime. Montesquieu believed that harsh punishment undermined morality and that a better way to prevent crime was to appeal to an individual's sense of decency and what was morally and socially right.

This social contract applied to minors as well as to adults. Youth were expected to obey the rules established by society and to suffer the consequences if they did not. The social contract was important to the reform movement in that it emphasized community responsibility, in essence lessening the power of the king, just as his advocating a separation of powers had done.

Beccaria

An Italian economist, Milanese aristocrat, jurist and criminologist, the Marchese di Cesare Bonesana Beccaria (1738–1794), was influenced by Montesquieu. At the core of Beccaria's philosophy was Montesquieu's social contract.

■ Beccaria was the founder of the **classical view of criminality** stressing the social contract, the prevention of crime and the need to make any punishment fit the crime committed.

A basic assumption of Beccaria was that people are rational and responsible for their acts. In 1764 he wrote his best known work, *An Essay on Crimes and Punishments,* outlining his philosophy. Among the principles he advocated, which characterizes the classical view of criminality, are the following (Barnes and Teeters, 1959, p. 322):

- All social action should be based on the utilitarian concept of the greatest good for the greatest number.
- Crime is an injury to society, the only rational measure of which is the extent of the injury.
- Preventing crime is more important than punishing those who commit crime. To do so the public must be educated about what the laws are, their support for the law enlisted, and virtue rewarded.
- Secret accusations and torture should be abolished. Those accused of crimes should have speedy trials and be treated humanely before, during, and after the trial.
- The purpose of punishment should be to deter crime, not to obtain revenge for an offended society. It is not the severity of the punishment, but the certainty and swiftness that will result in deterring crime. Penalties must fit the crime, with crimes against property being punished by fines or imprisonment for those who cannot pay the fine. Capital punishment should be abolished as life imprisonment is a better deterrent.

▌ Imprisonment should be more widely used but improved by having better physical facilities and separating prisoners by age, sex, and degree of criminality.

The four individual rights of those accused of crimes that were advocated by Beccaria were included in the French Code of Criminal Procedure in 1808 and the French Penal Code of 1810:

1. Individuals should be regarded as innocent until proven guilty.
2. Individuals should have the right to employ legal counsel and to cross-examine the state's witnesses.
3. Individuals should not have to testify against themselves.
4. Individuals should have the right to a prompt, public trial, usually by a jury.

Howard

Yet another reformer was John Howard (1726–1790) who was appointed sheriff of Bedfordshire, England, in 1773. In this position he became painfully aware of the inhuman conditions under which people were confined. Howard undertook a study of England's prisons and also traveled to other countries to study their prisons.

▌ **Howard is often thought of as the father of prison reform.**

One institution that greatly impressed Howard was the Hospice (hospital) of San Michele in Rome, commonly referred to as St. Michael. Built in 1704 by Pope Clement XI, the Hospice was one of the first institutions designed exclusively for youthful offenders. Incorrigible youth under age 20 ate and worked in silence in a large central hall, but slept in separate cells. The emphasis was on reading the Bible and hard work. An inscription placed over the door by the Pope is still there: "It is insufficient to restrain the wicked by punishment unless you render them virtuous by corrective discipline."

▌ **The first institution for the treatment of juvenile offenders, the Hospice of San Michele, was established in Rome in 1704.**

The Pope stated the facility's purpose was "For the correction and instruction of profligate youth, that they who when idle were injurious, may when taught become useful to the state" (Griffin and Griffin, 1978, p. 7).

Most of the conditions of confinement Howard found were shocking, and he detailed them in his study *The State of Prisons in England and Wales* (1777), which eventually led Parliament to correct many of the abuses. Howard put forth four principles for reform: (1) abolition of fees, (2) a reformatory regime, (3) secure and sanitary conditions and (4) systematic inspections.

To this day the John Howard Society continues to promote his ideas. This nonprofit organization, located in Chicago, provides support to inmates and their families, and promotes community understanding of prisons and the problems of prisoners and prison administrators alike. The Society also offers technical assistance to correctional institutions.

Peel

Despite the efforts of reformers such as Montesquieu, Beccaria and Howard, during the nineteenth century, execution was still common. In fact, the death penalty was imposed for over 200 crimes in England during this time. Among the most important reforms during the nineteenth century were those proposed by Sir Robert Peel (1788–1850), often called the father of modern policing.

As England's home secretary, one of the first steps Peel took was to abolish the death penalty for over a hundred offenses. Peel also advocated returning to the Anglo-Saxon principle of individual community responsibility for preserving law and order. As part of his proposal, he called for London to have a group of citizens appointed and paid for by the community to serve as police officers, creating the Metropolitan Police of London.

Peel's principles for reform called for local responsibility for law and order and appointed, paid civilians to assume this responsibility.

▮ Peel's reforms resulted in the passage of the Metropolitan Police Act of 1829, creating the Metropolitan Police of London.

Many principles introduced by Peel are still being practiced not only in England but also in the United States. The establishment of the Metropolitan Police marked the beginning of separate components—police, courts, corrections—within the criminal justice system.

Lombroso

Toward the end of the eighteenth century, opposition to the classical view increased. Among the leading opponents was Italian physician Cesare Lombroso (1835–1909).

Lombroso maintained that criminals were born with a predisposition to crime and needed exceptionally favorable conditions in life to avoid criminal behavior. As the originator of the **positivist view of criminality,** that is, transferring emphasis from the crime itself to the criminal behavior, Lombroso has been called the father of modern criminology. He firmly believed that criminals were literally "born," not made—that the primary cause of crime was biological. He was writing at the same time Charles Darwin's theory of evolution was becoming widely circulated and was probably greatly influenced by Darwin's ideas (late 1800s). Although some of Lombroso's work was later found to be flawed, he had started people thinking about causes for criminal behavior other than free will.

▮ Building on Lombroso's idea that environmental influences affected criminal behavior, some scholars developed the positivist view of criminality based on the concept of **determinism.**

As noted by Snarr (1992, p. 47):

Determinism maintains that human behavior is the product of a multitude of environmental and cultural influences. The view regards crime as a consequence, not of a single but of many factors. Among the influences considered were the population density, the economic status, and the legal definition of crime. The multiple-factor causation theory brought the positivist view into direct conflict with the complex free-will notion of the rejection of pain and the seeking of pleasure concept.

THE DEVELOPMENT OF JUVENILE JUSTICE IN THE UNITED STATES

The justice system developed in England served as the basis for the juvenile justice system in America, and the system continued to evolve in response to the unique conditions present in this country.

From the Colonial Period to the Industrial Revolution

The United States inherited much of its law from the Anglo-Saxon law of England. Hence, the colonists brought with them much of the English criminal justice system as well, including poor laws and the forced apprenticeship system for poor and neglected children. Before 1800, under common law, children under age seven were presumed incapable of criminal intent; children over 14 were treated as adults. In between these ages intent had to be proven. As in England, youth who committed serious crimes were handled by the adult criminal justice system.

Age, by definition, has always been a consideration in juvenile justice. Blackstone (1776, p. 23) summarized the law on the responsibility of youth in these words: "Under seven years of age indeed an infant cannot be guilty of a felony; for then a felonious discretion is almost an impossibility in nature; but at eight years old he may be guilty of a felony." He goes on to say that under age 14, although by law a youth may be adjudged incapable of discerning right from wrong (*doli incapax*), it appeared to the court and the jury that he *could* discern between good and evil (*doli capax*) (italics in original).

In the early years of colonization, the fundamental mode of juvenile control was the family, with the father given absolute authority over all family matters. For example, early laws prescribed the death penalty for children who disobeyed their parents.

In 1646 the Colonial Puritan philosophy was enacted into law when Massachusetts passed the Stubborn Child Law, which was the first **status offense,** that is, an act that is illegal for minors only. The law stood, unrevised, for over three hundred years.

Up until the end of the eighteenth century, the family was also the main economic unit, with family members working together farming or in home-based trades. Children were important contributors to these family-based industries. The privileged classes found apprenticeships for their children to learn marketable skills. The children of the poor, in contrast, were often bound out as indentured servants.

The Industrial Revolution, beginning at the end of the eighteenth century, changed forever the face of America. Families flocked to the cities to work in the factories, and child labor in these factories replaced the apprenticeship system.

For the next twenty years child labor was used increasingly. During this revolution, children made up 47 to 55 percent of the cotton mill workforce (Krisberg and Austin, 1993, p. 15). As the country became more industrialized, the social control once exerted by the family weakened. Children in the workforce had to obey the demands of their bosses, often in conflict with the demands of their parents. In addition, poverty was increasing for many families. This combination of poverty and weakened family control set an "ominous stage" with some Americans fearing a growing "dangerous class" and seeking ways to "control the wayward youth who epitomized this threat to social stability" (Krisberg and Austin, 1993, p. 15).

Colonial America handled juveniles much like petty thieves. After a warning, shaming or corporal punishment, the offender would return to the community. If accused of a major criminal act, the juvenile would proceed through the justice system as an adult. Trials and punishment were based on age, and any one over seven years was subject to the courts.

Toward the end of the eighteenth century, as noted, the belief was that wrongdoers chose to commit crimes of their own free will. Sufficient pain should be administered to offset the pleasure derived from committing the crime. The result was corporal punishment, hard labor and similar tactics to reinforce this assumption.

The following section summarizes the prevailing philosophy, treatment and sociopolitical policies in effect during the seventeenth through eighteenth centuries in the United States. Highlights of the several periods of reform discussed in this chapter and the next are adapted from materials of the Center for the Assessment of the Juvenile Justice System (Hawkins et al., 1980).

Highlights of Colonial Period and Industrial Revolution Reform

Philosophy

▐ Consensual belief that all children were inherently sinful and in need of strict control and/or punishment when necessary. Most nonconforming children were of lower-class parentage; middle-class families protected their children from bad influences by controlling the behavior of less fortunate youth.

Treatment

▐ Misbehaving children were generally controlled by familial punishment.
▐ External, community punishment and control was necessary only when the parents failed in their duties.

Policies

- ■ Communal legal sanctions were guided by the British tradition of common law, allowing children over seven years of age to receive public punishment.
- ■ Children could be punished publicly for several status offenses such as rebelliousness, disobedience and sledding on the Sabbath. Thus, a separate system of justice was set up for children and adults.
- ■ Several institutions were created that cared for orphaned and neglected children: almshouses and orphanages.

Developments in the Early Nineteenth Century

In the 1700s and the early 1800s, it was thought that the family, church and other social institutions should handle juvenile delinquents. During that period jail was the only form of incarceration, and it was primarily used for detention pending trial.

As time progressed and mobility and town sizes increased, the traditional forms of social control began to break down. To accommodate these changes, communities created institutions for children where they could learn good work and study habits, live in a disciplined and healthy environment, and develop "character."

In the United States during the nineteenth century, and continuing into the early twentieth century, juveniles were handled by various civil courts and public institutions such as welfare agencies. Increasing industrialization, urbanization and immigration created severe problems for families and their children.

■ Five distinct, yet interrelated, social institutions developed in response to poor, abused, neglected, dependent and delinquent children brought before a court: indenture and apprenticeship, mixed almshouses (poorhouses), private orphanages, public facilities for dependent children and jails.

Throughout history, until the late nineteenth century, all wrongdoers, regardless of age, were punished rather than "treated." Often the punishment was a kind of community-based correction.

Such community-based corrections involved dispositions that reflected (1) compensation and restitution by offenders to their victims; (2) indenture of offenders to the victims' families when they could not provide restitution and compensation; (3) assignment to the public works such as quarries, mines, construction of roads and buildings and other public services and (4) banishment or execution.

The 1800s were a period of concern and social reform. The reformers were instrumental in changing laws and public policy as they affect children. New York, Pennsylvania and Massachusetts established the first halfway houses in America in the early 1800s (Keller and Alper, 1970, p. 7). In 1803 the New York City mayor attempted a project to assist young ex-convicts, but the project was dropped for lack of funds and interest. In 1817 the Society for the Prevention of Pauperism was founded in New York City. Its objectives were to determine the major cause of pauperism and to have children confined in a building separate from prisons for adult criminals.

▮ A committee report in 1818 listed "juvenile delinquency" as a major cause of pauperism—the first public recognition of the term *juvenile delinquency.*

Several other significant events occured in the 1800s that altered the administration of juvenile justice (Griffin and Griffin, 1978, p. 20):

- ▮ 1818—Juvenile delinquency defined
- ▮ 1825—First House of Refuge established in United States
- ▮ 1847—State reform and industrial schools founded
- ▮ 1869—First official use of probation (Massachusetts)
- ▮ 1869—Agent of Board of state Charity empowered to investigate cases and attend meetings of the court
- ▮ 1870—First use of separate trials for juveniles (Massachusetts)
- ▮ 1877—Separate dockets and records established for juveniles (Massachusetts)
- ▮ 1880—First probation system applicable to juveniles instituted
- ▮ 1898—Segregation of children under 16 awaiting trial (Rhode Island)
- ▮ 1899—First juvenile court established (Illinois)

The institutions created by the reformers were houses of refuge, reform schools and foster homes.

Houses of Refuge

In 1823 the New York Society for the Reformation of Juvenile Delinquents was founded. In 1825 this society opened the New York House of Refuge, the first reformatory in the United States.

The House of Refuge was to care for children who were vagrants or who had been convicted of a criminal offense. This was the predecessor of today's training schools. Children were placed in these homes by court order and usually stayed until they reached the age of maturity.

▮ In 1825 the New York House of Refuge opened to house juvenile delinquents, defined in its charter as "youths convicted of criminal offenses or found in vagrancy."

The managers of the House believed that children's behavior would change through vigilant instruction. Children who misbehaved should be punished by losing certain rewarded positions or by whippings. The managers took the position that the public had the responsibility of disciplining children where natural parents and guardians refused to do so. The labor of the House was contracted out for a fee to local businesses. Youths were given apprenticeships and training in practical occupations.

■ *At the New York House of Refuge, children learned various trades and also engaged in physical activity.*

In 1827 Pennsylvania followed New York's lead, establishing the Philadelphia House of Refuge, an institution designed to separate juvenile delinquents and poor urchins from adult criminals.

The authority of the state to send children to such houses of refuge was upheld in 1838 in Pennsylvania in *Ex parte Crouse*. In this case a mother claimed that her daughter was incorrigible and had her committed to the Philadelphia House of Refuge. The girl's father sought her release, but was denied by the court, which stated:

> The object of the charity is reformation, by training its inhabitants to industry; by imbuing their minds with principles of morality and religion; by furnishing them with means to earn a living; and above all, by separating them from the corrupting influence of improper associates. To this end, may not the natural parents, when unequal to the task of education, or unworthy of it, be superseded by the parens patriae, or common guardian of the community?

However, many of these houses of refuge were, in effect, prisons with harsh discipline including severe whippings and solitary confinement. Krisberg and Austin (1993, p. 17) note that: "[F]rom the onset, the special institutions for juveniles housed together delinquent, dependent, and neglected children—a practice still observed in most juvenile detention facilities today."

Houses of refuge were operated by private philanthropic societies in many of the largest cities of the northeastern states. A typical day at the house began at sunrise and followed a highly disciplined, regimented routine. Morning prayers were followed by one and one-half hours of school and then by work routines until the noon eating break. After eating, youths returned to work until 5:00 P.M. At 5:00 P.M. they ate, had one and one-half hours of school followed by prayers, and then returned to their cells and the rule of silence (Pickett, 1969, p. 49). Confinements were lengthy, and escapes were frequent. There was public disapproval of the harsh disciplinary treatment and health hazards. By 1860, 20 other such institutions opened in the United States.

Krisberg and Austin (1993, p. 16) suggest: "Although early 19th-century philanthropists relied on religion to justify their good works, their primary motivation was protection of their class privileges. Fear of social unrest and chaos dominated their thinking. The rapid growth of a visible impoverished class, coupled with apparent increases in crime, disease, and immorality, worried those in power."

Although the statutes for these facilities did not change, they did recognize a need for treatment and the state's responsibility of *parens patriae*.

Reform Schools

By the middle of the nineteenth century, the more progressive states began to develop new institutions—*reform schools*. Reform schools were intended to provide discipline in a "homelike" atmosphere where education was emphasized.

▌ Reform schools emphasized formal schooling, but they also retained large workshops and continued the contract system of labor.

From 1859 to 1890 many houses of refuge were replaced by the reform school movement. The Boston House of Reformation was one of the earliest. Most reform schools were large congregate institutions with strictly regimented work schedules. Also stressed were physical conditioning and learning a trade. Other states such as Ohio, Maine, Rhode Island and Michigan followed Massachusetts in the reform school concept.

In many respects, however, reform schools were indistinguishable from the houses of refuge. They drew their inmates from a variety of sources and confined diverse populations.

Foster Homes

While many states were building reform schools, New York in 1853 emphasized the need to place neglected and delinquent children in private or *foster homes* which frequently were located in rural areas. At the time, the city was viewed as a place of crime and bad influences, in contrast with the clean, healthy, crime-free country. Placement in the rural area was consistently viewed by the Children's Aid Society of New York as in the best interest of the child.

The foster home was supposed to be the family surrogate used in all stages of the juvenile justice process. For a variety of reasons this concept faltered.

Personality conflicts between foster parents and juvenile clients often caused disruption. Some foster parents were convicted of various abuses and neglect. And there was inadequate, and sometimes a total lack of, accrediting and monitoring of foster home licenses. However, the New York City concept of foster care is still used as the primary placement option for minor delinquency.

The Child Savers

Many reforms swept through the United States in the nineteenth century, including the child-saving movement, which began around the middle of the 1800s. The **child savers** believed children's environments could make them "bad." These wealthy, civic-minded citizens attempted to "save" unfortunate children by placing them in houses of refuge and reform schools.

These reformers were shocked that children could be tried in a criminal court, like adults, and be sentenced to jail with hardened criminals. The reformers believed society owed more to its children than the guarantee of justice. They believed society also must be sensitive and responsive to children's health, safety and welfare.

■ The child savers' philosophy was that the child was basically good and was to be treated by the state as a young person with a problem.

Further, society's role was not just to ascertain whether the child was guilty or not guilty. Children's contact with the justice system should not be a process of arrest and trial, but should seek answers to what the children are; how they have become what they are; and what society should do in the children's best interest, as well as society's best interest, to save them from wasted lives. The child savers' motivating principles were as follows (Task Force Report, 1976, p. 6):

■ Children, because of their minority status, should not be held as accountable as adult transgressors.
■ The objective of juvenile justice is to help the youngster, to treat and rehabilitate rather than punish.
■ Dispositions should be predicated on an analysis of the youth's special circumstances and needs.
■ The system should avoid the punitive adversary and formalized trappings of adult criminal process with all of its confusing rules of evidence and tightly controlled procedures.

The child savers were not entirely humanitarian, however, viewing the poor children as a threat to society. These children needed to be reformed to conform, to value hard work and to become contributing members of society.

Anthony Platt, author of *The Child Savers,* did extensive research on this period and the reform movement. He (1968, p. 176) writes:

The child savers should in no sense be considered libertarians or humanists:

1. Their reforms did not herald a new system of justice but rather expedited traditional policies which had been informally developing during the nineteenth century.

▌ *Prisoners, including women and children, leaving on a van named the Black Maria in New York to sail to Blackwell's Island where they will be confined. Engraving from an American newspaper of 1868.*

2. They implicitly assumed the "natural" dependence of adolescents and created a special court to impose sanctions on premature independence and behavior unbecoming youth.
3. Their attitudes toward "delinquent" youth were largely paternalistic and romantic, but their commands were backed up by force. They trusted in benevolence of government and similarly assumed a harmony of interest between "delinquents" and agencies of control.
4. They promoted correctional programs requiring longer terms of imprisonment, long hours of labor and militaristic discipline, and the inculcation of middle-class values and lower-class skills.

The child-saving movement was not so much a break with the past as an affirmation of faith in certain aspects of the past.

The Introduction of Probation

One especially important reformer was John Augustus (1784–1859). Augustus was a prosperous Boston shoemaker with several employees in his shop. One August morning in 1841 he was in court when a wretched looking man was brought into court and charged with being a drunkard. Augustus spoke briefly with the man and then provided the man's bail on the provision he sign a pledge to never drink spirits again and to return to court at a set time as a reformed man.

For the next 18 years, Augustus spent much time visiting the courts, showing an interest in prisoners and bailing out misdemeanants who could not pay the fines themselves. He would help offenders find work or a place to live. His own home was filled with people he bailed out.

■ John Augustus was the first probation officer.

When Augustus and a defendant returned to court, he would report on the progress of the defendant's rehabilitation and recommend a disposition in the case. These recommendations were usually accepted by the court.

During the first year of his work, Augustus assisted ten drunkards, who because of his help received only small fines instead of imprisonment. Augustus later assisted other types of offenders, young and old, men and women. From 1841 to 1851 Augustus provided bail for 1,102 men and women, some as young as eight years old (Bartollas and Conrad, 1992, p. 95). As he continued his work, he was able to report that out of 2,000 cases, only ten failed to appear and jumped bail or probation. Later he and his wife established a house of refuge.

Several aspects of the system used by Augustus remain a basic part of modern probation. He thoroughly investigated each person he considered helping. He considered the previous character of the person, his age and likely future influences. Augustus not only supervised each defendant but also kept a careful case record, which he submitted to the court. After he died in 1859, probation work in Massachusetts was left to volunteers. Augustus' work was continued by Rufus Cook, chaplain to the county jail, who represented the Boston Children's Aid Society.

■ *John Augustus was the first probation officer in the United States.*

Highlights of Early 1800's Reform

Philosophy

■ Poverty was a crime that could be eliminated by removing children from offending environments and reforming their unacceptable conduct.

Treatment

■ Nonconforming children were controlled by external institutions, such as houses of refuge and reformatories created by paternalistic child savers.

■ Public education was used to "Americanize" foreign and lower-class children.

■ Private groups were organized to rescue children from poor and unfit environments.

Policies

■ Local and state governments became providers of new care and treatment for neglected and delinquent children.

■ Joint sharing of construction and supervision costs for institutions was assumed by private and public agencies.

■ The *parens patriae* tradition, correctional separation policies for adult and youthful offenders and indeterminate sentencing for juvenile inmates were adopted in several states.

■ Statutory definitions of juvenile delinquency were expanded to include a new series of status offenses, such as begging, cheating and gambling.

Developments in the Late Nineteenth Century

The Civil War (1861–1865) was followed by the Reconstruction Period and massive industrialization. Many children were left fatherless by the war, and many families moved to the urban areas seeking work. Many children were exploited in the "sweat shops." Others roamed the streets in gangs while their parents worked in the factories.

As American urbanization and industrialization increased and the immigrant population grew, crime also rose. In the nineteenth and early twentieth centuries, America chose to remove criminals and wrongdoers by placing them in *locked facilities* until they could be reformed to return to society and lead law-abiding lives. A great building boom occurred, and prisons, reformatories and industrial training schools became the instruments to satisfy society's need for reforming offenders.

In 1866 the first specialized institution for male juveniles was authorized in Washington, D.C. This House of Corrections consisted of several cottages containing some 60 or more beds. Throughout most of its existence the House of Corrections served a dual function, accepting youth convicted of federal crimes, as well as those convicted in Washington, D.C., courts.

In 1869 Massachusetts provided for the appointment of a State Board of Charities to investigate cases involving children tried before the courts. In 1878

■ *Larned City Prison in Kansas, 1886.*

the Massachusetts legislature enacted the first probation statute for a paid probation officer for the court of criminal jurisdiction of the city of Boston. It authorized the mayor to hire a probation officer who would be supervised by the superintendent of police.

■ **In 1878 the position of probation officer was officially recognized as an arm of the court.**

The legislation authorized a probation officer to investigate cases and recommend probation for "such persons as may reasonably be expected to be reformed without punishment." Probation was available, in this court system, to everyone: young, old, men, women, felons and misdemeanants.

Other developments took place as well. The 1870s saw the beginning of state reformatories, including the New York State Reformatory at Elmira, which opened in 1877.

In 1887 in New York City, the Neighborhood Guild was the first settlement house to open in the United States. It was an outgrowth of the London movement of Toynbee Hall (Stroup, 1960, pp. 43–45). Earlier organizations had been formed for similar objectives, such as the Young Men's Christian Association (YMCA, 1851) and the Young Women's Christian Association (YWCA, 1861). Their purpose was to provide recreation and counseling services to youths who needed them to "keep normals normal," thereby preventing delinquency.

The American settlement houses were designed to improve the entire neighborhood. They provided economic security, employment, recreation, better lighting, social welfare and other social benefits. These improvements were sometimes considered only peripheral to efforts to control and prevent delinquency and crime.

By the end of the 1800s, reform schools introduced vocational education, military drill and calisthenics into the institutions' regimen. As noted by Mennel (1973, p. 104): "The routines were designed as much to reinforce the authoritarian type of control for which reform schools had been traditionally noted as they were to improve the physical condition of the inmates."

At the same time, some reform schools changed their name to "industrial schools" and later to "training schools," to emphasize the "treatment" aspect of corrections. For example, the Ohio Reform Farm School, opened in 1857, later became the Boy's Industrial School, and was renamed again to the Fairfield School for Boys.

In 1898, 20 years after Massachusetts authorized the first paid probation officer, Vermont passed legislation for the probation officer to serve all courts in a particular county. Rhode Island followed Massachusetts and Vermont, but placed restrictions on who could be granted probation. This violated a basic tenet of the positivist school: judge the offender, not the offense. The restriction in the law excluded from probation persons convicted of treason, murder, robbery, arson, rape and burglary. The probation law, which applied to both children and adults, also introduced the concept of a state-administered probation system. Rhode Island provided a state agency, the Board of Charities

▮ *The dining hall at Darkhurst Reformatory.*

and Correction, and appointed a state probation officer and deputies "at least one of whom should be a woman" (Glueck, 1933, p. 231).

The Juvenile Court Movement

A juvenile court movement in the 1890s provided citizen participation in community-based corrections. This citizen participation through the Parent Teacher Association (PTA), founded in 1897, induced the Cook County Bar Association to write the law to establish a juvenile court in Chicago (Hunt, 1973).

The first juvenile court was created by the Illinois Juvenile Court Act in 1899, as titled an "Act to Regulate the Treatment and Control of Dependent, Neglected and Delinquent Children." Key features of this Act included the following:

■ Defined a delinquent as anyone under age 16.
■ Separated children from adults in institutions.
■ Set special, informal procedural rules for juvenile court.
■ Provided for use of probation officers.
■ Prohibited the detention of children under age 12 in a jail or police station.

■ In 1899 the Illinois legislature passed a law establishing a juvenile court that became the cornerstone for juvenile justice throughout the United States.

As noted by Springer (1986, p. 4):

The Illinois act divested the criminal courts of jurisdiction over persons under age 16 and substituted a paternalistic system which viewed criminally active juveniles as victims of their environments who were not responsible for their criminal acts.

As a consequence of this kind of thinking, juvenile courts operated under a medical model, giving "individualized treatment" to the ailing victims of the slings and arrows of a bad environment. The welfare of the child was the guidepost of the new social court, and it was thought that ministering to the welfare of the individual child would cure or rehabilitate the child and, ultimately, benefit society.

However, as Flicker (1990, p. 32) states:

[I]t could be argued that the most reprehensible feature of the Illinois contribution to juvenile justice is the continued erosion of distinctions between juveniles who commit criminal acts, thereby demonstrating objectively that they are a present threat to community safety, and those who are themselves victims as abused, neglected, or dependent children.

The 1899 Illinois Act provided public policy, social reform and a structured way to reform children in trouble, as well as to care for children needing official protection. The law created a public policy, based on the **medical model**, to retard the social and moral decay of the environment, family and youth. Concern was raised regarding the motives and intents of the reformers and the amount of energy being expended in seeking legislation on behalf of juveniles.

In Chicago, at the same time, a competing campaign was being launched to improve housing and living conditions, protect women in the workplace, advance and promote the public welfare and provide stronger labor laws for children. All the reformers' efforts, however, were directed at restoring and controlling children. They emphasized parental authority, home education, domesticity and rural values, which they perceived to be in decline (Platt, 1968, p. 176).

When the adjudicative process of the juvenile justice system was first established, the system conducted business in an administrative fashion. The process, set up within the juvenile court, was to be special to that court. The juvenile court was *not* to function as an adult criminal court. The Juvenile Court Act that established the first juvenile court in Chicago gave "original jurisdiction in *all* cases coming with the terms of this act." As noted by Springer (1986, p. 21): "This important change divested the adult criminal courts of all criminal jurisdiction over children under age 16. . . . From July 1, 1899, there were no more criminals under 16 in Illinois."

■ The first juvenile courts functioned as administrative agencies of the circuit or district courts and were mandated as such by legislative action.

As a special court, juvenile courts were to be separate, with separate records, and to use informal procedures. This meant that several important parts of the criminal trial, such as the indictment, pleadings and jury (unless the jury was demanded by the interested party or ordered by the judge), were to be eliminated.

The court based its findings on the administrative purpose and scope of the Juvenile Court Act. The Act was incorporated in some state statutes to be construed liberally, so that the care, custody and discipline of children would approximate as nearly as possible the care that could be given by individual parents.

The setting common to administrative hearings is strikingly different from the setting of a court hearing. The adversary function of the criminal court was perceived to be incompatible with the procedural safeguards of the juvenile court, which are focused on the treatment and welfare of children. The procedural safeguards of the juvenile court were intended to reflect the basic philosophy of the court that its duty as parent (*parens patriae*) was to help rather than punish children. Those involved in the administrative process of adjudicating did not recognize any constitutional rights, since children were legally wards of the state. Despite this, juvenile court was initially perceived as far more humane than the criminal court.

■ The vision of the child savers and the founders of the juvenile court was the rehabilitative ideal of reforming children instead of punishing them.

A six-year-old sentenced to the House of Refuge on Blackwell's Island, New York City, for vagrancy pleads unavailingly for mercy for his first offense. Engraving from an American newspaper of 1868.

Some scholars contend that the system was set up to take advantage of children. Disputing the benevolent motives of the founders of the juvenile court, especially in the adjudication procedure, scholars have suggested that the civil liberties and privacy of the juvenile court diminished through the process. They accuse the middle class of promoting the child-saving movement to support its own interest.

Other scholars contend that the development of the juvenile courts and the adjudication function represents neither a great social reform in processing juveniles, nor an attempt to diminish juveniles' civil liberties and control them arbitrarily. Rather, it represents another example of the trend toward bureaucracy and an institutionalized compromise between social welfare and the law. Sutton (1985, p. 142) suggests that the juvenile court "was primarily a shell of legal ritual within which states renewed and enacted their commitment to discretionary social control over children."

The law creating the juvenile court in Illinois was the first time probation and a probation officer were formally made *specifically* applicable to juveniles. The Illinois Juvenile Court Act stipulated:

The court shall have authority to appoint or designate one or more discreet persons of good character to serve as probation officers during the pleasure of the court . . . it shall be the duty of the said probation officer to make such investigation as may be required by the court; to be present in court in order to represent the interests of the child when the case is heard; to furnish to the court such information and assistance as the judge may require; and to take such charge of any child before and after trial as may be directed by the court.

▋ Probation, according to the 1899 Illinois Juvenile Court Act, was to have both an investigative and a rehabilitation function.

The Act further states delinquency could be treated as follows:

In case of a delinquent child the court may continue the hearing from time to time and may commit the child to the care and guardianship of a probation officer duly appointed by the court and may allow said child to remain in its own home, subject to the visitation of the probation officer; such child to report to the probation officer as often as may be required and subject to be returned to the court for further proceedings, whenever such action may appear to be necessary, or the court may commit the child to the care and guardianship of the probation officer, to be placed in a suitable family home, subject to the friendly supervision of such probation officer; or it may authorize the said probation officer to board out the said child in some suitable family home.

The law implies that probation officers superseded parental rights. Societal conditions sometimes dictated the functions of the probation officer. For example, when an influx of immigrants who were not regarded as satisfactorily caring for their children arrived, probation officers stepped in. When such children got into trouble, they often became wards of the juvenile court under the watchful eye of a probation officer.

In 1899, with the Illinois Act, the nation's criminal justice system finally recognized that it owed a different duty to children than to adults and that impressionable and presumably salvageable youths should not be mixed in prisons with hardened criminals. The development of juvenile courts is considered the first transformation of the juvenile justice system.

Highlights of Late Nineteenth Century Reform

In the nineteenth century, children were protected from confinement in jails, prisons and institutions by the opening of houses of refuge. Responsibilities shifted back and forth between the private and public sectors. Chicago, as early as 1861, provided a Commission at the local level to hear and determine petty cases of boys from 6–17-years old. Suffolk County (Boston) in 1870 and New York in 1877 provided separate dockets and records as well as separate trials for juveniles under age 16. By statute, in 1869, Massachusetts stipulated that an agent of the State Board of Charities should attend children's trials, protect their interests and make recommendations about them to the judge. Between 1878 and 1898 Massachusetts established a statewide system of probation to aid the court in juvenile matters, a method of corrections currently in every state in the United States.

The same period saw the regulation of child labor, the development of special services for handicapped children and the growth of public education.

There was a growing acceptance of public responsibility for the protection and care of children. However, no legal machinery yet existed to handle juveniles in need of special care, protection and treatment as wards of the state, rather than as criminals.

Philosophies

- ■ Increasing number of youth problems as by-products of rapid urbanization: poverty, immigration and unhealthy environments.
- ■ Individual treatment and control of juvenile offenders could improve their behavior.

Treatment

- ■ Several private organizations were created to assimilate foreign and lower-class youth into American culture.
- ■ Locked facilities were constructed across the nation.
- ■ Orphan asylums became popular ways to house and mold the conduct of those children left homeless by the Civil War and/or neglected by unfit parents.

Policy

- ■ State and local governments across the nation expanded their involvement in the lives of neglected and delinquent children: adoption of new educational/assimilation tools (vocational, industrial and manual training schools) for institutionalized and lower-class youth, passage of immigration restriction laws and assumption of a stronger role in creating financing and administering reform institutions.

The Evolution of Child, Parent and State Relationships

Developments with the evolving juvenile justice system in the United States had a direct effect on the relationships between children and their parents, children and the state and parents and the state. The National Juvenile Justice System Assessment Center has summarized the major developments and influences on these relationships in Table 1–1.

Table 1–1 covers up to the end of the nineteenth century, and the Puritan Period in the table overlaps the Colonial Period and early nineteenth century as discussed in this chapter. The table also omits the Illinois Juvenile Court Act from the Refuge Period. These differences serve to illustrate that the developments described and neatly categorized in the table are actually fluid, overlapping and ongoing. The twentieth century will be added to the table in Chapter 2.

TABLE   **Juvenile Justice Developments and Their Impact**
1-1

Period	Major Developments	Precipitating Influences	Child/State	Parent/State	Parent/Child
Puritan 1646– 1824	Massachusetts Stubborn Child Law (1646)	A. Christian view of child as evil B. Economically marginal agrarian society	Law provides: A. Symbolic standard of maturity B. Support for family as economic unit	Parents considered responsible and capable of controlling child	Child considered both property and spiritual responsibility of parents
Refuge 1824– 1899	Institutionalization of deviants, New York House of Refuge established (1824) for delinquent and dependent children	A. Enlightenment B. Immigration and industrialization	Child seen as helpless, in need of state intervention	Parents supplanted as state assumes responsibility for correcting deviant socialization	Family considered to be a major cause of juvenile deviancy

SOURCE: Hawkins, J. David; Paul A. Pastor, Jr.; Michelle Bell; and Sheila Morrison. *Reports of the National Juvenile Justice Assessment Center: A Topology of Cause-Focused Strategies of Delinquency Prevention.* Washington, D.C.: U.S. Government Printing Office, 1980.

SUMMARY

The Code of Hammurabi was the first comprehensive description of a system used by society to regulate behavior and at the same time punish those who disobeyed the rules. The main principle of this Code was that the strong shall not injure the weak. It established a social order based on individual rights. It is the origin of the legal principle of *lex talionis,* that is, an eye for an eye.

A significant influence on the development of juvenile justice was the concept of *parens patriae,* which came from the Feudal Period of England. *Parens patriae* is the right and responsibility of the government to take care of minors and others who cannot legally take care of themselves.

Bridewells were the first houses of corrections in England. They confined both children and adults considered to be idle and disorderly. As time progressed, conditions in the bridewells and other places of confinement became so deplorable that several individuals demanded reform.

Among the key reformers of the Enlightenment were Montesquieu, Beccaria, Howard, Peel and Lombroso. Montesquieu's philosophy centered around the social contract whereby free, independent individuals agree to form a community and to give up a portion of their individual freedom to benefit the security of the group. Beccaria was the founder of the classical view of criminality stressing the social contract, the prevention of crime and the need to make any punishment fit the crime committed.

Another reformer was John Howard, often thought of as the father of prison reform. Howard brought to England from Rome a model of the first institution for treating juvenile offenders, the Hospice of San Michele (Saint Michael), established in 1704. The father of modern policing was Peel, whose reforms resulted in the passage of the Metropolitan Police Act of 1829, creating the Metropolitan Police of London.

In opposition to the classical view of criminality, another reformer, Lombroso, believed that environmental influences affected criminal behavior, leading scholars to develop the positivist view of criminality based on the concept of determinism.

The colonists brought much of the English criminal justice system with them to America. During this time five distinct, yet interrelated, social institutions developed in response to poor, abused, neglected, dependent and delinquent children brought before a court: indenture and apprenticeship, mixed alms-houses (poorhouses), private orphanages, public facilities for dependent children and jails.

A committee report in 1818 listed "juvenile delinquency" as a major cause of pauperism—the first public recognition of the term *juvenile delinquency*. In 1825 the New York House of Refuge opened to house juvenile delinquents, who were defined in its charter as "youths convicted of criminal offenses or found in vagrancy." By the middle of the nineteenth century many states either built reform schools or converted their houses of refuge to reform schools. The reform schools emphasized formal schooling, but they also retained large workshops and continued the contract system of labor.

The middle of the nineteenth century also included the child-saving movement. The child savers' philosophy was that the child was basically good and was to be treated by the state as a young person with a problem. Another important reformer during this time was John Augustus, the first probation officer. In 1878 the position of probation officer was officially recognized as an arm of the court.

In 1899 the Illinois legislature passed a law establishing a juvenile court that became the cornerstone for juvenile justice throughout the United States. The first juvenile courts functioned as administrative agencies of the circuit or district courts and were mandated as such by legislative action. The vision of the child savers and the founders of the juvenile court was the rehabilitative ideal of reforming children instead of punishing them. Probation, according to the 1899 Illinois Juvenile Court Act, was to have both an investigative and a rehabilitative function.

■ Discussion Questions

1. The justice system has been defined as "justice that applies to children and adolescents, with concern for their health, safety, and welfare under sociolegal standards and procedures." Is this definition adequate?

2. Under the principle of *parens patriae,* how does the state (or the court) accept the role of "father"? Are all households administered and managed alike?

3. Is the current system of justice for juveniles functioning under the same concepts as the Code of Hammurabi, that is, "an eye for an eye"? If not, what is different?

4. What changes, if any, have occurred in the juvenile justice system since the founding of a court process in Illinois in 1899?

5. Who are the present "child savers"? What states, associations and individuals have contributed to the present child-saver philosophy?

6. What do you consider to be the major milestones in the evolution of juvenile justice?

7. Is it possible for one system to effectively and fairly serve both children who need correction and those who need protection?

▮ References

Barnes, Harry E., and Negley K. Teeters. *New Horizons in Criminology,* 3rd ed. Englewood Cliffs, N.J.: Prentice Hall, 1959.

Bartollas, Clemens, and John P. Conrad. *Introduction to Corrections,* 2nd ed. New York: Harper Collins, 1992.

Blackstone, William. *Commentaries on the Laws of England,* vol. 4. Oxford: Clarendon, 1776.

de Scheveinitz, Karl. *England's Road to Social Security.* Philadelphia: University of Pennsylvania, 1943.

Flicker, Barbara Danziger. *Standards for Juvenile Justice: A Summary and Analysis,* 2nd ed. New York: Institute for Judicial Administration, 1990.

Gay, Peter. *The Age of Enlightenment.* New York: Time, 1966.

Glueck, Sheldon, ed. *Probation and Criminal Justice.* New York: MacMillan, 1933.

Griffin, Brenda S., and Charles T. Griffin. *Juvenile Delinquency in Perspective.* New York: Harper & Row, 1978.

Grunhut, Max. *Penal Reform.* New York: Clarendon, 1948.

Hawkins, J. David; Paul A. Pastor, Jr.; Michelle Bell; and Sheila Morrison. *Reports of the National Juvenile Justice Assessment Center: A Topology of Cause-Focused Strategies of Delinquency Prevention.* Washington, D.C.: National Institute for Juvenile Justice and Delinquency Prevention, U.S. Government Printing Office, 1980.

Hunt, G. Bowdon. "Foreword." In *A Handbook for Volunteers in Juvenile Court,* by Vernon Fox. Special Issues of *Juvenile Justice.* February 1973.

Keller, Oliver J., and Benedict S. Alper. *Halfway Houses: Community-Centered Corrections and Treatment.* Lexington, Mass.: D.C. Heath, 1970.

Kocourek, Albert, and John H. Wigmore. *Source of Ancient and Punitive Law, Evolution of Law, Selected Readings on the Origin and Development of Legal Institutions,* vol. 1. Boston: Little, Brown, 1951.

Kramer, S. N. *The Sumerians.* Chicago: University of Chicago Press, 1963.

Krisberg, Barry, and James F. Austin. *Reinventing Juvenile Justice.* Newbury Park, Calif.: Sage Publications, 1993.

LaMonte, John L. *The World of the Middle Ages: A Reorientation of Medieval History.* New York: Appleton-Century-Crofts, 1949.

Mennel, Robert M. *Thorns and Thistles: Juvenile Delinquency in the United States 1824–1940.* Hanover, N.H.: University Press of New England, 1973.

Oran, Daniel. *Oran's Dictionary of the Law.* St. Paul, Minn.: West Publishing, 1983.

Pickett, Roberts. *House of Refuge: Organs of Juvenile Justice in New York State.* Syracuse, N.Y.: Syracuse University Press, 1969.

Platt, Anthony M. *The Child Savers: The Invention of Delinquency.* Chicago: University of Chicago Press, 1968.

Rendleman, Douglas R. "*Parens Patriae:* From Chancery to the Juvenile Court." In *Juvenile Justice Philosophy,* edited by Frederick L. Faust and Paul J. Branington. St. Paul, Minn.: West Publishing, 1979, pp. 58–96.

Snarr, Richard W. *Introduction to Corrections,* 2nd ed. Dubuque, Iowa: Wm. C. Brown, 1992.

Springer, Charles E. *Justice for Juveniles.* Washington, D.C.: U.S. Department of Justice, Office of Juvenile Justice and Delinquency Prevention, 1986.

Stojkovic, Stan, and Rick Lovell. *Corrections: An Introduction.* Cincinnati, Ohio: Anderson Publishing, 1992.

Stroup, Herbert H. *Social Work.* New York: American Book, 1960.

Sutton, John R. "The Juvenile Court and Social Welfare: Dynamics of a Progressive Reform." *Law & Society Review* 19 (1985) 1:142.

Task Force Report on Juvenile Justice and Delinquency Prevention. *Juvenile Justice and Delinquency Prevention.* Washington, D.C.: U.S. Government Printing Office, 1976.

Webb, Sidney, and Beatrice Webb. *English Local Government: English Poor Law History,* Part I. New York: Longmans, Green, 1927.

Zietz, Dorothy. *Child Welfare: Services and Perspective.* New York: John Wiley, 1969.

■ Case

Ex parte Crouse, 4 Whart. 9 (Pa. 1838).

The Evolution of the Juvenile Justice System in the Twentieth Century

If you want the present to be different from the past, study the past.

Baruch Spinoza (1632–1677)

▌ Do You Know?

How Progressive Era proponents viewed crime? What model they refined?
How social workers became affiliated with the first juvenile courts?
When and how probation officers became affiliated with the juvenile court?
What resulted from the 1909 White House Conference on Youth?
What act funded federal programs to aid children and families?
What the 1951 Congress accomplished in juvenile justice?
Which state first separated status offenses from delinquency? When?
What effect isolating offenders from their normal environment might have?
When the Youth Service Bureau was established? Its function?
What new approach for dealing with delinquency emerged in the late 1960s?
What was the major impact of the 1970 White House Conference on Youth?
Under what department the OJJDP is assigned?
What the JJDP Act of 1974 established? Its two main goals?
What the Four Ds of juvenile justice refer to?
What juvenile delinquency liability might be limited to?
Where corrections institutions were built in the 1980s? Why?
What was established by the following key cases: *Breed v. Jones, In re Gault, Kent v. United States, McKeiver v. Pennsylvania, Nicholl v. Koster, Schall v. Martin, In re Winship, Witter v. Cook County Commissioners*?

▌ Can You Define the Following Key Terms?

decriminalization, deinstitutionalization, deserts, deterrence, diversion, double jeopardy, due process, just deserts, justice model, net widening, PINS, preventive detention

INTRODUCTION

Chapter 1 described the development of the juvenile justice system up to the twentieth century. In the early 1900s, several changes were made in juvenile justice, including the establishment of the first juvenile courts. Numerous theories on the causes of delinquency also emerged during this time. During the first half of the twentieth century, the federal government became actively involved in the problem of juvenile delinquency. According to Flicker (1990, p. 29):

> The development of the current juvenile justice system, often heralded as a courageous and innovative reform movement, is permeated with confused concepts, grandiose goals, and unrealized dreams. The system has failed in many ways. Yet it really is wonderful in many ways, too—a social institution that cares, a separate court to deal exclusively with juvenile and family problems, a blending of public and voluntary programs, a body of law focused on the best interests of the child, and a correctional authority organized for the rehabilitation of offenders. The system's inability to achieve its noble ideals can be understood best by examining its history.
>
> The most significant fact about the history of juvenile justice is that it evolved simultaneously with the child welfare system. Most of its defects and its virtues derive from that fact.

The juvenile justice and the child welfare systems continue their simultaneous evolution to the present day. Trends and issues in the twentieth century are the dual focus of this chapter.

THE PROGRESSIVE ERA

The first quarter of the twentieth century is often referred to as the Progressive Era or the Age of Reform. The Progressive Era was another major reform era affecting youth and the juvenile justice system in the United States. According to the Progressives, children were not bad, but they were made so by society and the environment in which they grew up. Progressives believed the family was especially influential and that parents were responsible for bringing their children up "properly"—meaning to be obedient and to work hard.

The reformers were optimistic, college-educated people who believed that individualized treatment based on the inmate's history was critical. They were also concerned with their own futures, as noted by Krisberg and Austin (1993, p. 27): "During the Progressive Era, those in positions of economic power feared that the urban masses would destroy the world they had built. . . . From all sectors came demands that new action be taken to preserve social order, and to protect private property and racial privilege."

> ■ The Progressives further developed the medical model established by the Illinois Court Act, viewing crime as a disease that could be treated and cured by social intervention.

The Progressives, fearing that the urban masses might destroy their privileged world, demanded reforms to preserve the social order, to protect the privileged classes and to maintain racial separation. According to Krisberg and Austin (1993, p. 27):

> The times demanded reform, and before the Progressive Era ended, much of the modern welfare state and the criminal justice system were constructed. Out of the turmoil of this age came such innovations as widespread use of the indeterminate sentence, the public defender movement, the beginning of efforts to professionalize the police, extensive use of parole, the rise of mental and I.Q. testing, scientific study of crime. . . .

Krisberg and Austin (1993, p. 31) contend: "The thrust of Progressive Era reforms was to found a more perfect control system to restore social stability while guaranteeing the continued hegemony [predominance or authority] of those with wealth and privilege." For example, in their efforts to control youthful behavior, Illinois in 1901 added noncriminal behavior to its definition of delinquency.

The First Juvenile Courts

Although a formalized juvenile justice system was desperately needed, the reformers gained governmental control and order over a wide range of youthful conduct that previously had been handled informally and would continue to be so handled. That is, the juvenile court received formal sanction for its informal process of dealing with youths.

In an early critique Breckenridge and Abbott, two prominent members of the Progressive Era, evaluated the records of the first juvenile courts in Cook County, Illinois, from 1899 to 1909. They also took in-depth interviews with parents of boys who had come before the court in 1903 and 1904. (A similar approach with parents of girls was limited because there were not enough cases and because girls were typically brought before the court on issues involving immorality.) The stereotype of delinquent youths that had come before the court in its first ten years of existence was that delinquents were children of poor immigrants.

Breckenridge and Abbott's evaluation (1912, pp. 42–43) noted: "children who do wrong can be found in every social stratum, but those who become wards of the court are the children of the poor." Their findings confirmed that the juvenile court constituted a powerful means of social control by the dominant class: "Children in families of great wealth may be guilty of much more serious offenses than are the children of the poor but the offenses of the latter bring them more quickly within the realm of the law" (pp. 42–43).

During the first half of the twentieth century, several interpretations of the cause of delinquency gained prominence. The earliest theories explored biologi-

▮ *Judge Benjamin Lindsay presided in juvenile court in Denver, Colorado, from 1900 to 1927.*

cal and psychological factors. In fact, physical and psychological examinations of children who were brought before the court were standard orders of the juvenile court process. The disposition by judges frequently included individual counseling and psychological therapy.

Slowly, this approach was replaced with social milieu and environmental explanations of the causes of delinquency. Delinquency prevention was attempted by reorganizing the social environment, both physically, through housing renewal, and socio-economically, through social welfare. Significant in this context is a philosophical shift from assigning personal responsibility for delinquency to social responsibility. Consequently, the federal government was increasingly drawn into the process of juvenile delinquency prevention.

Commonwealth v. *Fisher* (1905) defended the juvenile court ideal, reminiscent of the holding of the court in the Crouse case of 1838:

> To save a child from becoming a criminal, or continuing in a career of crime, to end in maturer years in public punishment and disgrace, the legislatures surely may provide for the salvation of such a child, if its parents or guardians be unwilling or unable to do so, by bringing it into one of the courts of the state without any process at all, for the purpose of subjecting it to the state's guardianship and protection.

Rieffel (1983, p. 3) notes that early juvenile courts believed that:

▮ Delinquency is preventable and curable.
▮ Special informal court procedures best serve the juveniles involved, by providing a supportive atmosphere in which to resolve problems.
▮ Since both criminal and non-criminal misbehavior are but symptoms of an unhealthy environment, the distinction between them is of minimal significance.

The juvenile court is the product of the Progressive Era reformers, who believed children were not fully developed humans. Thus, unlike adult criminals, they were incapable of being fully responsible for antisocial and criminal behavior. Further, children were thought to be malleable and more capable of rehabilitation than adults. The reformers clearly believed that criminal court procedures were inappropriate for children and that institutions ought to treat them rather than simply hold them.

Social workers served the juvenile court and held this same philosophy.

■ **In the first juvenile courts social workers were probation officers.**

Social workers' basic responsibility was to the juvenile court and the youths brought before it. They collected facts about youths' misbehavior, including the history of their families, school performance, church attendance, and neighborhood. They also made recommendations for disposition to the judge. And they provided community supervision and casework services to the vast majority of children adjudicated by the juvenile courts.

Social work and the juvenile justice system movement flourished from within, focusing on youths and their families. The movement gradually became more concerned with professionalism in the intake process and correctional supervision. This went unnoticed from without until the early 1960s.

The official position of a probation officer for juveniles was contested in two early landmark court cases.

■ Two cases, *Nicholl v. Koster* (1910) and *Witter v. Cook County Commissioners* (1912), established probation officers as necessary assistants to the juvenile court.

A California decision, *Nicholl v. Koster* (1910), provided identity to the probation officer and outlined the responsibilities of the office. The situation arose when the city of San Francisco refused to pay the salary of an assistant probation officer because the auditor claimed the probation officer's duties were properly the role of the sheriff. The *Nicholl* decision observed that the duties of a probation officer:

> are of a character not before imposed upon sheriffs. The probation officer is required to inquire into the antecedents, character, family history, environment, and cause of delinquency of every child brought before the court, to be present in court and represent the interests of such child upon the hearing as to its being a delinquent, to give the court such information and assistance upon that hearing as the court may require, to take charge of the child before and after the hearing if so ordered, and in some circumstances, he is required to act in a capacity similar to that of a guardian of such child.

In a second case, *Witter v. Cook County Commissioners* (1912), the issue was the firing of the head juvenile court probation officer, who had three years' service and authority to hire and fire. It was concluded, however, that the court had that power. The uniqueness of *Witter* is that the court described the position of a probation officer, as well as the duties and responsibilities that position served for the court:

> The neglected, dependent, or delinquent child ordinarily has no means to employ counsel. It would be impossible for the court to make personal investigation of each case so as to act intelligently, and it is essential that the court act only upon a thorough investigation of facts and a consideration of every circumstance that will enable the court to enter a just decree. Accordingly, it has been deemed wise to provide by statute the duty of the probation officer to make such investigation as may be required by the court, to be present in court in order to represent the interest of the child when the case is heard, to furnish to the court such information and assistance as the judge may require, and to take such charge of any child, before and after trial, as may be directed by the court. The investigation to be made by the probation officer is the investigation of the court through that officer as his assistant, by whom he performs the judicial duties and exercises judicial power. Whenever a minor is a party to a proceeding in any court, it is the duty of that court to see that the minor is properly represented by guardian or next friend. Courts of Chancery have always appointed guardian ad litem for minors who are parties to suits and controlled them by compelling performance of their duties. The probation officer is practically a guardian ad litem for each child brought into the court and has enlarged duties under any statute. Like attorneys, Masters in Chancery, receivers, commissioners, referees, and other similar officers, probation officers are mere assistants of the court in the performance of judicial functions.

▌ The *Nicholl* and *Witter* decisions established the basic dual functions of probation officers: providing legal and social services.

Federal Government Concern and Involvement

The earliest federal interest in delinquency was the 1909 White House Conference on Youth.

▌ A direct result of the White House Conference on Youth was the establishment of the U.S. Children's Bureau in 1912.

According to Olson (1982): "[The Children's Bureau] marked the first genuine commitment of the federal government to assist troubled youth." In addition, in 1912 the first child labor laws were passed by Congress.

Early Efforts at Diversion: The Chicago Boy's Court

Diversion is the official halting of formal juvenile proceedings against a youthful offender, and instead, treating or caring for the youth outside the formal juvenile justice system. In 1914, a diversion from juvenile court was founded in the origin of the Chicago Boy's Court. This court was an extralegal form of probation. Judge Jacob Baude (1984, pp. 9–14), a Chicago municipal court judge, says that the court was founded to process and treat young offenders without labeling them as criminals: "While the facility of probation is available to the court, it is used at a minimum because before one can be admitted to probation he must be found guilty. Having been found guilty, he is stamped with a criminal record and then telling him to go out and make good is more likely to be a handicap than an order."

The Boy's Court version of diversion used four community service agencies: The Holy Name Society (a Catholic church agency), the Chicago Church Foundation (predominantly Protestant), the Jewish Social Service Bureau and the Colored Big Brothers for the diversion program. The court released juveniles to the supervision and authority of these agencies. After a sufficient time to evaluate each youth's behavior, the agencies reported back to the court that the individual had made satisfactory adjustments. The court took the evaluation and, if satisfactory, the judge officially discharged the individual. No record was made.

Highlights of Progressive Era Reform

The philosophical beliefs about juvenile justice policy started to dissolve in the late 1800s. Policy makers and practitioners differed on the causes of delinquency, the most effective treatment for unacceptable behavior and who should be responsible for organizing and regulating juvenile justice. Clearly, the progress of industrialization and social modernization dictated someone or some agency should be responsible but at what governmental level—local, state or federal?

The act establishing the first juvenile court in Chicago stated that the purpose of the court was to regulate the treatment and control of "dependent, neglected, and delinquent children," equating poor children with delinquent children. Nowhere did the act mention punishment. Since then, legislatures have revised certain critical elements of juvenile court practices almost annually. Specialized rules of juvenile procedure were set forth by a growing number of judicial bodies.

Philosophies

- Adolescence was accepted as a unique period of biological and emotional transition from child to adult that required careful control and guidance.
- Misbehavior by middle-class youth was to be expected and controlled by concerned families, but lower-class youth were to be reformed via public efforts.

Treatment

- Children were primarily treated by public efforts that were guided by new public policies and research.

Policies

- State juvenile courts were created to adjudicate youths separately from adults, thereby expanding the *parens patriae* precedent.

▮ The federal government began providing direction for youth services by sponsoring conferences, stimulating discussions, passing child-labor legislation and creating the Children's Bureau as the first national child-welfare agency.

THE NEW DEAL ERA

The aftermath of World War I, the Great Depression and World War II occupied much of the government's attention during the 1920–1960 period as it sought to help citizens cope with the pressures of the times. However, by 1925 all but two states had juvenile court systems and the U.S. Children's Bureau and the National Probation Association issued a recommendation for *A Standard Juvenile Court Act* in 1925.

The Great Depression of the 1930s was economically devastating for American families.

▮ Passage of the Social Security Act in 1935 was the beginning of major federal funding for programs to aid children and families.

As a result, in 1935 the Social Security Act established and supported public welfare agencies that served families and youths. The National Youth Administration provided work relief and employment for young people ages 16 to 25 years. Then, in 1936, the Children's Bureau began administering the first federal subsidy program, providing child welfare grants to states for the care of dependent, neglected, exploited, abused and delinquent youths (Simmons et al., 1981, p. 18).

The federal government passed the Juvenile Court Act in 1938, adopting many features of the original Illinois act. Within ten years every state had enacted special laws for handling juveniles, establishing the juvenile court movement. Schmalleger (1993, p. 514) contends that the juvenile court movement was based upon the following five identifiable philosophical principles:

1. The belief that the state is the "higher or ultimate parent" of all the children within its borders.
2. The belief that children are worth saving, and the concomitant belief in the worth of nonpunitive procedures designed to save the child.
3. The belief that children should be nurtured. While the nurturing process is underway, they should be protected from the stigmatizing impact of formal adjudicatory procedures.
4. The belief that justice, to accomplish the goal of reformation, needs to be individualized; that is, each child is different, and the needs, aspirations, living conditions, and so on, of each child must be known in their individual particulars if the court is to be helpful.
5. The belief that the use of noncriminal procedures are necessary in order to give primary consideration to the needs of the child. The denial of due process

could be justified in the face of constitutional challenges because the court acted not to punish, but to help.

In the 1940s a number of conferences on children and youths were held, but most of the energy for public support and public programs was directed toward the war and reconstructing families after the war.

█ In 1951 Congress passed the Federal Youth Corrections Act and created a Juvenile Delinquency Bureau in the Department of Health, Education and Welfare.

Despite the federal assistance in youth-oriented programs, juvenile delinquency continued to rise. The result was passage of the Federal Youth Corrections Act and assignment of the newly created Juvenile Delinquency Bureau (JDB) under HEW. The positioning of the JDB within the Department of Health, Education and Welfare is significant. It reflects the prevalence of the medical model at this time as well as the emphasis on prevention as a key to dealing with the growing delinquency problem.

Also in the 1950s psychological therapists such as Carl Rogers became influential, introducing psychological counseling as a way to treat juveniles. Group counseling was used in most juvenile institutions during the 1950s.

The Youth Counsel Bureau

In the early 1950s, developments in youthful diversionary programs included New York City's Youth Counsel Bureau. This bureau was established to handle delinquents who were not deemed sufficiently advanced in their misbehavior to be directed to court and adjudicated. Referrals were made directly to the bureau from police, parents, school, court and other agencies. The bureau provided a counseling service and discharged those whose adjustments appeared promising. There was no court, police or any record labeling the youth delinquent (Glaser et al., 1969, pp. 145–155).

Highlights of New Deal Era Reform

During this period the juvenile court was perceived as a means for attaining certain social ends. The court continued this philosophy and delivery of legal protection until after World War II.

A growing belief developed that the court and the juvenile system was carrying its own brand of stigma that was harmful to juveniles under its jurisdiction. That stigma was applied by processes that did not amount to due process of law.

By the late 1940s the gap in the juvenile court operation, between the theoretical assistance given to youths and the actual punitive practices, became more obvious. Legal challenges to the informality and lack of safeguards were brought. Many critics asserted that the court applied legal sanctions and procedures capriciously.

Philosophies

▮ Controlling and improving societal rather than individual conditions might decrease the incidence of youthful crime.

▮ Children were to be gently led back to conformity, not harshly punished.

Treatment

▮ Children were handled primarily by juvenile courts.

Policies

▮ The juvenile court system was adopted by every state in the nation.

▮ The federal government broadened its role with youth by passing legislation to improve family and youth circumstances during the Depression, creating federal juvenile legislation and supporting the protection of children's basic constitutional rights.

THE GREAT SOCIETY ERA

The next 20 years in the United States saw radical changes occurring in society as well as in the juvenile justice system, particularly the juvenile courts.

The 1960s

In 1960 the United States Attorney General reported that delinquency and crime were costing the American public more than $20 million per year. In addition, the poor, lower-class delinquents were now joined by youths with middle- and upper-class backgrounds. Rural youths also entered the statistics of youth delinquency and crime.

Shortly after the release of the Attorney General's report, Congress enacted the Juvenile and Youth Offenses Act of 1961, providing federal monies to delinquency prevention programs and to community social agencies and institutions. The Act ceased in 1967, having spent $47 billion to combat juvenile delinquency but with no decline of juvenile delinquency.

In the 1960s the American family underwent significant changes that directly affected social work and its liaison between the juvenile, the family and the court. Divorces increased, with more children living in one-parent households. Births to unmarried women increased, and more women started to enter the labor force. This affected the family structure and prompted a reorganization of social work philosophy and service.

The Great Society of the 1960s advanced causes for families and children, providing federal monies to attack poverty, crime and delinquency. The 1960s also saw a proliferation of community-based correctional facilities including group homes and halfway houses.

Further, the 1960s saw racial tensions at an all-time high with leaders such as Malcolm X and groups such as the Black Muslims and the Black Panthers demanding "power to the people," referring to the masses. As noted by Krisberg and Austin (1993, p. 44): "The riots of the mid-1960s dramatized the growing gap between people of color in the United States and their more affluent 'benefactors.' "

Civil rights efforts during the 1960s helped broaden concerns for all children, especially those coming under the jurisdiction of juvenile courts. Rieffel (1983, p. 3) suggests:

> Juvenile law, perhaps more than any other aspect of law, reflects the stumbling and confused nature of our society as its values and goals evolve.
>
> So it was in the 1960s, when American society put itself through an extraordinary period of self-examination, that a great many problems were identified in the way we handle juvenile crime.

During this time two policies affecting youths and the juvenile justice system were established—decriminalization and due process.

Decriminalization

Decriminalization refers to legislation to make status offenses, such as smoking and violating curfew, *non*criminal acts.

■ In 1961 California was the first state to separate status offenses from the delinquent category.

■ *During the 1960s Martin Luther King, Jr. led many civil right marches like this one in Albany, GA.*

New York followed California. In 1962 the revised New York Family Court Act created a new classification for noncriminal misconduct—**PINS,** Person in Need of Supervision. Other states (Illinois in 1965 and Colorado in 1967) followed suit, adopting such labels as CINS, CHINS (Children in Need of Supervision), MINS (Minors in Need of Supervision), JINS (Juveniles in Need of Supervision) and FINS (Families in Need of Supervision). These new labels were intended to reduce the stigma of being labeled a delinquent, in effect, decriminalizing a whole broad category of status offenses.

Due Process

Legal challenges in the 1960s, seriously and publicly questioning whether the juvenile justice system—the juvenile court in particular—truly was a benign parent, went as far as the U.S. Supreme Court. Society began to demand that children brought before the juvenile court for matters that had the equivalent of criminal sanctions receive due process protection. The Supreme Court was clearly protecting juveniles from the court's paternalism and from the support systems of the court that held the same paternalistic attitude.

Due process is difficult to define, yet a cherished American ideal. Oran (1985, p. 105) notes: "The *Due Process Clause* of the U.S. **Constitution** requires that no person shall be deprived of life, liberty, or property without *due process of law.* The Supreme Court regularly changes these *due process* requirements, and they vary in detail by situation, but their central core is that a person should always have **notice** and a real chance to present his or her side in a legal dispute and that no law or government procedure should be **arbitrary** or unfair" (italic and bold in original).

Due process and the philosophy of the juvenile court have come into conflict when due process factors emphasize protecting juveniles. The court became concerned about due process in *Haley v. Ohio* (1948). It was specifically concerned about the admissibility of a confession taken from a 15-year-old boy on trial for first-degree murder. It was held that the due process clause barred use of the confession. Due process became a clear concern in *Kent v. United States* (1966).

The Kent *Decision*

Morris Kent, a 16-year-old with a police record, was arrested and charged with housebreaking, robbery and rape. Kent admitted the charges and was held at a juvenile detention facility for almost a week. The judge then transferred jurisdiction of the case to an adult criminal court. Kent received no hearing of any kind.

In reviewing the case, the Supreme Court decreed: "As a condition to a valid waiver order, petitioner [Kent] was entitled to a hearing, including access by his counsel to the social records and probation or similar reports which are presumably considered by the court, and to a statement of the reasons for Juvenile Court's decision." *Kent* was interpreted as setting the minimum due process requirements for transfer from juvenile to criminal court.

■ The procedural requirements for waiver to criminal court were articulated by the Supreme Court in *Kent v. United States.*

Kent established that juveniles have the right to a hearing on the question of transfer and the right to be represented by legal counsel. Upon request, a juvenile's legal counsel must be given access to the social record that the court has compiled on the juvenile. If jurisdiction is waived, the juvenile must be given a statement of the reasons for the waiver.

According to Arnold and Brungardt (1983, p. 24): "The impact of the *Kent* decision went far beyond the relatively narrow legal issue—conditions of waiver to criminal court—that it addressed. It served as a warning to the juvenile justice system that the juvenile court's traditional laxity toward procedural and evidentiary standards would no longer be tolerated by the highest court in the land."

An appendix to the *Kent* decision contained the following criteria established by the Supreme Court for states to use in deciding on transfer of juveniles to adult criminal court for trial. The court was to consider:

1. The seriousness of the alleged offense and whether the protection of the community requires waiver.
2. Whether the alleged offense was committed in an aggressive, violent, premeditated or willful manner.
3. Whether the alleged offense was against persons or against property, greater weight being given to offenses against persons, especially if personal injury resulted.
4. The prospective merit of the complaint.
5. The desirability of trial and disposition of the offense in one court when the juvenile's associates in the alleged offense are adults who will be charged with crimes in the adult court.
6. The sophistication and maturity of the juvenile as determined by consideration of his or her home, environmental situation, emotional attitude and pattern of living.
7. The record and previous history of the juvenile.

The Gault Decision

The juvenile court and its process became a national issue in the *Gault* decision (1967). This case was instrumental in changing almost completely the adjudication process into a deliberately adversarial process. *In re Gault* concerned a 15-year-old boy, already on probation, who was committed in Arizona as a delinquent after being apprehended upon a complaint of lewd remarks on the telephone.

Gault was taken into custody at 10:00 A.M., for allegedly making obscene phone calls to a neighbor. No steps were taken to notify his parents. When Mrs. Gault arrived home about 6:00 P.M., she found her son missing. She went to the detention home and was told why he was there and that a hearing would be held the next day. At the hearing, a petition was filed with the juvenile court making general allegations of "delinquency." No particular facts were stated.

The hearing was held June 9 in the judge's chambers. The complaining neighbor was not present, no one was sworn in, no attorney was present and no record of the proceedings was made. Gault admitted to making part of the phone call in question. At the end of the hearing, the judge said he would consider the matter.

▌ The *Gault* decision requires that the due process clause of the Fourteenth Amendment apply to proceedings in state juvenile courts, including the right of notice, the right to counsel, the right against self-incrimination and the right to confront witnesses.

Gault was held in the detention home for two more days and then released. Another hearing was held on his delinquency on June 15. This hearing also had no complaining witnesses, sworn testimony, counsel or transcript. The probation officer's referral report listed the charge as lewd phone calls and was filed with the court. The report was not made available to Gault or his parents. At the end of the hearing the judge committed him to the State Industrial School until age 21. Gault received a six-year sentence for an action for which an adult would receive a fine or a two-month imprisonment.

The United States Supreme Court overruled Gault's conviction on the grounds that:

▌ Neither Gault nor his parents had notice of the specific charges against him.

▌ No counsel was offered or provided to Gault.

▌ No witnesses were present, thus denying Gault the right of cross-examination and confrontation.

▌ No warning of Gault's privilege against self-incrimination was given to him; thus no waiver of that right took place.

In delivering the Court's opinion, Justice Fortas stated:

Where a person, infant or adult, can be seized by the State, charged and convicted for violating a state criminal law, and then ordered by the State to be confined for six years, I think the Constitution requires that he be tried in accordance with the guarantees of all provisions of the Bill of Rights made applicable to the States by the Fourteenth Amendment. Undoubtedly this would be true of an adult defendant, and it would be a plain denial of equal protection of the laws—an invidious discrimination—to hold that others subject to heavier punishments could, because they are children, be denied these same constitutional safeguards. I consequently agree with the Court that the Arizona law as applied here denied to the parents and their son the right of notice, right to counsel, right against self-incrimination, and right to confront the witnesses against young Gault. Appellants are entitled to these rights, not because "fairness, impartiality and orderliness—in short the essentials of due process"—require them and not because they are "the procedural rules which have been fashioned from the generality of due process," but because they are specifically and unequivocally granted by provisions of the Fifth and Sixth Amendments which the Fourteenth Amendment makes applicable to the States.

Due process, in *Gault,* was held to embrace adequate written notice; advice as to the right to counsel, either retained or appointed; confrontation and cross-examination. The Court refrained from deciding whether a state must provide appellate review in juvenile cases or a transcript or recording of the findings.

With the emphasis on constitutional requirements, the Supreme Court set standards for the handling of juveniles. Thus, the *Gault* decision provided the standard of due process for juveniles.

Effects of Kent *and* Gault

Since *Kent* and *Gault,* police and others have been more cautious in referrals. A California appellate court was asked to review the decision of a juvenile court (*In re Daniel,* 1969). The court ruled that a 16-year-old boy who admitted selling marijuana was in danger of leading an idle, wayward, "dissolute life." Although the decision was reversed for lack of sufficient evidence, the appellate court expressed no concern that the juvenile was taken into custody with neither warrant nor probable cause and was referred to the court under "waywardness," which needs less proof to establish than a criminal act. Since there was some indication of criminal conduct in this case, the alleged criminal conduct furnished the basis for referral.

The juvenile was not adjudicated a ward of the state on the petition that he violated a criminal act, but rather was referred because he was in danger of leading an idle, dissolute, lewd or immoral life, supported by some evidence— however slight—that he had engaged in criminal conduct. This suggests that the police agency making the referral, in absence of probable cause, relied on "protective jurisdiction," which permits a youth to be taken into custody for his own safety and welfare, rather than on the stringent rules of due process and probable cause. In this case law enforcement officers' attempts to make a referral based on a youth's "dissolute life" were not successful. Nonetheless, police agencies may use this approach to referral because it requires less proof than does establishing that a youth has committed a criminal act.

The President's Commission

The President's Commission on Law Enforcement and Administration of Justice, in 1967, gave evidence of "disenchantment, with the experience of the juvenile court" (President's Commission, 1967; p. 17). It criticized lack of due process, law enforcement's poor relationship to youth and the handling of juveniles and the corrections process of confining status offenders and children "in need" to locked facilities.

According to the President's Commission (1967, p. 69): "Institutions tend to isolate offenders from society, both physically and psychologically, cutting them off from schools, jobs, families, and other supportive influences and increasing the probability that the label of criminal will be indelibly impressed upon them." The Commission, therefore, recommended community-based corrections should be considered seriously for juvenile offenders.

▪ Isolating offenders from their normal social environment may encourage
   the development of a delinquent orientation and, thus, further
   delinquent behavior.

The issues raised by the President's Commission indicated a need to integrate
rather than isolate offenders, to reduce rather than simplify the delinquent label.
The resulting community-based correctional programs, such as probation,
foster care and group homes, represent attempts to respond to these issues by
normalizing social contacts, reducing the stigma attached to being institutionalized and providing opportunities for jobs and schooling.

This Commission also strongly endorsed diversion for status offenders and
minor delinquent offenses. In addition, the Commission recommended establishing a national youth service bureau and local or community youth service
bureaus to assist the police and the courts in diverting youth from the juvenile
justice system.

These community-centered referral programs began in 1967 with the
establisment of the federal Youth Service Bureau. This Bureau was to act as a
central coordinator of community services for youths and to provide services
lacking in the community or neighborhoods, particularily for less seriously
delinquent juveniles and those in need of public service.

▪ In 1967 the President's Commission established a Youth Service Bureau
   to coordinate community-centered referral programs.

The target population for this Bureau was both delinquent and nondelinquent
juveniles (President's Commission, 1967, p. 83).

Local youth service bureaus were to divert from the juvenile justice system
minor offenders whose behavior was rooted in ... is at home, in school or
in the community. They were also to deter from ... linquent behavior children
who had not committed criminal acts, but who had similar problems that might
lead them to do so if they did not receive help. While a broad range of services
and certain mandatory functions were suggested for youth service bureaus,
individually tailored work with troublemaking youngsters was proposed as a
primary goal.

As envisioned by the Commission, youth service bureaus were not part of the
juvenile justice system. The bureaus would provide necessary services to youths
as a substitute for putting them through the juvenile justice process; that is to
say, they would avoid the stigma of formal court involvement.

▪ The three main functions of local youth service bureaus were defined as
   diversion, resource development and system modification.

Diversion included accepting referrals from the police, the courts, schools,
parents and other sources, and working with the youth in a voluntary,
noncoercive manner through neighborhood-oriented services. *Resource develop-*

ment included offering leadership at the neighborhood level to provide and develop a variety of youth assistance programs, as well as seeking funding for new projects. *System modification* included seeking to change or modify those attitudes and practices that discriminate against troublesome youths and, thereby, contribute to their antisocial behavior in schools and community institutions (National Council on Crime and Delinquency, 1971, pp. 3–4).

The Youth Service Bureau Organizational Chart, shown in Figure 2–1, outlines the functions and referral targets for youth service bureau operations.

To meet the unique needs and deal with the unique problems of each community, the organization and programming of local youth service bureaus were to remain flexible. A high degree of adaptability was seen as helpful to bureau staffs in obtaining favorable public support, counteracting the opposition of powerful community groups and securing funding support from the community. Ideally, as Figure 2–1 indicates, a youth service bureau would have a wide range of community service agencies to which it could make referrals. In reality, some of these agencies might not exist in a youth service bureau area. In such cases, the bureau would provide the necessary services itself.

Bureaus developed throughout the country in response to different needs of communities, existing youth programs, types of sponsorships and sources of funding. When the juvenile courts turn cases over to a bureau, the court involvement ceases, and the bureau accepts responsibility for diversion. The bureau emphasizes to the youths and their parents that no label or stigma is attached to receiving assistance from a youth service bureau. Further, no type of juvenile record is kept on those who accept services.

Many youth service bureaus that were established when the concept initially became popular did not survive the federal funding cuts during the Carter and Reagan administrations. Most eliminated bureaus were relatively new agencies that had not yet established themselves within the funding structure. Evaluations of the effectiveness of the bureaus indicated that it was impossible to prove they had diverted any significant number of youths from juvenile court involvement. Without such proof, the bureaus could not justify their existence as delinquency prevention or reduction agencies.

Those bureaus that have endured have turned their focus to providing employment activities for juveniles who are employable, particularly during summer months. They have also concentrated on providing health, recreation or educational referrals or services.

The Task Force on Juvenile Delinquency and Youth Crime of the President's Commission on Law Enforcement and Administration of Justice (1967) advocated *prevention* as the most promising and important method of dealing with crime.

■ In the late 1960s a new approach for dealing with delinquency emerged: the *prevention* of crime before youths engage in delinquent acts.

In 1968 the historic Delinquency Prevention and Control Act was passed. One provision of this Act was to reform the juvenile justice system nationally.

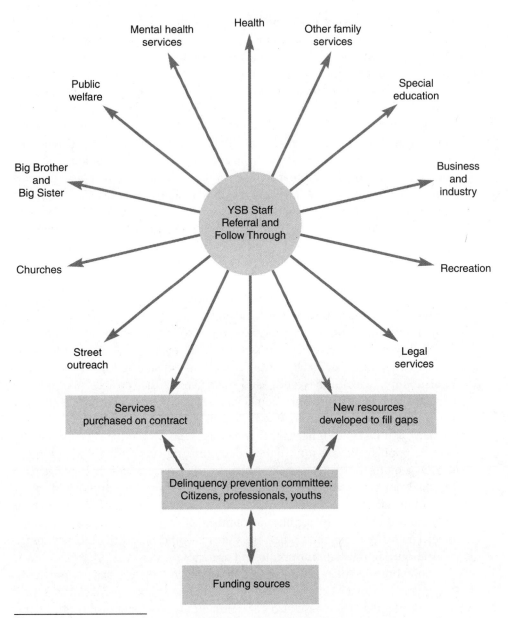

▮ FIGURE 2–1   Youth Service Bureau Organizational Chart

Linking Youth to Services: Noncoercive; operates from neighborhood centers; open door policy; involves child, family, and neighborhood in identifying and solving problems; coordinates services, refers and follows through as advocate of child.

Develops New Resources: Purchases urgently needed services not otherwise available; promotes new or expanded services and facilities to fill gaps.

Modifies Systems: Constructively intervenes in delinquency-breeding attitudes and practices.

SOURCE: National Council on Crime and Delinquency, *The Youth Service Bureau* (Paramus, NJ: NCCD Center, 1971) p. 9. Reprinted by permission.

Highlights of Great Society Era Reform

The combination of serious, stigmatizing results achieved without due process safeguards led the U.S. Supreme Court in the 1960s to impose new requirements in determining when a juvenile could be made a ward of the state.

Since its inception, the juvenile court was guided by a welfare concept. When the U.S. Supreme Court took issue with its procedures, juvenile court moved from the simple family atmosphere to a more adversarial system. The treatment of juveniles changed to a criminal approach, which dispenses punishment and places youths in locked facilities.

Philosophies

- Dissent arose among professional child-welfare workers and policymakers about the causes of and treatment for juvenile delinquency.
- Consensus arose among the public and policymakers that the traditional agents of control—family, police, schools and courts—could not curb the rise of delinquency.

Treatment

- The juvenile court system was revised to include due process, deinstitutionalization, decriminalization and diversion programs.
- Community-based therapy, rather than institutionalization, became the preferred method of treatment.

Policies

- The federal executive branch expressed its concern about crime and delinquency by appointing the President's Commission on Law Enforcement and Administration of Justice.
- Large-scale federal financial and programmatic grants-in-aid were made available to states and localities for delinquency prevention and control programs.
- A federal agency was created to administer juvenile justice and delinquency prevention grants and to coordinate the federal youth-serving effort—the Office of Juvenile Justice and Delinquency Prevention (OJJDP).

While the Supreme Court questioned the juvenile court on due process procedures, the juvenile court also came under severe criticism because its philosophy of helping all juveniles rather than punishing delinquents led to indiscriminate mixing of neglected or abused children, status offenders and violent offenders. Public policy has since been developed to separate neglected and abused juveniles from the delinquents, but status offenders have continued to be in contact with violent criminal delinquents.

THE 1970s
■▬▬▬▬

The 1970s brought further challenges to the juvenile justice system. The effectiveness of correctional treatment of juveniles had been called into question. A growing body of empirical evidence cast serious doubt that social casework, the linchpin of correctional treatment along with probation and parole, helped rehabilitate youths (Hellum, 1979).

Rehabilitation was the major premise on which the creation of the juvenile justice system rested. Research found that correctional "treatment," especially in institutions, was often unnecessarily punitive and sometimes sadistic. The modern reformers became appalled that noncriminal youths and status offenders could easily find their way into the same institutions as seriously delinquent youths. This spawned a rapid growth in community-based alternatives to institutionalization, as well as national interest in juvenile justice.

The White House Conference on Youth

National interest in the problems of youth was again expressed in 1970 at the White House Conference on Youth. This conference warned: "Our families and children are in deep trouble. A society that neglects its children and fears its youth cannot care about its future" (White House Conference on Youth, 1972, p. 346). The message from the Conference was interpreted as a need for special federal assistance to identify the needs of families.

■ The major impact of the White House Conference on Youth was that it hit hard at the foundation of our system for handling youths including unnecessarily punitive institutions.

Beginning in 1971 a series of federal cases tried to specify minimum environmental conditions for juvenile institutions.

In 1971 the Institute of Judicial Administration began planning a juvenile justice standards project. The American Bar Association became a cosponsor of the project in 1973, creating the Institute of Judicial Administration/American Bar Association Joint Commission on Juvenile Justice Standards.

By 1972 there was a cooperative effort among federal administrations to focus on programs for *preventing* delinquency and *rehabilitating* delinquents outside the traditional criminal justice system. In 1974 Congress created the Office of Juvenile Justice and Delinquency Prevention (OJJDP) under the Department of Justice. The Congress also passed the Juvenile Justice and Delinquency Prevention (JJDP) Act. The provisions of the 1974 Act are too extensive to list, but the thrust of the Act was directed towards alternatives to incarcerating status offenders (U.S. Code para. 5633). The intent was "to provide a unified rational program to deal with juvenile delinquency prevention and control within the context of the total law."

■ The Office of Juvenile and Delinquency Prevention (OJJDP) was
assigned under the Department of Justice rather than the Department of
Health, Education and Welfare (HEW).

Consequently, the prevention philosophy of HEW was replaced with more
emphasis on the legal process.

The landmark JJDP Act, passed by Congress in 1974, required that in order
for states to receive federal funds, incarceration and even temporary detention
be used for young people only as a last resort.

■ The Juvenile Justice and Delinquency Prevention Act of 1974 had two
key goals: deinstitutionalization of status offenders and
separation/removal of juveniles from adult facilities. The Act made funds
available to states who removed status offenders from prisons and jails
and who created alternative voluntary services to which status offenders
could be diverted.

The Act was amended in 1976, 1977 and 1980. According to Decker (1984,
pp. 37–38), amendments to the JJDP Act in 1977:

1. Broadened the functions of State Planning Agency Advisory groups to include
   the private business sector;
2. Involved alternate youth programs and people with special experience in
   school violence and vandalism programs, including social workers;
3. Gave states the opportunity to participate in grant programs for deinstitutionalization;
4. Required monitoring of all states with state juvenile detention and correctional
   facilities to determine their suitability for status offenders.

Clearly, deinstitutionalization was one of the Four Ds described by sociologist
LaMar Empey (1978) as characterizing the second transformation of the
juvenile justice system, the first transformation having begun with the 1899
Illinois Juvenile Court Act.

■ The "Four Ds" of juvenile justice are deinstitutionalization, diversion,
due process and decriminalization.

Deinstitutionalization

Deinstitutionalization refers to providing programs for juveniles in a
community-based setting rather than in an institution.

In the early 1970s Massachusetts undertook what some considered a
"radical" experiment in deinstitutionalization. Jerome Miller, state commissioner
of youth services and head of the Massachusetts Department of Youth Services,
closed every juvenile institution in the state. As noted by Schmalleger (1993,
p. 535):

Deinstitutionalization was accomplished by placing juveniles in foster care, group homes, mental health facilities, and other programs. Many were simply sent home. The problems caused by hard-core offenders among the released juveniles, however, soon convinced authorities that complete deinstitutionalization was not a workable solution to the problem of delinquency. The Massachusetts experiment ended as quickly as it began.

Although total deinstitutionalization ended in Massachusetts, hundreds of juveniles were successfully moved into community-based programs. The successes of this experimentation in deinstitutionalization by Massachusetts, as well as the availability of federal funds for such programs, were encouraging to those wanting to reform the juvenile justice system.

Diversion

The juvenile due process requirements from *Kent* and *Gault,* combined with rising costs of courts and correctional facilities, resulted in wider use of community-based alternatives to treat youths before and after adjudication. The trend was to make greater use of diversion programs in the 1970s. Young offenders were placed in remedial education, drug abuse programs, foster homes and in out-patient health care and counseling facilities.

As noted by Blomberg (1980, p. 572): "A major conceptual rationale underlying the diversion concept was that reducing offender insertion into the justice system would avoid the danger assumed to be associated with criminal stigmatization and criminal association, thereby reducing the likelihood of subsequent crime by the offender." In other words, the theoretical premises behind diversion lay with labeling theory and differential association theory. Many studies have focused on the problems produced by labeling and the resulting stigma from involvement with juvenile justice.

Lemert (1981, p. 37) indicated that diversion arose in large part as a corrective for the perceived evils and shortcomings in juvenile justice. Most labeling theorists claim that once labeled, the stigma attached to delinquency leads to further delinquency; difficulty in changing delinquent behavior; and unfavorable school, vocational and employment opportunities.

Some research indicates that labeling does *not* always have negative consequences. Police coercion, involving telling juveniles they would be committed to a juvenile authority if they continued to get into trouble, may deter misbehavior and deter future delinquency. Labeling, stigma and contact with the juvenile justice system can have both negative and positive effects.

Net Widening

Diversion does not necessarily mean less state social control over juveniles. It has had the negative consequences of transferring state power from juvenile courts to police and probation departments. What has actually happened is that more diversion "to" other programs or agencies has occurred than true diversion "away" from the system. This is called **net widening.**

■ Many youngsters who earlier would have been simply released were instead referred to the new system of diversionary programs that had sprung up. This process is referred to as *net widening*.

In net widening, police have set up diversion projects in their own departments, hired their own personnel and programmed cases to fit law enforcement needs. This development is opposed to diversion's original purpose, to lessen state power in the control of juveniles.

The Dallas Youth Services Program

The Dallas Police Department provides an example of net widening. The Youth Services Program (YSP) is a unit of the Dallas Police Department's Youth Section. Manned by both police officers and civilian counselors, the YSP has 14 counselors supervised by a counseling psychologist. The YSP, which is voluntary, has two major goals according to Collingwood et al. (1980, p. 94): "To divert juveniles from the juvenile justice system and to reduce recidivism." It serves youths taken into custody from ages 10 to 16, who are either felons or misdemeanants and who may be first offenders or repeat offenders.

The YSP has two subprograms: a three-hour lecture awareness program for first offenders and a counseling unit for more serious offenders. Together these provide two more options for the police investigating officer, in addition to the former choices of simply sending youths home or referring them to the juvenile court. It is the investigating officer who decides if a particular youth could benefit from a referral to the YSP.

The counseling unit provides a form of correctional treatment by enhancing physical fitness, interpersonal skills and study skills. It uses a three-stage, six-month process:

1. Intake and counselor assessment.
2. Direct treatment, providing 16 hours of skill training over four weeks (parents receive training in parenting skills during this same period).
3. Follow-up with homework assignments or behavioral contracts.

The program incorporates several treatment strategies in its eclectic approach. Social network development (control theory) is evident, as is the effort to provide constructive activities and recreation. Finally, use of behavioral contracts is derived from learning theory and behavior modification.

The YSP makes modest claims of effectiveness at this point, since controlled comparisons over significant time spans have not been completed.

■ The successes of the Youth Services Program have been traced to three factors: (1) the police-based nature of the program, (2) the use of counseling in a law enforcement setting and (3) the skills approach to training and treatment.

"The employment and utilization of counselors within a law enforcement setting," claim Collingwood et al. (1980, p. 94), "has brought an emphasis upon helping youth instead of upon just the legal processing of a juvenile."

Diversion has been advocated as reducing the court's caseload, but more importantly, children seem to respond more readily to the treatment provided by community-based services than to the correctional services available through the court.

Critics of Diversion

Diversion is not without its critics. Although diversion programs have greatly expanded during the past decade, the number of young people committed to institutions has not decreased appreciably. It appears to many professionals and scholars that the increase in diversion programs is net widening and that children who in the past would not have been formally handled are so handled now. As noted by Lemert (1981, p. 41):

> That many youths who are diverted are not free from the heavy hand of the juvenile justice system is highlighted when diversion is made conditional. A frequent condition for referral to a diversion program is the juvenile's admission of an offense. In reality, this is an outgrowth of police discretion, in which contrition is a prerequisite for leniency from the police. Parents or even siblings may be required to participate in counseling, in order for the youth to be diverted. If juveniles perform well in the program, no further legal action is taken, but if they are uncooperative, they may be returned to court for further processing. Some of the methods used in police diversion programs, such as weekly reporting by juveniles and officer "tracing" of youth's activities, are reminiscent of old-style informal police probation, now grown large and strengthened by official sanction.

The diversion apparatus has in many cases become a prevention apparatus, receiving the bulk of referrals from parents, schools and welfare agencies, as opposed to the police, intake or the court. The referrals are, by and large, younger juveniles with minor offenses and without prior records, girls and status offenders.

Not only does diversion widen the net, but it adds to the dangers of violating rights of due process and fundamental fairness. Critics emphasize that due process and fairness are violated because referrals usually occur *before* adjudication. Thus, it is often never established that referred youngsters are actually guilty of any offense, which might make them properly the subjects of conditional placement. Diversion violates a fundamental principle that youths who have not done anything illegal have a right to be left alone.

Critics of diversion suggest that net widening has created a gap between rhetoric and what is actually happening. Instead of weakening state control, the correctional structure has become stronger. The nets of control are wider (Austin and Krisberg, 1981), and confinement is not reduced (Scull, 1984).

For nearly 20 years, juvenile diversion and its labeling-theory orientation have received attention. The philosophical, legal, theoretical and practical strengths and weaknesses of diversion have been debated. Little research has addressed the effectiveness of limiting official intervention in the lives of diverted and nondiverted youth. However, one fact exists:

> ■ Diverted youths tend to remain in the justice system longer than
> nondiverted youths.

Problems with Diversion

Diversion is a discretionary decision that often is not part of any record. Because diversion is personalized, treatment may be inconsistent from one youth to the next. Diversion is problematic in that it may reflect individual class or social prejudices. It removes juveniles from any penalties with no exposure to the judicial process of the juvenile court. Further, informal diversion is usually unsystematic.

Due Process

As in the 1960s, the 1970s saw juveniles' rights being addressed and the juvenile court becoming more like the adult court in several important ways. The juvenile rights addressed were standard of proof, right to jury trial and double jeopardy. Whether the court was dealing with status offenders, youths who had committed violent crimes or protecting abused or neglected children, it no longer had free reign. The juvenile court must grant many aspects of due process to the youths who come under its jurisdiction.

The Standard of Proof in Juvenile Proceedings

In re Winship (1970) concerned a 12-year-old New York boy charged with having taken $112 from a woman's purse. He was adjudicated a delinquent based on a *preponderance of the evidence* submitted at the hearing. He was committed to a training school for 18 months with extension possible until he was 18-years old, a total possible sentence of six years. The question raised was whether New York's statute allowing juvenile cases to be decided on the basis of a preponderance of evidence was constitutional.

Gault had already established that due process required fair treatment for juveniles. The Court held that: "The Due Process Clause protects the accused against conviction except upon *proof beyond a reasonable doubt* of every fact necessary to constitute the crime with which he is charged" (italics in original). New York argued that its juvenile proceedings were civil, not criminal; but the Supreme Court said the standard of proof beyond a reasonable doubt not only played a vital role in the criminal justice system, it also ensured a greater degree of safety for the presumption of innocence of those accused of crimes.

> ■ *In re Winship* established proof beyond a reasonable doubt as the
> standard for juvenile adjudication proceedings, eliminating lesser
> standards such as a preponderance of the evidence, clear and convincing
> proof and reasonable proof.

In re Winship (1971) Chief Justice Warren Burger wrote in his dissenting opinion:

> What the juvenile court systems need is less not more of the trappings of legal procedure and judicial formalism; the juvenile court system requires breathing room and flexibility in order to survive the repeated assaults on this court. The real problem was not the deprivation of constitutional rights but inadequate juvenile court staffs and facilities.

The Right to a Jury Trial

The move toward expanding juvenile's civil rights was slowed by the ruling in *McKeiver* v. *Pennsylvania* (1971) where the Court ruled that juveniles do not have the right to a jury trial. This case involved a 16-year-old Pennsylvania boy charged with robbery, larceny and receiving stolen goods, all felonies in Pennsylvania. He was adjudicated a delinquent. The question for the Court to decide was whether the due process clause of the Fourteenth Amendment guaranteeing the right to a jury trial applied to adjudication of a juvenile court case.

In *McKeiver,* the Court held that *Gault* and *Winship* demonstrated concern for the fundamental principle of fairness in justice, with the fact-finding elements of due process necessary and present for this fairness. The Court emphasized in *McKeiver:* "one cannot say that in our legal system the jury is a necessary component of accurate fact finding. There is much to be said for it, to be sure, but we have been content to pursue other ways for determining facts."

The Court realized the juvenile court had not been successful. But it also concluded that the juvenile court should not become fully adversarial like the criminal court. Requiring a jury might put an end to "what has been the idealistic prospect of an intimate informal protective proceeding." Installing a jury in juvenile proceedings would not enhance fact finding, nor would it remedy the defects of the system. Requiring jury trials for juvenile courts could also result in delays, as well as in the possibility of public trials.

■ *McKeiver* established that a jury trial is not a required part of due process in the adjudication of a youth as a delinquent by a juvenile court.

This decision, in effect, took issue with making juvenile proceedings a full adversary system. The Court left open the possibility for state courts to experiment, inviting them to try trial by jury in juvenile proceedings, but refusing to require them to do so.

Double Jeopardy

Double jeopardy was the issue in *Breed* v. *Jones* (1975). The Supreme Court ruled, that defendants may not be tried twice for the same offense. Breed was 17 when apprehended for committing acts with a deadly weapon. He was adjudicated in a California juvenile court, which found the allegation true. A dispositional hearing determined there were not sufficient facilities "amenable to the care, treatment and training programs available through the facilities of the juvenile court," as required by the statute. Breed was transferred to the criminal court where he was again found guilty. Breed argued that he had been tried twice for the same offense, which constituted double jeopardy. The Supreme Court agreed and reversed the conviction.

■ A juvenile cannot be adjudicated in juvenile court and then tried for the same offense in an adult criminal court (*Breed* v. *Jones*, 1975).

Beginning in 1976, the majority of states enacted legislation making it easier to transfer youth to adult courts. The number of incarcerated youths increased as did the proportion of minority youth in public correctional facilities.

Decriminalization

In 1977, the American Bar Association Joint Commission on Juvenile Justice Standards voted to eliminate uniquely juvenile offenses, that is, status offenses such as cigarette smoking or consumption of alcohol.

■ According to the American Bar Association, juvenile delinquency liability should include only such conduct as would be designated a crime if committed by an adult.

The referral of status offenses to juvenile court has been viewed by many as an ineffective waste of valuable court resources. These critics believe resources could best be used for the more serious recidivist delinquents the court has to deal with.

The Issue of Right to Treatment

Also in the 1970s two conflicting types of cases emerged: one type attempted to establish a "right to treatment," the other to establish the "least restrictive alternative." *Martarella* v. *Kelley* (1972) established that if juveniles who are judged to be "in need of supervision" are not provided with adequate treatment, they are deprived of their rights under the Eighth and Fourteenth Amendments. *Morales* v. *Turman* (1973) ruled that juveniles in a Texas training school have a statutory right to treatment. And, in *Nelson* v. *Heyne* (1974), the Seventh U.S. Court of Appeals also confirmed juveniles' right to treatment:

> When a state assumes the place of a juvenile's parents, it assumes as well the parental duties, and its treatment of its juveniles should, so far as can be reasonably required, be what proper parental care would provide. . . . Without a program of individual treatment, the result may be that the juvenile will not be rehabilitated, but warehoused.

The U.S. Supreme Court has not yet declared that juveniles have a right to treatment. And, as noted by Senna and Siegel (1993, p. 690):

The American Bar Association supports decriminalizing status offenses such as smoking cigarettes.

In recent years, however, progress in the movement for a legal right to treatment seems to have been curtailed. . . .

The future of the right to treatment for juveniles remains uncertain. Minimum standards of care and treatment have been handled on a case-by-case basis, but some courts have limited the constitutional protections regarding the right to treatment. In light of the current hard-line approach to juvenile crime, the courts probably will not be persuaded to expand this constitutional theory further.

Development of Standards for Juvenile Justice

In 1977 the tentative draft of the Institute of Judicial Administration/American Bar Association *Juvenile Justice Standards* was published in 23 volumes. In 1978 Washington State began extensive legislative revision of their juvenile justice system based, in part, on these standards. It was found that following implementation of the new legislation (Rieffel, 1983, pp. 36–37, italics in original):

▌ Sentences were considerably more uniform, more consistent and more proportionate to the seriousness of the offense and the prior criminal record of the youth.

▌ While the overall level of severity of sanctions was reduced during the first two years, there was an increase in the certainty that a sanction of some kind would be imposed.

▌ There was a marked increase in the use of incarcerative sanctions for the violent and serious/chronic offender, but nonviolent offenders and chronic minor property offenders were less likely to be incarcerated and more apt to be required to pay restitution, do community service, or be on probation.

▌ Compliance with the sentencing guidelines was extremely high; nevertheless, differential handling of minorities and females still existed.

▌ There was a better record of holding juveniles accountable for their offenses.

▌ While the new legislation completely eliminated the referral of *status offenses,* it did not eliminate the referral of *status offenders.* Runaways were more likely to be contacted for delinquent acts, for example.

▌ Recontacts by law enforcement officials showed an increase, although whether as a result of increased commission of offenses, or as a result of increased law enforcement confidence in the system remains unclear.

From 1979 to 1980, 20 volumes of these standards received American Bar Association approval. The standards related to the following: adjudication; appeals and collateral review; architecture of facilities; corrections administration; counsel for private parties; court organization and administration; dispositional procedures; dispositions; interim status; the release, control, and detention of accused juvenile offenders between arrest and disposition; juvenile delinquency and sanctions; juvenile probation function; intake and predisposition investigative services; juvenile records and information systems; monitoring; planning for juvenile justice; police handling of juvenile problems; pretrial court proceedings; prosecution; rights of minors; transfer between courts; youth service agencies. A summary and analysis of the project and the standards was released in 1990, reviewing the progress of the application of the standards (Flicker, 1990).

In the 1970s the rising fear of youth crime and rebelliousness coincided with a growing disillusionment with the effectiveness of the juvenile justice system. The result has been a much harsher attitude toward youth crime and a call to "get tough" with youthful lawbreakers in the 1980s and 1990s. At the same time, during the 1970s the medical model of viewing unlawful behavior began to shift to what is often called a **justice model.** The issues involved and how they are viewed in each model are summarized in Table 2–1.

THE 1980s

By the 1980s the "best interests" of society gained ascendency over those of youth. In the 1980s the OJJDP became increasingly conservative. Emphasis shifted to dealing with hard-core chronic offenders. Also in the 1980s state and

TABLE 2-1   **Comparison of the Medical and Justice Models**

Issue	Medical Model 1930–1974	Justice Model 1974–Present
Cause of crime	Disease of society or of the individual.	Form of rational adaptation to societal conditions.
Image of offender	Sick; product of socio-economic or psychological forces beyond control.	Capable of exercising free will; of surviving without resorting to crime.
Object of correction	To cure offender and society; to return both to health; rehabilitation.	Humanely control offender under terms of sentence; offer voluntary treatment.
Agency/institution responsibility	Change offender; reintegrate back into society.	Legally and humanely control offender; adequate care and custody; voluntary treatment; protect society.
Role of treatment and punishment	Voluntary or involuntary treatment as means to change offender. Treatment is mandatory; punishment used to coerce treatment; punishment and treatment [are] viewed as same thing.	Voluntary treatment only; punishment and treatment not the same thing. Punishment is for society's good, treatment is for offender's good.
Object of legal sanctions (sentence)	Determine conditions that are most conducive to rehabilitation of offender.	Determine conditions that are just re: wrong done, best protect society and deter offender from future crime.
Type of sentence	Indeterminant, flexible; adjust to offender changes.	Fixed sentence (less good time).
Who determines release time?	"Experts" (parole board for adults, institutional staff for juveniles).	Conditions of sentence as interpreted by Presumptive Release Date (PRD) formula.

SOURCE: D. F. Pace, *Community Relations Concepts*, 3rd ed. Copyright © 1993, p. 127. Copperhouse, Placerville, Calif. Reprinted by permission.

federal concerns tended to center on problems created by procedural informality and the broad discretion of the juvenile court. The adversary system of legal process took over the sedate environment and process of the "family" court that was directed to consider the "best" interest of the child's health, safety and welfare. The courts returned to a focus on what was right according to the law.

According to Krisberg (1990) the conservative swing added two more "Ds" to our juvenile justice system: **deterrence** and **just deserts.** *Deterrence* views punishment as a means to prevent future lawbreaking. It does so in several ways, the most obvious being locking someone up so they can do no further harm to society. Such incarceration may result in further deterrence by

(1) serving as a lesson to the incarcerated person that "crime does not pay" and (2) providing this same message to the law-abiding public.

Deserts, or *just deserts* as it is often called, views punishment as a kind of justified revenge—the offending individual gets what is coming. This is the concept of *lex talions,* or an "eye for an eye" expressed in the Code of Hammurabi centuries ago.

In 1982, 214 long-term public institutions in the United States were designated either "strict" or "medium" custody training schools. This number included some original training schools, as well as smaller, high-security institutions built to either replace or augment them.

■ Many training schools and high-security institutions were built in rural areas or close to small rural towns so the inmates could be trained in agriculture.

Most of the schools involved agricultural training, which was thought to be reformative. This training focus by necessity located the schools in rural areas. An unanticipated outcome of this location policy was removal of the corrections problem from community awareness. Later lack of awareness proved to be a stumbling block when the emphasis shifted to addressing the problems of corrections within the community setting, as discussed in Chapter 12.

Three States' Innovations for the Juvenile Justice System

The efforts of Massachusetts, Utah and Georgia to improve their juvenile justice system began in the 1960s and 1970s and produced some impressive results by the 1980s. Massachusetts embarked in 1972 in a bold new direction in revamping its juvenile justice system. It is now considered to have one of the model systems of youth corrections in the country. In the late 1970s, Utah altered its approach to youth corrections. It borrowed heavily from Massachusetts' experience and adopted a similar approach to handling juveniles who break the law. Reforms in Massachusetts and Utah involved:

■ Closing the large training schools.
■ Establishing a few small, high-security treatment units for violent youths and those who persist in committing serious crimes.
■ Developing a diverse network of community-based programs that allow for individual treatment and appropriate security. These programs are largely offered by private providers under contract with the state.
■ Unlocking the once sunk costs to run the training schools and reinvesting them to finance community programs.

Results have been impressive both in terms of youth and public protection and in developing humane services. In 1987, the Hubert H. Humphrey Institute of Public Affairs, Center for the Study of Youth Policy, completed a report on the reforms entitled "Reinvesting Youth Corrections Resources: A Tale of Three States" (Schwartz, 1987).*

Massachusetts

In 14 years, juvenile justice in Massachusetts was transformed from an institution-based system of large, custody-oriented training schools to a predominantly community-based model in which 90 percent of the young people served are in small, nonsecure programs designed to address the complex needs of this troubled population.

- Approximately 2,000 young people are in Department of Youth Services programs on any given day.
- Approximately 65 percent of the youth in these programs reside at home, either under caseworker supervision or enrolled in a variety of nonresidential programs, including educational, vocational, counseling and employment-related services. They are monitored by outreach workers.
- Thirty percent are in residential settings ranging from group homes to secure treatment facilities to the state's Homeward Bound program, more widely known as the "Forestry Camp."
- The remaining five percent are in foster homes.
- The Violent Offenders Project, a program consisting of a secure treatment phase and a nonsecure residential phase followed by intense supervision upon return to the community, is successful in significantly curtailing delinquent activities of youth who complete the program.
- Only 15 percent of the new adult inmates committed to the adult prison system in Massachusetts in 1985 were graduates of the juvenile system. This compares with 35 percent in 1972.

Utah

Before 1977, Utah relied heavily on incarceration as a primary response to the juvenile crime problem. The state's single juvenile corrections facility was the Youth Development Center, a century-old, 450-bed training school. In addition to young people convicted of felonies, including violent and chronic offenders, the school was used to house "runaways" and "ungovernables," who were also under the jurisdiction of the juvenile court. Because the state lacked alternatives to incarceration, the Youth Development Center was Utah's principal resource for handling youth committed to the state.

Between 1977 and 1983, a revolution occurred in Utah's juvenile corrections system (Table 2–2). The Utah system today includes:

- Two 30-bed high-security units for violent and chronic offenders.
- Three regional nonsecure observation and assessment centers.

---

*Edward J. Loughman, Commissioner of the Massachusetts Department of Youth Services, described the Massachusetts experience. Utah's segment was written by Russell Van Vleet, Director of Court Services, Second District Court of Salt Lake City; Andrew Rutherford, Co-Director, Institute of Criminal Justice in the Faculty of Law, University of Southampton, England; and Ira Schwartz. Georgia's experience was described by the Honorable Chief Justice of Georgia Supreme Court, Thomas O. Marshall. The report contains executive summaries, key events and current activity and progress.

TABLE   Youth Corrections in Utah 1976–1986
2–2
■

	1976	1980	1986
Secure beds	450	200	60
Community program slots	0	100	250
Youth in jail	700	230	109

■ A wide range of community-based programs provided by private organizations and county governmental entities. These programs include locked and unlocked residential programs offering a continuum of supervised and rehabilitative care.

The results of these reforms were:

■ *Utah's new system is more humane.* Children are not being abused, staff members are qualified and caring, and programming is individualized. Incarceration is used sparingly and is reserved for youth who are violent and chronic offenders.

■ *Utah's new system is more effective.* Juveniles sentenced to Youth Corrections have extensive and serious criminal histories including many violent offenses. However, according to a study by the National Council on Crime and Delinquency (NCCD), these juveniles showed a 66 percent drop in the number of new arrests in the year following their commitment to the Youth Corrections program. In its report, the NCCD states: "The recidivism data for Youth Corrections offenders strongly indicate that the imposition of appropriate community-based controls on highly active serious and chronic juvenile offenders does reduce the incidence of subsequent criminal behavior."

■ *Utah's new system is more cost-effective.* The two secure facilities, three regional observation and assessment centers, and community-based programs are operated at the same expenditure level as was the single training school facility.

■ *Utah's new system provides better protection for the public.* The runaway rate for young people in the old Youth Development Center averaged 25 percent. There have been *no* runaways from the two secure facilities for violent and chronic offenders.

Georgia

Georgia's juvenile justice system has been in a process of evolutionary change since the early 1960s. At that time, there were relatively few specialized juvenile court judges, and incarceration was the primary means of handling Georgia's young people in trouble with the law. Over 25 years, Georgia developed a specialized, statewide system—separate and distinct from the adult system—for dispensing justice and providing treatment for Georgia's youth.

■ In 1966, only 27 of Georgia's juvenile courts were served by specialized juvenile court judges, and only four of those judges served full time. By 1986, there were separate juvenile court judges in 62 of the state's counties.

∎ In the early 1960s, judges had two options for juveniles—commitment to a youth development center or probation. By 1986, a wide variety of options was available, including group homes, community treatment centers, day schools, wilderness programs, contract homes, private psychiatric programs and regional youth development centers.

∎ Until the late 1970s, Georgia ranked among the top ten states in incarceration of juveniles. In 1970, 92 percent of children committed to the state were in institutions. By 1985, 59 percent were in alternative programs.

∎ As late as 1975, 2,000 youths were held in Georgia jails because the state lacked facilities for young offenders. By 1986, the number of youth held in adult jails had been reduced to 73.

At the same time that some states were moving in what would appear to be the "best interests of the child," significant state and federal court decisions reflected the conservative wave of "get tough" with youthful lawbreakers. One such case, *Schall* v. *Martin* (1984), clearly reflected the Supreme Court's more restrictive approach to the rights of youths in trouble with the law.

Schall v. *Martin* and Preventive Detention

On December 13, 1977, at 11:30 P.M., Gregory Martin was arrested on charges of robbery, assault and criminal possession of a weapon. Because of the lateness of the hour and because he lied about his address, Martin was kept in detention overnight. The next day he was brought before the family court for an initial appearance, accompanied by his grandmother. The family court judge noted that he had lied to the police about his address, that he was in possession of a loaded weapon and that he appeared to lack supervision at night. In view of these circumstances, the judge ordered Martin detained until trial under section 320.5(3)(6) of the New York State code. Section 320.5 authorizes pretrial detention of accused juvenile delinquents if "there is a substantial probability that they will not appear in court on the return date or there is a serious risk that they may before the return date commit an act which if committed by an adult would constitute a crime."

While Martin was in pretrial detention, his attorneys filed a habeas corpus petition demanding his release. The petition charged that his detention denied him due process rights under the Fifth and Fourteenth Amendments. The suit was a class action suit on behalf of all youths being held in preventive detention in New York. The New York appellate courts upheld Martin's claim, stating that most delinquents are released or placed on probation; therefore, it was unfair to confine them before trial. Indeed, later at trial, Martin was adjudicated a delinquent and sentenced to two years probation.

The prosecution appealed the decision disallowing pretrial detention to the Supreme Court for final judgment. The Supreme Court reversed the decision and *Schall* v. *Martin* (1984) established the right of juvenile court judges to deny youths pretrial release if they perceived them to be dangerous. The Supreme Court held that **preventive detention** serves the legitimate objective of protecting both the juvenile and society from pretrial crime. Pretrial detention need not be considered punishment merely because the juvenile is eventually released or put on probation.

■ In *Schall* v. *Martin* (1984) the Supreme Court upheld the state's right to place juveniles in preventive detention.

Associate Justice William H. Rehnquist, writing for the majority, stated two principle interests upholding the New York statute for preventive detention. The first was that of "protecting a juvenile from the consequences of his criminal activity." The second, of course, was protecting the public. In other words, even before being tried, youths may be sent to jail to wait and see if the court is going to incarcerate them.

■ Preventive detention fulfills a legitimate state interest of protecting society and juveniles by detaining those who might be dangerous to society or to themselves.

In *Schall,* the Court reiterated its belief in the fundamental fairness doctrine and in the doctrine of *parens patriae,* indicating it was trying to strike a balance between the juvenile's right to freedom pending trial and the right of society to be protected.

The Supreme Court decision was not unanimous. In a dissenting opinion, Associate Justice Thurgood Marshall wrote: "[I]t is difficult to take seriously the majority's characterization of preventive detention as merely a transfer of custody from a parent or guardian to the state. Surely there is a qualitative difference between imprisonment and the condition of being subject to the supervision and control of an adult who has one's best interests at heart."

Nonetheless, all 50 states have similar language allowing preventive detention in the scope of their juvenile codes. But no code mentions "corrections," incarceration, confinement or any reference to a locked facility.

Schall also established a due process standard for detention hearings. This standard included procedural safeguards, such as a notice, a hearing and a statement of facts given to juveniles before they are placed in detention.

The Court further stated that detention based on prediction of future behavior did not violate due process. Many decisions made in the justice system, such as the decision to sentence or grant parole, are based partly on predicting future behavior. These decisions have all been accepted by the Court as legitimate exercises of state power.

Some Effects of Preventive Detention

The effects of preventive detention were described in a May 27, 1985, *Newsweek* article entitled "Justice":

▮ In August 1984, a 15-year-old California girl arrested for assaulting a police officer hanged herself after four days of isolation in a local jail.

▮ In 1982 a 17-year-old boy was taken into custody and detained for owing $73 in unpaid traffic tickets, only to be tortured and beaten to death by his cellmates.

▮ In a West Virginia jail a truant was murdered by an adult inmate; in an Ohio jail a teenage girl was raped by a guard.

▮ In December 1982, 15-year-old Robbie Horn hanged himself in a Kentucky jail where he had been held for only 30 minutes. His offense: arguing with his mother.

During the last few years, however, the classical view has "come back into style." It has also become easier for youths to be treated as adult offenders, particularly if they are over a certain age (usually 14 or 15) and have committed a serious crime such as murder, robbery or rape. Over 80,000 youths are currently being held in institutions, both public and private. According to Siegel and Senna (1988, p. 85): "Since 1980, three juvenile offenders who were waived to the adult court have been executed, and today there are more than 30 on death row. The death penalty for juvenile offenders is an extremely controversial issue."

On June 26, 1989, the Supreme Court ruled that the death penalty for 16- and 17-year-olds is not necessarily "cruel and unusual punishment" and that juveniles may be executed. The decision of whether to apply the death penalty to juveniles is now in the hands of the individual states (*Stanford* v. *Kentucky* and *Wilkins* v. *Missouri*).

STILL EVOLVING

The juvenile justice system continues to evolve. Table 2–3 adds the twentieth century to the National Juvenile Justice System Assessment Center's summary of developments in juvenile justice, which was presented in Chapter 1. Although the table presents developments and relationships in neat categories, in reality, as seen in these two chapters, considerable overlap exists. In addition, the observation of Krisberg (1990, p. 157) is of relevance: "Although the conservative revolution in juvenile justice was motivated by the concepts of deterrence and deserts, the emergence of a 'get tough' philosophy also produced another 'D' in the world of juvenile justice—disarray."

The Office of Juvenile Justice and Delinquency Prevention, suggests (*OJJDP Annual Report, 1990*, p. v): "As we enter the last decade of the twentieth century, the challenge of improving America's juvenile justice system to prevent and address delinquency more effectively continues to demand our best efforts. Our children and our Nation deserve no less."

TABLE 2–3   Juvenile Justice Developments and Their Impact

Period	Major Developments	Precipitating Influences	Child/State	Parent/State	Parent/Child
Puritan 1646–1824	Massachusetts Stubborn Child Law (1646)	A. Christian view of child as evil B. Economically marginal agrarian society	Law provides: A. Symbolic standard of maturity B. Support for family as economic unit	Parents considered responsible and capable of controlling child	Child considered both property and spiritual responsibility of parents
Refuge 1824–1899	Institutionalization of deviants; New York House of Refuge established (1824) for delinquent and dependent children	A. Enlightenment B. Immigration and industrialization	Child seen as helpless, in need of state intervention	Parents supplanted as state assumes responsibility for correcting deviant socialization	Family considered to be a major cause of juvenile deviancy
Juvenile court 1899–1960	Establishment of separate legal system for juveniles—Illinois Juvenile Court Act (1899)	A. Reformism and rehabilitative ideology B. Increased immigration, urbanization, and large-scale industrialization	Juvenile court institutionalizes legal irresponsibility of child	*Parens patriae* doctrine gives legal foundation for state intervention in family	Further abrogation of parents' rights and responsibilities
Juvenile rights 1960–[1980]	Increased "legalization" of juvenile law—*Gault* decision (1966); Juvenile Justice and Delinquency Prevention Act (1974) calls for deinstitutionalization of status offenders	A. Criticism of juvenile justice system on humane grounds B. Civil rights movements by disadvantaged groups	Movement to define and protect rights as well as provide services to children	Reassertion of responsibility of parents and community for welfare and behavior of children	Attention given to children's claims against parents; earlier emancipation of children

SOURCE: Hawkins, J. David; Paul A. Pastor, Jr.; Michelle Bell; and Sheila Morrison. *Reports of the National Juvenile Justice Assessment Center: A Topology of Cause-Focused Strategies of Delinquency Prevention.* Washington, D.C.: U.S. Government Printing Office, 1980.

SUMMARY

In the first quarter of the twentieth century, the Progressives further developed the medical model established by the Illinois Court Act, viewing crime as a disease that could be treated and cured by social intervention. In the first juvenile courts social workers were probation officers. Two cases, *Nicholl v. Koster* (1910) and *Witter v. Cook County Commissioners* (1912), established probation officers as necessary assistants to the juvenile court. The *Nicholl* and *Witter* decisions established the basic dual functions of probation officers: providing legal and social services.

Federal government concern and involvement also began during this period. A direct result of the White House Conference on Youth was the establishment of the U.S. Children's Bureau in 1912. Passage of the Social Security Act in 1935 was the beginning of major federal funding for programs to aid children and families. Then, in 1951, Congress passed the Federal Youth Corrections Act and created a Juvenile Delinquency Bureau in the Department of Health, Education and Welfare.

In 1961 California was the first state to separate status offenses from the delinquent category, in effect, decriminalizing them. Also during the 1960s, the due process rights of youth aroused concern and resulted in several landmark cases. The procedural requirements for waiver to criminal court were articulated by the Supreme Court in *Kent v. United States*. The *Gault* decision requires that the due process clause of the Fourteenth Amendment apply to proceedings in state juvenile courts, including the right of notice, the right to counsel, the right against self-incrimination and the right to confront witnesses.

Another emphasis for reform was concern with isolating offenders from their normal social environment. It was felt such isolation may encourage the development of a delinquent orientation and, thus, further delinquent behavior. In 1967 the President's Commission established a Youth Service Bureau to coordinate community-centered referral programs. The three main functions of the local youth service bureaus were defined as diversion, resource development and system modification. In the late 1960s a new approach for dealing with delinquency emerged—the prevention of crime before youths engage in delinquent acts.

In the 1970s, the major impact of the White House Conference on Youth was that it hit hard at the foundation of our system for handling youths including unnecessarily punitive institutions. Another major change was the assignment of the Office of Juvenile Justice and Delinquency Prevention under the Department of Justice rather than the Department of Health, Education and Welfare.

The Juvenile Justice and Delinquency Prevention (JJDP) Act of 1974 made federal delinquency prevention funds available to states who removed status offenders from prisons and jails and who created alternative voluntary services to which status offenders could be diverted. This act had two key goals: deinstitutionalization of status offenders and separation/removal of juveniles from adult facilities.

During the last half of the twentieth century the Four Ds of juvenile justice were deinstitutionalization, diversion, due process and decriminalization. Although diversion was heralded by many, it also had some negative aspects. Many youngsters who earlier would have been simply released were instead being referred to the new system of diversionary programs that had sprung up. This process is referred to as *net widening*. Many of the diversionary programs did achieve success. The successes of the Dallas Youth Services Program have been traced to three factors: (1) the police-based nature of the program, (2) the use of counseling in a law enforcement setting and (3) the skills approach to training and treatment. Nonetheless, diverted youths tend to remain in the justice system longer than nondiverted youths.

The 1970s also saw juveniles' rights being addressed. *In re Winship* established proof beyond a reasonable doubt as the standard for juvenile adjudication proceedings, eliminating lesser standards such as a preponderance of the evidence, clear and convincing proof and reasonable proof. *McKeiver* established that a jury trial is not a required part of due process in the adjudication of a youth as a delinquent by a juvenile court. *Breed* v. *Jones* established that a juvenile cannot be adjudicated in juvenile court and then tried for the same offense in an adult criminal court (double jeopardy).

By 1977 the American Bar Association endorsed decriminalization of status offenses, urging that juvenile delinquency liability should include only such conduct as would be designated a crime if committed by an adult.

In the 1980s many training schools and high-security institutions were built in rural areas or close to small rural towns so the inmates could be trained in agriculture. The hope was that such training would produce productive citizens.

In *Schall* v. *Martin* (1984) the Supreme Court upheld the state's right to place juveniles in preventive detention. Preventive detention was perceived as fulfilling a legitimate state interest of protecting society and juveniles by detaining those who might be dangerous to society or to themselves.

■ Discussion Questions

1. How may diversion result in "widening the net" of juvenile justice processing?
2. What are the rationales on which police diversion of juveniles is based in your community and state?
3. What are the major types of police diversion programs in your area and state?
4. What impact has diversion had on the efficiency of processing cases in the juvenile justice system? In your state?
5. What evidence suggests that diversion programs are effective in reducing juvenile recidivism? What, if any, findings contradict this evidence? Do you know of a diversion program that is working or one that has failed? Why?
6. Does the public understand the principle of diversion? Do they knowingly support it?
7. What are the advantages and disadvantages of diversion?

■ References

American Bar Association Joint Commission on Juvenile Justice Standards. Juvenile Justice Section. Washington, D.C., n.d.

Arnold, W. R., and T. Brungardt. *Juvenile Misconduct and Delinquency.* Boston: Houghton Mifflin, 1983.

Austin, James F., and Barry Krisberg. "Wider, Stronger and Different Nets: The Dialectics of Criminal Justice Reform." *Journal of Research in Crime and Delinquency* 18 (1981):165–96.

Baude, Jacob M. "Boy's Court: Individualized Justice for the Youth Offender." *Federal Probation* 12 (June 1984):9–14.

Blomberg, Thomas G. "Widening the Net: An Anomaly in the Evaluation of Diversion Programs." In *Handbook of Criminal Justice Evaluation,* edited by Malcolm W. Klein and Katherine S. Tielmann. Beverly Hills, Calif.: Sage Publications, 1980.

Breckenridge, Sophoniska P., and Edith Abbott. *The Delinquent Child and the Home.* New York: Random House, 1912.

Center for the Study of Youth Policy. *Reinvesting Youth Corrections Resources: A Tale of Three States.* "Juvenile Corrections: The Massachusetts Experience," Edward J. Loughran, pp. 8–9; "Reinvesting Youth Corrections Resources in Utah," Russell Van Vleet, Andrew Rutherford, and Ira M. Schwartz, pp. 20–21; "Building a Juvenile Justice System for Georgia's Future," Chief Justice Thomas O. Marshall, pp. 34–36. Minneapolis, Minn.: Hubert H. Humphrey Institute of Public Affairs, University of Minnesota, 1987.

Collingwood, Thomas R. et al. "Juvenile Diversion: The Dallas Police Department Youths Service Program." In *Effective Correctional Treatment,* edited by Robert R. Ross and Paul Gendreau. Toronto: Butterworths, 1980, pp. 93–100.

Decker, Scott H. *Juvenile Justice Policy.* Beverly Hills, Calif.: Sage Publications, 1984.

Empey, LaMar. *American Delinquency: Its Meaning and Construction.* Homewood, Ill.: Dorsey, 1978.

Flicker, Barbara Danziger. *Standards for Juvenile Justice: A Summary and Analysis,* 2nd ed. New York: Institute for Judicial Administration, 1990.

Glaser, Daniel; James A. Inciardi; and Dean V. Babst. "Later Heroin Use by Marijuana Using, Heroin Using, and Non-Drug Using Adolescent Offenders in New York City." *International Journal of the Addictions* 4 (June 1969):145–55.

Hellum, F. "Juvenile Justice: The Second Revolution." *Crime and Delinquency* 25 (1979) 3:299–317.

"Justice." *Newsweek,* 27 May 1985.

Krisberg, Barry. "The Evolution of the Juvenile Justice System." Appeared in *The World & !,* April 1990, pp. 487–503. Reprinted in *Criminal Justice 92/93,* 16th ed., edited by John J. Sullivan and Joseph L. Victor. Guilford, Conn.: Dushkin Publishing 1992, pp. 152–159.

Krisberg, Barry, and James F. Austin. *Reinventing Juvenile Justice.* Newbury Park, Calif.: Sage Publications, 1993.

Lemert, Edwin M. "Diversion in Juvenile Justice: What Has Been Wrought." *Journal of Research in Crime and Delinquency* 18 (Jan. 1981) 1:37, 41.

National Council on Crime and Delinquency. *The Youth Service Bureau.* Paramus, N.J.: NCCD Center, 1971.

OJJDP Annual Report, 1990. Washington, D.C.: Office of Juvenile Justice and Delinquency Prevention, 1990.

Olson, Gayle Clark. "The Role of the Federal Government in Juvenile Delinquency Prevention and Control." Unpublished manuscript distributed at the 1982 Academy of Criminal Justice Sciences held in Louisville, Ky.

Oran, Daniel. *Law Dictionary for Nonlawyers,* 2nd ed. St. Paul, Minn.: West Publishing, 1985.

The President's Commission on Law Enforcement and Administration of Justice. *The Task Force Report: Juvenile Delinquency and Youth Crime.* Washington, D.C.: U.S. Government Printing Office, 1967.

Rieffel, Alaire Bretz. *The Juvenile Justice Standards Handbook.* Washington, D.C.: American Bar Association, 1983.

Schmalleger, Frank. *Criminal Justice Today,* 2nd ed. Englewood Cliffs, N.J.: Prentice Hall, 1993.

Schwartz, Ira M. *Reinvesting Youth Corrections Resources: A Tale of Three States.* Minneapolis, Minn.: Hubert H. Humphrey Institute of Public Affairs, University of Minnesota, 1987.

Scull, Andrew T. *Decarceration.* 2nd ed. Cambridge: Polity Press, 1984.

Senna, Joseph J., and Larry J. Siegel. *Introduction to Criminal Justice,* 6th ed. St. Paul, Minn.: West Publishing, 1993.

Siegel, Larry J., and Joseph J. Senna. *Juvenile Delinquency.* 3rd ed. St. Paul, Minn.: West Publishing, 1988.

Simmons, Constance C. et al. *Major Issues in Juvenile Justice and Training: Grants in Aid of Local Delinquency Prevention and Control Services.* Washington, D.C.: U.S. Government Printing Office, 1981.

The White House Conference on Youth. Washington, D.C.: U.S. Government Printing Office, 1972.

■ Cases

Breed v. Jones, 421 U.S. 519, 533, 95 S.Ct. 1779, 1787, 44 L. Ed. 2d 346 (1975).

Commonwealth v. Fisher, 213 Pa. 48, 62 A. 198, 199, 200 (1905).

In re Daniel, 274 Cal. App. 2d 749, 754, 79 Cal. Rptr. 247, 250 (1969).

In re Gault, 387 U.S. 1, 19–21, 26–28, 87 S.Ct. 1428, 1439–1440, 1442–1444, 18 L. Ed.2d 527 (1967).

Haley v. Ohio, 332 U.S. 596, 68 S.Ct. 302, 92 L. Ed. 224 (1948).

Kent v. U.S., 383 U.S. 541, 86 S.Ct. 1045, 16 L. Ed.2d 84 (1966).

Martarella v. Kelley, 349 F. Supp. 575 (S.D.N.Y. 1972).

McKeiver v. Pennsylvania, 403 U.S. 528, 547, 91 S.Ct. 1976, 1987, 29 L. Ed.2d 647 (1971).

Morales v. Turman, 364 F.Supp. 166 (E.D. Tex. 1973).

Nelson v. Heyne, 491 F.2d 352 (7th Cir. 1974).

Nicholl v. Koster, 157 Cal. 416, 108 P. 302 (1910).

Schall v. Martin, 467 U.S. 253, 104 S.Ct. 2403, 81 L. Ed.2d 207 (1984).

Stanford v. Kentucky, 109 S.Ct. 2969 (1989).

Wilkins v. Missouri, 109 S.Ct. 2969 (1989).

In re Winship, 397 U.S. 358, 90 S.Ct. 1068, 25 L. Ed.2d 368 (1970).

Witter v. Cook County Commissioners, 256 Ill. 616, 100 N.E. 148 (1912).

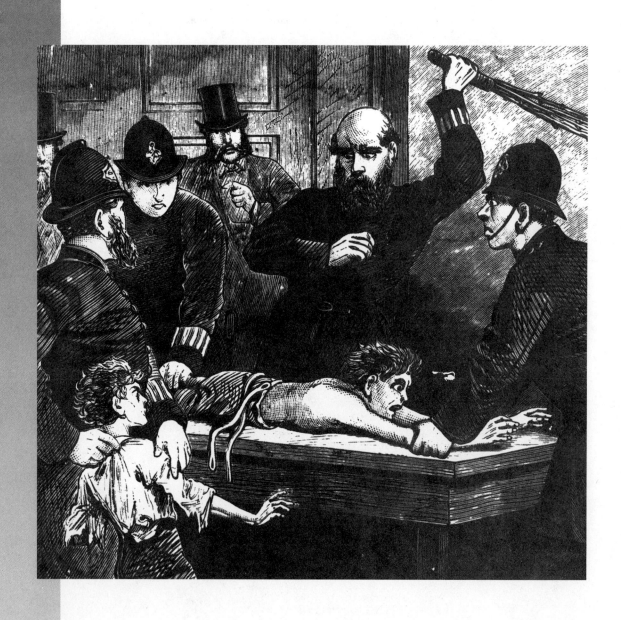

Justice Through the Ages: Philosophical and Legislative Roots

Injustice anywhere is a threat to justice everywhere.

Martin Luther King, Jr. *(1929–1968)*

▌ *Do You Know?*

What proponents of the classical view and those of the positivist view advocate for offenders?

How classical theorists suggest the system deal with delinquency?

How the conservative philosophy and the liberal philosophy of juvenile justice differ?

What function is served by punishment according to the Durkheimian perspective? The Marxist perspective?

The five main purposes of the Uniform Juvenile Court Act?

Where youths involved in juvenile justice proceedings may be detained?

What a petition in the juvenile justice system is?

If juvenile hearings involve a jury?

If juvenile hearings are open to the public?

What rights children involved in the juvenile justice system have?

What is needed in addition to determining that a child has committed the alleged acts in order to detain him or her?

Whether an order of disposition or other adjudication in a juvenile court is criminal or noncriminal?

If juveniles involved in juvenile justice proceedings can be fingerprinted or photographed?

▌ *Can You Define the Following Key Terms?*

classical view of the world, disposition, distributive justice, hearing, petition, positivist view of the world, referee, retributive justice, social justice, summons

INTRODUCTION

This concluding chapter of the first section looks at the two competing world views that have existed throughout the centuries and how these two views have influenced approaches to those who break the law. It then looks at the role of punishment from a sociological perspective, followed by an examination of how justice has been viewed throughout the ages.

The chapter concludes with an in-depth look at the legislative underpinnings of the juvenile justice system contained in the Uniform Juvenile Court Act. This Act not only continues to influence all components of the system, it graphically illustrates the interconnectedness of those components.

TWO COMPETING WORLD VIEWS

For centuries, fervent debate has centered on who or what is responsible for crime. Two distinct and opposing views exist. The **classical view of the world** holds that humans have free will and are responsible for their own actions. The **positivist view of the world** holds that humans are shaped by their society and are the product of environmental and cultural influences. The classical view focuses on crime; the positivist view on the criminal.

Classical theorists believed delinquency was the result of free will. Consequently, they advocated harsh and immediate punishment, so that offenders would be "unwilling" to commit future crimes. According to Trojanowicz and Morash (1987, pp. 43–44):

> Because offenders were viewed as being very rational, the pleasure-pain principle was invoked as the major method of dealing with them. The pleasure-pain principle proposed that if the punishment for the particular act produced negative consequences that were more severe than the pleasures derived from committing the act, potential offenders would be discouraged from being deviant. Offenders were presumed to be rational enough and to have enough "good sense" to choose right from wrong, since most of their behavior was supposedly guided by the desire to seek pleasure and to avoid pain. If the punishment produced enough pain, the potential offenders would decide not to become involved in unlawful behavior. The punishment was also supposed to fit the crime, and such factors as offender age or background characteristics were not to be considered.

■ Proponents of the classical view advocate punishment for offenders.

Several aspects of the classical view are represented in the juvenile justice system. Classical theory suggests that the threat of punishment will lower youths' tendency to delinquency. If the punishment is severe enough, youths will avoid delinquent activity, a process known as *deterrence*. The effectiveness of deterrence is uncertain. Many law violators believe they will never be caught, and if they are, they believe they can "beat the rap." Those who violate the law under the influence of drugs may believe they are invincible. Punishment is no threat to them. Juveniles may also resist the threat of punishment because of peer pressure. Being rejected by the gang would be worse than getting caught by the police. Also, many juveniles know the differences between juvenile and adult court and believe they will receive less severe punishment because of their age.

Classical theory also advocates *incapacitation* as a consequence for criminal activity. Institutionalization is not intended to rehabilitate offenders, but to keep them away from law-abiding society. Classical theory holds that criminal offenders should be sanctioned merely because they deserve punishment, and that punishment should be founded on what the offender deserves. Critics say this "just deserts" approach is actually a desire for revenge. Many states have criminal sentencing laws that set the punishment for a particular crime, ensuring that all offenders of that crime be punished equally.

Since the first juvenile court in 1899, the juvenile justice system has opposed deserts-based punishment. Incarcerated juveniles were usually given short sentences (one to three years maximum) and sent to a nonpunitive, rehabilitation-oriented institution. Recently, however, deserts-based sentences have been given to serious delinquents. As noted by Siegel and Senna (1988, p. 87): "While juvenile justice philosophy in general rejects punishment that fits the crime and embraces consideration of individual needs, fear of violent, serious juvenile offenders has caused some states to rethink their priorities and create more punitive policies in juvenile justice."

■ Classical view theorists suggest that deterrence, incapacitation and, in some cases, just deserts punishment is the way to deal with delinquency.

Classical theorists' views conflict with those adhering to the *parens patriae* philosophy, which advocates reform as a more appropriate way to deal with delinquency. The positivist view theorists, who believe delinquent behavior is the result of a youth's biological makeup and life experiences, feel treatment should include altering one or more of the factors that contributed to the unlawful behavior.

■ Proponents of positivist view advocate rehabilitation for offenders.

Positivist theorists stress community treatment and rehabilitation rather than incapacitation. For years, the *parens patriae* attitude prevailed, with youths shielded from being labeled and punished as criminals. However, the reemergence of the classical theory to deal with delinquency has resulted in frequent use of secure incarceration. A study by Charles Murray and Louis Cox found that seriously delinquent youths who experienced incapacitation were less likely to commit delinquent behavior upon their release than youths with similar backgrounds who were treated in community-based rehabilitation-oriented programs.

Throughout the ages, societies have embraced one view or the other, with many individuals taking a middle position but tending toward one view or the other. Whichever view is held affects how punishment and justice are viewed.

Conservative and Liberal Philosophies of Justice and Punishment

The conservative attitude is to "get tough," "stop babying these kids," and "get them off the streets." This is reminiscent of the child saver's efforts to "contain" certain children.

▌ The conservative philosophy of juvenile justice is "get tough on juveniles"—to punish and imprison them.

Such conservative philosophies accept retribution as grounds for punishment. The conservative view also believes in imprisonment to control crime and antisocial behavior. Rehabilitative programs may be provided during incarceration, but it is imprisonment itself, with its attendant deprivations, that must be primarily relied on to prevent crime, delinquency and recidivism. Correctional treatment is not necessary.

In contrast, the liberal philosophies of juvenile justice is "treatment, not punishment" for youths who are antisocial and wayward.

▌ The liberal philosophy of juvenile justice stresses treatment and rehabilitation, including community-based programs.

Liberal ideologies tend to favor community corrections because, as Sutherland and Cressey note (1966, p. 51):

> [T]he person or personality is . . . a part of the kinds of social relationships and values in which he participates; he obtains his essence from rituals, values, norms, rules, schedules, customs, and regulations of various kinds which surround him; he is not separable from the social relationships in which he lives . . . criminal and delinquent is not just a product of an individual's contacts with certain kinds of groups; it is in a real sense "owned" by groups rather than by individuals.

Yet another way to look at offenders and approaches to them is to examine the relationship between those who break the law and law-abiding citizens within a society and the role punishment plays in this relationship.

SOCIOLOGICAL PERSPECTIVE ON PUNISHMENT

Garland (1991) describes two sociological perspectives on punishment, which can be seen influencing the criminal justice system—the Durkheimian perspective and the Marxist perspective.

Punishment and Social Solidarity—The Durkheimian Perspective

Emile Durkheim (1858–1917), a pioneer in sociology, argued that punishment is a moral process to preserve the shared values of a society, that is, its "collective conscience." When individuals deviate from this collective conscience, society is outraged and seeks revenge to restore the moral order. As Garland (p. 123) notes: "Punishment thus transforms a threat to social order into a triumph of social solidarity." Garland (p. 127) also notes: "As Durkheim makes clear, an act of punishment is also a sign that authorities are in control, that crime is an aberration, and that the conventions that govern social life retain their force and vitality."

■ The Durkheimian perspective sees punishment as revenge and as a way to restore and solidify the social order.

Two key elements of Durkheim's perspective are (1) that the general population is involved in the act of punishing, giving it legitimacy, and (2) it is marked by deeply emotional, passionate reactions in response to crime. The question arises, however, especially in modern times, as to whether we do, in fact, have a collective conscience. This issue and others is addressed in the Marxist perspective.

Punishment and Class Power—The Marxist Perspective

Rather than viewing punishment as a means of providing social solidarity, Karl Marx (1818–1883) saw punishment as a way to enhance the power of the upper class and an inevitable result of capitalism. Marx referred to the lower class as a "slum proletariat" made up of vagrants, prostitutes and criminals. "In effect, penal policy is taken to be one element within a wider strategy of controlling the poor; punishment should be understood not as a social response to the criminality of individuals but as a mechanism operating in the struggle between social classes" (Garland, p. 128).

■ The Marxist perspective sees punishment as a way to control the lower class and preserve the power of the upper class.

This rationale was doubtless operating throughout the Middle Ages, Renaissance, Reformation and into the nineteenth century. Society was divided into a small ruling class, a somewhat larger class of artisans and a vastly larger class of peasants. Intimidation through a brutal criminal law was an important form of social control.

Flicker (1990, p. 38) sees this rationale operating in the development of our juvenile justice system:

> The unfortunate historical fact is that the juvenile justice system . . . began with the right observation and the wrong conclusion. Manifestly, poor people are more likely to beg, steal, and commit certain other crimes related to their social and economic status than affluent people. Although socially unacceptable, crime could be seen as a response to poverty. It was a way to get money. The preferred solutions—jobs, vocational training, financial assistance for the unemployable— required a constructive community attitude toward the disadvantaged. But a combination of Calvinism, prejudice, and social Darwinism confused cause and effect—idleness, inferiority, and criminality were seen as causing poverty, rather than the reverse. Therefore progressive elements in the community, the social reformers, felt justified in saving impoverished children from the inexorable path of crime by investigating their homes and families, attempting to imbue them with principles of Christian morality, and, if unsuccessful, removing them to a better environment.
>
> Cultural, ethnic, economic, and class bias combined to blind the zealous ladies bountiful and their male counterparts to the injustice of their cause.

JUSTICE

Aristotle warned that no government can stand that is not founded on justice. As a nation, America is firmly committed to "liberty and justice for all." But is this the reality?

Centuries ago, Aristotle wrote about the *just* as that which is lawful (universal justice) and that which is fair and equal (particular justice). According to Aristotle (Ross, 1952, pp. 378–379):

> Of particular justice and that which is just in the corresponding sense, one kind is that which is manifested in distributions of honour or money or the other things that fall to be divided among those who have a share in the constitution. . . .
>
> This, then, is what the just is—the proportional; the unjust is what violates the proportion. Hence one term becomes too great, the other too small, as indeed happens in practice; for the man who acts unjustly has too much, and the man who is unjustly treated too little, of what is good.

■ Distributive justice provides an equal share of what is valued in a society to each member of that society. This includes power, prestige and possessions.

Distributive justice or **social justice** is frequently ignored but must certainly be considered in any discussion of justice. Usually, however, the focus is on **retributive justice**, that is, justice being served by some sort of punishment for wrongdoing, harkening back to the ancient concept of "an eye for an eye" (*lex talionis*). When this is the case, the issue becomes whether it is more effective to punish offenders or to treat them—the justice versus the medical model.

Hawkins and Alpert (1989, p. 79) note:

> The construction of a just system of criminal justice in an unjust society is a contradiction in terms. . . .
>
> However just in applying its rules, retributive justice cannot be ultimately just unless distributive justice is. . . .

Too frequently distributive and retributive justice are not differentiated and critics claim that retributive justice has failed when, in effect, it has no power over the failure. As noted by Hawkins and Alpert (1989, p. 79): "The criminal justice system is often blamed for injustice which resides at the distributive level."

Merton (1957, n.p.) views crime as being caused by the frustration of the lower socioeconomic levels within an affluent society that denies them legal access to social status and material goods. He views this denial as not only unjust but also as a root of many social ills, including crime. Merton further suggests that this is especially true of our "underprivileged youth" who need not only groceries, but "groceries for growing."

That distributive injustice exists was acknowledged by President Clinton in his January 25, 1994, State of the Union address:

> I urge you to consider this: As you demand tougher penalties for those who choose violence, let us also remember how we came to this sad point. In our toughest neighborhoods, on our meanest streets, in our poorest rural areas, we have seen a stunning and simultaneous breakdown of community, family, and work, the heart and soul of civilized society. This has created a vast vacuum which has been filled by violence and drugs and gangs. So I ask you to remember that even as we say no to crime, we must give people, especially our young people, something to say yes to.

In a similar vein, in a paper on justice for juveniles, Springer (1986, p. 76) suggests:

> It is beyond the scope of this paper to discuss social justice, what Aristotle called "distributive justice," but it is within its scope to make mention of the sad consequences of our inability to provide a decent social environment for what would appear to be a growing segment of our youthful society.
>
> This is not the place to engage in discourse on the dire ends of poverty, class divisions, urbanization, industrialization, urban blight, unemployment, breakdown of religion, breakdown of the family, and all of the other established criminogenic factors. It is the place, however, to recognize, at least, that the criminal justice system is the least effective means of crime prevention and social control. If we are interested in a relatively crime-free society, we must look elsewhere than the courts.

Breed (1990, p. 68) shares Springer's view: "When half of our nation's children live in poverty and one-third grow up ignorant, we have in fact developed a third world underclass within this major nation." Breed, like Springer, suggests (p. 68):

Crime and delinquency will be reduced only to the degree that we are willing to address wider social problems, such as maintaining and supporting the family unit—nurturing, housing, nutrition, education, health care and parent training.

If we are unwilling to address basic prevention issues, then we are not going to reduce crime. Our concern must be to keep children out of harm's way, instead of concentrating on caring for them after they have been harmed. We must recognize that investing in children is not a national luxury and not a national chore, but a national necessity.

Consider finally the statement of Krisberg and Austin (1993, p. 51) at the conclusion of their discussion of historical approaches to juvenile delinquency:

Not surprisingly, juvenile justice reforms have inexorably increased state control over the lives of the poor and their children. The central implication of this historical analysis is that the future of delinquency prevention and control will be determined largely by ways in which the social structure evolves. It is possible that this future belongs to those who wish to advance social justice on behalf of young people rather than to accommodate the class interests that have dominated this history.

Against this background, turn your attention now to the legislation that is at the heart of the juvenile justice system, the Uniform Juvenile Court Act.

THE UNIFORM JUVENILE COURT ACT

In 1968, the National Conference of Commissioners on Uniform State Laws drafted the Uniform Juvenile Court Act. Although titled a "court" act, the Act includes provisions affecting the police and corrections. The Act provides a context within which the discussion of police, courts and corrections can be set and also illustrates the interconnectedness of the parts of the system.*

The discussion in this section focuses on the main sections of the Act. It must be remembered that each state has made its own modifications to this Act. It is important to familiarize yourself with the specific provisions in your state.

Purposes of the Act

The Uniform Juvenile Court Act was drafted:

1. To provide for the care, protection, and wholesome moral, mental, and physical development of children coming within its provisions;
2. Consistent with the protection of the public interest, to remove from children committing delinquent acts the taint of criminality and the consequences of criminal behavior and to substitute therefore a program of treatment, training, and rehabilitation;

---

*Copies of all Uniform and Model Acts and other printed matter issued by the Conference may be obtained from: National Conference of Commissioners on Uniform State Laws, 645 N. Michigan Avenue, Chicago, IL 60611.

3. To achieve the foregoing purposes in a family environment whenever possible, separating the child from his parents only when necessary for his welfare or in the interest of public safety;

4. To provide a simple judicial procedure through which this Act is executed and enforced and in which the parties are assured a fair hearing and their constitutional and other legal rights recognized and enforced; and

5. To provide simple interstate procedures which permit a resort to cooperative measures among the juvenile courts of the several states when required to effectuate the purposes of this Act.

■ The Uniform Juvenile Court Act was drafted to provide for the care, protection and development of youth, without the stigma of a criminal label, by a program of treatment, training and rehabilitation, in a family environment when possible; as well as to provide a simple judicial procedure and simple interstate procedures.

Definitions

The Act includes the following definitions:

- A *child* is "an individual who is under the age of 18 years or under the age of 21 years who committed an act of delinquency before reaching the age of 18 years."
- A *delinquent act* is "an act designated a crime under the law." It includes local ordinances, but does not include traffic offenses.
- A *delinquent child* is "a child who has committed a delinquent act and is in need of treatment or rehabilitation."
- An *unruly child* refers to children who are subject to compulsory school attendance but are habitually truant; who habitually disobey reasonable and lawful commands of their parents, guardians, or other custodians; or who have committed an offense applicable only to a child and, because of the preceding, need treatment or rehabilitation.

The Act notes that: "The 'unruly child' category is needed to limit the disposition that can be made of a child who is in need of treatment or rehabilitation, but who has committed no offense applicable to adults. The 'unruly child' is usually unmanageable and in need of supervision but not to the extent that he should be institutionalized with delinquent children."

- A *deprived child* is one who "is without proper parental care or control, subsistence, education as required by law, or other care or control necessary for his physical, mental, or emotional health, or morals, and the deprivation is not due primarily to the lack of financial means of his parents, guardian, or other custodian; or who has been placed for care or adoption in violation of the law; or who has been abandoned by his parents, guardian, or other custodian; or is without a parent, guardian, or legal custodian."

▋ A *custodian* is "a person, other than a parent or legal guardian, who stands *in loco parentis* to the child or a person to whom legal custody of the child has been given by order of a court."

Probation Services

The Act describes how probation officers can be appointed and notes that:

> A competent probation staff is essential to achieving the objectives of the juvenile court system. The staff must be adequately trained, working loads must be limited, and conditions must be provided that permit the giving of the required time and attention called for by each individual case.
>
> A probation service may be established on either a local or a statewide basis. Competent authorities disagree on the relative merits of the two alternatives. The National Council of Juvenile Court favors a local system, stressing the importance of having these services provided by court personnel responsible to and under the direction of the juvenile court judge, since he is responsible for the successful conduct of the juvenile program. Proponents of the statewide system stress the frequent inadequacy of local resources to provide the needed minimum service required and contend that better probation service is provided by a state system, and that the prospect of the judge successfully achieving the objectives of the court's program is therefore enhanced.

According to guidelines set forth in the Act, probation officers should:

▋ Make investigations, reports and recommendations to the juvenile court.
▋ Receive and examine complaints and charges of delinquency, unruly conduct or deprivation of children.
▋ Supervise and assist children placed on probation.
▋ Make appropriate referrals to other private or public agencies if needed.
▋ Take into custody and detain children who are under their supervision or care as delinquent, unruly or deprived children, if the children's health or safety is in danger. Arrange to have children removed from the jurisdiction of the court.

Probation officers do *not* have the powers of law enforcement officers. The Act notes that: "The primary role of the probation officers is the care and protection of the child, and in delinquency cases, his treatment and rehabilitation as well. Incompatible roles such as the power of arrest, conducting the accusatory proceeding in juvenile court, representing the child in court, have been excluded."

Referees

A juvenile judge may appoint a lawyer to serve as a part-time or full-time **referee.** Referees are helpful when a judge's caseload is more than can be effectively handled. The referee is assigned simple, routine cases. Before a referee hears a case, he or she must inform the parties involved that they are entitled to have the matter heard by the judge. If they want a judge, they get one.

Transfer from Criminal Court

If during a criminal proceeding it is learned that the defendant is under age 18 or was under age 18 at the time the offense occurred, the case is transferred to juvenile court.

Venue and Transfer

Usually, proceedings take place in the county where the juvenile lives. If a proceeding involving a juvenile begins in a different county, the court may ask that the proceedings be transferred to the county where the juvenile lives. Likewise, transfer can be made if the child's residence changes before the proceedings.

Custody and Detention

Children can be taken into custody by court order, under the laws of arrest, by a law enforcement officer if there are "reasonable grounds to believe that the child is suffering from illness or injury or is in immediate danger from his surroundings . . . or to believe that the child has run away. . . ." The Act notes that: "The taking of a child into custody is not an arrest, except for the purpose of determining its validity under the constitution of this state or of the United States."

Technically youth are not arrested; they are simply taken into custody.

Section 14 deals with detention of children:

A child taken into custody shall not be detained or placed in shelter care prior to the hearing on the petition unless his detention or care is required to protect the person or property of others or of the child or because the child may abscond or be removed from the jurisdiction of the court or because he has no parent, guardian, or custodian or other person able to provide supervision and care for him and return him to the court when required, or an order for his detention or shelter care has been made by the court pursuant to this Act.

The trend is to not hold children in confinement unless it seems necessary to assure their appearance in court.

Once children are taken into custody, they should either be released to their parents, guardians or custodians; brought before the court; or delivered to a detention or shelter care facility, or to a medical facility if needed. This is to be done "with all reasonable speed and without first taking the child elsewhere." The parent, guardian or custodian and the court must be promptly given a written notice stating the reason the child was taken into custody.

The Act provides in Section 16 that:

■ A delinquent can be detained only in (1) a licensed foster home or a home approved by the court; (2) a facility operated by a licensed child welfare agency; (3) a detention home or center for delinquent children that is under the direction or supervision of the court or other public authority, or of a private agency approved by the court; or (4) any other suitable place or facility, designated or operated by the court.

The final omnibus or "catchall" clause in this provision of the Act weakens the effectiveness of the Act.

Section 16 further specifies that delinquents may be kept in a jail or other adult detention facility only if the preceding are not available, the detention is in a room separate from adults and it appears that public safety and protection reasonably requires detention. The Act requires that the person in charge of a jail inform the court immediately if a person under age 18 is received at the jail. The Act further stipulates that deprived or unruly children "shall not be detained in a jail or other facility intended or used for the detention of adults charged with criminal offenses or of children alleged to be delinquent." The intent of this section is to protect children from the harm of exposing them to criminals and the "degrading effect of jails, lockups, and the like."

Section 17 states that if a child is brought before the court or delivered to a detention or shelter care facility, an investigation must be made immediately as to whether detention is needed. If the child is not released, a petition must be filed promptly with the court. In addition, an informal detention hearing should be held within 72 hours to determine if detention is required. A written notice of the time, place and purpose of the hearing is given to the child and, if possible, the parents or guardians. Before the hearing begins, the court must inform the people involved of their right to counsel—court appointed if they cannot afford to pay private counsel and of the child's right to remain silent during the hearing.

Petitions

■ A petition states the facts necessary to bring a child into the juvenile justice system.

The **petition** is similar to the complaint in the adult system. It sets forth:

■ The facts that bring the child within the jurisdiction of the court, with a statement that it is in the best interest of the child and the public that the proceeding be brought and, if delinquency or unruly conduct is alleged, that the child is in need of treatment or rehabilitation.

■ The name, age and residence address, if any, of the child on whose behalf the petition is brought.

■ The names and residence addresses, if known to petitioner, of the parents, guardian or custodian of the child and of the child's spouse, if any.

■ If the child is in custody and, if so, the place of detention and the time it occurred.

Any person, including law enforcement officers, may make a petition, but it will not be filed until the court or someone authorized by the court determines and endorses that the filing of the petition is in the best interest of the public and the child.

Several states have separated delinquency from status offenders and children in need of the court's protection. A delinquency petition such as that illustrated in Figure 3–1 may be issued. The same procedure is used with children in need of protection or services (CHIPS), as illustrated in Figure 3–2.

Summons

After the petition is filed, the court fixes a time for a hearing. If the youth is in detention, the hearing must be within ten days of the filing of the petition. When the hearing date is set, summonses are issued to the child, if 14 years or older, the parents, guardians or custodians, and to any other people to appear before the court. The **summons** is accompanied by the petition and clearly states that the person is entitled to a lawyer.

The summons should be served at least 24 hours before the hearing if the person is within the state at a known address. If the address is not known or the person lives out of the state, the summons can be sent by registered or certified mail at least five days before the hearing.

Figure 3–3 illustrates a typical summons. In place of the phrase "alleging that the above-named child is a delinquent," any appropriate phrase may be substituted, for example, "alleging that the above-named child is a truant/runaway."

A typical listing of the rights of the parents/guardians and the youths that appears on the back of the summons is illustrated in Figure 3–4.

Sometimes the court elects to issue a Notice in Lieu of Summons to be sent along with the petition to the parents or guardians. This is a somewhat less formal, less intimidating process. A sample form is illustrated in Figure 3–5.

STATE OF _____   DISTRICT COURT

COUNTY OF _____   _____ JUDICIAL DISTRICT

In the Matter of the Welfare of

_____   DELINQUENCY PETITION
          Child.
                                         Court File No._____

Your petitioner states on information and belief that the above-named child, a resident
of _____ County, State of _____, with post office address of
_____, and being then of the age of _____,
with date of birth on _____ , did on or about _____,
in _____ County, State of _____, violate _____ Statutes §260.015;
_____X_____ Subd. 5(a), in that the child has violated a state or local law
_____ Subd. 5(b), in that the child has violated a federal law or law of another
state and committed the following act of delinquency:

(PROBABLE CAUSE ON PAGE TWO)

The name, residence and post office address of the child's parents, guardian and spouse, if any, and
of the person having custody or control over the child, and if no parent or guardian can be found,
of the nearest known relative are:

Name   Relationship   Address   County

Mother's county of residence: Father's county of residence:

Your petitioner, being duly sworn deposes and says that has read the petition, the probable cause
and attached pages, if any, and knows the contents are true to the best of your petitioner's
information and belief.

Subscribed and sworn to before me this   _____
_____day of _____, 1989.   Petitioner

                                         Endorsed pursuant to JCR 19.02, Subd. 2:
_____
          NOTARY PUBLIC
                                         _____

                                         Assistant _____ County Attorney

∎ FIGURE 3–1 Sample Delinquency Petition

STATE OF _____   DISTRICT COURT

COUNTY OF _____   _____ JUDICIAL DISTRICT

In the Matter of the Welfare of

                                                     CHILD IN NEED OF PROTECTION
                                                          OR SERVICES PETITION

           Child.   Court File No.
                                                            Co. Atty. File No.

Petitioner, alleges that:

The first name, date of birth, residence and post office address of the above-named child are as follows:

Name   Date of Birth   Address   County

Child's county of residence:

The child in need of protection or services within the meaning of _____ Statutes §260.015, Subd. 2a:

The name, residence and post office address of the child's parents, guardian and spouse, if any, and of the person having custody or control over the child, and if no parent or guardian can be found, of the nearest known relative, are:

Name   Relationship   Address   County

Mother's county of residence: Father's county of residence:

This petition, including attached reports and exhibits, if any, consists of pages.

Your petitioner, being first duly sworn, deposes and says that has read the petition, probable cause, and attached pages, if any, and knows the contents are true to the best of your petitioner's information and belief.

Subscribed and sworn to before me this   _____
_____ day of _____, 1989.
                                                     Petitioner

_____

■ FIGURE 3–2 Sample CHIPS Petition (Includes Status Offenders)

```
STATE OF _____                    DISTRICT COURT

COUNTY OF _____            _____ JUDICIAL DISTRICT


In the Matter of the Welfare of:              S U M M O N S

_____
          (child)                        File No.


    To the above-named child, residing at _____

_____ and to _____

residing at _____

the person(s) having custody or control of the child:

    A petition was filed with this court on _____

alleging that the above-named child is a delinquent.    A copy of

that petition is attached to this summons.

    This court has set _____ at _____ M.

as  the  time,  and  the  Juvenile  Hearing  Room, _____County

Courthouse, _____, _____, as the place

of a hearing to be held in the above-entitled matter.

    EACH OF YOU IS HEREBY SUMMONED AND REQUIRED TO APPEAR BEFORE

THIS COURT AT THE HEARING.

    FAILURE TO APPEAR ON THIS SUMMONS WILL RESULT IN A WARRANT

FOR YOUR ARREST.


Dated: _____        _____
                                     Judge of District Court


    A statement of the nature of the hearing to which you are
summoned  and  your  rights  with  respect  thereto  appears  on  the
reverse side of this Summons.
```

▌ FIGURE 3–3 Sample Summons

STATEMENT OF RIGHTS

The hearing will be held for the purpose of determining whether the child admits the _____ alleged in the petition.   If the child denies the delinquency alleged in the petition or if he exercises his right to remain silent, the court will schedule a hearing at a later date for the purpose of considering evidence in the matter.   If the child admits the _____ alleged in the petition, the court will then have the power to determine what should be done with or about the child, including the power to:

(1) Counsel the child and his parents, guardian or custodian.
(2) Place the child on probation in his own home under conditions prescribed by the court.
(3) Transfer legal custody of the child under supervision of the court.
(4) Transfer legal custody of the child by commitment to the _____ Corrections Authority.
(5) Order restitution for any property damage done by the child.
(6) Order special treatment or care for the child's physical or mental health.
(7) Recommend to the commissioner of highways that the child's driving license be canceled.

In connection with these proceedings, the person(s) having custody or control of the child have the following rights:

(1) To be represented by a lawyer at all stages of the proceedings.   If you cannot afford to retain a lawyer, you are entitled to have a lawyer appointed for you at county expense.
(2) To introduce evidence at the hearing.
(3) To cross-examine witnesses testifying against the child.
(4) To inspect any report filed with the court, and if it is admitted in evidence, to cross-examine the preparer of such report.
(5) To obtain a transcript of the proceedings.
(6) To appeal decisions of the juvenile court.
(7) To have subpoenas issued by the court on your behalf requiring the attendance and testimony of witnesses, or the production of papers.

The child has the same rights as the person(s) having custody or control of the child, except that:

(1) His right to an appointed lawyer at county expense shall be measured by whether his parents can afford to retain a lawyer.   The child is also entitled to an appointed lawyer if his parents can afford to retain a lawyer but their interests and his appear to the court to conflict, or if the parents refuse to provide a lawyer.

(2) The child has the right to remain silent at all stages of the proceedings prior to a determination that he is a delinquent.   His right to remain silent includes the right not to be interrogated by a representative of the state except in the presence of one of his parents, and the right to consult with a laywer prior to making any statements. If he chooses to make any statements, they may be used in the proceedings against him.

If you desire to retain a lawyer, you should do so immediately, so you will be ready at the hearing.

If you desire to be represented by a lawyer, but cannot afford the cost, you must immediately notify the court that you want an appointed lawyer.

■ FIGURE 3–4 Listing of Youths' Rights During the Hearing

The Hearing

According to Section 24: "Hearings under this Act shall be conducted by the court without a jury, in an informal but orderly manner, and separate from other proceedings." The prosecuting attorney presents the evidence supporting the petition. The **hearing** may be recorded electronically or minutes may be kept. Most hearings are not open to the public. The child may be excluded from the hearing while the charges are being made.

```
STATE OF _____              DISTRICT COURT

COUNTY OF _____        _____ JUDICIAL DISTRICT


                                        NOTICE IN LIEU
  _____                 OF SUMMONS
  |                       |
  |                       |           File No.
  |                       |
  |_____|


  _____
  |                       |
  |                       |
  |                       |
  |_____|
```

RE: In the Matter of the Welfare of_____, Child

You are hereby notified that a petition (a copy of which is attached) has been filed in this court alleging that the above-named child is delinquent;

That the court has set a hearing on this petition on _____ in the Probate-Juvenile Courtroom, _____ County Courthouse, _____, _____, __. **You are required to be present at least 15 minutes prior to your scheduled time to speak with your court appointed attorney.**

You are entitled by law to have a summons served upon you requiring your appearance at the hearing. Service of such summons has been dispensed with for your convenience. If you appear in court for the hearing fixed in this notice, you will be deemed to have waived issuance and personal service of a summons. If you do not appear, a summons will be served upon you by personnel of the sheriff's office.

                                   _____
                                   Court Administrator
                                   _____, _____

Dated: By_____
                                                              Deput y
_____

State of _____   **CLERK'S CERTIFICATE OF MAILING**
County of _____

I hereby certify that at the city of _____, _____ on the date hereof, I mailed a copy of the foregoing Notice in Lieu of Summons to each of the persons whose names appear thereon by depositing the same in the U.S. mail at _____, _____ with postage prepaid addressed to each of said persons at the addresses shown thereon.

                        IN WITNESS WHEREOF, I have hereunto set my
                        hand and seal of this Court, at _____,
                        _____ this

                        _____, Court Administrator

                        By _____
                                                       Deputy

▮ FIGURE 3–5 Sample Notice in Lieu of Summons

■ Hearings in juvenile court do not involve a jury. They are not open to the public.

The Child's Rights

As seen in Figure 3–4, children have specific rights during a hearing.

■ Children have the same rights as adults, except trial by jury and, in some states, the right to bail.

Children are entitled to have a lawyer present at all stages of any proceedings under the Act and, if unable to afford private counsel, to have the court provide counsel. The due process requirement of the appointment of counsel for needy children charged with delinquency was established by *Kent* v. *United States* and *In re Gault,* discussed in Chapter 2.

Children are also entitled to introduce evidence and to tell their side of the story, as well as the right to cross-examine adverse witnesses. Children charged with delinquency need not be witnesses against themselves. According to Section 27: "A confession validly made by a child out of court is insufficient to support an adjudication of delinquency unless it is corroborated in whole or in part by other evidence."

■ Children have the right to an attorney at all stages of the proceedings, the right to introduce evidence and tell their side of the story, the right to cross-examine witnesses and the right to remain silent during the hearing.

Disposition

After hearing the evidence on the petition, the court makes its findings, or **disposition.** If the court finds that the child is not deprived or that the allegations of delinquency or unruly conduct have not been established, it dismisses the petition and the child is discharged.

If a court finds on proof beyond a reasonable doubt that the child is delinquent or unruly, it proceeds immediately or at a postponed hearing to hear evidence as to whether the child is in need of treatment or rehabilitation.

As noted by Arthur (1976, p. 43):

A disposition is not simply a sentencing. It is far broader in concept and in application. It should be in the best interest of the child, which in this context means effectively to provide the help necessary to resolve or meet the individual's definable needs, while, at the same time, meeting society's needs for protection.

▌ It is not sufficient to find the child has committed the alleged acts. The court must also determine that the child is in need of treatment or rehabilitation.

If the court then finds from clear, convincing evidence that a child is deprived or in need of treatment or rehabilitation, the court decides on the proper disposition of the case.

Deprived children may be permitted to remain with their parents or guardians subject to specific conditions and limitations. Temporary legal custody may be given to any individual the court finds qualified to receive and care for the child. Children may be placed in an agency or other private organization licensed or authorized to receive and provide care for children, for example, the Child Welfare Department.

A child found to be *delinquent* may be placed on probation or placed in an institution, camp or other facility for delinquent children.

A child found to be *unruly* may receive any disposition authorized for a delinquent child except commitment to the state institution to which commitment of delinquent children is made. The order of disposition committing a delinquent or unruly child to an institution is in effect for two years or until the child is discharged.

A delinquent or unruly child thought to be suffering from *mental retardation* or *mental illness* may be committed for a period not exceeding 60 days to an appropriate institution, agency or individual for study. If the child is determined to be committable under state laws, the court may order the child detained. If the child is not committable, the court proceeds with the disposition of the child as appropriate.

If a child is or is about to become a *nonresident* of the state, the court may defer hearing on the need for treatment or rehabilitation and ask that the juvenile court of the child's new or prospective residence accept jurisdiction of the child. Likewise, the *resident child received from another state* should be accepted by the child's new or prospective residence. These provisions facilitate cooperative action between the courts of the two states involved.

▌ An order of disposition or other adjudication in a juvenile court is *not* a conviction of a crime.

Section 33 states that: "A child shall not be committed or transferred to a penal institution or other facility used primarily for the execution of sentences of persons convicted of a crime." The Comment regarding this section states:

> Although several states permit commitment or transfer of a delinquent child to a penal institution, its constitutionality is in serious doubt since it permits confinement in a penal institution as a product of a non-criminal proceeding. Such legislation has been held invalid in a number of states. See *In re Rich,* 125 Vt. 373, 216 A. 2d 266 (1966).

Transfer to Other Courts

After a petition alleging delinquent conduct designated a crime or public offense under state law is filed with a juvenile court, the court may transfer the offense to a different court if:

█ The child was 16 years or older at the time of the conduct.
█ Written notice is given to the child and parent at least 3 days before the hearing.
█ The court has reasonable grounds to believe that the child committed the act, is not amenable to treatment or rehabilitation as a juvenile through available facilities, or is not committable to an institution for the mentally retarded or mentally ill, AND the interests of the community require that the child be placed under legal restraint or discipline (emphasis in original).

No statements made by the child before being transferred may be used against him or her in the criminal proceedings following the transfer. As the Comments note:

> First, a child may make statements unaware that he may be transferred for criminal prosecution. Fairness requires that these not be used against him in a criminal prosecution. See *Harling* v. *United States,* 295 F 2d, 161 (1961) stating, ". . . if admissions obtained in juvenile proceedings before waiver of jurisdiction may be introduced in an adult proceeding after waiver, the juvenile proceedings are made to serve as an adjunct to and part of the adult criminal process. This would destroy the Juvenile Court's *parens patriae* relation to the child and would violate the non-criminal philosophy which underlies the Juvenile Court Act."
>
> Second, a child should not be handicapped in presenting his case against transfer by the prospect that what is presented may be used against him in the criminal prosecution. Otherwise, the proceeding becomes in effect a discovery procedure for the state. Since whether or not to transfer is one of the most important decisions the juvenile court makes, the hearing should be a full and unrestricted one.

If the case is not transferred, the judge who conducted the hearing on the transfer may not preside at the hearing on the petition. Likewise, if the case is transferred and the judge who conducted the hearing on the transfer is also the judge in the court to which the case is transferred, he or she is disqualified from presiding during prosecution of the case.

Some states, for example Illinois, have mandatory adult court requirements for 14-, 15-, and 16-year-olds for certain major offenses. The prosecuting attorney makes the decisions in other major crime situations.

Court Files and Records

Juvenile records are open to inspection by only the judge, officers and professional staff of the court; the parties to the proceedings and their counsel and representatives; a public or private agency or institution providing supervision or having custody of the child under court order; a court and its probation and other officials or professional staff and the attorney for the defendant.

Section 55 states that: "Law enforcement records and files concerning a child shall be kept separate from the records and files of adults. Unless a charge of delinquency is transferred for criminal prosecution, the interest of national security requires, or the court otherwise orders in the interest of the child, the records and files shall not be open to public inspection or their contents disclosed to the public."

Juvenile records may be sealed if:

1. [Two] years have elapsed since the final discharge of the person.
2. Since the final discharge the person has not been convicted of a felony, or of a misdemeanor involving moral turpitude, or adjudicated a delinquent or unruly child and no proceeding is pending seeking conviction or adjudication.
3. The person has been rehabilitated. This is to protect a "rehabilitated youth from the harmful effects of a continuing record of the adjudication of delinquency."

Fingerprinting and Photographing Children

▮ Children involved in juvenile justice system proceedings may be fingerprinted or photographed under specific conditions.

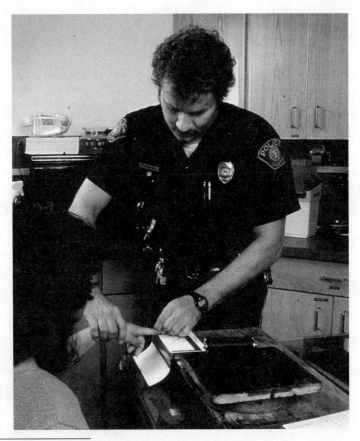

▮ *Youths taken into custody may be fingerprinted, but the files must be kept separate from the adult fingerprint files.*

Section 56 specifies that law enforcement officers may take and file finger-prints of children 14 years and older involved in the crimes of murder, non-negligent manslaughter, forcible rape, robbery, aggravated assault, burglary, housebreaking, purse snatching and automobile theft. Children's fingerprint files should be kept separate from adult files and should be kept locally—not sent to a central state or federal depository unless in the interest of national security. The fingerprints should be removed from the file and destroyed if the child is adjudicated not to be delinquent or if the child reaches age 21 and has not committed a criminal offense after reaching age 16.

If latent fingerprints are found during an offense and law enforcement officers have probable cause to believe they are the prints of a particular child, they may fingerprint the child, regardless of age or the offense. If the comparison of the latent and inked prints is negative, the fingerprint card is to be immediately destroyed.

Section 56 also specifies that, without a judge's consent, children should not be photographed after being taken into custody unless the case is transferred to another court for prosecution. A form such as that in Figure 3–6 may be used.

THE JUVENILE AND ADULT JUSTICE SYSTEMS COMPARED

The juvenile justice system not only evolved into a system separate from the adult system but also the terms used became tailored to fit the juvenile system. The main differences in terminology are summarized in Table 3–1. Although the table refers to "court" terms, notice that all components of the juvenile and adult system are directly affected.

SUMMARY

Proponents of the classical view advocate punishment for offenders. They suggest that deterrence, incapacitation and, in some cases, "just deserts" punishment is the way to deal with delinquency. In contrast, proponents of the positivist view advocate rehabilitation for offenders. These two opposing world views often translate into either a conservative philosophy of juvenile justice calling for "getting tough on juveniles"—punishing and imprisoning them—or a liberal philosophy of juvenile justice stressing treatment and rehabilitation, including community-based programs.

Punishment can be viewed from a sociological perspective as well as a philo-sophical perspective. For example, the Durkheimian perspective sees punish-ment as revenge and as a way to restore and solidify the social order. The Marxist perspective sees punishment as a way to control the lower class and preserve the power of the upper class. This is closely related to the concept of distributive justice. Distributive justice provides an equal share of what is valued in a society to each member of that society. This includes power, prestige and possessions.

```
TO:    JUVENILE COURT JUDGE - _____ COUNTY


FROM: _____    RE:_____
                 Police Department                  Juvenile           D.O.B.


THE ABOVE NAMED JUVENILE IS CURRENTLY IN CUSTODY AND UNDER INVESTIGATION.  IT IS

REQUESTED THAT WE BE ALLOWED TO TAKE A PICTURE OF SAID JUVENILE FOR THE FOLLOWING

REASONS:
```

```
THE NEGATIVE, IF ANY, AND ALL PRINTS WILL BE RETAINED BY OUR JUVENILE DIVISION IN ITS

SEPARATE RECORDS UNTIL SUBJECT IS EIGHTEEN YEARS OF AGE AND AT THAT TIME ALL NEGATIVES

AND PRINTS WILL BE DESTROYED.  NO ONE WILL BE PERMITTED TO RECEIVE OR TO MAKE COPIES OF

THE NEGATIVE OR PRINTS EXCEPT OUR POLICE DEPARTMENT.  VIOLATIONS OF THE FOREGOING ARE A

MISDEMEANOR, OR CONTEMPT OF COURT, OR BOTH.


                                      _____
                                                Chief of Police


                                      _____
                                      By:                         Date

                                      For the Court

                                      _____
                                                Judge/Referee      Date

Original:  Police Department
Copy:      Clerk of Juvenile Court
```

▮ **FIGURE 3-6 Photograph Release Form**

TABLE   The Language of Juvenile and Adult Courts
3–1

Juvenile Court Term	Adult Court Term
Adjudication: decision by the judge that a child has committed delinquent acts.	Conviction of guilt
Adjudicatory hearing: a hearing to determine whether the allegations of a petition are supported by the evidence beyond a reasonable doubt.	Trial
Adjustment: the settling of a matter so that parties agree without official intervention by the court.	Plea bargaining
Aftercare: the supervision given to a child for a limited period of time after he or she is released from training school but while he or she is still under the control of the juvenile court.	Parole
Commitment: a decision by the judge to send a child to training school.	Sentence to imprisonment
Delinquent act: an act that if committed by an adult would be called a crime. The term does not include such ambiguities and noncrimes as "being ungovernable," "truancy," "incorrigibility," and "disobedience."	Crime
Delinquent child: a child who is found to have committed an act that would be considered a crime if committed by an adult.	Criminal
Detention: temporary care of an allegedly delinquent child who requires secure custody in physically restricting facilities pending court disposition or execution of a court order.	Holding in jail
Dispositional hearing: a hearing held subsequent to the adjudicatory hearing to determine what order of disposition should be made for a child adjudicated as delinquent.	Sentencing hearing
Hearing: the presentation of evidence to the juvenile court judge, his or her consideration of it, and his or her decision on disposition of the case.	Trial
Juvenile court: the court that has jurisdiction over children who are alleged to be or found to be delinquent. Juvenile delinquency procedures should not be used for neglected children or for those who need supervision.	Court of record
Petition: an application for a court order or some other judicial action. Hence, a "delinquency petition" is an application for the court to act in a matter involving a juvenile apprehended for a delinquent act.	Accusation or indictment
Probation: the supervision of a delinquent child after the court hearing but without commitment to training school.	Probation (with the same meaning as the juvenile court term)
Residential child care facility: a dwelling (other than a detention or shelter care facility) that is licensed to provide living accommodations, care, treatment, and maintenance for children and youths. Such facilities include foster homes, group homes, and halfway houses.	Halfway house

continued

TABLE   **The Language of Juvenile and Adult Courts,** *continued*
3–1

∎

Juvenile Court Term	Adult Court Term
Shelter: temporary care of a child in physically unrestricting facilities pending court disposition or execution of a court order for placement. Shelter care is used for dependent and neglected children and minors in need of supervision. Separate shelter care facilities are also used for children apprehended for delinquency who need temporary shelter but not secure detention.	Jail
Take into custody: the act of the police in securing the physical custody of a child engaged in delinquency. The term is used to avoid the stigma of the word "arrest."	Arrest

SOURCE: Reprinted by permission from *Crime and Justice in America: A Human Perspective,* by Harold J. Vetter and Leonard Territo. Copyright © 1984 by West Publishing Co. All rights reserved.

The evolution of the juvenile justice system has been influenced not only by differing world views and approaches to youthful offenders, but also by a major piece of legislation passed in 1968, the Uniform Juvenile Court Act. The Uniform Juvenile Court Act was drafted to provide for the care, protection and development of youth, without the stigma of a criminal label, by a program of treatment, training and rehabilitation, in a family environment when possible; as well as to provide a simple judicial procedure and simple interstate procedures.

A delinquent can be detained only in: (1) a licensed foster home or a home approved by the court; (2) a facility operated by a licensed child welfare agency; (3) a detention home or center for delinquent children that is under the direction or supervision of the court or other public authority or of a private agency approved by the court or (4) any other suitable place or facility, designated or operated by the court.

A petition states the facts necessary to bring a child into the juvenile justice system. Hearings in juvenile court do *not* involve a jury. They are not open to the public. Children have the same rights as adults, except trial by jury and, in some states, the right to bail. Children have the right to an attorney at all stages of the proceedings, the right to introduce evidence and tell their side of the story, the right to cross-examine witnesses and the right to remain silent during the hearing.

It is not sufficient to find a child has committed the alleged acts. The court must also determine that the child is in need of treatment or rehabilitation. An order of disposition or other adjudication in a juvenile court is *not* a conviction of a crime.

Children involved in juvenile justice system proceedings may be finger-printed or photographed under specific conditions.

▌ Discussion Questions

1. Do you take the position of those who hold a classical view or those who hold a positivist view? Do you hold the same view for children as you do for adults?
2. Do you feel distributive justice is required for the United States to truly provide "liberty and justice for all"?
3. What instances of the Durkheimian or Marxist perspective of punishment can you cite from the historical overview of juvenile justice?
4. Why did the Uniform Juvenile Court Act come into existence? Has it had much impact on the various state juvenile court acts?
5. Should all states adopt the Uniform Juvenile Court Act and abolish their own? What are the advantages and disadvantages of one national act?
6. A juvenile, age 14, is brought before the juvenile court for allegedly repeatedly refusing to obey his parents' orders to be home before ten o'clock at night. Would such behavior fall within the scope of most juvenile courts?
7. What is the most important purpose of the Uniform Juvenile Court Act?
8. Why does the Act not differentiate between treatment of abused or neglected children, status offenders and youths who commit serious, violent crimes?
9. Given that the Act was passed in 1968, is it time for the Act to be revised?
10. Does your state have its own Juvenile Court Act? If so, how does it differ from the federal act?

▌ References

Arthur, Lindsay. "Status Offenders Need a Court of Last Resort." *Boston University Law Review* 20 (1976):43.

Breed, Allen F. "America's Future: The Necessity of Investing in Children." *Corrections Today,* February 1990, pp. 68–72.

Flicker, Barbara Danziger. *Standards for Juvenile Justice: A Summary and Analysis,* 2nd ed. New York: Institute for Judicial Administration, 1990.

Garland, David. "Sociological Perspectives on Punishment." In *Crime and Justice: A Review of Research,* vol. 14, edited by Michael Tonry. Chicago: The University of Chicago Press, 1991, pp. 115–165.

Hawkins, Richard, and Geoffrey P. Alpert. *American Prison Systems: Punishment and Justice.* Englewood Cliffs, N.J.: Prentice Hall, 1989.

Krisberg, Barry, and James F. Austin. *Reinventing Juvenile Justice.* Newbury Park, Calif.: Sage Publications, 1993.

Merton, Robert K. *Social Theory and Social Structure,* Rev. Ed. New York: Free Press, 1957.

Ross, W. D. (trans.) "Nicomachean Ethics." *Aristotle: II.* Chicago: Encyclopedia Britanica, 1952.

Siegel, Larry J., and Joseph J. Senna. *Juvenile Delinquency,* 3rd ed. St. Paul, Minn.: West Publishing, 1988.

Springer, Charles E. *Justice for Juveniles.* Washington, D.C.: U.S. Department of Justice, Office of Juvenile Justice and Delinquency Prevention, 1986.

Sutherland, Edwin H., and Donald R. Cressey. *Principles of Criminology,* 7th ed. Philadelphia: J. B. Lippincott, 1966.

Trojanowicz, Robert C., and Merry Morash. *Juvenile Delinquency: Concepts and Control,* 4th ed. Englewood Cliffs, N.J.: Prentice-Hall, 1987.

▮ Cases

Harling v. United States, 295 F.2d 161 (D.C.Cir. 1961).

In re Gault, 387 U.S. 1, 19–21, 26–28, 87 S.Ct. 1428, 1439–1440, 1442–1444, 18 L.Ed.2d 527 (1967).

Kent v. United States, 383 U.S. 541, 86 S.Ct. 1045, 16 L.Ed.2d 84 (1966).

In re Rich, 125 Vt. 373, 216 A.2d 266 (1966).

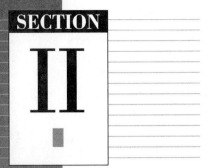

Our Nation's Youth: A Challenge to the Justice System

The moral test of government is how it treats those who are in the dawn of life, the children.

Hubert H. Humphrey (1911–1978)

Before examining our contemporary juvenile justice system, it is important to understand those who are served by this system—our youth. One of the extreme challenges facing the system is the "one-pot" approach to juvenile justice, evident throughout history. That is, those who are poor, who are neglected, who commit minor status-type offenses and those who commit vicious, violent crimes are currently lumped into the same judicial "pot." But their needs and the approaches to meet those needs are drastically different.

The section begins with a discussion of normal growth and development, including physical, psychological and sociological influences (Chapter 4). Then the critical roles played by the family and by the school during the formative years of our youth are highlighted (Chapter 5). This is followed by a look at children who are victimized—neglected or abused—and are in need of assistance and protection (Chapter 6). According to a three-year study released 12 April 1994 by the Carnegie Corporation, a philanthropic New York agency, as many as *half* our nation's 12 million infants and toddlers face at least one risk factor that could harm their future. David A. Hamburg, president of Carnegie Corporation stated: "So this is a high-stakes game we are playing with our children, and hence with the future of our nation."*

Next the development of youth who victimize others is explored (Chapter 7). The Bureau of Justice Statistics reports that although youths age 15 to 19 make up only 9 percent of the population, they account for 15 percent of all violent crimes and 32 percent of property crimes.** To successfully deal with such youths, while at the same time protecting society, is a large challenge for the juvenile justice system.

The section concludes with a discussion of gangs in the United States (Chapter 8), including the purposes they serve and the threat they pose.

---

*"Quiet Crisis: Half of Tots Face Problems." Reported by Associated Press. [Cited 13 April 1994.] Available from Prodigy Interactive Services Co., White Plains, NY.
**Bureau of Justice Statistics, *Report to the Nation on Crime and Justice,* 2nd ed. (Washington, D.C.: U.S. Department of Justice, 1988), p. 41.

Growth and Development: The First Eighteen Years

There is no characteristic of adolescence whose germ may not be found in childhood, and whose consequences may not be traced in maturity and old age.

Frederick Tracy

▍ Do You Know?

At what age most individuals legally become adults?

What ages are most critical in child development?

What is required for learning?

What kind of reinforcement is usually best?

What a self-fulfilling prophecy is?

What role labeling plays in the growth and development of our youth?

How primary and secondary deviance differ?

What danger occurs by labeling a child as deviant?

What types of children with special needs may be involved in the juvenile justice system?

Which children may be at risk of not developing "normally"?

What adolescence is? What occurs during this time?

What is happening to the "American Dream"?

▍ Can You Define the Following Key Terms?

attention deficit hyperactivity disorder, crack children, EBD, fetal alcohol syndrome, labeling, learning disability, primary deviance, secondary deviance, self-fulfilling prophecies

INTRODUCTION

$\mathbf{A}$t the heart of the juvenile justice system are the children and youth being served. This chapter provides a very brief overview of what rights our youth ideally enjoy and how they normally grow and develop, as well as a look at children with special needs and children at risk of not developing "normally." This is followed by a discussion of adolescence and the unique challenges and stresses of this developmental stage. Included in the discussion is the problem of teen pregnancy.

The challenges facing today's youth are tremendous, as noted by Louv (1990, p. 5):

> Today's children are living a childhood of firsts. They are the first day-care generation; the first truly multicultural generation; the first generation to grow up in the electronic bubble, the environment defined by computers and new forms of television; the first post-sexual revolution generation; the first generation for which nature is more abstraction than reality; the first generation to grow up in new kinds of dispersed, deconcentrated cities, not quite urban, rural, or suburban.

YOUTH AND *PARENS PATRIAE*

Under the principle of *parens patriae* the state is to protect its youth. The age at which a child becomes an adult is legally established by each state.

■ **Eighteen is the most common age for individuals to legally become adults.**

Table 4–1 summarizes the age at which young people are officially considered adults in each state. Note the range from 16 to 19 years of age.

Until they become adults, it is generally understood that youth need special assistance. In fact, the Joint Commission on Mental Health of Children (1970, pp. 3–4) lists the following as children's *rights:*

■ The right to be wanted.
■ The right to be born healthy.
■ The right to live in a healthy environment.
■ The right to satisfaction of basic needs.
■ The right to continuous loving care.
■ The right to acquire the intellectual and emotional skills necessary to achieve individual aspirations and to cope effectively in our society.

110

TABLE **Age at Which U.S. Criminal Courts Gain Jurisdiction over**
4–1   **Young Offenders**

Age 16	Age 17	Age 18		Age 19
Connecticut	Georgia	Alabama	Nebraska	Wyoming
New York	Illinois	Alaska	Nevada	
N. Carolina	Louisiana	Arizona	New Hampshire	
	Massachusetts	Arkansas	New Jersey	
	Michigan	California	New Mexico	
	Missouri	Colorado	N. Dakota	
	S. Carolina	Delaware	Ohio	
	Texas	D. of Columbia	Oklahoma	
		Florida	Oregon	
		Hawaii	Pennsylvania	
		Idaho	Rhode Island	
		Indiana	S. Dakota	
		Iowa	Tennessee	
		Kansas	Utah	
		Kentucky	Vermont	
		Maine	Virginia	
		Maryland	Washington	
		Minnesota	W. Virginia	
		Mississippi	Wisconsin	
		Montana	Federal Districts	

SOURCE: Linda A. Szymanski, "Upper Age of Juvenile Court Jurisdiction Statutes Analysis" (Washington, D.C.: National Center for Juvenile Justice, March 1987).

■ The right to receive care and treatment through facilities which are appropriate to their needs and which keep them as closely as possible within their normal social setting.

Such rights are essential to our youths' growth and development.

CHILD DEVELOPMENT

Child development usually deals with children from birth to adolescence and concerns their physical, intellectual, emotional (personality) and social growth as they adjust to the demands of society.

The study of child development is relatively new, beginning at the end of the nineteenth century. Pioneers in the field included psychologist John B. Watson who believed that environment dominated development, that children could be shaped and molded as desired. Another pioneer, Arnold Gesell, held the opposing view that biology dominated. As the study of child development evolved, many researchers stressed the importance of both. "Development," according to Hall et al. (1986, p. 2), "is an intricate process in which heredity, culture, and personal experience interact to produce the final pattern of a life. . . . No single theory has been able to explain all aspects of the process satisfactorily, but each has contributed to our understanding of human development."

Behavior and an individual's sociability is learned very early in life and becomes ingrained in the individual's character structure. According to Caticchio (1990, p. 7):

> If the child [during the first 18 months of life] experiences being treasured and important to those around him, then his basic sense of self as having value is repeatedly and predictably reinforced. . . .
>
> If his experiences are primarily ones in which he is related to as a burden—to be seen and not heard—all the successes in his later life will give only brief respite from a basic sense of inferiority and inadequacy which was repeatedly reinforced by thousands of incidents, big and small, over many years, with the most important people who will ever relate to him. . . .
>
> Being treasured during these first few months and years has much more to do with a child's *basic* sense of self-esteem than will all the magnificent structures he may build in later life (italic in original).

Caticchio (p. 9) also suggests that if very young children are not nurtured by their parents, the children will feel alienated and isolated:

> The non-nurturing patterns, if sustained both in time and substance, lead the child to be withdrawn, or hostile and aggressive. These traits, in turn, make him a less enjoyable person, reinforcing others' lack of interest or caring about him. He begins to *not* be a very nice person.

The Critical First Three Years

Child development experts state that the first three years of life lay the foundation for all that follows.

▮ The period from birth to age three is the most formative time of a child's life.

During this time, with attentive parents or older brothers or sisters, children learn the concept of consequences—rewards and punishments. They also begin to distinguish right from wrong and to develop what is commonly called a *conscience.*

Table 4–2 summarizes some of the basic needs of children if they are to grow and develop. Unfortunately, for too many of our nation's children, this is *not* the reality. Their healthy development is hindered by inadequate medical care, poverty, violence and disintegrating families.

According to a Carnegie study ("Developmental Risk," 1994): "Millions of infants and toddlers are so deprived of medical care, loving supervision and intellectual stimulation that their growth into healthy and responsible adults is threatened." Specifically,

> The report notes that 3 million children, nearly one-fourth of all American infants and toddlers, live in poverty. Divorce rates, births to unmarried women and

TABLE   **What Children Need for Healthy Growth and Development**
4–2

Need	Comments
Choices and challenges	Children need the chance to explore and learn, to stretch to their limits.
Healthy and safe surroundings	Children need to feel secure and protected from harm, supported when confronted with strange or frightening experiences.
Independence	Children need to develop their own personality and self-confidence, to know that others have faith in their ability to do things for themselves.
Love	Children need to be loved—physically and emotionally. They need to feel wanted, appreciated, a part of a family unit. They need hugs.
Direction	Children need to know the rules, their boundaries and what will happen if they overstep these boundaries. They need to know how to interact with others and to get along.
Respect and recognition	Children need to be accepted for who they are and to be praised for their accomplishments.
Encouragement	Children need to be supported and helped to grow and develop.
Nurturing	Children need not only nutritious food, but attention to their mental and emotional growth and development as well.

single-parent households have all soared in the past 30 years, and children in single-parent households, it points out, are more likely to experience behavioral and emotional problems than those in two-parent households. The number of children entering foster care jumped by more than 50 percent from 1987 to 1991, rising to 460,000 from 300,000.

David A. Hamburg, Carnegie president, states ("Developmental Risk," 1994): "What could be more important than a decent start in life? All the rest depends on this foundation. . . . If a poor start leaves an enduring legacy of impairment, then high costs follow. They may show up in various systems: health, education, justice. We call them by many names: disease, disability, ignorance, incompetence, hatred, violence. By whatever name, these outcomes involve severe economic and social penalties for the entire society."

Other findings of the Carnegie study include the following:

■ One in every three abused children is less than one year old.
■ More than half of women with children under one year old are working.
■ American children are among the least likely in the world to be immunized.
■ An increasing number of very young children grow up witnessing knifings, shootings and beatings as *everyday events* (italics in original).

According to the Carnegie study, scientific evidence points to the criticality of the first three years of life in development of the human brain. Research in molecular biology and neurology show that what children experience in the first few years affects how many brain cells develop and how many connections are formed between them. Early environmental stimulation increases the number of cells and interconnections. Research also shows that stress early in life may activate hormones that actually impair learning and memory.

Between the ages of one and three normal conflicts arise between parents and their children: toilet training, eating certain vegetables, going to bed at a certain time, staying within prescribed boundaries, and the like. How these conflicts are resolved will establish the pattern for how the child will deal with conflict later in life.

The Next Ten Years

Building on the foundation of the first three critical years, children continue to grow and develop physically, mentally and emotionally. During this time they are continuously learning.

The Learning Process

Understanding the process of learning behavior, either as a group or individually, requires an understanding of the psychological principles involved and the social conditions under which learning happens.

The basic formation of individual personalities and character usually takes place in the family. Through a series of learning experiences within this intimate circle, individuals gradually form attitudes, values and behaviors that they generally retain throughout life.

Adults often forget about the difficult learning experiences of early childhood. They remember them only by observing the blundering adaptations of children. Everyone has tried to learn a skill and failed without knowing why, or has tried to teach others and found them slow to understand. Remember learning how to tie your shoes or ride a bike—or teaching a child to do these things? Such experiences demonstrate that learning is not automatic. Where the principles of learning are not understood and conditions are not correctly arranged, little learning occurs.

Because most learning is not accomplished in one trial, teaching requires great patience. No one immediately walks, talks or performs motor skills without repeating them time and again. Under appropriate conditions children learn to talk, to walk, to have good manners and to suppress socially unacceptable words heard and behaviors seen in play groups. To learn, children must want something, notice something, do something and get something. What they get can be positive or negative.

■ Learning requires drive, a cue, a response and reinforcement.

To use a classic example: a child sees fire, is curious, and touches it. The child is burned and learns not to touch fire again.

Learning research suggests that positive reinforcement or rewards are much stronger than negative reinforcement or punishments. Unfortunately, too often inappropriate behaviors are noticed and punished rather than appropriate behaviors noticed and rewarded. Children learn what not to do—or get caught doing—but are often not taught what they should be doing.

■ **Praise is usually better than punishment when teaching children. Accentuate the positive.**

The message for parents, teachers and all adults who work with children is to reward children for doing good things and acting in socially accepted ways.

To go a step further, learning is reflected in behavior. Youths' behavior depends on how they see, interpret and react to the world around them. Physical, psychological and social influences directly affect their behavior. This behavior within a specific environment provides the stimulus for choice. If this choice is achieved through self-awareness, imagination, conscience and independent will, the response is likely to be one that reflects responsibility to self and to society. The complex interaction of these variables is illustrated in Figure 4–1.

A strong advocate of individual responsibility for behavior is Samenow (1989, p. 18) who writes: "The environment from which a person comes is less crucial than the choice the individual makes as he responds to his environment." Samenow supports this position by presenting numerous instances of families in which one child is antisocial, but the other children in the family or in similar circumstances are not. He notes: "Children do not get pressured haplessly into a life of crime. They make deliberate choices to do so."

Smetanka (1993, p. 1A) describes the choices of an eight-year old girl left alone, supperless, by her mother who went out drinking. The hungry child got

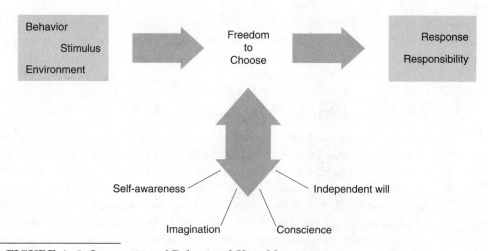

■ **FIGURE 4–1 Interaction of Behavioral Variables**

out the phone book and looked up the number to order pizza. When it came, she paid for it with money she had saved. The question posed by Smetanka is: "Is she a victim or a survivor?"

The Institute of Child Development at the University of Minnesota is studying children who overcome large obstacles and thrive despite living in poverty or with other large personal problems. Such children are considered *resilient,* defined as one who "has the capacity to spring back, to successfully adapt in the face of adversity" (Smetanka, 1993, p. 16A). A noted child psychiatrist, E. James Anthony, suggests the following analogy: Imagine three dolls, one made of glass, one of plastic, and one of steel. If struck with a hammer, the glass doll shatters, the plastic doll is scarred, but the steel doll proves invulnerable, reacting only with a metallic ping (Gelman, 1991, p. 44). That's resiliency. A profile of the resilient child suggests that such children are caring, independent, hopeful about the future, good at expressing their feelings and "most of all, they have a strong relationship with at least one caring adult."

The importance of adult support is stressed by Attorney General Reno: "[I]t is essential that we view a child's life as a continuum and provide a consistent support system for those times when the family is unable to provide that support on its own" (Wilson, 1993, p. 2).

Labeling

A psychological phenomenon important as children grow and learn is that of **labeling.** It is human nature to apply labels to things, that is, to name them. But when dealing with individuals, it is important to restrict the labeling to specific behaviors rather than to the person exhibiting these behaviors.

Children are born into a society in which situations are predefined and corresponding rules of conduct developed. People who conform to the established standards and codes and perform in acceptable ways are called "law-abiding" and given other positive labels. Conversely, people who do not conform to acceptable behavior are called "deviants" and given other negative labels.

Much has been made of the power of positive thinking. Logically, the power of negative thinking can be just as powerful. People are talked into believing what or who they are. If individuals are constantly called "stupid," this could retard their intellectual growth.

Labeling and Self-Fulfilling Prophecies

In a frequently cited research study, psychology majors were given three groups of laboratory rats. They were told in advance how smart each group was. The first set consisted of super-smart rats who would be able to master a maze with no difficulty; therefore, they should have ample rewards along the way and a huge piece of cheese at the end. The second set consisted of rats of average ability who would not be able to make use of the clues along the way; they should have an average amount of cheese at the end. The third group consisted of rats of below-average intelligence who had little hope of finding their way through the maze; a simple picture of some cheese at the end would do.

At the end of the day, all the super-smart rats were munching away at the cheese at the end of the maze; some of those with average intelligence had found their way to the end; and the below-average rats were aimlessly milling around in the maze, with none of them yet at the end. Imagine the students' surprise when the professor told them the rats were all of the same intelligence. It was how they were treated, based on how they were labeled, that made the difference.

A similar experiment using three classes of second graders has often been used to illustrate the effects of labeling. The teachers were told that one group was brilliant, one group was of average intelligence, and one group was below average. The "brilliant" group made tremendous gains in learning during a six-week period; the "average" group made some gains; and the "below-average" group actually lost ground. In reality, all three groups were of the same intelligence, but the teachers treated them differently, expecting large gains from the "brilliant" group and paying little attention to the "below-average" group. What they expected is exactly what they got.

■ Self-fulfilling prophecy occurs when people live up to the labels they are given.

Behavior mirrors self-image. Actions reflect the feelings of self at the time. Too often, parents' conceptions of their children become **self-fulfilling prophecies.**

■ Children and adolescents in particular incorporate labels as part of their self-image.

Regardless of social class or environment, children have a strong natural inclination to believe those they respect. What is said to them makes a difference. A 16-year-old boy who appeared in juvenile court was admonished by a court judge who called the youth a "menace" to society. The judge further stated that the boy was the kind of "kid" who gave "good" kids a bad name. This insensitive judge did not know there was a computer error and the "kid" was not the ruthless figure he was labeled. The event, however, was so traumatic for the 16-year-old that he wrote in a note, "The judge is right, I am no good." He signed it and then shot himself. It was the third suicide of a youth who appeared before the same judge.

Consequences of Labeling

Before formalized law enforcement, neighbors watched over neighbors, and if an incident occurred that needed public service, a "hue and cry" was raised. For example, if a neighbor saw a stranger removing a cow, he would pursue the thief yelling, "Stop, thief!" and arouse all the other neighbors to join the chase. If the thief abandoned the animal out of sight of the crowd, and an innocent person stopped to hold the cow and was mistakenly labeled as the thief by the pursuers, he was probably hanged.

The same thing can happen to youths who commit status offenses. They are automatically labeled "delinquent" and subject to the discipline of the juvenile court. If the court decides to teach such youths "a lesson," they can be placed in a locked facility for something as petty as a curfew violation. The youths are not hanged as the innocent man with the cow, but the consequences can be almost as devastating.

The same thing can happen if a youth is referred to as a "criminal," a "thief" or "no good." It is possible for youths to accept a particular label. For example, people who are identified as "deviant" may act in a way society considers to be deviant.

There are many kinds of deviant behavior. Crime is one; delinquency is another. Practices of various religious cults deviate from the norm. In fact, deviance has been identified in many areas of human activity: sex, eating habits, dress, speech, politics and earning a living. A half century ago Darrow (1934, p. 2) noted: "That certain things are forbidden does not mean these things are necessarily evil, but rather that politicians believe there is a demand for such legislation from the class of society that is most powerful in political action."

Primary and Secondary Deviance

Edwin Lemert (1951, p. 22) formulated some major assumptions of the labeling perspective. He related deviance to processes of social differentiation and social definition, stating:

> We start with the idea that persons and groups are differentiated in various ways, some of which result in social penalties, rejection, and segregation. These penalties and segregative reactions of society or the community are dynamic factors which increase, decrease, and condition the form which the initial differentiation or deviation takes.

Lemert also distinguished between **primary** and **secondary deviance.** *Primary deviance* is the original act that is defined as deviant by others. More important, however, is *secondary deviance,* an adaptation to society's reaction to primary deviation in terms of rules, social identity and processes in fixing a person in a deviant category.

▮ Primary deviance is an original act that violates society's rules.
Secondary deviance is an act that results because society has labeled the individual a deviant.

For example, if nondelinquents commit a status offense, such as violating curfew or being truant from school, the juvenile justice system may adjudicate such youths as delinquents and place them in a social category along with all other delinquents. The delinquent label then places a stigma on these youth that can force isolation. The alternative to isolation is to associate with other delinquents.

The harmful consequences that may result from negative labeling are stressed because it is a known fact that while growing up, nearly all children get into trouble regardless of their social status. It is not just inner-city youth or youth living in poverty who break the rules of society. It is almost *all* our youth who do so.

■ Labeling theorists state that when a deviant label is attached to particular individuals they become stigmatized and are left little opportunity to be rewarded for conformist behavior. The label becomes a self-fulfilling prophecy.

Fortunately, it is also a fact that most children grow up to be law-abiding, sociable and productive citizens, having developed responsible behavior through the maturation process.

Barriers to Achievement

Numerous obstacles can hinder growth and development, not only during the pre-adolescent period but also throughout life. Some of these barriers are illustrated in Figure 4–2. Some barriers are the result of lack of prenatal care. One-fourth of pregnant mothers receive no physical care of any sort during the crucial first trimester of pregnancy. About 20 percent of handicapped children would not be impaired had their mothers had one physical exam during the first trimester, which could have detected potential problems (Hodgkinson, 1991, p. 10). In addition, every year about 350,000 children are born to mothers who were addicted to cocaine during pregnancy. Those who survive birth have strikingly short attention spans, poor coordination and worse, as discussed shortly.

Another large barrier to achievement while children are growing up may be fear. Some children are constantly afraid. They may fear not belonging, not being accepted, not meeting adult expectations. Children are especially afraid in school. They fear failing, being kept back, being called stupid, feeling stupid and, more recently, they may fear physical harm, as will be discussed shortly. Such fears are most pronounced in children from deprived, poor families with low social status.

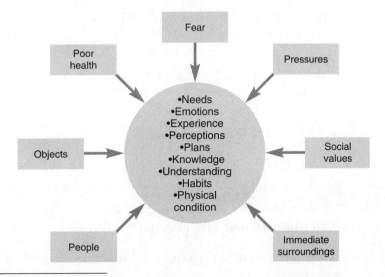

■ **FIGURE 4–2 Barriers to Achievement**
Behavior depends upon how individuals see, interpret and react to the world around them.

Pressures such as wanting to belong to "the" group, to get good grades, or to make an athletic team may mount to the point where they inhibit achievement of any kind. A desire for money and possessions is yet another type of barrier if it becomes too high a priority. Closely related to this is the use of drugs, including alcohol. Substance abuse usually lessens achievement in many areas.

Other barriers to achievement exist in one's immediate surroundings. Youths who grow up in homes without books or magazines, with no nutritious food, and living in unsanitary conditions in run-down neighborhoods may have difficulty accomplishing much more than simply surviving.

Still other obstacles hindering growth and development are faced by children with special needs.

CHILDREN WITH SPECIAL NEEDS

The majority of children in our country are "normal," but thousands of other children have special needs.

▪ Children with special needs include those who are emotionally/behaviorally disturbed, who have learning disabilities, who have an attention deficit hyperactivity disorder, or who have behavior problems resulting from prenatal exposure to drugs, including alcohol, or to the Human Immunodeficiency Virus (HIV).

Emotionally/Behaviorally Disturbed Children

One challenging segment of youth are children who are emotionally/behaviorally disturbed (**EBD**) children. Usually emotionally/behaviorally disturbed youth have one or more of the following behavior patterns:

▪ Severely aggressive or impulsive behavior.
▪ Severely withdrawn or anxious behaviors, pervasive unhappiness, depression or wide mood swings.
▪ Severely disordered thought processes that show up in unusual behavior patterns, atypical communication styles and distorted interpersonal relationships.

Such children may have limited coping skills and may be easily traumatized.

Youth with Attention Deficit Hyperactivity Disorder

Attention deficit hyperactivity disorder is a common childhood disruptive behavior disorder affecting from 5 to 10 percent of all children, with boys four times as likely to be affected as girls. Attention deficit hyperactivity disorder is characterized by the following behaviors:

- Heightened motor activity (fidgeting and squirming).
- Short attention span.
- Distractibility.
- Impulsiveness.
- Lack of self-control.

Such behaviors can greatly interfere with learning and are usually unnerving for parents, teachers and other adults.

Youth with Learning Disabilities

From 5 to 10 million children in the United States experience some form of **learning disability.** The Association for Children with Learning Disabilities (ACLD) describes a learning disabled child in the following way (n.d., p. 4): "A learning disability person is an individual who has one or more significant deficits in the essential learning processes."

According to the ACLD (p. 3): "The most frequently displayed symptoms are short attention span, poor memory, difficulty following directions, inadequate ability to discriminate between and among letters, numerals, or sounds, poor reading ability, eye-hand coordination problems, difficulties with sequencing, disorganization and numerous other problems." Such children are often discipline problems, are labeled "underachievers," and are at great risk of becoming drop-outs.

Although usually associated with school, the consequences of learning disabilities go well beyond school. Behaviors that may be problematic include the following:

- Responding inappropriately.
- Saying one thing, meaning another.
- Forgetting easily.
- Acting impulsively.
- Demanding immediate gratification.
- Becoming easily frustrated and then engaging in disruptive behavior.

Other behaviors commonly accompanying learning disability include the following (ACLD, p. 8):

- An inability to read and interpret environment and people.
- An inability to adequately interpret their problems and needs.
- Little thought about the results of their actions—poor judgment.
- Inability to set realistic priorities and goals.
- Inappropriate conclusions due to deficient reasoning ability.
- Illogical reasons for their actions—sometimes even contradicting what was previously stated.
- Inability to develop meaningful social relationships with others; usually these children are loners.
- Inability to draw appropriate conclusions due to poor reasoning.
- Childish and bossy behavior.

Youth with learning disabilities are usually frustrated, have experienced failure after failure and lack self-esteem.

Youth Exposed to Drugs or HIV Prenatally

"Intrauterine exposure to drugs is the epidemic of the 1990s. Drug abuse is not new. . . . But the threat today is like a tidal wave" (Brazelton, 1990, p. 1). According to the National Institute on Drug Abuse, as reported in Sautter (1992, p. K2):

▐ The number of drug-exposed children born each year ranges from 375,000 to 739,000—possibly 18% of all newborns in the United States.
▐ Nearly 5% have been exposed to cocaine, from which crack is derived.
▐ Nearly 17% have been exposed to marijuana.
▐ Nearly 73% have been exposed to alcohol.
▐ By the year 2000 as many as *four million* drug-exposed children will be attending school (italic in original).

Children exposed to cocaine while in the womb, the so-called **crack children,** may exhibit social, emotional and cognitive problems. As noted by Downing (1990, p. 9):

These children, exposed to the damaging effects of cocaine (commonly in its less expensive and highly-addictive crystalized form: crack) while still in the womb, are already showing up in significant numbers in kindergarten classes and preschool programs in New York and Los Angeles. . . .

They may over-react to—or fail to respond to—the stimuli of a classroom. They may have difficulty forming attachments. They may not be capable of structuring their own play or playing with other children.

Typically, these kids don't socialize well, don't work well in groups, and stimulate too easily or do not respond at all—they can be either hyperactive or lethargic.

Griffith (1992, p. 30) cautions against stereotyping such children, however, noting that: "[T]he media have sensationalized the problems these children present and have shown worst-case scenarios as if they were the norm."

A closely related problem is **fetal alcohol syndrome** (FAS). Burgess and Streissguth (1992, p. 24) suggest: "Fetal alcohol syndrome (FAS) is now recognized as the leading known cause of mental retardation in the western world." They estimate that one in 500 to 600 children is born with fetal alcohol syndrome and one in 300 to 350 children has fetal alcohol effects, including the following:

▐ Children are impulsive and have poor communication skills.
▐ Children are not able to predict consequences or to use appropriate judgment in daily life.
▐ Small children may exhibit a high level of activity and distractibility.
▐ Adolescents may suffer frustration and depression.

Another group of children with special needs are those prenatally exposed to HIV. Scott et al. (1989, p. 1791) note: "Today, a disproportionate number of children with HIV infection come from low-income, minority families in our inner cities and acquire the virus from maternal transmission." According to Seidel (1992, p. 39), such children may experience:

▐ Deficits in both gross and fine motor skills.
▐ Reduced flexibility and muscle strength.

■ Cognitive impairment including decreased intellectual levels, specific learning
disabilities, mental retardation, visual/spatial deficits, and decreased alertness.
■ Language delays.

A great number of these children with special needs entered grade school in
the early 1990s and will be adolescents toward the end of the decade. Early
intervention and support is imperative.

CHILDREN AT RISK

Research suggests that some other groups of children may also be at risk as they
grow and develop because of relationships within their family or because of
drugs.

■ Children who *may* be at risk as they grow and develop are children of
immigrants, those who are adopted, those whose parents are divorced,
those whose mothers or fathers are incarcerated and those who are on
drugs.

Immigrants' Children

In addition to language barriers, immigrants experience other problems. Often
families are disrupted with some members being left behind. Another problem,
role reversal, commonly occurs as children more readily learn English and
become translators for their parents, in effect, gaining control. Further, native
customs and values may differ greatly from what is accepted in the United
States. For example, Day (1992, p. 15) reports: "More than one Southeast Asian
family has been investigated for child abuse after health professionals noted the
skin lesions caused by traditional coin rubbing treatment." (*Coining*, thought to
have healing powers, consists of rubbing warm oil and coins across the skin,
and sometimes produces long, red bruises.) Finally, immigrants may also be
subjected to prejudice and discrimination.

Children Who Are Adopted

Studies have shown that adopted children are more likely to become involved
with the social services and juvenile justice systems. A study in Minnesota, for
example, showed that although only 1 or 2 percent of children in Minnesota are
adopted, 10 percent are in state juvenile residential treatment centers and 7
percent are in the county's petty offender program (Hopfensperger, 1988, p. 1A).

Psychologists suggest that part of the reason may be an intensified identity
crisis so common during adolescence. This seems to be particularly problematic
with children who are of a different racial background than their adoptive
parents.

Children Whose Parents Are Divorced

One study (Wallerstein and Corbin, 1986) of father-child relationships after divorce looked at the amount of financial child support provided and its relationship to educational opportunity. This 10-year longitudinal study of 60, largely white, middle-class Northern California families, included 131 children between the ages of two and eighteen at the time of the divorce. This study found that not only did child support payments seldom increase even as the cost of living increased, it also found that such payments often stopped immediately when the legal obligation was fulfilled, usually when the youth became eighteen. Unfortunately, it is at this age that youths aspiring to further education need the most financial support. The study concluded (p. 124): "[I]t is surely tragic that the economic and psychological burdens of divorce not only fall upon children during their growing up years, but may affect them detrimentally throughout their entire adult lives."

Divorce has a shattering effect on families with young children, particularly if the mother has limited education or job skills. According to Hodgkinson (1991, p. 10), some 15 million children are being reared by single mothers—whether divorced or never married. In addition, when mothers go back to work to support the family, the children may be left unsupervised: "At least two million school-age children have no adult supervision at all after school. Two million are being reared by *neither* parent" (Hodgkinson, 1991, p. 10).

Children Whose Mothers or Fathers Are Incarcerated

A study by the National Council on Crime and Delinquency (NCCD), conducted in 1992 (NCJA, 1993), found that more than half of those women in jails and prisons had not seen their children while incarcerated. Typically, the women had histories of physical and sexual abuse and were drug users. Over one-third were serving sentences for drug offenses.

Eighteen percent of the women reported their children having learning or school-related problems; 16 percent reported their children having behavior problems. The study also found that these women tended to underestimate the severity of their children's problems.

Further, children whose mothers have been incarcerated seem to be more likely to be incarcerated themselves if the relationship with their mother is damaged (NCJA, 1993, pp. 1–2, 4).

Another study found that one child in fifty under age 15 may have a parent in jail. The researchers reported that: "Possible medical consequences to children of inmates include exposure to tuberculosis, hepatitis, the AIDS virus or other infections acquired by the parent while incarcerated. . . . Besides poverty, one of the strongest risk factors for juvenile delinquency is a parent who has a criminal history" ("1 In 50 Under Age 15," 1993).

Children Who Are On Drugs

The tremendous impact of drug use on the growth and development of our youth is vividly stated by Moore (n.d., p. 1): "One of the worst aspects of drug use may be its attraction to youths in urban ghettos, for it robs many of their chance for upward mobility. With that, some of the promise and justice of a democratic society is lost."

In a speech to the Child Welfare League of America, former Surgeon General Joycelyn Elders said children are "out in an ocean surrounded by the sharks—drugs, alcohol, homicide, suicide . . . and we've been sitting on the beach sipping from our fountains of 'just say no' . " She said it is easier for many children to find drugs than it is to find hugs ("Quiet Crisis," 1994).

ADOLESCENCE

■ Adolescence refers to youth ages 12 to 19 or 20.

In adolescence children go through puberty, experiencing hormonal changes. During this time adolescents seek independence, yet at the same time can be very much influenced by their peers. Each generation produces a distinct adolescent subculture, with a common language, clothing, music and standards. The result is what is often referred to as a *generation gap*.

According to Canning (1992), adolescence is characterized by:

■ Rapid growth and sexual maturity—self-image, self-centeredness, wondering about body changes, sexuality, intimacy, and sexual identity.
■ Consciousness of self in relation to other people—peer pressure and the shift of the primary support system from parents to friends.
■ Mood swings of high and low feelings—changeable, intense and often confused feelings; outlets for high energy are needed.
■ Experimentation—examining the myth of invulnerability, beginning to learn from experience (doubt advice), developing abstract thinking vs. concrete thinking, new freedoms.
■ Re-evaluation of values—rebelling against "what-is"—search for values that fit lifestyles.
■ Search for identity—a negative identity is better than no identity at all, internal vs. external control, recognition as an individual, seeking independence.
■ Self-image—the need to be valued, to feel worth, to be viewed as capable and contributing.

That adolescence is no longer typified by the carefree lifestyle of the 1950s, depicted in the television program *Happy Days,* is underscored by the large percentage of high school seniors who report worrying about social problems, as shown in Table 4–3. Almost 91 percent of the class of 1993 reported worrying about crime and violence! As shown in the table, this has been of concern to the majority of seniors for the past decade. On a positive note, fear of the chance of nuclear war has greatly lessened, reflecting the dramatic changes that have taken place in the world.

Adolescence is a difficult time of life, not only for youths themselves, but also for their families, schools, neighborhoods and, increasingly, the police. It is a period of stress and social strain.

TABLE 4–3   What U.S. High School Seniors Worry About, 1983–1993

Question: "Of all the problems facing the nation today, how often do you worry about each of the following?

	Class of 1983 (N = 3,339)	Class of 1985 (N = 3,286)	Class of 1987 (N = 3,370)	Class of 1989 (N = 2,849)	Class of 1991 (N = 2,595)	Class of 1993 (N = 2,807)
Chance of nuclear war	66.6%	64.5%	58.3%	52.4%	41.5%	28.8%
Population growth	31.5	25.7	26.6	29.6	30.6	38.9
Crime and violence	85.4	82.3	81.9	86.3	88.1	90.8
Pollution	53.0	46.9	45.2	55.9	72.1	72.8
Energy shortages	49.9	33.7	28.1	27.9	38.2	29.8
Race relations	45.5	43.4	44.2	53.6	59.4	75.4
Hunger and poverty	59.1	69.7	62.2	64.1	66.4	71.1
Using open land for housing or industry	31.9	30.4	30.5	30.8	33.8	32.9
Urban decay	19.5	17.9	18.5	19.8	21.7	25.3
Economic problems	73.5	60.4	55.6	57.6	63.9	71.8
Drug abuse	68.7	69.1	75.4	79.5	79.5	75.5

Note: These data are from a series of nationwide surveys of high school seniors conducted by the Monitoring the Future Project at the Survey Research Center of the Institute for Social Research from 1975 through 1992. The survey design is a multistage random sample of high school seniors in public and private schools throughout the continental United States. All percentages reported are based on weighted cases; the N's that are shown in the tables refer to the number of weighted cases.

Response categories were "never," "seldom," "sometimes," and "often." [Percent responding "often" or "sometimes" are reported in the table.] Readers interested in responses to this question for 1975 through 1979 should consult previous editions of Sourcebook. For survey methodology and definitions of terms, see Appendix 6 [of the Sourcebook].

SOURCE: U.S. Department of Justice, Bureau of Justice Statistics, *Sourcebook of Criminal Justice Statistics, 1993* (Washington, D.C.: U.S. Government Printing Office [1993]), p. 221.

■ Adolescence brings biological, psychological, emotional and social changes, often resulting in stress.

The influence of social change in shaping adolescent behavior is second in importance only to psychological change. The mind must adjust to the conditions, pleasures and pressures of society that influence growth and development to adulthood. This is seldom done smoothly.

Juveniles often pretend to be adults in different ways and activities, but becoming an emotionally mature, socially accepted adult requires a struggle. From a social standpoint, many never succeed. Adolescents may try to look like adults, talk like adults or take on what they believe to be adult ways, but unfortunately they remain quite immature. At the same time that they imitate adult behavior, juveniles also strive for individuality, independence and freedom, which they believe they can achieve by disassociating themselves from society and their parents. Such a position between imitation and disassociation, can generate a great deal of psychological stress.

Typical stressors for adolescents have been suggested by Daniel J. Anderson, President of Hazelden Foundation (1986, p. 5C), which provides a wide range of services related to chemical dependency:

▌ *Families with single parents or both parents working, placing more demands on young people.*
▌ Children never getting a chance to be bored because they are in every scheduled event possible.
▌ Children who are bored because they watch many hours of television each day.
▌ Families that do not provide nutritionally balanced meals for children.
▌ Adults who make statements and act in ways damaging to a child's self-image.
▌ Parents who expect their children to be young adults before they can be.

Anderson (1986) asserts: "These are just some of the possible areas of adolescent stress. As parents or teachers it would be helpful to identify stress in our children's lives, and the place to start would be to ask the children."

Adolescents do communicate messages about their disturbances in growth and development. However, adults frequently do not heed these messages. No matter what social position, class or status, adults often fail to listen to children.

Adolescents in lower socioeconomic classes struggle to succeed academically and financially. Without scholarship assistance, college may be unaffordable. The need to balance education with earning an income can be exhausting and disheartening. More affluent adolescents commonly face pressure to gain admission to the highest ranked colleges. If they don't get into Harvard, Yale or the like, they may be considered failures, especially if their parents attended such schools.

Life for some adolescents is often lonely and depressing. Parents are involved in demanding careers, travel a lot and leave child care to paid help or the extended family. They seldom do things as a family. When young people become bored with the happenings around them or with life in general, they often turn to antisocial or unlawful activity or to self-destruction.

Ruby Takanishi (1994, p. 11), executive director of the Carnegie Council on Adolescent Development, stresses that good health is critical to not only physical but psychological development: "If you have a toothache or a stomachache, or are worried about staying alive in a violence-prone neighborhood, even the most wonderful education won't get you very far." She cites the following statistics:

Over a quarter of 10- to 18-year-olds live in poor or near-poor families. . . . The rates of physical, sexual, and emotional abuse have risen swiftly. Pregnancy rates and births outside of marriage are the highest among industrialized nations.

About 20 percent of people with AIDS are 20–29-year-olds, many infected during adolescence. More kids are experimenting with drugs earlier. Suicide rates are sharply higher. And up to 33 percent of adolescents suffer some form of depression.

Although it is sometimes thought that youth with problems exist primarily in the inner-city, this is simply not the case.

According to Hawkins (1985, p. 51) thousands of middle class youth are "wasting their formative years . . . killing time in discos, video parlors, shopping centers, and other hangouts." Hawkins explains: "Upset with their parents and tired of school, many of these teens band together, substituting peers for family. Police describe the activity as 'rat packing' . "

When this same phenomenon occurs in urban areas, the result would be called a *gang* rather than a rat pack. Hawkins (p. 54) notes that authorities fear that these rat packers: "will become tomorrows criminals or consign themselves to aimless lives. Ill-prepared for a complex society, they may pass on a confused legacy to their children" resulting in an even less desirable next generation.

Teen Pregnancy

One important change within our culture has been a more open attitude toward sex and at least a tolerance of sexual intimacy outside of marriage. In many instances, marriage is no longer a requirement to live together. According to recent polls, the majority of teenage males and females have engaged in sexual intercourse by age 19 (Caldas, 1994, p. 405). The result is a large increase in teenage pregnancy. Data from the National Center for Health Statistics reports that in 1990 533,484 American girls under age 20 gave birth (Ventura et al., 1993).

When teenagers become pregnant, not only is their own growth and development affected, the situation into which they bring their newborn children often is unsuited for the healthy growth and development of these children. Teenage pregnancy has created an "underclass" of poor young women with small children. These women have no training and limited resources.

Caldas (1994, p. 403) reports that 60 percent of teen families live in poverty. Even more devastating, however, is "strong evidence for the intergenerational transfer of poverty to the children of single-parent families."

Some seldom mentioned facts about teen pregnancy are set forth by Males (1994, pp. 408–409):

▐ The large majority of all "teenage" pregnancies are caused by adults. Men older than high school age account for 77% of all births among girls of high school age (ages 16–18) and for 51% of births among girls of junior high school age (15 and younger). Men over age 25 father twice as many "teenage" births as do boys under age 18.

▐ A large majority of all pregnant teenagers have histories of rape, sexual abuse, and physical abuse.

▐ Poverty is the key indicator of early pregnancy.

Males notes that adults model one behavior and preach a different behavior. He suggests (p. 408): "Attempting to contrive and preach 'values' that contradict the values adults practice is an exercise in futility." He concludes: "The problem is not that teenagers are confused or that they reject the values of adults around them, but that they copy them only too well."

According to former Surgeon General Joycelyn Elders, the government spent $34 billion in 1992 on Aid to Families with Dependent Children (AFDC), Medicaid and food stamps for families begun by adolescent parents. Elders noted: "[T]he children of adolescent parents are more likely to become adolescent parents themselves, perpetuating the cycle" ("Teen Moms," 1994).

The Fading of the "American Dream"

As youths develop and approach adulthood, they need to have feelings of self-worth and of hope for their future. Our society places great pressure on individuals to be "successful." As noted by Eitzen (1992, p. 566):

> The highly valued individual in American society is the self-made person—that is, one who has achieved money, position, and privilege through his or her own efforts in a highly competitive system. Economic success, as evidenced by material possessions, is the most common indicator of who is and who is not successful. Moreover, economic success has come to be the common measure of self-worth.
>
> Competition is pervasive in American society, and we glorify the winners. . . . What about the losers in that competition? How do they respond to failure? How do we respond to them? How do they respond to ridicule? How do they react to the shame of being poor? . . . They may respond by working harder to succeed, which is the great American myth. Alternatively, they may become apathetic, drop out, tune out with drugs, join others who are also "failures" in a fight against the system that has rejected them, or engage in various forms of social deviance to obtain the material manifestations of success.

Eitzen (1992, p. 584) notes: "Some young people act in antisocial ways because they have lost their dreams." He compares an individual's economic situation with a boat, noting that it is assumed that just as "a rising tide lifts all boats" a rising economy will elevate the financial status of everyone. This was generally true from 1950 to 1973, with a steady rise in the average standard of living. In the past 20 years, however, this has not been true. As noted by Eitzen: ". . . [S]ince 1973 the water level was not the same for all boats, some boats leaked severely, and some people had no boat at all."

■ The "American Dream" is fading for many youth.

Homes, college education, things formerly taken for granted are now out of reach for millions of Americans. In addition, says Eitzen (p. 587): "Children, so dependent on peer approval, often find the increasing gap in material differences between themselves and their peers intolerable. This may explain why some try to become 'somebody' by acting tough, joining a gang, rejecting authority, experimenting with drugs and sex, or running away from home."

Smith (1993, p. 10) stresses that: "[O]ptimal growth cannot occur when young people do not regard their future as worthwhile." He suggests that many young people lack faith in the future because "the traditional ladder of success has uneven, broken, and even missing rungs." Youth who have no faith in the future are less likely to fear the consequences of using illegal means to obtain what appears to be out of reach through legal means.

A large part of the responsibility for assuring that our youth feel they have a promising future and a stake in our society rests with the family and with the school, the focus of the next chapter.

SUMMARY

The juvenile justice system exists to serve the children and adolescents of our country. Eighteen is the most common age for individuals to legally become adults, no longer under the jurisdiction of the juvenile court. Until that time it is expected that the state will assure the healthy growth and development of its children.

The period from birth to age three is the most formative time of a child's life. For children to learn they require drive, a cue, a response and reinforcement. Praise is usually better than punishment when teaching children. The positive needs to be accentuated.

Great care must be taken when using labels with children. Self-fulfilling prophecies occur when people live up to the labels they are given. Children and adolescents in particular incorporate labels as part of their self-image. An act that violates society's rules is known as *primary deviance*. Acts that result because society has labeled the individual as deviant are known as *secondary deviance*. Labeling theorists state that when a deviant label is attached to particular individuals they become stigmatized and are left little opportunity to be rewarded for conformist behavior. The label becomes a self-fulfilling prophecy.

Children with special needs include those who are emotionally/behaviorally disturbed, who have learning disabilities, who have an attention deficit hyperactivity disorder or who have behavior problems resulting from prenatal exposure to drugs, including alcohol or HIV. Children who *may* be at risk as they grow and develop are children of immigrants, those who are adopted, those whose parents are divorced, those whose mothers or fathers are incarcerated and those who are on drugs.

Adolescence refers to youth ages 12 to 19 or 20. Adolescence brings biological, psychological, emotional and social changes often resulting in stress. It may also bring a fading of the "American Dream" for many youth.

▮ Discussion Questions

1. What is meant by the chapter opening quote?
2. The adult world stresses material and financial gain, social status and winning at any cost. Can children adjust to or understand this attitude? What values should be communicated to children regarding these attitudes?
3. What are common labels for different youths used in local high schools, e.g., nerd? How can the labels hurt youths?
4. Can labels be beneficial? What might be some positive effects of labeling?
5. How can a youth overcome negative labels?

131

6. Should status offenders be labeled delinquent? Does a court appearance by a status offender stigmatize the offender?
7. At what age do individuals become adults in your state?
8. Do you know any children who have special needs or who may be at risk for not developing "normally"? If so, have they managed to overcome their particular problem?
9. Do you recall your adolescent period? How would you characterize it? What were stressors for you?
10. Do you believe the "American Dream" is attainable for those willing to sacrifice and to work hard?

■ References

"1 in 50 Under Age 15 May Have a Jailed Parent." Reported in (Minneapolis/St. Paul) *Star Tribune,* 10 August 1993, p. 1A.

Anderson, Daniel J. "Stress in Children is Overlooked." (Minneapolis/St. Paul) *Star-Tribune 24 March 1986 p. 5C.*

Association for Children with Learning Disabilities. "Taking the First Step to Solving Learning Problems." Pittsburgh, Penn.: Association for Children with Learning Disabilities, pamphlet, n.d.

Brazelton, T. Berry. *Identifying the Needs of Drug-Affected Children: 1990 Issue Forum.* Washington, D.C.: Office for Substance Abuse Prevention, U.S. Department of Health and Human Services, 1990.

Burgess, Donna M., and Ann P. Streissguth. "Fetal Alcohol Syndrome and Fetal Alcohol Effects: Principles for Educators." *Phi Delta Kappan,* September 1992, pp. 24–30.

Caldas, Stephen J. "Teen Pregnancy: Why It Remains a Serious Social, Economic, and Educational Problem in the U.S." *Phi Delta Kappan,* January 1994, pp. 402–405.

Canning, Miles (ed.). "Both Sides of Adolescence." Richfield, Minn.: Storefront/Youth Action, 1992.

Caticchio, John A. *Putting Humpty Back Together.* Wayzata, Minn.: Vivere Publications, 1990.

Darrow, Clarence. *Crime: Its Causes and Treatment.* London: Watts, 1934.

Day, Thomas W. "Cross-Cultural Medicine at Home." *Minnesota Medicine,* March 1992, pp. 15–17.

"Developmental Risk Called High for U.S. Children: Study Raises Fears They Won't Be Responsible Adults." *New York Times,* reported in (Minneapolis/St. Paul) *Star Tribune,* 12 April 1994, p. 1A.

Downing, David. "Coming Soon to a Classroom Near You: 'Crack Kids.' " *Advocate,* 5 October 1990, p. 9.

Eitzen, Stanley. "Problem Students: The Sociocultural Roots." *Phi Delta Kappan,* April 1992, pp. 584–590.

Gelman, David. "The Miracle of Resiliency." *Newsweek Special Edition,* Summer 1991, pp. 44–47.

Griffith, Dan R. "Prenatal Exposure to Cocaine and Other Drugs: Developmental and Educational Prognoses." *Phi Delta Kappan,* September 1992, pp. 30–34.

Hall, Elizabeth; Michael E. Lamb; and Marion Perlmutter. *Child Psychology Today,* 2nd ed. New York: Random House, 1986.

Hawkins, Steve L. " 'Rat Pack' Youth: Teenage Rebels in Suburbia." *U.S. News & World Report,* 11 March 1985, pp. 51–54.

Hodgkinson, Harold. "Reform versus Reality." *Phi Delta Kappan,* September 1991, pp. 9–16.

Hopfensperger, Jean. "New Wave of Adopted Children Confronting Special Problems." (Minneapolis/St. Paul) *Star Tribune,* 7 November 1988, pp. 1A, 9A.

Lemert, Edwin. *Social Pathology.* New York: McGraw-Hill, 1951.

Louv, Richard. *Children's Future.* Boston: Houghton Mifflin, 1990.

Males, Mike. "Poverty, Rape, Adult/Teen Sex: Why 'Pregnancy Prevention' Programs Don't Work." *Phi Delta Kappan,* January 1994, pp. 407–410.

Moore, Mark. *Drug Trafficking.* Washington, D.C.: National Institute of Justice, n.d.

National Criminal Justice Association. "Many Mothers Serving Time Never See Their Children, Says NCCD Report." *Juvenile Justice,* July 1993, pp. 1–2, 4.

"Quiet Crisis—Half of Tots Face Problems." Reported by Associated Press. [Cited 13 April 1994.] Available from Prodigy Interactive Services Co., White Plains, NY.

Samenow, Stanton E. *Before It's Too Late: Why Some Kids Get into Trouble—and What Parents Can Do about it.* New York: Times Books, 1989.

Sautter, R. Craig. "Crack: Healing the Children." *Phi Delta Kappan Special Report,* November 1992, pp. K1–K12.

Scott, Gwendolyn B. et al. "Survival of Children with Prenatally Acquired Human Immunodeficiency Virus Type I Infection." *New England Journal of Medicine,* 321 (1989):1791–1796.

Seidel, John F. "Children with HIV-Related Developmental Difficulties." *Phi Delta Kappan,* September 1992, pp. 38–56.

Smetanka, Mary Jane. "New Hope for 'At-Risk' Children: Schools Learning to Help Kids Build on Inborn Resilience." (Minneapolis/St. Paul) *Star Tribune,* 1 November 1993, pp. 1A, 16A.

Smith, Robert L. "In the Service of Youth: A Common Denominator." *Juvenile Justice,* 1, (Fall/Winter 1993) 2:16–22.

Takanishi, Ruby. "Young Lives in the Balance: Participant Interview." *The Participant.* New York: TIAA/CREF, April 1994, pp. 10–11.

"Teen Moms Are Found to Feed Cycle of Welfare." Associated Press, reported in (Minneapolis/St. Paul) *Star Tribune,* 3 June 1994, p. 7A.

Ventura, Stephanie J.; Joyce A. Martin; and Thomas Dunn. "Advance Report of Final Natality Statistics, 1990." *Monthly Vital Statistics Report.* National Center for Health Statistics, February 1993, supp.

Wallerstein, Judith S., and Shauna B. Corbin. "Father-Child Relationships After Divorce: Child Support and Educational Opportunity." *Family Law Quarterly,* 20 (Summer 1986) 2:109–128.

Wilson, John J. "A National Agenda for Children: On the Front Lines with Attorney General Janet Reno." *Juvenile Justice* (Fall/Winter 1993) 2:2–8.

The Family and the School: Two Powerful Influences on Youths' Development

What you live, you learn. What you learn, you practice. What you practice, you become. What you become is a pattern. Patterns create consequences.

Author unknown

Do You Know?

Why the structure and interaction patterns of the home are important?
What are characteristics of a healthy family?
What *adult supremacy* refers to?
What common values might be passed on to our youth?
What the principle of *in loco parentis* refers to?
What is the likely result of succeeding in school?
What educational practices may encourage failure?
How students might respond to failure in school?
Whether failure in school and delinquency are linked?
What have been identified as the two most important problems facing local public schools?
How many children are born at risk of being educationally disadvantaged?
How might negative norms and behavior be offset?
What rights students have within the school?
What standard has been set by the Supreme Court for cases involving students' rights?

Can You Define the Following Key Terms?

adult supremacy, educare, *in loco parentis*, Norman Rockwell family

INTRODUCTION

$\mathbf{T}$wo of the most powerful influences on the growth and development of our youth are the family and the school, both of which have undergone tremendous changes in the past few decades. The preceding chapter on how children and adolescents develop should have made obvious the importance of these two institutions. This chapter takes an in-depth look at the family, at practices such as spanking, at values that might be instilled in our youth and at how the disintegration of the family is affecting society as a whole, including the juvenile justice system.

The second major influence, the school, has also undergone significant changes and is facing new challenges, including increased crime and violence as well as more children entering school not ready to learn. This chapter looks at common educational practices that might promote failure, how students might react to that failure and what link this has with delinquent behavior. It then discusses what steps schools have taken and what more might be done to enhance student learning and success. The chapter concludes with a brief discussion of students' constitutional rights within the school setting.

THE IMPORTANCE OF FAMILY

The preceding discussion on growth and development should make amply clear the vital role the family has in healthy growth and development. The *OJJDP Annual Report, 1990* (p. vi) notes: "Strong families are the foundation of a sound society. America is blessed with many. They teach the moral values that develop respect for one's own responsibilities and for the rights of others."

In November 1989, the General Assembly of the United Nations adopted several articles outlining the "rights of the child" (U.N., 1989). The importance of the family was stressed in the preamble of this declaration of rights. The United Nations recognized that:

■ [T]he family, as the fundamental group of society and the natural environment for the growth and well-being of all its members and particularly children, should be afforded the necessary protection and assistance so that it can fully assume its responsibilities within the community . . .

■ [T]he child, for the full and harmonious development of his or her personality, should grow up in a family environment, in an atmosphere of happiness, love and understanding . . .

■ [T]he child should be fully prepared to live an individual life in society, and be brought up in the spirit of the ideals proclaimed in the Charter of the United

Nations, and in particular in the spirit of peace, dignity, tolerance, freedom, equality, and solidarity.

These powerful statements convey not only the importance of the family, but also the values that the family is to instill in children as it nurtures them and teaches them to be individuals as well as contributing members of society.

The family is a significant force in the growth and development of children. The National Council of Juvenile and Family Court Judges dedicated its Metropolitan Court Judges Committee Report on Deprived Children (1985, p. 2) to:

> the goal of preserving and strengthening American families. Only by securing stable and nurturing family structures—with capable and caring parents and safeguarded and well-cared-for children—can our nation hope to surmount the tragedies of millions of children who are deprived primarily because of family failure.
>
> The efforts of skilled and committed judges, legislators, law enforcement officers, health and child care workers, doctors, teachers, attorneys, volunteers and others involved in the lives of deprived children can do little without a rekindled national awareness that the family is the foundation for the protection, care and training of our children.

The closing statement of the Judges Committee report (pp. 41–42) makes amply clear the critical role of the family:

> Both parents—natural, adopted or foster parents or parent substitutes—must actively demonstrate the love, trust, care, control and discipline which result in secure, emotionally happy and healthy children. It is the role of society to engender within its citizens the awareness of what it is to be a good parent. No public or private agency, child care, social worker, teacher or friend can replace the parents in the child's mind. To the extent that family life is damaged or failing, our children, their children and the nation will suffer. The high calling of "parenthood" must be more adequately recognized, respected and honored by our society. Therein lies the future of our nation.

___

■ **The structure and interaction patterns of the home influence whether children learn social or delinquent behavior.**

___

In general, the family can have a positive impact on insulating children from antisocial and criminal patterns, providing it can control rewards and effectively maintain positive relationships within the family unit. Delinquency is highest when family interaction and controls are weak.

Family relationships are much more complex than relationships between two people. A family of five, for example, has 10 one-to-one relationships, 10 three-person relationships, and 5 four-person relationships for a total of 25 separate relationships. Parker et al. (1989, p. 109) note that the larger the family becomes, the more complicated the relationships become. A family with eight children has a total of 1,011 different relationships.

THE FAMILY AS THE FIRST TEACHER

The family is usually the first teacher or model in behavior and misbehavior. It is the first social institution to affect children's behavior and to provide knowledge of and access to the goals and expectations of the broad society. However, if the integration process between parents and children is deficient, the children may fail to learn appropriate behaviors. In the learning process, children should develop a sense of right and wrong. The home becomes their first classroom, and parents serve as their first educators.

Canning (1992) emphasizes that:

▮ We need to find out what it is our children want and need; not what they don't like (p. 10).
▮ All of us have a life-long need for acceptance and positive strokes from others (p. 11).
▮ Our children face a world we don't fully understand and a future that we know will be different from our past (p. 15).
▮ Natural, normal development is characterized by the individual seeking independence from parents, finding an identity separate from the family, and making decisions based upon a developing sense of autonomy (p. 18).

Some psychologists who study families see the role of the family as *peoplemaking*. In this process four main areas of learning are important (Parker et al., 1989, p. 110):

▮ *The home is a child's first classroom. This grandfather is active in an early childhood reading readiness program.*

1. Feelings of self-worth.
2. Communication patterns.
3. Rules about how people should feel and act.
4. Link to society—the ways members relate to other people and institutions.

Children need to feel wanted and loved. They need to be able to communicate openly and clearly with others. They need to know what is expected of them and what to expect of others. And they need a sense of belonging to their family, their community and the broader society.

■ In healthy families, self-esteem is high, communication is direct and honest, rules are flexible and reasonable and members' attitudes toward the outside world are trusting and optimistic.

According to Parker et al. (1989, p. 110):

> Conversely, troubled families promote feelings of low self-worth, have distorted patterns of communication, have rigid, non-negotiable rules, and promote a blaming or fearful view of society.

Effective communication involves much more than simply talking and listening. It involves not only factual statements but feelings and attitudes. It may require reviewing and adjusting beliefs; it may involve identifying problems and searching for solutions. Figure 5–1 illustrates this process.

AMERICAN CHILD-REARING RIGHTS AND PRACTICES

Physically punishing children is generally supported in the United States. The familiar adage "Spare the rod, and spoil the child" attests to the traditional American view that it is parents' responsibility to teach their children right from wrong. Before children can reason, physical measures may be relied upon. The question becomes not so much whether such physical coercion is appropriate, but rather what *degree* of physical coercion is appropriate. In other words, when does punishment become abuse? Is a slap on the hand the same as a slap to the face? Is a "paddling" through clothing with a bare hand the same as a beating with a belt on a bare bottom? Or is physical coercion ever justified?

In 1994 an American teenager, Michael Fay, was found guilty of vandalizing some cars in Singapore. He was sentenced to serve time in jail as well as to receive six blows with a cane. Despite pleas for clemency from President Clinton, many, many American citizens supported the punishment. According to a Prodigy poll, 75 percent of the 60,000 members responding said Fay should be flogged. Another 57% said U.S. courts should use flogging. In an article applauding the flogging of Michael Fay, a student at New York University, Wu (1994, p. 25A) wrote:

> [T]here is something simplistic and powerful about using whacks on the behind as corporal punishment, a back-to-the-basics method that may be the answer to the growing violence in this country.

∎ FIGURE 5–1 The Communication Process

Too many 18-year-olds are running wild, waving guns, pointing them at people. Too many young people are bad and, most dangerously, too many are fearless. They roll their eyes at lectures, laugh at teachers when suspended and think of a night in jail as an adventure. They brag about their badness and bravery to friends. To the average 18-year-old, everything is like a TV sitcom.... at eighteen you live in a world without consequences.

So, here's to Michael Fay from one 18-year-old to another. "Take it like a man, sonny. You've done something bad, so face up to your consequences. Remember the pain, the humiliation and fear. Let's hope you've learned your lesson."

Such reasoning is often used by parents in justifying the use of spanking to discipline their children.

The Spanking Controversy

A three-year violence prevention project conducted in Minnesota by Murray Straus, head of the Family Research Laboratory at the University of New Hampshire, suggests that parents seldom accomplish the positive results they hope for by spanking. In addition, the study found that spanking may have much less desirable impacts (Walsh, 1994, p. 1B):

Children who are spanked are much more likely to be aggressive with other children. . . . They are also more likely to grow up to be aggressive adults.

Walsh (p. 8B) reports on other negative effects spanking may have:

Straus said that spanking has been shown to be related to lower income and occupational achievement for children who go on to graduate from college and that it may inhibit the development of self-confidence. "Spanking," said Straus, "leaves children feeling powerless and depressed."

Straus also conducted the second National Family Violence Survey, funded by the National Institute of Mental Health. The findings of this and other studies are described in his upcoming book, *Beating the Devil Out of Them: Corporal Punishment in American Families.* In another article West (1994, p. 13) reports that Straus confirms the harmful effects of spanking:

Children who are spanked a lot are from two to five times more likely to be physically aggressive as children, to become juvenile delinquents as adolescents and, as adults, to suffer from depression, according to Straus. "The only people we allow to be hit are children," he says. "If you hit your neighbor, that would be a physical assault. That's a crime."

Despite such findings, spanking remains an issue. And, according to Straus' research, 90 percent of parents spank their toddlers (West, 1994, p. 13). Supporting the *reasonable* use of spanking, Dr. Den A. Trumbull, an Alabama pediatrician and authority on parental discipline, says spanking is a useful, harmless tool if used properly, especially for children ages two to six who are openly defiant of their parents. Dr. Trumbull also stresses using praise liberally for good behavior.

West (1994, p. 14) notes that researchers say: "[M]ost studies conducted on corporal punishment provide more heat than light. The research generally is loaded with more editorial comment than original data and more study is needed." West also notes that researchers generally accept two statements regarding parenting as true:

1. Most people tend to raise their children the way they were raised, good or bad.
2. Extreme levels of physical punishment are bad.

Adult Supremacy

Force and violence toward children, including physical punishment, has been characterized as **adult supremacy.** In this relationship power is sanctioned by legal rules with the effect being to subordinate one person—within limits—to the arbitrary authority of another person.

■ Adult supremacy subordinates children to the absolute and arbitrary authority of parents.

The dangers of adult supremacy were noted over 80 years ago by Ledlie (1907, p. 449):

The right of control based on family law produces subordination, not a mere obligation. It represents a power over free persons and a power which curtails the freedom of those subject to it, because the person in whom power vests is entitled to exercise it, up to a certain point, in his own interests alone, to exercise it, in a word, as he chooses.

Adults have a legally protected right to bodily integrity, free from assault, but children do not, except in extreme circumstances. Parents are authorized to use force against their children because society believes adults are older and presumably wiser, and because the right to rear one's child as one chooses is held to be fundamental.

Courts give parents wide latitude in disciplining their children so they learn to respect authority. Such discipline, says Maurer (1974, p. 614), "always suggests action in the interest of order, rule, or control by authority."

Another explanation for adult supremacy, including violence and force against children, is given by Foster (1974, p. 4), who feels it is inherited from "a common law concept of status derived from a feudal order which denied children legal identity and treated them as objects or things, rather than persons." He notes that in the United States up until about 1900, the only person in the family who had any legal rights was the father. The status of children today is akin to the status of women and blacks before their emancipation. When issues arise regarding children's moral and legal rights, "there is a conflict between the principles of subordination and equality which are characteristics of a society that traces its origins to a patriarchal culture" (p. 6). This conflict indicates "paternalistic measures may be more protective of ancient paternal prerogatives than of the best interest of minors" (p. 55).

The power vested in parents brings to mind Acton's maxim that power tends to corrupt and absolute power corrupts absolutely—a thought-provoking idea, considering that children are the most powerless group in the world, both physically and politically.

Socialization

Children should learn in the home that others have rights which they must respect. They should learn about social and moral values; to consider others' property, possessions and individual self; to manage their own affairs and to take responsibility for their actions.

The family, in the socialization process, is also concerned with ways to suppress or eliminate behavior considered undesirable. Behavior that does not conform to social standards is disturbing to group members and is seen as a threat to the cohesiveness and psychological integrity of the group. When children display unacceptable behavior, the family rushes to correct them to get rid of the undesirable behavior. It would be far more effective to teach them socially acceptable patterns, such as honesty and fair play.

It is partly because of the failure of families to teach children basic conformity to social values and standards that children look for alternative groups. This search for alternatives can produce the subculture group, or gang, and misbehavior.

Children develop their sense of being worthwhile, capable, important and unique individuals from the attention and love given to them by their parents.

They can develop a sense of worthlessness, incapability, unimportance and facelessness from a lack of attention and love, or from physical or sexual abuse. The development of social cognition as perceived by psychologists is outlined in Table 5–1.

Note that the development begins during the end of the critical first three years and for most children is completed during adolescence.

TABLE 5–1   Development of Social Cognition

	Understanding Self	Understanding Others	Understanding Friends	Understanding Social Roles	Understanding Society
Preoperational Period (About age 2–7)	Understands concrete attributes Understands major emotions, but relies on situation	Understands concrete attributes, including stability of behavior	One-way assistance (age 4–9)	Can generalize role (age 4) Understands person can change role and remain same person	Feels no need to explain system (age 5–6)
Concrete Operational Period (About age 7–12)	Understands personal qualities Relies on inner feelings as guide to emotions Understands shame and pride	Understands personal qualities	Fairweather cooperation (age 6–12)	Understands that people can occupy two roles simultaneously	Understands social functions observed or experienced (age 7–8) Provides fanciful explanations of distant functions (age 9–10) Has acquired concrete knowledge of society
Formal Operational Period (After about age 12)	Capable of complex, flexible, precise description Understands abstract traits Establishes identity	Capable of complex, flexible, precise description	Intimate sharing (age 9–15)		Can deal with abstract conception of society, government, and politics (by age 15)

SOURCE: Elizabeth Hall, Michael E. Lamb, and Marion Perlmutter, *Child Psychology Today*, 2nd ed. (New York: Random House, 1986), p. 562. Reprinted with permission of McGraw–Hill.

One important aspect of socialization is passing on the values of society. As noted by Pace (1991, p. 108): "The future of this nation depends upon the values they [our youth] are forming. They obviously will be the future decision-makers of our society."

VALUES

Values are extremely important in any society. Values reflect the nature of the society, what is most important. Values describe how individuals are expected to behave. Throughout the ages, societies have embraced certain values, taught these values to their children and punished those who did not adhere to them. When youth do not accept the values of society, conflict is inevitable.

Families, schools and the broader community need to examine their values and, if found to be "good," teach these values to our youth. Canning (1992, p. 36) suggests the following as common values in most communities:

- ▮ Equality: All people have the same rights.
- ▮ Honesty: Telling the truth; meaning what you say.
- ▮ Promise-Keeping: Keeping your promises; keeping your word.
- ▮ Respect: Treating everyone, including yourself, with dignity.
- ▮ Responsibility: Carrying out your obligations or duties and answering for your own actions.
- ▮ Self-Control: Being able to control your own actions.
- ▮ Social Justice: Being fair to all people.

▮ **Common values that might be passed on to our youth include equality, honesty, promise-keeping, respect, responsibility, self-control and social justice.**

Unfortunately, in many families, no values or negative values, such as the use of violence to resolve disputes, are passed on. This is one focus of the next chapter.

Criminologist James Q. Wilson said in a speech about fighting crime that the approach must be to regain our "moral sense":

Obviously criminals are not inclined to follow the golden rule. . . . The question is not what our values ought to be. Every reasonable person knows what they ought to be. But what is the best way to inculcate them?" (von Sternberg, 1994, p. 9B).

One cause of this lack of a "moral sense" in many of our youth is the disintegration of the traditional family.

THE DISINTEGRATION OF THE TRADITIONAL FAMILY

Unquestionably, the family has undergone great changes over the years. What began as an extended family, with two or three generations of a family living together, gradually became a nuclear family consisting of parents and their children. When the children grew up, they moved out and started their own family. Changes that have occurred in contemporary American society have been more problematic, including more single-parent families, blended families, adoptive families and dysfunctional families.

Eitzen (1992, p. 588) notes the changes that have occurred in American families: "These trends indicate widespread family instability in American society—and that instability has increased dramatically in a single generation." Hodgkinson (1991, p. 10) reports that: "The **Norman Rockwell family**—a working father, a housewife mother and two children of school age—constitutes only 6 percent of U.S. households . . . " (bold added).

More than 60 percent of all children born in the 1990s will spend at least some time in a single-parent household before reaching age 18. The magnitude of the collapse of family structure is historically unprecedented and is at the root of many social and economic problems.

A major study of children from one-parent families, conducted by the National Association of Elementary School Principals, has found 30 percent of the two-parent elementary school students were ranked as high achievers, compared with only 17 percent of the one-parent children. At the other end of the scale, 23 percent of the two-parent children were low achievers versus 38 percent of the one-parent children. There were more clinic visits among one-parent students, and their rate of absence from school ran higher. One-parent students were consistently more likely to be late, truant and subject to disciplinary action. One-parent children were found to be more than twice as likely to drop out of school altogether.

The Census Bureau found in the 1990s that two-thirds of all people in female-headed families with children under 18 get benefits from a welfare program (Aid to Families with Dependent Children, General Assistance, Supplemental Security Income, Medicaid, food stamps, rent assistance). Further, of all never-married mothers, more than 80 percent receive some kind of government check. The federal government spends more than a hundred billion dollars every year on assistance to families. But this aid does not come close to providing households with the security most intact families enjoy.

In the early 1980s during the New Hampshire primary campaign, Jimmy Carter stated: "The steady erosion and weakening of our families" required the development of a new "pro-family policy." The next four years saw proposal after proposal meet opposition and, in most cases, defeat. Among the legislation were bills regulating abortion, adolescent pregnancy, child and foster care and a lowered age limit for charging juveniles as adults.

Others continue to recognize the needs of children and families. According to Smith (1993, p. 10):

> The problems plaguing our young—alienation, isolation, dependency, and delinquency—are related to the gradual but progressive deprivation of opportunities to participate in family and community life. Children are expected to mature at progressively younger ages at the same time that youth are increasingly treated as children.

The first item on Attorney General Janet Reno's "National Agenda for Children" is families:

First, we need to develop family preservation ·programs that offer support to families *before* they are in a crisis situation so they are much more likely to stay together through life's difficulties. We've got to make sure that our parents are old enough, wise enough, and financially able to take care of their children. We've got to make a major effort against teen pregnancy in America. And we've got to offer parenting skill courses in every school so that children who have been raised without quality support from parents learn how to give it to their own children (Wilson, 1993, p. 2).

THE ROLE OF THE SCHOOL

Schools have a responsibility for the students who attend under the principle of *in loco parentis.*

▮ The principle of *in loco parentis,* meaning "in place of parents," gives certain social and legal institutions the authority to act as a parent might in situations requiring discipline or need.

The school is one such institution. Most youngsters have education as their "sole occupation."

The U.N. Convention on the Rights of the Child said of schools that "education should be directed at developing the child's personality and talents, preparing the child for active life as an adult, fostering respect for basic human rights and developing respect for the child's own cultural and national values and those of others" (U.N., 1989, Article 29, p. 9).

Schools tend to stress academic learning, yet a decade ago a leading psychologist, Howard Gardner, set forth his theory of multiple intelligences. Gardner (1983, p. 69) warned, however:

There is a universal human temptation to give credence to a word to which we have become attached, perhaps because it has helped us to understand a situation better. . . . [I]ntelligence is such a word; we use it so often that we have come to believe in its existence, as a genuine tangible, measurable entity, rather than as a convenient way of labeling some phenomena that may (but may well not) exist.

Gardner believes that each individual may have several different "intelligences": linguistic, musical, logical-mathematical, spatial, bodily-kinesthetic and personal. Not all intelligences are equally developed in any single person, but the potential in each area exists. The challenge to educators is to discover which "intelligences" are most developed in each student and to capitalize on these strengths. Being able to praise children for nonacademic accomplishments strengthens the teacher-student relationship and should promote learning and understanding.

The Importance of Success in School

The importance of succeeding in school was emphasized by noted educator William Glasser (1969, p. 5) in his classic work *Schools Without Failure:* "I believe that if a child, no matter what his background, can succeed in school, he has an excellent chance for success in life. If he fails at any stage of his educational career—elementary school, junior high, high school, or college— his chances for success in life are greatly diminished."

■ **Children who succeed in school have a greater probability of succeeding in other areas of their lives.**

A serious obstacle to achieving academically is an anti-achievement ethic in many schools. What is perceived as "cool" is skipping school, misbehaving in class, smarting off to teachers and others in authority. What is "uncool" is to get good grades. In a senior high school in a crime-infested ward of Washington, D.C., according to Suskind (1994): "Teachers call what goes on here the 'crab bucket symdrome.' When one crab tries to climb from a bucket, the others pull it back down." Students are often torn between wanting to be accepted by their peers and wanting to succeed in school. Academic success in many schools assures social ostracism.

Another reason children do so poorly in school is because they see nothing of relevance to them. Over two decades ago, Father John Culkin (1966, p. 51) noted:

> The schools are no longer dealing with the student of 1900 whose sources of information were limited to the home, church, school, and neighborhood gang. Today's student comes equipped with a vast reservoir of facts and vicarious experiences gleaned from the news media. All the analogies comparing the mind to a blank page or an empty bucket died with Edison. The teacher is now in

■ *Children who experience success in school are likely to also experience success in life; those who experience failure in school are likely to also experience failure in life.*

competition with a host of rival communicators, most of them are smarter, richer, and considerably more efficient. Relevance and competence are educational tactics against which students have not devised a defense.

And that was nearly 30 years ago. Consider how much the media has advanced and what teachers now have to compete against. In addition to sometimes lacking relevance, several school practices actually encourage failure.

HOW SCHOOLS PROMOTE FAILURE

Glasser notes (1969, p. 59): "Probably the school practice that most produces failure in students is *grading*. If there is one sacred part of education, revered throughout almost the entire United States as utilitarian and necessary, it is A-B-C-D-F grading." He continues (p. 60):

> Today, grades are the be-all and end-all of education. The only acceptable grades are good ones, and these good grades divide the school successes from the school failures. Grades are so important that they have become a substitute for education itself. Ask your own small child what is most important in school and he will tell you, "Grades." . . . Grades have become moral equivalents. A good grade is correlated with good behavior, a bad grade with bad behavior, a correlation that unfortunately is very high.

In many schools what Glasser condemned 30 years ago continues to be standard practice.

A second educational practice Glasser says helps produce failure is *objective testing*. Such testing is usually based on memorization of facts, many of which students see as irrelevant. Only the "successful" student will continue to memorize these often irrelevant facts to continue to receive good grades.

Closely related to objective testing is the common educational practice of *grading on a normal curve*. By definition, in this system, 50 percent of the students must be below average!

According to Glasser (p. 72): "The fourth poor educational practice, closed-book examinations, is based on the *fallacy* that *knowledge remembered is better than knowledge looked up*." Living in the information age, it is critical that students learn to use references, not to simply memorize often irrelevant facts.

Another common school practice contributing to student failure is *tracking*, grouping students either by ability level or achievement and often labeling the high achieving group the "college-bound" or "college preparatory" group. Some negative consequences of tracking are outlined by Siegel and Senna (1988, pp. 305–6):

∎ *Self-fulfilling prophecy.* Low-track students, from whom little achievement and more misbehavior are expected, tend to live up to these often unspoken assumptions about their behavior.

∎ *Stigma.* The *labeling* effect in a low track leads to loss of self-esteem, which increases the potential for academic failure and troublemaking both in and out of school.

■ *Student subculture.* Students segregated in lower tracks develop a value system that often rewards misbehavior rather than the academic success they feel they can never achieve.

■ *Future rewards.* Low-track students are less inclined to conform. Because they see no future rewards for their schooling, their futures are not threatened by a record of deviance or low academic achievement.

■ *Grading policies.* Low-track students tend to receive lower grades than other students, even for work of equal quality, based on the rationale that students who are not college-bound are less bright and do not need good grades to get into college.

■ *Teacher effectiveness.* Teaching high-ability students takes more of an effort to teach in an interesting and challenging manner than teaching lower-level students.

■ **Educational practices that may encourage failure include the A-B-C-D-F grading system, objective testing, grading on a curve, having closed-book tests and tracking students.**

The educational practices discussed are not an indictment of the schools, but a partial explanation of why so many students fail in school and how this failure affects not only their school performance but also their behavior in all other areas of their lives.

Canady and Hotchkiss (1989, p. 68) offer the following comments:
Perhaps identifying and teaching the best students was once a valid function of the schools. After all, until fairly recently the American economy did not need large numbers of highly educated workers. However, when 15 million children are at risk of academic failure and of joining the ranks of the chronically unemployed, that time has clearly passed. To help such children become productive citizens, schools must shift their focus from sorting and selecting to teaching and learning.

They suggest that current grading policies and practices are often counterproductive for students at all ability levels. Twelve specific, counterproductive grading procedures are discussed (pp. 68–71):

1. Varying grading scales. A score of 75 percent correct can be a C in one system and an F in another.
2. Worshipping averages. A student who arrives late for a test and as a result does not finish it may receive a score that can lower the grade for the entire grading period. Additionally, no one works at peak performance at all times. This problem might be reduced by allowing students to drop their worst grade in a grading period.
3. Using zeros indiscriminately. One or two zeros can drop a student's grade a whole level. And frequently the zeros are not related to academics. Some teachers, for example, give zeros for negative behavior, lack of classroom participation and lack of punctuality.
4. Following the pattern of assign, test, grade and teach. All too often students are given an assignment and told to be ready for a test on the

material the next day. After the test, the teacher discusses where the students made mistakes.

5. Failing to match testing to teaching. Some teachers pride themselves on the difficulty of their tests. They may stress recall during class discussions and then test for application and analysis.

6. Ambushing students. The infamous "pop quiz" is an example of ambushing students to "keep them on their toes." According to Canady and Hotchkiss (p. 70): "Pop quizzes are simply punitive measures that teachers employ when they suspect that their students have not learned the material."

7. Suggesting that success is unlikely. High school teachers often warn their students that they've come into the "big time" and won't be given so many As and Bs or that they'll find it much harder to get good grades now.

8. Practicing "gotcha" teaching. Teachers sometimes have their own hidden objectives that they don't share with their students. It's up to the students to guess what's important to learn.

9. Grading first efforts. This is very similar to the assign, test, grade, teach procedure. "The standard practice, from kindergarten through college, seems to be to assign grades first and then to give feedback (p. 71)."

10. Penalizing students for taking risks. Students may register for an advanced course and find that it is "over their heads." Often such students are not allowed to change their registration.

11. Failing to recognize measurement error. Frequently teachers assign the same weight to homework, pop quizzes, papers, tests and major projects.

12. Establishing inconsistent criteria. One teacher may penalize students for late papers; another teacher may not. One teacher may count off for spelling errors in an essay test; another teacher may not. One teacher may count off for guessing on multiple-choice or true/false tests; another teacher may not.

Canady and Hotchkiss (p. 71) conclude: "We are not advocating lowering standards. Rather, we wish to raise expectations for success by expanding students' chances to succeed."

Student Response to Failure

When students fail to meet expectations of teachers or parents, they may become involved in delinquent groups of youths who share similar experiences of abuse or failure. The group provides the needed outlet for frustration and anger. Some students skip school or drop out completely. Other youths run away. Some seek escape in alcohol and other drugs or attempt suicide.

▮ Students' responses to failure include skipping school, joining gangs, dropping out of school, drinking, doing drugs, performing delinquent acts and even suicide.

THE LINK BETWEEN DELINQUENCY AND THE SCHOOLS

Glasser suggests that the school must take a large part of the responsibility for the delinquency problem. Glasser (1969, p. 2) describes a group counseling session with seven girls:

> These girls had all been in trouble with the law. Their juvenile offense was incorrigibility. Refusing to obey their parents, the school authorities, or the local juvenile curfew ordinances, they had, for example, stayed out all night, associated with people of whom their parents disapproved, cut school on many occasions, and dabbled in illegal drugs, alcohol, and sex. Although not hard-core delin-quents, they had already been put into a local custodial institution; further trouble would lead them to the state reform school. Of the seven girls in the group, five firmly believed that they were failures in life and that they could not reverse this failure; the other two thought they might succeed in the school but had little confidence in success anywhere else. The five said that they would only go through the motions in school, that they had no hope of learning anything that would be valuable now or later in their lives. They realized that without a good education they were handicapped, but when I asked them whether they would work hard in school now that they recognized the gravity of their situation, they said they would only try hard enough to pass. Having accepted school failure, they would make no effort that might lead to success in school.
>
> The girls also described their failure to make warm, constructive relationships with their families or their teachers; they even lacked warm feelings for each other, although they had lived together for several months. As they were resigned to school failure, so were they resigned to the lack of important human relationships. Although they were not happy in the institution they were living in, they predicted that they would do poorly at home, mostly because they had no confidence in their chances of succeeding in school. They readily admitted that most of their problems at home with their parents concerned school failure and their association with in-school or out-of-school failures.

■ The link between failure in school and delinquency is strong.

Hodgkinson (1991, p. 10) notes: "Today, more than 80% of America's one million prisoners are high school dropouts (costing taxpayers upwards of $20,000 each per year)." He concludes (p. 16): "America's children are truly an 'endangered species'."

Siegel and Senna (1988, p. 300) have cited six theories that might explain the link between delinquency and the schools. These theories parallel those set forth to explain delinquency in general society.

   ■ *Classical Theory.* People commit crime because of poor social control. The school can educate youths about the pains of punishment and through disciplinary procedures teach youths that behavior transgressions lead to sanctions. Education can stress moral development.
   ■ *Positivist (Individual) Theory.* The school can compensate for psychological and biological problems. For example, youths with low IQs or learning disabilities can be put in special classes to ease their frustration and reduce their delinquency proneness.

▌ *Social Structure Theory.* The school is a primary cause of delinquency. Middle-class school officials penalize lower-class youths, intensifying their rage, frustration, and anomie (alienation or unrest).

▌ *Social Process Theory.* A lack of bond to the school and nonparticipation in educational activities can intensify delinquency proneness. The school fails to provide sufficient definitions toward conventional behavior to thwart delinquency.

▌ *Labeling Theory.* Labeling by school officials solidifies negative self-images. The stigma associated with school failure locks youths into a delinquent career pattern.

▌ *Social Conflict Theory.* Schools are designed to train lower-class youngsters for menial careers and upper-class youths to be part of the privileged society. Rebellion against these roles promotes delinquency.

Just as the family sometimes does not succeed in providing a nurturing, caring environment or in controlling children, likewise the school is sometimes nonsupportive and lacking in discipline and control.

PROBLEMS FACING SCHOOLS

How can our schools deal with students who are disruptive, incorrigible, thieving and violent? Why have teachers and students been viciously beaten, raped, stabbed and shot? And why do so many school programs focus on problems such as delinquency, truancy, alcoholism and drugs?

Many schools face serious problems with crime. And many schools do not provide realistic programs for underachievers and marginal students. They lack counseling at a personal level, teachers who are willing to reach out to students and adequate community and school evening and weekend activities for students.

Gallup Poll collaborated with Phi Delta Kappa, a professional education organization, in producing "The 26th Annual Phi Delta Kappa/Gallup Poll of the Public's Attitudes Toward the Public Schools" considered by most as a continuing source of reliable information about opinions on significant school questions. According to the poll (Elam et al., 1994, p. 42): "For the first time ever, the category 'fighting, violence, and gangs' shares the number one position with 'lack of discipline' as the biggest problem confronting local public schools . . . only a year after inadequate financing and drug abuse were most frequently mentioned."

▌ The 26th Gallup Poll identified "fighting, violence, and gangs" and "lack of discipline" as tied for being the biggest problems facing local public schools.

From 1969 to 1985 discipline was the number one problem every year except 1971. In 1986 the drug problem claimed the number one spot until 1992 when it tied with finances for the top spot. Table 5–2 provides a summary of the results from 1990 to 1994.

TABLE 5–2 Phi Delta Kappa/Gallup Poll Results, 1990–1994

Question: "What do you think are the biggest problems with which the public schools in this community must deal?"

	1990				1991				1992			
	National	No children in school	Public school parents	Non-public school parents	National	No children in school	Public school parents	Non-public school parents	National	No children in school	Public school parents	Non-public school parents
Use of drugs	38%[a]	40%	34%	39%	22%	24%	17%	13%	22%	26%	17%	18%
Lack of discipline	19	19	17	25	20	20	18	31	17	18	15	19
Lack of proper financial support	13	18	17	21	18	15	26	11	22	20	25	25
Difficulty in getting good teachers	7	6	10	10	11	11	11	6	5	4	7	5
Poor curriculum/ poor standards	8	9	7	6	10	11	8	15	9	9	8	15
Large schools/ overcrowding	7	6	10	16	9	8	11	7	9	6	13	16
Parents' lack of interest	4	5	3	3	7	7	8	10	5	5	5	4
Pupils' lack of interest/truancy	6	7	3	3	5	6	5	(b)	3	3	2	2
Integration/busing	5	5	4	6	5	4	5	10	4	4	4	5
Low teacher pay	6	5	6	8	4	5	3	(b)	3	2	3	2
Fighting/violence/ gangs[c]	2	2	2	(b)	3	4	4	1	9	9	9	6
Lack of family structure	3	3	3	2	3	3	4	8	3	4	2	3
Lack of needed teachers	3	3	3	1	3	3	4	3	2	2	3	1
Moral standards	3	4	2	1	3	3	1	5	4	6	2	3
Drinking/alcoholism	4	4	4	3	2	2	3	(b)	2	2	1	3
Crime/vandalism	5	7	4	1	2	2	2	2	3	3	3	4

continued

TABLE 5–2 Phi Delta Kappa/Gallup Poll Results, 1990–1994, continued

Question: "What do you think are the biggest problems with which the public schools in this community must deal?"

	1993				1994			
	National	No children in school	Public school parents	Non-public school parents	National	No children in school	Public school parents	Non-public school parents
Use of drugs	16%	17%	14%	9%	11%	11%	13%	7%
Lack of discipline	15	15	15	19	18	18	17	22
Lack of proper financial support	21	19	24	13	13	12	16	9
Difficulty in getting good teachers	5	4	7	3	3	4	2	2
Poor curriculum/poor standards	9	9	8	18	3	2	3	2
Large schools/overcrowding	8	6	11	10	7	5	11	10
Parents' lack of interest	4	5	4	3	3	4	2	3
Pupils' lack of interest/truancy	4	3	4	4	3	3	3	5
Integration/busing	4	4	4	4	3	3	2	2
Low teacher pay	3	4	3	2	—	—	—	—
Fighting/violence/gangs[c]	13	12	14	17	18	19	16	17
Lack of family structure	—	—	—	—	5	5	3	4
Lack of needed teachers	—	—	—	—	—	—	—	—
Moral standards	3	3	3	9	—	—	—	—
Drinking/alcoholism	—	—	—	—	—	—	—	—
Crime/vandalism	—	—	—	—	4	5	4	3

Note: For a discussion of public opinion survey sampling procedures, see Appendix 5 [of the report].

[a] Column totals add to more than 100 percent because of multiple responses.

[b] Less than one-half of 1 percent.

[c] Category worded as "fighting" prior to 1991.

SOURCE: U.S. Department of Justice, Bureau of Justice Statistics, *Sourcebook of Criminal Justice Statistics, 1992* (Washington, D.C.: U.S. Government Printing Office, [1992]), p. 163; and Stanley M. Elam, Lowell C. Rose, and Alec M. Gallup. "The 26th Annual Phi Delta Kappa/Gallup Poll of the Public's Attitudes Toward the Public Schools," *Phi Delta Kappan*, September 1994, p. 41–56. Data for 1994: ©1994, Phi Delta Kappa, Inc.

As significant as the preceding problems are, of even greater importance to the juvenile justice system is the amount of crime and violence existing in our nation's schools.

Crime and Violence in the Schools

Research suggests that unchecked, disruptive behavior in the playgrounds, parking lots, halls and classrooms of our schools breeds violence. McConaghy (1994, p. 655) cautions: "Just as conditions in rundown and disorderly neighborhoods in urban centers invite a criminal invasion . . ., allowing disorderly behavior in schools leads to bullying, sexual assault, and verbal abuse of teachers."

In support of McConaghy's observation, a nationwide survey of victimization by the Bureau of Justice Statistics identified the location of victimization by frequency (Crowe, 1991, p. 19):

Location	Victimization of Children and Teenagers
Street, park, or playground	36%
At or in school	24
At or near home	14
Parking lots	9
Commercial, office	6
Transit	1
Unknown or other	11

Another survey, the National Crime Victimization Survey, School Crime Supplement, indicates approximately 18 percent of students had been victimized at school. Table 5–3 presents the data by student and school characteristics.

■ *A student talks with a police officer who, with his dog, was there to ensure an orderly exit as the school closed early due to fights.*

TABLE 5–3   Victimization at School, 1989

▮

	Total Number of Students	Percent of Students Reporting Victimization at School		
		Total	Violent[a]	Property[b]
Student Characteristics				
Sex				
Male	11,166,316	9%	2%	7%
Female	10,387,776	9	2	8
Race				
White	17,306,626	9	2	7
Black	3,449,488	8	2	7
Other	797,978	10	2	8
Hispanic origin				
Yes	2,026,968	7	3	5
No	19,452,697	9	2	8
Not ascertained	74,428	3[c]	(d)	3[c]
Age				
12 years	3,220,891	9	2	7
13 years	3,318,714	10	2	8
14 years	3,264,574	11	2	9
15 years	3,214,109	9	3	7
16 years	3,275,002	9	2	7
17 years	3,273,628	8	1	7
18 years	1,755,825	5	1[c]	4
19 years	231,348	2[c]	(d)	2[c]
Number of times family moved in last 5 years				
None	18,905,538	8	2	7
Once	845,345	9	2[c]	7
Twice	610,312	13	3[c]	11
3 or more	1,141,555	15	6	9
Not ascertained	51,343	5[c]	5[c]	(d)
Family income				
Less than $7,500	2,041,418	8%	2%	6%
$7,500 to $9,999	791,086	4	1[c]	3
$10,000 to $14,999	1,823,150	9	3	7
$15,000 to $24,999	3,772,445	8	1	8
$25,000 to $29,999	1,845,313	8	2	7
$30,000 to $49,999	5,798,448	10	2	8
$50,000 and over	3,498,382	11	2	9
Not ascertained	1,983,849	7	3	5
Place of residence				
Central city	5,816,321	10	2	8
Suburbs	10,089,207	9	2	7
Nonmetropolitan area	5,648,564	8	1	7
School Characteristics				
Type of school				
Public	19,264,643	9	2	8
Private	1,873,077	7	1[c]	6
Not ascertained	416,372	6	3[c]	4[c]

continued

TABLE   Victimization at School, 1989, *continued*
5–3

▊

		Percent of Students Reporting Victimization at School		
Grade in school	Total Number of Students	*Total*	*Violent*[a]	*Property*[b]
6th	1,817,511	10	3	8
7th	3,170,126	9	2	8
8th	3,258,506	9	2	8
9th	3,390,701	11	3	9
10th	3,082,441	9	2	7
11th	3,223,624	8	2	7
12th	3,171,819	6	1	5
Other	439,364	5	3[c]	3[c]

Note: The National Crime Victimization Survey (NCVS) is conducted by the U.S. Bureau of the Census for the U.S. Department of Justice, Bureau of Justice Statistics. These data are national estimates derived from the School Crime Supplement (SCS) conducted as part of the 1989 NCVS. The findings are based on a nationally representative sample of 10,449 youth who were interviewed from January to June 1989. Eligible respondents for the SCS were household members between the ages of 12 and 19, who had attended school any time during the 6 months preceding the interview, and were enrolled in a school that would advance them toward the receipt of a high school diploma. The SCS focused on personal crimes of violence and theft that were committed inside a school building or on school property only. These data are estimates derived from a sample and therefore subject to sampling variation. For survey methodology and definitions of terms used in the National Crime Victimization Survey, see Appendix 7 [of the report].
[a]Includes the crimes of rape, robbery, simple, and aggravated assault.
[b]Includes personal larceny, with and without contact, and motor vehicle theft.
[c]Estimate is based on 10 or fewer sample cases.
[d]Less than 0.5 percent.
SOURCE: U.S. Department of Justice, Bureau of Justice Statistics, *Sourcebook of Criminal Justice Statistics,* 1992 (Washington, D.C.: U.S. Government Printing Office [1992]), pp. 1–2.

Zawitz et al. (1993, p. 27) cite the following facts about crime occuring in our schools:

▊ Public school students (22%) are substantially more likely than students in private schools (13%) to indicate some level of fear of attack at school.

▊ Sixteen percent of respondents claimed that a student had attacked or threatened a teacher at their school in the six months before the interview.

Martin (1994, p. 36) describes the existence of crime and violence in a somewhat more graphic way:

▊ There are more than 3 million crimes committed each year in or near our nation's 85,000 public schools.

▊ About 9 percent of eighth-graders carry a gun, knife, or club to school at least once a month, according to a recent study by the University of Michigan which estimates that there are approximately 270,000 guns in schools on an average day.

IN DEFENSE OF THE SCHOOLS

Martin (1994, p. 39) describes some measures schools have taken, including having drive-by shooting drills, fencing in their campuses, adding metal detectors, conducting locker searches, banning the wearing of overcoats and backpacks that could conceal weapons and adding uniformed and armed security guards or police officers. Martin suggests that such measures are merely treating symptoms rather than focusing on the causes and notes (p. 40): "Since the causes of increased teen violence are societal—hopelessness, family break-down, media violence, the drug culture, demographics—treating them requires nothing less than curing American society."

This view is shared by Frymier (1992, p. 32) who claims: "Problems that most children face lie outside the school rather than inside, on the street rather than on the playground, and in the living room rather than in the classroom." In a similar vein, McClellan (1994, p. 4) cites statistics from the Center for the Study of Social Policy that indicate that of 1.7 million families started in 1990: "45 percent are at risk because the mother was in her teens, the parents were unmarried, or the mother had not completed high school."

■ Approximately 45% of children being born are at risk of being educationally disadvantaged.

Says McClellan: "Many of the factors that disadvantaged children face—poverty, family composition—are beyond the schools' realm of influence."

The Need for Positive Values

Just as the family must promote positive values, so must our schools. As U.S. Supreme Court Justice Powell stated (1972, p. 41): "We are being cut adrift from the type of humanizing authority which in the past shaped the character of our people. . . . The more personal forms we have known in home, church, school and community which give direction to our lives."

Along with a weakening of the family structure is a diminishing emphasis on ethics and values in the schools, especially the public schools. The Thomas Jefferson Research Center, a nonprofit institution studying America's social problems, reports that in 1775 religion and morals accounted for more than 90 percent of the content in school texts. By 1926 it was 6 percent. In the 1980s it was almost nonexistent. A study of third grade reading books showed that references to obedience, thoughtfulness and honesty began to disappear after 1930 (U.S. Congress, p. 11).

The findings of the Jefferson Research Center are reiterated by former Chief Justice Warren Burger (1981, p. 2): "Possibly some of our problem of behavior stems from the fact that we virtually eliminated from public schools and higher education any effort to teach values of integrity, truth, personal accountability and respect for others' rights."

■ One of the most effective ways to offset negative norms and behavior is to promote positive values in our schools.

Promoting positive values in the schools is difficult in a pluralistic society. Increased use of curriculum materials that promote both the incentive and the resources for confronting problems of moral commitment and choice is a necessary first step. As noted by the National School Safety Center (1988, p. 3):

> While schools cannot be expected to shoulder the full responsibility for socializing thus-far unsocialized youth, the educational system is, nonetheless, an anchor around which the family, community, church, and public and private social service agencies can build a cooperative network to reduce and eventually eliminate negative gang activity.

Although the Center is referring to only gang activity, this same concept applies to the role of the educational system in building a cooperative network to reduce and eventually eliminate other forms of negative juvenile behavior as well.

HOPE FOR THE FUTURE

Attorney General Reno (Wilson, 1993, pp. 2–3) has three of her seven items on the "National Agenda for Children" focused on education. She recommends **educare** programs that she defines as: "safe, constructive child care for all children." Such programs should be linked with "expanded and improved Head Start programs" so that children can begin the learning process during the critical first three-year period. Reno also supports conflict resolution programs in the schools, freeing up teachers' time to teach and developing truancy prevention programs in all elementary schools.

Another way to enhance and support the schools' efforts is to involve parents. Most teachers agree that children are much more likely to do well in school if parents become actively involved in their children's education. A recent National PTA survey, reported by Elam et al. (1993, p. 149), indicated that over 95 percent of the parents surveyed favored parental involvement in the school, as summarized in Table 5–4.

Also encouraging is the focus on the schools by the Clinton administration. Six very lofty goals have been proposed for attainment by the year 2000. The National PTA asked respondents to prioritize the goals. The results are summarized in Table 5–5.

STUDENTS' RIGHTS WITHIN THE SCHOOL

One final area of concern to the juvenile justice system is protecting students' rights within the school. Until the past decade, the landmark case in student rights was *Tinker v. Des Moines Independent Community School District* (1969),

TABLE   Importance of Parental Involvement in Education
5–4

∎

Question: "How important do you think it is to encourage parents to take a more active part in educating their children?"

	National Totals	No Children in School	Public School Parents	Nonpublic School Parents
Very important	96%	97%	95%	95%
Fairly important	3	2	5	5
Not too important	1	1	*	*
Not at all important	*	*	*	*
Don't know	*	*	*	*

*Less than one-half of 1%.

SOURCE: National PTA survey reported in Stanley M. Elam, Lowell C. Rose, and Alec M. Gallup, "The 25th Annual Phi Delta Kappa/Gallup Poll of the Public's Attitudes Toward the Public Schools," *Phi Delta Kappan*, October 1993, p. 149. © 1993 Phi Delta Kappa.

which established the fact that students have constitutional rights that must be protected in the school.

∎ Students have full constitutional rights within the school, including freedom of speech as well as the right to be free from illegal search and seizure.

Under *Tinker*, students' rights could not be removed unless exercising them would "substantially interfere with the work of the school or impinge upon the rights of other students." This standard changed in 1985. According to Rose (1988, p. 589), the Supreme Court set a new standard for cases involving student rights, a standard of *reasonableness*:

> The change has increased the discretion of school officials in such areas as search and seizure, student publications, and student expression. In establishing the new standard, the Court seems to be giving school officials broad latitude in structuring an environment in which students can both learn and develop "socially appropriate behavior."

∎ The Court requires only that schools' actions in restricting students' constitutional rights be "reasonably related to legitimate pedagogical concerns."

This puts great responsibility on school administrators' judgment and is likely to greatly reduce the likelihood of court intervention into school-related matters. Rose calls the standard a "minimum scrutiny" standard. The standard is based on three cases: *New Jersey v. T.L.O.* (1985), *Bethel School District #403 v. Fraser* (1986) and *Hazelwood School District v. Kuhlmeier* (1988). In all three cases, students claimed their constitutional rights were violated.

TABLE   National Educational Goals for the Year 2000
5–5

Question: "How high a priority do you think each goal should have for the remainder of the decade?"

	Priority Assigned					National Totals	
						Very High	
	Very High	High	Low	Very Low	Don't Know	1993	1990
By the year 2000, all children in America will start school ready to learn.	41%	48%	8%	1%	2%	41%	44%
By the year 2000, the high school graduation rate will increase to at least 90%.	54	38	6	1	1	54	45
By the year 2000, American students will leave grades 4, 8, and 12 having demonstrated competency in challenging subject matter, including English, mathematics, science, history, and geography. In addition, every school will insure that all students will learn to use their minds well so that they may be prepared for responsible citizenship, further learning, and productive employment in a modern economy.	59	33	6	1	1	59	46
By the year 2000, American students will be first in the world in science and mathematics achievement.	45	43	9	2	1	45	34
By the year 2000, every adult American will be literate and will possess the knowledge and skills necessary to compete in a global economy and to exercise the rights and responsibilities of citizenship.	54	37	7	1	1	54	45
By the year 2000, every school in America will be free of drugs and violence and will offer a disciplined environment conducive to learning.	71	19	7	2	1	71	55

SOURCE: National PTA survey reported in Stanley M. Elam, Lowell C. Rose, and Alec M. Gallup, "The 25th Annual Phi Delta Kappa/Gallup Poll of the Public's Attitudes Toward the Public Schools," *Phi Delta Kappan*, October 1993, p. 140. © 1993 Phi Delta Kappa.

In *New Jersey* v. *T.L.O.,* a teacher observed two girls, one of whom was T.L.O., smoking cigarettes in a girl's restroom in violation of the school's rules. The girls were accompanied to the school administrator's office where T.L.O. denied smoking at all. The administrator requested T.L.O.'s purse, inspected it, found cigarettes, marijuana and marijuana paraphernalia. Further examination disclosed money and change amounting to $40.98, and a letter from T.L.O. to a friend asking for her help to sell marijuana in school. The administrator contacted the police, who referred the matter to the juvenile court.

The court ruled there was a violation of search and seizure. Upon appeal, the Supreme Court overturned the ruling, saying that schools can make rules for administration of the school, and there was no violation of Fourth Amendment protection.

▮ *Although students have full constitutional rights within the school, school administrators can make and enforce rules to assure a safe, effective educational environment. This includes the right to search students' lockers.*

In *Bethel School District #403* v. *Fraser,* a student was suspended from school for three days and had his name removed from a list of candidates for graduation speaker because he used sexually explicit language in his campaign speech. The student brought suit, claiming his First Amendment right to free speech had been violated, but the Court said it was constitutional for a school "to prohibit the use of vulgar and offensive terms in public discourse," and it left the determination of this with the school board.

In *Hazelwood School District* v. *Kuhlmeier,* a principal prohibited publication of two pages of a student newspaper because he felt the articles were inappropriate. One article was on student pregnancies, written from the point of view of three pregnant students; each gave a positive account of the experience. The other article was on the impact of divorce on students and included comments attributed to specific individuals; the principal considered this to be inappropriate. The Court upheld the prohibition as constitutional.

These three cases set the standard governing a school's restriction of students' constitutional rights.

SUMMARY

Both the family and the school are powerful influences on the development of youth. The structure and interaction patterns of the home influence whether children learn social or delinquent behavior. In healthy families, self-esteem is high, communication is direct and honest, rules are flexible and reasonable and members' attitudes toward the outside world are trusting and optimistic.

In some families, the concept of adult supremacy may threaten sound relationships. Adult supremacy subordinates children to the absolute and arbitrary authority of parents. Common values that might be passed on to our youth include equality, honesty, promise-keeping, respect, responsibility, self-control and social justice.

The schools also play a vital role in the development of our youth. They are given this responsibility through the principle of in loco parentis, meaning "in place of parents." This principle gives certain social and legal institutions, including the schools, the authority to act as a parent might in situations requiring discipline or need. It is similar to parens patriae, only at the local level.

Children who succeed in school have a greater probability of succeeding in other areas of their lives. However, several educational practices may encourage failure, including the A-B-C-D-F grading system, objective testing, grading on a curve, having closed-book tests and tracking students. Students' responses to failure may include skipping school, joining gangs, dropping out of school, drinking, doing drugs, performing delinquent acts and even suicide. The link between failure in school and delinquency is strong.

Our schools face several problems. The 26th Gallup Poll identified fighting, violence, and gangs and lack of discipline as tied for being the biggest problems facing local public schools. Also problematic is the number of children coming to school not ready to learn. Approximately 45 percent of children being born are at risk of being educationally disadvantaged.

One positive way to offset negative norms and behavior is to promote positive values in our schools. Another is to involve parents in the educational process. And, if students are to be taught respect for others, their own constitutional rights should be respected within the school. Students do have full constitutional rights, including freedom of speech as well as the right to be free from illegal search and seizure. However, the Court requires only that schools' actions in restricting students' constitutional rights be "reasonably related to legitimate pedagogical concerns."

■ Discussion Questions

1. Do you believe controlled spanking in certain circumstances is justified? Were you spanked as a child?
2. What values do you feel should be passed on to the next generation?
3. Do you have personal experiences with an educational practice that promoted failure rather than success?
4. Did you ever skip school when you were young? If you did, do you remember why? Why do youths become truants? Is truancy the responsibility of the school, parents or youths?
5. Why should an individual be forced to get an education? Is refusing to go to school a delinquent act? Why or why not?
6. Should schools be forced into continually having to accept disruptive and incorrigible students? What are some alternatives? Do you think this matter is best resolved in the juvenile court? If not, where?

7. Do schools contribute to the problem of youths who are disruptive, antisocial, incorrigible and truant? How?

8. Do society, schools and parents expect too much from youths who display unacceptable behavior in and out of school? How can such behavior be adjusted? Should the youths be put into the juvenile justice system?

9. How can teachers become more sensitive to the problems of youth?

10. What were teachers like in your school? Did you ever feel like rebelling or staying away from school? Why? What could be changed?

■ References

Burger, Warren E. "Annual Report to the American Bar Association." Houston: 8 February, 1981, p. 2.

Canady, Robert Lynn, and Phyllis Riley Hotchkiss. "It's a Good Score! Just a Bad Grade." *Phi Delta Kappan,* September 1989, pp. 68–71.

Canning, Miles (ed.). "Both Sides of Adolescence." Richfield, Minn.: Storefront/Youth Action, 1992.

Crowe, Timothy D. *Habitual Juvenile Offenders: Guidelines for Citizen Action and Public Responses.* Washington, D.C.: Office of Juvenile Justice and Delinquency Prevention, October 1991.

Culkin, Father John. "I Was a Teenage Movie Teacher." *Saturday Review* 16 July 1966, p. 51.

Eitzen, Stanley. "Problem Students: The Sociocultural Roots." *Phi Delta Kappan,* April 1992, pp. 584–590.

Elam, Stanley M.; Lowell C. Rose; and Alec M. Gallup. "The 25th Annual Phi Delta Kappa/Gallup Poll of the Public's Attitudes Toward the Public Schools." *Phi Delta Kappan,* October 1993, pp. 137–152.

Elam, Stanley M.; Lowell C. Rose; and Alec M. Gallup. "The 26th Annual Phi Delta Kappa/ Gallup Poll of the Public's Attitudes Toward the Public Schools." *Phi Delta Kappan.* September 1994, pp. 41–56.

Foster, H. "A 'Bill of Rights' for Children." In *Child Abuse and Neglect,* 1974.

Frymier, Jack. *Growing Up Is Risky Business, and Schools Are Not To Blame.* Bloomington, Ind.: Phi Delta Kappa, 1992.

Gardner, Howard. *Frames of Mind: The Theory of Multiple Intelligences.* New York: Basic Books, 1983.

Glasser, William. *Schools Without Failure.* New York: Harper & Row, 1969.

Hodgkinson, Harold. "Reform versus Reality." *Phi Delta Kappan,* September 1991, pp. 9–16.

Ledlie, J. *Sohm's Institute of Roman Law.* 1907. Out of print.

Martin, Deirdre. "Teen Violence: Why It's on the Rise and How to Stem Its Tide." *Law Enforcement Technology,* January 1994, pp. 36–42.

Maurer, D. "Corporal Punishment." *American Psychologist.* September 1974.

McClellan, Mary. "Why Blame Schools?" *Research Bulletin of the Center for Evaluation, Development, and Research,* No. 12. Phi Delta Kappa, March 1994.

McConaghy, Tom. "School Violence: Not Just in the U.S." *Phi Delta Kappan,* April 1994, pp. 654–655.

Metropolitan Court Judges Committee Report. *Deprived Children: A Judicial Response.* Washington, D.C.: U.S. Government Printing Office. 1986.

National School Safety Center. *Gangs in Schools: Breaking Up Is Hard to Do.* Malibu, Calif.: Pepperdine University Press, 1988.

OJJDP Annual Report, 1990. Washington, D.C.: Office of Juvenile Justice and Delinquency Prevention, [1990].

Pace, Denny F. *Community Relations Concept.* Placerville, Calif.: Copperhouse Publishing, 1991.

Parker, L. Craig, Jr.; Robert D. Meier; and Lynn Hunt Monahan. *Interpersonal Psychology for Criminal Justice.* St. Paul, Minn.: West Publishing, 1989.

Powell, Lewis F., Jr. "What Justice Powell Says Is Wrong with America." *U.S. News & World Report.* 28 August 1972, p. 41.

Rose, Lowell C. " 'Reasonableness'—The High Court's New Standard for Cases Involving Student Rights." *Phi Delta Kappan,* April 1988, pp. 589–592.

Siegel, Larry J., and Joseph J. Senna. *Juvenile Delinquency.* 3rd ed. St. Paul, Minn.: West Publishing 1988.

Smith, Robert L. "In the Service of Youth: A Common Denominator," *Juvenile Justice* 1 (Fall/Winter 1993) 2:16–22.

Suskind, Ron. "Tormented for Learning." *The Wall Street Journal,* 26 May 1994.

United Nations. Convention on the Rights of the Child. Adopted by the General Assembly of the United Nations, 20 November 1989.

U.S. Congress, House Committee on Education and Labor. *Hearing before Subcommittee on Elementary, Secondary, and Vocational Education on H.R. 123.* 96 Congress, 1st Session, 24 April 1979.

von Sternberg, Bob. "Expert: 'Moral Sense' Must Be Regained to End Crime." (Minneapolis/ St. Paul) *Star Tribune,* 28 April 1994, p. 9B.

Walsh, James. "To Hit Is to Harm, Anti-Spanking Project Stresses." (Minneapolis/St. Paul) *Star Tribune,* 12 April 1994, pp. 1B, 8B.

West, Nancy. "Should a Child Be Spanked?" *Parade Magazine,* 17 April 1994, pp. 12–14.

Wilson, John J. "A National Agenda for Children: On the Front Lines with Attorney General Janet Reno." *Juvenile Justice* 1 (Fall/Winter 1993) 2:2–8.

Wu, Amy. "Flogging May Be Cure for Teenage Violence." (Minneapolis/St. Paul) *Star Tribune,* 17 April 1994, p. 25A.

Zawitz, Marianne W. et al. *Highlights from 20 Years of Surveying Crime Victims: The National Crime Victimization Survey, 1973–1992.* Washington, D.C.: U.S. Department of Justice, October 1993.

■ Cases

Bethel School District #403 v. *Fraser,* 478 U.S. 675, 106 S.Ct. 3159, 92 L.Ed.2d 549 (1986).

Hazelwood School District v. *Kuhlmeier,* 484 U.S. 260, 108 S.Ct. 562, 98 L.Ed.2d 592 (1988).

New Jersey v. *T.L.O.,* 469 U.S. 325, 105 S.Ct. 733, 83 L.Ed.2d 720 (1985).

Tinker v. *Des Moines Independent Community School District,* 393 U.S. 503, 89 S.Ct. 733, 21 L.Ed.2d 731 (1969).

Youth Who
Are Victims

The cycle of abused and neglected children who have become abusing and neglecting parents with their children in turn being abused, neglected, running away, acting out and often ending up before the courts has not been broken.

Metropolitan Court Judges Committee

▌ Do You Know?

Which age group has the highest victimization rate?
How many children live in poverty?
What are two consequences for children who live in poverty?
What are believed to be the two leading causes of child abuse?
How extensive the problem of child neglect and abuse is?
What the major cause of death of young children is?
What the three levels of abuse are?
How many states have banned corporal punishment for children?
What the likely result of violence is for children?
What five categories of missing children have been identified in the NIS-MART study?
What two federal agencies have concurrent jurisdiction for missing and exploited children?
What the leading cause of suicide is?

▌ Can You Define the Following Key Terms?

child abuse, collective abuse, extrafamilial sexual abuse, individual abuse, institutional abuse, intrafamilial sexual abuse, neglected, runaways, seesaw model, thrownaways

INTRODUCTION

Youth are victimized in many ways. Kaplan (1991, p. K6) notes that a child drops out of public school every eight seconds of every school day. Another runs away from home every 26 seconds. Almost every minute daily a teenager has a baby, and every three minutes four children are abused or neglected. In addition, in a single year:

- 3,392 young people were dying from firearms-related injuries, many of them at the hands of the 135,000 schoolchildren who daily toted guns into the halls of learning.
- The infant mortality rate of the U.S., 19th in the world, was worse than those of Singapore, Hong Kong, Spain, or Ireland.
- The economically backward Hashemite Kingdom of Jordan and the Czech and Slovak Federal Republic, reeling from 40 years of totalitarian excesses, had better records than the U.S. in immunizing their children against polio.

Equally disturbing, the Center for the Study of Social Policy, University of Minnesota, reported that the 1980s were "a terrible decade for children," with increases in the percentages of children in poverty, incarcerated juveniles, out-of-wedlock births and violent deaths (Spencer and Spolar, 1991, p. A-3).

A report of the Metropolitan Court Judges Committee (1985, p. 41) placed a large portion of the responsibility on the family:

The concept of "family" as the foundation of our society is undergoing new and significant pressures. Never before has our pluralistic society included families with such vast numbers of single parents, ethnic and cultural variables, working mothers, and latch key children. Never have the costs of providing child care, medical care and education been so high. Never have adverse influences and values outside the home or through television been so great. It is often against tremendous odds that many families are able to fulfill their traditional and vital functions. . . . The cycle of abused and neglected children who have become abusing and neglecting parents with their children in turn being abused, neglected, running away, acting out and often ending up before the courts has not been broken. The cycle of teenage pregnancies and teenage mothers without partners or providers, leading to dependence upon welfare and social services, and often to another generation of abused or neglected children continues.

The bleak existence of many of our country's youth is also described by McClellan (1994, p. 1):

In 1991, the most recent year for which data are available, Fordham University's Index of Social Health reached its lowest point since it was first compiled in 1970. The number of children living in poverty has grown steadily to over 20%, more than double that of other major industrialized nations. Especially hard hit are 44% of African-American children and 38% of Hispanic children. By eighth grade, 7 out of 10 children have consumed alcohol. In 1990, 9% of all babies born in the U.S.—360,645 children—had teenage mothers. 22,000 infants were abandoned in U.S. hospitals the next year. Perhaps most distressing is the amount of violence pervading many children's lives. Nearly 4,000 children are murdered each year among 10- to 17-year-olds, the arrest rate for murder more than doubled from 5.4 youths per 100,000 in 1983 to 12.7 in 1991.

Yet another report released early in 1994 by the Annie E. Casey Foundation, a philanthropy for poor children, "Kids Count Data Book," states that nearly 4 million American children, 84 percent of whom are Latino and Black, are growing up welfare-dependent in poor neighborhoods. Among the emerging trends threatening large numbers of youth, the report documents the following ("Millions of Kids," 1994, p. 7):

> The number of teen-agers who died violently rose by 13 percent from 1985 to 1991, from 62.8 per 100,000 to 71.1 per 100,000. In contrast, the accidental death rate for 15–19-year-olds dropped by 15 percent, while homicides doubled.
>
> The number of juveniles arrested for violent crimes jumped from 305 per 100,000 in 1985 to 457 per 100,000 in 1991—a 50-percent increase.
>
> The percentage of students who graduate from high school on time fell from 71.6 percent to 68.8 percent during 1985–91.
>
> The poverty rate dipped slightly, declining from 20.8 percent to 20 percent. But one-fourth of all children under the age of 6 live in poverty—over half of them in families headed by women.
>
> One out of every 4 black children lives in a severely distressed neighborhood, as does 1 of every 10 Latino children and 1 out of every 63 white children.
>
> Births to single, teen-age mothers are on the rise in every state except Maryland, New Jersey and New York.

Finally, a study conducted by the National Institute of Justice (Widom, 1992, p. 5) concluded: "Childhood victimization represents a widespread, serious social problem that increases the likelihood of delinquency, adult criminality, and violent criminal behavior. Poor educational performance, health problems, and generally low levels of achievement also characterize the victims of early childhood abuse and neglect."

This chapter discusses such victimization, including children who are victims of crime and violence, of poverty, of neglect, and of abuse—emotional, physical and sexual. It examines violence in our society and the cycle of violence being perpetuated. This is followed by a discussion of the dire results of abuse and violence: youth who are delinquents, runaways, thrownaways, missing and even suicidal.

CHILDREN AND YOUTH AS VICTIMS OF CRIME

One of the most obvious ways youth are victimized is by becoming a victim of crime. The preceding chapter noted the amount of victimization occurring in our nation's schools, with 9 percent of students experiencing a victimization during a six-month period in 1989. The U.S. Department of Justice reports the following school violence statistics:

∎ Over 300,000 high school students are assaulted every month in schools.

∎ Each month 2,400,000 students have personal property stolen.

∎ Over 200,000 students remain home each day because of fear of violence.

FBI statistics from 1993 depict the same grim picture. Every school day nationwide:

∎ 160,000 students skip classes because they fear physical harm.

∎ 1 in 5 carries some type of weapon.

∎ 1 in 20 carries a gun.

Children and youth are also frequent victims of crime outside of school. According to the FBI, in 1994, 5,000 youth under age 19 will die from guns and an additional 50,000 will be injured by guns. According to Louis Sullivan, Health and Human Services Secretary in 1991: "The leading killer of young black males is young black males." Such killings are often gang-related, as discussed in Chapter 8.

In a study on teenage victims, Whitaker and Bastian (1991, p. 1) report:

> From 1985 to 1988, persons age 12 to 19 were victims of 1.9 million violent crimes and 3.3 million crimes of theft annually. Teenagers were much more likely than adults to be victims of crimes of violence. On average, every 1,000 teenagers experienced 67 violent crimes each year, compared to 26 for every 1,000 adults age 20 or older.

Table 6–1 shows the specific data for this time frame.

Victimization data for 1992 shows this trend continuing, with those under age 25 having higher victimization rates than older persons (Bastian, 1993, p. 2), as shown in Table 6–2.

∎ **Youth are victims of crime more often than those over age 25.**

∎ *Police investigate the scene of a homicide of a 15-year old shot while riding his bike on a city street.*

TABLE   Average Annual Victimization Rates by Age and Type of Crime,
6–1   1985–1988

Type of Crime	Age of Victim		
	12–15	16–19	20 or older
Victimization Rate			
Crimes of violence	61.6	72.4	26.0
Rape	.9	2.3	.6
Robbery	9.2	10.0	4.8
Aggravated assault	13.1	22.2	7.2
Simple assault	38.3	37.9	13.4
Crimes of theft	113.6	122.5	62.4
Personal larceny			
With contact	3.3	3.0	2.6
Without contact	110.3	119.5	59.8
Number of Victimizations			
Crimes of violence*	834,623	1,056,961	4,383,799
Rape	11,800	32,884	101,501
Robbery	125,159	146,622	802,978
Aggravated assault	177,916	324,344	1,217,205
Simple assault	519,748	553,111	2,262,116
Crimes of theft	1,540,112	1,788,546	10,522,143
Personal larceny			
With contact	44,516	44,500	433,951
Without contact	1,495,597	1,744,046	10,088,192
Number of persons in age group	13,554,626	14,594,898	168,699,541

Note: Detail may not add to total because of rounding. The victimization rate is the annual average of the number of victimizations for 1985–1988 per 1,000 persons in each age group.
*Annual average for 1985–1988.

SOURCE: Catherine J. Whitaker and Lisa D. Bastian, *Teenage Victims: A National Crime Survey Report,* NCJ–128129 (Washington, D.C.: Bureau of Justice Statistics, May 1991), p. 1.

VICTIMS OF POVERTY

According to Eitzen (1992, p. 587): "A significant proportion of people— 13.5% in 1990 and rising—are officially poor." And a significant number of those living in poverty are children.

"Nearly one child in four is born into poverty," says Cowley (1991, p. 18), "a formidable predictor of lifelong ill health, and a growing number lack such basic advantages as a home, two parents and regular access to a doctor." He notes (p. 21): "Kids under 5 suffer more poverty than any other age group in America." (See Figure 6–1.)

TABLE   **Victimization Rates by Age, 1992**
  6–2
  ∎

	Crimes of violence						Crimes of theft
	Total	Total*	Robbery	Assault			
				Total	Aggravated	Simple	
Sex							
Male	101.4	38.8	8.1	30.1	12.0	18.1	62.6
Female	81.8	25.9	3.9	21.1	6.1	15.0	55.9
Age							
12–15	171.0	75.7	9.8	64.8	20.1	44.7	95.3
16–19	172.7	77.9	15.4	60.9	26.3	34.5	94.8
20–24	177.0	70.1	11.4	56.0	18.1	38.0	106.9
25–34	111.1	37.6	7.7	29.4	9.3	20.1	73.4
35–49	75.1	21.2	3.8	17.1	6.8	10.2	53.9
50–64	43.3	10.0	2.8	7.1	2.3	4.8	33.3
65 or older	21.1	4.8	1.5	3.1	1.3	1.8	16.3
Race							
White	88.7	29.9	4.7	24.6	7.8	16.8	58.8
Black	110.8	50.4	15.6	33.5	18.3	15.2	60.4
Other	88.3	23.7	5.1	18.6	5.3	13.3	64.6
Ethnicity							
Hispanic	100.1	38.1	10.6	26.9	10.0	16.8	61.9
Non-Hispanic	90.3	31.4	5.4	25.3	8.9	16.4	58.9
Family Income							
Less than $7,500	136.7	64.4	11.1	52.0	23.1	28.8	72.3
$7,500–$9,999	94.4	40.3	11.5	28.8	9.3	19.5	54.1
$10,000–$14,999	85.9	34.3	7.1	26.6	9.0	17.6	51.6
$15,000–$24,999	88.1	34.1	5.4	27.8	9.7	18.1	54.0
$25,000–$29,999	93.3	35.6	6.3	29.3	6.3	23.0	57.6
$30,000–$49,999	83.3	26.6	4.8	20.9	6.6	14.3	56.6
$50,000 or more	92.2	21.2	3.7	16.9	5.5	11.4	71.0
Residence							
Central city	116.5	43.2	10.8	31.5	12.1	19.4	73.3
Suburban	84.8	28.2	4.4	23.1	7.3	15.8	56.5
Nonmetropolitan areas	72.4	25.2	2.7	22.1	7.8	14.3	47.2

Note: Victimizations per 1,000 persons age 12 or older.
*Includes data on rape not shown separately.

SOURCE: Lisa D. Bastian, *Criminal Victimization 1992: A National Crime Victimization Survey Report,* Bureau of Justice Statistics Bulletin (Washington, D.C.: October 1993), p. 6.

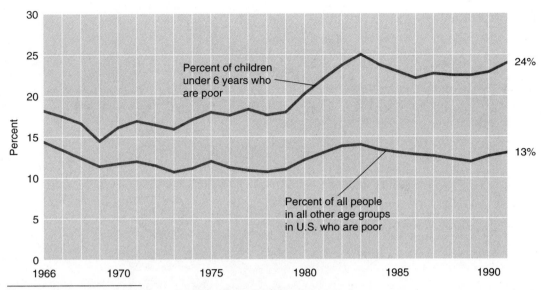

■ **FIGURE 6–1 Percentage of Those Living in Poverty**
Young children endure more poverty than any other age group in the population.
SOURCE: National Center for Children in Poverty, Columbia University, *Five Million Children: 1993 Update* (New York: [1994]).

■ Nearly one-fourth of our children live in poverty.

The result (Cowley, p. 21):

> Poor children are more likely to suffer from low birth weight, more likely to die during the first year of life, more likely to suffer hunger or abuse while growing up and less likely to benefit from immunizations or adequate medical care.

Home conditions of poverty and economic deprivation or uncertainty can expose children to ills ranging from malnutrition to extreme psychopathology. This country has pockets of squalor found on tenant farms, in migrant camps and in the tenements of large cities. A report of the Task Force on Juvenile Justice and Delinquency Prevention, (1977, p. 794) stated:

> [A]n increase in crime is highly probable in the remainder of this century. More crimes may be committed as our population continues to grow; as the process of urbanization continues and more of our largest cities become ghettos composed largely of the poor, the young, and the black; as the inhibitions and restraints imposed by religious morality continue to weaken in an increasingly secularized society; as women and teenagers feel increasingly free to go their own way in a society liberated from the prejudices of the past; as increasing economic affluence brings the difference between the well-to-do and those caught in the "culture of poverty" into sharper focus; as the material goods of a growing middle income group increase and become more vulnerable to criminal acts; as higher professional standards make employment more difficult for millions of inadequately educated citizens and contribute to a widening cultural gulf between white and minority group citizens; as the employment opportunities for the illiterate, uneducated and undereducated in post-industrialized society decline relative to the opportunities for those trained in professional and technical skills; and as the

∎ *This young boy lives with his family of eight in a tiny two-bedroom house in California's San Joaquin Valley, an area suffering from the state's worst poverty rate: 33.2 percent for children and 22.6 percent overall.*

process of bureaucratization alienates an increasing number of citizens from the administration of justice and makes the larger police departments in urban centers more efficient but less responsive to the needs of the population they serve, and less adaptable to a rapidly changing social environment.

The recitation of trends associated with crime is likely to continue to the end of this century and appears to be very accurate. Many of these trends result in increased economic poverty for millions of youth.

∎ Economic poverty may remove children from the culture at large and deprive them of the stimulation to grow as most children do.

It takes more than economic relief to lift families from a pattern of irresponsibility or depravity. Social agencies in every community know certain families that can be counted on to produce more than their share of school failures, truancy, sexual deviation, alcoholism, disorderliness and disease. They are also all too familiar with the inadequate personalities who become parents of other inadequate personalities in a recurring sequence that led early geneticists to talk about heredity and social incompetence.

■ *Harlem, New York, in April 1988. The picture says it all.*

It must be remembered, however, that poverty alone cannot be blamed for delinquency. Many children raised in extreme poverty grow up just fine.

The Children's Defense Fund has suggested: "We must make it un-American for any child to grow up poor, or without adequate child care, health care, food, shelter, or education" (Kaplan, 1991, p. K1). Unfortunately, as Kaplan notes (p. K7), the universal, gilt-edged rhetorical support for such care is hollow at the core: "[T]he jury of public opinion is still debating whether children are actually a valued national resource or just another neglected minority." Two possible reasons for this lack of action are that children don't vote and they don't contribute to political campaigns.

■ Two of the most serious consequences of poverty for children are homelessness and increased risk of lead poisoning.

Homelessness

In 1990 the percentage of families making up the homeless population rose to 34 percent. The number of children who are homeless on any given night ranges from 68,000 (U.S. General Accounting Office) to half a million (National Coalition for the Homeless).

Being homeless places great stress on families and may result in child neglect or abuse. The homeless children also experience the stress and are likely to exhibit some of the following general tendencies (Linehan, 1992, p. 62): "[A]cting out, restlessness, aggressive behavior, depression, school behavioral problems, learning problems, regressive behavior (especially in younger children), inattentiveness, hyperactivity, and persistent tiredness and anxiety." Linehan also notes that: "A child living in a shelter is vulnerable to physical, mental, and emotional maladies because the whole experience tends to erode the child's primary protective structure—the family."

In addition to these general tendencies, four conditions often characterize homeless children's experiences (Linehan, pp. 62–64):

▌ Constant moving—results in a lack of roots, viewing life as temporary, becoming restless, being easily frustrated, and having limited attention spans.
▌ Frequent change of schools—results in falling behind academically as well as an unwillingness to form friendships or to participate in extracurricular activities.
▌ Overcrowded living quarters—results in either withdrawal or aggressiveness.
▌ Lack of access to basic resources (food, clothing, transportation)—results in deprivations with far-reaching effects.

Some homeless youth are entirely on their own, including **runaways** and **thrownaways** (their family has kicked them out). Stevens and Price (1992, p. 18) report that more than 300,000 school-age children are homeless each year. Difficulties facing such youth are discussed later in the chapter.

Victims of Lead Poisoning

Children who live in poverty are also much more likely than others to be exposed to lead from old paint and old plumbing fixtures and from the lead in household dust. Other sources of lead are old water systems, lead crystal and some imported cans and ceramics. According to Eitzen (1992, p. 587), 16 percent of white children and 55 percent of black children have high levels of lead in their blood, a condition leading to irreversible learning disabilities and other problems.

Stevens and Price (1992, p. 18) report some three to four million children exposed to damaging levels of lead. The gravity of this problem was stated by the Public Health Service: "[L]ead poisoning remains the most common and societally devastating environmental disease of young children" (Needleman, 1992, p. 35).

Babies exposed to low doses of lead before birth often are born underweight and underdeveloped. Even if they overcome these handicaps, when they go to school they face more obstacles (Cowley, 1991, p. 20):

[L]ead-exposed kids exhibit behavioral problems, low IQ and deficiencies in speech and language. And research has shown that teenagers with histories of lead exposure drop out of school seven times as often as their peers.

According to Needleman (1992):

Being poor increases a child's risk radically. The ATSDR [Agency for Toxic Substances and Disease Registry] estimates that 7% of well-off white children have elevated blood lead levels; for poor whites, the proportion is 25%. Of poor African-American children, 55% have elevated levels. More than half of African-

American children who live in poverty begin their education with the potentially handicapping condition. Lead exposure may be one of the most important—and least acknowledged—causes of school failure and learning disorders.

Cowley (1991) suggests that according to some experts lead poisoning is the nation's "foremost environmental hazard."

Poverty is also often associated with other problems such as child neglect and abuse.

CHILDREN WHO ARE NEGLECTED

Often the families from which **neglected** children come are not only poor, they are disorganized. They have no set routine for family activity. The children roam the streets at all hours. They are continually being petitioned to juvenile court for loitering and curfew. The family unit is often fragmented by death, divorce or desertion of parents.

Broken homes often deprive children of affection, recognition and a sense of belonging unless there is a strong parent to overcome these responses and provide direction. If a child's protective shield is shattered, the child may lose respect for moral and ethical standards. The broken home, in and of itself, does not cause delinquency. But it can nullify or even destroy the resources needed for handling the emotional problems of youths in a constructive way. Children from broken homes may suffer serious damage to their personalities. They may develop aggressive attitudes and strike out. They may feel punishment is preferable to no recognition. Even when marriages are intact, both parents frequently work. Consequently, many parents spend less time in the home interacting with their children.

Some children are stunted in their growth by being raised in a moral vacuum, where parents ignore them. Even more problematic are parents who do not conform in their behavior to moral and ethical standards or who have different values than the dominant moral order, who set poor examples for their children. Such parents cannot ignore the probability that their children may model their actions.

> ■ The homes of neglected children frequently are disorganized, broken and have parents who ignore the children or who set a bad example for them.

Parents at times deliberately refrain from discipline in the mistaken belief that authoritative restrictions inhibit children's self-expression or unbalance their delicate emotional systems. At the other extreme are parents who discipline their children injudiciously, excessively and frequently, weighing neither transgression nor punishment. Parents' warped ideas, selfish attitudes and twisted values can lead to their children becoming delinquents.

Family policies that are inconsistent, or that emphasize too much leniency or excessive punishment, may produce a form of retaliation by children that is often directed at society in general.

Children's behavior develops from what they see and interpret happening around them. If children are exposed to excessive drinking and use of drugs, illicit sex, gambling and related vices by parents or adult role models, they may repeat these behaviors.

Neglected children often do not have adequate food, clothing, shelter, medical care, supervision, education, protection or emotional support necessary to ensure physical, mental and emotional health. They may also suffer emotional harm through disrespect and denial of self-worth, unreasonable or chronic rejection and failure to receive necessary affection, protection and a sense of family belonging. Other victims of neglect are described by Cowley (1991, p. 18), including the thousands who die from preventable accidents, the millions who go unvaccinated against common childhood diseases and the millions more poisoned by cigarette smoke or household lead. He concludes that: "American children remain the most neglected in the developed world."

Cowley (1991, p. 20) cautions: "Cigarette smoke not only poisons developing fetuses—causing a quarter of all low birth weights and a tenth of all infant deaths—but disables children who breathe it growing up."

Another large contributor to neglect is crack. Will (1994, p. 25A) reports on the increase in cases of child abuse and neglect handled by the Legal Aid Society in New York, going from 3,310 cases in 1984 to over 24,000 in 1989. He suggests this is the direct result of crack: "What happened? Crack did, beginning in 1985. Sixty percent of abuse and neglect cases involve drug allegations."

Even more devastating, however, are the traumatic accidents maiming or killing children: "No disease, drug or environmental hazard rivals traumatic injuries as a killer of children. Every year mishaps claim the lives of 8,000 American youngsters and permanently disable 50,000" (Cowley, 1991, p. 20). Some of these mishaps result from safety hazards in the home. An estimated 90 percent of permanent childhood injuries could have been prevented by adequate supervision. Often the lack of supervision is the direct result of a parent high on drugs or alcohol.

Certainly not all neglect is intentional. It may be the result of parent immaturity or lack of parenting skills. It may also be the result of a parent's physical, psychological or mental deficiencies. Other parents who neglect their children may do so because they cannot tolerate stress, they cannot adequately express anger or they have no sense of responsibility.

Indicators of Neglect

Among the *physical indicators* of child neglect are frequent hunger, poor hygiene, inappropriate dress, consistent lack of supervision (especially in dangerous activities or for long time periods), unattended physical problems of medical needs and abandonment. The *behavioral indicators* of neglect may include begging, stealing food, extending school days by arriving early or leaving late, constant fatigue, listlessness or falling asleep in school, alcohol or drug abuse, delinquency, stealing and reporting that no one is at home to care for them (Bennett and Hess, 1994, p. 401).

Consequences of Neglect

As noted by Springer (1986, p. 75):

> It is generally accepted that maternal deprivation and infant neglect can result in neurological maldevelopment. Even given fulfillment of all chemical needs, mammalian nervous systems fail to develop properly absent appropriate sensory and emotional stimulations. Surrogate mothers in the form of colored television sets tending to [hold] captive infants in cages called playpens can result in the same kind of crippling that results from deprivation of chemical nutrients.
>
> The human brain is undeveloped at birth. For it to develop properly the infant must be fondled, touched, picked up, rocked, and carried. . . .
>
> [U]nloved children do not develop properly and are higher-risk candidates for entry into the juridicial [sic] justice system.

█ For children's brains to develop properly, children need handling and love.

Springer (1986, p. 75) cites the testimony of James W. Prescott before the Standing Senate Committee on Health, Welfare, and Science:

> Human infants and animals who are deprived of sensory stimulation during the formal period of brain development develop a biological system of brain functioning and structure which predisposes these organisms—these animals, these children—to pathologically violent behavior.

A study by the National Institute of Justice (Widom, 1992, p. 1) suggests that neglect can lead to future violent behavior and that "far more attention needs to be devoted to the families of children whose 'beatings' are forms of abandonment and severe malnutrition."

Other children need assistance because the "beatings" are physical and violent.

CHILDREN WHO ARE EMOTIONALLY OR PHYSICALLY ABUSED

Throughout history children have been subjected to physical violence. Infants have been killed as a form of birth control, to avoid the dishonor of illegitimacy, as a means of power, as a method of disposing of retarded or deformed children and as a way of ensuring financial security.

Historical Roots of Abuse

In Greece, a child was the absolute property of the father and property was divided among the male children. The father would raise the first son and expose subsequent children to the elements.

Under Roman law the father had the power of life and death (*patria potestas*) over his children and could kill, mutilate, sell or offer them as a sacrifice.

In the industrial, urban and machine age the exploitation of child labor was common. Children of all ages worked 16 hours a day usually with irons and chains to their ankles to keep them from running away. They were starved, beaten and dehumanized with the result being many died from exposure in the workplace or from occupational diseases or committed suicide.

Before the first juvenile court, in 1871, the Society for the Prevention of Cruelty to Children was formed as a result of church workers removing a severely beaten and neglected child, Mary Ellen, from her home under the law that protected animals.

The first Child Protection Service was founded in 1875. Some 50 years later the Social Security Act authorized public funds for child welfare.

In the 1940s, advances in diagnostic x-ray technology allowed physicians to detect patterns of healed fractures in their young patients. In 1946 Dr. John Caffey, a pediatric radiologist, suggested the novel idea that the multiple fractures in the long bones of infants had "traumatic origin," perhaps willfully inflicted by parents. Two decades later, Dr. C.H. Kempe and his associates coined the phrase *battered child syndrome* based on clinical evidence of maltreatment. In 1964 individual states began enacting mandatory child abuse laws using Dr. Kempe's definition of a battered child and by 1966, 49 states had enacted such legislation.

The Causes of Abuse

Most emotional and physical **child abuse** is committed by parents or those caring for children. Parker et al. (1989, p. 118) contend:

> Overall, abusing parents are inadequate parents and caregivers. Their troubled past, history of failure, unstable marriage or relationship, and low self-esteem, coupled with inadequate preparation as parents and caregivers force the child into an early life of pain, fear, inadequate bonding, and fear of intimacy.

The American Medical Association (AMA) (1985, p. 797) states that vulnerable families have several identified characteristics that correlate with child maltreatment:

▮ Low income.
▮ Socially isolated (no external support systems).
▮ Husbands and wives resort to violence on one another.
▮ Individuals were exposed to abnormal child-rearing practices and were maltreated as children.
▮ Parental expectations inconsistent with the child's developmental abilities.
▮ Stressors such as alcohol and drug misuse, inadequate housing (e.g., overcrowding) and mental illness.

In a survey regarding attitudes toward what causes child abuse, the two leading responses were violence between husbands and wives and poverty. The survey results are summarized in Table 6–3.

TABLE Attitudes Toward the Causes of Child Abuse in the United States, 1991
6–3

Question: "To what extent do you think that _____ contributes to child abuse?"

		Sex		Region			
	Total	Male	Female	East	Midwest	South	West
Violence between husbands and wives	58%	50%	66%	61%	60%	56%	56%
Poverty	45	42	48	52	42	45	43
Violence on television	28	19	36	22	34	27	24
Violence in movies	25	18	33	24	27	27	22
Racial discrimination	24	23	25	25	19	24	29
Heavy-metal rock music	20	15	24	16	24	22	16
Parents hitting or spanking children	19	15	23	25	18	17	18
Sex discrimination	14	14	14	14	10	13	21
Teachers hitting or spanking children	12	7	18	21	10	9	13
Toy guns or war toys	11	7	14	13	10	12	9
Death penalty for murderers	8	8	8	8	7	8	8
Contact sports	4	3	6	5	3	5	5

Note: Percent responding "a great deal."

SOURCE: U.S. Department of Justice, Bureau of Justice Statistics, *Sourcebook of Criminal Justice Statistics, 1992* (Washington, D.C.: U.S. Government Printing Office [1992]), p. 240.

■ The two leading causes for child abuse are believed to be violence between husbands and wives and poverty.

A **seesaw model** to conceptualize the causes of child abuse has been developed by Ostbloom and Crase (1980). This model illustrates both functional and nonfunctional families and two critical factors: stress and resources. In the functional family the resources are available to cope with daily stressors, resulting in a "balanced" family, as illustrated in Figure 6–2. In the nonfunctional family, resources are insufficient to deal with the stresses and they become overpowering, as illustrated in Figure 6–3.

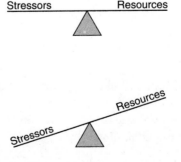

■ **FIGURE 6–2 (top) The Balanced, Functional Family, and FIGURE 6–3 (bottom) The Unbalanced, Nonfunctional Family**

To bring such families back into balance, stressors must be removed, or resources to cope with the stressors must be increased—or both.

Vulnerable Children

The AMA (1985, p. 797) has also identified characteristics of children that increase their risk of being abused:

▍ Premature birth.
▍ Birth of a child to adolescent parents.
▍ Colic, which renders infants difficult to soothe.
▍ Congenital deficiencies or abnormalities.
▍ Hospitalization of the neonate [newborn], who lacks parental contact.
▍ Presence of any condition that interferes with parent-child bonding.

Indicators of Emotional Abuse

Physical indicators of emotional abuse may include speech disorders, lags in physical development and a general failure to thrive. *Behavioral indicators* of emotional abuse may include such habit disorders as sucking, biting and rocking back and forth, as well as conduct disorders such as antisocial, destructive behavior. Other possible indicators are sleep disorders, inhibitions in play, obsessions, compulsions, phobias, hypochondria, behavioral extremes and attempted suicide (Bennett and Hess, 1994, p. 401).

Indicators of Physical Abuse

Among the *physical indicators* of physical abuse are unexplained bruises or welts, burns, fractures, lacerations and abrasions. Such physical injuries may be in various stages of healing. Among the *behavioral indicators* of physical abuse are being wary of adults, being apprehensive when other children cry, showing extreme aggressiveness or extreme withdrawal, being frightened of parents and being afraid to go home (Bennett and Hess, 1994, p. 401).

Indications of physical abuse may also be provided by the parents, including contradictory explanations for a child's injury; attempts to conceal a child's injury or to protect the identity of the person responsible; routine use of harsh, unreasonable discipline inappropriate to the child's age or behavior and poor impulse control (Bennett and Hess, 1994, p. 401).

The Seriousness of the Problem

The 1990 Annual Fifty State Survey conducted by the National Committee for Prevention of Child Abuse found that almost a million children are victims of child abuse and neglect (DeWitt, 1992, p. 1).

ten Bensel et al. (1985, p. 1) show the extent of the problem of child abuse and neglect:

An estimated 4 or 5 million children are neglected or physically or sexually abused each year, with an additional 2 million vulnerable as runaways or missing.

■ *Emotional or mental abuse can be as devastating as physical abuse.*

Abused children often suffer severe physical and emotional damage from family violence, unreasonable corporal punishment, verbal harassment, alcoholic and substance abuse and sexual or other exploitation.

■ Child abuse has been identified as the biggest single cause of death of young children.

A report on a symposium, "Joint Investigations of Child Abuse" (1993, p. 2), notes: "In 1991 at least four children a day died at the hands of their caretakers. Physical abuse accounted for most of the fatalities—60 percent—and neglect for 36 percent. . . . Almost half the known deaths involved children who were previous or current clients [of the child welfare system]."

An unofficial Prodigy Poll reported 3 million cases of child abuse and neglect in 1993. According to this poll some 1,300 children died, 40 percent of whom were known to child protection workers.

The abuse is sometimes inflicted by those outside the family, but more tragically and commonly it is inflicted in the homes by a child's natural parents or members of the immediate family.

Many children desperately need help and protection. Children requiring foster care often suffer deprivation. Children who are habitually truant, or who have run away from home or who are homeless or chemically dependent are also at risk of being exploited for prostitution, pornography, theft or drug trafficking. Chronically incorrigible children—those who are found so unreasonably disobedient of the proper guidance or protection of parents or guardians that custodial supervision is called for—must also be considered to be at risk.

THREE LEVELS OF ABUSE

Thus far in the discussion, child abuse has been discussed primarily as an act between individuals. In reality, however, three separate levels of abuse exist.

▐ The three levels of abuse are collective, institutional and individual.

Collective abuse is seen in the poverty and other forms of social injustice previously discussed. As noted millions of children live in poverty in our country. Children are eating and drinking contaminated food and water. Many are exploited for child pornography. Constant violence blares forth from television sets across the country. Child care is often grossly inadequate, and physical punishment of children is widely sanctioned. The collective attitude of most Americans tends to deny and ignore the natural and legal rights of children.

Institutional abuse of children includes the approved use of force and violence against children in the schools and in the neglect and denial of children's due process rights in institutions run by different levels of government.

However, the use of corporal punishment in schools has been declining, with "paddling" decreasing from 1,415,540 in 1982 to 613,514 in 1990 (Benshoff, 1993, p. 4B).

▐ Corporal punishment for children has been banned in 26 states.

Individual abuse is what is normally thought of when child abuse is discussed. This is one (or more) individuals who emotionally or physically abuse a child. Individual abuse includes child sexual abuse.

Child Abuse and the Link with Delinquency

Child abuse has also been directly linked with delinquency, as will be discussed shortly. When delinquent behavior occurs, it may bring about further abuse, resulting in a vicious cycle and ever worsening behavior, as illustrated in Figure 6–4.

Children and adolescents who have a pattern of delinquency that emanates from the home imitate similar behavior of parents or other family members. In extreme cases children have been taught how to commit crimes. Because

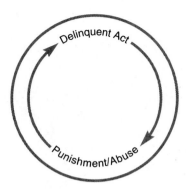

■ **FIGURE 6–4 The Delinquency/Abuse Cycle**

children do not receive the same penalties as adults, some parents actually teach their children to be pickpockets, pimps and to commit associated crimes.

In *Unraveling Juvenile Delinquency,* the Gluecks (1950) reported that 85 percent of the delinquents released from a Massachusetts correctional institution were from families in which other members were delinquent. The research was conducted in the late forties and early fifties, when families were less fragmented than families now. In 45 percent of the delinquent cases, the mother of the offender had a criminal record; in 66 percent the father had a criminal record.

The Cost of the Problem

The Metropolitan Court Judges Committee (1985, pp. 7–8) notes the high costs of child neglect and abuse:

> The immediate economic costs to society of child abuse and neglect are staggering. Initial costs for child protective services for each case opened are estimated to average $10,000. Long-term costs for psychological or medical care for sexual abuse or severe neglect and abuse cases can be much higher.
>
> Temporary foster care costs $5,000 to $15,000 a year. Home-based services average $50 a visit and 40 visits a year are common. At a conservative estimate of only $15,000 in costs per average case, and counting only the 650,000 cases actually serviced nationwide, annual costs amount to $10 billion.

The Committee's estimate does not include substantial law enforcement, hospital or court costs, nor the costs of future crime and child abuse perpetrated by the abused victim. Further, the committee's figures are in 1985 dollars.

CHILDREN WHO ARE SEXUALLY ABUSED

Every year roughly 100,000 cases of child sexual abuse are reported. Couple this with experts' estimates that more than 90 percent of child molestations are not reported to the criminal justice system (Holmes et al., 1993, p. 77), and the magnitude of the problem is apparent. Some experts feel that as many as 50 percent of young women have been sexually abused before their eighteenth birthday.

Langan and Harlow (1994, p. 1) report that only 12 states gather rape information in sufficient detail to distinguish child victims from adult victims. The victims in these 12 states numberd 20,824, or 20 percent of the national total. In addition, 51 percent of female rape victims in these 12 states were under age 18, while females under 18 made up 25 percent of the 1992 U.S. female population. If these 12 states are typical, child rape is indeed a serious problem.

Sexual abuse is often classified as intrafamilial or extrafamilial. **Intrafamilial sexual abuse** is sexual abuse by a parent or other family member. **Extrafamilial sexual abuse** involves a friend or stranger. According to Duvall (1991, p. 109): "The sad, ugly truth in today's society is: with 85 to 90% of all the sexually abused children, the offender is someone the child knows, loves or trusts. The place most people remember as a safe haven is most likely the very place children are being raped; anally, orally, and vaginally; by someone they know, love or trust."

Gomes-Schwartz and Horowitz (1988, p. 3) conducted research that supported the hypothesis that: "[F]amily disruption combined with poverty may increase the likelihood that a child will be sexually abused."

Indicators of Sexual Abuse

Rarely are *physical indicators* of sexual abuse seen. Two possible indicators, especially in preteens, are venereal disease and pregnancy.

Among the possible *behavioral indicators* of sexual abuse are being unwilling to change clothes for or participate in physical education classes; withdrawal, fantasy or infantile behavior; bizarre sexual behavior, sexual sophistication beyond age or unusual behavior or knowledge of sex; poor peer relationships; delinquent or runaway; reports of being sexually assaulted (Bennett and Hess, 1994, p. 401).

As with physical abuse, the behavior of parents may also provide indicators of sexual abuse. Such behaviors may include jealousy and overprotectiveness of a child. A parent may hesitate to report a spouse who is sexually abusing their child for fear of destroying the marriage or for fear of retaliation. Intrafamilial sex may be preferred to extramarital sex (Bennett and Hess, 1994, p. 401).

VIOLENCE

The pervasiveness of violence in the United States, not only toward children, but among adults, might, in part, be explained by our country's historical reliance upon force and violence in its international relations, frequently engaging in military hostilities without a formal declaration of war. In addition,

American history is rooted in the genocide of native Americans, the slavery of African-Americans and in white male supremacy. These historical roots may, in part, explain the prevalence of violence.

According to Craig (1992, p. 67): "For some children, family violence is so severe that it results in intervention by public authorities. For many other youngsters, it remains a secret destroyer that slowly permeates the fabric of self and distorts the content of all relationships."

Roth (1994, p. 1) notes that: "The level of violent crime in this country has reached high, though not unprecedented levels. . . . Violence falls most heavily on ethnic minority males and occurs most often in urban areas." Roth has developed a matrix that organizes the risk factors underlying violent behavior, contained in Table 6–4.

Roth (pp. 5–6) presents two illustrations of how violence resulted in the death of a child and then shows how the matrix helps to explain what happened.

The first illustration involved Dave, Evelyn and their ten-month-old son Jason. Evelyn had just turned 20 when Jason was born, and Dave had just lost his job. The family was struggling, and Dave became moody and argumentative. During some of the arguments over money, Dave would slap Evelyn, but always begged forgiveness. He also began to resent Jason. Evelyn, hoping to help the situation, went back to work as a waitress. Her first day back at work Dave "hit bottom," overwhelmed by feelings of humiliation and rejection with his new role as baby-sitter. Jason's crying made it worse. And nothing Dave did could stop the crying. When Jason wet on Dave, Dave lost control, filled the bathtub with scalding water and held Jason in the tub by his arm and leg, causing third-degree burns over 35 percent of his body according to the medical examiner's report.

The second illustration involves a beer bash in a "tough blue-collar suburb" involving two friends who had begun drinking heavily as teenagers, Andy and Bob. In this tough town, Bob was known as one of the toughest, almost always winning his fights. He had recently lost his job for missing work and had recently spent time in jail following a bar brawl. At this particular beer bash, Bob began making passes at Andy's sister who resisted the passes and finally slapped him. Several party goers began laughing at Bob. Andy, wanting to protect his sister, came at Bob. As they began to fight, Andy's older brother told them to "take it outside," which they did. The crowd followed, cheering them on. Bob got a tire iron out of his car's trunk and knocked Andy out, then proceeded to get in his car and drive over him two times. Andy died in the hospital four hours later from massive internal injuries.

Roth uses these two examples to demonstrate the risk factors in operation, as shown in Table 6–5.

Violence and the Media

The influence of violence in the media is often blamed for the amount of violence in society. Recall that in Table 6–3, over one-fourth of the respondents believed that violence on television or in the movies was a cause of child abuse.

TABLE   **Matrix for Organizing Risk Factors for Violent Behavior**
6–4

Units of Observation and Explanation	Proximity to Violent Events and Their Consequences		
	Predisposing	*Situational*	*Activating*
Social Macrosocial	Concentration of poverty Opportunity structures Decline of social capital Oppositional cultures Sex role socialization	Physical structure Routine activities Access: weapons, emergency medical services	Catalytic social event
Microsocial	Community organizations Illegal markets Gangs Family disorganization Pre-existing structures	Proximity of responsible monitors Participants' social relationships Bystanders' activities Temporary communication impairments Weapons: carrying, displaying	Participants' communication exchange
Individual Psychosocial	Temperament Learned social responses Perceptions of rewards/penalties for violence Violent deviant sexual preferences Social, communication skills Self-identification in social hierarchy	Accumulated emotion Alcohol/drug consumption Sexual arousal Premeditation	Impulse Opportunity recognition
Biological	Neurobehavioral* "traits" Genetically mediated traits Chronic use of psychoactive substances or exposure to neurotoxins	Transient neurobehavioral* "states" Acute effects of psychoactive substances	Sensory signal processing errors

*Includes neuroanatomical, neurophysiological, neurochemical, and neuroendocrine. "Traits" describe capacity as determined by status at birth, trauma, and aging processes such as puberty. "States" describe temporary conditions associated with emotions, external stressors, etc.

SOURCE: Jeffrey A. Roth, *Understanding and Preventing Violence*, National Institute of Justice, Research in Brief. (Washington, D.C.: February 1994), p. 7. Adapted from Reiss, Albert Jr., and Jeff A. Roth. eds., *Understanding and Preventing Violence*, Washington, D.C.: National Academy Press, 1993, p. 297.

TABLE   Examples of Possible Risk Factors in Two Murders
6–5
■

Units of Observation and Explanation	Proximity to Violent Events and Their Consequences		
	Predisposing	*Situational*	*Activating*
Social Macrosocial	1. Low neighborhood social interaction. 2. Neighborhood culture values fighting, drinking, sexual prowess.	1. No child care providers in neighborhood. 2. No local emergency medical services.	
Microsocial	1. Dave began hitting Evelyn months ago. 2. Widespread expectations of wild drinking parties at Andy's house.	1. Baby cries. Dave unable to cope. 2. Charlene humiliates Bob by resisting his advances.	1. Baby wets Dave. 2. Older brother says "take it outside," crowd goes outside to watch and cheer.
Individual Psychosocial	1. Dave has low self-esteem. 2. Bob develops adolescent pattern of drinking and violent behavior.	1. Dave humiliated by Evelyn's new job, his own lack of parenting skills. 2. Threats to Andy's family status, Bob's personal status.	
Biological	2. Possible familial traits of alcoholism and antisocial behavior in Bob's family.	2. Andy, Bob, and bystanders under alcohol influence.	
Murder 1: 10-month-old baby scalded to death by father; no witnesses.	*Murder 2:* 20-year-old male beaten and intentionally run over by automobile; many witnesses.		

SOURCE: Jeffrey A. Roth, *Understanding and Preventing Violence,* National Institute of Justice, Research in Brief (Washington, D.C.: February 1994), p. 8. Adapted from Reiss, Albert Jr., and Jeff A. Roth, eds., *Understanding and Preventing Violence,* Washington, D.C.: National Academy Press, 1993, p. 297.

The AMA is asking Congress to pass legislation requiring every TV set sold in this country to have a microchip that would allow parents to block programming containing violence. The AMA is also urging that advertisers boycott programs showing violence. Dr. Robert McAfee, AMA president-elect, stated during hearings on violence in the media:

Violence in general is clearly an enormous and at least partially avoidable public health problem in this country today. . . . [P]articularly alarming is the prevalent depiction of violent behavior on television, especially in terms of its "role-modeling" capacity to potentially promote "real-world violence" (NCJA, 1993, p. 3).

The Convention on the Rights of the Child also stresses the important role played by the media in "disseminating information to children that is consistent with moral well-being and knowledge and understanding among peoples, and respects the child's cultural background" (United Nations, Article 17, p. 5).

The media glamorizes "materialism, violence, drug and alcohol use, hedonistic lifestyles, and easy sex" (Eitzen, 1992, p. 588).

An article by Gordon Witkin, "Kids Who Kill" (p. 181), reports: "Today's kids are desensitized to violence as never before, surrounded by gunfire and stuffed with media images of Rambos who kill at will." The article notes another significant change: "By far the biggest difference in today's atmosphere is that the no-problem availability of guns in every nook of the nation has turned record numbers of everyday encounters into deadly ones."

Surveys concerning violence on television generally conclude that too much violence is shown and that it adversely affects children. In one survey, three-fourths of the people responding felt that television had more influence on children than their parents had (Milavsky, n.d., p. 1). Further, the American Psychological Association asserts that children see, on the average, 8,000 murders and 100,000 other violent acts on television before they finish elementary school (Martin, 1994, p. 38).

Other individuals contend that there is insufficient data to clearly implicate violence on television with violence in society. Milavsky (n.d., p. 3), for example, states:

> We cannot be sure that our common belief in television's impact on violence is correct. However, since an effect cannot entirely be ruled out, both those who produce television programs, and those who watch them, must be alert to the possibility of a causal link between violent television and violent behavior.

The American Psychological Association Commission on Violence and Youth takes a stronger position, stating (n.d., p. 33): "Children's exposure to violence in the mass media, particularly at young ages, can have harmful lifelong consequences." The Commission noted:

> Aggressive habits learned early in life are the foundation for later behavior. . . . A longitudinal study of boys found a significant relation between exposure to television violence at 8 years of age and antisocial acts—including serious, violent criminal offenses and spouse abuse—22 years later.

The Cycle of Violence

Paisner (1991, p. 35) warns:

> Violence is learned behavior. Children who have witnessed abuse or have been abused themselves are *1,000* times more likely to abuse a spouse or child when they become adults than are children raised in a home without violence (italic in original).

Violence is, indeed, self-perpetuating. When adults teach children by example that those who are bigger and stronger can force their wishes on others who are smaller through violence, the lesson is remembered. In addition, family violence has been directly linked with delinquency, especially violent offenses, as discussed in the next chapter. The cycle of violence is illustrated in Figure 6–5.

According to Goldschmidt (1992, p. 66) two-thirds of adult felons currently in our corrections system were abused as children.

Halvorsen (1993, p. 7A) notes that: [M]any American homes are not safe havens for children, but instead are training grounds for criminals. . . . [C]hildren are harmed by the sights and sounds of violence—and not just by physical blows that might rain down on them."

Violence often leads to more violence. Children who are abused are more likely to be delinquents and violent themselves.

The connection between children's histories of neglect or abuse and subsequent delinquency, crime and other problems has been largely ignored by our

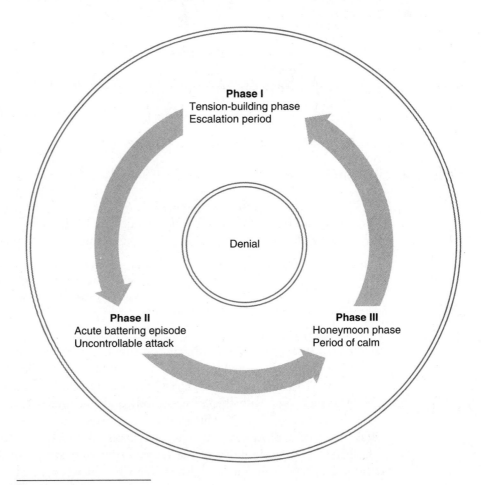

FIGURE 6–5 The Cycle of Violence

juvenile justice and social service systems. This is difficult to understand, given that those who experience violent, abusive childhoods are more likely to become child or spouse abusers than those who have not.

Although child abuse is more prevalent in families in lower socioeconomic groups, family violence, abuse and neglect can be found across the spectrum of society, including families of all social and economic backgrounds. Children are lied to and lied about, mutilated, shot, stabbed, burned, beaten, bitten, sodomized, raped and hanged.

Figure 6–6 illustrates a model of intrafamily violence, the variables affecting it, individual characteristics of family members, precipitating factors, social variables and the consequences for the child, the family and society.

CHILD ABUSE AND NEGLECT LAWS

Laws regarding child abuse and neglect have been passed at both the federal and the state level.

■ Typically, child abuse/neglect laws have three components:
1. Criminal definitions and penalties.
2. A mandate to report suspected cases.
3. Civil process for removing the child from the abusive or neglectful environment.

Federal Legislation

In 1974 the federal government passed P. L. 93–247, the Federal Child Abuse Prevention and Treatment Act. It was amended in 1978 under P. L. 95–266. The law states in part that any of the following elements constitutes a crime:

> The physical or mental injury, sexual abuse or exploitation, negligent treatment, or maltreatment of a child under the age of eighteen, by a person who is responsible for the child's welfare under circumstances which indicate the child's health or welfare is harmed or threatened.

Nonetheless, federal courts have also ruled that parents are free to strike children because "the custody, care and nurture of the child resides first in the parents" (*Prince* v. *Massachusetts* [1944]) and is a fundamental liberty interest of the parents. This fundamental right to "nurture" has been supplanted by the U.S. Supreme Court with the "care, custody and management" of one's child (*Santosky* v. *Kramer* [1982]). This shift from "nurture" to "management" could herald a return to older laws, such as that expressed in *People* v. *Green* (1909): "The parent is the sole judge of the necessity for the exercise of disciplinary right and of the nature of the correction to be given." The court need only determine if "the punishment inflicted went beyond the legitimate exercise of parental authority."

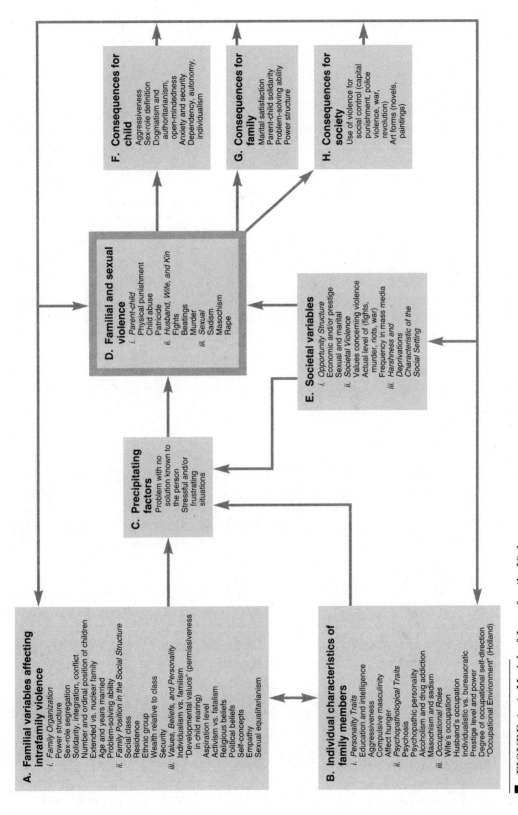

A. Familial variables affecting intrafamily violence

i. Family Organization
Power structure
Sex-role segregation
Solidarity, integration, conflict
Number and ordinal position of children
Extended vs. nuclear family
Age and years married
Problem-solving ability
ii. Family Position in the Social Structure
Social class
Residence
Ethnic group
Wealth relative to class
Security
iii. Values, Beliefs, and Personality
Individualism vs. familism
"Developmental values" (permissiveness in child rearing)
Aspiration level
Activism vs. fatalism
Religious beliefs
Political beliefs
Self-concepts
Empathy
Sexual equalitarianism

B. Individual characteristics of family members

i. Personality Traits
Education and intelligence
Aggressiveness
Compulsive masculinity
Affect hunger
ii. Psychopathological Traits
Psychosis
Psychopathic personality
Alcoholism and drug addiction
Masochism and sadism
iii. Occupational Roles
Husband's occupation
Wife's occupation
Individualistic vs. bureaucratic
Prestige level and power
Degree of occupational self-direction
"Occupational Environment" (Holland)

C. Precipitating factors

Problem with no solution known to the person
Stressful and/or frustrating situations

D. Familial and sexual violence

i. Parent-child
Physical punishment
Child abuse
Patricide
ii. Husband, Wife, and Kin
Fights
Beatings
Murder
iii. Sexual
Sadism
Masochism
Rape

E. Societal variables

i. Opportunity Structure
Economic and/or prestige
Sexual and marital
ii. Societal Violence
Values concerning violence
Actual level of (fights, murder, riots, war)
Frequency in mass media
iii. Harshness and Deprivations
Characteristic of the Social Setting

F. Consequences for child

Aggressiveness
Sex-role definition
Dogmatism and authoritarianism, open-mindedness
Anxiety and security
Dependency, autonomy, individualism

G. Consequences for family

Marital satisfaction
Parent-child solidarity
Problem-solving ability
Power structure

H. Consequences for society

Use of violence for social control (capital punishment, police violence, war, revolution)
Art forms (novels, paintings)

■ **FIGURE 6–6 Model of Intrafamily Violence**

SOURCE: Suzanne K. Steinmetz and Murray A. Straus, *Violence in the Family* (New York: Dodd, Mead, 1974), pp. 18–19.

193

Up to the present time, the courts' role has been to decide what and when, and to what degree, physical punishment steps beyond "the legitimate exercise of parental authority," or what is "excessive punishment." They always begin with the presumption that parents have a legal right to use force and violence against their own children. In *Green,* seventy marks from a whipping was held excessive and unreasonable, even though the parent claimed he was not criminally liable because there was no permanent injury and he had acted in good faith. But the assumption remained that the parent had an unquestionable right "to administer such reasonable and timely punishment as may be necessary to correct growing faults in young children."

Current laws protect parents, and convictions for child abuse are difficult to obtain because of the circumstantial evidence, the lack of witnesses, the husband-wife privilege and the fact that an adult's testimony frequently is sufficient to establish a reasonable doubt. All too frequently, the Court determines the punishment to be "reasonable," never scrutinizing the age-old presumption that hitting children is permissible.

A determination of "reasonableness' was made in *Ingram* v. *Wright* (1977), regarding the use of physical punishment of children by teachers. The Florida statute specified that the punishment was not to be "degrading or unduly severe." One student was beaten by 20 strokes with a wooden paddle; another was beaten by 50 strokes.

State Laws

Since the 1960s every state has enacted child abuse and neglect laws. On the whole, states offer a bit more protection to children by statute than the federal government.

Legal definitions vary from state to state. California, for example, declares it illegal for anyone to willfully cause or permit any child to suffer or for any person to inflict unjustifiable physical or mental suffering on a child or to cause the child to "be placed in such situations that its person or health is endangered" (California Penal Codes, Sec. 273A).

Alaska defines abuse broadly: "The infliction, by other than accidental means, of physical harm upon the body of a child." Other state statutes are much less broad. For example, Maryland's statute states that a person is not guilty of child abuse if the defendant's intentions were good, but his or her judgment was bad. The defendant in *Worthen* v. *State* (1979) admitted he had punished his two-year-old stepdaughter because she was throwing a temper tantrum, "but sought to explain as not having exceeded the bounds of parental propriety." The jury found him guilty of assault and battery for the multiple contusions about the girl's face, ribs, buttocks and legs, but the appellate court ordered a new trial because the trial court in the jury instructions had omitted the defense of good intentions and also the defense that he had not exceeded the bounds of parental authority. What is "reasonable" varies from state to state, from one judge or court to another and from jury to jury.

Unfortunately, federal and state laws are often not enough to protect our children and youth. Another category of our young who are victimized are children who are missing and exploited, often by choice because of intolerable conditions in the home.

MISSING AND EXPLOITED CHILDREN

The Missing Children's Act was passed in 1982 and the Missing Children's Assistance Act in 1984. The Missing Children's Assistance Act of 1984 defines a "missing child" as:

> Any individual, less than 18 years of age, whose whereabouts are unknown to such individual's legal custodian—if the circumstances surrounding the disappearance indicate that (the child) may possibly have been removed by another person from the control of his/her legal custodian without the custodian's consent; or the circumstances of the case strongly indicate that (the child) is likely to be abused or sexually exploited (*Annual Report on Missing Children 1990,* p. ix).

During the period 1985–1990, the National Incidence Studies of Missing, Abducted, Runaway, and Thrownaway Children in America (NISMART) conducted a telephone survey of 30,000 households and did an analysis of the FBIs data, police records and residential facilities and institutions, as well as community and professional services, to determine the scope of the missing children problem. The first findings of NISMART were released in May 1990. Among the key findings was that: "What has in the past been called the missing children problem is in reality a set of at least five very different, distinct problems" (Finkelhor et al., 1990, p. 4).

■ The five categories of missing children included in the NISMART study are runaways; thrownaways; nonfamily abducted children; family abducted children; and lost, injured or otherwise missing children.

NISMART used two types of definitions within each of the five distinct problem areas: *broad scope* and *policy focal* definitions. Broad scope definitions are more general, defining the problem the way the family might define it. Policy focal definitions, on the other hand, define the problem from the point of view of the police or other social agencies, being restricted to more serious episodes where children truly are at risk and need immediate intervention. All broad scope and policy focal definitions in the following discussions are from this report. NISMART's data is summarized in Table 6–6.

A major conclusion of the study was that: "Many of the children in at least four of these categories were not literally missing. Caretakers did know where they were. The problem was in recovering them" (Finkelhor et al., 1990, p. 4).

Runaways

When adolescents cannot cope with a relationship in a family, they may perceive their only recourse to be running away. Historically, running away has

TABLE   NISMART Estimates of Missing Children in Five Categories
6-6

Category	Number of Children in 1988
Family Abductions	
Broad scope	354,100
Policy focal	163,200
Nonfamily Abductions	
Legal definition abductions	3,200–4,600
Stereotypical kidnappings	200–300
Runaways	
Broad scope	450,700
Policy focal	133,500
Thrownaways	
Broad scope	127,100
Policy focal	59,200
Lost, Injured, or Otherwise Missing	
Broad scope	438,200
Policy focal	139,100

Note: Because of definitional controversies, each problem is estimated according to two possible definitions.
These estimates should not be added or aggregated.
SOURCE: David Finkelhor, Gerald Hotaling, and Andrea Sedlak, *Missing, Abducted, Runaway, and Thrownaway Children in America. First Report: Numbers and Characteristics, National Incidence Studies, Executive Summary.* (Washington, D.C.: Office of Juvenile Justice and Delinquency Prevention, May 1990), p. 4.

been defined as a behavioral manifestation of psychopathology. In fact, the American Psychiatric Association has classified the "runaway reaction" as a specific disorder. Benalcazar (1982) cites numerous investigations that describe runaways as insecure, depressed, unhappy and impulsive, with emotional problems, low self-esteem and an unmanageable personal life. Running away may compound their problems. Many become streetwise and turn to drugs, crime, prostitution or other illegal activities. Typical runaways report conflict with parents, alienation from them, rejection and hostile control, lack of warmth, affection and parental support.

Runaways have a distinct age pattern. The police estimate that both male and female youngsters start runaway activity at approximately age 12 and reach a peak at age 14 or 15. At 16 a change usually occurs. The number of males who leave home declines sharply, while the number of females rises. The decline continues for males at 17, but the trend continues to climb for females. This decline in males and climb in females correlates significantly with maturity.

When males are absent from the home at age 12, the absence is usually one day or less. This is also true of females. Females, however, are more prone to recidivism and usually stay away longer. The older the runaways are, the longer they tend to stay away. And because females mature faster and can become self-sufficient faster, they stay away longer.

Broad scope runaways were children who left home without permission and stayed away overnight. In 1988 there were an estimated 446,700 broad scope

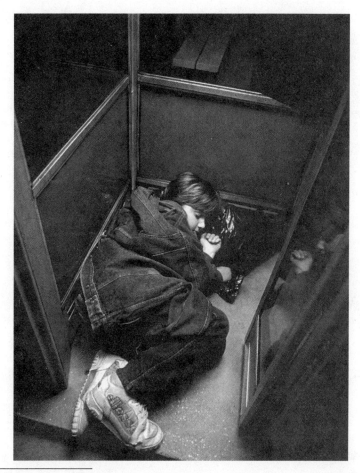

■ *Running away from home is seen as a solution to problems at home or school by many youths.*

runaways from households. An additional 450,700 were broad scope runaways from facilities. The policy focal definition added the condition that the youth had no familiar or secure place to stay. There were an estimated 129,500 policy focal runaways from households. Runaways from juvenile facilities were also considered to be policy focal, so the joint number of policy focal runaways from households and juvenile facilities was estimated to be 133,500 in 1988.

The NISMART project's researchers observe: "[T]oday, we know that when many children run, it is often to escape from a protracted and painful family conflict or from physical, sexual or psychological abuse. We also know what may lie in wait for the long-term runaway: homelessness, drugs, crime, sexual exploitation, and suicide" (Sweet, 1990b, p. 17).

Problems reported by youth seeking services from runaway and homeless youth centers included family problems such as emotional conflict at home, parents who were too strict and physical abuse and neglect. The National Council of Juvenile and Family Court Judges has stated: "We know that many [youths] who are on the streets are there as a result of sound rational choices they have made for their own safety and welfare, such as avoiding physical abuse, sexual abuse, or extreme neglect at home."

The two most frequently mentioned personal problems were a poor self-image and depression. Table 6–7 summarizes the results of this survey.

As noted by Sweet (1990a, p. 1):

> Of all the youth at risk, runaways pose one of the most serious dilemmas for the juvenile justice system. Although not all runaways come to the attention of the system, juvenile justice professionals are responsible for protecting and intervening on their behalf. As the risks for victimization, illegal drug use, and delinquency continue to rise for runaway youth, the need remains crucial for the juvenile justice system to play its part in ensuring their safety.

Thrownaways

A broad scope thrownaway child faces one of four situations:

1. Told to leave.
2. Not allowed back after having left.
3. No effort to recover runaway.
4. Abandoned or deserted.

According to NISMART findings, there were an estimated 127,100 broad scope thrownaways in 1988, including 112,600 from the household survey and 14,500 based on the community professionals study.

A policy focal case was a thrownaway who was without a secure and familiar place to stay during some portion of the episode. All abandoned children were considered to fall within this category. There were an estimated 59,200 policy focal thrownaways in 1988.

TABLE 6–7   Problems Reported by Youth Seeking Services from Runaway and Homeless Youth Centers, 1990

Type of Problem	Total	Female	Male
*Family Problems**	(N = 30,373)	(N = 17,170)	(N = 13,203)
Emotional conflict at home	41%	43%	39%
Parent too strict	21	24	18
Parental physical abuse	20	23	18
Parental neglect	20	19	21
Parent drug or alcohol problems	18	19	17
Family mental health problems	11	12	11
Parental domestic violence	10	10	10
Parental unemployment	9	9	9
Wants to live with other parent	6	7	6
Parental sexual abuse	7	9	2
Physical or sexual abuse by other family member	5	6	3
Physical or sexual abuse by nonfamily member	4	5	2
No parent figure	4	4	5
Parent is homosexual	1	2	1
None of the above	16	13	19

continued

TABLE   Problems Reported by Youth Seeking Services from Runaway and Homeless
6–7   Youth Centers, 1990, *continued*

Type of Problem	Total	Female	Male
*Individual Problems**	(N = 30,388)	(N = 17,180)	(N = 13,208)
Poor self-image	49%	51%	46%
Depressed	43	48	36
School attendance or truancy	33	33	33
Bad grades	31	30	33
In trouble with justice system	19	13	27
Drug abuse	15	13	17
Alcohol abuse	13	13	13
Possibly suicidal	12	15	8
Cannot get along with teachers	13	10	17
Learning disability	7	5	10
Custody change	5	5	5
Pregnant or suspects pregnancy	4	7	0
Other health problems or handicap	4	4	4
Homosexual or sexual identity issue	2	2	3
Prostitution	1	2	1
Venereal disease	1	1	0
None of the above	19	19	20

Note: These data were collected by the U.S. Department of Health and Human Services and are for the period Oct. 1, 1989 to Sept. 30, 1990. The data were collected in response to Section 361 of the Runaway and Homeless Youth Act, Title III of the Juvenile Justice and Delinquency Prevention Act of 1974, as amended, including amendments and renumbering under the Anti-Drug Abuse Act of 1988 (P.L. 100-690). The Runaway and Homeless Youth Act is administered by the Family and Youth Services Bureau, within the Administration for Children, Youth and Families, Office of Human Development Services, Department of Health and Human Services.

These data are derived, in large part, from the Youth Information Forms that are filled out by basic center staff for each youth receiving shelter or ongoing services. In fiscal year 1990, there were 338 basic centers located in the 50 States, the District of Columbia, Puerto Rico, the Virgin Islands, Guam, the Northern Mariana Islands, and Palau. It is important to note that center submission of the data to the U.S. Department of Health and Human Services was voluntary. Approximately 60 percent of the centers reported at least partial data. Both the response rate and the nonrandom nature of the sample should be kept in mind when interpreting these data. The U.S. Department of Health and Human Services defines a runaway youth as a "person under 18 years of age who absents himself or herself from home or place of legal residence without the permission of parents or legal guardian." A homeless youth is defined as a "person under 18 years of age who is in need of services and without a place of shelter where he or she receives supervision and care."

*Because multiple responses are permitted, totals exceed 100 percent.

SOURCE: U.S. Department of Justice, Bureau of Statistics, *Sourcebook of Criminal Justice Statistics, 1992* (Washington, D.C.: U.S. Government Printing Office, [1992]), p. 589.

Nonfamily Abduction

NISMART used both legal and stereotypical definitions in this area. The legal definition of nonfamily abduction was the coerced, unauthorized *taking* of a child into a building, a vehicle or a distance of more than 20 feet; *detaining* a child for more than one hour; or *luring* a child for the purpose of committing another crime. Under this definition, from 3,200 to 4,600 cases were known to the police.

The stereotypical kidnapping required one of five circumstances:

1. Gone overnight.
2. Transported 50+ miles.
3. Ransom.
4. Intent to keep.
5. Killed.

In 1988 between 200 and 300 stereotypical kidnappings occurred, according to NISMART estimates.

Researchers studying missing children have estimated that the number of children kidnapped and murdered by strangers is between 52 and 158 a year (Speirs, 1989, p. 1). The highest rate of all age groups is teenagers, between ages 14 and 17. This is quite different from the estimates that thousands of children face this fate each year. Researchers have also found that girls are at greater risk than boys, as are racial minorities.

Family Abduction

The broad scope definition of family abduction is a situation where a family member (1) took a child in violation of a custody agreement or decree; or (2) in violation of a custody agreement or decree failed to return a child at the end of a legal or agreed-upon visit, with the child being away at least overnight. There were an estimated 354,100 such abductions in 1988.

The policy focal abduction involved one of three additional aggravating conditions: concealment, transportation out of state or intent to permanently alter custody. An estimated 163,200 policy focal family abductions (46% of the broad scope) occurred in 1988.

"Parental kidnapping—the unlawful taking of a child by one parent from the legal custody of the other—is one of the most troubling and intractable problems in the missing children arena" (*Missing and Exploited Children*, 1988, p. 39). Not only is parental kidnapping illegal, it can result in the abducted child becoming a pawn or a "bargaining chip" to reduce support obligations or even to "extort a reconciliation."

Although often the parent/kidnapper truly has the child's best interests at heart, the risks to the kidnapped child are great:

> Factors that are proven contributing causes to child abuse and neglect—such as financial difficulties, stress, worry, and isolation—are often present in abduction scenarios. Fearing discovery, for example, many abducting parents move from job to job and are reluctant to place their children with babysitters, relatives, or daycare centers or even to enroll them in school. Even if there is little risk of abuse or neglect, parental kidnapping is almost certain to intensify and prolong the psychological trauma and stress to a child caused by the divorce or separation of his or her parents (*Missing and Exploited Children*, 1988, pp. 39–40).

Lost, Injured or Otherwise Missing

The broad scope definition of lost, injured or otherwise missing children varied with the child's age, whether the child had any disabilities and the time missing.

TABLE   Lost, Injured or Otherwise Missing: Broad Scope Definition
6–8

Age	Time Missing
0–2	Any
3–4	2 hrs
5–6	3 hrs
7–10	4 hrs
11–13	8 hrs
14–17	Overnight
Disabled	Any
Injured	1 hr

SOURCE: David Finkelhor, Gerald Hotaling, and Andrea Sedlak, *Missing, Abducted, Runaway, and Thrownaway Children in America. First Report: Numbers and Characteristics, National Incidence Studies. Executive Summary.* (Washington, D.C.: Office of Juvenile Justice and Delinquency Prevention, May 1990), p. 17.

Table 6–8 summarizes the requirements for children to fall within this definition.

There were an estimated 438,200 broad scope lost, injured or otherwise missing children in 1988. Policy focal cases were broad scope incidents serious enough that the police were called. There were an estimated 139,100 policy focal lost, injured or otherwise missing children in 1988, or 32 percent of the broad scope children.

Responsibility for Investigating Missing and Exploited Children

Primary responsibility for investigating missing and exploited children falls at the local and state level, but the federal government is also involved. According to *Missing and Exploited Children* (1988, pp. 22–26), two government agencies in particular have responsibilities in the area and come at the problem from very different perspectives.

■ The Department of Health and Human Services through its Administration for Children, Youth and Families (ACYF) and the Justice Department through OJJDP have concurrent jurisdiction for missing and exploited children.

Both these agencies' authority comes from the 1974 Juvenile Justice and Delinquency Prevention (JJDP) Act, amended in 1978 by the Runaway and Homeless Youth (RHY) Act. The RHY Act took a "social welfare, emergency care" approach to the problem of runaways, playing down the law enforcement solutions. This approach is the focus of the ACYF.

ACYF's approaches to locating, detaining, and returning runaway children do not involve law enforcement or juvenile justice authorities. Instead, they focus on such activities as having shelter staff encourage runaways to contact home; using "runaway switchboards" to exchange messages between runaways and their families; and utilizing mental health programs to provide crisis counseling (and, in some cases, longer term counseling) to assist reunification efforts (*Missing and Exploited Children,* 1988, p. 23).

The OJJDP focus is very different, focusing on the challenges runaways present to law enforcement and the juvenile justice system, but hampered by the OJJDP emphasis on deinstitutionalization:

> However well motivated the thinking behind this policy [deinstitutionalization], the fact remains that secure custodial care has often been the only practical, effective means for protecting runaways themselves, and for protecting communities from the problems of juvenile prostitution, drug abuse, theft, and other criminal acts committed by runaway youngsters seeking to support a day-to-day, hand-to-mouth existence (*Missing and Exploited Children,* 1988, p. 25).

Clearly, these two approaches are often at odds with each other. Coordination between the two agencies is vital if the runaway problem is to be effectively addressed.

YOUTHS AND SUICIDE

Suicide rates for America's teens have more than tripled from 1960 to 1988, from 3.5 per 100,000 to 11.3. However, as noted by suicidologist Adina Wrobleski (1989, p. 29):

> Teenagers kill themselves the least of all age groups, but get most of the attention because it always seems more tragic when a young person's life is cut short. Even though young people from 15 to 24 years old make up the smallest number of suicides . . . their suicide rates rose quickly from the 1950s to 1980s.

Wrobleski reports that from 1980 to 1985 there was a great deal of attention and publicity about "epidemic," "cluster" and "copy-cat" suicides. In that five-year span about 200 young people died in what were described as "clusters." However, during that same time span, some 11,000 teenagers committed suicide alone. Wrobleski notes that receiving great publicity was a single study by Phillips in 1986 claiming that three fictionalized television programs about teenage suicide led to approximately 80 "extra" teenage suicides. Three other studies by others did *not* agree.

At least one-fourth of high schools students report having suicidal thoughts and behavior, as summarized in Table 6–9.

▮ The leading cause of suicide is untreated depression.

Sometimes the depression may not be readily apparent. The individual may try to cover it up with overactivity, preoccupation with trivia or acting out behavior, such as delinquency, use of drugs or sexual promiscuity.

TABLE   **High School Students Reporting Suicidal Thoughts and Behavior**
6-9

■

	Suicidal thoughts		Made specific suicide plans		One or more suicide attempt(s)		Suicide attempt required medical attention	
	1990	*1991*	*1990*	*1991*	*1990*	*1991*	*1990*	*1991*
Total	27%	29%	16%	19%	8%	7%	2%	2%
Sex								
Male	20	21	12	13	6	4	2	1
Female	34	37	20	25	10	11	2	2

Note: Students were asked whether they had thought seriously about attempting suicide during the 12 months preceding the survey, whether they had made a specific plan to attempt suicide, whether they had actually attempted suicide, and whether the suicide attempt(s) resulted in an injury or poisoning that had to be treated by a doctor or nurse.

SOURCE: U.S. Department of Justice, Bureau of Justice Statistics, *Sourcebook of Criminal Justice Statistics, 1992* (Washington, D.C.: U.S. Government Printing Office, [1992]), p. 319.

SUMMARY

Our youth are victimized in many ways. Youth are victims of crime more often than those over age 25. In addition, nearly one-fourth of our children live in poverty. Two of the most serious consequences of poverty for children are homelessness and increased risk of lead poisoning.

Youth are also victimized by neglect and abuse. The two leading causes for child abuse are believed to be violence between husbands and wives and poverty. An estimated 4- to 5-million children are neglected or physically or sexually abused each year, with an additional 2 million vulnerable as runaways or missing. The three levels of abuse are collective, institutional and individual. Use of corporal punishment for children has been banned in 26 states.

Violence often leads to more violence. Children who are abused are more likely to be delinquents and violent themselves. They are also likely to run away, becoming part of the "missing and exploited children" problem. The five categories of missing children included in the NISMART study are runaways; thrownaways; nonfamily abducted children; family abducted children and lost, injured or otherwise missing children.

The Department of Health and Human Services through its Administration for Children, Youth and Families (ACYF) and the Department of Justice through OJJDP have concurrent jurisdiction for missing and exploited children. Children and youth who do not receive appropriate assistance may become suicidal. The number one cause of suicide is thought to be untreated depression.

▌ Discussion Questions

1. What causes parents or custodians of children to abuse them?
2. Does your state law contain two or more of the following components?

∎ Nonaccidental physical injury
∎ Physical neglect
∎ Emotional abuse or neglect
∎ Sexual abuse
∎ Abandonment

3. Of all abuses, which one has the most lasting effect? Why?
4. How can society cope with abuse and strive to control it?
5. What protection does a child have against abuse? Should the court remove parental rights in abuse cases?
6. Do courts act in the best interest of the child when they allow abused children to remain with the family?
7. How does abuse at a low socioeconomic status differ from that at a high socioeconomic level?
8. Are the definitions of *child abuse* and *child neglect* the key elements in determining the volume of child abuse cases in various jurisdictions? How is the volume of cases determined?
9. In your area, how are children protected from abuse? Can the system be improved? How?
10. Why did the NISMART project have two different definitions for each of the five categories of missing children? Did you find these two definitions helpful or confusing?

∎ References

American Medical Association. "AMA Diagnostic and Treatment Guidelines Concerning Child Abuse and Neglect." *JAMA* 254 (1985) 6: 796–800.

American Psychological Association. *Violence & Youth: Psychology's Response,* vol. 1. *Summary Report of the American Psychological Association Commission on Violence and Youth.* n.d.

Annual Report on Missing Children, 1990. Washington, D.C.: Office of Juvenile Justice and Delinquency Prevention.

Bastian, Lisa D. *Criminal Victimization 1992: A National Crime Victimization Survey Report.* Bureau of Justice Statistics Bulletin, October 1993.

Benalcazar, B. "Study of Fifteen Runaway Patients." *Adolescence* 17 (Fall 1982): 553–66.

Bennett, Wayne M., and Kären M. Hess. *Criminal Investigation,* 4th ed. St. Paul, Minn.: West Publishing, 1994.

Benshoff, Anastasia. "Schools to Shelve Paddles." *The Rockford Register Star,* 16 October 1993, p. 4B.

Cowley, Geoffrey. "Children in Peril." *Newsweek Special Issue,* Summer 1991, pp. 18–21.

Craig, Susan E. "The Educational Needs of Children Living with Violence." *Phi Delta Kappan,* September 1992, pp. 67–71.

DeWitt, Charles B. "From the Director." National Institute of Justice, Research in Brief, October 1992, p. 1.

Duvall, Ed, Jr. "What Is Happening to Our Children?" *Law and Order,* November 1991, p. 109.

Eitzen, Stanley. "Problem Students: The Sociocultural Roots." *Phi Delta Kappan,* April 1992, pp. 584–590.

Finkelhor, David; Gerald Hotaling; and Andrea Sedlak. *Missing, Abducted, Runaway, and Thrownaway Children in America. First Report: Numbers and Characteristics, National Incidence Studies, Executive Summary.* Washington, D.C.: Office of Juvenile Justice and Delinquency Prevention, May 1990.

Glueck, Sheldon, and Eleanor Glueck. *Unraveling Juvenile Delinquency.* Cambridge: Harvard University Press, 1950.

Goldschmidt, Neil. "Saving Our Children Is First Step Toward Solving Society's Problems." *Corrections Today,* April 1992, pp. 66–68.

Gomes-Schwartz, Beverly, and Jonathan Horowitz, with Albert P. Cardarelli. *Child Sexual Abuse Victims and Their Treatment.* Washington, D.C.: U.S. Department of Justice, Office of Juvenile Justice and Delinquency Prevention, July 1988.

Halvorsen, Donna. "Children Who Witness Abuse Bear Scars, Experts Say," (Minneapolis/St. Paul) *Star Tribune,* 8 November 1993, p. 7A.

Holmes, Ronald M.; Stephen T. Holmes; and Jerrie Unholz. "Female Pedophilia: A Hidden Abuse." *Law and Order,* August 1993, pp. 77–79.

"Joint Investigations of Child Abuse: Report of a Symposium." U.S. Department of Justice and U.S. Department of Health and Human Services, July 1993.

Kaplan, George. "Suppose They Gave an Intergenerational Conflict and Nobody Came." *Phi Delta Kappan Special Report,* May 1991.

Langan, Patrick A., and Caroline Wolf Harlow. "Child Rape Victims." *Crime Data Brief.* Washington, D.C.: Bureau of Justice Statistics, June 1994.

Linehan, Michelle Fryt. "Children Who Are Homeless: Educational Strategies for School Personnel." *Phi Delta Kappan,* September 1992, pp. 61–66.

Martin, Deirdre. "Teen Violence: Why It's on the Rise and How to Stem its Tide." *Law Enforcement Technology,* January 1994, pp. 36–42.

McClellan, Mary. "Why Blame Schools?" *Research Bulletin,* no. 12, Phi Delta Kappa, March 1994.

Metropolitan Court Judges Committee Report. *Deprived Children: A Judicial Response.* Washington, D.C.: U.S. Government Printing Office. 1986.

Milavsky, J. Ronald. *TV and Violence.* National Institute of Justice, Crime File Study Guide, n.d.

"Millions of Kids Seen Facing a High-Risk Future." *Law Enforcement News,* 15 May 1994, p. 7.

Missing and Exploited Children: The Challenge Continues. Washington, D.C.: U.S. Attorney General's Advisory Board on Missing Children, December 1988.

National Criminal Justice Association. "AMA Calls for Measures to Shield Children from TV Violence." *Juvenile Justice,* July 1993, pp. 3–4.

Needleman, Herbert L. "Childhood Exposure to Lead: A Common Cause of School Failure." *Phi Delta Kappan,* September 1992, pp. 35–37.

Ostbloom, Norman, and Sedahlia Jasper Crase. "A Model for Conceptualizing Child Abuse Causation and Intervention." *Social Case Work: The Journal of Contemporary Social Work,* March 1980, pp. 164–172.

Paisner, Susan R. "Domestic Violence: Breaking the Cycle." *Police Chief,* February 1991, pp. 35–38.

Parker, L. Craig, Jr.; Robert D. Meier; and Lynn Hunt Monahan. *Interpersonal Psychology for Criminal Justice.* St. Paul, Minn.: West Publishing, 1989.

Roth, Jeffrey A. *Understanding and Preventing Violence.* National Institute of Justice, Research in Brief, February 1994.

Speirs, Verne L. *Preliminary Estimates Developed on Stranger Abduction Homicides of Children.* OJJDP, Juvenile Justice Bulletin, January 1989.

Spencer, Rich, and Christine Spolar. "1980s 'Terrible' for American Children." *Washington Post,* 1 February 1991, p. A-3.

Springer, Charles E. *Justice for Juveniles.* Washington, D.C.: U.S. Department of Justice, Office of Juvenile Justice and Delinquency Prevention, 1986.

Stevens, Linda J., and Marianne Price. "Meeting the Challenge of Educating Children at Risk," *Phi Delta Kappan,* September 1992, pp. 18–23.

Sweet, Robert W., Jr. "From the Administrator." OJJDP, Update on Statistics, November 1990(a), p. 1.

————"Missing Children: Found Facts." National Institute of Justice, Reports, November/December 1990(b), pp. 15–18.

ten Bensel, Robert et al. "Child Abuse and Neglect." *Juvenile and Family Court Journal.* Reno: National Council of Juvenile and Family Court Judges, 1985.

———"Research: Aftermath of Physical Punishment." *The Last Resort* 9:2 (November/December 1980). Cited in "Child Abuse and Neglect," p. 4.

Whitaker, Catherine J., and Lisa D. Bastian. *Teen Victims: A National Crime Survey Report,* NCJ–128129. Washington, D.C.: Bureau of Justice Statistics, May 1991.

Widom, Cathy Spatz. *The Cycle of Violence.* National Institute of Justice, Research in Brief, October 1992.

Will, George F. "Child Abuse and Neglect Cases Soared with Advent of Crack." (Minneapolis/St. Paul) *Star Tribune,* 1 May 1994, p. 25A.

Witkin, Gordon. "Kids Who Kill." *U.S. News and World Report,* 8 April 1991, pp. 26–32. Reprinted in *Criminal Justice 92/93,* 16th ed., edited by John J. Sullivan and Joseph L. Victor. Guilford, Conn.: Dushkin Publishing, 1992, pp. 181–185.

Wrobleski, Adina. *Suicide: Why? 89 Questions and Answers About Suicide.* Minneapolis, Minn.: Afterwords, 1989.

▌ Cases

Ingram v. *Wright,* 430 U.S. 651, 97 S.Ct. 1401, 51 L.Ed.2d 711 (1977).

People v. *Green,* 155 Mich. 524, 532, 119 N.W. 1087 (1909).

Prince v. *Massachusetts,* 321 U.S. 158, 166, 64 S.Ct. 438, 442, 88 L.Ed. 645 (1944).

Santosky v. *Kramer,* 455 U.S. 745, 753, 102 S.Ct. 1388, 71 L.Ed.2d 599 (1982).

Worthen v. *State,* 42 Md.App. 20, 399 A.2d 272 (1979)—The International Year of the Child.

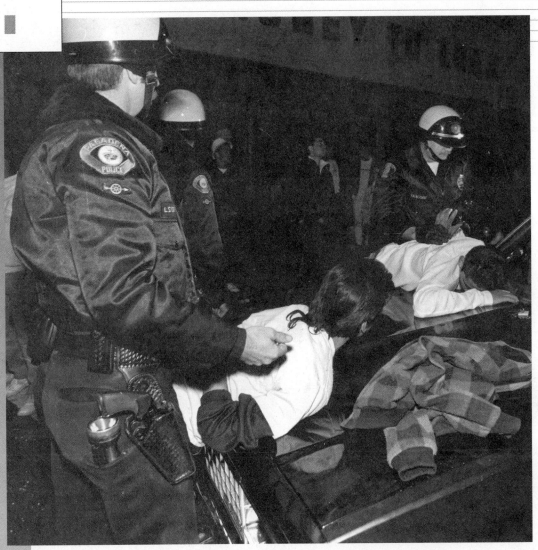

Youth Who Break the Law and Those Who Victimize

The greatest future predictor of violent behavior is a previous history of violence. Without systematic and effective intervention, early aggression commonly will escalate into later violence and broaden into other antisocial behavior.

American Psychological Association Commission
on Violence and Youth

Do You Know?

How researchers measure the nature and extent of youthful offenses?
How prevalent delinquency is according to self-report?
What acts are classified as status offenses in most states?
What delinquency offenses result in the highest number of juvenile arrests?
What positivist theories of the causes of juvenile delinquency have been formulated? What the main thesis of each is?
What is a major characteristic of juvenile delinquents?
What a psychopath is?
How the public health model views violence in the United States and what should be done about it?

Can You Define the Following Key Terms?

acting out, antisocial personality disorder, chronic juvenile offender, conduct disorder, contagion, delinquent, ephebiphobia, psychopathic behavior, serious juvenile offender, sociopathic behavior, Uniform Crime Report, violent juvenile offender

INTRODUCTION

Some actions discussed in the last chapter, such as running away from home, not only place youngsters at risk of being victimized, they also violate the law and, therefore, put the youngsters at risk of being arrested.

This chapter looks at the sources of information about ways in which youth break the law as well as the range of offenses that might be committed by juveniles. This range goes from minor status offenses, such as violating a curfew law, to major violent crimes, such as rape and murder. The chapter looks at theories on the causes of delinquency. It also returns to the widespread problem of violence in our society and the effects it is having on our youth. The chapter concludes with a discussion of violence as a public health problem and a change in perspective.

MEASURING THE AMOUNT OF JUVENILE OFFENSES COMMITTED

Just how serious is the problem of youth breaking the law in the United States?

> Researchers use three methods to measure the nature and extent of unlawful acts by juveniles: official data, self-report data and victim surveys.

Official Data

Official data is information and statistics collected by the police, courts and corrections on the local, regional and national level. One widely used official source of delinquency statistics is the **Uniform Crime Reports** collected by the FBI. The FBI surveys over 15,000 police agencies every year.

The *Uniform Crime Reports* (UCR) divide crimes into Part I and Part II. Part I includes the eight major crimes: homicide and non-negligent manslaughter, forcible rape, robbery, aggravated assault, burglary, larceny, arson and motor vehicle theft.

The UCR's arrest statistics help look at the extent of the delinquency problem. The statistics must be interpreted cautiously, however. The data represent only youths who have been arrested. Many are never caught. It has been estimated that between 80 and 90 percent of our children under 18 commit some offense for which they could be arrested, but only about 3 percent of them are. In addition, multiple arrests of the same youth for different crimes are counted separately. The total number of arrests does not equal the number of youths who have been arrested, because chronic offenders have multiple arrests.

Report to the Nation on Crime and Justice (1988, p. 41) notes that: "Most crimes are committed by males, especially by those under age 20." Using data presented in the UCR, this same report (p. 42) contends that: "Young people make up the largest proportion of offenders entering the criminal justice system."

Official statistics have several problems, such as how the data is collected, variations in interpretation and police bias in arrest decision making. In addition, official statistics do not provide information about the personality, attitudes and behavior of delinquents. This comes from self-reports.

Self-Reports

Self-report studies let youths personally reveal information about their violations of the law. Different formats of self-reports include one-to-one interviews, surveys and anonymous questionnaires. According to Siegel and Senna (1988, p. 35): "When truancy, alcohol consumption, petty theft, and soft drug use are included in self-report scales, delinquency appears almost universal."

■ According to self-report studies, delinquency is almost universal.

Victimization Data

A third source of information about the extent of the delinquency problem is victimization data. The Bureau of Justice Statistics of the U.S. Department of Justice, working with the U.S. Census Bureau, conducts annual house-to-house surveys of victims of crimes. This National Crime Survey (NCS) has surveyed about 50,000 households, including about 100,000 individuals each year for the past decade.

Trojanowicz and Morash (1987, p. 34) note the following trends evident from the NCS:

■ Today's youths are no more seriously delinquent than youths 10 years ago.
■ From 1973 to 1981, there has been little change in the rate of juveniles committing rape, robbery, assault, and personal larceny (purse snatching and pocket picking).
■ There has been little or no change in the types of people who are victimized by juveniles.
■ Juvenile offenders primarily victimize other juveniles, and they victimize males about twice as often as females.

STATUS OFFENDERS

Status offenses are based solely on the offenders' age and are unique to juveniles. The age governing status offenses ranges from 16 to 19, but in most states it is 18. Anyone above the legal age engaging in the same behaviors would not be committing an offense.

■ Status offenses include actions such as violating curfew, habitual truancy, running away, incorrigibility, ungovernable conduct, being beyond the control of parents, being wayward, using tobacco and drugs and drinking alcohol.

Table 7–1 summarizes the status offenses that are tracked by the FBI. Note that the number of runaway and ungovernability cases decreased while the number of truancy cases and liquor law violations increased.

The runaway problem was discussed in the previous chapter. However, running away is a status offense in most communities so that the juvenile justice system has jurisdiction in the matter and can act "in the best interest of the child."

In 1974 the federal government enacted a law that urged the decriminalization of incorrigible offenses such as truancy and running away. To insure the continued flow of federal funds for youth programs, states changed their laws to prevent the prolonged incarceration of noncriminal minors.

U.S. News & World Report (1985) describes youths fitting into the status offense category:

In Canoga Park, California, in the San Fernando valley is a staging area for troubled youths. Fifteen-year-old Mike kept coming home late. One night his

TABLE 7–1   Percent Change in Petitioned Status Offense Cases

Offense	Number of Cases			Case Rates*		
	1986	1990	Pct. Chg.	1986	1990	Pct. Chg.
Status Offense Totals	84,400	86,900	3%	3.2	3.4	6%
Runaway	15,600	12,900	–17	0.6	0.5	–15
Truancy	21,700	24,600	13	0.8	1.0	17
Ungovernable	16,700	11,500	–31	0.6	0.5	–29
Liquor	24,100	29,000	20	0.9	1.1	24
Other	6,300	8,800	40	0.2	0.3	44

Note: Detail may not add to totals because of rounding. Percentage calculations are based on unrounded numbers.

*Case Rate = Cases per 1,000 youth at risk

SOURCE: Jeffrey A. Butts and Eileen Poe, *Offenders in Juvenile Court, 1990*, OJJDP, Update on Statistics, December 1993, p. 8.

father slapped him so hard that one of the boy's eardrums was shattered. Now he lives with other teenagers, shuffling between different homes, sometimes sleeping in cars, all-night gas stations or even caves.

Upset over a curfew imposed by her parents, Karen, 13, stayed away from home for two months.

Jim, 17, has missed more than 60 days of school this year, attending classes only to see his friends. His mother and school officials have all but given up.

In Chicago, 4,000 homeless youths who wander the streets are from affluent suburbs. The Denver suburbs were shocked when a 14-year-old boy pleaded guilty to stabbing his mother. His lawyer says the woman, a successful real-estate broker, "ignored him until the pressure blew him up."

A problem closely related to running away is truancy. Several approaches to this problem have been tried. Suburban Houston's Spring Branch Independent School District, for example, holds parents responsible for absent teenagers. After phone calls and visits to the families of truants, the district files charges. Both parents can be fined up to $100 per day for a child's chronic truancy. But even monetary penalties haven't ended the problem. The school district averages four to six court cases per month to enforce attendance rules.

Truancy is the most frequent offense for those under age 15, probably because after that age those who would be truant have simply dropped out of school. The most frequent offense for those 16 or older is liquor violations.

One of the most common violations falling under the *other* category is curfew violations. Curfew laws are enacted so that police officers can maintain control over youths during the nighttime when they are more likely to be getting into trouble. Frequently, youths who violate curfews are simply warned. Other times they are held at the police station until their parents come for them. Fines are used by some departments. Curfew ordinances have been challenged in several communities as being unconstitutional because they discriminate against those who are not yet legally adults.

Table 7–2 shows the distribution of status offenses by age at referral.

Vandalism

Vandalism is usually a mischievous, destructive act done to get attention, for revenge or to vent hostility.

TABLE 7–2   Offense Characteristics by Age at Referral, 1990

Offense	Age 15 or Younger	Age 16 or Older
Runaway	18%	11%
Truancy	41	11
Ungovernable	17	9
Liquor	13	60
Other	11	10
Total	100%	100%

Note: Detail may not total 100% because of rounding.

SOURCE: Jeffrey A. Butts and Eileen Poe, *Offenders in Juvenile Court, 1990,* OJJDP, Update on Statistics, December 1993, p. 8.

Philip Zimbardo, a Stanford psychologist, reported in 1969 on some experiments testing the broken-window theory. He arranged to have two comparable automobiles without license plates parked with their hoods up on a street in the Bronx, New York, and on a street in Palo Alto, California. The car in the Bronx was attacked by "vandals" within ten minutes of its "abandonment."

The first to arrive were a family—father, mother and young son—who removed the radiator and battery. Within 24 hours, virtually everything of value had been removed. Then random destruction began. Windows were smashed, parts torn off, upholstery ripped. Children began to use the car as a playground. Most of the adult "vandals" were well-dressed, clean-cut whites.

The car in Palo Alto sat untouched for more than a week. Then Zimbardo smashed part of it with a sledgehammer. Soon passerbys were joining in. Within a few hours, the car had been turned upside down and utterly destroyed. Again, the "vandals" appeared to be primarily respectable white adults. Commenting on this research, Wilson and Kelling (1982, pp. 29–38) state:

> Untended property becomes fair game for people out for fun or plunder, and even for people who ordinarily would not dream of doing such things and who probably consider themselves law-abiding. Because of the nature of community life in the Bronx—its anonymity, the frequency with which cars are abandoned and things are stolen or broken, the past experience of "no one caring"—vandalism begins much more quickly than it does in staid Palo Alto, where people have come to believe that private possessions are cared for, and that mischievous behavior is costly. But vandalism can occur anywhere once communal barriers—the sense of mutual regard and the obligations of civility—are lowered by actions that seem to signal that "no one cares."

Rowdy children sometimes send a message of personal problems by vandalism. Destructive behavior can occur because children lack ways of communicating a need for help.

A Key Issue

Should the term *juvenile delinquency* encompass both those youths who commit serious, violent crimes and those who commit status offenses? Incorporating crimes and status offenses is a key issue in juvenile justice.

JUVENILE DELINQUENTS

A juvenile **delinquent** is a youth who commits an act that would be a crime were it to be committed by an adult. The term is intended to avoid the stigma of the label of *criminal*. The term should not be applied to status offenders.

As noted previously, just who qualifies as a "youth" varies from state to state. No one nationally recognized age places youths into the juvenile justice system. Some states consider juveniles to be age 16 or under, others have established 19 as the legal age. The majority of states, however, have established age 18, as was seen in Table 4–1.

Definitions

The National Coalition of State Juvenile Justice Advisory Groups, in its 1992 annual report to the President, the Congress and the Office of Juvenile Justice and Delinquency Prevention (pp. 13–14), includes the following definitions:

█ **Serious juvenile offender**—A juvenile who has been convicted of a Part I offense as defined by the FBI *Uniform Crime Reports,* excluding auto theft or distribution of a controlled dangerous substance, and who was 14, 15, 16, or 17 years old at the time of the commission of the offense.

█ **Chronic juvenile offender**—A youth who has a record of five or more separate charges of delinquency, regardless of the gravity of the offenses.

The Coalition (p. 14) lists the following criteria most often mentioned as characterizing serious or chronic offenders:

█ A delinquency adjudication prior to the age of thirteen.
█ Low family income.
█ Between the ages of eight and ten being rated troublesome by teachers and peers.
█ Poor school performance by age ten.
█ Psychomotor clumsiness.
█ Having a sibling convicted of a crime.

Table 7–3 shows the number of offenses committed by youth in 1990 and shows the change since 1986. Property crimes continue to head the list, accounting for well over half the number of offenses committed in 1990.

█ The most frequent delinquency offenses were property crimes, with larceny-theft being the most common followed by burglary. The third most frequent delinquency offense was simple assault.

█ *The police have great discretion when dealing with juveniles. They may take them into custody or simply give them a talking to.*

TABLE 7-3   Delinquency Cases by Offense, 1990

Offense	Number of Cases	Percent Change 1986–90	Percent Change 1986–90
Total Delinquency	1,264,800	4%	10%
Person	239,700	14	29
Criminal Homicide	2,700	29	64
Forcible Rape	4,400	7	–5
Robbery	28,900	22	9
Aggravated Assault	60,100	21	48
Simple Assault	120,800	11	27
Other Violent Sex Offenses	7,300	9	18
Other Person Offenses	15,600	9	44
Property	731,700	4	8
Burglary	141,400	6	1
Larceny-Theft	318,300	0	3
Motor Vehicle Theft	68,600	0	63
Arson	6,900	2	17
Vandalism	91,700	11	10
Trespassing	48,400	–1	–4
Stolen Property Offenses	27,800	17	–2
Other Property Offenses	28,600	19	37
Drug Law Violations	68,200	–13	–7
Public Order	225,200	3	6
Obstruction of Justice	82,200	1	9
Disorderly Conduct	55,100	14	14
Weapons Offenses	28,800	14	43
Liquor Law Violations	17,400	10	–18
Nonviolent Sex Offenses	12,100	–2	0
Other Public Order	29,600	–19	–17
Violent Crime Index*	96,000	21	31
Property Crime Index**	535,300	2	8

Note: Detail may not add to totals because of rounding.
*Violent Crime Index includes criminal homicide, forcible rape, robbery, and aggravated assault.
**Property Crime Index includes burglary, larceny-theft, motor vehicle theft, and arson.
SOURCE: Jeffrey A. Butts and Eileen Poe, *Offenders in Juvenile Court, 1990,* OJJDP, Update on Statistics, December 1993, p. 2.

Table 7–4 illustrates the types of offenses engaged in by those age 15 or younger and those 16 or older. Delinquency rates tend to increase dramatically as age increased, as shown in Figure 7–1.

According to Regnery (1991, p. 165): "Juveniles do commit crimes at a rate significantly higher than the rest of the population. In fact, 16-year-old boys commit crimes at a higher rate than any other single age group. These are criminals who happen to be young, not children who happen to commit crimes."

Arrest data show that the intensity of criminal behavior slackens after the teens, and it continues to decline with age.

TABLE Type of Offense Committed by Age at Referral, 1990
7–4
■

Offense	Age 15 or Younger	Age 16 or Older
Person	20%	18%
Property	62	53
Drugs	3	8
Public Order	15	21
Total	100%	100%

Note: Detail may not total 100% because of rounding.

SOURCE: Jeffrey A. Butts and Eileen Poe, *Offenders in Juvenile Court, 1990,* OJJDP, Update on Statistics, December 1993, p. 3.

Burglary

Burglary is usually committed for quick financial gain, often to support a drug habit. It is the most accessible route to money for unemployed juveniles. In 1990 juveniles committed 141,400 burglaries.

Arson

Arson, like vandalism, sends a message through a delinquent act. For many children, setting fires is a symbolic act, often a symptom of underlying emotional or physical stress. Children who do not abandon normal childhood experiments with fire frequently are crying for help, using fire as an expression of their stress, anxiety and anger. What turns these troubled youths into repeat firesetters, according to psychologist Kenneth R. Fineman, is positive reinforcement for their incendiary activities. With "fire success," these youngsters have the "urge to burn," as their firesetting acts provide them with a sense of power and control otherwise lacking in their lives (Wooden, 1985, p. 40–45). Juvenile firesetters usually take out their hostility on school property. According to government figures, arson is the most expensive crime inflicted on schools.

PROFILE OF DELINQUENCY

No one personality is associated with delinquency. However, some characteristics are common among delinquents. Those who become delinquent are more likely to be socially assertive, defiant, ambivalent about authority, resentful, hostile, suspicious, destructive, impulsive and lacking in self-control.

Shea (1987) has suggested a profile of the delinquent as a male adolescent who has committed at least 50 felonies, who began crime at age five or six, and whose family is frustrated and exhausted. He typically is skipping school or has dropped out, and his friends have the same profile. The probability of chemical abuse is 75 percent. He is impulsive, irresponsible and unwilling to see or understand how his actions affect others.

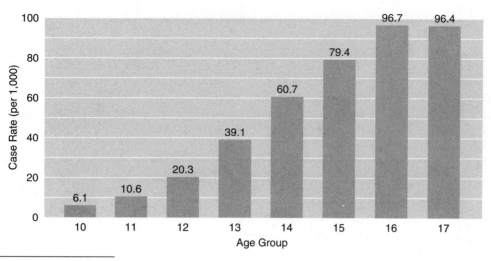

▮ **FIGURE 7–1 Delinquency Case Rates by Age at Referral, 1990**

SOURCE: Jeffrey A. Butts and Eileen Poe, *Offenders in Juvenile Court, 1990*, OJJDP, Update on Statistics, December 1993, p. 3.

Konopka's (1966, p. 112) classic in-depth study, *Adolescent Girls in Conflict,* describes a 17-year-old girl who shows impulsive, irresponsible behavior:

> If we don't have money, we rob people. I helped. I knew the boy we robbed. I had gone with him. He was a show-off. He always talked about how much money he had.
>
> Did I think about whether he had worked for it? Oh, you don't think of that! You just think you need money. What did I want and need money for? Clothes . . . but I never bought clothes. I just drank. I used the money for drinking.

Sometimes the impulsiveness and irresponsibility goes even further, resulting in acting out or in psychopathic behavior, as discussed shortly.

Wolfgang's classic long-term study of delinquents in Philadelphia found that from 6 to 8 percent of male juveniles were responsible for over 60 percent of the serious juvenile offenses. His studies also showed that by the third arrest, a delinquent was almost guaranteed a life of crime.

Delinquency is a focus of the juvenile justice system. More energy and effort is spent by those within the system on delinquency than any other responsibility. The United States generates more after-care programs than any other country. Delinquency and its causes are usually examined *after the fact,* with research on preventing delinquency getting little attention.

What causes delinquency?

CAUSES OF DELINQUENCY

Do children frequently grow up to be like their parents because they have inherited something from their parents, or is it because of the way their parents have raised them? This question is especially relevant when related to children who become delinquents.

Attempts to answer the question "Why do youths become delinquent?" have resulted in extensive research. The vast array of theories that have developed range from the very conservative to what some may consider outlandish.

Recall the *classical view* developed by Cesare Beccaria. Beccaria's treatise did not emphasize the causes of criminal behavior. He assumed individuals choose to do wrong or right, and if the individual chooses to do wrong, he must suffer the consequences. Outside influences such as the social system, community or economic status had little bearing regardless of biological, psychological or social variables. In short, the classical school maintained that there were no "causes" of crime or delinquency other than one's free will and ability to choose right or wrong.

A refinement of classical theory, developed by Cohen and Felson, is the *routine activity theory*. This theory states that the volume and distribution of predatory crime (where the offender tries to steal an object directly) are highly correlated with three variables found in everyday American life:

1. The availability of suitable targets (homes containing easily sold goods).
2. The absence of capable guardians (homeowners, neighbors, friends, relatives).
3. The presence of motivated offenders (unemployed teenagers, etc.).

The presence of these three variables increases the chances of a predatory crime occurring. This approach gives equal weight to the roles of victim and offender. It also suggests that the opportunity for criminal action depends on the victim's lifestyle and behavior.

The *positivist view* was developed by Cesare Lombroso. This theory takes into consideration the criminal's personal and background characteristics. Positivist theory sees delinquents as being "victims of society." Trojanowicz and Morash (1987, p. 44) state: "In effect, offenders are "sick," and their behavior merely reflects the various determinants in each person's background. The determinants would be the offender's biological, psychological, sociological, cultural, and physical environments." The founders of the positivist view began the scientific inquiry into *causes* of delinquent and criminal behavior.

How often have you heard of a terrible crime and thought, "The person who did that must have been crazy"? The law recognizes insanity, temporary and otherwise. Many respected authorities on delinquency believe the mental or physical makeup of the offender is the cause of misbehavior in youths. One aspect of positivist theory is that outside forces may compel an individual to behave a certain way. No "free will" is involved. The earliest attempts to understand juvenile delinquency from a positivist viewpoint focused on the biological and psychological aspects of behavior.

In examining these two basic schools of thought, it is easy to see where the tension lies—whichever theory you perceive as logical, loopholes remain. The purely classical approach is easily accepted because most people make their decisions based on thought. The idea that people should be held accountable for actions that they take seems logical. But are all decisions made via such logic?

The positivist theory makes sense for others. It seems quite possible that "outside influences" are at play when no other explanation presents itself. How can you explain the suicide of a 12-year-old who has no history of depression or other problems? How can you explain the violent ax murders of mother, father and siblings by a 15-year-old who has a reputation throughout the community as being polite and quiet, just like every other kid?

Modern positivist research on the causes of crime and delinquency centers on such areas as biology, sociology and psychology.

▮ Positivist theories of the causes of juvenile delinquency include biological, behavioral, sociological and psychological theories.

These theories provide a base to understand juvenile behavior and related offenses.

Biological Theories

Biological theorists contend that criminals are born, not made. The classic studies of Lombroso (1913) and Garofalo (1915) support a biological causation for deviant behavior and suggest that individuals who do not conform to society's laws and regulations are biologically inferior. Lombroso, for example, attributed criminality to the "atavistic" characteristics of offenders. That is to say, criminals are evolutionary throwbacks to primitive cultures, and criminality can be identified by the presence of physical "stigmata," such as supernumerary nipples or unusual skull size. The assumption is that criminals are biologically abnormal and different from or inferior to law-abiding citizens.

▮ Biological theorists state that how a person acts is basically a result of heredity.

The biological theorists who followed Lombroso in the early twentieth century studied families to determine the influence of heredity on criminal behavior. Many of the assumptions of the theorists and researchers were either inappropriate or invalid, such as illegitimacy causing a genetic strain that predisposes one to criminal behavior. These early biological theorists focused on the relationship between physical characteristics and one's propensity to do crime. All early theories have been refuted by more current research.

Some researchers feel a genetic mishap may cause one member of a family to deviate from the norm. For example, Richard Speck, convicted of killing eight Chicago nurses, showed an unusual genetic structure—he had one extra male chromosome. Speck is not the only convicted criminal to display such a genetic abnormality.

Further, Hernstein and Wilson (1983, p. 19) state that: "Criminologists have long known about the correlation between criminal behavior and [low] I.Q., but many have discounted it for various reasons." Nonetheless the correlation does exist, and IQ is thought to be greatly influenced by heredity.

According to Hernstein and Wilson (1983, pp. 18–19), the most compelling evidence of biological factors for criminality comes from studies of twins and of adopted boys. The twins studies rest on the fact that identical twins come from a single fertilized egg and share identical genes; fraternal twins, in contrast, come from two separately fertilized eggs that have about half their genes in common. If identical twins are clearly more similar in a trait than fraternal twins, it is probable that the trait has high inheritability.

About a dozen studies of criminality have been based on this theory, with more than 1,500 pairs of twins being studied in the United States, the Scandinavian countries, Japan, West Germany, Britain and elsewhere. Hernstein and Wilson (1983, pp. 17, 20) note that: "[T]he result is qualitatively the same everywhere. Identical twins are more likely to have similar criminal records than fraternal twins." Further, they note: "[E]ssentially the same results are found in studies of adopted children. . . . Recent studies show that the biological family history contributes substantially to the adoptees' likelihood of breaking the law."

As way of illustration, they describe the research conducted by Sarnoff Mednick, a psychologist at the University of Southern California, along with other associates in the United States and in Denmark. The researchers found that:

> Boys with criminal biological parents and noncriminal adopting parents were more likely to have criminal records than those with noncriminal biological parents and criminal adopting parents. . . . The risk was unrelated to whether the boy or his adopting parents knew about the natural parents' criminal records, whether the natural parents committed their crimes before or after the boy was given up for adoption, or whether the boy was adopted immediately after birth or a year or two later.

Table 7–5 summarizes the data from these adoption studies.

Modern biological theorists possess the scientific rigor, and they look to biochemical relationships, endocrine imbalances, chromosomal complements, brain wave activity and other biological determinants of behavior.

TABLE   Cross-Fostering Analysis
7–5

Are Adoptive Parents Criminal?	Are Biological Parents Criminal?	
	Yes	*No*
Yes	24.5% (of 143)*	14.7% (of 204)
No	20.0% (of 1,226)	13.5% (of 2,492)

*The numbers in parentheses are the numbers of cases in each cell, for a total sample of 4,065 adopted males.

SOURCE: S. A. Mednick et al., "Genetic influences in criminal convictions: Evidence from an adoption cohort," *Science* (1984), p. 224. Copyright 1984 by the AAAS.

▮ Modern studies of the genetic relationship to crime support the
proposition that criminality and violence may be inherited.

"Like father like son" is a cliche accepted without question. Children inherit
their parents' build, hair color, eyes, allergies and physical conditions. It is
reasonable to believe that a violent disposition can be inherited. The inherited
traits may predispose an individual to crime or violence.

Harvard researcher Anne Liese Pontus found that one-third of the criminals
she studied were inflexible and could not respond to, withdraw from or
conclude a dangerous situation. These were criminals who tended to be
recidivists. Their actions and responses indicated that once the behavior
(burglary, robbery, assault) was initiated they had to carry it out. Such behavior
was related to brain dysfunction.

Habitually aggressive delinquents have brain wave abnormalities at the rate
of five times the normal population, according to research conducted in 1987
by Charlotte Johnson and William Pelman. The results of brain wave abnormalities include hostility, destructiveness, hyperactivity and poor impulse
control.

▮ Violence and aggression have been associated with the presence or
absence of certain chemicals in the brain.

The biological theories attempt to identify the factors associated with a
tendency to violence and aggression. As more and better diagnostic techniques
are developed, the evidence may increase. The fact that biological explanations
are supported by research cannot be ignored in looking at the causes of
delinquent and antisocial behavior.

Behavioral Theories

A counter position to biological theory is behavioral theory, which contends
that criminals are made, not born. Behavioral theorists argue that human
physical and psychological development is not fixed by biological inheritance.
People become who they are because of their *life experiences*.

As children grow and develop, they learn from their family about the rules
that govern their conduct. Any wrongdoing or mischief reflects what was
learned and manipulated to whatever gain might be desired, without taking into
account the risk or punishment that might result. If children who misbehave are
corrected by their parents, they are likely to conform to society's expectations; if
they are not corrected, they are likely to ignore society's rules and laws. (The
influence of the family is discussed in detail in Chapter 5.)

This learning process provides the experience for decision making in later
years, that is, for either conforming to or challenging rules and laws in an adult
world. In this development process, children learn a sense of right and wrong
from their environment: family, neighbors, peers, teachers and the media.

▌ Behavioral theorists state that how a person acts is learned and that
attitudes and values of the social mores are acquired through
conditioning.

The behavioral position has tremendous implications for the family unit, as well
as for the educational system.

Sociological Theories

Sociological theorists take the behavioral position one step further. Socialization
provides children with accepted behavior repertoires and endows them with the
basic values of their social milieu. In the socialization process children may also
learn antisocial values, if such values are important in their social and cultural
environment. In such instances socialization actually contributes to delinquent
behavior.

▌ Sociological theorists state that society conditions its members to behave
in certain ways.

Socialization begins in the family. Preschoolers, for example, discover that
when they get into mischief, words and symbols become tangible. A word like
no becomes associated with more severe action if the disruptive behavior
continues. Any object can become a tool for dispensing pain.

To youths, however, society's laws often are not seen as applicable. Laws are
part of the adult world, a world adolescents tend to ignore. It is a period
sometimes referred to as "socialized" delinquency because it is characterized by
stealing and truancy in the company of "bad" companions.

Although delinquency often begins when children first enter schools, its
most serious manifestations usually occur in adolescence. As noted earlier,
self-report data suggests that most youth at one time or another test the limits,
shoplift, steal from their mother's purse or engage in similar petty thefts. Such
behavior is usually outgrown without intervention from the juvenile justice
system if the parents administer appropriate discipline. Unfortunately, not all
youth outgrow these tendencies to misbehave. As Eitzen (1992, p. 585) states:
"Some children are angry, alienated, and apathetic. A few are uncooperative,
rude, abrasive, threatening, and even violent. Some abuse drugs. Some are
sexually promiscuous. Some belong to gangs. Some are sociopaths." Eitzen goes
on to state: "My strong conviction is that children are *not* born with sociopathic
tendencies; problem children are socially created" (italic in original).

The Gluecks (1950) also favor a sociological causation for delinquency. Their
extensive studies of delinquent boys had as one result a *predictive index*. The
accuracy of this index was tested in the 1950s, and of 220 predictions, 209
were accurate. The social factors in their index included how they were
disciplined and supervised, how much affection was shown in the home and
the cohesiveness of the family.

According to Sprinthall and Collins (1984, p. 344), the Gluecks' study had and continues to have important implications about the causes of serious delinquent behavior of teenagers:

▮ Delinquent behavior starts prior to adolescence. During adolescence the antisocial acts increase in seriousness and frequency.

▮ The home environment—especially the quality of the mother-son relationship—is a major causative factor.

▮ The actual economic status of delinquency-prone families is lower than that of nondelinquent families, even though there is no difference in the level of parental employment.

▮ There is virtually a 100% rate of school dropout for the delinquents.

▮ Follow-up studies indicate that in adulthood almost one-third of the delinquents engage in serious crimes.

Psychological Approaches

Many delinquent youths have to deal with poor home lives and destructive relationships. Such an environment can lead to a disturbed personality structure marked by negative, antisocial behavior. While many delinquents do not show significant psychological disturbances, enough do suffer from problems to allow psychological factors to be considered in the theory of delinquency.

No field of study has established stronger inroads in the explanation of delinquency than psychology. Psychology and psychiatry have a wide range of categories into which offenders can be classified. Classification and categorization are major elements of the postadjudicatory process in the juvenile and adult justice systems. Clearly, this is why criminal behavior is linked so often with psychological defects.

In psychoanalytical perspectives violence is an expression of tension or psychic energy built up as a result of the faulty emotional development of an individual and the absence of appropriate outlets for the pressure. This pressure is particularly apparent in adolescents. Adolescence is normally a time of inner tensions, excessive energy and ambiguity. It is a time when the individual is neither child nor adult. Youths still have childish needs and a desire for dependency though they have adult expectations imposed by self or others. If the emotional foundation is weak, the result can be catastrophic. A poor emotional foundation for an adolescent or an adult may be the result of the faulty psychological development of the child.

▮ A major characteristic of juvenile delinquents is that they act out their inner conflicts.

In **acting out,** youths freely express their impulses, particularly hostile ones. Acting out is the free, deliberate, often malicious indulgence of impulse, which frequently leads to aggression as well as other manifestations of delinquency, such as vandalism, cruelty to animals and sometimes even murder. Acting out essentially reflects an absence of self-control and a desire for immediate gratification.

Such lack of self-control may result from an early history of severe parental rejection or deprivation, or from witnessing or being the victim of severe physical abuse and violence. Children strike back against a world they perceive as hostile. Acting out may also give adolescents a sense of importance, a way to overcome feelings of inadequacy and inferiority.

Adolescents who act out come from all socioeconomic levels and are not psychopathic according to conventional classifications. They may have a clear sense of conscience and be capable of strong feelings of loyalty to a gang. But their impulses are stronger than their consciences. The acting out may be a form of defense against feelings of anxiety produced by an awareness of guilt.

Closely related to this theory is learning theory. If an individual learns and maintains behavior that produces the results society wants and expects, the result is reinforced behavior. When an individual "learns" that violence produces submission and reduces defiance, the person relies on this learning when faced with frustration or having difficulty succeeding. The learning models may be parents, peers, the mass media, those in entertainment and trusted adults.

Delinquency and Drugs

The relationship between delinquency and drug use is also well established. Not only do some drugs lower inhibitions so that youths are apt to engage in behavior they would not do while not under the influence of the drugs but also the need for money to buy drugs may lead to thefts and burglaries. Table 7–6 summarizes the availability of drugs to high school seniors; Table 7–7 shows the reported illegal drug use by high school seniors in 1991.

Other Theories on Causes of Delinquency

Siegel and Senna (1988, pp. 92–96) suggest some other possible causes of delinquency.

■ Delinquency may also result from biochemical factors, including diet, or from neurological dysfunction, including learning disabilities.

Biochemical Factors

Biochemical research focuses on the connection between youths' antisocial behavior and their biochemical makeup. Diet, blood chemistry, hormonal imbalances and allergies all affect body function and the central nervous system. These physical factors can influence behavior and have been linked to antisocial behavior. Diet is of particular interest, because an unusually high consumption of artificial food colorings, milk and sweets may negatively affect behavior.

Neurological Dysfunction

Neurological research focuses on the brain and nervous system. Children with abnormal EEGs at birth may develop other neurological problems later, such as low IQ.

TABLE High School Seniors' Perceptions of Availability of Drugs
7–6

Question: "How difficult do you think it would be for you to get each of the following types of
    drugs, if you wanted some?" (Percent saying drug would be "fairly easy" or "very easy" for them
    to get[a])

Type of drug	Class of 1989 (N = 2,806)	Class of 1990 (N = 2,549)	Class of 1991 (N = 2,476)	Class of 1992 (N = 2,586)	Class of 1993 (N = 2,670)
Marijuana	84.3%	84.4%	83.3%	82.7%	83.0%
Amyl and butyl nitrates	26.8	24.4	22.7	25.9	25.9
LSD	38.3	40.7	39.5	44.5	49.2
PCP	28.9	27.7	27.6	31.7	31.7
Some other psychedelic	28.2	28.3	28.0	29.9	33.5
Cocaine powder	53.7	49.0	46.0	48.0	45.4
"Crack"	47.0	42.4	39.9	43.5	43.6
Cocaine	58.7	54.5	51.0	52.7	48.5
Heroin	31.4	31.9	30.6	34.9	33.7
Some other narcotic (including methadone)	38.3	38.1	34.6	37.1	37.5
Amphetamines	64.3	59.7	57.3	58.8	61.5
Crystal methamphetamine (ice)	NA	24.1	24.3	26.0	26.6
Barbituates	48.4	45.9	42.4	44.0	44.5
Tranquilizers	45.3	44.7	40.8	40.9	41.1
Steroids	NA	NA	46.7	46.8	44.8

[a]Answer alternatives were: (1) probably impossible, (2) very difficult, (3) fairly difficult,
(4) fairly easy, and (5) very easy.

SOURCE: U.S. Department of Justice, Bureau of Justice Statistics, *Sourcebook of Criminal Justice Statistics,* 1993 (Washington, D.C.:
U.S. Government Printing Office [1993]), p. 230. Adapted from: Lloyd D. Johnston, Jerald G. Bachman, and Patrick M.
O'Malley, *National Survey Results on Drug Use from the Monitoring the Future Study, 1975–1993,* U. S. Department of Health and
Human Services, National Institute on Drug Abuse (Washington, DC: U.S. Government Printing Office, 1994).

TABLE Reported Illegal Drug Use by High School Seniors, 1991
7–7

Drugs	Used within the last:	
	12 months	30 days
Marijuana	23.9%	13.8%
Stimulants[b]	8.2	3.2
Inhalants	6.6	2.4
Hallucinogens	5.8	2.2
Cocaine (other than crack)	3.2	1.2
Other opiates[b]	3.5	1.1
Sedatives[b]	3.6	1.5
Tranquilizers[b]	3.6	1.4
Crack	1.5	.7
Heroin	.4	.2

[a]Including the last 30 days.
[b]Includes only drug use which was not under a doctor's orders.

SOURCE: *Drugs and Crime Facts* (Washington, D.C.: Bureau of Justice Statistics, 1992), p. 25.

Mark and Ervin (1970) argue that all behavior "filters through the central nervous system," and that, therefore, studying the relationship between the brain and violence is the best way to study criminal behavior. According to Springer (1986, p. 74):

> As one psychiatrist said, "I can't counsel lead poisoning out of this young man's brain." It is difficult to counsel a poisoned brain; and it is difficult to counsel a maldeveloped brain that exists because of deprivation or insufficiency of groceries during childhood, a result of failure to give children what is their due.

A study of inmates on death row showed that a significant number had neurological handicaps due to head injuries they suffered as children. Studies suggest behavior is highly correlated to EEG functions, and abnormal EEGs are thought to correlate to poor impulse control, inadequate social ability, hostility, temper tantrums, destructiveness and hyperactivity. Of particular concern is a neurological pattern known as *minimal brain dysfunction* (MBD). One type of MBD is *learning disabilities* (LDs). Learning disabilities are defined by the National Advisory Committee on Handicapped Children (Post, 1981):

> Children with special learning disabilities exhibit a disorder in one or more of the basic psychological processes involved in understanding or using spoken or written languages. They may be manifested in disorders of listening, thinking, talking, reading, writing, or arithmetic. They include conditions which have been referred to as perceptual handicaps, brain injury, minimal brain dysfunction, dyslexia, developmental aphasia, etc. They do not include learning problems which are due to visual, hearing or motor handicaps, to mental retardation, emotional disturbance, or to environmental disadvantages.

Studies show that arrested and incarcerated children have a much higher LD rate than children in the general population, highlighting the relationship between learning disabilities and delinquent behavior. Approximately 10 percent of all youths have learning disorders; however, the occurrence of learning disorders in adjudicated delinquents ranges from 26 to 73 percent (Zimmerman et al., 1981).

■ Other factors commonly cited as contributing directly to delinquency include poverty, unemployment, breakdown of religion, breakdown of the family, effects of the media (TV, movies, music), peer pressure and, most importantly, being abused as children.

According to ten Bensel (*Child at Risk,* p. 41), national expert on child abuse and neglect, studies have shown that virtually "all violent juvenile delinquents have been abused children," that "all criminals at San Quentin prison . . . studied had violent upbringings as children," and that "all assassins . . . in the United States during the past 20 years had been victims of child abuse."

All of the theories considered here ask the same basic question: "Are criminals made or born?" Hernstein and Wilson (1983, p. 17) suggest that the answer is "Both": "The causes of crime lie in a *combination* of predisposing biological traits channeled by social circumstance into criminal behavior. The traits alone do not inevitably lead to crime; the circumstances do not make criminals of everyone; but together they create a population responsible for a large fraction of America's problem of crime in the streets."

▮ Criminal behavior probably is the result of both heredity and life experiences.

This sentiment is echoed by Wilson (1983, p. 86):

[W]e now have available an impressive number of studies that, taken together, support the following view: Some combination of constitutional traits and early family experiences account for more of the variation among young persons in their serious criminality than any other factors, and serious misconduct that appears relatively early in life tends to persist into adulthood. What happens on the street corner, in the school, or in the job market can still make a difference, but it will not be as influential as what has gone before.

Also of great importance is how the serious, chronic offenders are treated by the juvenile justice system. According to Crowe (1991, pp. 26, 27):

It is a basic fact that many serious habitual juvenile offenders are not placed in pretrial detention or sentenced to institutional programs because they are too difficult to handle. This poses two serious issues:

▮ Protection of the public from the progressively violent offender.
▮ Protection of the public and property from the habitual who commits an estimated 10–20 offenses for every time he or she is caught.

These troubled, problem, or delinquent children are officially invisible until they commit an extremely serious crime. Such crimes are almost always also extremely violent.

VIOLENT JUVENILE OFFENDERS

The National Coalition of State Juvenile Justice Advisory Groups, in its 1992 annual report (pp. 13–14), includes the following definition:

Violent juvenile offender—a youth who has been convicted of a violent Part I offense, one against a person rather than property and who has a prior adjudication of such an offense, or a youth who has been convicted of murder.

The Coalition (pp. 15–16) notes that violent offenders showed "an exceptionally high incidence of head injuries and a history of serious physical or sexual abuse."

A *New York Times* article (Applebome, 1987, p. 16) included the observation that today's juvenile offenders are younger and the crimes they commit are more serious. Sgt. Richard J. Paraboschi of the Newark Police Department's Youth Aid Bureau was quoted as saying, "A ten-year-old is now like a 13-year-old used to be. And the 16-year-olds are going on 40." Similarly, Justice Richard Huttner, State Supreme Court in Brooklyn, stated, "When I was first on the bench in

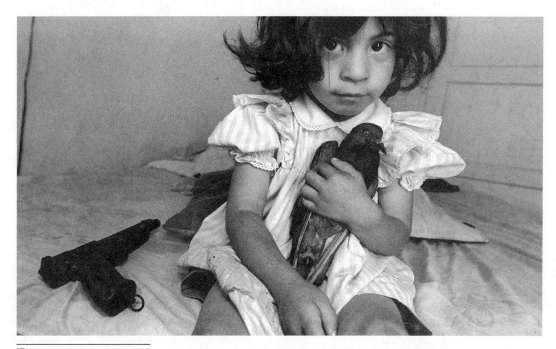

■ *A three-year-old Los Angeles girl plays with a BB gun. She knows how to load and fire it. Guns are a natural part of the lives of many children who, like this girl, live in the Watts area of Los Angeles.*

1978, if I had one gun case a year it was a lot. Now from what I hear it's not unusual to have one or two in a week."

Violent crime in Detroit is so common at present that even murders sometimes rate only a brief mention in the back pages of newspapers. Reasons for the increase in the seriousness of the offenses and the decrease in the age of the offenders range from the problems of increasing gang activity and drug use in the elementary schools to the heightened level of violence in society in general and to increasing stress on families, especially in economically deprived areas.

The *New York Times* article included statements from juvenile judges and their perception of the problem. Justice Huttner, former head of New York City's Family Court, said: "[T]hey used to be kids arrested for stealing Twinkies from a grocery store. Now it's different. An 11- or 12-year-old is not big enough to rob most people, but with a gun it's a different story." According to Judge Tom Rickhoff, San Antonio District Court: "When you see a 10-year-old in your court you almost want to reach out and pat them and tell them they'll be all right, but these are exceptionally dangerous people."

Other recent newspaper headlines confirm these sentiments:

■ Armed, Young, and Dangerous: Juvenile-crime surge reveals a system in disarray—*Arizona Republic*, 30 January 1994.
■ St. Paul teen killed as four robbers [ages 18, 20, 21, and 22] flee—(Minneapolis/St. Paul) *Star Tribune*, 7 October 1993.

▮ 4 teens charged in tourist's death; boys 13, 14 had criminal records—*The Tallahassee Democrat,* 7 October 1993.

▮ Youths major players in tragedy on streets—(Minneapolis/St. Paul) *Star Tribune,* 11 October 1993.

▮ Cops seize gas can [from a car driven by a thirteen year old suspect] in St. Paul arson that killed 5 kids—(Minneapolis/St. Paul) *Star Tribune,* 12 March 1994.

The scene pictured in "Kids Who Kill" (Witkin, 1991, p. 181–182) graphically portrays the deadliness of some youth:

The datelines change daily, but the stories are chillingly similar. In Washington, D.C., 15-year-old Jermaine Daniel is shot to death by his best friend. In New Haven, Conn., Markiest Alexander, 14, is killed in a drive-by shooting. In St. Louis, Leo Wilson, 16, is robbed of his tennis shoes and Raiders jacket and then shot dead. In New York, a 14-year-old boy opens up with a semiautomatic pistol in a Bronx schoolyard, wounding one youngster and narrowly missing another, apparently in a dispute over a girl. . . .

During every 100 hours on our streets we lose more young men than were killed in 100 hours of ground war in the Persian Gulf. . . . Where are the yellow ribbons of hope and remembrance for our youth dying in the streets?

FBI statistics from 1993 indicate that between 1982 and 1993 juvenile robbery arrests were up 22 percent, juvenile assault arrests were up 95 percent and juvenile murder arrests were up 128 percent.

The International Association of Chiefs of Police (IACP) convened a summit to examine the problem of violent crime in the United States and possible solutions. The report of this summit (IACP, 1993, p. 59) stated: "The American people are also suffering from a startling level of violent crime committed by juveniles and young adults." The report cited a 1992 study showing that although the proportion of males 18- to 24-years-old decreased (the most violence-prone portion of the population), violent crime increased. That is, fewer teenagers and young adults were accounting for a greater proportion of crime. In addition, the perpetrators were younger. The figures from the 1980s into the early 1990s showed the criminal homicide arrest rates rose a startling 217 percent for 15-year-old males.

Martin (1994, p. 36) suggests two main reasons for the rise in teen violence: "[A] shift in adolescent attitudes toward the value of life and the ready availability of handguns."

Rosenfeld and Decker (1993, p. 14) report: "Adolescents and young adults in the United States are at high risk for interpersonal violence. Risk among young African Americans is at epidemic levels."

The national Youth Risk Behavior Survey conducted in 1990 found that students who reported four or more fights made up less than 2 percent of all students surveyed, but they accounted for nearly one-half of all the fights during the 30 days before the survey (Center for Disease Control, 1992).

The Link Between Violence and Later Violent Criminality

The evidence linking child abuse and neglect and violence in the home to later violent criminality is growing. This link is supported by Wilson in his interview with Attorney General Reno (1993, p. 6), who notes: "Our [OJJDP's] Causes and Correlates study confirms that there is a direct link between physical child abuse and neglect and subsequent violent delinquency, and more significantly, that the amount of domestic violence to which a juvenile is exposed or victimized by is directly proportional to the violent conduct in which the juvenile later engages."

A study sponsored by the National Institute of Justice, found that: "[C]hildhood abuse increased the odds of future delinquency and adult criminality overall by 40 percent" (Widom, 1992, p. 1). According to this study: "[B]eing abused or neglected as a child increased the likelihood of arrest as a juvenile by 53 percent, as an adult by 38 percent, and for a violent crime by 38 percent."

Duvall (1991, p. 109) suggests the dire consequences of not attending to the problem of child abuse:

> Children are our biggest asset for the future. If society doesn't wake up and hear the screams and see the tears, the next time they see these abused victims may be on the front page of newspapers, or worse yet, holding a pistol in your face. This is a national problem and unless addressed soon, on a united front, we are in for a very violent future.

In his State of the Union address 25 January 1994, President Clinton stated: "Violent crime and the fear it provokes are crippling our society, limiting personal freedom, and fraying the ties that bind us."

The National Coalition of State Juvenile Justice Advisory Groups' 1992 annual report lists the following causes of serious, violent and chronic juvenile crime:

▌ Abuse and neglect.
▌ Economic, social, and educational conditions.
▌ Drugs and other substances.
▌ Gangs.
▌ Accessibility of weapons.

Martin suggests similar causes for violence (1994, p. 37):

▌ Hopelessness and exposure to violence.
▌ Weakening of the family unit.
▌ Media celebration of violence.
▌ Drug culture leading to gun culture.

According to the American Psychological Association: "Social forces such as prejudice, economic inequality, and attitudes toward violence in the mainstream American culture interact with the influences of early childhood to foster the expression of violence" (p. 6). The Association describes several developmental experiences that violent youth frequently share (p. 21):

> [Y]outh at greatest risk of becoming extremely aggressive and violent tend to share common experiences that appear to place them on a "trajectory toward violence." These youth tend to have experienced weak bonding to caretakers in infancy and

ineffective parenting techniques, including lack of supervision, inconsistent discipline, highly punitive or abusive treatment, and failure to reinforce positive, prosocial behavior. These developmental deficits, in turn, appear to lead to poor peer relations and high levels of aggressiveness.

Additionally, these youth have learned attitudes accepting aggressive behavior as normative and as an effective way to solve interpersonal problems. Aggressive children tend to be rejected by their more conforming peers and do poorly in school, including a history of problems such as poor school attendance and numerous suspensions. These children often band together with others like themselves, forming deviant peer groups that reinforce antisocial behaviors. The more such children are exposed to violence in their homes, in their neighborhoods, and in the media, the greater their risk for aggressive and violent behaviors.

CONDUCT DISORDER

A term appearing frequently in discussion of the problems of youth is **conduct disorder**—a "nice term for the anger exploding among more and more teenagers" (Hallinan, 1994, p. 9A). The American Psychiatric Association states that this disorder is characterized by prolonged antisocial behavior and can range from truancy to fistfights. Hallinan cites formal surveys indicating that from 2 to 6 percent of American youths—between 1.3 and 3.8 million—have such a conduct disorder. As noted by Hallinan (1994, p. 9A): "Two influential studies—one in 1988 and one in 1991—concluded that conduct disorder is a lifelong disability for which there currently is no cure."

The American Psychiatric Association (1987, pp. 344–346) has described the **antisocial personality disorder.** This disorder exists in individuals at least age 18, who show evidence of a conduct disorder before age 15 as well as a pattern of irresponsible and antisocial behavior since the age of 15. It occurs in about 3 percent of American males and less than 1 percent of American females. Table 7–8 lists the behaviors indicative of conduct disorders and irresponsible, antisocial behavior.

The Association asserts (p. 343): "In early adolescence these people characteristically use tobacco, alcohol, and other drugs and engage in voluntary sexual intercourse unusually early for their peer group. . . . Almost invariably there is a markedly impaired capacity to sustain lasting, close, warm, and responsible relationships with family, friends, or sexual partners." The Association lists the following predisposing factors:

▮ Attention-deficit hyperactivity disorder and conduct disorder during prepuberty.
▮ Absence of consistent parental discipline.
▮ Abuse as a child.
▮ Removal from the home.
▮ Growing up without parental figures of both sexes.

TABLE 7-8 Antisocial Personality Disorder

A. Current age at least 18.

B. Evidence of Conduct Disorder with onset before age 15, as indicated by a history of *three* or more of the following:

   (1) was often truant

   (2) ran away from home overnight at least twice while living in parental or parental surrogate home (or once without returning)

   (3) often initiated physical fights

   (4) used a weapon in more than one fight

   (5) forced someone into sexual activity with him or her

   (6) was physically cruel to animals

   (7) was physically cruel to other people

   (8) deliberately destroyed others' property (other than by fire-setting)

   (9) deliberately engaged in fire-setting

   (10) often lied (other than to avoid physical or sexual abuse)

   (11) has stolen without confrontation of a victim on more than one occasion (including forgery)

   (12) has stolen with confrontation of a victim (e.g., mugging, purse-snatching, extortion, armed robbery)

C. A pattern of irresponsible and antisocial behavior since the age of 15, as indicated by at least *four* of the following:

   (1) is unable to sustain consistent work behavior, as indicated by any of the following (including similar behavior in academic settings if the person is a student):

     (a) significant unemployment for six months or more within five years

     (b) repeated absences from work unexplained by illness in self or family

     (c) abandonment of several jobs without realistic plans for others

   (2) fails to conform to social norms with respect to lawful behavior, as indicated by repeatedly performing antisocial acts that are grounds for arrest (whether arrested or not), e.g., destroying property, harassing others, stealing, pursuing an illegal occupation

   (3) is irritable and aggressive, as indicated by repeated physical fights or assaults (not required by one's job or to defend someone or oneself), including spouse- or child-beating

   (4) repeatedly fails to honor financial obligations, as indicated by defaulting on debts or failing to provide child support or support for other dependents on a regular basis

   (5) fails to plan ahead, or is impulsive, as indicated by one or both of the following:

     (a) traveling from place to place without a prearranged job or clear goal for the period of travel or clear idea about when the travel will terminate

     (b) lack of a fixed address for a month or more

   (6) has no regard for the truth, as indicated by repeated lying, use of aliases, or "conning" others for personal profit or pleasure

   (7) is reckless regarding his or her own or others' personal safety, as indicated by driving while intoxicated, or recurrent speeding

   (8) if a parent or guardian, lacks ability to function as a responsible parent, as indicated by one or more of the following:

     (a) malnutrition of child

     (b) child's illness resulting from lack of minimal hygiene

     (c) failure to obtain medical care for a seriously ill child

     (d) child's dependence on neighbors or nonresident relatives for food or shelter

     (e) failure to arrange for a caretaker for young child when parent is away from home

     (f) repeated squandering, on personal items, of money required for household necessities

   (9) has never sustained a totally monogamous relationship for more than one year

   (10) lacks remorse (feels justified in having hurt, mistreated, or stolen from another)

D. Occurrence of antisocial behavior not exclusively during the course of Schizophrenia or Manic Episodes

SOURCE: American Psychiatric Association, *Diagnostic and Statistical Manual of Mental Disorders,* 3rd ed. (Washington, D.C.: American Psychiatric Association, 1987), pp. 344–346. Reprinted with permission.

PSYCHOPATHIC OR SOCIOPATHIC BEHAVIOR

Psychopathic or **sociopathic behavior** refers to chronic asocial behavior rooted in severe deficiencies in the development of a conscience.

The failure to develop feelings of guilt is usually attributed to the absence or neglect of a strong identification with stable parental figures, or to having parents who have problems with social values. The failure to develop a conscience begins with the use or exploitation of children by parents. The children are encouraged to carry out the parents' own forbidden impulses and wishes. This encourages children in their own antisocial behavior. Such patterns of behavior usually originate with an overly dominant mother and child who believes in acting out maternal wishes.

Psychopaths are remarkable for emotional blandness, particularly about actions that profoundly shock normal individuals.

■ Psychopaths are virtually lacking in conscience. They do not know right from wrong.

They may, however, profess to recognize and speak smoothly about devotion to accepted values, and they can be charming in casual personal contacts.

Psychopaths often make glib promises and resolutions. Meanwhile, they may be stealing from the person or company they work for, or from the person they are talking to at a particular time. They are profoundly egocentric and never see their own responsibility for anything that goes wrong. Although most psychopaths have normal intelligence, their thinking is essentially superficial. Despite an ability to learn, they do not profit by the lessons of their own experience, so their behavior is out of step with what they abstractly know. In fact, they not only seem indifferent to the consequences for other people of what they do, but they do not seem concerned about the almost certain unfortunate consequences for themselves. They are incurably, unrealistically optimistic. Table 7–9 illustrates some common characteristics of a psychopath.

THE PUBLIC HEALTH MODEL AND THE LAW ENFORCEMENT PERSPECTIVE

One innovative approach to violence is to view it not just as a problem to be dealt with by the criminal justice system, but as a threat to our national health. When violence is viewed in this way, it makes sense to adopt the approach used in our public health system. A basic principle of the public health response to problems is to target those most in need and use its resources there.

**TABLE
7–9**   **Characteristics of a Psychopath**

1. Glibness/superficial charm
2. Grandiose sense of self-worth
3. Need for stimulation/proneness to boredom
4. Pathological lying
5. Conning/manipulative
6. Lack of remorse or guilt
7. Shallow affect
8. Callous/lack of empathy
9. Parasitic lifestyle
10. Poor behavioral controls
11. Promiscuous sexual behavior
12. Early behavior problems
13. Lack of realistic, long-term plans
14. Impulsivity
15. Irresponsibility
16. Failure to accept responsibility for own actions
17. Many short-term marital relationships
18. Juvenile delinquency
19. Revocation of conditional release
20. Criminal versatility

SOURCE: R. D. Hare, "Characteristics of a Psychopath." In *Unmasking the Psychopath,* edited by W. H. Reid, D. Dorr, J. I. Walker, and J. W. Bonner III (New York: W. W. Norton, 1986), p. 18. © 1991, Multi-Health Systems, Inc., 908 Niagara Falls Boulevard, North Tonawanda, NY 14120-2060 (800-456-3003). Reproduced by permission. All rights reserved.

■ Viewing violence as a public health problem, practitioners have targeted "adolescent and young black males who live in the neighborhoods with the highest levels of violence" (Rosenfeld and Decker, 1993, p. 37.)

All too often, however, as noted by Astroth (1994, p. 411):

It is common today to hear that almost half of all young people between the ages of 10 and 17 are at risk of school failure, substance abuse, delinquency, and teenage pregnancy. Today's mythology that most or all youths are "at risk" scatters valuable resources and dilutes efforts to help the minority of youths who are genuinely troubled.

Astroth argues: "U.S. teenagers today are, by nearly every important measure, *healthier, better educated, and more responsible* than teens of the past" (italic in original). They are, in fact, for the most part much healthier than the adults who label them "at risk." Astroth suggests that American adults are suffering from **ephebiphobia**—"a fear and loathing of adolescence" (p. 412). He notes that throughout history adults have felt youth were getting out of control. As far back as Socrates' day, adults bemoaned the behavior of their youth:

The children now love luxury. They have bad manners, contempt for authority, they show disrespect for elders, love chatter in place of exercise. They no longer rise when their elders enter the room. They contradict their parents, chatter before company, gobble up their dainties at the table, cross their legs, and tyrannize over their teachers.—Socrates (500 B.C.)

Astroth (p. 412) concludes: "Unfortunately, the notion of "youth at risk" has become a lens through which we view *all* young people, so that today adolescence is seen as some incurable social disease."

Another contribution from the public health model is the metaphor of **contagion** as a way to explain the spread of violence. As noted by Rosenfeld and Decker (1993, p. 46):

> Violence is a "contagious" social process. Acts of violence tend, under certain circumstances, to spread rapidly within high-risk areas and groups. . . . Some analyses locate the source of high rates of violence in subcultures of violence that encourage people—young males in particular—to use physical force as a way of commanding respect and settling conflicts. Others view violence as spread through cycles of revenge and retaliation among perpetrators and victims linked to one another in "social and moral networks."

This second explanation of the rapid spread of violence as a kind of retaliation or self-help can be viewed as an indication that those engaging in the violence have no faith in the system. They perceive that justice is not to be obtained through the system. This was vividly illustrated in the public's rush to buy guns following the Los Angeles riots resulting from the Rodney King verdict in 1992.

A further consideration when considering a public health approach to the violence problems is how law enforcement views violence. According to Rosenfeld and Decker (1993, pp. 45–46): "From the perspective of law enforcement, the single most important fact about the social reality of violence in our society: the persons at highest risk for violence—and therefore with the greatest need for prevention—are criminal offenders." They note the challenges facing those attempting to deal with the violence problem:

> It is inherently difficult in our society, with its heavily armed population, traditions of self-protection, a popular culture saturated with violent images and examples—and a criminal justice system that institutionalizes violent retribution in the form of capital punishment—to shape sensible and effective anti-violence policies and programs. These barriers confront both public health and law enforcement responses to violence. An additional policy barrier, however, derives from the distinct intellectual traditions of the two approaches. Law enforcement is part of the classical tradition that conceives of human action as a product of rational and moral choice. Public health is rooted in positivist conceptions of human behavior as "caused" by external forces that, in principle, are subject to modification.

How these conflicting philosophies translate into programming for both prevention and treatment of delinquency is discussed in Section Four. The table in Appendix A summarizes the influences on delinquency discussed in this chapter.

SUMMARY

Researchers use three methods to measure the nature and extent of unlawful acts by juveniles: official data, self-report data and victim surveys. According to self-report studies, delinquency is almost universal. One reason is that status offenses are often included as being acts of delinquency. Status offenses include such actions as violating curfew, habitual truancy, running away, incorrigibility, ungovernable conduct, being beyond the control of parents, being wayward, using tobacco and drugs and drinking alcohol. The most frequent delinquency offenses were property crimes, with larceny-theft and burglary being most frequent. The third most frequent delinquency offense was simple assault.

Positivist theories of the causes of juvenile delinquency include biological, behavioral, sociological and psychological theories. Biological theorists state that how a person acts is basically a result of heredity. Modern studies of the genetic relationship to crime support the proposition that criminality and violence may be inherited. Violence and aggression have also been associated with the presence or absence of certain chemicals in the brain.

Behavioral theorists state that how a person acts is learned, and that attitudes and values of the social mores are acquired through conditioning. A major characteristic of juvenile delinquents is that they act out their inner conflicts.

Delinquency may also result from biochemical factors, including diet, or from neurological dysfunction, including learning disabilities. Other factors commonly cited as contributing directly to delinquency include drug use, poverty, unemployment, breakdown of religion, breakdown of the family, effects of the media (TV, movies, music), peer pressure and, most importantly, being abused as children. Criminal behavior probably is the result of both heredity and life experiences.

The public health model stresses targeting those most in need of help, specifically adolescent and young black males living in violent neighborhoods.

Discussion Questions

1. What are the most common status offenses in your community?
2. Were you ever stopped (or arrested) for a status offense when you were a juvenile? Did you know anyone who was? How did you feel?
3. Do other countries have status offenses?
4. Have there been any instances of youths involved in serious, violent crime in your community in the past year?
5. Do you feel status offenders should be treated the same as youths involved in serious, violent crime?
6. When you think of juvenile delinquency and serious, violent crime, what comes to mind?
7. At what age does a juvenile become an adult in your state? Do you think the age is appropriate?

8. What is the difference between biological and genetic theories of causes of delinquency?
9. Is human development fixed by biological inheritance or by life experiences?
10. Is the sociological theory of the causes of delinquency an advancement of the behavioral theory? How? What is the main theme of the sociological theory?

▪ References

American Psychiatric Association. *Diagnostic and Statistical Manual of Mental Disorders,* 3rd. ed. Washington, D.C.: American Psychiatric Association, 1987.

American Psychological Association. *Violence & Youth: Psychology's Response.* (n.d.)

Applebome, Peter. "Juvenile Crime: The Offenders Are Younger and the Offenses Are More Serious." *New York Times,* 3 February 1987, p. 16.

Astroth, Kirk A. "Beyond Ephebiphobia: Problem Adults or Problem Youths?" *Phi Delta Kappan,* January 1994, pp. 411–413.

Center for Disease Control. "Physical Fighting Among High Schools Students—United States, 1990." *Morbidity and Mortality Weekly Report,* 41 (1992): 91–94.

Crowe, Timothy D. *Habitual Juvenile Offenders: Guidelines for Citizen Action and Public Responses.* Washington, D.C.: Office of Juvenile Justice and Delinquency Prevention, October 1991.

Duvall, Ed, Jr. "What Is Happening to Our Children?" *Law and Order,* November 1991, p. 109.

Eitzen, Stanley. "Problem Students: The Sociocultural Roots." *Phi Delta Kappan,* April 1992, pp. 584–590.

Glueck, Sheldon, and Eleanor Glueck. *Unraveling Juvenile Delinquency.* Cambridge, Mass.: Harvard University Press, 1950.

Hallinan, Joe. "The Age of Rage." Newhouse News Service. As reported in (Minneapolis/St. Paul) *Star Tribune,* 9 May 1994, p. 9A.

Hernstein, Richard J., and James Q. Wilson. "Are Criminals Made or Born?" In *Encyclopedia of Crime and Justice,* vol. 4, edited by Sanford H. Kadish. New York: Free Press, 1983.

International Association of Chiefs of Police. "Violent Crime in America: Recommendations of the IACP Summit." *Police Chief,* June 1993, pp. 59–61.

Konopka, Gisela. *The Adolescent Girl in Conflict.* Englewood Cliffs: Prentice Hall, 1966.

Mark and Ervin. *Violence and the Brain.* Hagerstown, Md.: Harper & Row, 1970.

Martin, Deirdre. "Teen Violence: Why It's on the Rise and How to Stem its Tide." *Law Enforcement Technology,* January 1994, pp. 36–42.

National Coalition of State Juvenile Justice Advisory Groups. *Myths and Realities: Meeting the Challenge of Serious, Violent, and Chronic Juvenile Offenders, 1992 Annual Report.* Washington, D.C.: 1993.

Post, Charles. "The Link Between Learning Disabilities and Juvenile Delinquency: Cause, Effect, and Present Solutions." *Juvenile and Family Court Journal,* 31 (1981):59.

Regnery, Alfred S. "Getting Away with Murder: Why the Juvenile Justice System Needs an Overhaul." In *Taking Sides: Clashing Views on Controversial Issues in Crime and Criminology,* 2nd rev. ed., edited by Richard C. Monk. Guilford, Conn.: Dushkin Publishing, 1991, pp. 164–170.

Report to the Nation on Crime and Justice. 2nd ed. U.S. Department of Justice, Bureau of Justice Statistics, March 1988.

Rosenfeld, Richard, and Scott Decker. "Where Public Health and Law Enforcement Meet: Monitoring and Preventing Youth Violence." *American Journal of Police,* 12 (1993), 3:11–57.

Shea, Cay. "A Current Look at the Chronic/Serious Juvenile Offender in Minnesota." Seminar presented at Minneapolis, Minn.: October 1987.

Siegel, Larry J., and Joseph J. Senna. *Juvenile Delinquency.* 3rd ed. St. Paul, Minn.: West Publishing, 1988.

Springer, Charles E. *Justice for Juveniles.* Washington, D.C.: U.S. Dept. of Justice, Office of Juvenile Justice and Delinquency Prevention, 1986.

Sprinthall, Norman A., and W. Andrew Collins. *Adolescent Psychology: A Developmental View.* New York: Random House, 1984.

ten Bensel, Robert. Testimony. Quoted in *Child at Risk,* 41. Office of Juvenile Justice and Delinquency Prevention, U.S. Dept. of Justice. Washington, D.C.: U.S. Government Printing Office.

Trojanowicz, Robert C., and Merry Morash. *Juvenile Delinquency: Concepts and Control.* 4th ed. Englewood Cliffs: Prentice Hall, 1987.

Widom, Cathy Spatz. *The Cycle of Violence.* National Institute of Justice, Research in Brief, October 1992.

Wilson, James Q. "Thinking about Crime." *The Atlantic,* September 1983, p. 86.

Wilson, James Q., and George L. Kelling. "The Police and Neighborhood Safety: Broken Windows." *The Atlantic Monthly.,* March 1982, pp. 29–38.

Wilson, John J. "A National Agenda for Children: On the Front Lines with Attorney General Janet Reno." *Juvenile Justice,* 1 (Fall/Winter 1993) 2:2–8.

Witkin, Gordon. "Kids Who Kill." *U.S. News and World Report,* 8 April 1991, pp. 26–32. Reprinted in *Criminal Justice 92/93,* 16th ed., edited by John J. Sullivan and Joseph L. Victor. Guilford, Conn.: Dushkin Publishing, 1992, pp. 181–185.

Wooden, Wayne S. "Arson Is Epidemic—and Spreading Like Wildfire." *Psychology Today,* January 1985.

Zimmerman, Joel; William Rich; Ingo Keilitz; and Paul Broder. "Some Observations on the Link Between Learning Disabilities and Juvenile Delinquency." *Journal of Criminal Justice,* 9 (1981): 9–17.

Youth Who Are
Gang Members

Street gangs prey upon their neighborhood much like a malignant growth which continues to spread through its host until only a wasted shell remains.

Los Angeles White Paper

Do You Know?

What the difference is between a gang, a street gang and a youth gang?
What separates a gang from a club?
Where street gangs may be found?
How street gangs acquire their power?
What are some causes of gangs?
How contemporary gangs can be classified?
What the most common gangs are?
What two well-known black street gangs are called?
What characteristics distinguish youth gangs?
How gangs are typically structured?
What basic functions are served by youth gangs?
How gang members can be identified?
What purpose is served by graffiti?
How gang members communicate?
What activities gangs typically engage in?
What might indicate gang activity?

Can You Define the Following Key Terms?

corporate gang, crew, expressive violence, gang, graffiti, hedonistic gang, instrumental gang, instrumental violence, predatory gang, representing, scavenger gang, socialized delinquency, street gang, tagging, territorial gang, turf, youth gang

INTRODUCTION

Youth gangs are an increasing problem of the juvenile justice system. As Harris (1985, p. 2) almost a decade ago noted:

> Gangs are now spreading through our society like a violent plague. Daily, countless news stories depict the tragedy of gang violence. The following excerpts document only the tip of the problem:
>
> ▮ Item . . . "A gang fight at a crowded park resulted in a seven-year-old girl being shot in the head, while picnicking with her family."
> ▮ Item . . . "Shot gun blasts from a passing car, intended for a rival gang member, strike a child on a tricycle."
> ▮ Item . . . "A shoot-out between rival gangs claimed the life of a high school track star as he jogged around the school track."

Harris further noted the danger of gangs (p. 1): "Gangs, almost by definition, are fractious, unruly, or downright criminal. Most of all, they do collectively what few of them would dare to do individually. . . . The level of every gang, big or small, is the level of its lowest, least law-abiding member."

This chapter examines the gang phenomenon, beginning with definitions that have been suggested for street gangs and youth gangs. A very brief history of gangs in the United States is followed by a discussion of the scope of the gang problem in the 1990s. Next the various causes of and classifications used for gangs are presented, with a close-up look at some of the major gangs, including the Crips and the Bloods. White gangs, female gangs, biker gangs and prison gangs are also discussed.

The characteristics of street gangs and the structure they typically exhibit is the next area of discussion, followed by a discussion of why youths join gangs and how they are recruited. Next you will be introduced to the outward trappings of gangs and how gang members might be identified, how they communicate, their symbols and their activities. The chapter concludes with a look at the relationship between gangs and drugs and with some common myths about gangs.

DEFINITIONS

The *Encyclopedia of Crime and Justice* (Kadish, 1983, p. 1673) states:

> Based on their distinguishing characteristics, youth gangs may be defined as follows: youth gangs are self-formed associations of youths distinguished from other types of youth groups by their routine participation in illegal activities. They

242

differ from other types of law-violating youth groups by manifesting better-developed leadership, greater formalization, more clearly defined identification with localities or enterprises, and a greater degree of deliberate intent in the conduct of crimes.

According to a Los Angeles White Paper, the following definition is accepted by law enforcement: "A gang is any group gathered together on a continuing basis to commit anti-social behavior."

Jackson and McBride (1985, p. 20) offer one of the most functional definitions of **gangs**:

■ "A gang is a group of people that form an allegiance for a common purpose, and engage in unlawful or criminal activity."

The Minnesota statute defining a gang is typical of many states:

Criminal gang means any ongoing organization, association, or group of three or more persons, whether formal or informal, that:

■ Has, as one of its primary activities, the commission of one or more of the offenses listed in section . . .
■ Has a common name or common identifying sign or symbol; and
■ Includes members who individually or collectively engage in or have engaged in a pattern of criminal activity.

The Minnesota statute also provides that if a gang member commits a felony, the sentence is to be three years longer than the statutory maximum for that crime.

■ A **street gang** is a group of individuals who meet over time, have identifiable leadership, claim control over a specific territory in the community and engage in criminal behavior.

Dart (1992, p. 96) suggests that street gangs are associations of individuals with the following characteristics in varying degrees:

■ A gang name and recognizable symbols.
■ A geographic territory.
■ A regular meeting pattern.
■ An organized, continuous course of criminality.

■ Criminal behavior is what separates a gang from a club such as the Boy Scouts.

Street gangs engage in criminal activity either individually or collectively. They create an atmosphere of fear and intimidation in a community. The term *street gang* is preferred by most local law enforcement agencies because it "includes juveniles and adults and designates the location of the gang and most of its criminal behavior."

■ The **youth gang**, for criminal justice policy purposes, is a subset of the street gang.

Spergel et al. (1990, p. 3) suggest:

The notion of *youth gang* incorporates two concepts: often a more amorphous "delinquent group" (e.g., a juvenile clique within a gang), and the better organized and sophisticated "criminal organization." The latter may be an independent group or clique of the gang and usually comprises older youth and young adults primarily engaged in criminal income-producing activity, most commonly drug trafficking (italic in original).

A BRIEF HISTORY

Gangs and gang violence are an integral part of American history. Organized groups for crime and antisocial behavior go back to Colonial times when John Hancock (the largest signature on the Declaration of Independence) amassed a fortune as an entrepreneur smuggling goods with his organized group. And, as noted by Gates and Jackson (1990, p. 20): "Young people of similar ethnic or social interests have banded together into gangs since the birth of our nation."

Street gangs have operated in the United States since the 1820s. Irish Americans in New York City organized the Forty Thieves, which murdered, robbed and mugged. These gang members came from areas of overcrowded, substandard housing, poor or nonexistent health care, broken homes and few opportunities to improve their situation.

The 1800s also had rural gangsters such as Jesse and Frank James. The 1920s and 1930s saw the rise of criminal syndicates, the Mafia or Cosa Nostra, and notorious gangsters such as John Dillinger, Machine Gun Kelly, Pretty Boy Floyd, Bonnie Parker and Clyde Barrow, George "Baby Face" Nelson and Ma Barker and her son Fred. These predecessors of today's gangs relied heavily on extortion, intimidation, robbery and violence to gain power and wealth.

CURRENT SCOPE OF THE GANG PROBLEM

Street gangs now exist across the country. From their beginnings on the East Coast, they have flourished in California, particularly the Los Angeles area, Chicago and other major U.S. cities. Los Angeles County has over 950 street gangs with an estimated membership of over 100,000 (Los Angeles White Paper, 1992, p. 1).

The Los Angeles and Chicago gangs have invaded other previously untouched areas of the country. As noted by Taylor (1991, p. 103): "The increase and spread of youth gangs in today's United States constitute a movement that must be recognized and understood. Gangs can no longer be defined in traditional, preconceived terms. Social and economic factors have redefined them, and their imperialistic spread is a multidimensional movement."

Miller (1991, p. 263) suggests: "Youth gangs in the 1980s and 1990s are more numerous, more prevalent, and more violent than in the 1950s, probably more so than at any time in the country's history." They are no longer confined to the two coasts and Chicago, but can be found in most major cities in the United States as well as in small towns and even rural areas. Among the attractions of the smaller towns are less competition from other gangs for the drug market as well as less rivalry and violence from such competition, resulting in more money and more power. Often the police presence is less also.

■ Street gangs can be found throughout the United States, not only in large cities, but in the suburbs, small towns and even rural areas.

A 1989 National Institute of Justice survey of law enforcement officials in 45 cities estimates the presence of 1,439 youth gangs and 120,636 gang members. Blacks and Hispanics together made up over 87 percent of the gang populations, far in excess of their representation in the general population (NIJ, 1992, p. 18). Many gangs were involved in serious crimes. The rate of violent offenses for gang members was three times as high as for nongang delinquents with juvenile gang members accounting for nearly 23 percent of index crimes in these jurisdictions. This survey also found illegal drugs associated with gangs.

The Los Angeles White Paper reported 771 gang-related deaths in 1991 and suggested: "Not only is the citizenry in mortal danger from street gangs, but the influence wielded by gangs has a trickle-down effect on all aspects of life for the residents of an area afflicted with a street gang" (p. 1).

Owens and Wells (1993, p. 25) write that: "According to the FBI, the Crips and the Bloods have now spread to more than 100 cities and count more than 40,000 members."

Further, according to Dart (1992, p. 96):

Violence perpetrated by street gangs is a principal—if not the major—social affliction affecting American communities today. In the last decade of the 20th century, gangs exist in virtually every community—suburban, as well as inner-city—in every metropolitan area. Rather than seeking socially acceptable means of achieving influence, gangs use violence, harassment, intimidation, extortion, and fear to control a neighborhood.

A report on the IACP Summit on violent crime in America describes the current gang problem as being partially responsible for the rise in violent crime (IACP, 1993, p. 61):

The rise of gangs has fueled much of the increase in violent crime. What were once loosely knit groups of juveniles and young adults involved in petty crimes have become powerful, organized gangs. There appear to be gangs intent on controlling lucrative drug trade through intimidation and murder, and also street gangs simply claiming "turf." Today, as never before, cities and neighborhoods, even those without long histories of youth gang activity, have been literally overrun by both types of gang violence. While gangs are not new, today's level of gang violence, organization, and sophistication is unprecedented.

The problem of gangs has escalated, in part, because of the easy availability of guns. Gates and Jackson (1990, p. 20) suggest: "The knives, clubs and occasional firearms once used by gang members have given way to semi- and fully automatic assault rifles—with devastating results." They also note: "[G]ang members are attacking peace officers at an alarming rate." For example, in Minneapolis, on 25 September 1992, 30-year patrol officer Jerome Haaf was shot in the back in an act attributed to a street gang (the Vice Lords) who wanted to assassinate a police officer.

Further, as noted by Jackson and McBride (1985, pp. 101–109): "Street gangs exist and function in the community from a base of strength gained through violent behavior." This is what makes them so terribly dangerous.

▮ Street gangs acquire their power in the community through their violent behavior.

Gang members are, in their own way, quite conservative, often believing in capital punishment. They know that if one of their gang members is killed, the likelihood of the killer being apprehended, let alone sufficiently punished, is very slim. Hence, they are likely to take vengeance into their own hands, resulting in the all-too-common gang shootings. Part of the reason for such violence is that gang members have little faith that "the system" will provide justice for the murdered gang member.

Law Enforcement News (1993, p. 13), in "Getting a Grip on Slippery Gang Problems," states: "Today's gangs exhibit a propensity for committing violent acts without remorse or regard for innocent bystanders, who are blithely referred to as 'mushrooms' in gang parlance."

Another way to view the seriousness of the problem is to see it through the words of a Los Angeles gang member (Shakur, 1993, pp. 69–70):

I was six years old when the Crips were started. No one anticipated its sweep. The youth of South Central were being gobbled up by an alien power threatening to attach itself to a multitude of other problems already plaguing them. An almost "enemy" subculture had arisen, and no one knew from where it came. No one took its conception seriously. But slowly it crept, saturating entire households, city blocks, neighborhoods, and eventually the nation-state of California.

Today, no school, library, institution, business, detention center, or church is exempt from being touched in some way by the gang activity in South Central. Per year, the gangs in South Central recruit more people than the four branches of the U.S. Armed Forces do. Crack dealers employ more people in South Central than AT&T, IBM, and Xerox combined. And South Central is under more aerial surveillance than Belfast, Ireland. Everyone is armed, frustrated, suppressed, and on the brink of explosion.

CAUSES OF GANGS

The National School Safety Center (1988, p. 2) notes that:

> Youth gangs are not a new phenomenon in America. Philadelphians convened in 1791 to decide how to deal with bands of young people disrupting that city, and officials in New York City admitted to having gang problems as early as 1825. Over the years, many other urban areas have experienced the unrest resulting from gangs of young people banding together for a variety of reasons. Such youths may just want to occupy time, fill an emptiness in their lives or experience a sense of belonging. Whatever the reason, when a gang evolves, communities almost always suffer serious consequences.

Jackson and McBride (1985, p. 8) and the Los Angeles White Paper state that gangs exist because of many social and economic factors, including cultural discord, ego fulfillment, traditional gang culture, racism, parental guidance, socioeconomic factors and lack of responsibility.

■ Gangs may result from cultural discord, ego fulfillment, racism, socioeconomic factors and family influences.

These combined factors may be pictured as spokes in a wheel. The more spokes, the stronger the wheel. The gang member's family unit is the hub of the wheel, supporting the rest. The following discussion of causes is adapted from the Los Angeles White Paper.

Racism

Racism played an early and important role in the formation of street gangs in California. The races did not mix. Although racism is most often associated with white people showing prejudice against nonwhites, in reality racism refers to the belief that one's own ethnic group is superior to all others. Racism often results in a particular group banding together, lending support to one another and excluding all other groups, sometimes even seeking to harm members of other groups. Black gangs were and still are totally black. White gangs tend to include whites only. Hispanic gangs may allow a sprinkling of blacks or whites to join. And violent rivalries between ethnic gangs are common.

Socioeconomic Pressure

Mexicans immigrating to California in the early part of the twentieth century were looked on as a source of unskilled, cheap labor. They were relegated to barrios, neighborhoods comprised almost totally of Hispanic populations and reinforced by a continuous flow of immigrants.

Before long, competition for jobs between the growing immigrant population and native Californians led to hatred and rivalries between the groups. Rivalries grew into neighborhood disputes. The same set of circumstances led to the formation of street gangs of African and Asian ancestry.

Family Structure

Probably the most important factor in the formation of a gang member is family structure. Investigators have found certain common threads running through most families having hard-core gang members.

A family containing gang members is quite often a racial minority on some form of government assistance. It often lacks a male authority figure. If a male authority figure is present, he may be a criminal or drug addict, therefore representing a negative role model. Typically, adult family members lack more than an elementary school education. Children live with minimal adult supervision.

When a child first encounters law enforcement authorities, the dominant figure (usually the mother) makes excuses for the child, normally in the form of accusations against society. Thus, children are taught early that they are not responsible for their actions and are shown how to transfer blame to society.

A second common type of family structure is one that may have two strong family leaders in a mother and father. Usually graduates from gangs themselves, they see little wrong with their children belonging to gangs.

A third common family structure involves parents who do not speak English. The children tend to adapt rapidly to the American way of life and, en route, lose respect for their parents and the "old ways." They quickly become experts at manipulating their parents, and the parents lose all control.

Many of these structures overlap.

Socialized Delinquency

Socialized delinquency is common among lower-class children who have been frustrated or hurt by a predominantly middle-class society. To youths, socialized delinquency is not delinquency at all. It is delinquency only in terms of middle-class standards. When individuals behave in ways sanctioned by the culture they belong to—the gang—they feel no guilt for their unlawful activities. The gang, in effect, becomes a surrogate family. Within this family, violence towards others is prevalent. One reason for this is that gang members were frequently neglected or abused as children.

A tragic example of socialized delinquency is that of Chicagoan Robert Sandifer, nicknamed "Yummy" because of his love of food. At age 11, he stood accused of killing a 14-year old neighbor. It is speculated that because Yummy became the focus of an extensive manhunt, he was killed by his own gang members. According to a *New York Times* article (Slain Boy, 8 September 1994, p. 7A): "Neglected and abused by his family, bounced from group homes to squad cars, and killed, police say, by his own street gang, Robert was buried Wednesday, a symbol of the nation's most troubled children."

TYPES OF GANGS

Contemporary gangs can usually be classified as one of three types.

■ Contemporary gangs may be classified as scavenger, territorial or corporate.

Taylor (1991, pp. 105–109) describes these three types of gangs:

Scavenger Gangs. Members of these gangs often have no common bond beyond their impulsive behavior and their need to belong. Leadership changes daily and weekly. They are urban survivors who prey on the weak of the inner city. Their crimes are usually petty, senseless, and spontaneous. Often acts of violence are perpetrated just for fun. They have no particular goals, no purpose, no substantial camaraderies. Scavenger gang members generally have the characteristics of being low achievers and illiterates with short attention spans who are prone to violent, erratic behavior. The majority come from the lower class and the underclass.

Territorial Gangs. A territorial gang, crew, group, or individual designates something, someplace, or someone as belonging exclusively to the gang. The traditional designation of territory as it relates to gangs is better known as *turf*.

When scavenger gangs become serious about organizing for a specific purpose, they enter the territorial stage. During this stage, gangs define themselves and someone assumes a leadership role. . . .

Gangs defend their territories in order to protect their particular business. The word is out on the street to everyone: "This is gang territory—stay away." . . .

Mobility through financial power is the distinguishing factor between the traditional definition of territory and the nontraditional concept of territory. . . . Prior to the windfall of illegal drug profits, territory as a concept was limited to the immediate neighborhood. Today, with the power of organized crime, technology, and escalating wages, territory can be intrastate, interstate, or international.

Organized/Corporate Gangs. These well-organized groups have very strong leaders or managers. The main focus of their organization is participation in illegal money-making ventures. . . . Discipline is comparable to that of the military, and goals resemble those of Fortune 500 corporations.

These organized/corporate gangs may have ties throughout the country, and, according to Saccente (1993, p. 28): "Since street gangs accumulate large sums of money, they must utilize legitimate businesses, financial institutions, family members, lawyers and other professions to process and hide their assets." He notes that viewing gangs as criminal organizations allows law enforcement to use the antiracketeering laws found in RICO statutes.

RICO (Racketeer Influenced and Corrupt Organization Act) was an important measure of the Organized Crime Control Act passed in 1970. The Act was designed to limit the activity of organized crime by defining racketeering to include conspiring to use racketeering as a means of making income, collecting loans or conducting business. Although aimed at organized crime, RICO statutes can also be applied to the illegal activities of gangs.

Another way of classifying gangs has been proposed by Huff (1989, pp. 528–529).

▮ Gangs may be classified as hedonistic, instrumental or predatory.

A **hedonistic gang** focuses on having a good time, usually by smoking pot, drinking beer and sometimes engaging in minor property crimes.

Instrumental gangs, in contrast, focus on money, committing property crimes for economic reasons rather than for the "thrill." Although some may sell drugs, this is not their primary activity. Members may also smoke pot and drink beer. This categorization fits well with the distinction between **instrumental violence** and **expressive violence.** As noted by Bell during a hearing before the House Select Committee on Children, Youth, and Families (1989, p. 79):

> Instrumental violence is where, if I don't have a watch and you have one, I'm going to use violence as an instrument to get your watch. That's a criminal justice kind of issue.
>
> Expressive violence has absolutely nothing to do with what I'm going to gain. It's, you know, you step on on my toe, I'm in a bad mood, I've had a head injury, have been in a family where there's violence. I've been violent all my life, I've been violent in schools, no one has ever said anything to me about it. I'm socializable, but I still pop off every so often. And then somebody commits a murder. That is the majority of the homicides in the country. Most of the violence in this country is expressive. It is not instrumental. You are not going to have solutions for expressive violence by addressing instrumental violence issues. It's just not going to happen.

Predatory gangs commit more violent crimes against persons, including robberies and street muggings. They are likely to use harder drugs such as "crack" cocaine, which contributes to their volatile, aggressive behavior.

The Los Angeles White Paper (1992) refers to street gangs as traditional (having a long heritage) or nontraditional (formed more recently). The following discussion is adapted from that paper.

▮ Street gangs are usually either traditional or nontraditional.

Traditional gangs are the typical Hispanic gangs found in barrios. Many times, members can trace the gang's heritage back to previous generations. An established system of traditional motivations have been formulated, and they are adhered to.

The nontraditional gang is also called a transitional gang. This type of gang has not been active long enough to have adapted long-standing traditions. Black street gangs of today still struggle with their gang identity.

Typically, gangs are structured around race or nationality.

▮ The most common gangs are Hispanic, black and Asian.

Hispanic Street Gangs

The structure of Hispanic street gangs is similar throughout the western United States. Codes of conduct have been established.

Leadership roles in Hispanic gangs are not formally recognized positions. Leadership positions are not usually assumed by any one individual permanently, but by any member who demonstrates unique qualities of leadership needed at a particular moment.

These street gangs lack a solid chain of command. They cannot operate efficiently as a unit. They divide themselves, according to age, into groups called *cliques.*

The gangs themselves usually adopt names that have some geographical significance in their neighborhood. Examples are "18th" (street) and "Lomas" (hills). A gang sees itself as the protector of its neighborhood. Gang wall writings or graffiti are an extension of the gang used to identify the boundaries of their turf. Gang members are loyal to the death. They are proud, even boastful, of their gang membership.

Female gang members have no inherent rights in the gang and belong only at the sufferance of their male counterparts. There are very few female gangs.

Black Street Gangs

Black street gangs have existed in the Los Angeles area for many years. From the 1920s through the 1960s, black street gangs went virtually unnoticed. In the early 1970s, a group of high-school aged "youths" began to terrorize local campuses and neighborhoods. This gang called themselves the Crips. Members extorted money from other students and were involved in violence. This type of activity grew, and in a matter of a few years, many neighborhoods had their own gangs. The violence of the groups was directed not only at rival gang members, but often at innocent nongang victims.

In the mid-1970s, a change occurred. The Crips built a reputation for being the strongest force among the black street gangs. Soon other gangs started renaming themselves, incorporating the word Crip into their new names. Although these gangs adopted the Crip name, they maintained their own leaders and membership and were independent.

Some of these rival gangs continued to fight among themselves, and a polarization of forces developed from these feuds. The black gangs divided themselves into Crips and Non-Crips. In gang terminology, the factions were called Bloods (Non-Crips) and Cuz (Crips).

▌ The Crips and the Bloods are rival black street gangs.

Black gang activity is no longer isolated in gang neighborhoods. The activities of such groups are not restricted to gang feuds but include crimes of various sorts in many areas of the country.

Asian Gangs

In the early 1900's, the Tongs (secret fraternal organizations) used boys as lookouts for the adult Tong members. These boys were called Wah Ching. After a period of time and as the Tongs became more legitimate, the need for the Wah Chings declined, but the Wah Chings themselves did not disband. They still operate, largely taking up where the Tongs left off.

Even though the Tongs presently are primarily benevolent societies, they will, when necessary, carry out violence through the agency of the Wah Chings. Eventually, because of excessive violence, the Chinese community itself spoke out against the Wah Chings. As differences of opinion developed within the Wah Chings, the group split into two factions. The older members became known as Yu Li, while the younger gang members retained the name Wah Ching.

Originally a member of the Yu Li, Joe Fong became disenchanted with the Yu Li and further fragmented the gang by forming the Joe Fong gang or Joe Boys. The 1967 massacre at the Golden Dragon restaurant in San Francisco's Chinatown was a result of the Joe Fong gang attacking the Wah Ching gang.

All three gangs (Yu Li, Joe Boys and Wah Chings) exist today and have spread to most major cities of the United States and Canada.

Unlike other groups, Chinese gang members do not have a particular dress code, so their identity as gang members is difficult to establish on sight.

One difficulty in dealing with Asian gangs is that most western police officers do not know how to translate names into English, making accurate record keeping and tracking of gang members difficult (Harlan, 1993, p. 51).

Ima (1992, p. 22) notes that refugee families face many issues that may contribute to youths joining gangs, including:

▮ Disrupted families—loss of a parent or family members.
▮ Role reversal—children become translators for their parents and, consequently, gain control over them.
▮ Disagreement on values and norms—youth accept American customs more rapidly than their parents.

Ima (p. 26) also notes several factors contributing to academic failure, which is also linked with gang membership, including family instability already mentioned, early marriage and childbearing, lack of access to jobs, language barriers and racism. Youth with dysfunctional families who are not succeeding in school are prime candidates for gangs.

The Home Invaders are young Asian males who work in groups, moving about the country brutalizing and robbing other Asian families. According to Burke (1990, p. 23): "The robberies are normally committed during the evening hours when confrontation is ensured. They rely upon intimidation and fear of retaliation to gain valuables."

Vietnamese gangs are also proliferating and posing a serious problem in that they are highly mobile and are especially vicious in their crimes against fellow Vietnamese.

Other Ethnic Gangs

Filipino neighborhood street gangs are similar in structure and operation to Hispanic groups. As a result, Filipino gangs gravitate toward Mexican gangs in their associations and friendships. The most common Filipino gangs are the Santanas, the Tabooes and Temple Street.

The Korean community also has very active gangs. The foremost is called the Korean Killers. It is unique in that it is primarily a theft-oriented gang.

White Gangs

The Justice Department estimates that three-quarters of the nation's known gangs are made up of minorities, primarily blacks and Hispanics, but the number of white youths in gangs is increasing. *Law Enforcement News* in "Getting a Grip on Slippery Gang Problems" (1993, p. 13) notes: "A number of jurisdictions report that youths from predominantly white, affluent suburbs are banding together in gangs, whose criminal activities are gradually escalating from graffiti and vandalism to beatings and drive-by shootings. In upper middle-class Westchester County, N.Y., . . . authorities estimate that 1,500 youths belong to as many as 70 gangs."

Stoner Gangs

One type of gang not discussed in the Los Angeles County White Paper is the stoner gang. According to Jackson and McBride (1985, pp. 42–45), stoner gangs consist of middle-class youths who are involved in drugs and alcohol (hence "stoned" much of the time), as well as into heavy metal rock music. Although they are not as apt to engage in the violent crimes often associated with other street gangs, they are often involved in satanism, which poses a unique problem to law enforcement and the juvenile justice system.

■ **Stoner gangs often practice satanism. They may mutilate animals, rob graves and desecrate human remains and churches.**

Stoners tend to wear colorful T-shirts, jeans and tennis shoes and to have long hair.

Biker Gangs

During the early 1980s law enforcement made biker gangs a priority and, as a result, many biker gang members found themselves in jail. As street gangs became more prominent, however, the focus of law enforcement shifted away from the biker gangs. According to Trethewy (1993, p. 95): "Street and biker gangs are cousins in crime." He notes that biker gangs are highly organized and that members pay club dues and follow club rules. Further: "Bikers use computers, cellular phones, complex surveillance equipment, sophisticated weaponry and pagers. They also enlist the support of popular movie and television personalities to spruce up their image."

Biker gangs also network with other gangs across the country, including prison gangs and hate groups such as the Aryan Brotherhood and the Ku Klux Klan.

Prison Gangs

The influence of the gang is also felt within the corrections portion of the juvenile justice system. The Youth Authority in Stockton, California, estimates that about 65 percent of its inmates belong to gangs (Rushing, 1993, p. 12):

> Far removed from the battlefields of the 'hood', gangsters in the California Youth Authority spill blood for the same things—rivalries, revenge, respect.
>
> Towering cyclone fences topped with razor wire surround the most serious criminals in the juvenile justice system, but they can't keep out the gang hatred that has cost so many lives on the street.

Those not affiliated with gangs prior to their confinement find that not belonging to a gang can be dangerous. As one 18-year-old said (Rushing, p. 13): "If you're claiming nothing [no gang affiliation], they'll be messing with you every day. They know you're not going to be doing nothing back, you know what I'm saying, because you got no backup to help you."

Females in Gangs

Ross (1993, pp. 8–9) notes that the numbers of girls in gangs is relatively small, but it is growing and the girls tend to be more violent. She includes the statement of a former female gang member: "You want to be where the men are, because that's where the power is. It's not enough anymore to just have dinner made. Now you have to go out and have a gun battle and go rip off a few cars, and come home and have dinner ready."

Females are used by gangs in a variety of ways. They may:

■ Serve as lookouts for crimes in progress.
■ Conceal stolen property or tools used in committing crimes.
■ Carry weapons for males who don't want to be caught with them.
■ Carry information in and out of prison.
■ Provide sexual favors (they are often drug dependent and are physically abused).

Like juveniles, females arouse less suspicion than male adults.

YOUTH GANGS—AN OVERVIEW

A report issued by the Metropolitan Court Judges Committee (1988, p. 48) summarizes the characteristic groups of youth gangs as follows:

▮ **Black Gangs.** Origins in Los Angeles, Chicago, New York, Miami, and other major urban ghettos. Crips, Bloods, Players, Untouchables, and Vice Lords are some of the more prominent gangs.

▮ **Jamaican Posses.** Immigrant Jamaicans in the U.S. with roots in Jamaica. Groups have been identified in New York, Boston, Philadelphia, Washington, D.C., Houston, Atlanta, Detroit, Seattle, and Anchorage among other locations.

▮ **Hispanic Gangs.** Origins in Los Angeles, valleys of California, New York (Puerto Rican), Miami (Mariel Cubans, Dominicans), Washington, D.C., and other urban barrios. Tend to use highly stylized graffiti lettering.

▮ **Asian Gangs.** Origins among recent emigrés from Viet Nam, Hong Kong, and Philippines. Activity centered in New York, New Orleans, Los Angeles and Orange County, California, Portland, Oregon, Seattle, San Francisco, and Houston.

▮ **Pacific Islander Gangs.** Primarily Samoans who have migrated to western urban areas, i.e., Los Angeles, San Francisco, Portland.

▮ **White "Stoner" Gangs.** Caucasian groups identified with heavy metal and punk Rock music preferences and with some British working class gangs. Sometimes involved with Satanic rites and symbols.

▮ **Neo-Nazi Gangs.** Tend to articulate white supremacy, racism, and Nazi symbols. Some call themselves "skinheads" and sport close-cut hair or shaved heads.

▮ **Motorcycle Gangs.** Dominantly Caucasians, branches of Hells Angels and other notorious motorcycle groups. Tend to be heavily involved with the manufacture and sale of methamphetamine.

CHARACTERISTICS OF STREET GANGS

According to Miller (1983, p. 1671), gangs can be distinguished from other forms of law-violating youth groups on the basis of five characteristics.

▮ Five characteristics that distinguish street gangs are leadership, organization, associational patterns, domain identification and illegal activity.

Miller details these five characteristics:

▮ Leadership in gangs is generally better defined and more clearly identifiable than in other types of law-violating youth groups.

▮ Compared to other types of groups, gangs tend to be more formalized or organized. . . . Organizational elements common to gangs include internal differentiation, hierarchical authority, and advanced planning.

▮ Relational bonds tend to be closer and affiliation more continuous in gangs than in other types of law-violating groups. . . . Gangs maintain specific criteria for membership eligibility that may be more or less formalized. Some gangs employ initiation rituals, often involving one or more criminal acts, as a precondition of membership.

▮ Youth gangs characteristically claim identification with and/or control over, particular locations, facilities, or enterprises. The best-known manifestation of this is the "turf" phenomenon.

▮ The principal characteristic that distinguishes both gangs and other types of law-violating groups from lawful groups is illegal activity. Offenses committed by gang members approximate the full range of street crime. . . . The most distinctive form of gang offense is gang-fighting, wherein two or more gangs or gang subunits engage one another in violent combat.

Davis (1982, p. 1) warns that gang activity:

is more lethal today than at any time in the twentieth century. . . . they have indeed become our most pervasive threat to date relative to criminal victimization. Epidemics of murders, stabbings, drug sales and "rip offs" by groups begin to identify a pattern. . . . [they] develop a lifestyle characterized by extortion, shootings, knifings, and dope deals. . . . Mutual excitement comes from pistol whippings or committing armed robberies.

GANG STRUCTURE

Varying levels of involvement can be found in most gangs.

▮ Most gangs contain leaders, hard-core members, regular members and fringe members or wannabes.

The leaders are usually the oldest members of the gang and have extensive criminal records. They may surround themselves with hard-core members, giving orders and expecting unquestioned obedience. The hard-core members are the ones who usually commit the crimes and are the most violent members of the gang. They have usually had to earn the right to become a true gang member through some sort of initiation or jumping in.

Kody Scott is a prime example of a hard-core member. He explains actions that led to his being accepted into a Los Angeles Crip gang (Shakur, 1993, p. 13):

In 1977, when I was thirteen, while robbing a man I turned my head and was hit in the face. The man tried to run, but was tripped by Tray Ball, who then held him for me. I stomped him for twenty minutes before leaving him unconscious in an alley. Later that night, I learned that the man had lapsed into a coma and was disfigured from my stomping. The police told bystanders that the person responsible for this was a "monster." The name stuck, and I took that as a moniker over my birth name.

"Monster" also describes the effect of being accepted into the gang (Shakur, 1993, p. 69):

My life was totally consumed by all aspects of gang life. I had turned my bedroom into a virtual command post, launching attacks from my house with escalating frequency. My clothes, walk, talk, and attitude all reflected my love for and allegiance to my set. Nobody was more important than my homeboys—nobody.

In fact, the only reason my little brother and I stayed close is because he joined the set. Anybody else I had nothing in common with.

On the fringes of most gangs are youth who aspire to become gang members, called *wannabes*. They dress and talk like the hard-core members, but they have not yet been formally accepted into the gang. Their progression from a high-risk youth to a wannabe to a hard-core gang member is illustrated in Table 8–1.

Another group of youth could be described as "potentials" or "could be's." Figure 8–1 shows the relationship of these youth to the gang. Many of these youth are what Dr. Cline (1979) would describe as "character-disturbed." His profile of a character-disturbed child is contained in Table 8–2. These characteristics are very similar to those outlined in Chapter 7 for individuals with behavior disorders, antisocial individuals and even psychopaths.

TABLE 8–1   **The Development and Path of a High-Risk Youth**

Ages	Risk Indicators
8	Youth plays outdoors a lot and is difficult to bring into the house.
9	Youth gets into mischief and neighborhood disputes.
10	Youth has first contact with police for petty thefts, vandalism, fire setting and animal abuse.
11	Youth engages in malicious and mischievous play; enters into delinquent networking (gang) activity; engages in stealing and destroying property.
12	Youth develops conflict with societal norms and values resulting in further peer and older youth criminal networking activity; experiments with drugs and alcohol; bullies younger children; is truant and unruly.
13–14	Youth's gang identity emerges as a result of community's failure to integrate youth into adult law-abiding society; commits residential burglaries and bicycle thefts; deals with stolen property; becomes runner for drug entrepreneur.
15–16	Youth's behavior characterized by loyalty to the gang; gang becomes family and provides education and experience. Youth commits burglaries and other thefts to finance drugs and alcohol; sells drugs; engages in auto theft and fraud. Youth's high truancy results in underachieving, leading to school dropout; becomes a social thrownaway; comes to the attention of the police.
16–17	**Gang member:** Youth, because of behavior, becomes *institutionalized* for violent acts: murder, rape, assault; is heavy drug and alcohol user. **Gang nonmember or loner:** Youth is highly socially dysfunctional; turns on family to vent frustration over inability to be socially stable; considers and may fulfill self-destruction.
18–20	**Gang member:** Youth goes from delinquent to more criminal associates; is intravenous drug abuser; commits crimes to satisfy addiction; is highly volatile; commits crimes against women and, if married, abuses spouse and children. **Gang nonmember:** Youth, if no criminal record or a gang dropout and from a highly dysfunctional family, has tendency to commit violent acts against women and children.

Hard-Core

These youths comprise approximately 5–10 percent of the gang. They have been in the gang the longest and frequently are in and out of jail, unemployed and involved with drugs (distribution or usage). The average age is early to mid twenties, however some hard-cores could be older or younger. Very influential in the gang.

Regular Members

Youths whose average age is 14–17 years old, however they could be older or younger. They have already been initiated into gang and tend to back up the hard-core gang members. If they stay in the gang long enough, they could become hard-core.

Claimers, Associates or "Wannabe's"

Youngsters whose average age is 11–13 years old, however age may vary. These are the youngsters who are not officially members of the gang but they act like they are or claim to be from the gang. They may begin to dress in gang attire, hang around with the gang or write the graffiti of the gang.

Potentials or "Could Be's"

Youngsters who are getting close to an age where they might decide to join a gang, live in or close to an area where there are gangs or have a family member who is involved with gangs. The potentials do not have to join gangs, they can choose alternatives and avoid gang affiliation completely. Generally, the further into a gang that someone is, the harder it is to get out.

▮ FIGURE 8–1 Gang Organizational Chart

WHY YOUTHS JOIN GANGS

Chapter 4 discussed the importance of feelings of belonging and self-worth. If youths do not get this support at home or at school, they will seek it elsewhere. The largest draw a gang has for its young members is a sense of belonging, of importance, of family. Rawles, a deputy director of Philadelphia's Crisis Intervention Network, contends that a gang "fills a vacuum in their lives. . . . Gangs offer kids a lot of things society doesn't offer, including status, a sense of self-worth and a place of acceptance" (Stover, 1986, p. 20).

"In a gang," says Dart (1992, p. 96), "troubled youths find the fellowship and sense of identity they lack; participation in gang activities leads to acceptance." This was also the conclusion of the National Coalition of State Juvenile Justice Advisory Groups (1992, p. 19): "Gangs seem to fill a desperate need on the part

TABLE   Profile of Character-Disturbed Child
8–2

1.	Lack of ability to give and receive affection
2.	Self-destructive behavior
3.	Cruelty to others
4.	Phoniness
5.	Severe problems with stealing, hoarding and gorging on food
6.	Speech pathology
7.	Marked control problems
8.	Lack of long-term friends
9.	Abnormalities in eye contact
10.	Parents appear angry and hostile
11.	Preoccupation with fire, blood or gore
12.	Superficial attractiveness and friendliness with strangers
13.	Various types of learning disorders
14.	A particular pathological type of lying—"primary process lying"

SOURCE: Foster Cline, M.D., *Understanding and Treating the Severely Disturbed Child*, 1979, p. 128. Evergreen Consultants, P.O. Box 2380, Evergreen, CO 80439. Reprinted with permission.

of many urban youths for stability, structure and a sense of belonging, and there is a major correlation between neighborhood poverty and social disorganization and gang activity."

■ Street gangs provide their members a feeling of belonging as well as protection from other youth. They may also provide financial power.

According to Hochhaus and Sousa (1988, p. 76): "Young people join gangs for the principle reasons of companionship, protection, and excitement, most likely through some form of peer pressure." Moriarty and Fleming (1990, p. 14) suggest that: "Gangs are likely to take shape wherever there's ethnic or racial change." Typically, when blacks or Hispanics move into a predominantly white neighborhood, the minority ethnic members will band together for support. This happens not only in the cities, but also in the suburbs, and not only within neighborhoods, but within schools. As noted by Spergel (1990, p. 171): "Youth gangs tend to develop during times of rapid social change and political instability. They function as a residual social institution when other institutions fail and provide a certain degree of order and solidarity for their members." Spergel also suggests:

> Race or ethnicity and social isolation interact with poverty and community disorganization to account for much of the gang problem. The gang is an important social institution for low-income male youths and young adults from newcomer and residual populations because it often serves social, cultural, and economic functions no longer adequately performed by the family, the school and the labor market.

To some members, the gang is also about money and power. Sgt. Jackson of the Los Angeles Police Department gang unit has said: "Their goal is money.

That's the most important thing in the mind of a gang member. He wants power, prestige, a chance to get out of the ghetto—and this all revolves around money. For him, that means selling drugs" (McGarvey, 1991, p. 27).

Jackson (1989, p. 315), in explaining why gangs are formed, describes what he calls: "The classic pioneering and as yet unsurpassed work on gangs"—*The Gang: A Study of 1,313 Gangs in Chicago,* by Frederic Thrasher in 1927. Thrasher's conclusion was that gangs were "a product of a breakdown or weakening of social controls, especially among newly arriving European immigrants who settled in Chicago's ganglands." Gangs created a social order where none existed. This can be a partial explanation for why so many Asian gangs are currently forming across the country.

In 1958 another researcher, Miller, studied lower-class gangs in Boston and concluded that "gangs are a natural outgrowth of a lower class culture in which the structure of social relations is composed on one's sex peer groups" (Jackson, 1989, p. 317). The typical family was female-dominated, lacking male role models. This void was filled by the gang.

A third explanation, according to Jackson (p. 318), is found in the work of the strain theorists, such as Cohen, who suggested:

> Working-class youth are unprepared for participation in middle class institutions. This leads to frustration and reaction formation, which, in turn, explains the genesis of the delinquent subculture, in which the values of middle class society are turned upside down. These values permit boys to gain status through non-utilitarian, malicious, negative behavior.

A fourth explanation for the existence of gangs is furnished by Matza's "control theory" of drift and bonding. Matza argues that youths drift into gangs because: "They exist in a state of suspension between childhood and adulthood, lack the rights and privileges of the latter, and seek out acceptance by their peers" (Jackson 1989, p. 318).

Yet another explanation focuses on the labeling theory previously discussed in Chapter 4. Youths who are simply "hanging out" together may be referred to as a gang often enough that they come to feel as if they *are* a gang.

Huff (1989, pp. 526–527) undertook a two-year study of youth gangs in Ohio (Cleveland and Columbus) and found that these gangs originated in three ways:

1. Breakdancing/"rappin" groups evolved into gangs as a result of inter-group conflict involving dancing, skating, and/or "rappin" competition.
2. Street corner groups similarly evolved into gangs as a result of conflicts with other "corner groups."
3. Street gang leaders already experienced in gang life moved to Ohio from Chicago or Los Angeles. These more sophisticated leaders were often charismatic figures who were able to quickly recruit a following from among local youth.

Huff also found that poverty and unemployment were equated with gang membership, noting that youth did not have "legitimate options" for buying stylish clothes or flashy cars and found the gang, crime, and selling drugs as an attractive option.

GANG RECRUITMENT

Transforming a youth into a gang member involves a slow assimilation. Once youths reach an age where they can prove themselves with peer leaders within the gang structure, they may perform some sort of rite of passage or ceremony called "jumping in." Or they may be "courted in," simply accepted into the gang without having to prove themselves in any particular way.

Often, gang members have minimal financial or worldly assets. Their most important possession becomes their reputation. A "hard look" or minor insult directed at a gang member by a rival gang member must be avenged. This attitude results in the blood baths often seen on urban streets.

OUTWARD TRAPPINGS OF THE GANG

Gangs establish **turf,** territorial boundaries, within which they operate and which they protect at all costs from invasion by rival gangs. Solidarity and neighborhood cohesiveness are intense. In fact, the greeting, "Where are you from?" is the challenge of the street (Los Angeles White Paper, 1992, p. 11). The inappropriate response may bring a severe beating or even death.

IDENTIFYING GANG MEMBERS

Law enforcement officers can deal more effectively with youths if they can identify those who are likely to be gang members.

■ Gang members may be identified by their names, symbols (clothing and tattoos) and communication styles, including graffiti and sign language.

Gang names vary from colorful and imaginative to straightforward. They commonly refer to localities, animals, birds, royalty and rebellion. As noted by the *Encyclopedia of Crime and Justice* (Kadish, 1983):

Localities can be streets (for example, the Tenth Streeters), neighborhoods (the Southsiders), housing projects (the Alazones Courts), and cities or towns (the Johnstown Gang). Popular animal names are the Tigers, the Panthers, the Cougars, the Leopards, the Cobras, the Eagles, and the Hawks. Royal titles include the Kings, the Emperors, the Lords, the Knights, the Barons, and the Dukes. Names denoting rebellion or lawlessness include the Rebels, the Outlaws, the Savages, and the Assassins. Gangs may be designated by the name of a leader or other important member such as "Joey and Them Kids" or "Garcia's Boys." A common combination is a local designation coupled with another category, for example, the West Side Majestic Warlords, the Third Street Rangers, and the Spring Hill Savages.

As noted by Wrobleski and Hess (1993, p. 460):

[G]ang symbols are also common. Clothing, in particular, can distinguish a particular gang. Perhaps best known is the typical attire of an outlaw motorcycle gang member: tattered Levis, scuffed boots, leather vests, and jackets with their own unique emblems. Sometimes "colors" are used to distinguish a gang, as dramatized in the film *Colors*. Gang members also use jerseys, T-shirts, and jackets with emblems.

Tattoos are also used by some gangs, particularly outlaw motorcycle gangs and Hispanic gangs. Black gang members seldom have tattoos.

GANG COMMUNICATION

Street gangs communicate primarily through their actions. Street gangs need and seek recognition, not only from their community, but also from rival gangs.

Verbal and nonverbal gang communication is ever present. Certainly the most observable gang communication is wall writings or **graffiti**.

Graffiti is an important part of the Hispanic gang tradition. It proclaims to the world the status of the gang and offers a challenge to rivals.

▮ Graffiti is commonly used to mark a street gang's turf.

Much valuable information relative to police work may be gained from gang graffiti. For instance one may be able to determine what gang is in control of a specific area by noting the frequency of the unchallenged graffiti. Throwing a *placa* on a wall corresponds to claiming a territory. Writing left unchanged

▮ *Wall writing or graffiti has been called the "newspaper of the street." It often marks a gang's "turf."*

reaffirms the gang's control. As one moves away from the center or core area of a gang's power and territory, more rival graffiti and cross-outs are observed.

The black and Hispanic styles of wall writings differ vastly. Black gang graffiti lacks the flair and attention to detail evidenced by Hispanic gang graffiti. Much of the black gang wall writing is loaded with profanity and expressions not found in the Hispanic graffiti.

Gang symbols in the form of graffiti usually appear throughout the turf and define boundaries. Such graffiti usually includes the gang name and the writer's name. It may also assert the gang's power by such words as *rifa,* meaning "to rule," or *P/V* meaning "Por Vida" (for life). In other words, the gang rules this neighborhood for life. The number 13 has traditionally meant that the writer used marijuana, but now it also can mean that the gang is from Southern California.

Slahor (1993, p. 55) describes another type of graffiti, called **tagging** which mimics gang graffiti, but often those doing the tagging are not members of gangs or involved in criminal activity (other than vandalism). As noted by Gross and Gross (1993, p. 258), tagging as a new form of graffiti has appeared in the last 25 years. They note: "The dominant visual impression of this phase includes words, though the graffiti only leaves a hint of words. . . . The words both reveal and conceal their identity. They reveal themselves to the insider or initiated but conceal themselves from the uninitiated." Gross and Gross identify two types of tagging: "[I]ndividual tagging or extended tagging called 'gang writing'." They note: "These two types of graffiti decorate the walls of modern civilization world-wide." They provide the tagging examples in Figure 8–2.

In some instances taggers band together into a **crew.** Sometimes the tagging becomes very serious and may even turn deadly. Ayres (1994, p. 4A) quotes a 17-year-old tagger: "I mean, like you tag this wall with spray real fast—sizzzzt! sizzzzt!—and nobody catches you and then another crew sees what you've done and tries to tag over you and you have to go after them—hey, like I say, it's a rush." Ayres notes that: "Many taggers now refer to themselves as 'tag bangers,' carrying guns, knives and clubs along with their marker pens and cans of spray

Youth in Brooklyn, New York, play with toy guns as a prelude to becoming gang members, when real guns will replace these toys.

Individual Tags

The following examples of individual tags were collected in 8 cities: Chicago, Billings, Fort Worth, San Marcos, San Antonio, El Paso, and Juarez, Mexico.

(1) Chicago, Illinois

Deciphering these tags, at best, would be a guess.

(2) Billings, Montana

Though rare in conservative small towns of the mid-northwestern United States, the example above demonstrates that they not only exist but in this case can be deciphered to reveal the word "slant."

(3) Denver, Colorado

From left to right the first three tags deciphered reveal the following letters/words: "MIR," "Vestige," and "Orion." The fourth's obscurity makes uninitiated deciphering impossible.

(4) Fort Worth, Texas

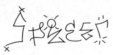

Deciphered the tag says, "Spicer."

(5) San Marcos, Texas

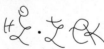

Deciphered the tag says, "hi-tek."

(6) San Antonio, Texas

The tags make uninitiated deciphering only guesswork.

■ FIGURE 8–2 Examples of Tagging

SOURCE: Daniel D. Gross and Timothy D. Gross, "Tagging: Changing Visual Patterns and the Rhetorical Implications of a New Form of Graffiti," *Et cetera*, Fall 1993, pp. 259–262. Reprinted from ETC: A Review of General Semantics, Fall 1993, with permission of the International Society for General Semantics.

(7) El Paso, Texas

Deciphered left to right the tags say, "the crow," "casper," and "the turtle."

(8) Juarez, Mexico

Deciphered the tags read,"sir eleven," and "eye."

Gang Writing

The three examples of gang writing were lifted from the walls of Fort Worth, San Antonio, and El Paso.

(1) Fort Worth, Texas

Deciphered the writing reads,"southside home girls."

(2) San Antonio, Texas

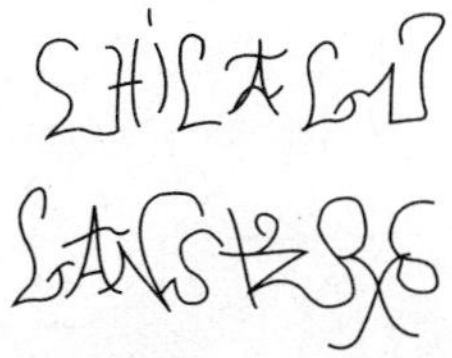

Deciphered the writing reads, "Chicago Gangsters."

(3) El Paso, Texas

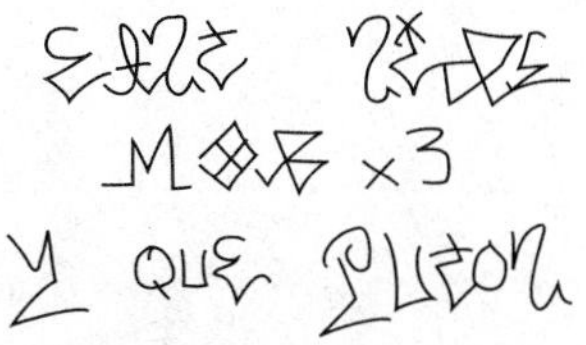

Deciphered the writing says: "Eastside Mob X3 Y Que Putos." (Translated: "Eastside mob 3rd generation" and in Spanish "and how tough.")

paint." What were once friendly neighborhood rivalries have turned into warfare over "tagger turf." The police in Los Angeles are looking for one tagger they believe is responsible for three murders.

In addition to marking territory, graffiti may show opposition for rival gangs by displaying a rival gang's symbols upside down, backwards or crossed out—a serious insult to the rival.

Another method of gang communication is that of flashing gang signs, or, hand signals. The purpose of these hand signals is to identify the user with a specific gang.

Hand signs communicate allegiance or opposition to another group. Most hand signs duplicate or modify signing used by the deaf and hearing impaired.

In addition to graffiti and hand signals, it is equally important for gang members to reinforce their sense of belonging by adopting a gang style of dress. There are two basic types of gang clothing. The first shows that the individual belongs to a gang without specifically identifying which one. Often certain color combinations are associated with specific gangs. The second type of gang clothing specifically identifies a gang. Such gang clothing may include jackets or sweatshirts with the gang name.

Representing also shows allegiance or opposition. Representing is a manner of dressing that uses an imaginary line drawn vertically through the body. Anything to the left of the line is representing left, anything to the right of the line is representing right, for example, a hat cocked to the right, right pant leg rolled up, and a cloth or bandana tied around the right arm.

Other important symbols may include certain hair styles, gold jewelry in gang symbols and certain cars. The following are symbols of the Disciples gang:

▮ Refer to themselves as "folk."

▮ Major insignia is the six-pointed star.

▮ *Hand signals are a common form of communication for gang members. Here four young girls flash their gang sign "LCB" for "Little Crip Bitches."*

- Dress to the right.
- Colors are black and blue.
- Earrings, if worn, are in the right ear.
- One glove may be worn on the right hand.
- One pocket, right side, is turned inside out, sometimes dyed one of the "colors."
- Right pant leg rolled up.
- Two fingernails on right hand painted gang colors.
- Hoods of sweatshirts dyed gang colors.
- Shoes or laces of right shoe of gang colors.
- Belt buckle worn loose on the right side.
- Bandana in gang colors worn on right side.

Gangs also use tattoos as a method of communication and identification. The traditional Hispanic gangs use tattoos extensively, and they are usually visible on arms, hands or shoulders. By contrast, black gang members are not enthusiastic about using tattoos to identify their members.

■ **Gang members communicate through graffiti, hand signals, clothing and tattoos.**

The following is a list of terms commonly used by gang members:*

- *A-K*—AK-47—assault rifle.
- *baller*—gang member who's making lots of money.
- *bent*—drunk.
- *cap*—a verbal comeback.
- *crab*—derogatory name for a Crip.
- *Cuz*—alternate name for a Crip, often used in greeting.
- *down*—to meet expectations.
- *five-O*—the police.
- *gangbanging*—doing things or hanging out with the gang.
- *gat*—gun.
- *hemmed up*—to be hassled or arrested by the authorities.
- *head up*—to fight one-on-one.
- *hoo ride*—drive-by-shooting.
- *hood*—short for neighborhood. Also called *turf*.
- *homeboy*—someone from the same neighborhood or gang. Also called a *homie*.
- *jacket*—reputation.
- *jet*—to leave.
- *jumped in*—being initiated into a gang. Sometimes entails getting beaten up as part of the initiation.
- *kickin' it*—hanging out with the gang.
- *peel*—kill.
- *rifa*—to rule.

---

*Many of these terms are from " 'Gangster' Rap Terminology," *Criminal Organizations*, 8 (1993) 2: 10.

∎ *set*—a neighborhood gang fitting within the Bloods or Crips.

∎ *smoke*—kill.

∎ *snaps*—money.

Regardless of the method of communication, gang messages are clear. Gang members are telling the world that their gangs or barrios are number one, the best. They also are expressing their commitment to turf and gang.

GANG SYMBOLS

Gangs have symbols or logos to identify themselves. Color is often significant. The following paragraphs describe the colors and symbols of a few gangs. Some typical markings of the Disciples, Vice Lords and Latin Kings, documented in Minneapolis, Minnesota, are shown in Figures 8–3 through 8–5.

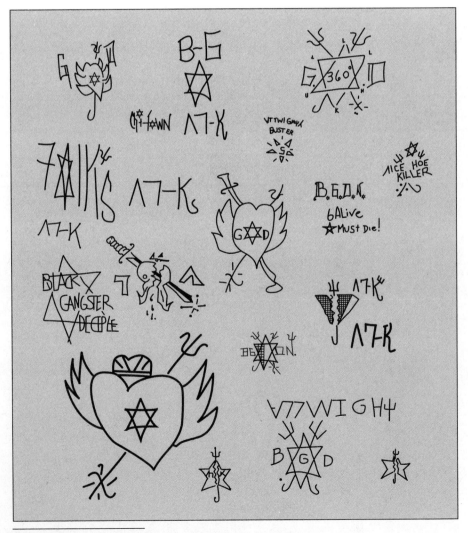

∎ **FIGURE 8–3 Black Gangster Disciples Symbols**

■ **FIGURE 8–4 Vice Lord Symbols**

■ **FIGURE 8–5 Latin Kings Symbols**

Black Gangster Disciples wear blue and black colors, represent to the right, and have as symbols a six-point star, flaming hearts and crossed pitchforks.

Vice Lords wear red and black colors, represent to the left and have as symbols a five-point star, a circle surrounded by fire, a half-crescent moon, a pyramid, top hat, cane, white gloves and martini glass.

The Latin Kings wear gold and black colors, represent to the left and have as a symbol a three- or five-point star.

Asian Gangs include the Hmong White Tigers, the Laotian Cobras and the Cambodian Night Creepers. These gangs usually wear no colors and show no representation. They are often deadly violent.

Native American Indian Gangs include the Death Warriors, the Naturals and the Club. They were formed primarily for neighborhood protection from other minority gangs.

Skinheads wear black boots and leather jackets and have as a symbol the swastika. Their heads are bald or very nearly bald.

TYPICAL GANG ACTIVITY

Traditions of solidarity and neighborhood cohesiveness run deep. Pride in one's neighborhood, however poor it may be, can be intense. Most gang members are unskilled and poorly educated.

■ Gang activity includes vandalism, arson, graffiti painting, stabbings and shootings, student extortion and teacher intimidation.

Gang activity, viewed from a juvenile justice perspective, is a study in violent crime. A perpetual cycle of violence by gang rivalries dates back many years. Gang members often do not know why they came to be rivals. One gang member stated, "I don't know why we fight them. We've fought 'em since my father's time."

Established law enforcement techniques work much better with black gang members than with Hispanics, since black gang members' personal freedom is often more important to them than their gangs. They may be more likely to deal or inform on their "homeboys" than Hispanic gang members are.

Often the activities of gangs are glamorized when, in fact, the members are just "hanging out" or acting like most teenagers do. As noted by Huff (1989, p. 530):

> Gang members actually spend most of their time engaging in exaggerated versions of typical adolescent behavior (rebelling against authority by skipping school, refusing to do homework, and disobeying parents; wearing clothing and listening to music that sets them apart from most adults; and having a primary allegiance to their peer group instead of their parents or other adults). They appear to "drift" into and out of illegal behavior. . . .
>
> [Illegal] activities committed by youth gangs during the course of this study [of Ohio gangs] include theft, auto theft, intimidation and assault in school and on the street, robbery, burglary, rape, group rape, drug use, drug sales, and even murder. . . . As one gang member said during his interview: "People may say there's no gangs 'cause they don't see no colors, but if they be robbin' people, shootin' people, and killin' people, they still a gang."

A gang's reputation is often enhanced by engaging in vicious, violent crimes. For example, as one individual said of the gangs in his community (McGarvey, 1991, p. 25): "You want to know about our gangs? Last week they killed a 21 year old. They cut off his head, put his body in a car and set fire to it. He was buried yesterday without his head."

INDICATORS OF GANG ACTIVITY

The telltale signs of gang activity will show up in a variety of ways.

■ Indicators of gang activity include graffiti, intimidation assaults, open sale of drugs, drive-by shootings and murders.

Gang affiliation might be verified in the following ways:

- Self-admission.
- Body tattoos of gang symbols.
- Jewelry or apparel associated with gangs.
- Written communications such as doodling on notebooks.
- Hand-signing.
- Vocabulary and use of monikers.
- Group photos including known gang members.
- Known gang associates.
- Reliable informants.

Other warning signs that an individual may be involved in a gang include abrupt changes in personality and behavior, newly acquired and unexplained money or, conversely, requests to borrow money, and "hanging around" behavior.

Clay and Aquila (1994, pp. 66) caution against overreacting to what appear to be the "trappings" of a gang. They cite a seminar on how to recognize gang graffiti and the facilitator's description of a new gang sign showing up in suburban school yards. A probation officer in attendance had the following discussion with the facilitator:

> "Is this [sign] usually painted in white on a brick wall?" The facilitator said that it usually was. The probation officer continued, "Is it usually on a wall where there are no windows?" The facilitator agreed again and asked whether the probation officer knew anything about this new gang. The officer didn't answer but continued his own line of questioning: "Is it usually about three feet off the ground, with white rectangles on either side of it on the ground?" At this point one of the other task force members chimed in with, "Yeah, I've seen that, too." Undaunted, the probation officer went on, "If you go about 20 yards away from the wall, I bet you will find a white stripe painted on the ground."
>
> All eyes were now riveted on the probation officer. "It's a strike zone!" he said. "It's used for wall ball. Kids throw a tennis ball against the wall, and it acts as your backstop."

Clay and Aquila conclude (p. 68): "When you set out to find signs of gang activity, an innocent drawing can become the symbol of some strange new gang."

GANGS' INFLUENCE ON THE SCHOOLS

Schools are a prime recruiting ground for gangs. They are also a market for illicit drugs and for extorting money from other students. Often gangs will stake out certain areas of a school as their turf. Stephens (1989, p. 16) cites the example of a Los Angeles high school where a gang had designated a certain public phone booth as its turf. When a nongang member student used the phone, the student was killed.

The Los Angeles White Paper (1992, p. 11) notes:

Gang activity on school campuses is evidenced by various symptoms. Acts of vandalism, arson and graffiti painting, although secretive in nature, are often considered gang involved. Stabbings and shootings between rival gangs take a toll of innocent students and teachers. Student extortion and teacher intimidation are also present. The presence of a sufficient number of gang members in a class effectively renders the teacher powerless to enforce discipline or to teach.

A key impediment in dealing with gang members is the inability to share information. The records of juveniles are often sealed. A presiding juvenile court judge in the Supreme Court of California, Orange County, issued a landmark order in 1989 to address this issue in that area:

Whereas, youth gangs clearly imperil the safety of both students and campuses, and;

Whereas, the Court has been informed that concerns about "confidentiality" have often hampered or prevented communication among educators, law enforcement, the District Attorney, and probation personnel; this lack of communication among the various professionals dealing with the same child impedes the solving and prosecution of crimes, as well as the evaluation and placement of juveniles who have committed crimes, depriving educators of information needed to insure safer schools.

Therefore it is ordered, that all school districts in Orange County, all police departments in Orange County, and the Orange County District Attorney may release information to each other regarding any minor when any person employed by such a department, office, or school district indicates that there is a reasonable belief that this minor is a gang member or at significant risk of becoming a gang member (Stephens, 1989, p. 17).

NARCOTICS AND GANGS

It is well known that most gang members abuse certain drugs such as alcohol, marijuana, phencyclidine (PCP) and cocaine. A recent phenomenon is the increasing number of gang members actually selling narcotics for monetary gain. As noted by Robbins (1988, p. 29A):

With the entrepreneurial savy of MBAs, the Bloods and Crips are making their way across the United States, and officials say there are few states they haven't reached. . . . Two California gangs, fanning out along the interstate highway system, are spreading a sophisticated pattern of violence and drug-dealing across the country. . . . [Minnesota Attorney General Hubert] Humphrey said the arrival of the Bloods and Crips gangs makes tougher laws necessary. "These drug gangs are the organized crime families of the 1990s," he said.

Authorities say members of the Crips and the Bloods have infiltrated cities from Alaska to Washington, D.C., selling cocaine and its derivative, crack.

According to the findings of the California State Task Force on Youth Gang Violence (1986), narcotics involvement has become a major factor in gang violence and gang recruitment. As Sgt. Jackson, Los Angeles Police Department, observes: "How can you tell a kid who's making $500 a week guarding a rock house that he really ought to be in school or that he ought to be getting up at 4 A.M. every day to ride his bicycle around the neighborhood to deliver the morning papers?"

Types of Drug-Involved Offenders

Chaiken and Johnson (1988) studied the types of adolescent drug-involved offenders and their typical drug use, problems and contact with the justice system. Their results are summarized in Table 8–3.

Chaiken and Johnson also studied the types of adolescent drug dealers (see Table 8–4). It appears from Chaiken and Johnson's studies that adolescents who sell drugs only occasionally and only in small amounts are most often involved in status type offenses, in contrast with those who sell drugs frequently in large amounts. The latter group of adolescents are often involved in violent crime. Among the adolescents who sell drugs frequently or in large amounts, three types have been identified: those who have less addiction and who have only moderate contact with the juvenile justice system; the "losers," who become addicted and have high contact with the criminal justice system; and the "winners," who usually can avoid becoming addicted and who also have minimal contact with the justice system.

TABLE 8–3   **Types of Drug-Involved Offenders**

▇

Type of Offender	Typical Drug Use	Typical Problems	Contact with Justice System
Occasional users	Light to moderate or single-substance, such as alcohol, marijuana, or combination use	Driving under influence; truancy; early sexual activity; smoking	None to little
Adolescents who sell small amounts of drugs	Moderate use of alcohol and multiple types of drugs	Same as adolescent occasional user; also, some poor school performance; some other minor illegal activity	Minimal juvenile justice contact
Adolescents who sell drugs frequently or in large amounts	Moderate to heavy use of multiple drugs, including cocaine	Many involved in range of illegal activities including violent crimes; depends on subtype (see Table 8–4)	Dependent on subtype (see Table 8–4)

SOURCE: Marcia R. Chaiken and Bruce D. Johnson, *Characteristics of Different Types of Drug-Involved Offenders* (Washington, D.C.: U.S. Department of Justice, National Institute of Justice, 1988).

TABLE   Types of Dealers Who Sell Drugs Frequently or in Large Amounts
8–4

Type of Dealer	Typical Drug Use	Typical Problems	Contact with Justice System
Lesser predatory	Moderate to heavy drug user; some addiction; heroin and cocaine use	Assaults; range of property crimes; poor school performance	Low to moderate contact with juvenile or adult justice system
Drug-involved violent predatory offenders— the "losers"	Heavy use of multiple drugs; often addiction to heroin or cocaine	Commit many crimes in periods of heaviest drug use including robberies; high rates of school dropout; problems likely to continue as adults	High contact with both juvenile and adult criminal justice system
The "winners"	Frequent use of multiple drugs; less frequent addiction to heroin and cocaine	Commit many crimes; major source of income from criminal activity; take midlevel role in drug distribution to both adolescents and adults	Minimal; low incarceration record

SOURCE: Marcia R. Chaiken and Bruce D. Johnson, Characteristics of Different Types of Drug-Involved Offenders (Washington, D.C.: U.S. Department of Justice, National Institute of Justice, 1988).

GANG MYTHS

This chapter has contained many generalizations about gangs and gang members from numerous sources. A fitting conclusion is to consider the following nine myths about gangs by Lorne Kramer, Chief of Police, Colorado Springs, Colorado.*

■ Myth 1–*The majority of street gang members are juveniles.* Juveniles, those who are 18 years or younger, actually compose a minority of gang membership. In Los Angeles County, juveniles represent only about 20 percent of gang members. Across the nation, the tenure of gang membership is increasing from as early as 9 to 10 years up to more than 40 years. Money, drugs, lax juvenile laws each are key factors in this transition to attract kids to gangs at younger ages.

■ Myth 2–*The majority of gang-related crimes involve gangs vs. gangs.* The reverse actually is true. In terms of gang-related homicides, more than half the time, innocent victims with no gang affiliation are killed or assaulted.

■ Myth 3–*All street gangs are turf-oriented.* Some gangs may not claim any specific turf, while other gangs may operate in multiple locations or even in very

*Courtesy of Lorne Kramer, Chief of Police, Colorado Springs, Colorado.

unsuspecting small cities. One Asian gang that operated crime rings from Florida to California had its headquarters in a small Pennsylvania town of less than 4,500 residents.

▌ Myth 4–*Females are not allowed to join gangs.* Females are joining gangs in record numbers and often are extremely violent. In times past, females were thought of simply as mules, transporters of weapons or drugs, or as innocent bystanders. Females now make up about 5 percent of gang members and this is increasing.

▌ Myth 5–*Gang weapons usually consist of chains, knives and tire irons.* Perhaps brass knuckles, knives and chains were the key weapons in the gangs of yesteryear, but today Uzis, AK–47's and semi-automatic firepower are the weapons of choice.

▌ Myth 6–*All gangs have one leader and are tightly structured.* Most gangs are loosely-knit groups and likely will have several leaders. If one member is killed, other potential gang leaders seem to be waiting in the wings.

▌ Myth 7–*Graffiti is merely an art form.* Graffiti is much more than an art form. It is a message that proclaims the presence of the gang and offers a challenge to rivals. Graffiti serves as a form of intimidation and control, an instrument of advertising.

▌ Myth 8–*One way to cure gang membership is by locking the gang member away.* Incarceration and rehabilitation of hard-core gang members has not proven effective. Changing criminal behavior patterns is difficult. Prisons often serve as command centers and institutions of higher learning for ongoing gang-related crime. Often prisoners are forced to take sides with one group or another simply for protection.

▌ Myth 9–*Gangs are a law enforcement problem.* Gangs are a problem for everyone. Communities need to develop systemwide programs to effectively address the gang problem in their areas.

Not merely a school problem either, gangs are a community problem and a national challenge. Responding to gangs requires a systematic, comprehensive and collaborative approach that incorporates prevention, intervention and suppression strategies. While each strategy has a specific vision and pressing mandate, the greatest hope is on the side of prevention, for only by keeping children from joining gangs in the first place will we be able to halt the rising tide of terror and violence that gangs represent.

SUMMARY

A street gang is a group of individuals who meet over time, have identifiable leadership, claim control over a specific territory in the community and engage in criminal behavior. Criminal behavior is what separates a gang from a club such as the Boy Scouts. The youth gang, for criminal justice policy purposes, is a subset of the street gang.

Street gangs are no longer confined to the large cities; they can be found throughout the country. They acquire their power in the community through their violent behavior. Gangs may result from cultural discord, ego fulfillment, racism, socioeconomic factors and family influences.

Contemporary gangs may be classified as scavenger, territorial or corporate. They may also be classified as hedonistic, instrumental or predatory. And they may be classified as traditional or nontraditional. The most common gangs are Hispanic, black and Asian. Two well-known rival black street gangs are the Crips and the Bloods.

Five characteristics that distinguish youth gangs are leadership, organization, associational patterns, domain identification and illegal activity. Most gangs contain leaders, hard-core members, regular members and fringe members or wannabes. Street gangs provide their members a feeling of belonging as well as protection from other youth. They may also provide financial power.

Gang members may be identified by their names, symbols (clothing and tattoos) and communication styles, including graffiti and sign language. Graffiti is commonly used to mark a street gang's "turf." Gang members communicate through graffiti, hand signals, clothing and tattoos. Gang activities involve vandalism, arson, graffiti painting, stabbings and shootings, student extortion and teacher intimidation.

Indicators of gang activity include graffiti, intimidation assaults, open sale of drugs, drive-by shootings and murders.

■ Discussion Questions

1. Are there gangs in your community? If so, do they cause problems for the police?
2. Have you seen any movies or TV programs about gangs? How are gang activities depicted?
3. What do you think are the main reasons individuals join gangs?
4. How does a youth gang differ from a group such as a Boy Scout troop or a school club?
5. How does a youth gang member differ from other juvenile delinquents?
6. Should convicted youth gang members be treated like other juvenile delinquents, including status offenders?
7. What factors might influence you to become a gang member? To not become a gang member?
8. Do you believe the juvenile justice system should support gang summits that claim to be working toward peaceful, lawful ways to improve the situation of gang members?
9. How do gangs of the 1990s differ from those of the 1960s and 1970s?
10. Do you think the gang problem will increase or decrease during the 1990s?

■ References

Ayres, B. Drummand, Jr. "The Addictive Art of Graffiti Tagging." *New York Times,* as reported in (Minneapolis/St. Paul) *Star Tribune,* 16 March 1994, p. 4A.

Bell. *Down These Mean Streets: Violence By and Against America's Children.* Hearings before U.S. House of Representatives, Committee on Children, Youth, and Families. 101st Congress, 1st sess., 16 May 1987, p. 79.

Burke, Tod W. "Home Invaders: Gangs of the Future." *Police Chief,* November 1990, pp. 23–25.

California Council on Criminal Justice, State Task Force on Youth Gang Violence. *Final Report.* January 1986.

Chaiken, Marcia R., and Bruce D. Johnson. *Characteristics of Different Types of Drug-Involved Offenders.* Washington, D.C.: U.S. Department of Justice, National Institute of Justice, Office of Communication and Research Utilization, 1988. NCH 108560.

Clay, Douglas A., and Frank D. Aquila. "Gangs and America's Schools." *Phi Delta Kappan,* September 1994, pp. 65–68.

Dart, Robert W. "Chicago's 'Flying Squad' Tackles Street Gangs." *Police Chief,* October 1992, pp. 96–104.

Davis, James R. *Street Gangs.* Dubuque, Iowa: Kendall/Hunt Publishing, 1982.

Gates, Daryl F., and Robert K. Jackson. "Gang Violence in L.A." *Police Chief,* November 1990, pp. 20–22.

"Getting a Grip on Slippery Gang Problems." *Law Enforcement News,* 31 December 1993, p. 13.

Gross, Daniel D., and Timothy D. Gross. "Tagging: Changing Visual Patterns and the Rhetorical Implications of a New Form of Graffiti." *Et cetera,* Fall 1993, pp. 251–264.

Harlan, Alan. "Battling Organized Asian Crime Gangs." *Law and Order,* February 1993, pp. 51–54.

Harris, Sidney J. "Gangs Make Martyrs of Losers." In *Understanding Street Gangs,* edited by Robert K. Jackson and Wesley D. McBride. Sacramento, Calif.: Custom Publishing, 1985.

Hochhaus, Craig, and Frank Sousa. "Why Children Belong to Gangs: A Comparison of Expectations and Reality." *High School Journal,* December/January 1988, pp. 74–77.

Huff, C. Ronald. "Youth Gangs and Public Policy." *Crime & Delinquency,* 35 (October 1989) 4: 524–537.

Ima, Kenji. *A Handbook for Professionals Working with Southeast Asian Delinquent and At-Risk Youth.* San Diego, Calif.: Southeast Asian Youth Diversion Project, June 1992.

International Association of Chiefs of Police. "Violent Crime in America: Recommendations of the IACP Summit." *Police Chief,* June 1993, pp. 59–60.

Jackson, Patrick. "Theories and Findings About Youth Gangs." *Criminal Justice Abstracts,* June 1989, pp. 313–329.

Jackson, Robert K., and Wesley D. McBride. *Understanding Street Gangs.* Sacramento, Calif.: Custom Publishing, 1985.

Kadish, Sanford H., ed. *Encyclopedia of Crime and Justice,* New York: Free Press, 1983.

Los Angeles County Sheriff's Department, Operation Safe Streets Gang Unit. *Street Gangs of Los Angeles County: A White Paper.* Revised 1 February 1992.

McGarvey, Robert. "Gangland: L.A. Super Gangs Target America." *American Legion Magazine,* February 1991, pp. 25–27, 60–61.

Metropolitan Court Judges Committee Report. Drugs—*The American Family in Crisis: A Judicial Response: 39 Recommendations.* 4 August 1988, p. 48.

Miller, Walter B. "Youth Gangs and Groups." In *Encyclopedia of Crime and Justice.* vol. 4, edited by Sanford H. Kadish. New York: Free Press, 1983, pp. 1671–1679.

Miller, Walter B. "Why the United States Has Failed to Solve its Youth Gang Problem." In *Gangs in America,* edited by C. Ronald Huff. Newbury Park, Calif.: Sage Publications, 1991, pp. 263–287.

Moriarty, Anthony, and Thomas W. Fleming. "Mean Suburban Streets: Youth Gangs Aren't Just a Big-City Problem Anymore." *The American School Board Journal,* July 1990, pp. 13–16.

National Coalition of State Juvenile Justice Advisory Groups. *Myths and Realities: Meeting the Challenge of Serious, Violent, and Chronic Juvenile Offenders, 1992 Annual Report.* Washington, D.C.: 1993.

National Institute of Justice. *Research and Evaluation Plan, 1992.* April 1992.

National School Safety Center. *Gangs in Schools: Breaking Up Is Hard to Do.* Malibu, Calif.: Pepperdine University Press, 1988.

Owens, Robert P., and Donna K. Wells. "One City's Response to Gangs." *Police Chief,* February 1993, pp. 25–27.

Robbins, William. "California Gangs Staking Claims Across the U.S." (Minneapolis/St. Paul) *Star Tribune,* 4 December 1988, p. 29A.

Ross, Martha. "Woman Warriors." *The Times/Bleeding Colors,* Special Edition, 26 September 1993, pp. 8–9.

Rushing, Rocky, ed. *The Times/Bleeding Colors.* Special Edition, 26 September 1993, pp. 12–13.

Saccente, D. D. "RAP to Street Gang Activity." *Police Chief,* February 1993, pp. 28–31.

Shakur, Sanyika. *Monster: The Autobiography of an L.A. Gang Member.* New York: Penguin Books, 1993.

Slahor, Stephenie. "Nipping in the Bud: The Task Force Approach to Gangs." *Law and Order,* May 1993, p. 55.

"Slain Boy, 11, Is Buried, a Sad Symbol for Nation." *New York Times,* reported in the (Minneapolis/St. Paul) *Star Tribune,* 8 September 1994, pp. 7A, 10A.

Spergel, Irving A. "Youth Gangs: Continuity and Change." *Crime and Justice,* 12 (1990): 171–275.

Spergel, Irving A.; Ronald L. Chance; and G. David Curry. "National Youth Gang Suppression and Intervention Program." OJJDP, Juvenile Justice Bulletin, June 1990.

Stephens, Ronald D. "Gangs, Guns and Drugs." *School Safety,* Fall 1989, pp. 16–17.

Stover, Del. "A New Breed of Youth Gang Is on the Prowl and a Bigger Threat Than Ever." *American School Board Journal,* August 1986, pp. 19–24.

Taylor, Carl S. "Gang Imperialism." In *Gangs in America,* edited by C. Ronald Huff. Newbury Park, Calif.: Sage Publications, 1991, pp. 103–115.

Trethewy, Steve. "Biker Gang Update." *Law and Order,* September 1993, pp. 95–98.

Wrobleski, Henry M., and Kären M. Hess. *Introduction to Law Enforcement and Criminal Justice,* 4th ed. St. Paul, Minn.: West Publishing, 1993.

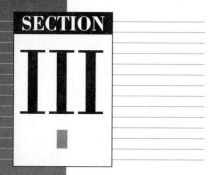

The Contemporary Juvenile Justice System

It should be clear that juvenile justice is not to reform the child but to form him.

Judge Emeritus Lindsay Arthur, Juvenile Court, Hennepin County, Minnesota

In the first section of this text you were introduced to how the juvenile justice system evolved and became distinct from the adult system. The juvenile system has retained, however, the three basic components of the adult system: law enforcement or the police, courts and corrections. The process usually begins with the police, who may turn the youth over to the juvenile court, who in turn may turn the youth over to the correctional component of the system. At any point in this process, youths may be diverted—one of the goals of the system. Figure III–1 illustrates not only the more complex flow of the system but also how it correlates to the adult system.

According to Crowe (1991, p. 36): "The system is designed intentionally to let juvenile offenders 'drop through the cracks'. " He suggests that this is probably all right because children naturally get into trouble and most deserve a "second chance." This results in what is often called the **funnel effect**; that is, at each point in the system fewer and fewer youths pass through.

Crowe suggests that since the police arrest only 100 out of every 1,000, or only 10 percent of the youths with whom they come into contact, the police are really more a part of the community than of the system. The system does appear to work for most juveniles, but where it breaks down is its ineffectiveness with the serious juvenile offender, as illustrated in Figure III–2.

Says Crowe (pp. 36–37):

The "funnel fallacy" teaches us a number of crucial lessons:

- **First**—the conventional conception of the role of the schools and police is not accurate.
- **Second**—that schools and police are fundamental to the community control of delinquency.

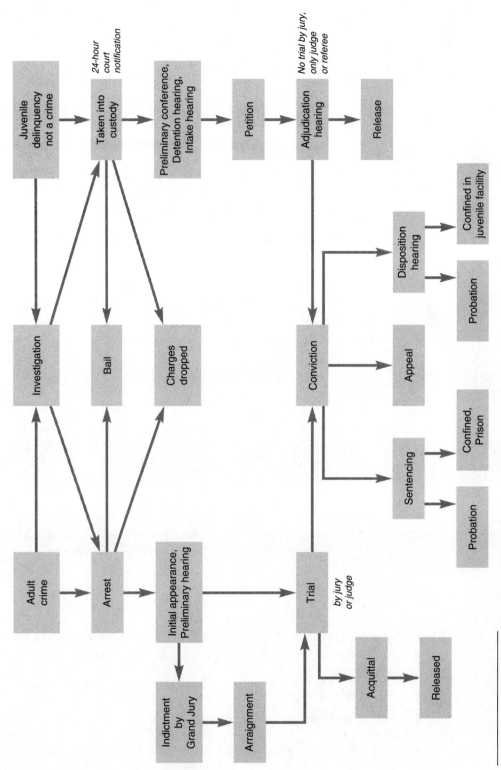

■ FIGURE III–1 Adult and Juvenile Justice Systems Flow

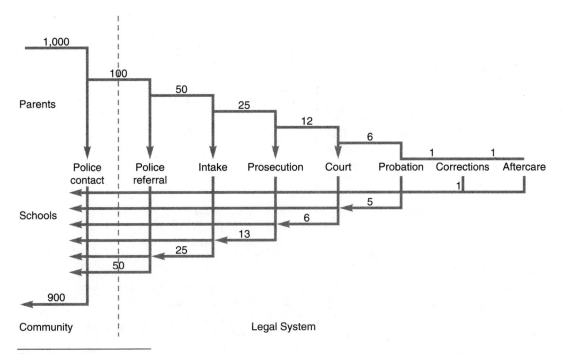

■ FIGURE III–2 The Funnel Fallacy—Processing and Dropout Rates of the Juvenile Justice System

Police really are primary participants in the community, instead of the juvenile justice system, since 90% of their contacts do not result in arrest.

SOURCE: Timothy D. Crowe, *Habitual Juvenile Offenders: Guidelines for Citizen Action and Public Responses,* Serious Habitual Offender Comprehensive Action Program (SHOCAP) (Washington, D.C.: Office of Juvenile Justice and Delinquency Prevention, October 1991), p. 36.

■ **Third**—school and police officials have more contact with our children than does anyone else, except **parents.**

■ **Fourth**—the juvenile justice system is irrelevant to the desire for the prevention and diversion of delinquency, because the schools and the police are not a significant part of the system. They are at the opening of the "funnel" and have been mistakenly excluded from the concept of the community's responsibility for controlling delinquency.

■ **Fifth**—parents, school officials, and police are the primary actors in the basic function of "parenting" in contemporary society.

■ **Sixth**—the contact and information that **could** be shared between parents, schools, and police are the **key** to the effective functioning of our juvenile justice system. They are the filtering point to the end of the "funnel" that feeds the legal system that has only one purpose—the effective control of individuals whom the community is unable to **control**! (bold type in original)

The OJJDP, the U.S. Department of Justice and the Federal Law Enforcement Training Center jointly sponsored a nationwide training program for juvenile officers. The 1,500 officers in attendance heard reports on several research projects and informal surveys related to juvenile justice. These research projects and informal surveys suggest the following breakdown of what actually happens in the juvenile justice system (Crowe, 1991, pp. 34–35):

- ▮ **Police contact**—for every 1,000 young persons in contact with police, 10 percent or **100** are arrested.
- ▮ **Police referral**—police commonly drop charges or reprimand and release about 50 percent of all juveniles who are arrested. Therefore, only **50** cases are filed with court intake.
- ▮ **Intake screening and referral**—of the 50 cases formally presented to the court intake, which is usually a detention counselor or state probation official, only about 50 percent or **25** are sent forward. The remainder are counseled and released or put on informal supervision. Few are actually placed in pretrial detention.
- ▮ **Prosecution screening**—unless a young offender has been arrested before or the immediate offense is serious, less than 50 percent of the cases, or **12** juveniles, will be referred to the court. The rest have charges dropped or are placed on deferred prosecution while attending treatment programs, as a condition of dropping charges.
- ▮ **Court trials**—less than 50 percent of cases presented result in the adjudication, or determination, of delinquent status. This means that only **6** accused delinquents will be found guilty and sentenced.
- ▮ **Court disposition**—most (5 out of 6) sentences will be for probation with some sort of supervision, which may include counseling or treatment. **One** juvenile will be incarcerated in a state reform school or a residential treatment program.
- ▮ **Probation**—the **5** juveniles placed on probation will generally see the probation counselor weekly or monthly and follow a set of rules that restrict the delinquent from certain locations, associations, or activities.
- ▮ **State corrections**—the **1** juvenile from the original 1,000 contacted by the police will serve a sentence in a state program.
- ▮ **After-care**—the **1** juvenile sentenced to a state program will probably be released eventually on parole, which is euphemistically referred to as after-care. (bold type in original)

This section looks at the contemporary juvenile justice system, beginning with the role of the police (Chapter 9). This is followed by the role of the juvenile court (Chapter 10) and juvenile corrections (Chapter 11). The section concludes with a discussion of the critical role of the broader community as part of the juvenile justice system (Chapter 12).

The section includes many references to government agencies involved directly and indirectly with juveniles. Most are under the U.S. Department of Justice through its Office of Justice Programs. The Office of Justice Programs coordinates the activities of these program offices and bureaus: the Bureau of Justice Statistics (BJS), the National Institute of Justice (NIJ), the Bureau of Justice Assistance (BJA), the Office of Juvenile Justice and Delinquency Prevention (OJJDP) and the Office for Victims of Crime (OVC). (See Figure III–3.) These offices often conduct joint efforts and programs.

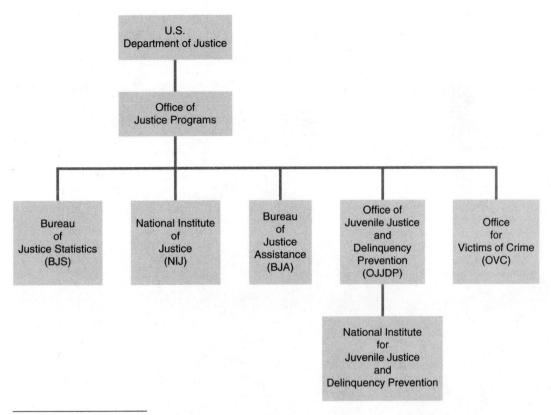

■ FIGURE III–3 Agencies of the U.S. Department of Justice Coordinated by the Office of Justice Programs

The Role of Law Enforcement

Children spend up to 25 percent of their waking hours in school. It has been estimated that 18 percent of their time is spent with their peers— other children. Another 18 percent of their waking hours may be spent in front of the television. Police are the only other significant parental type, albeit surrogate, in contact with our children.

Timothy D. Crowe

▌ *Do You Know?*

What factors affect how police officers resolve juvenile delinquency problems?
What street justice is?
Whether the police have discretionary power when dealing with juveniles?
What action police usually take when confronting juveniles?
What the five primary objectives of juvenile law enforcement are?
What the fundamental nature of the juvenile justice system is?
What "window of opportunity" exists with youth who are in detention?
What primary responsibility officers assigned a child abuse or neglect case have?
What the majority of police dispositions involve?
What predelinquent indicator often goes unnoticed?
What seems to be the most visible indicator of a future victim or offender?
How prevention methods have changed over the years and why?
What professionals are very important in delinquency prevention programs?
What the focus of Project DARE is? The TOP program?
What greatly influences youths' attitudes towards law and law enforcement?

▌ *Can You Define the Following Key Terms?*

detention, police-school liaison program, SHOCAP, station adjustment, street justice, window of opportunity

INTRODUCTION

J uvenile justice is basically concerned with three distinct types of youth: those who are victims, those who commit minor (status) offenses and those who commit serious crimes (delinquents). The police are charged with protecting youth, both victims and offenders, and with dealing fairly with them. Questions of what is in the best interest of the youth must be balanced with what is best for the community. Also the crime-fighting philosophy must be balanced with the service ideal.

This chapter looks at the various dispositions police officers can make when dealing with youth, be they victims or offenders. It discusses police discretion and whether the system is too lenient. The law enforcement portion of the juvenile justice system is examined from the time of taking into custody (arrest), to detention, to intake and, finally, to prosecution.

The issue of overrepresentation of minorities being processed by the system is discussed, followed by a more in-depth look at how law enforcement interacts with the various types of children and juveniles within its jurisdiction: neglected and abused children, status offenders, serious habitual offenders and gang members.

Next, prevention efforts undertaken by law enforcement are briefly reviewed, including such well-known programs as the DARE program. The chapter ends with a look at how law enforcement is changing and the challenges this is presenting.

POLICE DISPOSITIONS

Police dispositions involve all contacts police make concerning children's health, safety and welfare. The dispositions range from taking no action to referring the children to social service agencies or to the justice court. Police also deal with a wide range of youths, from those who need protection from abuse or neglect to those who have committed status offenses to those who have committed violent criminal acts. With status offenses the police have numerous alternatives that are guided by the community, the local system and individual officer discretion. The dispositions police make in violent criminal behavior are a different matter, however. The report, investigation and disposition in these cases follow a direct criminal justice scheme, and the police have limited alternatives and limited discretion.

■ In the disposition of matters related to children, how police resolve
matters depends on the officers' discretion and the specific incident.

Whether the police actually arrest a juvenile usually depends on several
factors, the most important being the seriousness of the offense. Other factors
affecting the decision include the following (Trojanowicz, 1978, p. 419):

> [T]he appraised character of the youth, which in turn is based on such facts as his
> prior police record, age, associations, attitude, family situation, the conduct of his
> parents, and the attitude of other community institutions such as his school. The
> external community may exert pressure on the police department which may
> affect the disposition of any case. Here attitudes of the press and the public, the
> status of the complainant or victim, the status of the offender, and the conditions
> which prevail in the available referral agencies (the length of the waiting list, the
> willingness of the social agencies to accept police referrals) are all of consequence.
> Internal police department pressure such as attitudes of co-workers and supervi-
> sors and the personal experience of the officer may also play an important part in
> determining the outcome of any officially detected delinquent offense. These
> factors also indirectly determine the officially recorded police and court delin-
> quency rates.

For example, conflict may occur between an officer's obsession for order and
a group of young individuals wanting to "hang around." How police respond to
such hanging around is influenced by the officer's attitude and the standards of
the neighborhood or community, rather than rules of the state. Each neighborhood or community and the officer's own feelings dictate how the police
perform in such matters.

Some areas may handle a delinquent act very differently from other areas.
For example, police investigating an auto theft in the suburbs and finding a
youth responsible will often simply send the youth home for parental discipline.
The youth will receive a notice of when to appear in court. In contrast, urban
juveniles—especially minority youths—who are caught stealing an automobile
are often detained in a locked facility. Sometimes, however, urban youths are at
an advantage. What rural law enforcement officers may perceive as criminal
behavior is often viewed as a prank by that officer's urban counterpart. Clearly,
justice for juveniles is not a neatly structured, impartial decision-making
process by which the rule of law always prevails and each individual is treated
fairly and impartially.

Sometimes police may "roust" and "hassle" youths who engage in undesirable
social conduct, but they probably will not report the incident; in this case,
street justice is the police disposition.

■ Street justice occurs when police decide to deal with a status offense in
their own way—usually by ignoring it.

POLICE DISCRETION AND THE INITIAL CONTACT

Between 80 and 90 percent of children under 18 commit some offense for which they could be arrested, yet only about 3 percent of them ever are ("Facts," 1988, p. 159). This is in large part due to the fact that they did not get caught. Further, those who do get caught have usually engaged in some minor status offense that can be better handled by counseling and releasing in many instances. Although the "counsel and dismiss" alternative is often criticized as being "soft" on juveniles, this approach is often all that is needed to turn a youth around.

In examining the question, "Is the juvenile justice system lenient?" Harris (1986, p. 105) notes: "[T]he question of leniency is irrelevant to the overwhelming preponderance of juvenile misconduct, which is not serious." Harris (1986, p. 107) also suggests:

> A view that law enforcement agencies react to the juvenile crime problem with leniency is rooted in two critical assumptions—namely, that police encounters with juveniles typically concern serious criminal behaviors and, further, that police frequently divert youths from traditional justice system processing. Three themes that contradict these conventional assumptions, but which emerge consistently from relevant literature are: one, that most juvenile behavior encountered by police officers is of a minor or insignificant nature; two, that serious criminal behaviors are typically referred for formal justice system process; and three, that extra-legal criteria and discretion are most likely to be introduced in cases involving behavior that is only a minor or even an ambiguous legal nature.

The Task Force on Juvenile Delinquency and Youth Crime, part of the President's Commission on Law Enforcement and Administration of Justice, highlighted several years ago the wide range of police discretion and the lack of guidelines for them to use (1967, p. 14):

> the range of police dispositions is considerable, and the criteria for selection of a disposition are seldom set forth, explicitly, ordered in priority, or regularly reviewed for administrative purposes. Inservice training designed to assist police in exercising their discretionary functions is unusual.

▪ Police officers have considerable discretionary power when dealing with juveniles.

Law enforcement officers who deal with children have a range of alternatives to take:

- ▪ Release the child, with or without a warning, but without making an official record or taking further action.
- ▪ Release the child, but write up a brief contact or field report to juvenile authorities, describing the contact.
- ▪ Release the child, but file a more formal report referring the matter to a juvenile bureau or an intake unit, for possible action.
- ▪ Turn the youth over to juvenile authorities immediately.
- ▪ Refer the case directly to the court, through the district or county attorney.

█ *Positive face-to-face contacts between police officers and youth are of tremendous importance.*

In some instances, youths engaging in delinquent acts are simply counseled. In other instances they are returned to their families, who are expected to deal with their deviant behavior. Sometimes they are referred to social services agencies for help. And sometimes they are charged and processed by the juvenile justice system.

█ The most common procedure is to release the child, with or without a warning, but without making an official record or taking further action.

As noted by Pindur and Wells (1988, p. 194): "For the vast majority of juveniles, the law enforcement agency is the initial point of contact with the system."

Figure 9–1 illustrates the flow of the juvenile justice system. Parents, schools and the police are the main sources of referral of youth into the juvenile justice system. Of these three sources, the police are, by far, the most common source of referrals.

Many police departments have a standard form for their juvenile reports. In the sample form (Figure 9–2) notice the youth may be arrested, released, turned over to another agency or referred to juvenile court.

In a few jurisdictions, if the child is not released without official record, he or she is automatically turned over to the juvenile authorities who make all further decisions in the matter. If the child is referred to court, another decision is whether police personnel should release or detain the child.

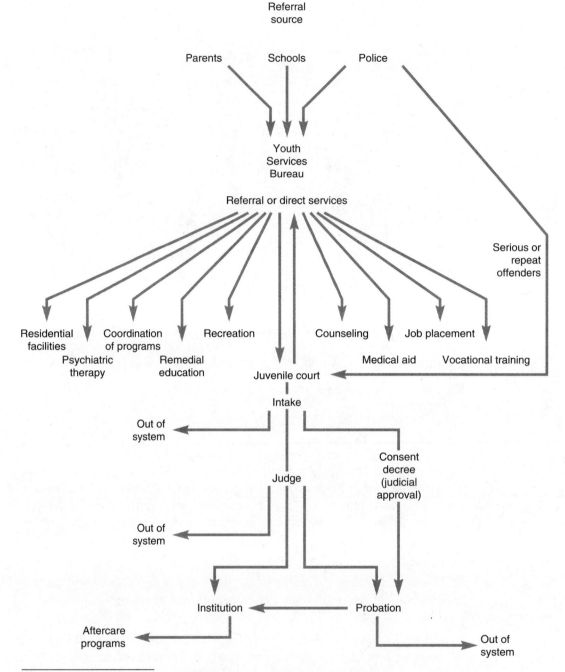

■ FIGURE 9–1 The Flow of the Juvenile Justice System

SOURCE: National Advisory Commission on Criminal Justice Standards and Goals, *Report of the Task Force on Juvenile Justice and Delinquency Prevention* (Washington, D.C.: Law Enforcement Assistance Administration, 1976), p. 9.

PERSON CHARGED 1. ARRESTED, HELD FOR PROSECUTION 2. SUMMONED/NOTIFIED OR CITED	SS:STATE STATUTE OR·ORDINANCE TT·FEDERAL TITLE OT·OTHER	SUPP

COMPLAINT NUMBER	POLICE DEPARTMENT JUVENILE REPORT	OFFENSE, INCIDENT, CHARGE		

DATE OCCURRED	TIME OCCURRED	LOCATION OF OCCURRENCE	

DATE RECEIVED	TIME RECEIVED	OFFICER(S)	APPROVED BY

NAME OF BUSINESS	ADDRESS	PHONE

VICTIM/COMPLAINANT (LAST) (FIRST) (MIDDLE)	HOME ADDRESS	PHONE

DEFENDANT (LAST, FIRST, MIDDLE)	STREET ADDRESS, CITY, STATE, ZIP	CTY.	PHONE

PSN	D.O.B.	AGE	HEIGHT	WEIGHT	EYES	HAIR	COMPLEXION	SEX	RACE	D.L. NO.

MOTHER'S NAME (LAST, FIRST, MIDDLE)	STREET ADDRESS, CITY, STATE, ZIP	BUSINESS PHONE	HOME PHONE

FATHER'S NAME (LAST, FIRST, MIDDLE)	STREET ADDRESS, CITY, STATE, ZIP	BUSINESS PHONE	HOME PHONE

CHILD LIVES WITH:
☐ Parents   ☐ Mother   ☐ Father   ☐ Other, who?

SCHOOL NAME	GRADE

DISPOSITION OF PROPERTY	DATE/TIME PARENTS NOTIFIED	NO. OF PRIOR CONTACTS	LIQUOR INVOLVED ☐ Yes ☐ No

MIRANDA GIVEN ☐ Yes ☐ No	DOES JUV. ADMIT OFFENSE ☐ Yes ☐ No	ATTITUDE:	RELEASE INFO. DATE: TIME:	BY WHOM: TO WHOM:

IF VEHICLE INVOLVED, MAKE, YEAR, MODEL	COLOR	LICENSE	STATE

REGISTERED OWNER, OR DRIVER, IF SAME AS DEF: LEAVE EMPTY	ADDRESS	CITY	STATE

ACCOMPLICES: (LAST) (FIRST) (MIDDLE)	2. (LAST) (FIRST) (MIDDLE)	3. (LAST) (FIRST) (MIDDLE)

ISN	UOC	STATUTE CHARGED └─┴─┘	ARREST DISPOSITION	CODE
ISN	UOC	STATUTE CHARGED └─┴─┘	ARREST DISPOSITION	CODE
ISN	UOC	STATUTE CHARGED └─┴─┘	ARREST DISPOSITION	CODE

5. RELEASED, NO FORMAL CHARGE D. JUVENILE HANDLED W/I DEPT. (R & R)	6. TURNED OVER TO OTHER AGENCY, WHO?	8. REFERRED TO JUVENILE COURT

■ **FIGURE 9–2 Police Juvenile Report Form**

OBJECTIVES IN HANDLING JUVENILES

Police officers usually follow a set of objectives in handling juveniles. In most jurisdictions, the law specifies that the first objective is to protect the juvenile. Second, officers are to investigate. Third, they are to determine the causes of the victimization or delinquency. These causes are usually exposed in a dialogue between the youth and authority. Fourth, every effort is made to prevent further victimization or delinquency. And fifth, the officers seek a proper disposition of the case.

■ The objectives of police officers handling juvenile cases are (1) to protect the juvenile, (2) to investigate, (3) to determine the causes of the victimization or delinquency, (4) to prevent further victimization or delinquency and (5) to properly dispose of the case.

Officers try to dispose of juvenile cases in a way that considers both the best interests of the juvenile and of the community. The intake process of the juvenile justice system requires the development of employee screening practices, certification standards and caseload guidelines. Caseworkers are or should be certified to practice on the basis of education, training and experience.

TAKEN INTO CUSTODY

In their initial contact with juveniles, the police are indirectly guided by the language of the Juvenile Court Act, which states that juveniles are "taken into custody," not arrested. This is interpreted to mean the police's role is to salvage and rehabilitate youth, a role indirectly sanctioned by many judges who condone or encourage settling disputes and complaints without referral to the court.

Police contact with children may result either from a complaint received or from apprehension at the time of an alleged offense.

When a juvenile is taken into custody, this is technically not considered an arrest. The law enforcement process for arrest is modified in most jurisdictions when juveniles are apprehended. Police officers should be concerned about the mental health of juveniles. They should be good listeners and try to discover the problem or reason for the juveniles' behavior.

It is paramount in administering juvenile justice that youths be protected by all sociolegal requirements. All actions must be in the best interest of the children. This is important whether the children involved are offenders or victims.

> ■ The fundamental nature of the juvenile justice system is rehabilitative rather than punitive.

Most states reflect this basic rehabilitative philosophy.

The Supreme Court has emphasized the full constitutional rights of persons under legal age. The protection, critical to the juvenile offender, is twofold:

1. At no point in any criminal investigation may the rights of the juvenile be infringed upon.
2. A crime by a juvenile must be proven beyond a reasonable doubt and all subsequent efforts by a state should be directed towards correlating and eliminating the cause of the crime rather than punishing the individual for having committed it.

Juveniles must be treated with consideration to build respect for authority. Officers must be firm but fair and show genuine interest. They must attempt to understand the juveniles' reasoning. In handling juveniles, if officers resort to vulgarity or profanity, lose their tempers, display prejudicial behavior or label juveniles as "liars" or "no good," this is usually counterproductive. Such actions are often followed by further disruptive conduct by the juvenile or by a lack of cooperation in any attempt to divert juvenile conduct.

According to Crowe (1991, p. 20) it now takes up to three times longer to detain (arrest) a juvenile than an adult because of public policy establishing so

■ *When police officers take a youth into custody, it is not technically an arrest, but the end result may be the same—incarceration.*

many safeguards for juveniles. Crowe also states that a detained juvenile is much less likely than an adult to receive official sanction. Given this situation, Crowe argues: "No wonder that uniformed police officers, who have 90 percent of the contact with juveniles, are more likely to exercise their discretion 'to do nothing' than to bother with a youngster who is just going to be released anyway."

If a youth is detained, the officers must remember that juveniles have the same constitutional rights as adults, including the right to remain silent, the right to counsel, the right to know the specific charge and the right to confront witnesses. As noted by the Minnesota POST (Police Officer Standards and Training) Board (1992, p. 72): "[A]lthough certain procedures of the juvenile justice system may differ from those of the adult system, peace officer duties and responsibilities for ensuring the rights of juveniles and thoroughly investigating the elements of juvenile criminal offenses is as great as or greater than their responsibilities of carrying out the same duties pertaining to adults."

Given the *parens patriae* philosophy underlying the juvenile justice system, it might be expected that the police would exercise extra care in dealing with youth. Krisberg and Austin (1993, p. 85) suggest the opposite: "Evidence suggests that youths are treated as harshly as their adult counterparts and with less respect for their constitutional rights. . . . Critics of police handling of juveniles attribute the tendency of police to ignore the civil rights of youths to the conflict of controlling crime while attempting to maintain a benevolent treatment approach."

Of the juvenile offenders taken into custody in 1990, almost two-thirds (64%) were referred to juvenile court jurisdiction. Slightly more than one-fourth (28%) were handled within the department and released—called **station adjustment.** Figure 9–3 shows the police dispositions of juvenile offenders taken into custody in 1990.

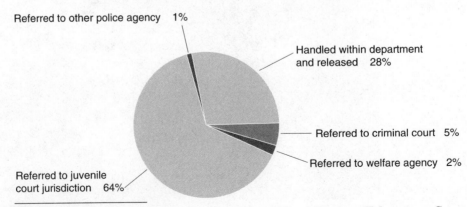

▮ **FIGURE 9–3 Police Dispositions of Juvenile Offenders Taken into Custody, 1990**

SOURCE: Howard N. Snyder, "Arrests of Youth, 1990", OJJDP, Update on Statistics, January 1992, p. 5.

Determining a Juvenile's Age

One problem of referral for juvenile authorities and the court, especially in a metropolitan area, is that it may be difficult to determine by appearance alone if an individual is a "juvenile." Youths may lie about or try to manipulate their age for practical reasons.

In a large city, for example, youths taken into custody or arrested for minor offenses such as disorderly conduct or prostitution often claim to be *over* the age limit, reasoning that if treated as adults they will simply be forced to spend a night in jail, hear a lecture by a judge and accept whatever penalty is disposed. If they identify themselves as juveniles, their detention usually is extended, and interference with their freedom and liberty may well be more substantial.

In small towns and in rural areas, the procedure for prereferral process is to release the youths to the custodians of the juvenile, allowing the custodians to dispense justice and relieve the workload of the court.

DETENTION

Krisberg and Austin (1993, p. 73) define **detention** as: "[T]he period in which a wayward youth is taken into custody by police and probation prior to a petition being filed and an adjudication hearing by the juvenile court." Detention is governed by two requirements of the JJDP Act: (1) removing all juveniles from adult jails and lockups, and (2) separating juvenile and adult offenders. The Act states:

> Provide that juveniles alleged to be or found to be delinquent and youths within the purview of paragraph (12) (i.e., status offenders and nonoffenders) shall not be detained or confined in any institution in which they have regular contact with adult persons incarcerated because they have been convicted of a crime or are awaiting trial on criminal charges.

In addition, state laws and department policy may affect who is detained and under what conditions. Most state statutes governing detention of juveniles are quite general. Among the common criteria used by states are (Krisberg and Austin, 1993, p. 73):

■ For the juvenile's protection, or for the protection of the person or property of others.
■ No parental care available for the juvenile.
■ To ensure a juvenile's presence at the juvenile court hearing.
■ The seriousness of the offense and the juvenile's record.

Harris (1986, p. 110) notes:

> Critics of juvenile justice leniency must also confront studies exposing the harsh conditions in detention facilities. Suicide and self-injury are no strangers to children's jails. . . .
> Given the harshness of the detention setting and relatively high rates of detention, one might wonder if some juveniles are detained for illegitimate purposes such as punishment.

RELEASE VS. DETENTION

Juvenile court statutes often require that once children have been taken into custody, they may be released only to their parents, guardians or custodians. Where such a law exists, a decision to detain automatically follows if the parents, guardians or custodians cannot be located. The child is placed in detention and must be referred to court. Thus, the police are removed from the referral process.

In most states police may take a child into custody for the child's own protection until appropriate placement can be made. A form such as that shown in Figure 9–4 may be used.

Standards to guide police personnel in the decision of release or detain may be formally prepared in written instructions by police administrators and court authority. In some states *mandatory referral* to juvenile authorities or even directly to court may be required for all crimes of violence, felonies and serious misdemeanors. Similarly, all juveniles on parole or probation may be referred. Some jurisdictions refer if the juvenile has had previous contact with the police.

The following key points must be considered when dealing with juveniles who commit status offenses (Community Research Associates, 1992, pp. 8–9):

1. Juveniles taken into custody for status offenses must be held nonsecurely until release or transfer.
2. Nonsecure custody requires five standards be met:
   - ∎ Any area where the juvenile is held must be an unlocked multipurpose area, such as a lobby, office, interrogation or report writing room.
   - ∎ In no event can the area be designed or intended for residential purposes.
   - ∎ The juvenile is not physically secured to cuffing rail or other stationary object.
   - ∎ Use of area(s) is limited to nonsecure custody only long enough for identification, investigation, processing, release to parents, or arranging transfer to appropriate juvenile facility or court.
   - ∎ The juvenile must be under continuous visual supervision until release.
3. Federal regulations prohibit secure holding of status offenders or nonoffenders in jails, lockups, or law enforcement facilities.
4. Written departmental policies and procedures for handling status offenders should be developed and followed.
5. Signs should be displayed in the juvenile holding area reminding officers of these policies and procedures.
6. Rollcall should routinely remind officers of Federal, State, and departmental requirements in the handling and custody of status offenders.
7. Handcuffing an offender to himself or herself and/or transporting him or her in a caged vehicle is not secure custody.
8. Any time a status offender is held in violation of these regulations, the incident should be documented with an explanation.
9. When dealing with an intoxicated juvenile, officer should determine whether emergency medical services are warranted.

DATE:_____

TIME TAKEN INTO CUSTODY_____

NOTICE OF 36 HOUR POLICE HEALTH AND WELFARE HOLD

I, _____, a duly authorized peace officer
in the State of _____, by reason of the authority vested in me by _____
Statutes §260.165, Subd. 1 (c) (2), have taken into custody the following child
(children):

Name	Age	Name	Age

Name	Age	Name	Age

and have placed the child (children) at:_____
                                                  Receiving Facility
Parents/Custodian_____Phone_____

Address_____

Having taken custody of this child (these children), I am now requesting that the

_____to assume custody on my behalf until
        Receiving Facility
such time as further action can be taken to safeguard the health or welfare of this

child (these children).

The child (children) shall not be released to the custody of his/her parent,
guardian, custodian or other suitable person unless:

1. The peace officer or his designate withdraws the health
   and welfare hold; or
2. The Juvenile Court orders release; or
3. 36 hours (excluding Saturdays, Sundays, or holidays) has expired
   without any court action being taken.

Person Accepting Child (Children)	Peace Officer Signature and Badge No.

Phone Number	Department or Precinct Phone No.

NOTE: THIS FORM DOES NOT TAKE THE PLACE OF A POLICE REPORT

Disposition (to be completed by the Receiving Facility):_____

_____

_____

White: Receiving Facility
Blue   _____County Welfare Department - Child Protection
Green   _____County Welfare Department - Court Unit
Canary   Police
Pink   Parents
Gold   Juvenile Court if child at Shelter Care Facility

■ FIGURE 9–4 Police Custody Report Form

10. A status offense is any offense that would not be a crime if committed by an adult.
11. Underage drinking and possession of alcohol by a minor are status offenses pursuant to JJDP Act requirements.
12. Officers should be knowledgeable of referral sources and phone numbers to inform both the parents and child whom to contact in seeking additional information and help.

The following key points must be considered when dealing with juveniles who commit delinquent acts (Community Research Associates, 1992, p. 14):

1. Federal regulations permit a 6-hour period of secure detainment in an adult jail or lockup for juveniles accused of committing criminal-type (delinquent) offenses.
2. No regular contact with adult offenders is allowed, thus separation from adult offenders must be maintained at all times. This means that juvenile and adult offenders cannot see or speak to one another (sight and sound separation). This separation may be achieved through time phasing use of an area to prohibit simultaneous use by juveniles and adults.
3. Records must be maintained documenting length of time a juvenile is in secure custody. (This may be critical in the event of a lawsuit.)
4. The 6-hour period for secure holding of accused delinquent offenders is limited to temporary holding for identification, processing, release to parents or guardian, or transfer to juvenile court officials or to juvenile facility. Any such holding should be limited to absolute minimum time necessary to complete these actions, not to exceed 6 hours and in no case overnight.
5. Written departmental policies and procedures for handling delinquent offenders should be developed and followed.

Figure 9–5 summaries the federal jail removal and separation requirements for juveniles. Table 9–1 summarizes the offenses charged in detained delinquency cases in 1986 and 1990 and the percent change.

From the study *Conditions of Confinement* undertaken by the OJJDP the *Research Summary* (1994, p. 1) reports:

Admissions to juvenile facilities rose after 1984 and reached an all-time high of nearly 690,000 in 1990. The largest increase was in detention, where admissions rose from just over 400,000 in 1984 to about 570,000 in 1990. The daily population of confined juveniles, based on Children in Custody (CIC) census 1-day counts, increased from about 50,800 in 1979 to about 65,000 in 1991.

The characteristics of confined juveniles also changed sharply in recent years. Between 1987 and 1991 the proportion of minorities among confined juveniles rose from 53 percent to 63 percent, with the biggest increases among blacks (37 percent to 44 percent) and Hispanics (13 percent to 17 percent). The percentage confined for crimes against persons rose from 22 percent to 28 percent, and those confined for property offenses declined from 40 percent to 34 percent.

The issue of disproportionate representation of minorities is discussed shortly. The conditions of confinement observed during the study are reported in Chapter 11.

Stewart (1990, p. 1) suggests that during detention police have "a **window of opportunity** . . . an opportunity to be an agency for change for youngsters who have by law come under its control. Drug testing can be used diagnostically to identify high-risk youth before they become established in the cycle of illicit

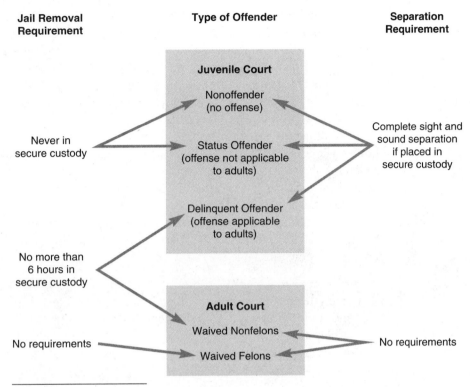

Jail Removal Requirement

Type of Offender

Separation Requirement

Juvenile Court

Nonoffender (no offense)

Status Offender (offense not applicable to adults)

Delinquent Offender (offense applicable to adults)

Never in secure custody

Complete sight and sound separation if placed in secure custody

No more than 6 hours in secure custody

Adult Court

Waived Nonfelons

Waived Felons

No requirements

No requirements

█ **FIGURE 9–5 Federal Jail Removal and Separation Requirements for Juveniles**

SOURCE: Timothy D. Crowe. *Habitual Juvenile Offenders: Guidelines for Citizen Action and Public Responses,* Serious Habitual Offender Comprehensive Action Program (SHOCAP), (Washington, D.C.: Office of Juvenile Justice and Delinquency Prevention, October 1991, p. 21.

TABLE 9–1   Percent Change in Detained Delinquency Cases, 1986 and 1990

█

Offense	Number of Cases		Percent Change
	1986	*1990*	
Total Delinquency	238,300	286,300	20%
Person	46,900	64,800	38
Property	117,500	135,300	15
Drugs	19,100	25,400	33
Public Order	54,900	60,900	11

Note: Detail may not add to totals because of rounding. Percentage calculations are based on unrounded numbers.

SOURCE: Jeffrey A. Butts and Eileen Poe, "Offenders in Juvenile Court, 1990," OJJDP, Update on Statistics, December 1993, p. 5.

drug use and crime" (boldface not in original). The strong link between illicit drug use and crime has been well established by research in the past decade. Dembo et al. (1990) report on an extensive three-year study of some 400 juveniles in a regional detention center in Tampa, Florida, and the role of drug use in their becoming involved in the juvenile justice system.

The study found that the older the juveniles became, the more involved with drugs they were, which is summarized in Table 9–2.

Urine tests were found to be a significant predictor of property misdemeanor crimes. Table 9–3 summarizes the offenses charged to the youths in the 18 months following their initial interview, with 44 percent having at least one referral for a property felony and 35 percent for a property misdemeanor.

In addition, 51 percent of those who tested positive for cocaine were rearrested or referred to juvenile authorities one or more times for a property misdemeanor. Cocaine use was clearly a predictor of property misdemeanor crimes, as shown in Table 9–4

∎ During detention, a window of opportunity exists to identify youths on drugs and, therefore, at risk of becoming repeat offenders. Such youth can be put into drug-treatment programs, hopefully averting the drug-crime-drug cycle.

Other windows of opportunity are discussed in chapter 14.

The Serious Habitual Offender Comprehensive Action Program (**SHOCAP**) suggests the following action steps at detention (Crowe, 1991, p. 48):

TABLE 9–2   **Urine Test Results at Initial Interview ($N = 399$)**

∎

Results	Percent
Positive for	
Marijuana	37%
Cocaine	10
Benzodiazepines (Valium)	<1
Opiates	<1
Any of above	41
Two or more of above	7

	Percent Positive by Age and (N)					
	10–12 (21)	13 (23)	14 (54)	15 (87)	16 (117)	17+ (97)
Positive for						
Any drug	24%	39%	28%	44%	44%	46%
Marijuana	24	39	24	40	39	41
Cocaine	0	4	4	6	14	15

SOURCE: Richard Dembo, Linda Williams, Eric D. Wish, and James Schmeidler, "Urine Testing of Detained Juveniles to Identify High-Risk Youth," NIJ, Research in Brief, May 1990, p. 2.

■ Establish a policy of separate and secure holding of all designated habitual offenders.

■ Provide a special close custody classification for all designated habituals to protect staff and other correctional clients.

■ Monitor and record all activities and transactions of designated habitual offenders.

TABLE 9–3   Referrals or Arrests by Category During 18-Month Follow-Up Period (N = 398)

Violent felonies	22%	Property felonies	44%	Drug felonies	13%
Murder, manslaughter, attempted murder or manslaughter, sexual battery, other felonious sex offenses, armed robbery, other robbery, aggravated assault or battery		Arson, burglary (breaking and entering), auto theft, grand larceny (excluding auto), receiving stolen goods		Felony violation of drug laws (excluding marijuana), felony marijuana offense	
		Property misdemeanors	35%	Drug misdemeanors	5%
Violent misdemeanors	21%	Petty larceny (excluding retail), retail theft (shoplifting), receiving stolen property (<$100), criminal mischief (vandalism)		Misdemeanor violation of drug laws (excluding marijuana), misdemeanor marijuana offense	
Assault and/or battery (not aggravated)					
Public disorder misdemeanors	13%				
Disorderly conduct (trespassing, loitering, prowling)					

Note: One youth who died after the initial interview is excluded. Percentages total to more than 100% because some had more than one arrest or referral.

SOURCE: Richard Dembo, Linda Williams, Eric D. Wish, and James Schmeidler, "Urine Testing of Detained Juveniles to Identify High-Risk Youth," NIJ, Research in Brief, May 1990, p. 5.

TABLE 9–4   Relationship of Cocaine Test Results to Property Crimes and Drug Sales

Referral/Arrest Information	Test Result at Initial Interview	
	Negative for Cocaine (359)	*Positive for Cocaine (39)*
Had 1+ referrals/arrests for:		
Property misdemeanor	33%	51%*
Property felony	43	56
Self-reported mean number of drug sale offenses committed in year prior to initial interview	28.6	108.4**

*p < .05
**p < .01

SOURCE: Richard Dembo, Linda Williams, Eric D. Wish, and James Schmeidler, "Urine Testing of Detained Juveniles to Identify High-Risk Youth," NIJ, Research in Brief, May 1990, p. 5.

INTAKE

The intake officer decides if a case should move ahead for court processing. This officer may release the juvenile to the parents with a warning or reprimand. Or the officer may release the youth on the condition that he or she enroll in a community diversion program or be placed on probation and be under the supervision of a juvenile court officer. As noted by Trojanowicz (1978, pp. 175–176):

> If the child is released at intake and no further processing takes place, there should still be a follow-up after any referral to a community agency by either the police or the intake unit. Follow-up facilitates not only the rendering of services to the child, but also promotes closer cooperation between the agencies involved.

For habitual offenders the Serious Habitual Offender Comprehensive Action Program (SHOCAP) suggests the following action steps at intake (Crowe, 1991, p. 48):

∎ Mandatory holding of all designated habituals who are brought in on new charges.
∎ Immediate notification of prosecutor of the intake of a habitual offender.
∎ Special follow-up and records preparation for the detention hearings for designated habituals.

If the intake officer determines that the case should move ahead for court processing, the officer will recommend that a petition (charge) be filed and will refer the case to the juvenile court prosecutor. In addition, if a petition is recommended, the intake officer determines if the youth is to be detained until further court action is taken or be released into the custody of the parents pending the hearing. When juveniles are detained, this decision is reviewed by a judge or court administrator at a detention hearing.

PROSECUTION

When the prosecutor receives the recommendation for petition by the intake officer, at least three options are available: dismiss the case, file the petition or determine that the charges are so serious that the case should be heard in adult court, waiving jurisdiction. If a petition is filed, this begins the formal adjudication process. Based on police reports, the county attorney may refer a juvenile to the screening unit of the juvenile court using a form such as that illustrated in Figure 9–6.

Circumstances may vary depending on the age and experience of the officer making the disposition. This exercise of individual authority, or street justice, may be repeated by court personnel, probation officers and correction workers. The rhetoric is the same for all within the system.

For prosecution of habitual offenders SHOCAP recommends these action steps (Crowe, 1991, pp. 48–49):

COUNTY ATTORNEY
REFERRAL TO SCREENING UNIT-JUVENILE SECTION

POLICE FILE NO.		DATE TYPED

NAME (FIRST, MIDDLE, LAST)	STREET ADDRESS, CITY, COUNTY, ZIP

HOME PHONE NO.	D.O.B.	PHYSICAL DESCRIPTION	HEIGHT	WEIGHT	EYES	HAIR	COMPLEXION	SEX	RACE

MOTHER'S NAME (FIRST, MIDDLE, LAST)	STREET ADDRESS, CITY, STATE, ZIP

FATHER'S NAME (FIRST, MIDDLE, LAST)	STREET ADDRESS, CITY, STATE ZIP

CHILD LIVES WITH: ☐ Mother ☐ Father ☐ Other, who?   SCHOOL NAME   GRADE

ALLEGED OFFENSE(S)

LOCATION OF OFFENSE(S)	DATE/TIME OF OFFENSE

VICTIM'S NAME	HOME ADDRESS	HOME PHONE NO.
	BUSINESS ADDRESS	BUS. PHONE NO.

DISPOSITION OF PROPERTY	DATE/TIME PARENTS NOTIFIED	NO. OF PRIOR CONTACTS	LIST PRIOR CONTACTS ON THE REVERSE SIDE

DOES JUV. ADMIT OFFENSE ☐ Yes ☐ No   ATTITUDE:

ARRESTING OFFICERS	INVESTIGATING OFFICERS	MIRANDA GIVEN ☐ Yes ☐ No

COMPANION NAME(S) THIS OFFENSE	D.O.B.	DISPOSITION

BRIEF DETAIL OF OFFENSES (WHO, WHAT, WHEN, WHERE, HOW)

(USE OTHER SIDE FOR ADDITIONAL INFORMATION AND COMMENTS)

EST. DAMAGE OR LOSS $ THE FOLLOWING ARE ATTACHED OR AVAILABLE
☐ Photos ☐ Statements ☐ Arrest Reports ☐ Property Invent. Sheets ☐ Prior Contacts List

DATE OF REPORT	POLICE DEPT. REPORTING	SIGNATURE OF OFFICER	PHONE NO.

NOTICE TO LAW ENFORCEMENT OFFICERS WHO PREPARE THIS REPORT: If the arresting or investigating officer wishes to discuss this matter with the assigned Probation Officer, please call _____ Please allow time for processing.   **BELOW FOR COUNTY ATTORNEY USE ONLY**

DATE RECEIVED	DATE REFERRED TO COURT SERVICES	DATE REFER TO ASS'T CO. ATTY.

FIGURE 9–6 County Attorney Referral Form

- File petition (charges) with the court based upon the highest provable offense.
- Resist the pretrial release of any designated habitual offender.
- Seek a guilty plea on all offenses charged.
- Vertically prosecute all cases involving designated habituals (assign only one deputy district attorney to each case).

∎ Provide immediate response to police and detention officials upon notification of the arrest of a designated habitual.

∎ Participate in interagency working groups and on individual case management teams.

∎ Share appropriate information with the crime analyst or official designated to develop and maintain profiles on habitual offenders.

∎ Establish a formal policy of seeking the maximum penalty for each conviction or adjudication of a designated habitual offender.

OVERREPRESENTATION ISSUES

The National Coalition of State Juvenile Justice Advisory Groups (1993, p. 35) notes: "Research confirms that from arrest through sentencing and incarceration, disproportionate representation and differential treatment are evident along the entire system continuum." The Coalition sets forth two points of view that may explain the disproportionate representation of minority juveniles in the system:

> One [view] urges that the problem rests with the system which employs, unintentionally or not, a "selection bias" that results in a disproportionate number of minority youth in the system. In other words, minority youth do not commit more crimes than any other youth; they merely get treated differently and more harshly at various points in the system. The other view posits that the nature and volume of offenses committed by minority youth are the real issue. In other words, minority youth commit more offenses, and more serious offenses, than other youth because of the social and economic conditions in which they are forced to live.

The Tofflers (1990, p. 3) suggest that it is "simple-minded" to blame poverty for the crime problem. They note that numerous societies throughout the world with extreme poverty do not have the crime problem anywhere approaching the magnitude of the United States. They also note, however: "[I]t is equally witless to assume that millions of poor, jobless young people—not part of the work-world culture and bursting with energy and anger—are going to stay off the streets and join knitting clubs."

Next turn your attention to a closer view of those who find themselves being processed by the system.

NEGLECTED AND ABUSED CHILDREN

Recall that according to ten Bensel et al. (1985, p. 1): "It is estimated that as many as four or five million children are neglected or physically abused each year, with an additional two million vulnerable as runaways or missing."

Bennett and Hess (1994, p. 384) note:

> Law enforcement agencies are charged with investigating all crimes, but their responsibility is especially great where crimes against children are involved.

Children need the protection of the law to a greater degree than other members of society because they are so vulnerable, especially if the offense is committed by one or both parents. Even after the offense is committed, the child may still be in danger of being further victimized. . . .

In most states, action must be taken on such reports within a specified time, frequently three days. If in the judgment of the person receiving the report it is necessary to remove the child from present custody, this is discussed with the responsible agency such as the welfare department or the juvenile court. If the situation is deemed life-threatening, the police may temporarily remove the child.

No matter who receives the report or whether the child must be removed from the situation, it is the responsibility of the law enforcement agency to investigate the charge. . . .

An officer may take a child into temporary custody, without a warrant . . . if there is an emergency or if the officer has reason to believe that to leave the child in the present situation would subject the child to further abuse or harm.

■ **The primary responsibility of police officers assigned to child neglect or abuse cases is the immediate protection of the child.**

Police officers must also balance the rights of children against those of the children's parents.

Among the service providers mandated to report incidents of suspected child abuse or neglect are child care providers, the clergy, educators, hospital administrators, nurses, physicians, psychologists and those in the social services.

The Minnesota POST Board (1992, pp. 128–129) suggests the following conditions that would lead an officer to place a child in protective custody:

- Maltreatment in the home which could cause the child permanent physical or emotional damage.
- Although the child is in immediate need of medical or psychiatric care, the parents refuse to obtain it.
- Child's age, physical, or mental condition renders the child incapable of self-protection.
- The physical environment of the home poses an immediate threat to the child.
- The parents cannot or will not provide for the child's basic needs.
- The parents may flee the jurisdiction.
- The parents abandon the child.

The National Institute of Justice (NIJ) undertook a study of the police and their response to abused children. The research first looked at the statutory framework for police actions in cases of child abuse and neglect. This was followed by a telephone survey conducted by the Police Foundation in the spring of 1988. The third portion of the study was site visits by Police Foundation staff for in-depth examinations of four agencies. The major findings of this study were as follows (Martin and Besharov, 1991, pp. 5–7):

- The vast majority of police agencies routinely report abuse and neglect to their local child protective service agencies.
- Over three-quarters of police agencies believe that child protective service agencies inform the police of all cases of sexual abuse brought to their attention; a smaller proportion believe they are being notified of all cases of physical abuse and neglect.

∎ Police and sheriff's departments conduct a large number of investigations of child abuse and neglect. A rough estimate, based on data from 59 urban agencies, suggests that they are informed of and investigate more than 200,000 cases annually.

∎ Of those cases that are closed by the police, nearly 40 percent of the sexual abuse cases and about a quarter of physical abuse and neglect cases result in the arrest of a suspected perpetrator. (Additional numbers of cases are investigated but not closed.)

∎ Nearly two-thirds of the police agencies surveyed have child abuse policies, about half of which recently had been adopted or updated.

∎ The vast majority of police agencies provide at least some training on identifying child abuse cases to all new recruits, and provide training on the handling of investigations to new child abuse investigators.

∎ About half of the police agencies with more than 250 officers have a squad of investigators who have received specialized training and work full time on investigating child abuse cases.

∎ In more than three-quarters of the police agencies, a specialized investigator is either on duty or on call 24 hours a day.

∎ The presence of a specialized child abuse squad, but not its organizational location, affects case dispositions. For example, agencies having a specialized sexual abuse squad close significantly more sexual abuse cases than do those without such a squad (but with a lower arrest rate).

∎ Eighty-one percent of the responding departments have interagency agreements regarding child abuse investigations. Fifty percent of agencies have written agreements with at least one other agency; thirty-one percent of agencies have informal agreements.

∎ Virtually all interagency agreements involve child protective services and the police; prosecutors and other law enforcement agencies are included in about two-thirds of the agreements; and about one-half involve the medical community. Participation by school, juvenile court, mental health, and private community service agencies is less widespread.

∎ Police practices across disparate jurisdictions are similar despite the variations in statutory provisions.

The findings suggest that police agencies should consider a variety of ways to improve their response to child abuse, including:

∎ a strong commitment by high-level administrators to improving the agency's response to child abuse;

∎ a written, agencywide child abuse policy;

∎ written interagency protocols;

∎ interagency teams to handle child abuse investigations;

∎ immediate telephone notification of the police by protective service agency workers regarding all sexual abuse cases and all cases of serious physical injury or danger;

∎ initial interviews conducted jointly with child protective agency workers, particularly in sexual abuse cases;

∎ patrol officers who are trained in the identification of abuse;

∎ specialized investigators, rather than patrol officers, to handle all cases;

∎ expertise in child exploitation and pornography investigations within the unit handling child abuse;

∎ child abuse specialists, skilled as investigators and comfortable interviewing young children;

■ sexual, ethnic, and language diversity within the unit;

■ child-friendly interview settings;

■ limited and selective use of videotaping and anatomical dolls by properly trained individuals; and

■ victim advocates available throughout the legal process, particularly in sexual abuse cases.

The study found that written policies dealing with the police response to child abuse increased departmental capabilities. About half (67 of the 122 agencies responding) had written policies. Table 9–5 summarizes the elements contained in these policies.

Youth Who Are Sexually Abused

Peters (1991, p. 21) urges that police departments have specialists in dealing with children who are sexually abused:

Neither police academies nor law schools cover such topics as understanding the psychological needs of victims as well as the dynamics of incest, recognizing the frequently vague symptoms of abuse and knowing how to elicit sensitive

TABLE   Contents of Written Child Abuse Policies
9–5

	Extent of Procedures and Guidelines in Percent (N = 67)
Notification of child protective agency	75%
Conducting initial investigation	64
Evidence collection	63
Follow-up investigations	49
When to take a child into protective custody	49
Obtaining medical diagnosis or treatment for victim	46
Handling protective custody (e.g., notifying parents, transporting child)	40
Statement of law enforcement responsibilities in joint investigation	37
Identifying cases of physical abuse	36
Specifying which cases to investigate jointly with child protection	34
Identifying cases of sexual abuse	30
Identifying neglect	30
Interviewing abuse victims	29
Resolving protective custody disagreements between law enforcement and child protection investigators	27
When to arrest	16
Interviewing alleged abuser	14
Looking for child abuse in spouse abuse cases	13

SOURCE: Susan E. Martin and Douglas J. Besharov, *Police and Child Abuse: New Policies for Expanded Responsibilities* (Washington, D.C.: National Institute of Justice, June 1991), p. 27.

information about sexual behavior from youngsters. The typical officer and the average prosecutor do not have an understanding of the child pornography underworld, juvenile prostitution, sex rings or ritualistic abuse.

Considering the probability that a sexually abused child will become a child abuser or engage in violent crimes, the importance of reducing this probability by effectively dealing with sexually abused children cannot be underestimated. Peters (1991, p. 23) stresses that law enforcement should treat child abuse as a significant issue: "Failure to assign high priority and competent professionals to child abuse cases, however, guarantees grim consequences, both in terms of current individual tragedies and future social implications."

Missing Children

The National Center for Missing and Exploited Children's (NCMEC) Investigator's Guide (Patterson, 1987, p. vii) notes:

> Missing child cases often involve a violation of the law and always involve the need to provide protection for the child. Even those youths who voluntarily leave home run the risk of becoming involved in criminal activity or exploitation through involvement in prostitution, child pornography, or with pedophile "protectors." Studies show that 85 percent of exploited children are missing when exploitation occurs.

The NCMEC provides two services to law enforcement agencies involved with investigating missing children cases. The first is an age progression program that creates photographs of the child approximating what the child would look like at the present time. The greatest age difference they have created is from age 6 to 31. Out of the 200 cases they have handled so far, 28 living children have been located (Strandberg, 1994, p. 47). In addition, they have identified several dead children.

The second service is called Project KidCare, which is provided in collaboration with Polaroid Corporation. This service consists of an educational packet and a high quality photo in a form the NCMEC and law enforcement consider ideal.

STATUS OFFENDERS

The majority of police dispositions involve status offenses.

■ Approximately 90 percent of police dispositions involve status offenders, according to the Uniform Crime Report.

The status offenders with whom the police make contact are often from middle socioeconomic families. This is especially true for runaways, incorrigibles and truants.

In making dispositions on juvenile matters, the police have found that the parents of the 1990s are often so absorbed with their own desires and problems they have little time to consider their children's needs. They tend to rely on church, school or civic groups to guide each child. They often pursue a policy of appeasement in the home rather than maintaining family discipline. In effect, these parents want society to be their baby-sitters. The increasing reliance on community services and parental emphasis on individual rights rather than responsibilities in the training and education of their children has, to a large extent, weakened the family and contributed to the growing delinquency problem. The Metropolitan Court Judges Committee Report (1985, p. 41) suggests that:

> The most glaring result of our nation's high divorce rate and single parent families is the lack of parental guidance. Children need both parents or at minimum a father or mother "figure," if not in the home, then at least nearby and available to provide additional nurturing and discipline. This is not the responsibility of teachers, coaches or neighbors.

Partly as a result of this lack of parental guidance, law enforcement is faced with the constant problem of making arrests on such charges as curfew violations, loitering, vagrancy and running away.

Curfew Violations and Loitering

When youths' behavior is such that the community wants them off the streets at night, a curfew is established for the public good. When youths hang around corners, walkways, alleys, streets and places of business without any purpose, their loitering must be controlled for the safety and security of the public. Both curfew violations and loitering can be offenses for those under legal age. (Loitering is also an adult offense in some states.)

Cruising and hanging out or loitering are frequent activities of juveniles. Such activities are not always harmless, however, as noted by Revering (1993, p. 39):

> The tragic death of a young Minnesota soldier who was beaten by a teenage mob recently in Colorado Springs, Colorado, is a glaring example of the violence that seethes beneath unchecked cruising and loitering problems. In each community where cruising and loitering have been allowed to escalate, youth gangs began to infiltrate and vandalism and violence became the norm.

In one community, a study of the citations issued for cruising and loitering revealed that 85 to 90 percent of the offenders were from outside the community (Revering, 1993, p. 40). Some communities combat this problem by antiloitering and anticruising ordinances. They also establish curfews targeted at juveniles to combat the problem during the evening hours.

In March, 1994, Orlando, Florida, passed an anticruising measure allowing Orlando police to write citations to any driver passing through downtown four times within two hours. They also passed a curfew law. The American Civil Liberties Union has threatened to sue Orlando, contending that such a law constitutes nightly house arrest and deprives parents of their right to set hours for their children.

The Civil Liberties Union was successful in getting a similar curfew lifted in March, 1994, in Dade County. The Circuit Judge Norman Gerstein wrote in the nine-page order halting enforcement of the one-month old curfew: "Juveniles, like adults, have constitutional rights under the Florida Constitution" (Yanez, 1994, p. 7B). The Metro-Dade Commission has said it will fight back.

Runaways

The police interest in runaways has resulted from public concern for the youths' safety and welfare, not because they have committed crimes. Youthful runaway behavior often is a precursor of future delinquent behavior and is usually—in most law enforcement agencies—the least investigated status offense.

Technically, runaways are individuals under the statutory age of an adult who leave home without authorized consent and who are reported to the police as missing. The object of the police search is to locate such youths and return them to their families. Generally, no police investigation, social service inquiry or school inquiry is conducted to determine the reasons these children left home, were truant because of this absence or why they continue to run away.

■ Running away is a predelinquent indicator, but its value often is not recognized by the parents, police, school, social agencies or the courts.

If the danger signal is ignored, society loses another battle in controlling antisocial behavior or criminal activity. Runaways may become violent, even killing others for survival, or turn to robbery, burglary, drug abuse and prostitution to meet their needs.

Because children run away for many reasons, police must be sensitive in their treatment of runaways. Police must treat runaways differently to account for their age, sex, family social order, paternal makeup (original, adopted or foster) or who represents control.

When the police take an initial complaint report on a runaway, the responsible adults seldom can give a reason for the youth leaving home. In middle-class families, with few exceptions, parents do not know why their child left home. They firmly believe their son or daughter was the victim of something evil, was under the influence of neighborhood children or that the fault lies with the school system.

Police experience has shown, without too much inquiry, that these so-called sinister happenings that parents fear seldom occur. They are a screen to the real problem. In most instances, police do not investigate why a child left home, nor do court services personnel unless the matter is disposed of in juvenile court, for a final disposition of "aftercare." This may be the result of priorities in personnel allocation, a lack of court support or a lack of support from state agencies.

> ■ If police dispositions are to be effective, the family must recognize the early signs of maladjustment in children. Running away is the most visible indicator of a possible future victim (assaulted, murdered) or involvement in criminal activity to support individual needs (prostitution, pornography, burglary, theft, robbery).

In its early stages, running away frequently can be corrected by cooperative policies and the parents. The parents must constantly be informed of the consequences of runaways and be advised of assistance available. Police officers can take a professional approach in their association with children and youth who get into minor offenses by being available and providing assistance to their needs. Officers know that children and youth want the opportunity to talk openly and freely about themselves and their lives to someone who will listen without judging and who are interested in them as individuals rather than as problems to be solved or disposed of in some manner.

When officers have handled matters directly with the youth and the family, without going through a formal process, it has totally remade the lives and personalities of a number of seemingly hopeless youth who could have become delinquents.

The Police as Mentors to Troubled Youth

Police committed to a mentoring relationship have an enormous impact on youth at risk of becoming chronic offenders. Carefully selected and trained police personnel can be the conduit to restoring youthful lives to productive relationships with families, schools and the community.

In dealing with troubled youth who are at risk of becoming juvenile offenders, mentoring is especially effective because it strikes directly at the individual's alienated condition. The youth's isolation and sense of meaninglessness is often dissolved over time through a long-term relationship characterized by respect. The youth's sense of powerlessness is eroded through a relationship with someone who helps clarify their choices and empowers them to make responsible decisions.

Police mentoring is the most effective means available for optimizing meaningful contact between society and alienated youth. As the youth begins to bond with a mentor, a new world view will crystallize, opening up a new range of perceived choices which reflects the values of their mentor and their community. Mentoring remains a single hope in reclaiming our troubled youth, our families, communities and society as a whole.

An opposite view of dealing with status offenders was set forth in the ninth recommendation to the President of the United States by former Attorney General William Barr (1992, p. 27):

> With respect to the larger group of juveniles, excessive leniency wastes the opportunity to salvage the youth and instead encourages them to become career criminals. As to the group of chronic offenders, excessive leniency fails to adequately protect society from these violent criminals. Tough, smart sanctions

tailored to the particular offender will both reduce the number of juveniles who become chronic offenders and better protect society from those who do.

Recommendation 9

Establish a range of tough juvenile sanctions that emphasize discipline and responsibility to deter nonviolent first-time offenders from further crimes.

One of the key challenges for a State juvenile justice system is to deter the youthful offender from further transgressions. For the vast majority of juveniles, this should be possible if we are smart in imposing sanctions. To this end, States should develop a range of tough but fair sanctions for nonviolent first-time juvenile offenders, where the emphasis is on instilling values of discipline and responsibility. These sanctions should include the option of institutional settings.

Barr also writes (p. 25):

To a large extent, the success or failure of the criminal justice system will depend upon its effectiveness in handling youthful offenders—ensuring that for the vast majority of juvenile offenders their first brush with the law is the last, and ensuring that the small group of chronic hardened youthful offenders are incapacitated for extended periods.

This "get tough" attitude has been criticized by some, however, such as Brodt and Smith (1991, p. 176) who suggest:

In practice, getting tough means "let's get tough" with the following groups: (1) blacks; (2) Chicanos; (3) the poor; (4) the uneducated; (5) youth from single parent families; (6) the unemployed; (7) illegitimate youth; (8) welfare families and (9) abused children.

Senna and Siegel (1990, p. 655), in discussing what to do with status offenders, state:

Since its inception, the DSO [deinstitutionalization of status offenders] approach has been hotly debated. Some have argued that early intervention is society's best hope of forestalling future delinquent behavior and reducing victimization. Others have argued that legal control over status offenders is a violation of youth's rights. Still others have viewed status-offending behavior as a symptom of some larger trauma or problem that requires attention. These diverse opinions still exist today.

SERIOUS, HABITUAL OFFENDERS

It is well documented that a large number of crimes are committed by a small number of repeat offenders. Colorado Springs Police Department instituted a Serious Habitual Offender/Directed Intervention (SHO/DI) Program aimed at this group of juvenile offenders.

Offenses classified by the FBI as violent crimes include homicide, forcible rape, aggravated assault and robbery. Juvenile arrests for violent crimes make up less than 1 percent of the total number of almost 10 million arrests for violent crimes ("Facts," 1988, p. 159). Nonetheless, the problem is serious. Pindur and

Wells (1988, p. 194) state: "Nearly 2,000 juveniles are arrested each year on murder charges and approximately 4,000 are arrested annually for rape. . . . Chronic, serious juvenile offenders often 'fall through the cracks' of the [juvenile justice] system because efforts are not coordinated."

As noted by the supervisor of the Crime Analysis Unit of the Colorado Springs Police Department (Kline, 1993, p. 32): "Looking the other way in the face of juvenile delinquency has spawned a generation of career offenders whose activities are far more vicious and sophisticated than the joy-riders and hubcap thieves of happier days." The goal of the program was threefold:

■ To develop trust and cooperation between agencies serving juveniles.
■ To identify and overcome real and perceived legal obstacles to cooperative efforts.
■ To build a credible interagency information process to identify and track habitual juvenile offenders.

Says Kline: "The ultimate goal was to 'incapacitate' the repeat offender, whether through detention, incarceration, probation or other means, so that for some period of time, his crimes would stop, and efforts could be made to change his ways."

One important component of the program was a court order signed by a juvenile judge allowing the police department to share information with the other component agencies in the juvenile justice system. Another important outcome of the program was a change in how the juvenile portion of the justice system was viewed. Traditionally, juvenile matters received low priority. "Kiddy Court" was not taken seriously, and beginning lawyers were assigned to prosecute juveniles. This practice was changed with the institution of the SHO/DI Program.

The Serious Habitual Offender Comprehensive Action Program (SHOCAP) of the Office of Juvenile Justice and Delinquency Prevention is aimed at juveniles who are a chronic, serious threat to a community's safety. As noted by Owens and Wells (1993, p. 26):

Through SHOCAP, the police department works with other juvenile-related agencies, including prosecutors, courts, corrections, the schools and human resources, to ensure a comprehensive and cooperative information and case management process that results in informed sentencing disposition. SHOCAP enables the juvenile and criminal justice system to focus additional attention on juveniles who repeatedly commit serious crimes, yet may somehow "fall through the cracks" of the system.

SHOCAP suggests the following action steps for management of habitual offenders for the police, including municipal and county law enforcement agencies (Crowe, 1991, p. 47):

■ Develop special crime analysis and habitual offender files.
■ Coordinate interagency activities and services for designated habitual offenders.
■ Prepare profiles of habitual offenders.
■ Conduct instantaneous radio checks of a juvenile's prior police contacts for patrol officers.

▮ Use field interrogation cards or juvenile citations to document reprimands and non-arrest situations.

▮ Institute directed patrol assignments to increase field contacts, assist in community control of probationers, and follow up on habitual truancy cases.

▮ Provide daily transmittal of all field interrogation or juvenile citation cards to probation authorities.

▮ Supply regularly updated lists of designated habitual offenders to all police officers.

Such action steps are important because although the habitual serious offenders make up a small portion of the juvenile offender population, they account for a great majority of the violent crimes that have paralyzed some communities with fear. As Barr (1992, p. 24) observed:

> The criminal justice system must recognize that some youthful offenders are simply criminals who happen to be young. Every experienced law enforcement officer has encountered 15- or 16-year-olds who are as mature and as criminally hardened as any adult offender. Although this group represents only a small fraction of our youth, they commit a large percentage of all violent crimes. As painful as this fact may be, public safety demands that law enforcement recognize and respond to this criminal element. The challenge for a State's juvenile justice system is to identify this group of hard-core offenders and to treat them as adults.

He recommends (p. 31):

▮ Increase the ability of the juvenile justice system to treat the small group of chronic violent juvenile offenders as adults.

▮ Provide for use of juvenile offense records in adult sentencing.

DEALING WITH GANGS AND GANG MEMBERS

The Director of the Bureau of Alcohol, Tobacco and Firearms, Stephen Higgins (1993, p. 46), stresses: "Despite the dedication of thousands of law enforcement officers nationwide, the gang epidemic shows no sign of abating; on the contrary it is increasing." Higgins (p. 47) notes:

> On January 9, 1992, then-Attorney General William P. Barr officially recognized street gangs as meeting the definition of organized crime and committed the investigative resources of both ATF and the FBI to augment the state and local authorities already battling this national crisis.

Gang activity is a chief concern for law enforcement and of vital interest to the general public. Police are determined to do something about gangs to satisfy the public need for peace and order. Though the police can make arrests whenever a gang member breaks the law, a gang has the advantage. Gangs can congregate and recruit without breaking the law. Only a small fraction of gang-related crimes can be solved by arrest. Thus, if an arrest is the only recourse, police soon feel helpless, and the public believe the police do nothing.

When this situation surfaces, the police do chase gang members away from where they congregate. Citizens and communities reinforce the police in this "no report activity," a use of informal social control. This type of police conduct is condoned by the public when the final disposition is looking out for the needs of the average citizen.

Jackson and McBride (1985, pp. 107–113) offer several suggestions for police patrol procedures when dealing with gangs. They stress that patrol offers law enforcement officers a chance to establish rapport with gang members, to communicate with them. They suggest:

> Even though an officer may find a street gang offensive to his or her sense of decency, the simple fact of the matter is that there is nothing illegal per se in belonging to a gang. Street gangs are not going to disappear just because society finds them repulsive. Furthermore, experience and studies have yet to show an instance in which a street gang was dissolved or put out of action solely because of suppressive police action. When police pressure is intensified on a street gang, its members typically go underground and become secretive, which may produce even greater problems. Therefore, start easy when working with a street gang.

Jackson and McBride note the paradox that gangs typically will not retaliate against police officers if they feel the officers are treating them firmly and fairly. They urge (p. 109): "Keep in mind that the police officer is probably the key authority figure with whom the gang member has dealt. As such, officers must themselves show their respect for the law by their behavior. The officer, whether he realizes it or not, is a *de facto* role model."

As early as the 1970s the Los Angeles Police Department saw the need for specialized units to deal with the gang problem. Their first such program was called Community Resources Against Street Hoodlums (CRASH). CRASH consisted of several specially trained units of patrol officers and detectives organized on a bureau or area level. CRASH put tremendous pressure on the Los Angeles gangs and resulted in many gang members being arrested. In 1988 the department instituted another program to focus specifically on the problem of narcotics and black street gangs. This program was called Gang-Related Active Trafficker Suppression (GRATS). As noted by Gates and Jackson (1990, p. 21): "The GRATS program targets street gangs involved in drug manufacturing, distribution and street sales. . . . During 1989, GRATS operations resulted in the arrest of 23,894 persons, including 8,574 identified street gang members."

The Anaheim Police Department has instituted a program to combat the graffiti problem using a computerized system called GREAT (General Reporting, Evaluating and Tracking). The department considers a tagging crew to be nothing short of a gang (Molloy and Labahn, 1993, p. 122): "The members of a crew associate with one another constantly; they share a common sign, symbol and name; and they have a common purpose of criminal anti-social behavior. They are a gang." The criteria the Anaheim police have established for a person to be a crew member includes the following:

- Self-admitted member.
- Information from an untested informant corroborated by independent information.
- Resides in or frequents the crew's area, wears common dress, uses or has common sign, symbol and/or tattoos, and associates with known members.

∎ Has several arrests in the company of known members with offenses consistent with membership.

∎ Maintains a close relationship with a member.

The Anaheim Police Department has also instituted an undercover school operation, "Operation GETUP" (Graffiti Enforcement Through Undercover Programs). This program resulted in 37 criminal cases filed against 17 suspects.

Another program also has the acronym GREAT—the Gang Resistance Education and Training program—developed by the Bureau of Alcohol, Tobacco and Firearms, the Federal Law Enforcement Training Center and the Phoenix Police Department. This program, similar to the DARE program, helps students say no, but in this case to gangs. The audience is older, focusing on seventh graders. Students are taught to set goals, resolve conflicts nonviolently, resist peer pressures and understand the negative impact gangs can have on their lives and on their community.

In 1987 the OJJDP established a research and development program to study the gang problem. As part of this program they conducted a national survey of youth gang problems and programs. This survey identified five strategies being used by organizations and cities to deal with the gang problem (Spergel et al., 1990, p. 2):

∎ *Suppression,* including such tactics as prevention, arrest, imprisonment, supervision and surveillance. (Most frequently employed—used by 44 percent.)

∎ *Social intervention,* including crisis intervention, treatment for youths and their families, outreach, and referral to social services. (Used by 31.5 percent.)

∎ *Social opportunities,* including the provision of basic or remedial education, training, work incentives, and jobs (4.8 percent).

∎ *Community mobilization,* including improved communication and joint policy and program development among justice, community-based, and grassroots organizations (8.9 percent).

∎ *Organizational development or change,* including special police units, vertical prosecution, vertical probation case management, and special youth agency crisis programs. The organizational development strategy modified the other four strategies (10.9 percent).

Owens and Wells (1993, p. 27) describe a developing OJJDP program component for SHOCAP called the Gang Offender Comprehensive Action Program or GO-CAP:

> Like SHOCAP, GO-CAP uses case management activity to pursue vigorous prosecution of all gang offenders via the Street Terrorism Act. . . .
>
> As a developmental component of SHOCAP, GO-CAP not only strengthens the city's Community-Oriented Problem-Solving Program, but shows promising applicability for most jurisdictions in the United States.

Saccente (1993, p. 31) urges law enforcement to view street gangs as criminal organizations and capitalize on laws against organized crime: "RICO, money-laundering and asset forfeiture laws, although different, have a common threat: they complement each other in their efforts to arrest and prosecute gang members and ultimately weaken the street gang structure."

Some gang experts, such as Hagedorn (1988, pp. 64–65), note concerns that law enforcement officers and officials fail to understand gangs:

The law enforcement paradigm defines gangs in a narrow and unchanging manner, which neglects the process of development which different age groups within gangs undergo and ignores or undervalues variations of all sorts. Gangs are not seen as young people struggling to adapt, often destructively, to a specific economic and social environment. Rather, gangs are treated as a major criminal problem and their members dehumanized as no more than aspiring "career criminals.". . . The fact that gangs today are overwhelmingly minority and most police departments overwhelmingly white, allows for racism to contribute to these stereotypes and results in even greater hostility on the street.

A recently released study on street gangs (Conly, 1993, pp. 48, 49) suggests the following:

In many urban communities there are tensions between police forces and the communities they serve. Law enforcement departments often feel hard pressed to find the staff time to meet the challenges in these communities, while residents are anxious for increased attention to their needs by law enforcement. Added to this problem is racial tension between members of law enforcement departments and minority communities.

In communities where gangs exist, residents have often retreated in fear, leaving the police and the gangs to battle each other. Nevertheless, the residents are not disinterested: they want the police to understand their problems while keeping the streets safe. In this regard, David Fattah, co-director of the House of Umoja in Philadelphia, observed that the role of the police in communities where there are gangs should be to show dignity and firmness without abuse. In his view, many law enforcement departments appear as military outposts in the community. If they were more approachable, "kids would go to them instead of some other group, like a gang."

Typical Law Enforcement Approaches to Gangs. Most law enforcement efforts are aimed primarily at crime control: gathering information; developing information systems; making arrests; and sharing information with others in the law enforcement community. Increasingly, they also include prevention activities:

■ Participating in community awareness campaigns (e.g., developing public service announcements and poster campaigns);
■ Contacting parents of peripheral gang members (through the mail or in personal visits) to alert them that their children are involved with a gang;
■ Sponsoring gang hotlines to gather information and facilitate a quick response to gang-related issues;
■ Organizing athletic events with teams of law enforcement officers and gang members;
■ Establishing working relationships with local social service agencies;
■ Making presentations on gangs in schools and community groups as a combined effort at prevention and information gathering;
■ Sponsoring school-based gang and drug prevention programs (e.g., DARE);
■ Serving as a referral for jobs and other community services.

PREVENTION STRATEGIES

Common sense suggests that it is better to prevent youth from becoming victims or victimizers. The thrust of the 1990s is toward proactive, problem-oriented policing, seeking causes for crime and allocating resources to attack those causes. Among the many preventive strategies available, one that costs nothing is fair and just treatment of juveniles during all contacts, whether the juvenile is a victim, a status offender, a delinquent or a gang member. Peace officers can serve as role models for personal responsibility and accountability and expect the same from the youths with whom they come in contact.

Other preventive efforts commonly engaged in by police departments include educational programs, recreation programs, crime prevention programs and diversion programs. However, juvenile delinquency prevention programs conducted by law enforcement reflect public policy and public attitudes. They often result as a reaction to a specific incident rather than from long-range preventive goals.

Early Efforts at Delinquency Prevention

When law enforcement first formally recognized the importance of actively promoting positive community relations, the approach selected was the best possible under the existing conditions. In an effort to "get the boys off the streets" and control gang activity, the New York police started the Police Athletic League (PAL). Youngsters, mostly males, were given instruction in boxing (for Golden Glove competition), basketball and baseball. Police sponsored athletic games and tournaments.

Law enforcement also promoted programs about subjects of interest to children and their parents, including a myriad of safety programs: bicycle, auto, household (poisons and related household hazards), guns and outdoor water.

∎ Initially, law enforcement sought to build a positive image rather than to develop constructive, lasting delinquency prevention programs.

Many law enforcement agencies continue to provide one-time and seasonal programs designed to address a particular problem rather than carefully planned, long-range programs.

Evolution of Prevention Programs

In the 1930s and 1940s, aside from PAL, law enforcement directed its energies toward school safety patrol programs. These programs were started with the assistance of civic and community groups for pedestrian safety. When conditions changed in the 1950s and 1960s, and mass busing of children to schools became the norm, the programs began to dissipate.

Frequently, delinquency prevention programs promoted by the police focused on matters common to children and of concern to parents, with no eye to the future. For example, in the 1960s cough medicine containing codeine, a morphine derivative, was being sold faster than druggists could stock the shelves. When law enforcement and parents became aware that such over-the-counter drugs could be purchased without a prescription, and that children of all ages were buying them, prevention programs pushed to stop future purchases. Eventually legislation restricted purchases of such cough medicine.

The "Get Tough" Trend

In recent years, many police departments have applied the prevention technique of "getting tough with juveniles." The effect of this technique often is to make the police the villain or "enemy," and it may alienate youths. Children no longer see law enforcement officers as "jolly cops." Instead, the police are more often viewed as enemies who are ignorant of the present and have no vision of the future.

This negative view of the police is explained by Pace and Curl (1985, p. 109):

> The law, to a young person, is often considered a "necessary evil." They do not understand the law, nor do they wish to learn about it. Rebellion against most laws, and especially those concerning the control of traffic, generates much hostility and animosity among the young.
>
> This hostility to law is naturally projected to police officers because they represent the negative forces that impose impossible sanctions. It is often said that the young do not like the police, and the feeling is often mutual. . . . In the short term, the feeling of hostility toward the police is real; however, this hostility will usually modify as the person gains maturity. Before maturation takes place, the mutual feeling of hostility between youth and the police only tends to create additional antagonism in their contacts. This feeling, in the long term, serves notice to the police that their behavior should be exemplary because they are being watched with an eye of some mistrust.

Law enforcement prevention programs cannot ignore this mistrust, or that sociological and behavioral causes and effects cannot be separated from crime. The objectives of law enforcement in delinquency prevention programs are to educate children and the community about existing and potential problems. Prevention programs must be flexible to adapt to changes in social values.

The International Association of Chiefs of Police and the National Sheriffs Association are valuable resources for prevention programs. Unconventional methods can evolve into conventionality by virtue of a changing, increasingly complex society. One unconventional program, started 30 years ago, the police-school liaison program, has become common in the 1990s.

Police-School Liaison Programs

A much publicized delinquency prevention plan was developed in 1958 in Flint, Michigan, with the cooperation of school authorities, parents, social agencies, the juvenile court officials, businesses and the police department. The foundation for the **police-school liaison program** was established many years before its inception, when people living in the community identified with different political, social, ethnic, economic and regional sections of large communities. A workable relationship through the public school system began.

Police-school liaison officers do not enforce school regulations, which are left to the school superintendent and staff. Instead, school liaison officers work with students, parents and school authorities to apply preventive techniques to problems created by antisocial youths who have not or will not conform to the community's laws and ordinances.

The techniques used by school liaison officers involve counseling children and their parents, referring them to social agencies to treat the root problems, referring them to drug and alcohol abuse agencies and being in daily contact in the school to check the progress of behavior. Often school liaison officers deal with predelinquent and early delinquent youths with whom law enforcement would not have been involved under traditional programs.

The police-school liaison program exemplifies those programs designed to alleviate problems encountered by the community through cooperative efforts of all citizens. However, budget reductions in a number of communities have adversely affected the police-school liaison program.

The Flint Program

The goals of the Flint Police-School Liaison Program are as follows:

- ▮ To reduce crime incidents involving school-age youths.
- ▮ To improve the attitudes of school-age youths and the police towards one another.
- ▮ To suppress by enforcement of the law any and all illegal threats that endanger the child's educational environment.

In the Flint program the liaison officers' home base is the middle or senior high school because these schools are more centralized and accessible. Also, the bulk of investigations and contacts with juveniles are at this level.

Liaison officers become acquainted with the building directors at the various schools and reassure them they are available should they be needed. They check the teen club activities at the schools and periodically appear at various club affairs to become familiar with their rules and procedures. At the same time they check for any loitering in and around the schools during these events and take steps to correct any matters that conflict with city ordinances. As a rule, school personnel supervise the social events. The officers do not become involved in matters pertaining to school policy, but they are available to give advice and help.

Liaison officers frequently patrol the elementary school areas until school starts in the morning, and also during the noon hour and after school. They watch for any suspicious people or automobiles and for infractions of safety rules regarding routes to and from school. They also check the middle school areas for anyone loitering around the building or grounds attempting to pick up students in the area.

As noted, liaison officers have no responsibility for school policy. They are, however, informed about anything indicating that a student is a potential delinquent or may be negatively influencing others. They are informed by the elementary schools about any groups that are troublemakers or who have been reprimanded for violation of the weapons policy. Officers must be alert and observe any students hanging around schools other than the one they attend. Generally, principals handle such situations without any further action. This is as it should be, because officers do not appear to be using their police authority in every incident that occurs. They frequently find that the schools have a rule the student is violating and school authorities take a dimmer view of the incident than the officers do. By coordinating all concerned, a better preventive program develops. Appendix B provides a detailed job description for a police-school liaison officer.

Many aspects of the police-school liaison program benefit students, the school and the community. The communication developed between the law enforcement agencies and school personnel provides information to guide young people. Respect for law enforcement agencies is built up in the minds of the youths. The police-school liaison officer becomes a friend to the juveniles. The effective preventive work of the police-school liaison program may be a considerable part of the answer to the problem of juvenile antisocial behavior.

Goals of Liaison Programs

▌ The goals of the police-school liaison program fall into two general categories: preventing juvenile delinquency and improving community relations.

Preventing Juvenile Delinquency

In seeking to prevent juvenile delinquency, police-school liaison programs focus on both preventive actions and official investigation of criminal activity, apprehension and court referral. Officers assigned to school liaison programs approach delinquency prevention through a variety of activities.

▌ *One goal of police-school liaison officers is to build student friendship and respect.*

Officers *act as instructors* before various school groups and classes, presenting material appropriate for discussion. Often youths get their ideas about how the police and the law function from street gangs, who are misinformed. Often a distorted, negative impression of the laws, their meanings and the police officers who enforce them are formed. Through class discussions and question and answer periods, students can gain a proper perspective.

Officers also *act as counselors* to students, either separately or with school personnel. Schools' counseling departments are often understaffed and overburdened. Many students are concerned about problems related to laws and their enforcement. Through teams made up of school administrators, counselors, health experts, police liaison officers and others, open lines of communication are formed to identify and treat troubled students. Using such teams, the workload of all is reduced. It is generally a more effective method of dealing with students. Officers need not wait until students have committed some overt act of antisocial behavior. They can counsel with and attempt to turn such youths away from antisocial behavior.

Officers also *maintain contacts with parents or guardians* of students exhibiting antisocial behavior, advising them of the acts, offering assistance and soliciting their help in coping with the problems. In doing so, officers open up new avenues of communication and improve the image of police officers. While officers are sympathetic to the problems of everyday life, at the same time they hope to create in parents an increased awareness of and sense of responsibility toward the laws and their enforcement.

Another important activity of liaison officers is *making public appearances*. Officers speak about preventing juvenile delinquency to various community organizations. They often present lectures and other types of programs aimed at preventing delinquency.

Furthermore, officers *maintain files* of information on students contacted. These files are used to determine the extent of delinquent behavior, as well as the types of students who are more apt to become delinquent. Many behavior patterns can be observed from analyzing these files, and more attention can then be directed to children at risk of becoming delinquent. The files can also indicate what types of diversionary program may be best suited to combat a given child's delinquent conduct.

Investigating complaints of criminal activity occurring within the school complex and the surrounding area is another activity of liaison officers. Thorough investigation and solution of these crimes, in itself, serves as a crime preventive measure and improves the police image. If it is found that the most effective way to deal with a youth is to petition him or her to juvenile court, liaison officers also take this action.

Finally, school liaison officers *maintain close contact with other police agencies* in the area and assist them whenever possible in investigating and apprehending suspects involved in criminal activity in the school or involving its students.

Improving Community Relations

The second general goal of police-school liaison programs focuses on community relations.

> ■ Community relations is projecting and maintaining an image of the
> police as serving the community, rather than simply enforcing laws.

Enhancing community relations is accomplished in several ways.

Public appearances are a key technique. Officers speak and present films or slide programs before many types of groups, such as PTAs, service groups, church fellowships, civic gatherings, youth clubs and civil rights groups. There is usually an interplay of ideas at such gatherings, and the officers sell the ideal of community service.

Another focus is *parent contacts*. Behavioral problems are often apparent in the school before they develop into more serious delinquent activity. Officers in the school know about such problems and can contact parents. They can work together with the parents to avoid any progression into serious delinquent behavior. Most parents take an interest in their children. This dissipates the age-old contest of parent versus school in control of children. Likewise, it affects their attitude toward anyone else in authority disciplining their children.

Possibly the most effective means of community relations at the officers' disposal are *individual contacts*. Officers have contact with many young people at every age level. In projecting an image of the "good guys," they influence the attitudes not only of those students counseled, but also of their friends and families. Many popular myths about laws and law enforcement officers are dispelled through this type of community relations.

Another important area is *liaison work with other interested agencies*. This includes contacts with juvenile courts, social agencies, mental health agencies, other schools and private organizations. Officers gain operational knowledge of each and learn to coordinate their efforts with these other agencies to better treat children.

Displaying interest indicates to these agencies that police are concerned with more than simply apprehension and detention in dealing with juvenile delinquency. Undoubtedly, teachers have a definite effect on their students' attitudes. Officers who help teachers with problem students improve teachers' image of the police. This, along with personally knowing a police officer, does much in long-range police-community relations and, as any preventive program must be, this preventive program is long range.

Finally, *recreational participation* is a type of interaction with youth that breaks down many walls of resentment. Officers who participate in organized athletics with youngsters build a rapport that is carried over into their other contacts with those youth.

The Importance of Teachers in Delinquency Prevention Programs

Since most delinquency prevention programs are based in schools or, at least, focus on school-age populations, it is critical that teachers be included in any delinquency prevention programs.

▮ Teachers are of vital importance to the success of any delinquency prevention program.

Pace and Curl (1985, p. 255) state:

> Teachers, next to parents, are society's most important transmitter of values, mores, and cultures. For many years, teachers, in internalizing their values, have been the most hostile group toward the police. Through their value system they have consistently rated police officers low on acceptance scales.

Pace and Curl suggest that teachers from all grade levels should be taken on ride-alongs so they could see the "consequences of their failures." They claim that if teachers would have this exposure, they might be "less willing to put the student 'out the schoolhouse door' because of poor academic performance."

Other Programs

Other well-known programs found throughout the country include the Officer Friendly program and the police dog McGruff ("Taking a bite out of crime") program. The McGruff program goes beyond delinquency prevention and seeks to help youth contribute positively to the community.

Sometimes the McGruff crime dog also promotes safety. For example, at Halloween, many police departments distribute trick or treat bags to children. These bags feature McGruff and list some tips for a safe Halloween.

Explorer Posts are also popular. These posts are an advanced unit of the Boy Scouts of America and include high school students between the ages of 14 and 18. Explorers wear uniforms similar to law enforcement officers and are taught several skills used in law enforcement such as firearms safety, first aid, fingerprinting and the like.

One school-based delinquency program sponsored by the Los Angeles Police Department is Project DARE.

▮ The Los Angeles Police Department and the Los Angeles Unified School District jointly sponsor the Drug Abuse Resistance Education (DARE) program.

The program is designed for elementary school children. It consists of 17 classroom sessions that are taught by experienced police officers. The focus is on teaching elementary age youths to say "no" to drugs, to resist peer pressure and to find alternatives to drug abuse.

On the opposite coast, a successful police-community prevention effort is that of the Rochester, New York, Police Department.

▮ Rochester's Teens on Patrol (TOP) program uses youths to patrol the city's parks and recreational areas in the summer.

Each summer about 100 youths are hired to keep order in the parks. At the same time they learn about police work. Many TOP participants have gone on to become police officers.

The Officer on the Street

The criticality of the officer on the street cannot be overlooked. Recall the earlier discussion of youths' hostility toward the law and police officers. Every law enforcement officer, no matter at what level, has an opportunity to be a positive influence on youths. It is ultimately the individual, one-on-one interactions on which youths' perception of the law and law enforcement will be based.

■ Youths' attitudes toward law and law enforcement are tremendously influenced by personal contacts with law enforcement officers. Positive interactions are a key factor in any delinquency prevention attempts.

■ *This canine officer and his partner "Books" have just completed a demonstration at an open house of a crime prevention association. Such contacts can do much to build good relationships between the police and the citizens they serve, including our youth.*

COORDINATION OF EFFORTS

The need for cooperative efforts when dealing with juveniles has been stressed in preceding chapters. Law enforcement needs to draw upon the expertise of psychologists, psychiatrists and social workers. They need the assistance of parents, schools, churches, community organizations and businesses.

Police officers need to be aware of the referral sources available in the community including not only the name of the resource agency but an address, phone number and contact person. Among the possible referral resources for the juvenile justice system are the following:

- Child welfare and child protection services.
- Church youth programs.
- Crisis centers.
- Detox centers.
- Drop-in centers or shelters for youth.
- Guardian *ad litem* programs.
- Human services councils.
- Juvenile probation services.
- School resources, including chemical dependency counselors, general counselors, nurses, school psychologists and social workers.
- Support groups such as AlAnon, Emotions Anonymous and Suicide Help Line.
- Victim/witness services.
- YMCA or YWCA programs.
- Youth Service Bureaus.

Ideally, police officers would serve on community boards and task forces that promote services for youth.

Working with the Schools

The importance of the schools has been noted in the preceding section. According to Nichols (1991, p. 21): "Although school authorities must accept their responsibility to have a plan, it is essential for police officials themselves to ensure preparedness for school-related crises." Nichols (p. 23) suggests:

> A good relationship among all agencies and their officials is a key component for the successful response to school crises. The police response to violence, hostage-taking, or any number of criminal incidents must be predicated on a standing relationship with school officials, other public safety authorities, the news media, and all other key personnel who may be involved.

RESPONDING TO A CHANGING SOCIETY

Policing today is at a critical point. People of different races, cultures and languages are coming into closer contact with each other, and enormous demands are being made on their understanding and tolerance. There is widening class divisions, more broken families and homelessness, a growing anger on the part of the disadvantaged and a rise in violence.

These are the signs of a society in transition, but they are also the seeds of social unrest. Like migration, social disorder is cyclical. What happens in the present can be a re-enactment of the past of social conflict that pitted different races and different generations of the same society against each other.

Policing is also cyclical. To be prepared for the future requires a strategic plan that anticipates changes likely to occur in the future. The police must be in partnership with the community. Policing must be proactive, identifying local crime and disorder problems. Problem-oriented policing means getting at root causes, analyzing the needs of the community and recognizing those factors that endanger the physical, mental and moral well-being of the citizen. But making the transition from a reactive, incident-driven style of policing to a more proactive, problem-directed style, or community-oriented policing, requires a comprehensive strategy that is directed to the officer on the street, intervening one-on-one in efforts to make the community safe.

To identify and solve problems, the police must be able to associate with the youth of a community, especially those who misbehave and are on the brink of criminal activity. An officer in the community has an understanding of its "trouble areas," and the environmental factors that have contributed to the personality and behavior of young offenders.

SUMMARY

Law enforcement is the initial contact in the juvenile justice system. Street justice occurs when police decide to deal with a status offense in their own way—usually by ignoring it. Police officers have considerable discretionary power when dealing with juveniles. The most common procedure is to release the child, with or without a warning, but without making an official record or taking further action.

The objectives of police officers handling juvenile cases are (1) to protect the child or youth, (2) to investigate, (3) to determine the causes of the victimization or the offense, (4) to prevent further victimization or delinquency and (5) to properly dispose of the case.

The fundamental nature of the juvenile justice system is rehabilitative rather than punitive. During detention, a window of opportunity exists to identify youths on drugs and, therefore, at risk of becoming repeat offenders. Such youths can be put into drug treatment programs, hopefully averting the drug-crime-drug cycle.

The primary responsibility of police officers assigned to child neglect or abuse cases is the immediate protection of the child. Approximately 90 percent of police dispositions involve status offenders, according to the Uniform Crime Reports. Running away is a predelinquent indicator, but its value often is not recognized by the parents, police, school, social agencies or the courts. If police dispositions are to be effective, the family must recognize the early signs of maladjustment. Running away may be such an indicator for a possible victim (assault, murder) or more serious offender, becoming involved in criminal activity to support individual needs (prostitution, pornography, burglary, theft, robbery). Ideally, child abuse and neglect and delinquency would be prevented rather than dealt with after the fact.

Initially, law enforcement sought to build a positive image rather than develop constructive, lasting delinquency prevention programs. Teachers are of vital importance to the success of any delinquency prevention program conducted in the schools. The Los Angeles Police Department and the Los Angeles Unified School District jointly sponsor the Drug Abuse Resistance Education (DARE) program. The Rochester Teens on Patrol (TOP) program uses youth to patrol the city's parks and recreational areas in the summer.

Youths' attitudes toward law and law enforcement are tremendously influenced by personal contacts with law enforcement officers. Positive interactions are a key factor in any delinquency prevention attempts.

▮ Discussion Questions

1. How are referrals handled in your state? Do police contribute the greatest percentage of referrals?
2. Do you believe police should make unofficial referrals, such as to community service agencies? What are the problems the police would face when referring youths to community service agencies?
3. Do the police display a helping attitude toward youths when they make their referrals?
4. Do you believe the social standing, race and age of juveniles influence the referral procedure?
5. Should acts of violence by a juvenile automatically be referred to a detention facility?
6. Which do you think is more effective: "street justice" by police or processing juveniles through the court system? Why?
7. Should the police be in the schools as a prevention method? Why or why not?
8. What police delinquency prevention programs are available in your area? Do they work? Why or why not?
9. Joe, a 13-year-old white male, has been apprehended by a police officer for stealing a bicycle. Joe took the bicycle from the school grounds shortly after a program at the school by the police on "Bicycle Theft Prevention." Joe admits to taking the bicycle, but says he only intended to "go for a ride" and was going to return the bicycle later that day. Joe has no prior police contacts that the officer is aware of. The bicycle has been missing for only an hour and is unharmed.

What should the officer do in handling the incident? Do you think the bicycle theft prevention program is worthwhile? Why or why not?

10. Do you have any personal experiences regarding juvenile prevention programs and police?

■ References

Barr, William P. *Combating Violent Crime: 24 Recommendations to Strengthen Criminal Justice.* Washington, D.C.: U. S. Department of Justice, July 28, 1992.

Bennett, Wayne, and Kären M. Hess. *Criminal Investigation.* 4th ed. St. Paul, Minn.: West Publishing, 1994.

Brodt, Stephen J., and J. Steve Smith. "Public Policy and the Serious Juvenile Offender." In *Taking Sides: Clashing Views on Controversial Issues in Crime and Criminology,* 2nd rev. ed., edited by Richard C. Monk. Guilford: Dushkin Publishing, 1991, pp. 171–180.

Community Research Associates. *Law Enforcement Custody of Juveniles* (Video Training Guide). Prepared for the Office of Juvenile Justice and Delinquency Prevention, March 1992.

Conly, Catherine H. *Street Gangs: Current Knowledge and Strategies.* Washington, D.C.: National Institute of Justice, August 1993.

Crowe, Timothy D. *Habitual Juvenile Offenders: Guidelines for Citizen Action and Public Responses.* Serious Habitual Offender Comprehensive Action Program (SHOCAP). Washington, D.C.: Office of Juvenile Justice and Delinquency Prevention, October 1991.

Dembo, Richard; Linda Williams; Eric D. Wish; and James Schmeidler. "Urine Testing of Detained Juveniles to Identify High-Risk Youth." NIJ, Research in Brief, May 1990.

"Facts About Youth and Delinquency." In *Criminal Justice 88/89,* edited by John J. Sullivan. Guilford, Conn.: Dushkin Publishing, 1988.

Gates, Daryl F., and Robert K. Jackson. "Gang Violence in L.A." *Police Chief,* November 1990, pp. 20–22.

Hagedorn, John M. *People and Folks: Gangs, Crime, and the Underclass in a Rustbelt City.* Chicago: Lakeview Press, 1988.

Harris, Patricia M. "Is the Juvenile Justice System Lenient?" *Criminal Justice Abstracts,* March 1986, pp. 104–118.

Higgins, Stephen E. "Interjurisdictional Coordination of Major Gang Investigations." *Police Chief,* June 1993, pp. 46–47.

Jackson, Robert K., and Wesley D. McBride. *Understanding Street Gangs.* Sacramento, Calif.: Custom Publishing, 1985.

Kline, E.M. "Colorado Springs SHO/DI: Working Smarter with Juvenile Offenders. *Police Chief,* April 1993, pp. 32–37.

Krisberg, Barry, and James F. Austin. *Reinventing Juvenile Justice.* Newbury Park, Calif.: Sage Publications, 1993.

Martin, Susan E., and Douglas J. Besharov. *Police and Child Abuse: New Policies for Expanded Responsibilities.* Washington, D.C.: NIJ, Office of Justice Programs, National Institute of Justice, June 1991.

Metropolitan Court Judges Committee Report. *Deprived Children: A Judicial Response.* Reno: National Council of Juvenile and Family Court Judges, 1985.

Minnesota POST Board. *Learning Objectives.* St. Paul, Minn.: 1992.

Molloy, Joseph T., and Ted Labahn. " 'Operation GETUP' Targets Taggers to Curb Gang-Related Graffiti." *Police Chief,* October 1993, pp. 120–125.

National Coalition of State Juvenile Justice Advisory Groups. *Myths and Realities: Meeting the Challenge of Serious, Violent, and Chronic Juvenile Offenders, 1992 Annual Report.* Washington, D.C.: 1993.

Nichols, David. "Preparing for School Crises." *FBI Law Enforcement Bulletin,* February 1991, pp. 20–24.

Office of Juvenile Justice and Delinquency Prevention. *Conditions of Confinement: Juvenile Detention and Corrections Facilities, Research Summary.* Washington, D.C.: February 1994.

Owens, Robert P., and Donna K. Wells. "One City's Response to Gangs." *Police Chief,* February 1993, pp. 25–27.

Pace, Denny F., and Beverly A. Curl. *Community Relations Concepts.* Sacramento, Calif.: Custom Publishing, 1985.

Patterson, John C. *Investigator's Guide to Missing Child Cases: For Law-Enforcement Officers Locating Missing Children,* 2nd ed. National Center for Missing and Exploited Children, October 1987.

Peters, James M. "Specialists a Definite Advantage in Child Sexual Abuse Cases." *Police Chief,* February 1991, pp. 21–23.

Pindur, Wolfgang, and Donna Wells. "An Alternative Model for Juvenile Justice." In *Criminal Justice 88/89,* edited by John J. Sullivan. Guilford, Conn.: Dushkin Publishing, 1988.

President's Commission on Law Enforcement and the Administration of Justice. *The Challenge of Crime in a Free Society.* Washington, D.C.: U.S. Government Printing Office, 1967.

Revering, Andrew C. "Cruising and Loitering: Preludes to Serious Crime." *Police Chief,* April 1993, pp. 39–40.

Saccente, D.D. "RAP to Street Gang Activity." *Police Chief,* February 1993, pp. 28–31.

Senna, Joseph J., and Larry J. Siegel. *Introduction to Criminal Justice.* 5th rev. ed., St. Paul, Minn.: West Publishing, 1990.

Spergel, Irving A.; Ronald L. Chance; and G. David Curry. "National Youth Gang Suppression and Intervention Program." OJJDP, Juvenile Justice Bulletin, June 1990.

Stewart, James K. "From the Director." In "Urine Testing of Detained Juveniles to Identify High-Risk Youth" by Richard Dembo et al. NIJ, Research in Brief, May 1990.

Strandberg, Keith W. "Age Progression and Kidcare." *Law Enforcement Technology,* February 1994, pp. 46–49.

ten Bensel, Robert et al. "Child Abuse and Neglect." *Juvenile and Family Court Journal.* Reno: National Council of Juvenile and Family Court Judges, 1985.

Toffler, Alvin, and Heidi Toffler. "The Future of Law Enforcement: Dangerous and Different." *FBI Law Enforcement Bulletin,* January 1990, pp. 2–5.

Trojanowicz, R. C. *Juvenile Delinquency: Concepts and Controls.* Englewood Cliffs, N.J.: Prentice Hall, 1978.

Yanez, Luisa. "Judge Lifts Curfew for Dade Teen-Agers." (Miami) *Sun-Sentinel,* 17 March 1994, p. 7B.

The Role of the
Juvenile Court

There is evidence in fact, that there may be grounds for concern that the child receives the worst of two possible worlds; that he gets neither the protections accorded adults nor the solicitous care and regenerative treatment postulated for children.

Justice Abe Fortas, *In re Gault*

▍ Do You Know?

If the juvenile court is primarily civil or criminal?

What three classifications of children are under juvenile court jurisdiction?

What two factors determine if juvenile court has jurisdiction?

What the most common jurisdictional age is for juveniles?

If juvenile courts deal only with juveniles?

What the three types of juvenile courts are?

What adjudication is?

How Supreme Court decisions have changed juvenile court procedure?

What a guardian *ad litem* is?

What two actions juvenile court may take on behalf of children in need?

What three phases occur when filing a petition?

What the functions of a court referee are?

What the trend is in disposition of juvenile cases?

What factors are considered in a juvenile sentencing law?

What mechanical jurisprudence is?

Who can certify a juvenile as an adult? What reverse certification is?

What dilemma the juvenile court faces?

▍ Can You Define the Following Key Terms?

adjudicate, adjudication, certification, disposition, guardian *ad litem*, jurisdiction, mechanical jurisprudence, restitution, reverse certification, waiver

INTRODUCTION

In the Unitited States, justice for juveniles is administered by a separate system with its own specific court. This system enforces and administers a blend of civil and criminal law, but theoretically the system is a civil system. A civil system was adopted by early juvenile courts to avoid inflicting on youths processed by the courts the stigma of a criminal conviction.

Juvenile court is bound more by the rules of the court, generally, than statutes. It covers a much broader variety of legal matters, and it is vastly more extensive than the adult criminal system.

▌ The juvenile justice system is basically a civil system, but it is evolving into the adversarial system typical of our adult criminal system.

This chapter examines the basic philosophy of the juvenile court, its jurisdiction, the types of juvenile courts and the characteristics exhibited in most such courts. This is followed by a discussion of the adjudication process from intake through the hearing to the final disposition. The role of guardian *ad litem* and court referees is also discussed. The issue of waiver and certification to adult court is examined, including the criticisms of some who feel such waivers are used too extensively.

Next the discussion focuses on the youth as they are being served by juvenile court, including those who are abused and neglected, the status offenders and the delinquents. The chapter concludes with a discussion of the issue of juvenile records, the dilemma facing juvenile courts and the criticisms that have been made of the juvenile courts.

BASIC PHILOSOPHY OF JUVENILE COURT

The basic philosophy underlying juvenile court is that of *parens patriae,* with the major goal being to "save" the children of the state. According to McCreedy (1975, p. 7):

> The state, as the child's substitute parent, was not supposed to punish the child for his misconduct, but to help him. To reach this noble goal, many of the procedures used in adult criminal proceedings were abandoned or replaced with procedures commonly used in non-criminal (civil) court proceedings. A whole new legal vocabulary and new methods of operations were developed to reflect the new philosophy and procedures used in the juvenile justice system.

Instead of a complaint being filed against the child, a *petition* was filed. No longer was the child to be arrested in the strict sense of the term. Instead, the child was given a *summons*. A *preliminary inquiry* or *initial hearing* replaced an arraignment on the charge. The child was not required to plead either guilty or not guilty to the alleged misconduct. Instead of being found guilty of a crime, the child was found *delinquent.* Moreover, adjudication of delinquency was not to be considered a conviction. None of the liabilities attached to a criminal conviction were to apply to a child found delinquent [italics in original].

The aim of the first juvenile court was to offer youth and adolescent offenders individualized justice and treatment rather than imparting justice and punishment. Just as the terminology used in the juvenile justice system differs from that used in the adult system (recall the comparison of terminology in Table 3–1), several characteristic features of the systems also differ, as summarized in Table 10–1.

JURISDICTION OF THE JUVENILE COURT

The **jurisdiction** of juvenile court refers to the types of cases it is empowered to hear. In almost every state in the United States, the jurisdiction of the juvenile court extends to three classifications of children: (1) those who are neglected,

TABLE 10–1   Comparison of Juvenile Court and Adult Criminal Court

Characteristic Feature	Juvenile Court	Adult Court
Purpose	Protect/treat	Punish
Jurisdiction	Based mainly on age	Based on offense
Responsible noncriminal acts	Yes (status offense)	No
Court proceedings	Less formal/private	Formal/public
Proceedings considered to be criminal	No	Yes
Release of identifying information to press	No	Yes
Parental involvement	Usually possible	No
Release to parental custody	Frequently	Occasionally
Plea bargaining	Less frequently; open admission of guilt more common	Frequently
Right to jury trial	No (*McKeiver* case)	Yes
Right to treatment Fourteenth Amendment	Yes	No
Sealing/expungement of record	Usually possible	No

SOURCE: Richard W. Snarr, *Introduction to Corrections,* 2nd ed. (Dubuque, Iowa: Wm. C. Brown Communications, Inc., 1992), p. 311. All rights reserved. Reprinted by permission.

dependent and abused because those charged with their custody and control mistreat them or fail to provide proper care; (2) those who are incorrigible, ungovernable, wayward and truant and (3) those who violate laws, ordinances and codes classified as penal or criminal.

▌ The jurisdiction of the juvenile court includes children who are in poverty, neglected or abused; who are unruly or commit status offenses and who are charged with committing serious crimes.

All fifty states have jurisdiction over the first and third categories. Only Idaho does not expressly provide for jurisdiction over children who are beyond the control of their parents or guardian.

According to Springer (1986, p. 44):

> The general purpose of the juvenile court is to do justice. Among the special purposes of the court are the following:
>
> To settle civil controversies that relate to the protection, care, and custody of abused, neglected, and endangered children. . . .
>
> To protect abused, neglected, and endangered minors by means of placement and protective orders.

Springer notes as a failing of the juvenile court system its "one-pot" jurisdictional approach, in which deprived children, status offenders and youths who commit serious crimes are put into the same "pot." Springer also notes that historically (p. 45):

> All three kinds of children were thought to be the products or victims of bad family and social environments; consequently, it was thought, they should be subject, as wards of the court, to the same kind of solicitous, helpful care. . . .

Thus, the common declaration of status was that of wardship; and, as mentioned above, street dancers, grave robbers and murderers wind up, theoretically at least, in the same "pot"—as wards of the court, subject to being treated by the paternal court in the manner that loving parents would or should treat their child.

Springer (1986, pp. 62–63) describes a proposed change in legislation that would remove deprived children from the delinquency jurisdiction of the court and make them subject to civil sanctions only. The legislation would also remove status offenders and those children whose parents could not control them from the delinquency jurisdiction of the court.

▌ Proposed civil legislation would provide for (1) protective jurisdiction over minors who are endangered or who are abused, neglected or abandoned; (2) jurisdiction over minors who commit offenses that only a minor can commit, such as truancy or breaking curfew; (3) jurisdiction over minors who are beyond control.

Under the proposed legislation, delinquent jurisdiction is reserved for juveniles who commit criminal offenses.

The proposed disposition of juveniles falling within the civil jurisdiction of the juvenile court are as follows (Springer, pp. 63–64):

1. In all cases in which minors are adjudicated to be within the court's civil jurisdiction, the court should within a reasonable time conduct a dispositional hearing to determine what actions to take. Minors within civil jurisdiction are entitled to care, guidance, and control within their own homes unless their best interests require otherwise.
2. If minors are removed from their homes or from their parents' control, the care should be as equivalent to that given in their homes as possible.
3. Except for emergency protection detention, minors within civil jurisdiction should not be detained except for violating probation or by direct court order. No minor under civil jurisdiction should be placed in any penal institution for youth or any reformatory, training center, general penal institution, or any secure residential facility to house or punish criminal offenders or delinquents.

The importance of differentiating between criminal and noncriminal conduct committed by juveniles and the limitation on the state's power under *parens patriae* was established over a hundred years ago in *People ex rel. O'Connell* v. *Turner* (1870). In this case Daniel O'Connell was committed to the Chicago Reform School by an Illinois law allowing the confinement of "misfortunate youngsters." The Illinois Supreme Court's decision was that the state's power of *parens patriae* could not exceed that of the parents except to punish crime. The court ordered Daniel to be released from the reform school.

Factors Determining Jurisdiction

In most states two factors determine the jurisdiction of the court.

■ Jurisdiction of juvenile court is determined by the offender's age and conduct.

The extended limit for exercise of the juvenile court's jurisdiction is determined by establishing a maximum *age,* below which children are deemed subject to the improvement process of the court. A "child" is generally defined as a person under the maximum age that establishes the court's jurisdiction. Age 18 is accepted in two-thirds of the states and in the District of Columbia.

■ The most common maximum jurisdictional age is 18.

The jurisdictional age, generally, is the same for all children and all forms of conduct. Some states, however, differentiate between delinquent and deprived. Connecticut, for example, has a jurisdictional age of 16 in cases of children alleged to be delinquent or "defective" and age 18 in cases of children alleged to be abused, dependent, neglected or "uncared for." Georgia has a jurisdictional age of 17 for delinquent or unruly children and 18 for deprived children.

The issue of jurisdiction and age was first questioned in 1905 by the Pennsylvania Supreme Court. Frank Fisher was adjudicated a delinquent in the

Philadelphia Juvenile Court. On appeal his lawyer challenged the constitutionality of the legislation establishing the court, urging in particular that Fisher was denied due process in the manner in which he was taken into custody and that he was denied his constitutional right to a jury trial for a felony. The Pennsylvania Supreme Court upheld a lower court's sanction. The court found that due process, or lack of it, simply was not at issue, since its guarantee applied to only *criminal* cases. The state could, on the other hand, place a child within its protection without any process at all if it saw fit to do so. Recall that in *Commonwealth* v. *Fisher,* 1905, the court stated: "To save a child . . . the legislature surely may provide for the salvation of such a child . . . by bringing it into the courts of the state without any process at all, for the purpose of subjecting it to the state's guardianship and protection." The court further stated:

> The natural parent needs no process to temporarily deprive his child of its liberty by confining it to his own home, to save it and to shield it from the consequences of persistence in a career of waywardness; nor is the state, when compelled as *parens patriae*, to take the place of the father for the same purpose, required to adopt any process as a means of placing its hands upon a child to lead it into one of its courts.

Similarly, the court argued, a jury trial could hardly be necessary to determine whether a child deserved to be saved. The court had the jurisdiction and responsibility of age and conduct, not due process.

Besides the jurisdictional age, *conduct* determines the juvenile court's jurisdiction. Although the definition of delinquency varies from state to state, the violation of a state law or local ordinance (an act that would be a crime if committed by an adult) is the main category. Youths who violate federal law or laws from other states; who are wayward, incorrigible or habitually truant or who associate with immoral people are incorporated under delinquency acts and subject to the jurisdiction of the juvenile court.

Other Cases Within Juvenile Court Jurisdiction

In addition to having jurisdiction over children who are in need of protection, who commit status offenses or who commit serious crimes, some juvenile courts have authority to handle other problems, such as adoptions, illegitimacy and guardianship.

The jurisdiction of the court is further extended by provisions in many states that it may exercise its authority over adults in certain cases involving children. Thus, in many states the juvenile court may require a parent to contribute to child support, or it may charge and try adults with contributing to the delinquency, neglect, abuse or dependency of a child.

▊ Juvenile courts may deal with child-related problems, such as adoptions, illegitimacy and guardianship. They may exercise authority over adults in certain cases involving children.

The state is the "higher or ultimate parent" of all the children within its borders. The rights of the child's own parents are always subject to the control of the state when in the opinion of the court the best interests of the child demand it. If the state has to intervene in the case of any child, it exercises its power of guardianship over the child and provides him or her with the protection, care and guidance needed.

Although the substantive justice system for juveniles is administered by a specialized court, a great deal of variation exists in the juvenile law of different jurisdictions. Before a court with juvenile jurisdiction may declare a youth a ward of the state, it must be convinced that a basis for that wardship exists. The possible bases for declaration of wardship include demonstrations that the child is abused or neglected, or has committed a criminal act (the same as committed by an adult) or a status offense.

Offenses Excluded from Juvenile Court Jurisdiction

Not all offenses committed by young people are within the jurisdiction of the juvenile court. There are no firm assurances a case will be heard in the juvenile court. The juvenile judge is given discretion to waive jurisdiction in a particular case and to transfer it to a criminal court if the circumstances and conduct dictate, as will be discussed later in this chapter.

In some states delinquency is not exclusively within the scope of the juvenile court. Jurisdiction in juvenile court may be concurrent with criminal court. Often this concurrent jurisdiction is limited by law to cases being handled by either court. Furthermore, certain offenses, such as murder, manslaughter or rape, may be entirely excluded from the jurisdiction of the juvenile court. In states with such laws, children charged with these offenses are automatically tried in criminal court.

Several states have specified offenses that are excluded from the jurisdiction of the juvenile court. Colorado statutes, for example, state:

> Juvenile court does not have jurisdiction over: children 14 or older charged with crimes of violence classified as Class 1 felonies; children 16 or older who within the previous two years have been adjudicated delinquent for commission of a felony and are now charged with a Class 2 or Class 3 felony or any nonclassified felony punishable by death or life imprisonment. . . .

Delaware excludes first degree murder, rape and kidnapping, unless the case is transferred to juvenile court from criminal court. Hawaii excludes Class A felonies in certain cases if the child is 16 years or older. Illinois excludes murder, criminal sexual assault, armed robbery with a firearm and possession of a deadly weapon in a school committed by a child 15 or older. Several other states exclude youths who have had previous problems with the law. (See Appendix C for each state's specific exclusions.)

TYPES OF JUVENILE COURTS

The phrase "juvenile court" really is a misnomer. Only in isolated cases have completely separate courts for juveniles been established. Where they have been, it has been primarily in the larger cities. Boston, for example, has a specialized court for handling juvenile matters, but its jurisdiction is less than citywide. A few states (Connecticut, Rhode Island and Utah) have separate juvenile court systems. Elsewhere throughout the country, juvenile court jurisdiction resides in a variety of courts: municipal, county, district, superior or probate. Some of these are multiple judge courts; others are served by a single judge.

> ∎ Throughout their history, juvenile courts have been separated into three types: designated courts, independent and separate courts, and coordinated courts.

Designated courts are those in municipalities, counties, districts and circuits that are designated to hear children's cases and while so functioning are called "juvenile court." The great majority of juvenile courts are designated courts and usually preside in counties.

Independent and separate courts are those whose administration is entirely divorced from other courts. Many of the separate and independent courts are presided over by judges from other courts, however, so their separateness and independence is more in name than in reality.

The last type of court with jurisdiction involving children is *coordinated courts*. These courts are coordinated with other special courts, such as domestic relations or family courts.

CHARACTERISTICS OF THE JUVENILE COURT

Although the juvenile court has had an uneven development and has manifested a great diversity in its methods and procedures, certain characteristics have appeared that are considered essential in its operation. As early as 1920, Evelina Belden of the United States Children's Bureau listed the following as the essential characteristics of the juvenile court:

- ∎ Separate hearings for children's cases
- ∎ Informal or chancery procedure
- ∎ Regular probation service
- ∎ Separate detention of children
- ∎ Special court and probation records
- ∎ Provisions for mental and physical examinations

Unfortunately, many juvenile courts do not have these characteristics. Critics argue that courts that do not have them cannot claim to be juvenile courts.

The standards for a juvenile court should consist of the procedures and standards in the Uniform Juvenile Court Act (see Chapter 3) for the court to be effective and meet its responsibilities.

In the United States the juvenile court varies from one jurisdiction to another, manifesting at present all stages of its complex development. It should not be overlooked that its philosophy, structure and functions are still evolving.

Rarely is the court distinct and highly specialized. In the more rural counties, it is largely rudimentary. Usually, it is part of a court with more jurisdiction. In Minnesota, for example, it is a part of the probate court. Judges hold sessions for juveniles at irregular intervals or when the hearings can be in clusters. Since there is great diversity, no simple structure or description of the juvenile courts of the United States can be given.

THE ADJUDICATION PROCESS

To **adjudicate** is to judge. Oran (1985, p. 11) defines an **adjudication** as "the formal giving, pronouncing, or recording of a judgment for one side in a lawsuit." *Adjudicative facts* are "The 'who, what, where, etc.,' facts about persons having a dispute before an *administrative agency*" (italics in original).

■ To adjudicate is to judge—to hear and decide a case.

In terms of the juvenile court, adjudication refers to the judge's determination (decision) that a youth is a status offender, a delinquent or neither.

Changes in the juvenile court interrelate with such factors as industrialization, urbanization, population shifts, the use of natural resources, the rapid acceleration of technology and the acceleration of transportation and communication. All have influenced the family and neighborhood, forcing communities to find new or additional sources of social control. This has given considerable impetus to a broader look at the juvenile court and its adjudication process.

In 1967 the U.S. Supreme Court decided a landmark juvenile justice case. For the first time in the history of the United States, the basic philosophy and practices of the juvenile court were reviewed. The Court concluded (*In re Gault*):

> While there can be no doubt of the original laudable purpose of the juvenile courts, studies and critiques in recent years raise serious questions as to whether actual performance measures well enough against theoretical purpose to make tolerable the immunity of the process from the constitutional guarantees applicable to adults. . . . There is evidence, in fact, that there may be grounds for concern that the child receives the worst of two possible worlds: that he gets neither the protections accorded to adults nor the solicitous care and regenerative treatment postulated for children.

■ A series of Supreme Court decisions has changed the juvenile court's procedures into a more adversarial approach

---

A brief review of these landmark cases is helpful at this point. *In re Gault* required that the due process clause of the Fourteenth Amendment apply to proceedings in state juvenile courts including the right of notice, the right to counsel, the right against self-incrimination and the right to confront witnesses.

In re Winship established proof beyond a reasonable doubt as the standard for juvenile adjudication proceedings, eliminating lesser standards such as a preponderance of the evidence, clear and convincing proof and reasonable proof.

McKeiver established that a jury trial is not a required part of due process in the adjudication of a youth as a delinquent by a juvenile court. *Breed* established that a juvenile cannot be adjudicated in juvenile court and then tried for the same offense in an adult court (double jeopardy).

Schall established that preventive detention fulfills a legitimate state interest of protecting society and juveniles by detaining those who might be dangerous to society or to themselves.

These Supreme Court decisions had a major impact on the adjudication process of the juvenile justice system. Some constitutional requirements have been applied to those parts of the states' juvenile proceedings that are adjudicative. In many cases, these changes have reflected a move towards a more adversarial system in the juvenile courts.

Guardian *Ad Litem*

Despite the trend toward a more adversarial approach, the juvenile justice system provides some safeguards against a full adversary system. One such safeguard provided in some states is the **guardian *ad litem.***

▮ A guardian *ad litem* is a representative of a juvenile, appointed by the juvenile court judge solely for the best interest of the child and to represent that interest on his or her behalf.

The guardian *ad litem* can be anyone the juvenile court judge determines will accept that responsibility and act in the child's best interest. The guardian *ad litem* fulfills this responsibility in all matters involving juveniles, whether they are neglected, abused, dependent or delinquent.

Forty-seven states have volunteer guardian *ad litem* programs called CASA— Court Appointed Special Advocate for Children. (*Casa* means home in Spanish.) One of the primary functions of a CASA is to conduct investigations as to the best placement in foster homes for children. Judge Forest Eastman, President of the National Council of Juvenile and Family Court Judges notes: "An effective CASA program can assure the court that a child is prospering in the ordered placement, and that no child will be lost in the system" (Sweet, 1987, p. 2).

Further, according to a Kentucky judge: "CASA's most important feature is that it is a people-to-people program. It matches caring, well-trained volunteers with children who otherwise might have no voice in determining their own future" (Sweet, 1987, p. 5).

CASAs work primarily in cases of child neglect, physical abuse, psychological abuse, sexual abuse, abandonment or when parents are unwilling or unable to care for their children. As noted by Sweet (1987, pp. 3–4):

The role of the CASA as a guardian ad litem is to investigate, evaluate, and recommend to the court what is truly in the child's best interests, both from a temporary and a long-term standpoint. The CASA serves as:

- ■ Investigator—determining all relevant facts through personal interviews and a review of records, documents, and clinical data.
- ■ Advocate—presenting the relevant facts before the court at hearings, through written reports, and direct testimony.
- ■ Facilitator or negotiator—ensuring that the court, social services, and legal counsel fulfill their obligations to the child.
- ■ Monitor of all court orders—ensuring compliance by all parties and bringing to the court's attention any change in circumstances that may require modification of the court order.

The intake hearing was introduced in Chapter 9 from the perspective of law enforcement and prosecution. Consider it now as the initial phase in the adjudication process.

THE INTAKE HEARING

In most jurisdictions the offender is referred immediately to juvenile authorities or an "intake unit." At the intake stage of the referral, an intake officer decides to adjust, settle or terminate the matter. The intake officer also makes referrals to other interests out of concern for the health, welfare and the safety of the child. This process in most states is called the "intake hearing." The purpose of these proceedings is not to adjudicate the affirmation (guilty) or denial (not guilty) of juveniles in the matter, but to determine if the matter requires the court's attention. The intake unit serves in an advisory capacity.

Another important function of the intake hearing is to provide an authoritarian setting in which a severe lecture or counsel may be administered to the youth so as to avoid future difficulties. Beyond a lecture, several other options are available to intake officers:

- ■ Write a reprimand.
- ■ Divert to another social agency.
- ■ Direct to the district/county attorney's office for a petition.
- ■ Dismiss the matter.

Intake cases are screened in the referral process by an officer appointed by the juvenile court. This officer is usually a probation officer or designated court personnel. Intake officers usually are not lawyers.

In matters handled by intake, the biggest disparity from state to state is in how abused, neglected and dependent children are helped, and in how the best interests of the child are defined. The amount and quality of social services available for implementing such help vary greatly. Two distinct kinds of court action may result.

■ **Court action on behalf of neglected, abused or dependent children may be noncriminal or criminal.**

The first action on behalf of neglected, abused or dependent children is *noncriminal.* It seeks to identify whether the child is in danger and, if so, what is needed for the child's protection. The parents may lose custody of the child, be required to pay child support or be ordered to make adjustments in care, custody and control. This type of action does not permit punitive sanctions against the parents, however.

A second option is *criminal* prosecution of the parents, on charges that they have committed a harmful act against the child or have failed to discharge their responsibility, thus placing the child in active danger. This action does not involve the status of the child. The scope of the court's position in these referrals is based on the juvenile court's responsibility for the welfare of the child under the philosophy of *in loco parentis.*

Referrals carry the same weight as a court process and are subject to rules of law and procedure to protect children. Referrals carry the necessary information to guide court personnel to proceed in a directed course, such as diversion or channeling to the proper authority.

THE THREE PHASES FOLLOWING FILING OF A PETITION

If a case involving a juvenile proceeds to court, a petition is filed. Following the filing, the court goes through three phases.

▮ The three phases following the filing of a petition are (1) the preliminary hearing or conference, (2) the adjudicatory hearing or trial and (3) the dispositional hearing or sentencing.

The *preliminary hearing* or conference satisfies those matters that must be dealt with before the case can proceed further. At this first hearing, the judge informs the parties involved of the charges in the petition and of their rights in the proceeding. If the case involves an abused, neglected or dependent child, a guardian is usually appointed to act as an advocate of the child. This person is often a representative of a social service or welfare agency. The hearing may also be used to determine whether an alleged delinquent should remain in detention or custody of juvenile authority. In the matter of detention, if the judge, with the assistance of a probation officer, determines that the child's behavior is a threat to the public, is a danger to himself and others or that the child will not return to court voluntarily, the judge can order the child to remain in custody. Dependent, neglected or abused children, as well as status offenders, may be placed in foster care or a residential shelter.

The *adjudicatory hearing* or trial is to determine if the allegations of the petition are supported by a "preponderance of evidence" (for status offenses) or by evidence that proves "beyond a reasonable doubt" that a delinquent act occurred. The child makes a plea, either an admission or denial of the allegations in the petition. If the allegations are sustained, the judge makes a finding of fact (that the child is delinquent, abused, neglected or otherwise in need of supervision), sets a date for a dispositional hearing and orders a social investigation or presentence investigation (PSI) or a predisposition report.

■ *A juvenile hearing is often informal and resembles a conference more than a trial.*

At the *dispositional hearing* the judge states what will happen to the youth, as discussed shortly.

COURT REFEREES

In many states the law provides for the juvenile judge to appoint referees. The judge may refer cases to these referees for hearings. The powers of the referee are limited by law. In some states that have referees, the referee is not empowered to make a final order, but acts as an advisor to the court.

■ The principal functions of referees are to act as hearing officers, to reduce testimony to findings of fact and to make recommendations on **disposition.**

The referee's recommendation may be modified, approved or rejected by the juvenile judge, but when approved or modified it becomes an order of the court.

Juvenile court referees are a valuable asset to the court, since they allow judges more time to focus attention on difficult cases. There are specific cases referees automatically hear and guidelines referees automatically follow. Judges normally would hear cases in which custody of a child is in question, as well as serious delinquency cases in which violence occurred. Referees also are not involved in matters where the question of jurisdiction of the court is in question, such as the transfer or certification of a juvenile to a criminal court.

The role of the referee is to assist the juvenile court judge, rather than to replace or become the judge.

DISPOSITION

Springer (1986, p. 50) says: "Disposition, called the 'heartbeat of the juvenile court,' is the euphemism used in juvenile court parlance to describe what is to be done for or to a child, once the child's status as poor, naughty, or criminal has been adjudicated by the court." The court has several options. It can:

∎ Dismiss the case with no charges at all.
∎ Refer the youth to a social service agency.
∎ Order that the youth make restitution.
∎ Put the youth on probation.
∎ Sentence the youth to a correctional facility.
∎ In some states order the death penalty.

∎ **The trend is toward deinstitutionalization of youth.**

The role of social services agencies is discussed in Chapter 12, that of probation and corrections in Chapter 11. The death penalty and restitution are discussed next.

Death Penalty

The United States is one of only three countries in the world that allows individuals who committed crimes while they were children to be executed. This practice has been disapproved by the United Nations Convention on the Rights of the Child. According to the National Coalition (1992, p. 27):

> As of May 1, 1992, there were 31 persons on death row under death sentences for juvenile crimes in this country. Since 1979 only eight juvenile executions have occurred worldwide—three in the United States. . . .

Greenfeld and Stephan (1993, p. 4) report that at the end of 1992 11 states and the federal system authorized age 18 as the minimum age for capital punishment. Those states were California, Colorado, Connecticut, Illinois, Maryland, Nebraska, New Jersey, New Mexico, Ohio, Oregon and Tennessee. Seventeen states authorized a minimum age for capital punishment *less* than age 18:

∎ Alabama (16)
∎ Arkansas (14)
∎ Georgia (17)
∎ Indiana (16)
∎ Kentucky (16)
∎ Louisiana (16)

- Mississippi (16)
- Missouri (16)
- Nevada (16)
- New Hampshire (17)
- North Carolina (17)
- Oklahoma (16)
- South Dakota (no minimum specified)
- Texas (17)
- Utah (14)
- Virginia (15)
- Wyoming (16)

The remaining states did not specifiy a minimum age authorized for capital punishment.

Restitution

An increasingly popular disposition of the juvenile court is **restitution,** that is, personally righting a wrong, restoring property or a right to a person unjustly deprived of the property or right. According to Schneider and Warner (1989, p. 1): "During the last decade, juvenile courts have shifted toward a philosophy of justice based on holding juveniles accountable to their crime victims through financial restitution (payment) or performing symbolic restitution (community service work)." They also note:

> One expert has argued that restitution is the only sanction available to juvenile courts that simultaneously seeks to increase public safety by reducing the likelihood of recidivism, holding juveniles accountable to victims, and increasing the capacity of the juvenile offender to outgrow delinquency and live a law-abiding adult life.

Table 10–2 summaries the major program components in restitution programs.
Feinman (1990, p. 3) stresses that any restitution program placing youths in paid or unpaid positions also assumes responsibilities for their safety and their behavior. Restitution programs must consider:

- Injuries sustained by the juvenile in a court-ordered placement.
- Injuries or harm done by the juvenile at the worksite.
- Loss or damages caused by the youth as a result of a crime committed at the workplace.

In the criminal justice system a crime is an act committed against the *state*. As victims' rights movements gain momentum, however, more attention is being paid to this group. One way this is happening is through restitution programs. Closely related to restitution is the victim-offender mediation program, modeled after the Victim Offender Reconciliation Program (VORP) originating in Canada in the mid-1970s. As noted by Hughes and Schneider (1990, p. 1), the purposes of the original VORP project were:

- To provide an alternative method of dealing with crime.
- To allow victim and offender an opportunity to reconcile and mutually agree on restitution.

TABLE   Major Restitution Program Components
10-2

Component	Number of Programs	Had Component in	
		1985	1986
Financial restitution	353	90%	92%
Community service	352	88	92
Victim-offender mediation	342	26	37
Victim services	329	38	49
Job information services	339	44	56
Work crews	337	41	47
Transportation	338	33	36
Job slots in private sector	340	24	32
Subsidies	341	21	25

Note: The number of programs varies depending upon the number that responded to each specific question.

SOURCE: Anne Larason Schneider and Jean Shumway Warner, *National Trends in Juvenile Restitution Programming,* Restitution Education, Specialized Training & Technical Assistance Program (RESTTA) (July 1989), p. 3.

▌ To use a third party to mediate and facilitate reconciliation.
▌ To deal with crime as a conflict to be resolved.

Hughes and Schneider (1990) report on the results of a survey mailed to 240 organizations involved in juvenile justice across the country known to be using mediation. Their response rate was more than 70 percent. The survey identified the purposes and goals of the respondents and compared these responses with those not using such a program. The results of this comparison are shown in Figure 10-1.

For all respondents, the most important goal was holding the offender accountable. The programs varied greatly in what type of restitution was required of the offender in the agreed-upon restitution contract, as summarized in Figure 10-2.

The perceived effectiveness of dispositional alternatives also varied, but all respondents rated restitution as most effective in reducing recidivism, rehabilitating offenders, increasing victim satisfaction, holding offenders accountable and being fair to offenders and victims. Mediation was rated second most effective in most instances. However, incarceration was seen as being more effective than mediation in increasing victim satisfaction. (See Figure 10-3.)

Support for mediation programs was highest among juvenile court judges, followed by family members. Least supportive were state legislators, but they, too, were on the positive side, as shown in Figure 10-4.

JUVENILE SENTENCING LAWS

The state of Washington passed a Juvenile Justice Act in 1977, which created a mandatory sentencing policy requiring juveniles ages 8-17 who are

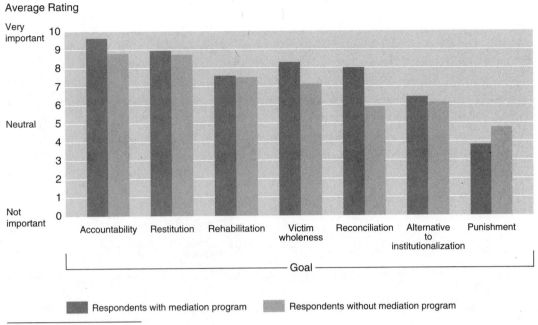

■ FIGURE 10–1 Mediation Program Goals

SOURCE: Stella P. Hughes and Anne L. Schneider, *Victim-Offender Mediation In the Juvenile Justice System,* Restitution Education, Specialized Training & Technical Assistance Program (RESTTA) (September 1990), p. 3.

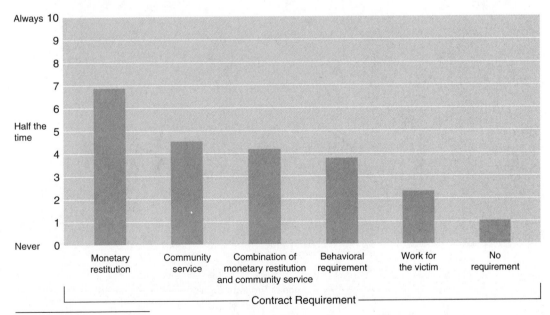

■ FIGURE 10–2 Frequency of Inclusion of Various Contract Requirements

SOURCE: Stella P. Hughes and Anne L. Schneider, *Victim-Offender Mediation In the Juvenile Justice System,* Restitution Education, Specialized Training & Technical Assistance Program (RESTTA) (September 1990), p. 6.

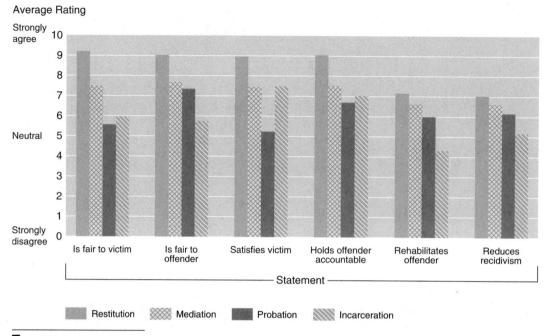

■ FIGURE 10–3 Perceived Effectiveness of Dispositional Alternatives

SOURCE: Stella P. Hughes and Anne L. Schneider, *Victim-Offender Mediation In the Juvenile Justice System,* Restitution Education, Specialized Training & Technical Assistance Program (RESTTA) (September 1990), p. 9.

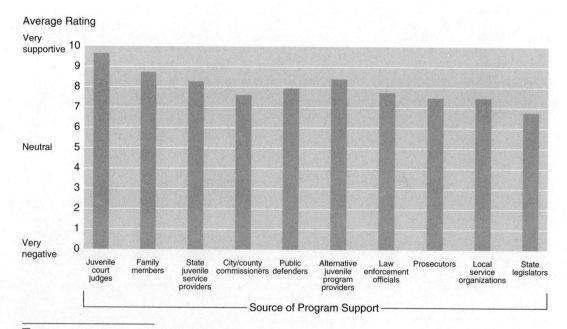

■ FIGURE 10–4 Amount of Support from Various Sources

SOURCE: Stella P. Hughes and Anne L. Schneider, *Victim-Offender Mediation In the Juvenile Justice System,* Restitution Education, Specialized Training & Technical Assistance Program (RESTTA) (September 1990), p. 7.

adjudicated delinquent to be confined in an institution for a minimum term. As noted in the Act:

> It is the intent of the legislature that a system be developed capable of having primary responsibility for being accountable for and responding to the needs of youthful offenders. It is the further intent of the legislature that youth, in turn, be held accountable for their offenses and that both communities and juvenile courts carry out their function consistent with this intent. (Section 13.40.010[2] Supp.1978)

To accomplish its goal, the Act includes a formal scoring sheet to determine how long an adjudicated youth must spend in confinement.

▌ **The mandatory sentencing policy in Washington is based on the juvenile's age, the current offense and the criminal history of the offender.**

To compute the score under the Washington system, the type of offense is plotted on the left side of Table 10–3 and the age of the juvenile is listed across the top. For example, a 15-year-old charged with first-degree arson (offense class A) would have a score of 250. This is multiplied by a weighting factor based on the youth's prior criminal record. If the youth had stayed out of trouble for 14 months, the 250 score would be multiplied by .6 for a score of 150. This final number would then be plotted on the grid in Table 10–4 to determine the sentence.

Systems such as these help guide judges in their sentencing and tend to make sentencing more equitable from one case to the next. A national survey of almost 1,000 randomly selected adults indicated that 78 percent believed the primary purpose of juvenile court should be treatment and rehabilitation of young offenders in contrast to the 12 percent who supported punishment (National Coalition, 1992, p. 38). Whatever the sentence, however, it should be individualized. Mechanical jurisprudence should be avoided in the juvenile justice system.

MECHANICAL JURISPRUDENCE

Legal philosopher H. L. A. Hart (1965, p. 125) expresses an underlying assumption in any government of laws:

> It is a feature of human predicament . . . whenever we seek to regulate, unambiguously and in advance, some sphere of conduct by means of general standards to be used without further official direction on particular occasions. . . . If the world in which we live were characterized only by the finite number of features, and these together with all the modes in which they could be made in advance for every possibility, we could make rules, the applications of which to particular cases never called for a further choice. Everything could be known, and for everything since it could be known, something could be done and specified in advance by rule. This could be a world for "mechanical jurisprudence."

TABLE 10–3   Adjudicated Offender Confinement Scoring Sheet, State of Washington

Offense Class*	Age at Current Offense(s)						Class Span	Criminal History (Months Since Last Involvement)			
	17	16	15	14	13	12		0–6	6–12	12+	More
A+	400	350	300	300	250	250	A+	.9	.8	.7	
A	300	300	250	250	225	200	A	.9	.8	.6	
B+	150	140	120	110	110	110	B+	.9	.7	.4	
B	54	52	50	48	46	44	B	.9	.6	.3	
C+	42	40	38	36	34	32	C+	.5	.3	.2	
C	30	28	26	24	22	20	C	.4	.3	.2	
GH+	26	24	22	20	18	16	GH+	.3	.2	.1	
GH	24	22	20	18	16	14	GH	.2	.1	.1	
M&V	10	8	6	4	4	4	M&V	.1	.1	.1	

*Offense class and crime types for the state of Washington are correlated as follows:

Offense Class	Offense Type (Examples)	Offense Class	Offense Type (Examples)
A+	Assault 1	C	Escape 2, forgery, theft 2
A	Arson 1, rape 1	GH+	Assault, simple
B+	Assault 2, burglary 1, rape 2, robbery 2	GH	Criminal trespass
B	Arson 2, burglary 2	M/V	Disorderly conduct, malicious mischief 3
C+	Assault 3, manslaughter 2, rape 3		

SOURCE: Wash. Rev. Code Ann., Title 9A, §§ 1-91 [1977] presented in Charles P. Smith, Paul S. Alexander, Garry L. Komp, and Edwin N. Lamert, Reports of the National Juvenile Justice Assessment Court, *A National Assessment of Serious Juvenile Crime and the Juvenile Justice System: The Need for a Rational Response*, vol. 3, Legislation, Jurisdiction, Program Interventions, and Confidentiality of Juvenile Records (Washington D.C.: U.S. Government Printing Office, 1980).

■ **Mechanical jurisprudence** suggests that everything is known and that, therefore, laws can be made in advance to cover every situation.

Unfortunately, the concept of mechanical jurisprudence is frequently applied to juvenile conduct and behavior, as illustrated in the following example from a report entitled "Karen's Kids" on the CBS television program *60 Minutes*.

The program reported a case of a mother found by the court to be mentally unstable, and who had her five children removed from home by a court order. The woman was hospitalized for mental illness and her children placed in a foster home until she recovered. The arrangement with the foster parents was to be short term, but it lasted for two years. During that time the foster parents petitioned the court to adopt the children. The hospitalized mother was asked to forfeit her parental rights so the adoption could proceed. The mother refused and wanted the children removed from the foster home. The social service agency proceeded to do so. The foster parents obtained a restraining order to

TABLE 10-4   Adjudicated Offender Sentence Grid, State of Washington

Points	Community Service Hours	Supervision	Fine	Confinement or Partial Confinement	Confinement Time	Time on Parole
1–9	5–25 hours	max. 3 mo.	max. $25			
10–19	20–35 hours	max. 3 mo.	max. $25			
20–29	30–45 hours	max. 6 mo.	max. $50			
30–39	40–65 hours	max. 6 mo.	max. $50			
40–49	50–75 hours	max. 6 mo.	max. $75			
50–59	60–69 hours	max. 9 mo.	max. $75	1–2		
60–69	70–100 hours	max. 9 mo.	max. $75	3–6		
70–79	80–110 hours	max. 1 yr.	max. $100	7–14		
80–89	90–130 hours	max. 1 yr.	max. $100	10–20		
90–109	100–150 hours	max. 1 yr.	max. $100	15–30		
110–119					60–90 days	max. 4 mo.
120–129					13–16 weeks	max. 4 mo.
130–139					15–20 weeks	max. 6 mo.
140–149					21–28 weeks	max. 6 mo.
150–169					30–40 weeks	max. 8 mo.
170–199					38–52 weeks	max. 8 mo.
200–229					12–15 mo.	max. 12 mo.
230–269					16–20 mo.	max. 12 mo.
270–309					20–25 mo. (2 yr.)	max. 12 mo.
310–349					24–30 mo.	max. 18 mo.
350–399					32–40 mo. (3 yr.)	max. 18 mo.
400 or Over					40–50 mo.	max. 18 mo.

SOURCE: Charles P. Smith, Paul S. Alexander, Garry L. Komp, and Edwin N. Lamert, Reports of the National Juvenile Justice Assessment Court, A National Assessment of Serious Juvenile Crime and the Juvenile Justice System: The Need for a Rational Response, vol. 3, Legislation, Jurisdiction, Program Interventions, and Confidentiality of Juvenile Records (Washington, D.C.: U.S. Government Printing Office, 1980).

ensure that the children would stay together. The children provided a deposition that they were very happy with the foster parents and that they did not want to return to their natural mother because she and her male friends physically abused them. The mother confirmed abusing the children, but denied knowing if any male friends had done so.

The two older girls, ages 11 and 13, were vehemently opposed to being removed from the foster parents and attempted suicide and running away. Despite this, the state social service agency's director ordered the children removed. The order was executed by uniformed sheriff's deputies, who removed the children despite pleas to the state agency by friends and neighbors. They also submitted pleas and requests to various bureaucrats and politicians with no success. The children were placed in five separate foster homes, the mother lost parental rights and the foster parents were discharged from the foster parent program. The two girls continued to run away from their new foster parents and attempted suicide twice. It would appear that in this instance that the court's inflexibility was *not* in the best interest of the children involved.

Mechanical jurisprudence is inappropriate in our justice system because everything cannot be known about any offense. Further, since delinquency includes a wide variety of different behaviors, there is no single common problem of delinquency but, instead, a series of separable problems each with its unique psychodynamic and social orientation.

WAIVER AND CERTIFICATION

The juvenile court may waive jurisdiction and transfer a case from the juvenile to the criminal court. Another possibility is that the court may decree that a juvenile should be certified as an adult (**certification**). When either case occurs, juveniles go through the same procedures and have the same constitutional rights as adults tried in a criminal court. **Waiver** or certification does not occur often. Recall that the procedural requirements for waiver to criminal court were articulated by the Supreme Court in *Kent* v. *United States*.

Certification is of paramount importance since it may result in far more severe consequences to the juvenile than if the juvenile had remained under the jurisdiction of the juvenile court. Appendix C describes the conditions involved in the waiver procedure in each state. The procedures followed differ from state to state.

▌ In some states the court makes the decision to certify a juvenile as an adult. In other states this is done by the prosecutor.

Davis (1985, pp. 4–3 to 4–5) outlines general guidelines for the certification procedure as follows:

▌ Most jurisdictions require the child be over a certain age and be charged with a particularly serious offense before jurisdiction may be waived.
▌ A number of states permit waiver of jurisdiction over children above a certain age, without regard to the nature of the offense charged.

■ Some jurisdictions place no limitations on waiver, permitting waiver without regard to the age of the child or the nature of the offense.

■ A number of states permit waiver based on a combination of other factors.

According to Harris (1988, pp. 655–656): "Legislatively mandated waiver and reduced ages of majority encourage the handling of greater numbers of juveniles within the criminal justice system. Determinate sentencing provisions, such as mandatory terms of incarceration for certain offenders, mimic provisions adopted by the criminal justice system in previous years." Despite such sentencing reforms, however, many perceive that when juveniles are waived to adult court, they are treated leniently. To determine if such was indeed the case, Harris asked prosecutors of one New Jersey county to rate the seriousness of the offenses of 500 juveniles and 500 adults charged with assault or robbery. The results of this study indicated that the crimes committed by juveniles were *not* as serious as those committed by adults, as indicated in Table 10–5. Juveniles

TABLE 10–5   **Characteristics of Assaults and Robberies by Crime and Court of Jurisdiction**

Characteristic	Assaults		Robberies	
	Juveniles	Adults	Juveniles	Adults
Weapon use	N = 225	N = 186	N = 249	N = 238
None	63.6%	4.3%	61.0%	25.6%
Objects	30.2	14.0	6.0	5.0
Knives	3.6	29.6	14.5	13.9
Gun	2.7	52.2	18.5	55.5
Extent of injury	N = 233	N = 223	N = 242	N = 214
None	14.6	24.2	42.6	61.7
Minor	9.4	3.1	13.2	10.7
Punched	73.0	40.4	40.9	19.2
Stabbed, shot	3.0	29.1	2.1	3.7
Killed	0.0	3.1	1.2	4.7
Number of victims	N = 238	N = 236	N = 246	N = 227
One	80.0	67.4	85.4	68.7
Two	16.0	20.3	13.0	25.1
Three	4.2	7.2	1.6	5.3
Four	0.0	4.7	0.0	0.4
Five or more	0.0	0.4	0.0	0.4
Value of victim loss (robberies only)			N = 216	N = 227
$ 0			26.9	15.7
$ 1–10			17.1	5.4
$ 11–50			21.3	16.2
$ 51–100			16.3	7.4
$ 101–200			10.2	22.1
$ 201–500			5.1	16.1
$ Over 500			3.2	17.2

SOURCE: Patricia M. Harris, "Juvenile Sentence Reform and its Evaluation: A Demonstration of the Need for More Precise Measures of Offense Seriousness in Juvenile Justice Research," *Evaluation Review,* (December 1988) 6:662. (Copyright Sage Publications, Inc.)

were much less likely to use a weapon, particularly guns. They were also less likely to cause injury. The value of victim loss in robberies was also less in the juvenile cases.

Table 10–6 summarizes the public's attitudes toward juvenile crime, justice and waiver to adult court. Although over half (57.4%) the respondents felt juveniles were entitled to the same due process as an adult, only 15.5 percent felt juveniles convicted of a crime should receive the same sentence as an adult.

TABLE 10–6   **Public's Attitudes Toward Juvenile Crime and Juvenile Justice, 1991**

	Strongly Agree	Somewhat Agree	Neither Agree nor Disagree	Somewhat Disagree	Strongly Disagree
A juvenile accused of a crime should receive the same due process as an adult.	57.4%	25.4%	0.7%	10.3%	6.1%
A juvenile convicted of a crime should receive the same sentence as an adult, no matter what the crime.	15.5	20.1	2.5	35.1	26.8
A juvenile charged with a serious property crime should be tried as an adult.	23.2	26.7	4.2	24.7	21.2
A juvenile charged with selling large amounts of illegal drugs should be tried as an adult.	40.5	21.6	2.4	20.4	15.0
A juvenile charged with a serious violent crime should be tried as an adult.	43.1	24.5	1.9	15.2	15.3
Juveniles should be sent to adult prisons for committing serious property crimes.	6.5	9.0	1.4	22.1	61.0
Juveniles should be sent to adult prisons for selling large amounts of drugs.	13.8	16.4	1.9	22.2	45.6
Juveniles should be sent to adult prisons for committing serious violent crimes.	22.0	20.2	2.5	21.7	33.6
Sending juvenile offenders to training schools discourages other young people from committing crimes.	23.4	27.4	4.4	24.5	20.2

Note: The Center for the Studies of Youth Policy conducted a national telephone interview survey during August and September 1991. The survey focused on public attitudes toward juvenile crime and juvenile justice. Approximately 50 percent of the sample was drawn from a national frame, excluding Alaska and Hawaii, of 1,200 listed household telephone numbers. The other 50 percent of the sample was generated using a random digit dialing procedure. After completing a weighting and adjustment procedure, the number of sample cases was 1,000. These data are estimates derived from a sample and, therefore, subject to sampling variation.

Percents may not add to 100 because of rounding.

SOURCE: *Sourcebook of Criminal Justice Statistics, 1992* (Washington, D.C.: U.S. Government Printing Office, 1993), p. 198.

A national survey conducted by *Parade* magazine in 1993 asked if a juvenile (13–16-years-old) charged with a violent crime should be tried in juvenile or adult court. Of those responding, only 28.8 percent favored juvenile court.

The National Coalition (1992, p. 26) reports: "[R]ecent studies show that juveniles are now receiving more severe sanctions in the adult court than youths with similar charges received in the juvenile court." In addition, according to the Coalition, violent youth required an average of 246 days to be transferred, convicted in and sentenced by the criminal court in comparison to an average of 98 days for juvenile court processing.

Reverse Certification

Some statutes automatically give jurisdiction to the criminal courts over juveniles who commit specified serious crimes, such as murder, but permit the criminal court to transfer the case to juvenile court. For example, New York statutes specify that juvenile court jurisdiction:

> Excludes children 13 or older charged with second degree murder and children 14 or older charged with second degree murder, felony murder, kidnapping in the first degree, arson in the first or second degree, assault in the first degree, manslaughter in the first degree, rape in the first degree, sodomy in the first degree, aggravated sexual abuse, burglary in the first or second degree, robbery in the first or second degree, attempted murder, or attempted kidnapping in the first degree, unless such case is transferred to the juvenile court from the criminal court.

■ When the criminal court has exclusive jurisdiction, it may transfer the case to the juvenile court by a process known as **reverse certification**.

YOUTH WHO COME BEFORE THE COURT

By this point you are well aware of the three types of children and youth served in the one-pot juvenile justice system.

Those Who Are Neglected or Abused

Participants at a conference of the National Committee for Prevention of Child Abuse discussed two kinds of intervention for deprived children: coercive and therapeutic.

■ Coercive intervention is out-of-home placement, detainment or mandated therapy or counseling. Therapeutic intervention is a recommendation of an appropriate treatment program.

Participants were in agreement that coercive intervention should be used with children only when necessary, either to protect society or to impose an effective treatment plan for the children.

Several policy recommendations came out of the conference, including the following (pp. 30–31):

▌ *Therapeutic intervention for all abused children who come to the attention of the court exhibiting problem behavior, regardless of the disposition of the case.* The present drift toward stricter delinquency statutes in some States, in which community protection is foremost and the best interest of the child standard is secondary, is based on an erroneous assumption. Protection of the community and rehabilitation of the child are not conflicting goals. . . . Among this group of abused children, there are two subgroups in particular in need of attention: the child exhibiting violent behavior and the sexually abused child.

▌ *Specific and different treatment within the correctional system of the young person who was abused.* . . . [M]uch of our Nation's delinquent population is in a debilitated condition—physically (neurologically), developmentally, and psychologically. . . . We know, for instance, that treatment for the abused child will have to take place over a long term. We know that corporal punishment, physical coercion, and violent or belittling language are inappropriate therapeutic tools; they add institutional abuse to the existing familial abuse.

▌ *Early intervention.* The optimal point of intervention with an abused delinquent would be before the abuse occurred. The earliest treatment intervention we can offer the young abused child would be aimed at keeping him from becoming a delinquent as a later reaction to the earlier abuse. The next opportunity for early intervention occurs when the young person comes to the attention of the court, before he becomes delinquent. Youth who enter the court as Minors ("Persons" or "Children" in different States) in Need of Supervision could be recognized as the abused children they often are and helped in such a way as to preclude further delinquent activity.

▌ *Attractive, benign broad-based intervention styles and services.* Services are needed that do not identify the clients as abusive, abused, or delinquent. Efforts to strengthen families, particularly the development and provision of services that could be called parent education are recommended.

▌ The National Committee for Prevention of Child Abuse recommends the following treatment for abused children: therapeutic intervention, specific and different treatment within the correctional system, early intervention and attractive, benign, broad-based intervention styles and services.

Status Offenders

Children and their families who are brought before the court for status offenses occupy a great share of the court's workload. Status offenders can try the patience of the court because such children often are considered as simply being "in need of supervision," resulting in a group of acronyms: CHINS (children in need of supervision), FINS (families in need of supervision), JINS (juveniles in need of supervision), and PINS (persons in need of supervision).

The juvenile court in some states has dispensed justice harsher for status offenders than for criminal law violators because status offenses are annoyances. There has always been a need to distinguish status offenses from delinquent acts. Often status offenses fall into a separate classification for the court to consider in its dispensing of justice. Recall that according to the American Bar Association, juvenile delinquency liability should include only such conduct as would be designated a crime if committed by an adult.

The referral of status offenses to juvenile court has been viewed by many as an ineffective waste of valuable court resources. Critics believe resources would best be used for the more serious recidivist delinquents the court has to deal with. Whether the court is dealing with status offenders or youths who have committed violent crimes or protecting abused or neglected children, it no longer has free reign. The juvenile court must grant many aspects of due process to the youth who come under its jurisdiction.

In 1990 juvenile courts formally handled about 86,900 status offenses. Forty percent of the status offenders were referred to juvenile court by law enforcement. A third of these cases (33 percent) involved liquor law violations, followed by truancy (28 percent). Table 7–2 summarized the status offenses by age at referral. As might be expected, the truancy rate drops as juveniles become older, but the liquor violations rise.

Figure 10–5 shows the procession of petitioned status offenders in 1990.

Over half the nonadjudicated cases were dismissed, and less than 1 percent were placed. Almost one-fourth received probation. In contrast, of those that were adjudicated, only 5 percent were dismissed, 17 percent were placed, and two-thirds were put on probation.

Sickmund (1990) reports on a study conducted by the OJJDP of the records of over 40,000 runaway cases processed between 1985 and 1986. This study

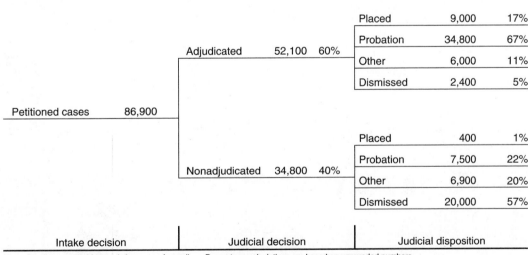

Note: Detail may not add to totals because of rounding. Percentage calculations are based on unrounded numbers.

■ **FIGURE 10–5 Juvenile Court Processing of Petitioned Status Offense Cases, 1990**

SOURCE: Jeffrey A. Butts and Eileen Poe, "Offenders in Juvenile Court, 1990," OJJDP, Update on Statistics, December 1993, p. 9.

indicated that 65 percent of the cases were referred by law enforcement. The next most frequent source of referral was relatives (26 percent). The percentage varied greatly, with law enforcement agencies from large counties having the greatest number of referrals, as shown in Figure 10–6.

According to the OJJDP study, courts handled 80 percent of the cases informally, with nearly three-fourths of the cases being dismissed at intake or referred to a juvenile court in another jurisdiction or a social service agency for service. Figure 10–7 shows the processing of runaway cases in varying size counties.

Delinquent Offenders

In 1990 juvenile courts handled 1,264,800 delinquency cases, a 10 percent increase from 1986. Eighty-five percent of the delinquency referrals were made by law enforcement. In 19 percent of the cases, the most serious charge was a person offense, 58 percent were property offenses, 18 percent public order offenses and 5 percent drug offenses. The juvenile courts transferred 2.7 percent of formally handled delinquency cases to criminal court compared to 1.9 percent in 1986 (Butts and Poe, 1993, p. 1). Table 7–3 showed the delinquency cases by offense. The processing of these delinquency cases is summarized in Figure 10–8. Compared to the processing of status offense cases, the percentage adjudicated and nonadjudicated are strikingly similar, as were the other judicial dispositions, especially the nonadjudicated cases.

Property cases were a major part of the juvenile court load according to an analysis of some 800,000 juvenile court records on delinquency referrals in

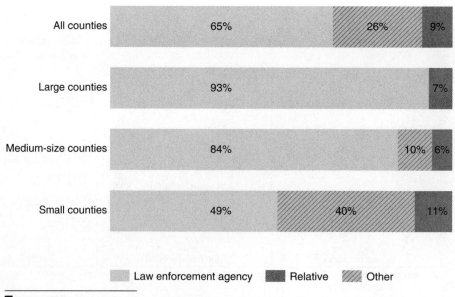

▮ **FIGURE 10–6 Source of Referral of Runaway Cases**

SOURCE: Melissa Sickmund, "Runaways in Juvenile Courts," OJJDP, Update on Statistics, November 1990, p. 5.

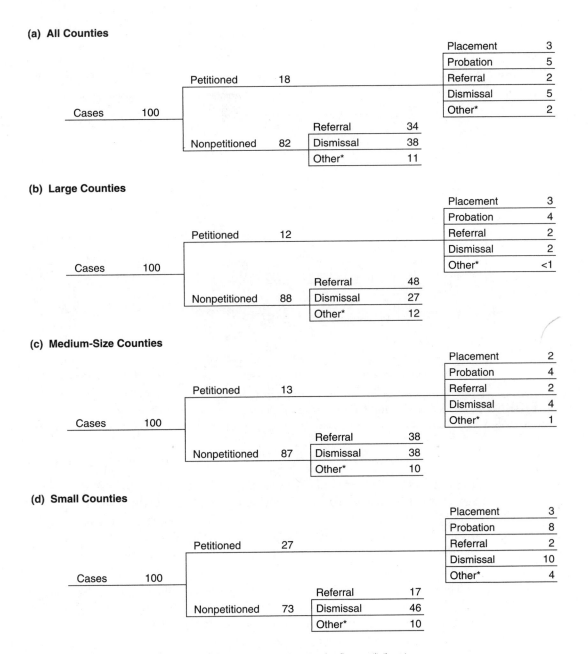

(a) All Counties

Cases 100

Petitioned 18

Placement	3
Probation	5
Referral	2
Dismissal	5
Other*	2

Nonpetitioned 82

Referral	34
Dismissal	38
Other*	11

(b) Large Counties

Cases 100

Petitioned 12

Placement	3
Probation	4
Referral	2
Dismissal	2
Other*	<1

Nonpetitioned 88

Referral	48
Dismissal	27
Other*	12

(c) Medium-Size Counties

Cases 100

Petitioned 13

Placement	2
Probation	4
Referral	2
Dismissal	4
Other*	1

Nonpetitioned 87

Referral	38
Dismissal	38
Other*	10

(d) Small Counties

Cases 100

Petitioned 27

Placement	3
Probation	8
Referral	2
Dismissal	10
Other*	4

Nonpetitioned 73

Referral	17
Dismissal	46
Other*	10

Note: Detail may not add to totals because of rounding. * Referrals to other agencies, fines, restitution, etc.

■ **FIGURE 10–7 Processing of 100 Typical Runaway Cases in Counties of Different Sizes, 1990**

SOURCE: Melissa Sickmund, "Runaways in Juvenile Courts," OJJDP, Update on Statistics, November 1990, p. 6.

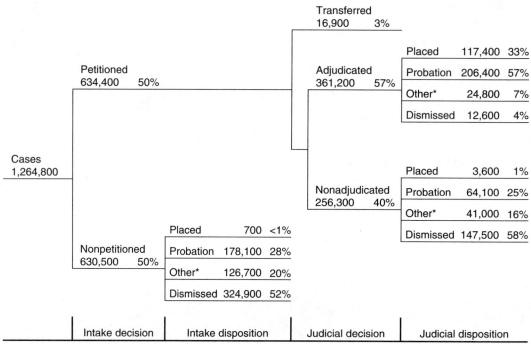

Note: Detail may not add to totals because of rounding. Percentage calculations are based on unrounded numbers. * Referrals to other agencies, fines, restitution, etc.

▌ **FIGURE 10–8 Juvenile Court Processing of Delinquency Cases, 1990**

SOURCE: Jeffrey A. Butts and Eileen Poe, "Offenders in Juvenile Court, 1990," OJJDP, Update on Statistics, December 1993, p. 6.

1985 and 1986. This analysis showed that property offenses increased through age 16 and then decreased for 17-year-olds. Shoplifting was the most common offense. Juveniles referred to court for motor vehicle theft were more likely to be detained than youths referred for other property offenses (Nimick, 1990). Figure 10–9 shows the percent of property cases attributable to male and female offenders.

The processing of property cases showed substantial differences. More than half of the burglary, larceny and motor vehicle theft cases were formally processed, but less than half of the shoplifting and vandalism cases were processed formally, as shown in Figure 10–10.

The National Center for Juvenile Justice (NCJJ) analyzed over 1.4 million case records to determine how juvenile courts' handling of violent offenders has changed from 1985 to 1989. The study included homicide, violent sex offenses, aggravated assault and robbery as violent offenses. Figure 10–11 depicts the offense characteristics of delinquency cases in 10 states in 1989.

This study found that the per capita rate of violent offense cases increased 18 percent from 1985 to 1989. The study also found that courts were more likely to file petitions in cases involving violent offenses (76 percent compared with 50 percent for nonviolent delinquent offenses). In addition violent offenders were more frequently detained (49 percent compared with 25 percent of nonviolent delinquent offenders). The study also found that about one-fourth of

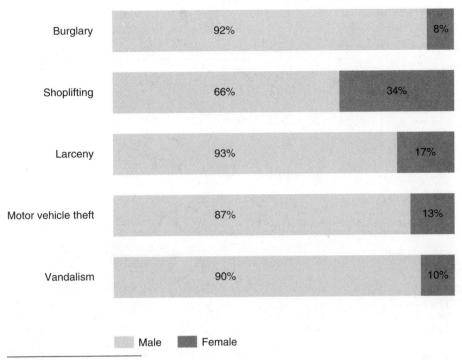

■ **FIGURE 10-9 Percent of Property Cases Attributable to Male and Female Offenders, 1990**

SOURCE: Ellen H. Nimick, "Juvenile Court Property Cases," OJJDP, Update on Statistics," November 1990, p. 2.

violent offenses cases were handled informally by juvenile courts. Seventy percent of these cases were dismissed, often for lack of evidence (Butts and Connors-Beatty, 1993).

THE CURRENT DILEMMA OF THE JUVENILE COURT

In the United States legislators have tremendous interest in the handling of juveniles and the rights guaranteed them by their birth. The "child savers" are still present, and those who wish to get tough with juveniles are continually lobbying for severe measures in all phases of the juvenile process. The U.S. Supreme Court is prepared to protect children and their parents against the custom of informality within the system.

■ The juvenile court's current dilemma hinges on its dual roles as a court of law and as a social service agency.

The juvenile court must gain strength in its judicial role and retain and develop only that part of its social service role necessary to administer individualized justice. As a court, even in the administration of individualized justice, it must express and reinforce the values of the society in which it functions.

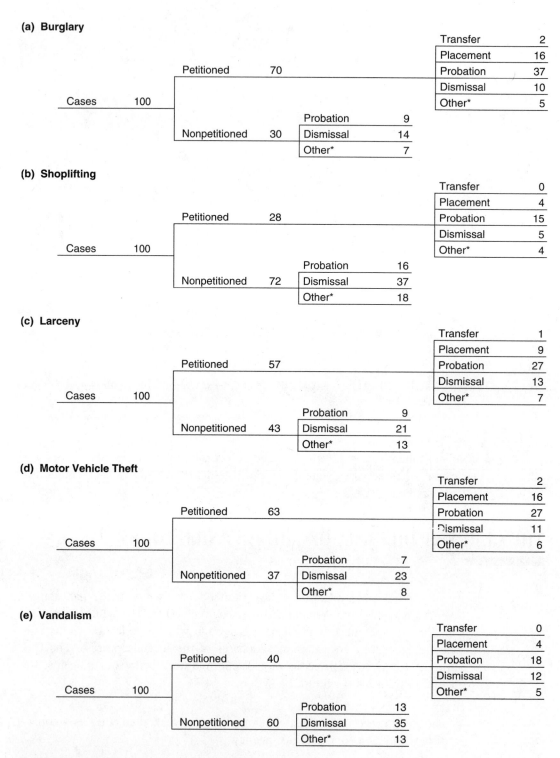

(a) Burglary

				Transfer	2
				Placement	16
		Petitioned	70	Probation	37
				Dismissal	10
Cases	100			Other*	5
			Probation	9	
		Nonpetitioned	30	Dismissal	14
			Other*	7	

(b) Shoplifting

				Transfer	0
				Placement	4
		Petitioned	28	Probation	15
				Dismissal	5
Cases	100			Other*	4
			Probation	16	
		Nonpetitioned	72	Dismissal	37
			Other*	18	

(c) Larceny

				Transfer	1
				Placement	9
		Petitioned	57	Probation	27
				Dismissal	13
Cases	100			Other*	7
			Probation	9	
		Nonpetitioned	43	Dismissal	21
			Other*	13	

(d) Motor Vehicle Theft

				Transfer	2
				Placement	16
		Petitioned	63	Probation	27
				Dismissal	11
Cases	100			Other*	6
			Probation	7	
		Nonpetitioned	37	Dismissal	23
			Other*	8	

(e) Vandalism

				Transfer	0
				Placement	4
		Petitioned	40	Probation	18
				Dismissal	12
Cases	100			Other*	5
			Probation	13	
		Nonpetitioned	60	Dismissal	35
			Other*	13	

Note: Detail may not add to totals because of rounding.   * Referrals to other agencies, fines, restitution, etc.

∎ **FIGURE 10–10 Processing of 100 Typical Cases of Different Property Offenses, 1990**

SOURCE: Ellen H. Nimick, "Juvenile Court Property Cases," OJJDP, Update on Statistics," November 1990, p. 5.

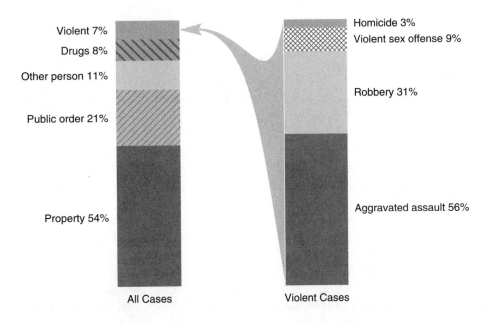

Note: Detail may not add to totals because of rounding.

■ **FIGURE 10–11 Offense Characteristics of Delinquency Cases in Ten States, 1989**

The data was collected from Alabama, Arizona, California, Maryland, Mississippi, Nebraska, Ohio, Pennsylvania, Utah and Virginia.

SOURCE: Jeffrey A. Butts and D. J. Connors-Beatty, "The Juvenile Court's Response to Violent Offenders: 1985–1989," OJJDP, Update on Statistics, April 1993, p. 2.

The facts of adjudication and disposition cannot be examined as if they are separate from each other. The juvenile court must be seen as a court—not as an administrative agency—designed in its adjudication to protect children from the traumatic experiences of a criminal trial and to balance the interests of the child and the community. It is not especially equipped to do welfare work. Whenever possible, it should be devested of jurisdiction and adjudication over cases in which the child is simply in need of aid. It should be governed by simple, specific rules, so that while children are receiving guidance and protection, their rights and the security of the community are not neglected.

CRITICISM OF THE JUVENILE COURT

Criticism of the operations of the nation's juvenile courts began in the 1950s. In 1949 lawyer-sociologist Paul Tappan published a volume on juvenile delinquency that drew together and raised for the first time a number of problems inherent in the work of the court:

■ The persistence in some courts of punitive practices, in contrast to rehabilitative theory.

▮ The abandonment of all semblance of regularized legal procedures or due process.

▮ The jurisdictional accretions by the court in the context of a preventive rationale.

The juvenile court has been criticized for its fundamental system. What most critics or people unfamiliar with the jurisdiction of the court fail to understand is that the scope of the court is varied and that criminal law, or law that refers to antisocial conduct, is only one part of the court's responsibility within its jurisdiction.

All courts within the juvenile justice jurisdiction exercise the principles of civil procedures, which emphasize notice and opportunity to defend. They also emphasize due process factors protecting juveniles who come under their authority, making dispositions for the child's best interest.

In effect, the juvenile court is less a law enforcement agency and more a social agency, handling truants, orphans, runaways and other misguided youths. It is, however, also responsible for youthful gang members, robbers, rapists and murderers. The court is seen as inadequate to satisfy the community's need to express its disapproval of antisocial conduct.

Attacks on the juvenile court's jurisdiction and procedures have been continually repelled, however. While shortcomings have been acknowledged, they have been characterized as the usual shortcomings one might expect in any novel and untried enterprise, and which faith, time and money surely would cure. For nine decades, therefore, the juvenile courts have been permitted to develop and mature, nurtured by judicial support and large doses of faith, if not money.

Both the IACP and the National Council of Juvenile Court Judges have expressed concern that the juvenile courts are becoming too formalized and are beginning to resemble the adult courts. This same concern was expressed by Chief Justice Warren Burger in his dissenting opinion in *In re Winship* (1970):

> My hope is that today's decision will not spell the end of a generously conceived program of compassionate treatment intended to mitigate the rigors and trauma of exposing youthful offenders to a traditional criminal court; each step we take turns the clock back to the pre-juvenile court era. I cannot regard it as a manifestation of progress to transform juvenile courts into criminal courts, which is what we are well on the way toward accomplishing.

A study conducted by Feld (1988) showed evidence of juvenile courts not meeting the requirements established in *In re Gault*. This study found that in three of the six states studied only about half the juveniles against whom petitions had been filed were represented by lawyers.

While the juvenile court has stood up to much criticism, some proposals for improvement have been put forth. Krisberg and Austin (1993, p. 184) suggest two changes that might improve our juvenile courts:

> Closed hearings have not been particularly successful in shielding youngsters from adverse publicity in high profile cases. Moreover, the seemingly hidden juvenile court operations have contributed to the public perception that the court is overly lenient. When open hearings have been tried there have been few negative consequences.

A corollary issue involves the quality of juvenile court judges. In many jurisdictions, assignment to the juvenile court is not a highly sought after judicial appointment. The juvenile court too often is a dead-end along the judicial career track. Even deeply committed judges may seek rotation out of juvenile court to assist their legal careers. Similar observations can be made about attorneys who practice in juvenile court. There are serious questions about the adequacy of legal training and the competence of lawyers in many juvenile courts.

SHOCAP believes that the judiciary offers only passive support for the "habitual juvenile offender" designation, but that the chief judge of a court may support the program by authorizing the sharing of information. Strategies that might be used include the following (Crowe, 1991, p. 49):

■ Authorize the inspection of records of the juvenile court, probation, protective services, prosecutor, school and police by the crime analyst or official designated to monitor the habitual offender.

■ Place limits on "deferred adjudication," especially for designated habitual offenders, who may also claim to have drug problems.

The National School Safety Center suggested a way to accomplish the first strategy described by SHOCAP. This center focuses national attention on cooperative solutions to problems disrupting the educational process. It emphasizes efforts to rid schools of crime, violence and drugs, and encourages programs to improve student discipline, attendance and achievement. The Center offers publications, visual aids and other resources to law enforcement officers, school personnel, court personnel and legislators. Table 10–7 presents the National School Safety Center's proposed "Model Interagency Juvenile Record Statute."

In 1988 the Bureau of Justice Statistics collaborated with SEARCH Group, Inc., to sponsor a national conference to consider merging adult and juvenile records: *Juvenile and Adult Records: One System, One Record?*" (January 1990). The proceedings showed a wide range of opinions on whether to merge the records or keep them separate. Representative statements from these various viewpoints follow.

In Favor of One Record

Marvin E. Wolfgang, Sellin Center for Studies in Criminology and Criminal Law: "The dual system of juvenile and criminal Justice that prevents the sharing of information and permits a serious, chronic violent juvenile to become a virgin offender after his 19th birthday is a strange cultural invention. . . . [H]owever, . . . highly selective sharing of a juvenile record should be used only to inform" (p. 18).

Reggie B. Walton, Deputy Presiding Judge of the D.C. Superior Court: "Judicial officers, strapped with the difficult responsibility of deciding whether an offender should be released or detained, must be put in the position to make the most informed decision possible" (p. 44).

Ken Moses, Inspector, Crime Scene Investigation Unit, San Francisco P.D.: "[S]ome jurisdictions keep juvenile prints out of the AFIS database, which, in my mind, is a major catastrophe. Any exclusion of criminal fingerprints from

TABLE   Model Interagency Juvenile Record Statute
10-7

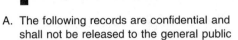

A. The following records are confidential and shall not be released to the general public except as permitted by this statute:
   1. Juvenile court records, which include both legal and social records (legal records include petitions, dockets, motions, findings, orders and other papers filed with the court other than social records. Social records include social studies and medical, psychological, clinical or other treatment reports or studies filed with the court);
   2. Juvenile social service, child protective service agency or multidisciplinary team records, whether contained in court files or in agency files (this includes all records made by any public or private agency or institution that now has or has had the child or the child's family under its custody, care or supervision);
   3. Juvenile probation agency records, whether contained in court files or in probation agency files;
   4. Juvenile parole agency records, whether contained in court files or in parole agency files;
   5. Juvenile prosecutor, state attorney, district attorney or county attorney records relating to juvenile cases;
   6. Juvenile law enforcement records, including fingerprints and photographs; and
   7. School records that are maintained by school employees on all students, including but not limited to, academic, attendance, behavior and discipline records.

B. Access to the records listed in Section A is permitted without court order for official use to the following:
   1. All courts;
   2. All probation or parole agencies;
   3. All attorneys general, prosecutors, state attorneys, district attorneys, county attorneys;
   4. All social service or protective service agencies or multidisciplinary teams;
   5. All law enforcement agencies;
   6. All schools attended by the minor; and
   7. All persons, agencies or institutions that have responsibility for the custody, care, control or treatment of the minor.

C. The juvenile court may issue an order releasing juvenile records to any person, agency or institution asserting a legitimate interest in a case or in the proceedings of the juvenile court.

D. Juvenile records may be sent to a central repository, which may be computerized. The central repository may be accessed by all agencies and organizations listed in Section B above.

E. The juvenile, the juvenile's parents and guardians and the juvenile's attorney may have access to the legal records maintained on the juvenile that are in the possession of the juvenile court without court order. The juvenile's attorney may have access to the social records maintained on the juvenile that are in the possession of the juvenile court and to the records listed in Section A above for use in the legal representation of the juvenile. The juvenile on whom records are maintained may petition the court to correct any information that is incorrect.

The National School Safety Center [1988] has proposed this model juvenile record-sharing statute for the stated purpose of "foster[ing] the sharing of information among those organizations and agencies that need information from juvenile records to adequately perform their jobs as they work in an official capacity with youths and their families." The focus of the statute is restricted to the sharing of records among child-serving agencies and does not concern itself with the broader issue of public access to juvenile records.

SOURCE: Used with permission from *The Need to Know: Juvenile Record Sharing.* Copyright 1989 by the National School Safety Center.

such a file is counterproductive, not only to society but also to the interests of juvenile justice" (p. 51).

Ronald D. Castille, Philadelphia D.A.: "[W]e ought to have liberal access to all records to make informed decisions about the disposition of both juvenile and adult cases" (p. 58).

Opposing One Record

Mark H. Moore, Professor of Criminal Justice at Harvard University: "[T]he proposal for 'one record, one system' would make a hash of either one or the other systems, and perhaps both of them, because they are founded on different philosophies" (p. 47).

Romae T. Powell, Georgia Juvenile Court Judge: "The juvenile justice system's goal is to use their records to rehabilitate, treat, supervise, protect and change children. . . . One record, one system, then, in my opinion, will destroy this mandate. . . ." (p. 38).

Howard N. Snyder, Director of Systems Research, National Center for Juvenile Justice, cautions: "[T]he considerations in merging juvenile and adult legal records are both technical and philosophical. The technical problems are easily addressed; the philosophical ones require us to take a careful look at why this nation has established a separate juvenile justice system" (p. 54).

SUMMARY

The juvenile justice system is basically a civil system, but it has evolved into the adversarial system typical of our adult criminal system.

The jurisdiction of the juvenile court includes children who are in poverty, neglected or abused; who are unruly or commit status offenses and who are charged with committing serious crimes. This jurisdiction is determined by the offender's age and conduct. The most common maximum jurisdictional age is 18.

Juvenile courts may also deal with child-related problems, such as adoptions, illegitimacy and guardianship. They may exercise authority over adults in certain cases involving children.

Throughout their history, juvenile courts have been separated into three types: designated courts, independent and separate courts and coordinated courts. Each type has as its primary function the adjudication of cases. To adjudicate is to judge—to hear and decide a case.

A series of Supreme Court decisions has changed the juvenile court's procedures into a more adversarial approach. One safeguard against such an adversarial system is the guardian *ad litem*. A guardian *ad litem* is a representative of a juvenile, appointed by the juvenile court judge solely for the best interest of the child and to represent that interest on his or her behalf.

Whether adversarial or not, court action on behalf of neglected, abused or dependent children may be noncriminal or criminal. If court action is to be taken and a petition is filed, the court goes through three phases: (1) the preliminary hearing or conference, (2) the adjudicatory hearing or trial and (3) the dispositional hearing or sentencing.

The work of the juvenile court is greatly aided by referees. The principal functions of referees are to act as hearing officers, to reduce testimony to findings of fact and to make recommendations on disposition.

In some states the court makes the decision to certify a juvenile as an adult. In other states this is done by the prosecutor. When the criminal court has exclusive jurisdiction, it may transfer the case to the juvenile court by a process known as reverse certification.

The mandatory sentencing policy in Washington state is based on the juvenile's age, the current offense and the criminal history of the offender. The trend in sentencing is toward deinstitutionalization of youth. No matter what the offense, mechanical jurisprudence should be avoided. Mechanical jurisprudence suggests that everything is known and, therefore, laws can be made in advance to cover every situation.

The juvenile court's current dilemma hinges on its dual roles as a court of law and as a social service agency. Solving this dilemma is a great challenge facing our juvenile courts.

▮ Discussion Questions

1. If to adjudicate is to hear and decide a case, why is this terminology used in criminal matters in juvenile court? Should the juvenile court have two separate courts for civil and criminal matters?
2. What changes to the adjudication process should be considered in your state? What would be the advantages or disadvantages of these changes?
3. Should a guardian *ad litem* be provided in addition to a defense counsel in all juvenile proceedings? Why or why not?
4. Are there inconsistencies in the justice dispensed by the juvenile courts in your area?
5. Should there be a separate justice system for juveniles, or should all juveniles be dealt with as in the adult system?
6. What types of behavior should the juvenile court deal with?
7. What criteria are used in decisions to waive juvenile court jurisdiction?
8. What are the major decision points in the adjudication process in juvenile court in your state? Are these decisions mechanical or determined by individual judges based on specific cases?
9. Does the public have the right to know what juveniles are committing crimes by publishing their names with the offense? Why or why not?
10. Should delinquency proceedings be secret?

▮ References

Belden, Evelina. *Courts in the United States Hearing Children's Cases*. U.S. Children's Bureau Publication No. 65. Washington, D.C.: U.S. Government Printing Office, 1920.

Butts, Jeffrey A., and D. J. Connors-Beatty. "The Juvenile Court's Response to Violent Offenders: 1985–1989." OJJDP, Update on Statistics, April 1993.

Butts, Jeffrey A., and Eileen Poe. "Offenders in Juvenile Court, 1990." OJJDP, Update on Statistics, December 1993.

Crowe, Timothy D. *Habitual Juvenile Offenders: Guidelines for Citizen Action and Public Response.* Serious Habitual Offender Comprehensive Action Program (SHOCAP). Washington, D.C.: Office of Juvenile Justice and Delinquency Prevention, October, 1991.

Davis, Samuel M. *Rights of Juveniles: The Juvenile Justice System.* New York: Clark Boardman, 1985.

Feinman, Howard. *Liability and Legal Issues in Juvenile Restitution.* Restitution Education, Specialized Training and Technical Assistance Program (RESTTA), May 1990.

Feld, Barry. "*In Re Gault* Revisited: A Cross-State Comparison of the Right to Counsel in Juvenile Court." *Crime and Delinquency,* 1988, pp. 34, 379–392.

Greenfeld, Lawrence A., and James J. Stephan. "Capital Punishment 1992." *Bureau of Justice Statistics Bulletin,* December 1993.

Harris, Patricia M. "Juvenile Sentence Reform and its Evaluation: A Demonstration of the Need for More Precise Measures of Offense Seriousness in Juvenile Justice Research." *Evaluation Review,* 12 (December 1988) 6:655–666.

Hart, H. L. A. *The Concept of Law.* Oxford: Oxford University Press, 1965.

Hughes, Stella P., and Anne L. Schneider. *Victim-Offender Mediation in the Juvenile Justice System.* Restitution Education, Specialized Training and Technical Assistance Program (RESTTA), September 1990.

Juvenile and Adult Records: One System, One Record? Proceedings of a BJS/SEARCH Conference conducted June 28–29, 1988. January 1990.

"Karen's Kids." *60 Minutes,* CBS. Aired December 1987.

Krisberg, Barry, and James F. Austin. *Reinventing Juvenile Justice.* Newbury Park, Calif.: Sage Publications, 1993.

McCreedy, K. R. *Juvenile Justice—System and Procedures.* Albany, N.Y.: Delmar Publishers, 1975.

National Coalition of State Juvenile Justice Advisory Groups. *Myths and Realities: Meeting the Challenge of Serious, Violent, and Chronic Juvenile Offenders, 1992 Annual Report,* Fall 1992.

Nimick, Ellen H. "Juvenile Court Property Cases." OJJDP, Update on Statistics, November 1990.

Oran, Daniel. *Law Dictionary for Nonlawyers.* 2nd ed. St. Paul, Minn.: West Publishing, 1985.

Schneider, Anne Larason, and Jean Shumway Warner. *National Trends in Juvenile Restitution Programming.* Restitution Education, Specialized Training and Technical Assistance Program (RESTTA), July 1989.

Sickmund, Melissa. "Runaways in Juvenile Courts." OJJDP, Update on Statistics, November 1990.

Springer, Charles E. *Justice for Juveniles.* Washington, D.C.: U.S. Department of Justice, Office of Juvenile Justice and Delinquency Prevention, 1986.

Sweet, Robert W., Jr. "CASA: Court Appointed Special Advocate for Children . . . A Child's Voice in Court." OJJDP, Juvenile Justice Bulletin, Updated from 1987.

Tappan, Paul. *Juvenile Delinquency.* New York: McGraw-Hill, 1949.

■ Cases

Breed v. *Jones,* 421 U.S. 519, 533, 95 S.Ct. 1779, 1787, 44 L.Ed.2d 346 (1975).

Commonwealth v. *Fisher,* 213 Pa. 48, 62 A. 198, 199, 200 (1905).

In re Gault, 387 U.S.1, 19–21, 26–28, 87 S.Ct. 1428, 1439–1440, 1442–1444, 18 L.Ed.2d 527 (1967).

Kent v. *U.S.,* 383 U.S. 541, 86 S.Ct. 1045, 16 L.Ed.2d 84 (1966).

McKeiver v. *Pennsylvania,* 403 U.S. 528, 547, 91 S.Ct. 1976, 1987, 29 L.Ed.2d 647 (1971).

People ex rel. O'Connell v. *Turner,* 55 Ill. 280, 8 Am.Rep. 645, (1870).

Schall v. *Martin,* 467 U.S. 253, 104 S.Ct. 2403, 81 L.Ed.2d 207 (1984).

In re Winship, 397 U.S. 358, 90 S.Ct. 1068, 25 L.Ed.2d 368 (1970).

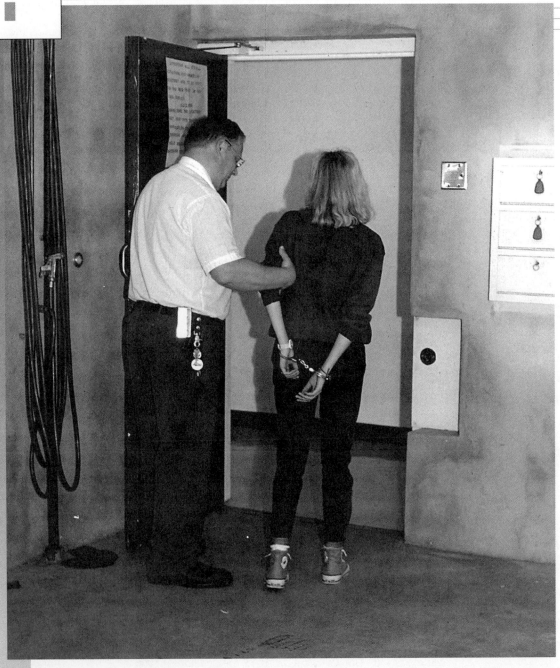

The Role of Corrections

[I]t is in the juvenile justice system that we will succeed or fail in reducing corrections populations . . . If we do not address juvenile corrections fully, these children will end up as tomorrow's clients in the adult system.

John J. Wilson

▌ Do You Know?

Whether juveniles have a right to treatment?
How the conservative and liberal approach treat juveniles?
What the most common disposition from the juvenile court is?
What the formal goal of probation is?
What the two main functions of a probation officer traditionally have been?
What the single greatest pressure on probation officers is?
What the essence of juvenile probation is? Its three common goals?
What the effect of isolating offenders from the community might be?
What kinds of nonresidential programs have been implemented?
What the five major categories of community-based corrections are?
What use has been recommended for foster homes?
What the most frequently used intermediate sanctions are?
What three justifications are given for putting juveniles in locked facilities?
What incarcerated groups are overrepresented?
How public and private correctional institutions differ?
If juvenile institutions model adult institutions in social organization? Culture?
How prison gangs differ from street gangs?
What parole is? Aftercare?

▌ Can You Define the Following Key Terms?

aftercare, boot camps, foster group homes, foster homes, group homes, intensive supervision, parole, probation, probation officer, shelters, shock incarceration, training schools

INTRODUCTION

Corrections serves several functions, with one of the most obvious being protecting the public by removing juvenile offenders from the community. Corrections has a dual function with these offenders, holding them accountable for their behavior and providing them with the education, vocational, personal and social skills needed to successfully return to the community. The complexities involved in juvenile corrections are summarized by Shumate (1991, p. 6):

> First, the system is expected to treat, rehabilitate and handle youths as victims. It is also expected to provide maximum assurances of due process guarantees at every turn. And there is the prevailing attitude of "lock'em up and throw away the key."
>
> Something as simple as the $64,000 Dollar Question, "What is a juvenile?" is still unresolved. The word continues to defy definition—across the nation answers range from 11 to 24 years of age.

This chapter focuses on the correctional portion of the contemporary juvenile justice system. It begins by looking at the most common disposition of the juvenile/family court—probation. This is followed by a discussion of several community-based correctional alternatives including day treatment alternatives and residential programs such as shelters, group homes, foster homes and camps.

Next, intermediate sanctions are explored, including electronic monitoring and boot camps. The chapter concludes with a discussion of youth who are institutionalized, who they are and the conditions under which they are confined.

AMERICAN CORRECTIONAL ASSOCIATION PUBLIC CORRECTIONAL POLICY ON JUVENILE CORRECTIONS

The following introduction to and statement about juvenile corrections from the American Correctional Association (ACA) provides an overview of what juvenile corrections officials and agencies should strive to do (1992, pp. 30–32):*

> *Introduction:* The correctional functions of the juvenile justice system (prevention, diversion, detention, probation, residential and aftercare) must provide specialized care and rehabilitative programs for young offenders in our society consistent with protection of the public. These functions of the juvenile justice system, although sharing in general the same overall purpose as adult corrections, have significantly different processes, procedures and objectives which require specialized services and programs.

---

*Reprinted from the October, 1992, issue of *Corrections Today*, with the permission of the American Correctional Association, Laurel, MD.

Policy Statement: Children and youth have distinct personal and developmental needs and must be kept separate and apart from adult offenders. The juvenile justice system must provide a continuum of services, programs, and facilities that assures maximum opportunity for rehabilitation. Each of these alternatives should provide programs which include the principle of accountability for behavior. The best interest of the individual youth must be the primary concern and should be balanced with the protection of the public and the maintenance of social order. To implement this policy, juvenile justice officials and agencies should:

A. Establish and maintain effective communication with all concerned with the juvenile justice system—executive, judicial, and legislative officials, prosecution and defense counsel, social service agencies, schools, police and families—to achieve the fullest possible cooperation in making appropriate decisions in individual cases and in providing and using services and resources;

B. Provide the least restrictive appropriate range of community and residential programs and services to meet individual needs, including education, vocational training, recreation, religious opportunities, individual and family counseling, medical, dental, mental health, and other specialized programs and services such as substance abuse, AIDS counseling and sexual offenders treatment;

C. Use family and community as preferred resources and include families whenever possible, in the decisionmaking processes at all stages in the continuum of services;

D. Exclude from placement in a secure facility serving adjudicated delinquent youth those individuals accused or adjudicated for status offenses; i.e., offenses which are not criminal if committed by an adult;

E. Operate a juvenile classification system to identify and meet the program and supervision needs of the juvenile offender, while actively considering the public's need for protection;

F. Provide a range of alternative nonsecure and secure short-term detention pending adjudication;

G. [Not use] [s]ecure pre-adjudication detention facilities . . . as a post-adjudication disposition alternative;

H. Provide planned transitional services for youth returning to community placement from residential care;

I. Establish written policies and procedures that will protect the rights and safety of the accused, the adjudicated, the victim, and the public in as balanced a manner as is possible;

J. Establish procedures to safeguard the accuracy and use of juvenile records and support limitations on their use according to approved national standards, recognizing that the need to safeguard the privacy and rehabilitative goals of the juvenile should be balanced with concern for the protection of the public, including victims; and

K. Implement evaluation and research procedures that will supply demographic, trends, and outcome information from which program effectiveness and systems operations can be measured.

THE RIGHT TO TREATMENT

The U.S. Supreme Court has apparently based the right to treatment on the principle that restriction of fundamental liberties through involuntary confinement must follow the "least restrictive alternative" available. This principle was stated by the Supreme Court in *Shelton v. Tucker* (1960):

> In a series of decisions this Court has held that, even though the governmental purpose be legitimate and substantial, that purpose cannot be pursued by means that broadly stifle fundamental personal liberties when the end can be more narrowly achieved. The breadth of legislative abridgement must be viewed in the light of less drastic means for achieving the same basic purpose.

Under this rationale, the state violates the individual's constitutional rights if it fails to confine and provide treatment in the least restrictive setting possible.

∎ The U.S. Supreme Court has never definitively ruled on whether there is a constitutionally based right to treatment. The state does violate the individual's rights if it fails to confine and provide treatment in the least restrictive setting possible.

Two opposing views exist as to just what this treatment should consist of.

Conservative and Liberal Philosophies of Corrections

The conservative attitude is to "get tough," "stop babying these kids" and "get them off the streets." Such conservative philosophies accept retribution as grounds for punishment. The conservative view also believes in imprisonment to control crime and antisocial behavior. Rehabilitative programs may be provided during incarceration, but it is imprisonment itself, with its attendant deprivations, that must be primarily relied on to prevent crime, delinquency and recidivism. Correctional treatment is not necessary.

∎ The conservative philosophy of juvenile justice is "get tough on juveniles"—to punish and imprison them.

In contrast, the liberal philosophy of juvenile justice is "treatment, not punishment" for youths who are antisocial and wayward. Liberal ideologies tend to favor community corrections because, as Sutherland and Cressey note (1966, p. 51):

> [T]he person or personality is . . . a part of the kinds of social relationships and values in which he participates; he obtains his essence from rituals, values, norms, rules, schedules, customs, and regulations of various kinds which surround him; he is not separable from the social relationships in which he lives. . . . criminal and delinquent is not just a product of an individual's contacts with certain kinds of groups; it is in a real sense "owned" by groups rather than by individuals.

∎ The liberal philosophy of juvenile justice stresses treatment and rehabilitation, including community-based programs.

PROBATION

Probation is the most widely used disposition of the juvenile or family court. Probation officers are in the unique position of serving both the court and the correctional areas of juvenile justice. Indeed, a **probation officer** is an officer of the court first and foremost. As noted by Hurst (1990a, p. 19):

> [C]ourts of juvenile and family jurisdiction remain institutions of hope, and juvenile probation is still a primary means by which that optimism is actualized. The court is a forum which assumes that children are capable of growing, developing, and changing, and that this growth and development can be directed toward social conformance by well-trained juvenile probation officers.

Many youths who break the law are given a second chance through probation. According to Oran (1985, p. 240), probation is "allowing a person convicted of a criminal offense to stay out of jail under supervised conditions (by a *probation officer*)."

■ Probation is the most common disposition of the juvenile court.

Probation is a guidance program to help juveniles overcome problems that may lead to delinquency and to keep an eye on juveniles who need supervision. It functions in the juvenile court as an alternative to a correctional facility and operates much like adult probation. Allen et al. (1979, p. 81) define probation as:

> A sentence which establishes the defendant's legal status under which his freedom in the community is continued or only briefly interrupted, subject to supervision by a "probation organization" and subject to conditions imposed by the court. The sentencing court retains the authority to modify the conditions of the sentence or resentence of the offender if he violates the conditions.

■ The formal goal of probation is to improve the delinquent's behavior—in short, rehabilitation.

Probation's goal of rehabilitation is sometimes short-circuited by a pervading preoccupation with *control*. Probation may reflect demands that the court "do something" about recurrent misconduct. It is organized to keep the delinquent in line, to prevent any further disturbing and inconveniencing trouble. The ultimate goal of reforming the delinquent's personality and conduct becomes subordinated to the exigencies of maintaining immediate control. Probationary supervision, consequently, takes on a decidedly short-term and negative character. Probation becomes a disciplinary regime to determine and inhibit troublesome conduct.

Often by the time a juvenile is placed on probation, the individual has a record of previous run-ins with the juvenile justice system, usually the police. The police regard probation as something juveniles "get away with" or "get off with." Many juveniles who receive probation instead of being sentenced to a correctional facility view it the same way. Some youths have stated, "I never see my P.O. [probation officer]. It's a joke! Don't ask me to tell you what he looks like, I can't remember. When I get done with this beef, I'll be cool, so I don't get hassled again."

The Probation Officer

▮ The probation officer has traditionally been responsible for two key functions: (1) personally counseling youths who are on probation and (2) serving as a link to other community services.

While counseling skills are viewed as significant, this has given way to probation officers filling the role of social service "brokers." In many jurisdictions the probation officer links "clients" with available resources within community service, such as vocational rehabilitation centers, vocational schools, mental health centers, employment services, church groups and other community groups like Girl Scouts, Boy Scouts and Explorers. This broad use of community resources has some inherent risks. Linking youths to one or more such groups may actually amplify a small problem into a much larger one. Overattendance by a youth in one or more of these groups may become an attention-getting device. Alternately, overprescription of community groups may reinforce the youth's or the community's perception of the problem as serious. In either case, further delinquency may well result.

Problems with Probation

Courts often attribute juveniles' troubles to something wrong with the youths or with their social milieu. The courts seldom sense that a juvenile's problems may be due to the court's program for guidance and control. In many cases probation officers simply do not have the training or skills to provide probationers with the kinds of assistance they might require.

Another factor is time. Even if probation officers possessed the skills necessary to do psychotherapy, vocational guidance and school counseling with diverse types of youths, caseloads dictate that they would not have the time to exercise these skills.

▮ Excessive caseloads are probably the single greatest pressure on probation officers.

In most probation offices, especially in large urban areas, certain characteristics pervade the personality of the office. Juveniles are viewed by their records, in terms of the trouble they have caused or gotten into. Records are not regarded as formulations assembled by various people in the juvenile justice system. That is to say, a juvenile's record is mechanically treated as a set of relevant facts instead of as a social production created by an organization.

The Current Role of Probation Officers

In many states probation officers determine whether the juvenile court has jurisdiction, especially at the intake portion of contact with a child. The probation representative also determines, to some degree, whether a formal or an informal hearing is called for.

Informal hearings have critics, because informal processing requires an explicit or tacit admission of guilt. The substantial advantages that accrue from this admission (the avoidance of court action) also act as an incentive to confess. This casts doubt on the voluntary nature and truthfulness of admissions of guilt. The process results in informal probation.

Informal probation can be a critical time in the life of a juvenile. If successful, the youngster may avoid further juvenile court processing and the potentially serious consequences. If the informal probation efforts are unsuccessful, the usual recourse is for the probation officer to request that a petition be filed to make the case official. This could result in the youth being confined in a locked or controlled facility for disciplinary action.

Probation and Filing Petitions

The probation officer may play an important role in each of the three phases a youth usually goes through after a petition is filed.

During the first phase, the preliminary hearing, the judge may determine with the assistance of a probation officer whether a child's behavior is a threat to the public or to self. If so, the judge will order preventive detention of the youth.

During the second phase, the adjudication hearing, the judge will usually order a social investigation, presentence investigation (PSI), or predisposition report. The probation officer is responsible for investigating and assessing the child's home, school, physical and psychological situation. The *predisposition* or *presentence investigation report* has the objective of satisfying the goal of the juvenile court, which is to provide services.

The Predisposition Report

The probation officer who conducts the investigation and completes the report seeks the best available information. The probation officer's report includes the sociocultural and psychodynamic factors that influenced the juvenile's behavior and provides a social history the judge can use to determine a disposition for the case. Judges' decisions can be greatly influenced by such reports.

The reports must be factual and objective—professional statements about a child's family, social and educational history, and any previous involvement with private or public agencies. The report also indicates the child's physical and mental health as reported by a court psychologist or psychiatrist.

A report typically includes (1) interviews with the child; (2) interviews with family members; (3) psychological and psychiatric examinations of the child and family members (usually just parents or custodians) and the results of tests and exams; (4) interviews with employers, youth workers and clergy when appropriate; (5) interviews with the complainant; (6) interviews with the police, their reports and any witnesses; (7) interviews with teachers and school officials; (8) a review of police, school and court records and (9) a recommendation of which treatment alternatives should be available in the case.

The probation officer must present the findings with supportive statements about the actual situation found in the investigation. Other than a recommendation, suppositions and opinions are to be avoided. The recommendation occasionally is not transcribed, but given as an oral presentation to the judge. The completed report should be comprehensive enough to help the judge make the best disposition available, based on the individual merits of the case and the service needs of the youth.

The Social History—A Close-Up Look

Purpose

The social history is a basic tool of the juvenile court. It helps probation officers gather and summarize the complete situation surrounding offenders who are appearing in juvenile court. The court uses this information to make dispositions. The facts of the report are as important as the recommendation.

The social history also follows children through their various placements. It is relied on by the various agencies that come in contact with children as a result of court action.

Preparation

A social history cannot be undertaken until ordered by the juvenile court judge. The juvenile court judge will not order a social history until a child has admitted to the allegations stated in the petition. The probation officer is expected to complete the social history in four to six weeks. The information is highly confidential, available to only the court and other court-designated persons or agencies.

The typical sections of a social history and what is often included are as follows (adapted from the Social History format of Anoka County, Minnesota).

Identifying Information.   The history begins with the child's name, address, date of birth, race, sex and parents' names and personal data.

People Contacted.   This includes the names and titles of all people and agencies contacted.

The Petition.   On __*date*__ a petition was signed by __*name*__ __*title*__ alleging that on or about the following dates __*name*__ did commit the following act of delinquency; (name and date of offense). (The above information should appear for each petition admitted to on the court date.) __*name*__ appeared in _____ Juvenile Court on __*date*__ . Subject admitted to the allegations of the petition. After due deliberation, the court continued the matter, requesting _____ Court Services to investigate the family history and environment.

Previous Difficulty

▮ *Legal Background.*   This section chronologically summarizes the offenses that have been referred to court services through the intake department or juvenile court prior to this court appearance and includes the date of any intake or court appearances and their dispositions. If local law enforcement agencies have had contact with the child and have not referred the matter to court, and this matter is alluded to in this section, there is a statement as to what kind of disposition resulted.

▮ *Other Agencies.*   This is a summary outlining what previous counseling has taken place, as well as any other contacts this individual has had with other helping agencies. This section includes dates that bracket the time span in which subject has had contact with these agencies as well as the approximate number of contacts. This section also summarizes why the particular agency was in contact with the child. (This section is optional and is deleted entirely if no agencies were involved.)

▮ *Placements.*   This section outlines the previous placements of the subject, including the dates, the agency that assisted in these placements and the reason for the placements. (This section is optional and is deleted if there were no previous placements.)

Present Family Situation.   This section describes the subject's family situation, including specific data as to the parents' date of birth, present employment, previous marriages and any other data deemed appropriate by the probation officer. This section also includes similar information about siblings residing in and out of the parental home. The section also discusses generally the child's present situation, describing the client's age, grade in school, placement in the family, etc.

Interview with Parents.   This section includes the parents' version of the offense; the parents' opinion as to the origin of the problem; any problems the family is having with the client, as well as a general statement about family interactions, including the type of discipline used in the family. This section also includes the parents' recommendation for their child.

Interview with Youth.   This section includes data the probation officer has gathered by interviewing the child, including the subject's version of the offense, description of home life, school life and/or employment life. This section also includes the child's recommendation as to the court's disposition. Optional information may include the juvenile's opinion of his brothers and sisters, his physical health, his religion, vocational adjustment, hobbies, interests and companions.

Education.   This section states where the subject is educationally, for example, grade, attendance and any extracurricular activities. It includes the last grades the subject has received and a statement as to whether these grades are consistent with previous performance. Any educational testing that has been conducted is also described. If the subject is a high school dropout, this section can be drastically condensed by stating the date the subject dropped out.

Additional Information.   This section summarizes information attached to the report, including chemical dependency evaluations and psychological information. This section also includes any *restitution*. Sometimes the probation officer gathers information and makes a recommendation about restitution.

Problem Assessment.   In this section the probation officer states his evaluation of the factors that led the child to involvement in delinquent acts. This may be very detailed and specific. Any recommendations made should relate to this section.

Recommendation.   This section states the probation officer's specific recommendations for a disposition. For example, the probation officer may recommend probation and restitution. Further, the probation officer should state why the recommendations best meet the treatment needs of the child.

Alternative Recommendations.   The probation officer should list, in numerical order, the alternatives and recommendations considered and why they were not recommended.

A form used by the probation officer taking notes is contained in Appendix D.

PROBATION AND DISPOSITION

A problem commonly encountered at the dispositional stage is the paucity of available alternatives for helping or treating a youngster. This can result from an inexperienced or uninformed probation officer who recommends treatment that is simply not available. Often a youngster is placed on or continued on probation because of a lack of viable alternatives.

After the dispositional hearing, if the court orders an individual placed on probation, certain procedures and commitments must be satisfied. An order must place the youth on probation, giving the probation officer authority for controlled supervision within the community. The terms of the probation are described in the order.

A violation of probation starts the judicial process over. It begins with a revocation hearing, where evidence and supportive information is presented before a juvenile judge. If the court decides to revoke the probation, the individual can be institutionalized.

In 1987 the National Center for Juvenile Justice (NCJJ) established the Juvenile Probation Officer Initiative (JPOI) to increase professionalism in juvenile probation. Thomas (1991, p. 62) notes: "The JPOI's fundamental principle is that it is not enough for officers to muddle through as best they can. In juvenile probation, proactive is better than reactive, dynamic is better than static, and science is better than art."

The JPOI has established a data base with the names, addresses and phone numbers of over 14,000 juvenile probation officers around the country. This list is used for mailing surveys, collecting data and disseminating information. The JPOI also provides technical assistance when requested.

In addition, the JPOI has developed *The Desktop Guide to Good Juvenile Probation Practices,* a reference book written by and for juvenile probation officers. The Guide, representing the collective experience of over 40 probation professionals, was sent at no charge to officers around the country. The following information (pp. 384–390) is a condensation and adaptation of this guide.

The mission of juvenile probation is "to assist young people to avoid delinquent behavior and to grow into mature adults and to do so without endangering the community" (p. 3). Effective probation officers have the following characteristics:

- ■ Strong, sustained commitment to people—viewing each probationer as an individual and conveying to them that they are cared about.
- ■ Family involvement.
- ■ Involvement with community agencies.
- ■ Informal community involvement—enlisting the support of community members to assist probationers.
- ■ Opportunistic supervision—picking the right time for intervention.

A national survey of juvenile probation professionals found that they regard basic interviewing techniques to be the most important skill for juvenile probation officers to possess upon hiring or to acquire early in their careers. Two other vital skills are information gathering and report preparation.

The National Advisory Committee (NAC) for Juvenile Justice and Delinquency Prevention recommends that probation departments prepare three-part predisposition reports (JPOI, p. 42):

1. Information concerning the nature and circumstances of the offense, and the juvenile's role, age and prior contacts.
2. Summary of information concerning:

- ■ The home environment and family relationships;
- ■ The juvenile's educational and employment status;
- ■ The juvenile's interests and activities;
- ■ The parents' interests; and
- ■ The results of medical or psychiatric evaluations.

3. Evaluation of the above, a summary of the dispositional alternatives available and the probation officer's recommendation.

Setting Conditions

An important responsibility of the probation officer is helping the court establish the conditions for probation. Two kinds of probationary conditions are usually established: mandatory and discretionary. Most mandatory conditions specify that probationers (1) may not commit a new delinquent act, (2) must report, as directed, to their probation officer and (3) must obey all court orders.

The discretionary conditions are more extensive, as illustrated by the discretionary conditions set forth in New Jersey Juvenile Statutes:

- ■ Pays a fine;
- ■ Makes restitution;
- ■ Performs community service;
- ■ Participates in a work program;
- ■ Participates in programs emphasizing self-reliance, such as intensive outdoor programs teaching survival skills, including but not limited to camping, hiking and other appropriate activities;
- ■ Participates in a program of academic or vocational education or counseling which may require attendance after school, evenings and weekends;
- ■ Be placed in a suitable residential or nonresidential program for the treatment of alcohol or narcotic abuse;

▮ Be placed in a nonresidential program operated by a public or private agency, providing intensive services to juveniles for specified hours, which may include education, counseling to the juvenile and the juvenile's family if appropriate, vocational counseling, work or other services;

▮ Be placed with any private group home (with which the Department of Correction has entered into a purchase of service contract).

The New Jersey statute also allows the court to set conditions for the probationer's parents and to revoke the juvenile's driving license as a condition of probation. Conditions may include such matters as the following:

▮ Cooperating with the program of supervision;
▮ Meeting family responsibilities;
▮ Maintaining steady employment or engaging or refraining from engaging in a specific employment or occupation;
▮ Pursuing prescribed educational or vocational training;
▮ Undergoing medical or psychiatric treatment;
▮ Maintaining residence in a prescribed area or in a prescribed facility;
▮ Refraining from consorting with certain types of people or frequenting certain types of places;
▮ Making restitution or reparation;
▮ Paying fines;
▮ Submitting to search and seizure;
▮ Submitting to drug tests.

A study conducted in Utah showed that for cases involving robbery, assault, burglary, theft, auto theft and vandalism, recidivism rates are lowered when juveniles agree or are ordered to pay restitution directly to their victims or through money earned from community service (Butts and Snyder, 1992, p. 1). California has the following conditions of probation (JPOI, p. 73):

A. That every juvenile lead a law-abiding life. No other conditions should be required by statute, but the probation officer should recommend additional conditions to fit the circumstances of each case. Development of standard conditions as a guide to making recommendations for probation is appropriate, so long as such conditions are not routinely imposed.

B. That they assist the juvenile in leading a law-abiding life. They should be reasonably related to the avoidance of further criminal behavior and not unduly restrictive of the juvenile's liberty or incompatible with his religion. They should not be so vague or ambiguous as to give no real guidance.

C. That they may appropriately include matters such as [those listed above for New Jersey].

Several constraints govern the setting of conditions. The conditions must be do-able, must not unreasonably restrict constitutional rights, must be consistent with law and public policy and must be specific and understandable. If the conditions are *not* met, probation can be revoked. This is normally accomplished by the probation officer reporting the violation of conditions to the juvenile court and a revocation hearing being conducted. Such hearings are also called *surrender hearings* or *violation hearings*.

Supervision

■ Supervision is the essence of probation.

As noted in the JPOI Guide (p. 79):

> The common thread that runs through all approaches to supervision is utility; that is, that juvenile justice intervention *must* be designed to guide and correct the naturally changing behavior patterns of youth. Unlike adult probation, juvenile supervision views a young offender as a developing person, as one who has not yet achieved a firm commitment to a particular set of values, goals, behavior patterns or lifestyle. As such, juvenile justice supervision is in the hopeful position of influencing that development and thereby reducing criminal behavior. . . .
>
> Probation departments [should] consider the converging interests of the juvenile offender, the victim, and the community at large in developing individualized case plans for probation. This approach to policy and practice resolves the habitual conflicts between rehabilitation vs. punishment, treatment vs. control, the community vs. the offender, and public safety vs. youth development. Probation must endeavor to not only protect the public and hold the juvenile offender accountable, it must also attempt to meet his needs (italic in original).

■ Probation often has three goals: (1) to protect the community from delinquency, (2) to impose accountability for offenses committed and (3) to equip juvenile offenders with required competencies to live productively and responsibly in the community.

These three goals should be reflected in the case plan/contract and offer the "balanced approach" illustrated in Figure 11–1.

Probation services should also provide a continuum from least restrictive and intensive to more restrictive and intensive supervision. **Intensive supervision** is highly structured and usually has the following features (JPOI, p. 87):

■ A greater reliance placed on unannounced spot checks; these may occur in a variety of settings including home, school, known hangouts and job sites.
■ Considerable attention directed at increasing the number and kinds of collateral contacts made by staff, including family members, friends, staff from other agencies and concerned residents in the community.
■ Greater use of curfew, including both more rigid enforcement and lowering the hour at which curfew goes into effect. (Other measures for imposing control included home detention and electronic monitoring.)
■ Surveillance expanded to ensure 7-day-a-week, 24-hour-a-day coverage.

Other components of intensive supervision are clear, graduated sanctions with immediate consequences for violations, restitution and community service, parent involvement, youth skill development and individualized and offense-specific treatment.

To determine if a probationer requires intensive supervision, the probation officer should have a classification procedure. Since intensive supervision is extremely time-consuming, it should be reserved for those probationers at

COMMUNITY PROTECTION

ACCOUNTABILITY

COMPETENCY
DEVELOPMENT

	GOALS	ACTION STEPS	START	COMPLETE
COMMUNITY PROTECTION	Learn to make better choices	Attend problem-solving group once a week	10-2	1-20
COMPETENCY DEVELOPMENT	Become well prepared for independent living	Design a "full-time job" budget to include rent, food, personal supplies, leisure activities	9-4	9-19
		Participate in emancipation class	9-5	10-5
ACCOUNTABILITY	Repay community for loss	Complete 40 hours of community service	9-4	12-7
	Repay victims for loss	Write victim apology letter and turn it in to counselor	10-5	10-31

MINOR'S SIGNATURE   DATE   JUVENILE COUNSELOR   DATE

PARENT/GUARDIAN SIGNATURE DATE   JUVENILE COURT REFEREE   DATE

▮ **FIGURE 11–1 Case Plan/Contract**

SOURCE: Juvenile Probation Officer Initiative (JPOI) Working Group, *Desktop Guide to Good Juvenile Probation Practice*, Washington, D.C.: Office of Juvenile Justice and Delinquency Prevention, May 1993, p. 84.

greatest risk of violating their probation. The National Institute of Corrections (NIC) Classification Project has been adapted by many juvenile court jurisdictions. NIC research suggests that an assessment of the following variables appear to be universally predictive of future delinquent behavior (JPOI, p. 81):

▮ Age at first adjudication.
▮ Prior delinquent behavior (combined measure of number and severity of priors).
▮ Number of prior commitments to juvenile facilities.
▮ Drug/chemical abuse.
▮ Alcohol abuse.
▮ Family relationships.

■ School problems.
■ Peer relationships.

The NIC calls for a reassessment every six months. After the assessment is completed, a case plan must arrange services so that the youth, the family and the community are all served. The National Council on Crime and Delinquency (NCCD) has a case planning strategy that involves the following components (JPOI, p. 83):

1. Analysis:

■ Identification of problem.
■ Identification of strengths and resources.

2. Problem prioritization based upon:

■ Strength—Is the problem an important force in the juvenile's delinquent's problems?
■ Alterability—Can the problem be modified or circumvented?
■ Speed—Can the changes be achieved rapidly?
■ Interdependence—Will solving the problem help resolve other problems?

This case plan is then reduced to a contract between the probation department, the juvenile offender and the family.

The probation officer must then convey this plan/contract to the juvenile and the parents and get consensus. The probation officer then monitors compliance with the contract.

Other Services

In addition to assessing the needs of probationers, devising a case plan/contract and supervising compliance with that contract, probation officers can also serve as a mature role model; they can also provide family counseling, crisis intervention and mediation. Mediation can be used in the following areas (JPOI, p. 95):

■ Diversion of cases at intake.
■ Settlement of cases by community groups.
■ Settlement of cases by the probation officer.
■ Settlement of disputes between a juvenile and the school.
■ Settlement of disputes between a juvenile and his/her family.
■ Settlement of restitution, custody and status matters.
■ Victim-offender reconciliation.

The role of the probation officer is demanding and challenging. The multifaceted role of the juvenile probation officer is illustrated in Table 11–1.

The Serious Habitual Offender Comprehensive Action Program (SHOCAP) says of probation (Crowe, 1991, p. 49):

Probation . . . services are commonly provided by employees of the court or the state. However, there have always been a significant number of private probation services. Some strategies are:

■ Institute intensive and continuous case management for designated habituals;
■ Adopt active community control concepts, including 24-hour home checks and limited house arrest;
■ Provide mandatory sanctions for each infraction of probation rules, including revocation of probation status.

TABLE   The Multifaceted Role of the Juvenile Probation Officer
11–1

Role	Description
Cop	Enforces judge's orders
Prosecutor	Assists D.A., conducts revocations
Father confessor	Establishes helpful, trustful relationship with juvenile
Rat	Informs court of juvenile's behavior/circumstances
Teacher	Develops skills in juvenile
Friend	Develops positive relation with juvenile
Surrogate parent	Admonishes, scolds juvenile
Counselor	Addresses needs
Ambassador	Intervenes on behalf of juvenile
Problem solver	Helps juvenile deal with court and community issues
Crisis manager	Deals with juvenile's precipitated crisis (usually at 2 A.M.)
Hand holder	Consoles juvenile
Public speaker	Educates public re: tasks
P.R. person	Wins friends, influences people on behalf of probation
Community resource specialist	Service broker
Transportation officer	Gets juvenile to where he has to go in a pinch
Recreational therapist	Gets juvenile to use leisure time well
Employment counselor	Gets kid a job
Judge's advisor	Court service officer
Financial advisor	Monitors payment, sets pay plan
Paper pusher	Fills out myriad of forms
Sounding board	Listens to irate parents, kids, police, teachers, etc.
Punching bag	Person to blame when anything goes wrong, kid commits new crime
Expert clinician	Offers or refers to appropriate treatment
Family counselor/marriage therapist	Keeps peace in juvenile's family
Psychiatrist	Answers question: why does the kid do it?
Banker	Juvenile needs car fare money
Tracker	Finds kid
Truant officer	Gets kid to school
Lawyer	Tells defense lawyer/prosecutor what juvenile law says
Sex educator	Facts of life, AIDS, and child support (Dr. Ruth)
Emergency foster parent	In a pinch
Family wrecker	Files petitions for abuse/neglect
Bureaucrat	Helps juvenile justice system function
Lobbyist	For juvenile, for department
Program developer	For kid, for department
Grant writer	For kid, for department
Board member	Serves on myriad committees
Agency liaison	With community groups
Trainer	For volunteer, students
Public information officer	"Tell me what you know about probation"
Court officer/bailiff	In a pinch
Custodian	Keeps office clean
Victim advocate	Deals with juvenile's victim

SOURCE: Adapted from: Juvenile Probation Officer Initiative (JPOI) Working Group, *Desktop Guide to Good Juvenile Probation Practice,* Washington, D.C.: Office of Juvenile Justice and Delinquency Prevention, May 1993, pp. 119–120.

Privatizing Juvenile Probation Services

Problems such as illegal drug use, street gangs, school violence, abused, homeless and runaway youth have strained the resources of the juvenile justice system. Given that probation departments are the single largest component of juvenile corrections, these departments especially feel the strain. One solution that has been proposed is privatization. To investigate this option, the OJJDP funded a three-year project called the Private Sector Probation Initiative. OJJDP chose the National Office for Social Responsibility (NOSR) to carry out the project. The Private Sector Probation Initiative Project developed seven steps for agencies to follow to transfer services from public to private sector operation (Donahue, 1989, p. 2):

Step 1. Prepare a comprehensive, realistic plan for accomplishing the transfer.

Specify the goals and expectations of the privatization process. Identify decisionmakers, define their roles, and establish a system for monitoring the conversion process.

Step 2. Enlist the help of the business and professional communities and form a public-private partnership.

Develop a working partnership between your agency and the business and professional leaders of your community. Get business leaders to contribute their management expertise to help you examine your agency's functions, goals, operating costs, and strengths and weaknesses.

Step 3. Assess your agency's existing organizational structure, procedures, and services.

Collect and analyze information about operating costs, staffing, service delivery systems, procurement procedures, legal requirements, liability issues, and the community and its political environment. This will help you structure future activities so they are consistent with ongoing goals and operations.

Step 4. Identify the juvenile probation functions most suited to privatization, and adjust or redesign probation components as needed.

Using the information gathered in step 3, with constructive advice from your partnerships, develop ideas for using privatization to improve your operations, then make plans for implementing the desired changes.

Step 5. Write clear, concise solicitations or Requests for Proposals. Select a contractor to carry out the privatized function.

Write a clear, concise solicitation or Request for Proposal that will attract bids from qualified contractors. Develop evaluation criteria and form a review team to select the contractor most responsive to your solicitation. Negotiate a contract that clearly spells out the contractor's responsibilities and expected performance standards.

Step 6. Implement the conversion of the probation function to contractor operation.

Following a predetermined timetable and procedure, transfer responsibility for management decisions, notify your staff and your clients of the transfer, turn over client files and other records, and train the staff. The foregoing will ensure a smooth transition of services.

Step 7. Establish a monitoring process to track the contractor's performance and evaluate the quality of services provided.

Identify the performance standards spelled out in the contract, develop indicators for measuring the contractor's performance against those standards, and work out a procedure and timetable for evaluating the results and taking remedial action when necessary.

The demonstration sites found that juvenile probation departments *can* successfully improve some functions by transferring them to the private sector.

COMMUNITY-BASED CORRECTIONS PROGRAMS

The community-corrections philosophy follows the juvenile justice rhetoric of treatment and restoration instead of punishment and decay. Krisberg et al. (1986, p. 36) suggest that: "Unless we structure our juvenile justice programs now, this new wave of adolescents will produce even higher levels of incarceration than is currently the case. As with overcrowding in adult prisons and jails, it is foolish to believe we can simply build enough new correctional facilities to stay ahead of this problem."

According to the President's Commission on Law Enforcement and Administration of Justice (1967, p. 69): "Institutions tend to isolate offenders from society, both physically and psychologically, cutting them off from schools, jobs, families, and other supportive influences and increasing the probability that the label of criminal will be indelibly impressed upon them." Community-based corrections therefore should be considered seriously for juvenile offenders.

▪ Isolating offenders from their normal social environment may encourage the development of a delinquent orientation and, thus, further delinquent behavior.

The issues raised by the President's Commission indicated a need to integrate rather than isolate offenders, to reduce rather than simplify the delinquent label. Community-based correctional programs, such as probation, foster care and group homes, represent attempts to respond to these issues by normalizing social contacts, reducing the stigma attached to being institutionalized and providing opportunities for jobs and schooling. The Commission recommended more use of community resources in working with juveniles (1967, p. 69):

Efforts, both private and public, should be intensified to:

▪ Involve young people in community activities.
▪ Train and employ youth as subprofessional aides.
▪ Establish Youth Services Bureaus to provide and coordinate programs for young people.
▪ Increase involvement of religious institutions, private social agencies, fraternal groups, and other community organizations in youth programs.
▪ Provide community residential centers.

The Commission was instrumental in persuading the federal government to provide funds for programs that emphasized probation and parole as measures replacing institutionalization. The programs made it possible to treat offenders in an open community on a much larger scale than before. Programs such as work release enabled delinquents to leave an institution and work in the community. Similar programs provided release to delinquents for education. Under these programs, they were provided conditional releases to halfway houses, prerelease centers and residential treatment facilities. Living in homes within the community, youths would go to work or school under some supervision and counseling. Pioneered in 1961 by the Federal Bureau of Prisons, under this program delinquents were released to four prerelease guidance centers in New York, Chicago, Detroit and Los Angeles.

Similar programs began in states and cities, such as Philadelphia's Youth Development Center, which provided conventional residential programs, and Opportunities Industrialization Centers (OIC), which involved group homes and a vocational training agency working together. Short-Term Adolescent Residential Training (START), in New York state, provided group counseling in the evening and work or school during the day. Short-Term Aid Youth (STAY) combined the same features as START, but youths went back to their own homes at night.

Several other nonresidential corrections programs have been implemented.

■ Nonresidential corrections programs include community supervision; family crisis counseling; proctor programs; and service-oriented programs, including recreational programs, counseling, alternative schools, employment training programs, and homemaking and financial planning classes.

Nonresidential Day Treatment Alternatives

Many state and local governments are turning to day treatment alternatives for delinquent juveniles because they appear to be effective and they are less costly than residential care. Alternatives might include evening and weekend reporting centers, school programs and specialized treatment facilities. Such programs can provide education, tutoring, counseling, community service, vocational training and social/recreational events.

Such programs tend to be successful because they can focus on the family unit and the youth's behavior in the family and the community. They are also effective from a legal standpoint in those states that require that youths be treated in the least restrictive environment possible.

Community-based corrections has supplemented, not replaced institutionalization. The community also sometimes provides residential, nonsecure facilities with accompanying programs.

Nonsecure Residential Programs

Residential programs are divided into five major categories.

▮ The five major categories of residential programs are shelters, group homes, foster homes, foster group homes and "other" types of nonsecure facilities.

Shelters

Shelters are nonsecure residential facilities where juveniles may be temporarily assigned, often in place of detention or returning home after being taken into custody or after adjudication while waiting for more permanent placement. Shelters usually house status offenders and are not intended for treatment or punishment.

Group Homes

The **group home** is a nonsecure facility with a professional corrections staff that provides counseling, education, job training and family-style living. The staff is small because the residence generally holds a maximum of 12 to 15 youths. Group home living provides support and some structure in a basically nonrestrictive setting, with the opportunity for a close, but controlled, interaction with the staff. The youths in the home attend a school in the community and participate in community activities in the area. The objective of the home is to facilitate reintegrating young offenders into society.

Group homes are used extensively in almost all states. Some are operated by private agencies under contract to the juvenile court. Others are operated directly by probation departments or some other governmental unit.

▮ *Group homes provide support for youths who need more support and supervision than probation or a foster home would provide, but less restriction than confinement would entail.*

Some, called "boarding homes," deserve special mention. Since these homes often accommodate as few as three or four youths, they frequently may be found in an apartment or flat in an urban setting. They are sometimes called a "Mom and Pop" operation because the adults serve as parent-substitutes. The adults are usually paraprofessionals whose strengths are personal warmth and an ability to relate to young people.

An example of a community-based residential treatment program is the program developed for Rutgers Medical School. Middlefield, in North Brunswick, New Jersey, is located in an old farmhouse on common grounds with a juvenile detention facility and a county jail for adults. In early 1980, Harriet Hollander developed a program for the Middlefield facility. At the time the facility had 12 residents, all males. Criteria for admission to the program included the following:

■ Be capable of social participation, i.e., show capacity to organize thoughts.
■ Possess minimal language skills to communicate ideas.
■ Have the potential to internalize behavior.

Unacceptable to the program were juveniles who had violent or aggressive behavior, or drug or alcohol addiction. The Middlefield program stressed psychoeducation and juvenile development, somewhat different from most group homes because of the focus on the individual rather than on the group. The program design was to "build responsibility in terms of actions; to help develop within the individual a good sense of values; and to give the boys direction in life" (Hollander, 1981). It emphasized offering both academic and vocational education with various community activities and trips. It also used Rutgers' Community Health Center and Alcoholics Anonymous for individual, group and family counseling.

Hollander (1981) stated the program was "a community-based treatment program built on a mental health model." This description places Middlefield in the category of programs that presumes some psychological disturbance or disorder to be the cause of delinquency. It, therefore, used psychological and mental health correctional strategies. Perhaps because of its focus on the individual and special blend of treatment approaches, the program did not produce the expectations it desired for a group home setting.

Foster Homes

Foster homes are intended to be family-like, as much as possible substitutes for natural family settings. Small and nonsecure, they are used at any of several stages in the juvenile justice process. In jurisdictions where a juvenile shelter is not available, foster homes may be used when law enforcement authorities take a juvenile into custody. The National Advisory Committee for Juvenile Justice and Delinquency Prevention (1980, p. 447) recommends that foster care become "the primary out-of-home placement for neglected juveniles and those involved in noncriminal misbehavior and a more utilized placement for delinquents."

▊ The National Advisory Committee for Juvenile Justice and Delinquency Prevention recommended foster homes for neglected juveniles and those charged with status offenses.

Foster care is not used as much for misbehaving children and those adjudicated youths in the area of community treatment as it is for children whose parents have neglected, abused or abandoned them. Social service agencies usually handle the placement in and funding of foster care programs. The police and courts coordinate their efforts through these agencies.

Foster Group Homes

Foster group homes are a blend of group home and foster initiatives. They provide a "real family" concept and are run by single families, not professional staffs. Foster group homes are nonsecure facilities that are usually acceptable to neighborhood environments and yet can give troubled youths a neighborhood-family type relationship.

In the United States, foster group homes can be found in various parts of the country.

Other Nonsecure Facilities

Correctional farms, ranches and camps for youth are usually located in rural areas. These facilities are an alternative to confinement or regimented programs. The programs with an outdoor or rural setting encourage self-development, provide opportunities for reform and secure classification and placement of juveniles according to their capabilities. Close contact with staff and residents instills good work habits.

According to the National Advisory Committee (1980, p. 431): "The camps and ranches . . . require a programmatic emphasis on outside activity, basic self-discipline and the development of vocational and interpersonal skills. . . . The camp provides a setting for juveniles to develop good work habits, learn to work, and develop skills. Further, residents perform useful and necessary work that benefits the community in general."

The Dilemma of Community Programs

Court dispositions are often compromises among the pressures to secure deterrence, incapacitation, retribution and rehabilitation. Community-based programs do not permit the freedom of dismissal or of suspended judgments, but neither do they isolate offenders from the community as institutions do. Community programs are sometimes perceived as being easy on youngsters and, thus, as not providing sufficient punishment or supervision to ensure deterrence, incapacitation and retribution. Nonetheless, commitment to such programs represents a considerable degree of restriction and punishment when compared to dismissal, suspended judgment or informal processing out of the system at an early stage.

■ *Camps and ranches allow youths to develop self-discipline and yet enjoy outdoor activities.*

INTERMEDIATE SANCTIONS

Intermediate sanctions include intensive supervision, house arrest with electronic monitoring and shock incarceration or boot camps.

■ Three common forms of intermediate sanctions are intensive supervision, electronic monitoring and boot camps.

Such sanctions provide swift, certain punishment, while avoiding the expense and negative effects of institutionalization. Intensive supervision was discussed previously.

Electronic Monitoring

Electronic monitoring (EM), sometimes referred to as *house arrest,* has been tried with some success in several jurisdictions. In fact, it is sometimes a key component in intensive probation and parole programs. According to the

Bureau of Justice Assistance monograph, *Electronic Monitoring in Intensive Probation and Parole Programs* (1989), electronic monitoring can be used to impose curfew, home detention (more restrictive than curfew, the offender must be home except when at work or at treatment) or home incarceration (the offender must be at home at almost all times). The use of EM has grown considerably, as illustrated in Figure 11–2.

The monograph (p. 3) suggests that electronic monitoring provides a "supervision tool that can satisfy punishment, public safety and treatment objectives." It can:

▮ Provide a cost-effective community supervision tool for offenders selected according to specific program criteria.
▮ Administer sanctions appropriate to the seriousness of the offense.

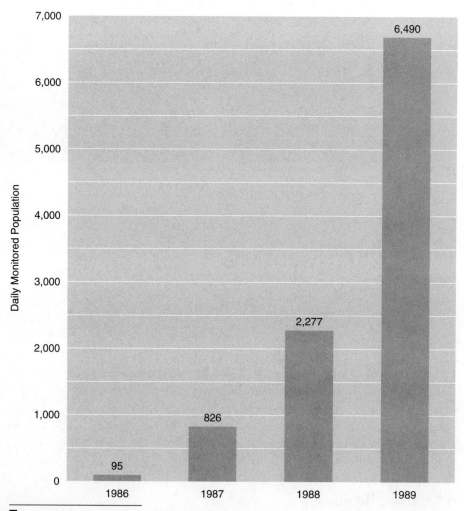

▮ **FIGURE 11–2 Estimated Daily Monitored Population in the United States, 1986–1989**

SOURCE: Marc Renzema and David T. Skelton, "Use of Electronic Monitoring in the United States: 1989 Update." *NIJ Reports* 222 (November/December, 1990): 1. Reprinted in NIJ, Research in Brief, n.d.

- Promote public safety by providing surveillance and risk control strategies indicated by the risk and needs of the offender.
- Increase the confidence of legislative, judicial and releasing authorities in Intensive Supervision Probation or Parole Program designs as a viable sentencing option.

Figure 11–3 (p. 400) illustrates the key decision points where EM can be used. The types of offenders who were likely to be monitored electronically are summarized in Table 11–2 (p. 401).

Renzema and Skelton (1990, p. 4) report that very little difference as far as being a good candidate for electronic monitoring was found among offense categories, with one exception. Those with major traffic offenses committed fewer technical violations and fewer new offenses than other offenders. Table 11–3 (p. 401) illustrates the outcome of electronic monitoring based on the age of the offender. Note that termination appears to become more successful as age increases.

Boot Camps

Use of boot camps as an intermediate sanction has also been growing. Also known as **shock incarceration, boot camps** stress military discipline, physical fitness, strict obedience to orders, as well as educational and vocational training and drug treatment when appropriate.

Most boot camps are designed for young, nonviolent, first-time offenders as a means of punishment and rehabilitation without long-term incarceration. According to MacKenzie (1990, pp. 6–7) conclusions emerging from NIJ research on boot camps include the following:

- Programs vary greatly, and any evaluation must begin with a description of the program and its objectives.
- There is some evidence that the boot camp experience may be more positive than incarceration in traditional prison.
- There is no evidence that those who complete boot camp programs are angrier or negatively affected by the program.
- Those who complete shock programs report having a difficult but constructive experience. Similar offenders who serve their sentences in a traditional prison do not view their experiences as constructive.
- Boot camp recidivism rates are approximately the same as those of comparison groups who serve a longer period of time in a traditional prison or who serve time on probation.
- Success may be contingent on the emphasis on rehabilitation—giving offenders the training, treatment and education needed to support new behavior—during incarceration and on aftercare during community supervision.

Table 11–4 (p. 402) shows the characteristics of shock incarceration programs in 14 states. New York, with the largest number of programs and participants, is concerned about maintaining the positive gains made during boot camp and has developed an "after shock" program to help offenders in their supervised return to the community.

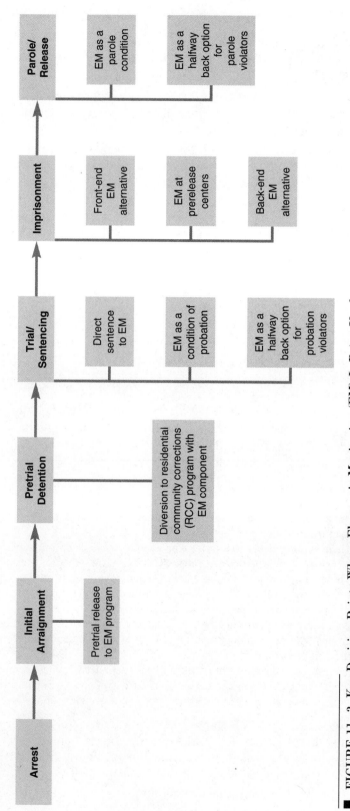

■ **FIGURE 11–3 Key Decision Points Where Electronic Monitoring (EM) Is Being Used**

SOURCE: Bureau of Justice Assistance, *Electronic Monitoring in Intensive Probation and Parole Programs.* Washington, D.C.: February 1989, p. 2.

TABLE   Monitored Offenders by Offense Category, 1987–1989
11–2

Offense Category	1987 % of Total Number	1988 % of Total Number	1989 % of Sample
Crimes against the person	5.6	9.7	11.8
Drug offenses	13.5	15.3	22.0
Frauds	3.3	3.8	2.3
Major traffic offenses	33.4	25.6	18.9
Property offenses	18.2	20.1	31.7
Sex offenses	2.8	4.0	1.4[a]
Weapon offenses	1.2	1.3	2.2
Multiple offenses	10.2	6.1	.9[b]
Other offenses	11.8	14.2	8.9

[a] Neither of the jurisdictions best known for the monitoring of sex offenders was included in the 1989 sample–this decline is likely an accident of sampling rather than a significant trend.
[b] The decline in "multiple offenses" is probably an artifact caused by form design. The 1989 form offered respondents an opportunity to precode responses and only limited space for multiple offenses.
SOURCE: Marc Renzema and David T. Skelton, "Use of Electronic Monitoring in the United States: 1989 Update," *NIJ Reports* 222 (November/December, 1990): 3. Reprinted in NIJ, Research in Brief, n.d.

TABLE   Type of Termination by Months on Monitoring, 1989 Sample
11–3

Duration of Monitoring	Successful Terminations[a]	Technical Violations[b]	New Offense Violations[c]
Month 1	271	94	16
Month 2	211	71	7
Month 3	170	43	6
Month 4	128	26	9
Month 5	67	16	3
Month 6	46	11	0
Months 7–12	66	12	6
Months 13–24	14	2	1
Total	973	275	48

[a] Successful Terminations are those in which the offender completed the assigned term or was removed for administrative reasons.
[b] Technical Violations include curfew violations, substance abuse violations, absconding, and other rule violations that caused the offender to be removed from monitoring. The usual but not invariable consequence of technical violations was incarceration.
[c] New Offense Violations were those in which the offender was arrested for an offense during electronic monitoring.
SOURCE: Marc Renzema and David T. Skelton, "Use of Electronic Monitoring in the United States: 1989 Update," *NIJ Reports* 222 (November/December, 1990): 4. Reprinted in NIJ, Research in Brief, n.d.

TABLE   Characteristics of Shock Incarceration Programs, May 1990
11–4

State	Year Programs Began	Number of Programs	Number of Participants (Male/Female)	Number of Days Served	Maximum Age Limit	First Felony?	Non-violent Only?
Alabama	1988	1	127 male[a]	90	none	no	no
Arizona	1988	1	150 male[a]	120	25	yes	no
Florida	1987	1	100 male[a]	90[b]	25	yes	no
Georgia	1983	2	250 male[a]	90	25	yes	no
Idaho	1989[c]	1	154 male	120	none	no	no
Louisiana	1987	1	87 male[a] 1 female	120	39	no	yes
Michigan	1988	1	120 male	120[d]	25	no	no
Mississippi	1985	2[a]	225 male[a] 15 female	110[e]	none	yes	yes
New York	1987	5[a]	1,500 male[a] 102 female	180	30	yes	yes
North Carolina	1989[c]	1	54 male	93	24	yes	yes
Oklahoma	1984	1	150 male	90[f]	25	yes	yes
South Carolina	1987	2	98 male[a] 13 female	90	24	yes	yes
Tennessee	1989[c]	1	42 male	120	30	yes	yes
Texas	1989	1	200 male	90	25	yes	no

[a]Indicates increase since May 1989.
[b]May 1989: Average 101.
[c]Program new since May 1989.
[d]May 1989: Average 90.
[e]May 1989: Average 180.
[f]May 1989: Average 120.

SOURCE: Doris Layton MacKenzie, " 'Boot Camp' Programs Grow in Number and Scope." *NIJ Reports* 222 (November/December 1990): 8.

A relatively new site for boot camps is the jail. Austin et al. (1993, p. 5) suggest that to be effective, a jail boot camp must address several key issues:

▮ Relief of crowding.
▮ Rehabilitation.
▮ Improving jail operations and community relations.

The possible goals to be met by jail boot camps vary greatly. Most often stressed are reducing recidivism, providing general education and drug education and developing good work skills, as summarized in Figure 11–4.

Table 11–5 (p. 404) summarizes the selection criteria and placement procedures used in 10 jail boot camps.

Most successful programs also have an aftercare component. Table 11–6 (p. 406) shows the services, aftercare and completion rates for 10 jail boot camps.

Having looked at the nonsecure facilities such as ranches, shelters and camps, focus now on the facilities serving the majority of youth who are not placed on probation or diverted from the system.

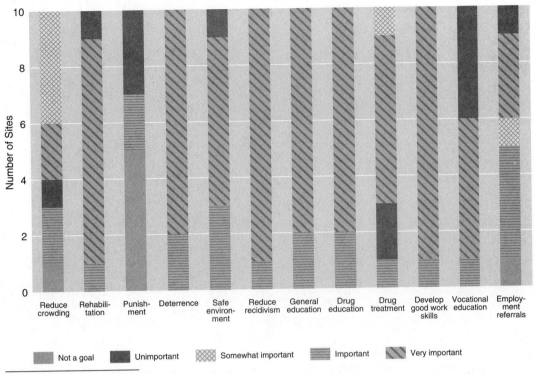

■ FIGURE 11–4 Jail Boot Camp Goals

SOURCE: James Austin, Michael Jones, and Melissa Bolyard, "The Growing Use of Jail Boot Camps: The Current State of the Art," NIJ, Research in Brief, October 1993, p. 4.

INSTITUTIONALIZATION

Some of the most secure institutions are merely storage facilities for juvenile offenders. Here juvenile delinquents often simply "do their time," with release based on conditions of overcrowding and, amazingly, inability of the system to "rehabilitate" the offender. Such nonconstructive time, when juveniles should be developing their values and planning their futures, can be devastating. Although lockups may be needed for a portion of the chronic, violent offenders, they serve as criminal training schools for other juveniles.

SHOCAP suggests the following for state correctional officers (Crowe, 1991, pp. 49–50):

. . . [S]tate juvenile corrections authorities are responsible for the housing and rehabilitation of adjudicated delinquents who are sentenced to either a definite or indefinite period of incarceration and/or treatment. Many state corrections agencies have had to classify custody levels and diagnose the treatment needs of juvenile offenders without the benefits of the detailed profiles that are being developed on serious habitual offenders. Therefore, some strategies are:

■ Provide all profile information to correctional authorities upon sentencing of a designated habitual offender;

TABLE 11–5 Jail Boot Camps: Selection Criteria and Placement Procedures

Selection Criteria	Travis, TX	New York City, Men	New York City, Women	Santa Clara, CA	Nassau, NY	New Orleans, LA	Harris, TX	Ontario, NY	Brazos, TX	Oakland, MI
Age	17–26	16–39	19 plus	18 plus	16–18	17–45	17–25	16–30	17–30	17 plus
Sex	Co-ed	Males	Females	Females	Males	Co-ed	Co-ed	Co-ed	Males	Males
First-time offenders	Yes	No	No	Yes	Yes	Yes	No	No	Yes	No
Nonviolent offenders	Yes	Yes	Yes	No	No	Yes	No	No	No	Yes
Other	N/A	Low classification	Low classification	Substance abuse	N/A	Multiple offender	N/A	N/A	N/A	N/A
Voluntary entry	For some	Yes	Yes	Yes	Yes	Yes	No	Yes	For some	Yes
Voluntary exit	No	Yes	Yes	Yes	Yes	Yes	No	No	No	Yes
Placement procedure	Judge recommends with jail approval; judge then sentences; jail also selects parole violators.	Jail selects, no other approval necessary; technical parole violators admitted upon referral to boot camp.	Jail selects, no other approval necessary; technical parole violators admitted upon referral to boot camp.	Jail selects, no other approval necessary.	Jail selects, no other approval necessary.**	Judge recommends with jail approval; judge then sentences.	Judge sentences, jail has no veto power.	Jail selects, no other approval necessary.	Judge recommends, jail approves.	Judge sentences, jail has veto power.

** Applicants screened by a board composed of correction staff, rehabilitation counselors, education counselor, clergy and probation staff.

SOURCE: James Austin, Michael Jones, and Melissa Bolyard, "The Growing Use of Jail Boot Camps: The Current State of the Art," NIJ, Research in Brief, October 1993, p. 6.

■ Share correctional case histories and diagnostic reports with the crime analyst or other officials designated to develop and maintain profiles of habitual offenders;

■ Develop special classification and custody levels for designated habitual offenders;

■ Limit placements of habituals to the most secure programs and keep them separate from juveniles of similar status;

■ Conduct special diagnostic and program activities to control behavior while in institutional programs and to assist in the eventual return to the community.

The trend toward "getting tough" on serious, habitual violent offenders has already been noted. Hurst (1990b, p. 49) suggests: "The trend is clearly toward punishment of juveniles in the adult criminal justice system, either through mandatory waiver of certain classes of offenders, exclusion of certain classes of offenders from the juvenile system, or through discretionary waiver from juvenile to adult criminal court."

The *OJJDP Annual Report, 1990* (p. 5) says an excess of 11,000 different facilities might hold juveniles. Of these 30 percent are specifically designed for juveniles. The remainder are adult jails, police lockups and state correctional facilities. Table 11–7 (p. 408) summarizes the estimates of the number of juvenile admissions to custody and in custody in recent years. On any given day nearly 100,000 youths reside in juvenile and adult facilities.

Table 11–8 (p. 409) shows the types of public and private facilities used for juveniles in 1989. Training schools were the most popular alternative for both public and private institutions. The public detention center was also extensively used.

DETENTION

Detention was discussed from a law enforcement perspective in Chapter 9. In 1989, the National Juvenile Detention Association (NJDA) developed and ratified a comprehensive national definition of juvenile detention (Smith, 1991, p. 56):

> Juvenile detention is the temporary and secure custody of children, accused or adjudicated of conduct subject to the jurisdiction of the family/juvenile court, who require a physically restricting environment for their own or the community's protection while pending legal action.
>
> Further, juvenile detention provides and maintains a wide range of helpful services which include, but are not limited to, the following: education, visitation, private communications, counseling, continuous supervision, medical and health care, nutrition, recreation and reading.
>
> In addition to advising the court on the proper course of action required to restore the child to a productive role in the community, detention also includes or provides a system for clinical observation and diagnosis, which complements the wide range of helpful services.

The NJDA clearly states that juvenile detention is to be reserved for juveniles who are violent and/or who pose a serious threat to community safety. According to Smith (1991, p. 58): "The weaker juvenile who is sentenced to a ten-day detention stay may be subject to violent acts, victimized by extortion and emotionally scarred." Smith (p. 60) concludes:

> Judges and probation officers who fall prey to the popular wisdom that espouses a get-tough policy on troublesome but non-dangerous teens are doing them a grave disservice. These youths need services, not time in detention centers. Detention is a preadjudicatory service for dangerous youths; to place chronic misdemeanants in that environment allows them to become victims of a system that should be their protector.

TABLE 11–6   Jail Boot Camps: Services, Aftercare and Completion Rates
∎

	Travis, TX	New York City, Men	New York City, Women	Santa Clara, CA	Nassau, NY
Services Provided					
Physical training and drill	3 hrs/wk	1 hr/day	1 hr/day	3.75 hrs/day	2 hrs/day
Work	6 hrs/wk	3 hrs/day	0	1.5 hrs/day	4 hrs/day
Vocational education	8 hrs/wk	3 hrs/day	2 hrs/day	2.5 hrs/day	0
Drug education counseling	4 hrs/wk	5 hrs/wk	2 hrs/day	1.5 hrs/day	4 hrs/day
General education	5 hrs/wk	12 hrs/wk	2 hrs/day	1.5 hrs/day	4 hrs/day
General counseling	Yes[a]	N/A	Yes[a]	1 hr/day	N/A
Other	Life skills, 4 hrs/wk	Community services	Community services, 5 hrs/wk	Personal hygiene, 1 hr/day	N/A
Aftercare special supervision	Yes	Yes	Yes	No	No
Type of supervision	Depends on risk level	Limited aftercare supervision for parole violators and conditional releases	Limited aftercare supervision for parole violators and conditional releases	N/A	N/A
Supervision provided by	Probation	Parole and probation	Parole and probation	N/A	N/A
Completion rate	47.7%	69.9%	71.4%	79.0%	67.8%[b]
Noncompletions	139	319	56	26	19
Medical/ psychol.	21	13	6	3	5
Disciplinary	114	126	23	16	7
Voluntary withdrawal	0	169	22	0	7
Other	4	11[d]	5[d]	7[e]	0

—continued

TABLE 11-6 Jail Boot Camps: Services, Aftercare and Completion Rates, *continued*

	New Orleans, LA	Harris, TX	Ontario, NY	Brazos, TX	Oakland, MI
Services Provided					
Physical training and drill	2 hrs/day	6 hrs/day	2 hrs/day	1 hr/day	4 hrs/day
Work	5 hrs/day	2 hrs/day	1/2 hr/day	6 hrs/day	8 hrs/day
Vocational education	3 hrs/day	2 hrs/day	2 hrs/day	Yes[a]	4 hrs/wk
Drug education counseling	1 hr/day	1 hr/day	4 hrs/day	1 hr/day	8 hrs/wk
General education	4 hrs/day	4 hrs/day	0	1 hr/day	6 hrs/wk
General counseling	N/A	Yes[a]	2 hrs/wk	1 hr/day	2 hrs/wk
Other	Community services, 1 hr/day	Life skills, 2 hrs/day	Health education, 2 hrs/wk	N/A	N/A
Aftercare					
special supervision	Yes	Yes	No	Yes	Yes
Type of supervision	Moderate	Intensive: Monitor devices, Halfway housing	N/A	Intensive	Moderate
Supervision provided by	Jail and probation	Probation	N/A	Jail and probation	Jail and probation
Completion rate	78.5%[c]	97.0%	92.6%	N/A	79.8%
Noncompletions	38	15	8	0	24
Medical/ psychol.	N/A	0	0	0	4
Disciplinary	N/A	0	8	0	9
Voluntary withdrawal	0	0	0	0	11
Other	38[f]	15[g]	0	0	0

[a] Par Hours not available.
[b] Reflects those still successfully enrolled in program; none have completed program to date.
[c] Reflects those still successfully enrolled in program; no 1992 completions to date.
[d] Legal.

[e] Sentence served prior to program completion.
[f] Includes medical and disciplinary; breakdown not available.
[g] Probation absconders.

SOURCE: James Austin, Michael Jones, and Melissa Bolyard. "The Growing Use of Jail Boot Camps: The Current State of the Art," NIJ, Research in Brief, October 1993, p. 7.

TABLE 11–7   Recent Estimates of the Number of Juvenile Admissions to Custody and in Custody

	Number of Facilities	Number of Juvenile Annual Admissions	Number in Custody, 1-Day Counts
Total	11,056	834,985[5]	99,617[5]
Public facilities[1]	1,100	619,181	56,123
Private facilities[1]	2,167	141,463	37,822
Adult jails[2]	3,316	65,263	1,676
State correctional facilities[3]	903	9,078	3,996
Police lockups[4]	3,570	Unknown	Unknown

Note: These data reflect a compilation of information from a number of separate statistical series. The definition of a juvenile differs in each data source. Also, the data on admissions do not represent individual youths taken into custody. However, these are the only data available to estimate the number of youths entering custody facilities.

[1] 1989 Census of Public and Private Juvenile Detention, Correctional and Shelter Facilities: Admissions for Calendar Year 1988; 1-Day Count Census Day was 2/15/89.
[2] Census of Local Jails, 1988: Admissions for FY 1988; 1-Day Count Census Day was 6/30/88; Juvenile is defined as a person of juvenile age as defined by State law even if tried as an adult in criminal court.
[3] Census of State Correctional Facilities, 1984. For this report, juveniles are all persons under the age of 18.
[4] Law Enforcement Management and Administrative Survey, 1987; Juvenile is defined as a person under juvenile court jurisdiction but would not include youths under 18 and under criminal court jurisdiction.
[5] Totals do not include juveniles admitted to police lockups.
SOURCE: *OJJDP Annual Report 1990* (Washington, D.C.: U.S. Department of Justice, [1990]), p. 6.

The *OJJDP Annual Report, 1990* (p. 115), suggests:

Many of these youth come from dysfunctional families, lack appropriate adult role models, have failed in school, lack vocational skills, and experience severely limited opportunities for lawful and gainful employment. They may also have behavioral and psychological problems such as high impulsivity, violent reactions to stress, sexual offending, depression, and drug- or alcohol-related problems.

CURRENT DETENTION CENTERS

The nation's original training and industrial reform schools have survived to the present under new names. They still function, however, under the same regimented format.

Detention centers, unlike group homes and shelters, are secure, locked facilities. The centers hold juveniles prior to and following adjudication.

TABLE 11-8   Juveniles in Public and Private Juvenile Facilities, 1989

■

Type of Facility	Juveniles in Facilities		
	Number	*Percent*	*Rate per 100,000** *
Public			
Detention centers	18,014	32%	70.0
Training schools	27,823	50	108.8
Ranches and camps	4,617	8	18.1
Shelters	646	1	2.5
Diagnostic centers	1,424	3	5.6
Halfway houses	3,599	6	14.1
Total public facilities	56,123	100	219.1
Private			
Detention centers	396	1	1.5
Training schools	7,352	19	28.8
Ranches and camps	4,826	13	18.9
Shelters	2,821	8	11.0
Diagnostic centers	477	1	1.9
Halfway houses	21,950	58	85.8
Total private facilities	37,822	100	147.9
Total	93,945		367.0

**Rate is calculated on U.S. Bureau of the Census estimates of the number of youth age 10 years to upper age of juvenile court jurisdiction in each State.

SOURCE: U.S. Department of Justice, Office of Juvenile Justice and Delinquency Prevention, *National Juvenile Custody Trends 1978–1989* (Washington, DC: U.S. Department of Justice, 1992), p. 8.

■ Formally, only three purposes justify putting juveniles in a locked facility: (1) to secure their presence at court proceedings, (2) to hold those who cannot be sent home and (3) to prevent juveniles from harming themselves or others, or from disrupting juvenile court processes.

In some areas, a detention center is incorporated in a jail. Finckenaur (1984, p. 132) visited an "all-purpose jail" in Tyler, Texas, and reported:

> On the upper floor of this jail (on a very humid day in late June, with the temperature soaring into triple figures) approximately a dozen juveniles were confined in a large bullpen cell. This cell was literally a "hot box," dark and without ventilation. Some of the juveniles were from out of state, and the average stay for most was somewhere around 45 days. Because these youths were confined in an adult facility, and because the sheriff was attempting to maintain physical separation of juveniles and adults, the youth had nowhere to go and nothing to do for just about the entire duration of their incarceration.

The National Advisory Commission on Corrections referred to the jailing of juveniles as a "disconcerting phenomenon." Because they are intended to be

▌ *Two youngsters share this cell in a youth detention facility. The mattress on the floor shows the overcrowded conditions.*

temporary holding facilities, jail and detention centers offer little or nothing in the way of correctional treatment.

Prior to adjudication, juveniles may stay from a day or more up to weeks. This raises the question of whether detention is appropriate before a juvenile is adjudicated delinquent. One rationale for detention prior to adjudication is that it serves as an informal punishment, advocated by those who believe in "getting tough on juveniles": "Teach them a lesson and give them a taste of jail" (Finckenaur, 1984, p. 152).

Some jurisdictions have formalized detention centers as jails for children. New Jersey, for example, permits sentencing juveniles who have been adjudicated delinquent for "repetitive disorderly person offenses" up to 60 days in detention centers (ACA, 1983, p. xvii).

TRAINING SCHOOLS

Training schools exist in every state except Massachusetts, which abolished them in the 1970s. They vary greatly in size, staff, service programs, ages and types of residents. Some training schools resemble adult prisons, with the same distinguishing problems of gang-oriented activity, homosexual terrorism and victimization, which often leads to progressive difficulties or suicide.

In California, for example, a compassionate law recognizes that many immature young men over 18 but under 21 will be abused if they are sent to adult jails or state prisons and would be more likely to survive if placed at the

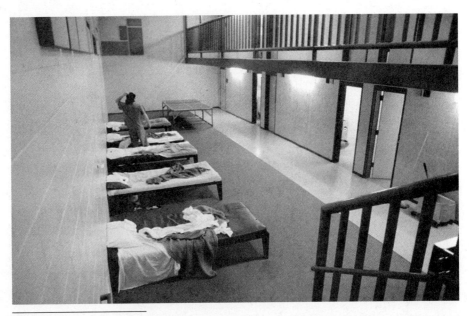

Some detention facilities are set up more like a dormitory.

youth authority. A report on the California Youth Authority describes the experiences of one young man not protected by the California law (Lerner, 1986, p. 21):

> Sam fits this description. Standing 5 foot, 6 inches and weighing 140 pounds, he was hardly one of the larger physical specimens . . . nor was he particularly street-wise or hardened. Sam was busted for stealing some stereo equipment. Sam is a classic institutional tragedy. He soon became a victim of "sexual pressure" by six inmates who threatened him with a "shank," or knife. He was then transferred to another facility where he fared no better. He had a reputation for caving in to sexual demands and was victimized sexually on a number of occasions. He told a counselor that inmates took Polaroid pictures of him being sexually abused, which they used to blackmail him. Sam, a white, 19-year-old from Modesto, successfully hanged himself from an air vent in his cell.

Most legislation requires training schools to provide both safe custody and rehabilitative treatment. A 1983 federal court case, however, rejected the idea of a constitutional right to treatment and training: "We therefore agree . . . that, although rehabilitative training is no doubt desirable and sound as policy and perhaps of state law, plaintiffs have no constitutional right to rehabilitative training" (*Santana v. Collazo*, 1983).

JUVENILES IN PUBLIC INSTITUTIONS

In 1991 over 57,000 youths were detained or committed in over 1,000 types of public short-term and long-term facilities, as summarized in Table 11–9.

TABLE   Juveniles Held in Public Juvenile Facilities, 1991
11-9

	All Facilities	Short-Term Facilities			Long-Term Facilities		
		Total	Institutional	Open	Total	Institutional	Open
Total juveniles	1,076	511	72	439	565	338	227
Total detained	18,467	17,890	705	17,185	577	156	421
Delinquent offenses[a]	17,214	16,693	291	16,402	521	110	411
Status offenses[b]	757	712	206	506	45	38	7
Abuse and neglect[c]	250	244	199	45	6	6	0
Offenses unknown[d]	246	241	9	232	5	2	3
Total committed	38,900	3,326	201	3,125	35,574	8,912	26,662
Delinquent offenses[a]	37,590	3,137	129	3,008	34,453	8,217	26,236
Status offenses[b]	998	135	52	83	863	500	363
Abuse and neglect[c]	221	39	20	19	182	173	9
Offenses unknown[d]	91	15	0	15	76	22	54

Note: "Detained" juveniles refer to those temporarily held awaiting adjudication, disposition, or placement; "committed" refers to placement following adjudication or any placement procedure.

[a]Offenses that would be criminal if committed by an adult.
[b]Offenses that would not be criminal for adults, such as running away, truancy, or incorrigibility.
[c]Also includes dependency, emotional disturbance, and mental retardation.
[d]Includes unknown or unspecified acts.

SOURCE: U.S. Department of Justice, Bureau of Justice Statistics, *Sourcebook of Criminal Justice Statistics, 1993* (Washington, D.C.: U.S. Government Printing Office, [1993]), p. 584.

Inmate Characteristics

An investigation of the characteristics of inmates of public long-term juvenile institutions shows a pattern not unlike that of America's jails and prisons. The disadvantaged and the poor make up a large percentage of the population. Other characteristics of the 49,322 juveniles confined in public institutions in 1987 and 1989 are summarized in Table 11-10.

■ The percentage of blacks and males in juvenile institutions far exceeds their proportions in the general population.

Some of the imbalance of males and blacks in juvenile institutions is doubtless because they tend to commit more serious offenses than females and whites. Also, blacks and males compile lengthier official records of delinquency than females and whites.

One project of an OJJDP and ACA partnership is a training curriculum in cultural differences for law enforcement and juvenile justice officials. The training curriculum is designed to reduce the overrepresentation of minority youths in the juvenile justice system.

■ *A facility for female offenders in upstate New York. Inmates are under constant surveillance in the mess hall.*

TABLE 11–10   Demographic Characteristics of Juveniles in Public Juvenile Facilities, 1987 and 1989

	1987	1989	Percent Change 1987–1989
Total juveniles	53,503	56,123	5%
Sex			
Male	46,272	49,443	7
Female	7,231	6,680	–8
Minority status			
Nonminority[a]	23,375	22,201	–5
Minority	30,128	33,922	13
Black[b]	20,898	23,836	14
Hispanic[c]	7,887	8,671	10
Other	1,343	1,415	5
Age on date of census			
9 years and younger	73	45	–38
10 to 13 years	2,811	3,276	17
14 to 17 years	43,898	44,894	2
18 years and older	6,721	7,908	18

[a]Includes whites not of Hispanic origin.
[b]Includes blacks not of Hispanic origin.
[c]Includes both whites and blacks of Hispanic origin.

SOURCE: U.S. Department of Justice, Office of Juvenile Justice and Delinquency Prevention, *Children in Custody 1989,* NCJ-127189 (Washington, D.C.: U.S. Department of Justice, January 1991), p. 3.

▮ *Most prison cells are stark. This juvenile is writing a letter to someone on the "outside."*

JUVENILES IN PRIVATE INSTITUTIONS

Whereas the earlier private institutions were products of philanthropic or religious impulse, the newer ones result from a more pecuniary, entrepreneurial drive. From the earliest days, private institutions attracted youths from more affluent backgrounds than those sent to public institutions. Many of the newer private institutions have chosen to emphasize their mental health and drug treatment programs. In this way they are able to capitalize on young people from families who have medical insurance or who are able to pay the costs of their children's confinement and treatment (Schwartz, 1987).

In 1991 the ACA surveyed juvenile corrections agencies on their use of private sector contracts, including all 50 states and the District of Columbia. The response rate was 98 percent. All respondents indicated they had at least one private sector contract (Levinson and Taylor, 1991, p. 242). Table 11–11 summarizes the types of private juvenile facilities being used and the characteristics of the youth being confined in such facilities in 1991. Of interest is the racial breakdown, with white offenders being in the majority in the private institutions.

TABLE **Private Juvenile Facilities and Youth Characteristics, 1991**
11–11

	Total	Detention Center	Shelter	Reception Center	Training School	Ranch/ Camp	Halfway House
Facilities[1]	2,032	44	309	22	81	80	1,496
Open	1,720	18	265	12	48	54	1,323
Institutional	243	25	38	6	29	24	121
Median capacity	10	10	11	12	52	47	10
Population	36,190	480	2,783	317	7,135	3,676	21,799
Sex							
Male	25,801	388	1,459	184	6,152	3,053	14,565
Female	10,389	92	1,324	133	983	623	7,234
Race							
White	20,524	207	1,670	170	2,993	2,079	13,405
Black	11,555	190	785	95	3,459	1,143	5,883
Hispanic	3,136	66	210	43	610	367	1,840
Other	975	17	118	9	73	87	671
Age							
Less than 10	632	4	94	6	44	27	457
10 to 12	2,696	17	254	25	322	215	1,863
13 to 15	18,134	303	1,569	199	2,986	2,093	10,984
16 to 17	13,089	152	854	82	3,284	1,144	7,573
18 or older	1,639	4	12	5	499	197	922
Reason for custody							
Delinquency	14,433	373	495	95	4,640	1,796	7,034
Person offense [b]	3,526	93	78	42	1,072	595	1,646
Property[c]	6,731	155	289	30	1,614	993	3,650
Alcohol offense	202	4	13	5	16	15	149
Drug offense	1,950	55	56	11	988	75	765
Public order[d]	387	23	22	4	119	38	181
Status offense	5,274	85	558	57	731	550	3,293
Nonoffender	9,915	22	763	91	1,077	778	7,184
Voluntary	6,568	0	967	74	687	552	4,288

[a]Includes 69 facilities that did not provide enough information to determine whether they had open or institutional environments.

[b]Includes murder, negligent and nonnegligent manslaughter, forcible rape, robbery, aggravated assault, assault, and sexual assault.

[c]Includes burglary, arson, larceny-theft, motor vehicle theft, vandalism, forgery, counterfeiting, fraud, stolen property, and unauthorized vehicle use.

[d]Includes disturbing the peace, prostitution, commercialized vice, weapons possession, minor traffic offenses, and curfew and loitering offenses.

SOURCE: U.S. Department of Justice, Bureau of Justice Statistics, *Sourcebook of Criminal Justice Statistics, 1993* (Washington, D.C.: U.S. Government Printing Office, [1993]), p. 586. Data provided to *Sourcebook* staff by the U.S. Department of Justice, Office of Juvenile Justice and Delinquency Prevention.

■ Compared to public correctional institutions, private correctional institutions confine more whites, more girls, more status offenders and more dependent and neglected youths. The inmates are younger and their stay is usually much longer.

Several reasons may account for this disparity. First, the population of private institutions probably includes a larger proportion of dependent and neglected children who have few family resources. For these youths, the institution becomes a surrogate home placement, which may last for several years. Second, because confinement is a profit-making activity, the private institutions are reluctant to discharge youths as long as their families can pay the bills. As a final proposition, private institutions are not forced to discharge to make room for new admissions, as is often the case in the public institutions. Public institutions often consider bed space as a criterion for release.

Objectives of Private Institutions

■ Private institutions offer much greater diversity in programs and structures than public institutions.

Private institutions also may have very strict rules that must be obeyed. For example, a private institution promoting itself as a placement option describes in its brochure the following requirements:

1. No coffee, tea, magazines, TV, radios, cigarettes, newspapers will be brought in the _____ Home.
2. No dresses or skirts above the knee. No pants or pants suits allowed.
3. No eye shadow of any kind.
4. Only two letters are written out, and those only to relatives or guardians.
5. All bags and boxes will be inspected on entering and leaving.
6. All money sent will be kept by the home and given as needed. No girl will be allowed to have money in her room.
7. If while at the home any girl should run away, her bags, clothes, etc., will not be sent home C.O.D. or express—they will be the property of the Home.
8. If anyone brings pants, eye make-up, or any of the items listed as not allowed, they will be taken up and destroyed.
9. No telephone calls will be made by the girls except in an emergency or of great importance.
10. Phone calls are permitted once a month from parents or guardians.
11. During the months of June, July, and August, all phone calls will be received only between 9:30 A.M. and 4:00 P.M. Monday through Friday.
12. Calls will be limited to five minutes unless an emergency.
13. No visiting in the girl's room—all visiting must be in a reception room or one of the visiting rooms.
14. Any girl that leaves the dorm with parents must have permission from one of the staff when she leaves and report in when returning.

15. The Home will not be responsible for the girls' actions when they are with parents.
16. All medical, dental, and other personal bills made by your daughter will be mailed to you, the parent or guardian, for payment.

SOCIAL STRUCTURE WITHIN CORRECTIONAL INSTITUTIONS

Correctional institutions—whether high or low security, locked or unlocked facilities, public or private, sexually integrated or segregated—often have an elaborate informal social organization and culture. The social organization includes a prestige hierarchy among inmates and a variety of inmate social roles. The inmate culture includes a complex of norms that indicate how inmates should relate to one another, to staff members and to the institutional regimen. According to Brown (1983, pp. 126–27):

> The institutional setting, with its large number of aggressive boys confined in tight quarters, served to encourage fighting.
>
> Fights were a daily occurrence. Somebody was upset about something. The reason did not matter, only the result. A wrong word, a wrong look, or being at the wrong place at the wrong time could create a confrontation. There was little to be done about it; either fight or be considered a "punk."
>
> Sometimes it was possible to find another way out, but not always. Usually it came down to a winner and a loser. Fighting was more than a way to vent frustration. It was also a means of gaining status and self-respect. . . . To be considered a "bad ass" was the highest compliment and afforded the greatest respect. A "rep" meant power and power meant control over people and situations. The top-ranked boys on campus and in a cottage had the fewest hassles. Other boys usually left them alone, choosing boys of lower rank on whom to take out their frustrations. Nobody wanted to lose a fight; it was a bad reputation and rank. Nonetheless, the time inevitably came when a face-off with a boy of similar or higher rank could no longer be avoided. It was then that ranking often changed and the power that accompanied rank sometimes shifted.

■ **The sociopolitical events produced in correctional institutions for youths are the same as those found in adult institutions.**

Upham, a juvenile correctional worker in Hennepin County's, Minnesota, juvenile jail, which houses the worst juvenile offenders, notes:

> This is their environment, especially if they're here a long time. . . . They make a lot of contacts, they get a lot of reinforcement for their negative behavior, they tell their war stories. . . . They stop growing in a way. They don't have normal experiences. They have this siege mentality. . . . They're not working on their careers. They're already in their careers here. Their careers are being in the system. Detention for some of these kids is not so bad an option. They're safe. They get three meals a day. They get rest. They get attention. They say they don't like it, but they keep coming back" (Brandt, 1993, p. 7B).

Violence can erupt when inmates cross racial lines in choosing their friends and allies. For example, Lerner (1986, pp. 23–24) describes a situation in a California institution:

> Pete, a tall white 18-year-old long-hair from Alhambra—doing two years in the California Youth Authority for stealing cars and some other petty stuff—got into trouble because he would not join the white clique. Instead he made the mistake of hanging out with some Blacks he knew from the streets, who liked him because he was a good athlete and enjoyed the same music they did.
>
> By doing this, Pete broke one of the unspoken rules of inmates at the Youth Authority: Stick to your own race. For a white to "kick back" with Blacks is an unacceptable affront to the inmates' unofficial rules which govern the living units. To punish him for his transgression, one day when he was sitting in the day room watching a televised football game, three whites sneaked up behind him and smacked him over the head with a sock of batteries. After doctors stitched his head, Pete was assigned to his cell 23 hours a day for his own protection.

A log book listing of cases of in-house violence serious enough to be taken to court reveals another glimpse of how brutal the world of young inmates can be:

> 1/9/85 Danny attacks Jeffrey while he is watching TV causing multiple fractures of the jaw which require a number of surgical procedures.
>
> 2/15/85 Jorge assaults Henry outside Evergreen Lodge with a sharpened flat metal bar with one end cut to be sharp. Henry had never had any problems with Jorge but became an enemy when he got in an argument with the head of Jorge's Southern Chicano Gang. The victim suffered lacerations on the skull and neck.
>
> 12/28/85 Stuart and Lee assault and injure Michael, an American Indian inmate, with an X-Acto knife, repeatedly slashing him and causing lacerations to his back, arms, thumbs, scalp and chest. Michael had allegedly made some racially derogatory remark.

Prison Gangs

Prison gangs are quite different from the street gangs described in Chapter 8. Jackson and McBride (1985, p. 55) say that prison gang members are "cold, calculating and purposeful" in contrast to street gang members, who operate "through pure emotion." Prison gangs also rely on anonymity, whereas street gangs thrive on notoriety. Street gang members are usually undisciplined and not sophisticated enough to fit into a prison gang until they have been through the entire juvenile justice system.

▉ Prison gangs are better disciplined, more calculating and more sophisticated than street gangs. They also rely on anonymity.

According to Jackson and McBride (1985, pp. 55–56):

> The prison gang will wait until the youthful offender has progressed through the juvenile justice system—from probation camps, reform schools and finally to prison. At this point the recruit has become wise in the ways of penal institutions and has matured sufficiently to be recruited into the prison gang. In today's justice system, only the worst of a very bad lot are sentenced to state prison, and they are the types that the prison gang is seeking.

. . . A phenomenon which both youth authorities and prison officials have noticed recently is a rift between prison gangs and the street gang members, in that the latter seem to be achieving an independence from the prison gangs.

. . . Some prisons are reporting that a number of street gangs have so many members at a particular institution that they are a force in themselves.

Male/Female Compared

The world of institutionalization is not significantly different for females in a locked facility than for their male counterparts. Violence, role identity and establishing power are equally important for self-preservation. In the Youth Authority facility of Ventura, California, a staff member relates (Lerner, 1986, p. 41):

Since judges are reluctant to send women to the Youth Authority except for the most serious crimes, those who do end up there are frequently in for violent offenses. The staff also consider many of them more dangerous than their male colleagues. As an example . . . a recent case of a young woman who tried to poison another female inmate by lacing her breakfast cereal with Ajax cleanser.

As at other Youth Authority facilities, there is also homosexual activity at Ventura. [T]wo young women had managed to elude the staff and bed down together for the night. Curiously, while male homosexuals are looked down upon by male inmates and seen as the bottom of the pecking order, . . . among women this is reversed and the lesbians often have considerable status among their peers. Another difference between male and female society . . . is that while the male code requires that no inmate snitch on another, "the women will tell on each other in a minute."

THE IMPACT OF INCARCERATION

Despite the diverse ideologies and strategies pursued by these various institutions, to a great extent, all generate an underlife that includes an informal social organization and an inmate code. While they are confined, youths are immersed in a culture that defines the institution, its staff and many of its programs in negative, oppositional terms. This perspective does not describe the experiences of the institution as beneficial to the "best interests" of the youths.

Several states have held that confinement that subjects those incarcerated to assaults and threats of violence constitutes cruel and unusual punishment. Juveniles who are victims of assaults by other inmates may sue for violation of their right to be reasonably protected from violence in the facility.

Further, if juveniles are kept in isolation (segregation) to protect them from assault, they may, nevertheless, suffer such sensory deprivation and psychological damage as to violate their constitutional rights. Confinement has frequently led to the ultimate self-destruction—suicide.

The impact of incarceration on juveniles often conflicts with the purpose of the juvenile justice system, which was expressly created to remove children from the punitive forces of the criminal justice system. Exposing juveniles to coercive institutional conditions may jeopardize their emotional and physical well-being.

REMOVING JUVENILES FROM ADULT JAILS AND LOCKUPS

Recall that one provision of the JJDP Act was that status offenders and nonoffenders (youth who are abused or neglected) should be removed from juvenile detention and correctional facilities. It further mandated that when youth were detained in the same facilities as adults that they were to be completely segregated. In 1985 the OJJDP awarded funds to Community Research Associates to help states develop strategies to keep juveniles out of adult jails. From this experience, eight plans that appear to work were identified (*OJJDP Annual Report, 1990*, p. 4):

■ Community commitment to keep juveniles out of adult jails.
■ Alternatives for juveniles who do not need to be in secure facilities.
■ Access to secure juvenile detention for those who do.
■ Objective criteria for detaining juveniles.
■ Capability of 24-hour intake in juvenile facilities.
■ Written policies and procedures for intake and detention services.
■ An effective system to monitor the system for keeping juveniles out of jails.
■ Local sponsorship and funding of intake and detention services.

CONDITIONS OF CONFINEMENT

Conditions of Confinement: Juvenile Detention and Corrections Facilities was a study commissioned by the OJJDP in 1988. The study was "the most comprehensive nationwide research ever conducted on the juvenile detention and corrections field" (Wilson, 1994, p. iii). The study included 984 public and private juvenile detention centers, reception centers, training schools and ranches, camps and farms in the United States. Excluded were youth halfway houses, shelters and group homes; police lockups, adult jails and prisons that hold juveniles tried and convicted as adults and psychiatric and drug treatment programs.

The study identified four areas with substantial deficiencies: living space, security, control of suicidal behavior and health care. Table 11–12 summarizes the conformance rates of facilities by topic areas.

Forty-seven percent of confined juveniles lived in crowded facilities (p. 7). The study also estimated that in one recent year there were 18,000 incidents of suicidal behavior and 10 suicides. Further, juvenile and staff injury rates were higher in crowded facilities, and juvenile-on-juvenile rates were higher for juveniles housed in large dormitories. Table 11–13 (p. 422) summarizes the incident rates and annualized estimates of incidents in juvenile facilities.

Three areas in which conditions of confinement appear adequate were (1) food, clothing and hygiene; (2) recreation and (3) living accommodations.

TABLE 11–12 **Summary of Public and Private Facilities' Conformance Rates by Topic Areas**

Topic Areas in Which Conditions Were Assessed	Percentage of Confined Juveniles in Facilities That Conform[a]	Percentage of Facilities That Conform[b]
Basic needs		
Living space (3 criteria)	24%	43%
Health care (6 criteria)	26	35
Food, clothing, and hygiene (4 criteria)	39	35
Living accommodations (4 criteria)	52	49
Order and security		
Security (3 criteria)	20	27
Controlling suicidal behavior (4 criteria)	25	51
Inspections and emergency preparedness (4 criteria)	67	55
Programming		
Education (4 criteria)	55	57
Recreation (1 criteria)	85	85
Treatment services (2 criteria)	68	60
Juvenile rights		
Access to community (5 criteria)	25	25
Limits on staff discretion (7 criteria)[c]	49	76

[a]This is the percentage of juveniles held in facilities that conform to all assessment criteria in each topic area.
[b]This is the percentage of facilities that conform to all the assessment criteria in each topic area.
[c]This excludes the assessment criteria on search authorization, which required facility administrators to authorize all searches. Only 14 percent of confined juveniles are in facilities that conform to this criterion. With this criterion included, only 6 percent of confined juveniles are in facilities that conform to all criteria.

SOURCE: Dale G. Parent et al. *Conditions of Confinement: Juvenile Detention and Corrections Facilities: Research Summary.* Washington, D.C.: Office of Juvenile Justice and Delinquency Prevention, February 1994, p. 6.

PAROLE

Parole is a planned release and is authorized by the correctional facility. Parole is unlike probation in authority and concept. Probation can be granted only by the juvenile court subject to the court's stipulations. It provides the individual freedom and continuity within the community. Parole is a release from confinement issued by the correction facility or a board upon recommendation by the correction facility. Each state has its own procedure for parole, as do federal corrections.

■ Parole is a supervised early release from institutionalization.

In Minnesota, the Department of Corrections parole agents supervise juveniles who have been sentenced to a correctional facility. The release of a juvenile from a correctional institution is the responsibility of a juvenile hearing officer.

TABLE   Incident Rates per 100 Juveniles and Annualized Estimates of Incidents in
11–13   Juvenile Facilities

Type of Incident	Rate per 100 Juveniles (Last 30 Days)	Estimated Incidents per Year
Injuries		
Juvenile-on-juvenile	3.1	24,200
Juvenile-on-staff	1.7	6,900
Staff-on-juvenile	0.2	106
Escapes		
Completed	1.2	9,700
Unsuccessful attempts	1.2	9,800
Acts of suicidal behavior	2.4	17,600
Incidents requiring emergency health care	2.0	18,600
Isolation incidents		
Short-term (1 to 24 hours)	57.0**	435,800
Longer-term (more than 24 hours)	11.0	88,900

**This does not include very-short-term isolation (up to 1 hour) used to control behavior or instill discipline. Such a practice is common in juvenile facilities and largely not documented, so it is impossible to measure its occurrence with any accuracy.

SOURCE: Dale G. Parent et al. *Conditions of Confinement: Juvenile Detention and Corrections Facilities: Research Summary.* Washington, D.C.: Office of Juvenile Justice and Delinquency Prevention, February 1994, p. 7.

The juvenile hearing officer uses a scale that incorporates the severity of the offense and the delinquent history. You looked at combining the severity of the offense and the offender's prior record in Chapter 10. Shenon (1986) provides an example of this type of sentencing, which was proposed by the American Legislative Exchange Council:

> Following is an example of a point system that might be used to sentence juvenile offenders under a proposal prepared for the Justice Department. The higher the point score, the more severe the punishment.
>
> John Doe, a troubled 13-year-old with one conviction in a burglary case, is convicted of another. Under the sentencing guidelines in his state, the sentence might be determined like this:
>
> ▌ Under the point system, first-degree burglary is a 50–point crime.   50
> ▌ John's previous conviction for burglary adds 20 points to the total.   +20
> ▌ Because his previous conviction was within the last year (an indication
>   that he may be a persistent lawbreaker), an extra 10 points are added.   +10
> ▌ Because John is only 13, his punishment should be less severe than
>   that for an older offender. The scores of 13-year-olds are therefore
>   multiplied by one-half. (The score for a 17-year-old might be multiplied
>   by 1.5, producing a larger point total and more serious punishment.)   ×0.5
>   Total   40

Under the sentencing guidelines, 40 points might correspond to a three-month sentence in a youth detention center.

Once back in the community, the juvenile is supervised by a parole officer, or probation officers are given added responsibility. The youth is required to abide by a set of rules and regulations, which, if violated, can return the youngster to a locked or secure facility. An example of a typical juvenile parole agreement and the rules, regulations and conditions under which it is granted is illustrated in Figure 11–5 (p. 424). The parole officer makes regular contacts and visits to the youth's residence, school or place of employment. One objective of the parole officer is to involve the family, school and community in facilitating the youth's rehabilitation and reintegration into the community. This is the same goal as that of probation officers.

AFTERCARE

Aftercare is supervision given youths for a limited time after they are released from a correctional facility but are still under the control of the facility or the juvenile court. SHOCAP suggests the following for parole/aftercare efforts for habitual offenders (Crowe, 1991, p. 50):

> . . .[M]any times the same agency handles intake, detention, probation, corrections, and after-care. After-care is a euphemism for parole which was intended to do more than guarantee good behavior on release. After-care counselors continue the treatment process as the young person re-enters life in the community. Some strategies are:
>
> ■ provide special placements of designated habitual offenders in after-care programs that provide the maximum intensive supervision;
> ■ share information regarding rules and case histories with school officials and police;
> ■ adopt active community control including limited forms of house arrest;
> ■ apply immediate sanctions for infractions of rules, including revocation where criminal offenses are committed.

According to Snarr (1992, pp. 337–338):

> In many jurisdictions, aftercare (parole) is an afterthought. It is the weakest link in the system and in great need of improvement. This could be done by thinking more in terms of providing continuing treatment. Many times little or no thought and planning are given to the transition when a youth is released from an institution or residential setting and faced with living back in the community.

Many juveniles being released from confinement and requiring aftercare come from dysfunctional or abusive homes and must be provided with alternative living arrangements. Other types of aftercare that can help youths make the transition back into the community include the following (Snarr, 1992, p. 338):

■ Home visits prior to release.
■ Living arrangement for the youth upon release.
■ A continuation of the treatment program and services within the community.
■ Identification of community support systems to include the family and social worker.
■ Availability of twenty-four-hour supervision.
■ A contract to achieve specific goals.
■ A gradual phasing out of services and supervision based on the youth's response, not on a predetermined schedule.

Minnesota Department of Corrections

JUVENILE PAROLE AGREEMENT

WHEREAS, it appears to the Commissioner of Corrections that

_____
(NAME)

☐   presently in custody at _____ , and

☐   presently on parole, and

WHEREAS, the said Commissioner, after careful consideration, believes that parole at this time is in the best interests of this said individual and the public.

Now, THEREFORE, be it known that the Commissioner of Corrections, under authority vested by law,   ☐ grants parole to,

☐ continues parole for, _____
                                          (NAME)

and does authorize his/her release from the institution with the parole plan which has been approved. Upon being paroled and released he/she shall be and remain in legal custody and under the control of the Commissioner of Corrections subject to the rules, regulations, and conditions of this parole as set forth on the reverse side of this agreement.

Signed this _____ day of _____ 19 ___ .

COMMISSIONER OF CORRECTIONS
BY:

_____
(HEARING OFFICER)

DISTRIBUTION:
Original — Central Office
2nd Copy — Parolee
3rd Copy — Agent
4th Copy — Inst. File

CR-00100-03

☐   **New Parole Agreement**

☐   **Restructured Parole Agreement**

▉ FIGURE 11–5 Juvenile Parole Agreement

STATEMENT OF RULES, REGULATIONS, AND CONDITIONS
UNDER WHICH PAROLE IS GRANTED

In consideration of the parole granted to me by the Commissioner of Corrections I do hereby accept such parole and agree to abide by the following terms and conditions:

1. I will report immediately upon arrival at my destination, either by mail, telephone, or personal visit, as directed by my supervising agent, who is:

    Name: _____ Telephone No.: _____
    Address: _____

2. I recognize that my liberty on parole is conditional and that I am subject to supervision by an assigned agent. Therefore I will:
    a) Obey all federal, state, and local laws and ordinances:
    b) Obtain approval from my supervising agent before:
        1. Purchasing or using any motor vehicle;
        2. Borrowing money, going into debt or doing any credit or installment buying;
        3. Changing my residence, employment, vocational or school programs;
        4. Getting married;
    c) Obtain permission of my supervising agent before leaving the state for any reason:
    d) Abide by the following special terms and conditions: _____
    _____
    _____
    _____
    _____
    _____
    _____
    _____

3. I will keep in close contact with my supervising agent and seek his/her guidance and assistance on any problems I meet. I will at all times follow instructions and contact him/her in the event of any difficulty. I will submit such reports as may be required and will reply promptly to any communications.

4. I will be guided and abide by such specific instructions as may be issued by the Commissioner of Corrections and/or supervising agent with regard to companions, hours, intoxicants, medical attention, family responsibilities, support of self, and court obligations.

5. I shall not possess or use narcotics or other drugs or drug preparations, except those prescribed for me by a physician.

6. I will not purchase or otherwise obtain, or have in my possession, any type of firearm or dangerous weapon without expressed permission in writing by my supervising agent.

7. I understand that the Commissioner of Corrections has the authority to place me in custody at any time and to revoke my parole in the event that I violate any of the terms or conditions hereof.
    My present expiration date is _____ .

8. I agree that if I am returned to a state correctional institution on replacement or hold status, institutional rules constitute a condition of my parole agreement and a violation of these rules while on replacement or hold status may result in the revocation of my parole.

9. I hereby do waive extradition to the State of Minnesota from any jurisdiction in or outside the United States where I may be found and also agree that I will not contest any effort by any jurisdiction to return me to the State of Minnesota.

I hereby certify that this parole agreement and statement of rules, regulations, and conditions has been read and explained to the parolee and he/she has agreed and consented to these rules, regulations, and conditions upon his/her release, this _____ day of _____ 19 ____.	I hereby certify that I fully understand this parole agreement and all the rules, regulations, and conditions set forth for me to comply with, and I hereby agree to be bound by all the rules, regulations, and conditions of this agreement. I certify that I have received a copy of this agreement.
_____ Institution Representative/Parole Agent	_____ 　　　　　　　　　　　　　　　　　　Parolee

The OJJDP funded a project to look at the aftercare needs of high-risk youth, which resulted in the project called "Intensive Community-Based Aftercare Programs." The goal was to reduce recidivism rates. As a first step to identify high-risk recidivists, the project developed a framework based on five principles (Altschuler and Armstrong, 1990, p. 170):

▮ Preparing youths for gradually increased responsibility and freedom in the community.
▮ Helping youths become involved in the community and getting the community to interact with them.
▮ Working with youths and their families, peers, schools and employers to identify the qualities necessary for success.
▮ Developing new resources and supports where needed.
▮ Monitoring and testing youths and the community on their abilities to interact.

The next step in the project was to identify three major program elements critical to successful aftercare programs: (1) "enabling" organizational characteristics, (2) continuous case management and (3) a functioning management information and evaluation capability.

An Example of Effective Aftercare

The Allegheny Academy, Pennsylvania, was designed for repeat juvenile offenders who failed in traditional probation programs but were not in need of, or likely to be helped by, institutionalization. Costanzo (1990, pp. 114–116) described how the program is run. Students are referred to the Academy by the judge or by their probation officer. The Academy is open daily and has a fleet of 15 passenger vans to provide safe, round-trip transportation for the juveniles. The juveniles come to the Academy after school and leave between 8 P.M. and 9 P.M., with a 10:30 P.M. curfew. On the weekend most arrive around noon. The students sleep at home and, with good behavior, can sometimes spend entire weekends at home.

While at the Academy, students study traditional school subjects, learn trades and receive counseling. A sports program is also available.

IMPORTANCE OF JUVENILE CORRECTIONS PARTNERSHIPS

The OJJDP has made a commitment to partner with juvenile corrections for three important reasons: (1) the improvement of the juvenile justice system is a major purpose of the JJDP Act, (2) the study "Conditions of Confinement" shows the need for improvement and (3) the increase in juvenile violence must be addressed. At the center of the OJJDP commitment is their Comprehensive Strategy for Serious, Violent and Chronic Juvenile Offenders. Acting administrator of the OJJDP, John Wilson (1994, p. 223), listed the following 10 goals for improvement:

▮ The cost of juvenile corrections must be reduced.
▮ Conditions of confinement must be improved.

■ Detention facility and training school populations must be decreased to their designed capacity.

■ Identification of treatment needs must be improved.

■ A continuum of program options must be established and made available to meet the needs of each juvenile in the system.

■ Inequality in the administration of juvenile justice must be eliminated. Disproportionate representation of minorities in secure confinement in the juvenile justice system must be erased.

■ Ensuring due process and quality legal representation for juveniles must be addressed.

■ Delinquency prevention must be a community priority.

■ Effective aftercare programs must be developed.

■ The use of alternatives to incarceration for nonviolent accused and adjudicated offenders must be increased.

SUMMARY

Although the U.S. Supreme Court has never definitively ruled on whether there is a constitutionally based right to treatment, the state does violate the individual's constitutional rights if it fails to confine and provide treatment in the least restrictive setting possible. What this treatment consists of is a subject of controversy. The conservative philosophy of juvenile justice is "get tough on juveniles"—to punish and imprison them. The liberal philosophy of juvenile justice stresses treatment and rehabilitation, including community-based programs.

Probation is the most common disposition of the juvenile court. The formal goal of probation is to improve the delinquent's behavior—in short, rehabilitation. The probation officer has traditionally been responsible for two key functions: (1) personally counseling youths who are on probation and (2) serving as a link to other community services. Excessive caseloads are probably the single greatest pressure on probation officers. Supervision is the essence of probation.

Probation often has three goals: (1) to protect the community from delinquency, (2) to impose accountability for offenses committed and (3) to equip juvenile offenders with required competencies to live productively and responsibly in the community.

Isolating offenders from their normal social environment may encourage the development of a delinquent orientation and, thus, further delinquent behavior. Community-based corrections therefore should be considered seriously for juvenile offenders.

Nonresidential corrections programs include community supervision; family crisis counseling; proctor programs; and service-oriented programs, including recreational programs, counseling, alternative schools, employment training programs and homemaking and financial planning classes.

The five major categories of residential programs are shelters, group homes, foster homes, foster group homes and "other" types of nonsecure facilities. The National Advisory Committee for Juvenile Justice and Delinquency Prevention recommended foster homes for neglected juveniles and those charged with status offenses.

Three common forms of intermediate sanctions are intensive supervision, electronic monitoring and boot camps.

Formally, only three purposes justify putting juveniles in a locked facility: (1) to secure their presence at court proceedings, (2) to hold those who cannot be sent home and (3) to prevent juveniles from harming themselves or others, or from disrupting juvenile court processes.

The percentages of blacks and males in juvenile institutions far exceed their proportions in the general population. Compared to public correctional institutions, private correctional institutions confine more whites, more girls, more status offenders, and more dependent and neglected youths. The inmates are younger and their stay is usually much longer. Private institutions offer much greater diversity in programs and structures than public institutions.

The sociopolitical events produced in correctional institutions for youths are the same as those found in adult institutions. Prison gangs are better disciplined, more calculating and more sophisticated than street gangs. They also rely on anonymity.

Parole is a supervised early release from institutionalization.

▮ Discussion Questions

1. How effective is probation in juvenile justice? What, if any, changes should be made in the juvenile probation process?
2. Should a juvenile have close supervision while on probation? If not, describe how you would supervise a youth who had committed a violent crime and was placed on probation, or one who was a status offender.
3. Should parents, custodians or guardians of youths be actively involved in a youth's probation? Why or why not?
4. Do you favor a system of state or local probation? What does your state have?
5. Is community corrections worthwhile? Does it work? What would you do to improve it?
6. Is there a difference in attitudes between a youth who has been confined and one who has been directed by programs in community corrections? What makes the difference?
7. Do community corrections give judges more options in sentencing youths? Is this an advantage or disadvantage?
8. Should violent offenders be subject to community corrections or directed to a secure facility? Why?
9. What are some potential alternatives to secure detention? What problems may be involved in expanding alternative programs?
10. Do you support a conservative or a liberal approach to treating juveniles? Why? Why do you think our society may be inclined to a "get tough on juveniles" attitude in the 1990s?

▮ References

Allen, Harry; Eric Carlson; and Evalyn Parks. *Critical Issues in Probation*. Washington, D.C.: U.S. Government Printing Office, 1979.

Altschuler, David M., and Troy L. Armstrong. "Designing an Intensive Aftercare Program for High-Risk Juveniles." *Corrections Today*, December 1990, pp. 170–171.

American Corrections Association. *Corrections Yearbook*. College Park, Md.: ACA, 1983.
———— "ACA Policy Statement." *Corrections Today,* October 1992, pp. 30–32.

Austin, James; Michael Jones; and Melissa Bolyard. "The Growing Use of Jail Boot Camps: The Current State of the Art." NIJ, Research in Brief, October 1993.

Brandt, Steve. "The In Crowd: Hennepin County's Jail for Juveniles Is Jammed." (Minneapolis/St. Paul) *Star Tribune,* 11 April 1993, pp. 1B, 7B.

Brown, W. K. *The Other Side of Delinquency*. New Brunswick, N.J.: Rutgers University Press, 1983.

Bureau of Justice Assistance. *Electronic Monitoring in Intensive Probation and Parole Programs*. Washington, D.C., February 1989.

Butts, Jeffrey A., and Howard N. Snyder. "Restitution and Juvenile Recidivism." OJJDP, Update on Research, September 1992.

Costanzo, Samuel A. "In Pennsylvania: Juvenile Academy Serves as Facility Without Walls." *Corrections Today,* December 1990, pp. 112–117.

Crowe, Timothy D. *Habitual Offenders: Guidelines for Citizen Action and Public Response*. Serious Habitual Offender Comprehensive Action Program (SHOCAP). Washington, D.C.: Office of Juvenile Justice and Delinquency Prevention, October 1991.

Donahue, Terrence S. "Privatizing Juvenile Probation Services: Five Local Experiences." OJJDP, Update on Programs, November/December 1989.

Finckenaur, James O. *Juvenile Delinquency and Corrections: The Gap Between Theory and Practice*. Orlando: Academic Press, 1984, p. 132.

Hollander, Harriet. *Relationship of Characteristics of Incarcerated Juveniles to Issues of Program Development and Staff Training: A Psycho-Education Model*. A Report Prepared by the Project on Psycho-Education and Juvenile Delinquency, College of Medicine and Dentistry of New Jersey, Community Health Center. Piscataway, N.J.: Rutgers Medical School, March 1981.

Hurst, Hunter. "Juvenile Probation in Retrospect." *Perspectives,* Winter 1990a, pp. 16–19.
———— "Turn of the Century: Rediscovering the Value of Juvenile Treatment." *Corrections Today,* February 1990b, pp. 47–50.

Jackson, Robert K., and Wesley D. McBride. *Understanding Street Gangs*. Sacramento, Calif.: Custom Publishing, 1985.

Juvenile Probation Officer Initiative (JPOI) Working Group. *Desktop Guide to Good Juvenile Probation Practice*. Washington, D.C.: Office of Juvenile Justice and Delinquency Prevention, May 1993.

Krisberg, B.; I. M. Schwartz; P. Litksy; and J. Austin. "The Watershed of Juvenile Justice Reform." *Crime and Delinquency,* 32(1), (1986), 5–38.

Lerner, Steve. *The California Youth Authority, Part Two: Bodily Harm*. Bolinas, Calif.: Common Knowledge Press, 1986.

Levinson, Robert B., and William J. Taylor. "ACA Studies Privatization in Juvenile Corrections." *Corrections Today,* August 1991, pp. 242, 248.

MacKenzie, Doris Layton. " 'Boot Camp' Programs Grow in Number and Scope." *NIJ Reports,* 222 (November/December 1990): 6–8.

National Advisory Committee for Juvenile Justice and Delinquency Prevention. *Standards for the Administration of Justice*. Washington, D.C.: U.S. Government Printing Office, July 1980, pp. 431–47.

OJJDP Annual Report, 1990. Washington, D.C.: Office of Juvenile Justice and Delinquency Prevention, 1990.

Oran, Daniel. *Law Dictionary for Nonlawyers*. 2nd ed. St. Paul, Minn.: West Publishing, 1985.

President's Commission on Law Enforcement and Administration of Justice. *The Challenge of Crime in a Free Society*. Washington, D.C.: U.S. Government Printing Office, 1967.

Renzema, Marc, and David T. Skelton. "Use of Electronic Monitoring in the United States: 1989 Update." *NIJ Reports,* 222 (November/December, 1990). Reprinted in NIJ, Research in Brief, n.d.

Schwartz, Ira M. *Reinvesting Youth Corrections Resources: A Tale of Three States*. Minneapolis: Humphrey Institute, Center for the Study of Youth Policy, 1987.

Shenon, Philip. "Federal Study on Youth Urges Fixed Sentences." *New York Times*, 29 August 1986.

Shumate, Denis J. "Juvenile Corrections: Clearing the Way for Public Support." *Corrections Today*, February 1991, pp. 6–8.

Smith, J. Steven. "A Lesson from Indiana: Detention Is an Invaluable Part of the System, But It's Not the Solution to All Youths' Problems." *Corrections Today*, February 1991, pp. 56–60.

Snarr, Richard W. *Introduction to Corrections*, 2nd ed. Dubuque, Iowa: Wm. C. Brown, 1992.

Sutherland, Edwin H., and Donald R. Cressey. *Principles of Criminology.* 7th ed. Philadelphia: J. B. Lippincott, 1966.

Thomas, Douglas W. "The Juvenile Probation Officer Initiative: Making a Tough Job a Little Easier." *Corrections Today*, February 1991, pp. 62–65.

Wilson, John J. "Developing a Partnership with Juvenile Corrections." *Corrections Today*, April 1994, pp. 74, 223–224.

—— foreword to Parent, Dale G. et al. *Conditions of Confinement: Juvenile Detention and Corrections Facilities: Research Summary.* Washington, D.C.: Office of Juvenile Justice and Delinquency Prevention, February 1994, p. iii.

■ Cases

Santana v. Collazo, 714 F.2d 1172, 1177 (1st Cir. 1983).

Shelton v. Tucker, 364 U.S. 479, 488, 81 S.Ct. 247, 252, 5 L.Ed.2d 231 (1960).

The Role of the Broader Community

Violence and crime have grown to an intolerable level that detrimentally impacts the lives of all citizens. This condition will continue unless, and until, all segments of our society assume their responsibilities and respond in a coordinated fashion.

IACP Summit on Violent Crime, 1993

▌ Do You Know?

How to define community?
What the broken window phenomenon refers to?
What community policing is?
How social work has influenced juvenile justice policy?
What parts of the juvenile justice system social work is involved in?
What the current emphasis in social services for youth is?
What type of intervention appears to hold the greatest promise?
What skill should be taught as a basic skill in the schools in the 1990s?
What benefits are derived from using volunteers in community-based corrections?

▌ Can You Define the Following Key Terms?

broken window phenomenon, community, community policing, integrated community

INTRODUCTION

The importance of the family and the schools in the development of our youth was stressed in the second section of this book. The importance of the community in the form of community corrections was described in Chapter 11. Unfortunately, in the 1990s many parents are too stressed, many schools are too impersonal and many communities are too disorganized to fulfill the basic need of children to belong. Estranged from family, friends, school and productive work, the seeds of discouragement and alienation are sown. The result, all too frequently, is antisocial behavior. Alienated youth often become angry, antisocial offenders.

The Office of Juvenile Justice and Delinquency Prevention *OJJDP Annual Report 1990* notes in its Foreword (p. v): "The answers to our problems [of delinquency] will not be found in Washington alone. If Pennsylvania Avenue and Capitol Hill are not joined by Main Street, U.S.A., the road ahead will be a dead end. But working together, we shall continue to take steps in the right direction."

Criminologists Miller and Ohlin (1985, n.p.) concur:

> Delinquency is a community problem. In the final analysis the means for its prevention and control must be built into the fabric of community life. This can only happen if the community accepts its share of responsibility for having generated and perpetuated paths of socialization that lead to sporadic criminal episodes for some youth and careers in crime for others.

In a report on the findings of a research conference, the National Committee for Prevention of Child Abuse, Gray (1986, p. 29) also states: "There must be continuing interchange among agencies and professionals in the justice system, the child abuse and neglect system and the schools, hospitals and mental health facilities. At present many sectors are dealing with a small piece of the same problem at different points in time or from varying vantage points."

This chapter focuses on the broader community and the role it plays in the juvenile justice system. It begins with looking at what a community is and how it can be a positive or negative influence on those growing up in it. Next, the current trend toward a justice system seeking to align itself more closely with the community is examined. The most common evidence of this trend is the implementation of community policing in departments across the country.

This discussion is followed by an in-depth look at the role of social workers and social services provided in the community. Just as probation officers were officers of the court as well as practitioners in corrections, so social workers may be an integral part of every aspect of the juvenile justice system, while at the same time being a part of the broader community.

Next, the role of the schools is considered, especially as it relates to dealing with the problems of violence and gangs. The chapter concludes with a discussion of how citizens, civic organizations and the community as a whole can contribute to solving the problems of crime and violence associated with our youth.

COMMUNITY DEFINED

Community can be thought of in several ways. It can refer to a specific geographic area, such as a small town or a suburb. It can be thought of as a group of people with common interests such as a community of worshippers in a congregation. In the legal sense, it refers to the area over which the police and the courts have jurisdiction.

In a more philosophical sense, according to Manning (1991, p. 33): "Community represents a sense of integration that people wish, hope, and envision as being a central part of their collective lives." In such an **integrated community** they feel ownership and take pride in what is right, responsibility for what is wrong. They also share values and agree on what is acceptable and unacceptable behavior and expect conformity to those expectations. Without such integration, the justice system is greatly hindered, as noted by Mastrofski (1991, p. 49):

> A basis for police action requires that a group of people—say a neighborhood—shares a definition of what constitutes right order, threats to it, and appropriate methods for maintaining it. To the extent that community implies a basis for citizens to work collectively with police to restore and preserve order, it also requires a sense of group identity or attachment—a "we-ness" derived from shared experience and integration.

Klockars (1991, pp. 247–248) suggests a sociological definition of community: "Sociologically, the concept of community implies a group of people with a common history, common beliefs, and understandings, a sense of themselves as 'us' and outsiders as 'them' and often, but not always, a shared territory."

In this chapter **community** will be used in both the legal, geographic sense as well as the philosophical, sociological sense.

■ Community is not only the geographic area over which the justice system has jurisdiction, it also refers to a sense of integration, of shared values, and a sense of "we-ness."

Children are very aware of their communities and how they feel about them. In an article describing what some Minnesota children think of their community, Monaghan (1994, p. 1E) states that the essays the children wrote on their neighborhoods and the community "are emphatically positive. What's needed, a majority say, is more of the same." Among the essays included in the article are the following:

Age 14, grade 8, St. James (a small town): The close bond between the people of my community is very special. We are a small community which keeps the relationships between people very close. We're like one giant family, working together to get things accomplished and enjoying together the things we have already accomplished.

Age 13, grade 7, St. Paul: Each neighborhood is special in its own way. My neighborhood is special because of the variety of people living here. Neighbors are friendly and watch out for each other. . . . Our neighbors work together recycling and taking good care of their houses. Every spring the neighborhood association has a cleanup day where we can get rid of all the old junk we don't want. It's a neat place to live and I hope it stays that way.

The positive outward appearance of the community is important to this second child as is the friendliness and caring of the people in the neighborhood. Unfortunately, not all communities generate such positive feelings. In a classic article, "Broken Windows," Wilson and Kelling (1982, p. 31) describe how a run-down neighborhood can promote crime:

Social psychologists and police officers tend to agree that if a window in a building is broken *and is left unrepaired,* all the rest of the windows will soon be broken. This is as true in nice neighborhoods as in run-down ones. Window-breaking does not necessarily occur on a large scale because some areas are inhabited by determined window-breakers whereas others are populated by

Two girls paint a window frame as part of Detroit's "Paint the Town" program. Thousands of volunteers paint hundreds of houses for elderly, low-income Detroit residents each year.

window-lovers; rather, one unrepaired broken window is a signal that no one cares, and so breaking more windows costs nothing. (It has always been fun.) (Italic in original.)

■ The **broken window phenomenon** states that if it appears "no one cares," disorder and crime will thrive.

The article on Minnesota children's attitudes is not all positive. Monaghan (1994, p. 1E) notes:

Behind their applause and celebration, a thundering negative rumbles.
It is crime.
It hangs over the more than 7,000 student essays like an angry, darkening cloud. . . .
Fear of gangs, rape, murder, kidnaping and shooting comes through clearly in essays from the country, the suburbs and the Twin Cities. For the citykids in the high-crime areas, though, the thunder about crime is the loudest and most frightening.

Monaghan shares part of an essay written by a 10-year-old Asian student from one of St. Paul's poorer neighborhoods: "The best thing about my neighborhood is that my school is near my house so if I get robbed on my way home I could just scream and my mom would hear me and come out."

Another inner-city youth's essay was equally poignant:

Age 9, grade 3, Minneapolis: I don't think that my community is a good place for kids to grow up because my brother got shot by a gang. He got shot four times in the head and about six times altogether. I don't think there should be any more gangs because they cause violence. I think there should be a program for kids in my community that has a gang free club in it. I want my community to be safe for kids.

An essay written by a suburban youth shows an awareness of how neighborhoods should be and a sense of helplessness about neighborhoods that are not this way:

Age 12, grade 6, Brooklyn Park (a suburb of Minneapolis): I think the best thing in my neighborhood is that everybody respects and gets along with everybody else. I just wish we could stop the violence and racism, but that probably will never change. I don't think hunger exists in my neighborhood, but it does affect the community, because when I'm in the car I can see people sitting on the sidewalks and that scares me. I just wish everybody and things could be OK.

The problems in our communities are enumerated by Inkster (1992, p. 28): "People of different races, cultures and languages are coming into closer contact with each other and enormous demands are being made on their understanding and tolerance. . . . There are widening class divisions, more broken families and homelessness, growing anger on the part of the disadvantaged, and a rise in violent crime." This does not imply, however, that communities must simply accept crime and violence. Consider the essay written by a youth who sees the crime and violence but who is able to make a positive from it—what was referred to as *resilience* earlier (Monaghan, 1994, p. 2E):

Age 14, grade 9, Mounds View (a suburb): Each day you hear that another horrifying crime has happened in the Twin Cities area. Robbery, a murder, cross-burning, abuse, rape or abduction, they turn people's lives inside out and upside down. Although these events are always tragic, one good thing comes from them. They bring the community together to help the people affected. People who don't even know the victims give their money, time, prayers, and support. It doesn't happen in all major cities, but I think that's the best thing about the Twin Cities area.

It is this sense of community values and the power of the community that has resulted in the awareness that the justice system cannot function alone, that it needs the support and *assistance* of the broader community. In an effort to obtain such support and assistance, many jurisdictions have implemented community policing.

COMMUNITY POLICING

Community policing takes many forms across the country. As noted by Miller and Hess (1994, p. xxv):

> Community policing offers one avenue for making neighborhoods safer. Community policing is not a program or a series of programs. It is a philosophy, a belief that working together, the police and the community can accomplish what neither can accomplish alone. The *synergy* that results from community policing can be powerful. It is like the power of a finely tuned athletic team, with each member contributing to the total effort. Occasionally heros may emerge, but victory depends on a team effort.

Wilson and Kelling (1989, p. 49) describe the types of changes that occur in a police department that institutes community policing:

> Community-oriented policing means changing the daily work of the police to include investigating problems as well as incidents. It means defining as a problem whatever a significant body of public opinion regards as a threat to community order. It means working with the good guys and not just against the bad guys.

In other words, community policing is proactive rather than reactive and it is problem driven rather than incident driven.

▮ **Community policing** is a philosophy embracing a proactive, problem-oriented approach to working with the community to make it safe.

Although community policing makes sense to many within the justice system, it is sometimes difficult for administrators to change. As noted by Wilson and Kelling (1989, p. 49): "While the phrase 'community-oriented policing' comes easily to the lips of police administration, redefining the police mission is more difficult. To help the police become accustomed to fixing broken windows as well as arresting window breakers requires doing things that are very hard for many administrators to do."

Wilson and Kelling (1989, p. 52) note that implementing community policing may also cause dissention within the ranks of the officers, who may have opposing views of the nature of police work, in what has been described as the conflict between the crime fighter function and the social service function: "In every department we visited, some of the incident-oriented officers spoke disparagingly of the problem-oriented officers as 'social workers,' and some of the latter responded by calling the former 'ghetto blasters'."

Yet another obstacle facing community policing, according to Wilson and Kelling (1989, p. 52), is lack of interagency cooperation:

> The problem of interagency cooperation may, in the long run, be the most difficult of all. The police can bring problems to the attention of other city agencies, but the system is not always organized to respond. In his book *Neighborhood Services,* John Mudd calls it the "rat problem": If a rat is found in an apartment, it is a housing inspection responsibility; if it runs into a restaurant, the health department has jurisdiction; if it goes outside and dies in an alley, public works takes over.

This lack of interagency cooperation is also stressed by Krisberg and Austin (1993, pp. 184–185): "The current organization of adolescent social and health services is characterized by rigidly drawn agency turfs and budgetary categories. This situation contributes to fragmented and often wasteful deployment of scarce public resources."

Among the most important "public resources" are social workers.

THE ROLE OF SOCIAL WORKERS AND SOCIAL SERVICES

Social workers are involved in community supervision programs for troubled youths and their families, in juvenile court-sponsored, community-based diversion programs and in school-based counseling programs. These programs are designed to help troubled youths who are in conflict with their families and need family dispute resolution and brief family therapy, as well as to help youths who are in conflict with the law.

The public interest in preventing delinquency and controlling youths and the interest in youth crime and rehabilitating youthful offenders are topics constantly discussed in communities and state legislatures across the country. Referral programs range from diversionary actions to socially designed programs in the "best interest of the child" and the best interest of the public safety.

Referral to adjustment and corrective programs under the guise of treatment is an issue of growing concern, due to increased demands for public and private services and limited available resources. As a result, legislators, policy makers and juvenile justice professionals are taking a hard look at the social services resources currently available and how they are being invested in youth referral programs. They are also asking if better ways exist to serve youths and protect the public.

Of great interest are the assessment and treatment of youths with emotional and behavioral problems. Many families experience child management problems at one time or another: incorrigibility, defiance, waywardness, temper tantrums, school disruptiveness, truancy and related problems. And many children experience neglect and abuse which, as already discussed, are often the prelude to delinquency.

The assessment of treatments and their underlying philosophies are debated by concerned groups that focus on child development. The active concern of one group is fear of violent juvenile crime. Many feel the juvenile courts are too lenient. They advocate a "get tough" attitude, emphasizing responsibility of actions and a system of accountability rather than the rehabilitation and treatment that is the hallmark of most existing state codes.

The public is also concerned about the inability of social services to properly investigate and treat cases of child physical and sexual abuse.

▌ Social workers have greatly influenced trends in juvenile justice policy in the areas of diversion, victim restitution, decriminalization of status offenders and deinstitutionalization.

Social workers are among the few involved in the juvenile justice system willing to disregard the jargon of "treatment," "control" or "punishment." They have accepted the challenge of trying to find the best approach to prevent the recurrance of mischievous or antisocial juvenile behavior.

Treger (1983, p. 8) has noted:

Social work is now the only profession in all parts of the justice system. Innovative programs in which social workers team up with the police, public defenders, legal aid lawyers, prosecutors, and magistrates have resulted in new relationships and opportunities for public service, new knowledge, and a workable model for system change. As a result of these new programs, social work's involvement in the justice system has been broadened and social justice has been extended, especially to minority and low income groups, many of whom are now diverted from the justice system into the social service system. . . .

Social workers in the justice system are now working with adjudicated and nonadjudicated people, juveniles, families, and adults who come to the attention of the system for a variety of reasons. They present a range of problems and predicaments, e.g., minor violations, personal, social bureaucratic problems, and the reluctance of agencies to provide services because of restrictive and inflexible policies.

▌ Social work functions in all aspects of the juvenile justice system.

Usually a combination of approaches is most effective.

Social work in different settings may provide a range of services that may include but by no means be limited to direct counseling with the individual juvenile. The broader role of social work within the context of juvenile facilities may include advocacy and brokerage on behalf of juveniles in their relations with family members, social agencies, school officials and potential employers.

Social work attempts by a variety of means to ease juveniles' passage through the most difficult stage of life and to prevent institutionalized youths from becoming brutal, embittered adults.

Needy, Neglected or Abused Children

Social work also addresses the needs of nondelinquent children and families. Since passage of the Social Security Act in 1935, the federal government has supported many services for children and families, from programs commonly called "welfare" to foster care maintenance and a range of adoption services.

In 1961, Congress amended part of the Social Security Act to provide states with substantial federal reimbursement for the cost of providing foster care to poor children (Gershenson, 1984). State child welfare departments, in association with the court, assigned more and more children to foster care and group homes.

In 1975 parents and advocates pressed through Congress the Education for All Handicapped Children Act, to grant all children the right to free and appropriate education in the least restrictive environment possible. Rather than removing handicapped children from home into special schools, these laws offered fiscal incentives to states in exchange for meeting federal standards.

In 1978 Congress passed the Indian Child Welfare Act, giving tribes greater control over the adoption and foster placement of their children and encouraging alternatives to placement by providing limited funds for service to Native American children and families.

After five years of testimony on foster care and adoption, in 1980 Congress passed the Adoption Assistance and Child Welfare Act, an important achievement for families at risk of extended or permanent separation. The Act requires that reasonable efforts be made to bring children who have been taken from their families for over 12 months back to the juvenile court. The court then reviews each case and makes a disposition for the best interests of the children and their families. Thus, children are no longer placed "in limbo" with no further review. The purpose of the Act is to assure that children and their families no longer suffer extended separation from each other without at least an annual review.

Current Emphasis

The federal emphasis on diverting status and minor offenders from the juvenile justice system stimulated development of social work and social welfare services in community-based services for delinquent and troubled youths. This philosophy emphasized the importance of a wide range of activities and programs, commonly referred to as community-based services.

■ The current emphasis in social services for youth is diversion to a wide range of community-based services and programs.

The term *community-based* refers to residential treatment centers, youth service bureaus, group or foster homes, halfway houses and adolescent units in psychiatric hospitals. These facilities vary in such important considerations as the degree of security provided, whether they are residential or nonresidential, the extent and nature of treatment provided and size.

Recent studies on the influence of social workers have focused on family interaction and family therapy. Family therapy with delinquents is relatively new. Drieland (1984, p. 87) reviewed 37 studies and reported that the results consistently showed positive effects.

∎ Studies suggest that family therapy is more effective in dealing with problems of youths than traditional juvenile justice intervention.

The social workers used behavioral and structural techniques in intrafamilial communication. This positive attention paid to the child was generally found to be more effective than probation.

An innovative service program that addresses family preservation, placement prevention, and family reunification issues was developed in Hennepin County, Minnesota, in August 1985. The program started working exclusively with families in which an adolescent had been approved for out-of-home placement. The basic purpose was to see if family-centered, home-based services are effective in reducing the number of out-of-home placements. A majority of the families had an extensive service history with the Child Welfare Division, and 40 percent of the children involved had a history of out-of-home placements.

All children exhibited a wide range of behavioral problems, including oppositional behavior both at home and at school. As a group, the parents lacked basic parenting skills. A significant number of family members also had a history of family violence and chemical dependency. Parents described their children's behavior as "out of control," and 70 percent were in favor of their child's placement.

At the conclusion of the research, the evidence indicated that family-centered, home-based services do provide an effective, viable alternative to substitute care and residential treatment for a significant proportion of children at risk of placement. The researchers cautioned, however, that maintaining this specialized program's effectiveness over time requires overseeing and monitoring (AuClaire and Schwartz, 1986).

Stern (1991) describes a Family Trouble Center in Memphis, Tennessee, which provides counseling and assistance for children who have been abused and their abusers. The Center provides anger management groups as well as support counseling for victims. It provides mediation through contracts and referral services to other agencies for protective shelter. In addition it provides alcohol and drug counseling and community outreach and education. One of its greatest strengths as a new resource, according to Stern (p. 73) "lies significantly in networking with existing agencies."

Another social service center is described by Snow (1992). This is the Child Advocacy Center in Marion County, Indiana. This center also serves as an advocate for abused children. Like the Family Trouble Center in Memphis, this center uses a multiagency approach. To make such an approach work, those operating the Marion County Child Advocacy Center offer the following suggestions (Snow, 1992, p. 287):

1. There should not be a "Director." Instead, consider having a "Coordinator." Workers often resist taking orders from a member of another agency.
2. Agencies involved must keep their work force stable. Workers must get to know one another if they are to develop relationships of coordination and cooperation.
3. Agencies must enter into the new relationship with open minds. Police, for example, often think of welfare workers as being "bleeding hearts," and of prosecutors as being unresponsive to police needs. To put such feelings aside takes strong leadership in each agency.
4. Insure that agencies don't attempt to take over each other's responsibilities once they learn each other's roles.

Another approach to providing services to youth proposed by the Clinton administration is a National Youth Service. This service would provide up to $10,000 to pay for college for young people who work a certain amount of hours in their community. Smith (1993, p. 13) poses this question: "Assume that Congress, in concert with the President, enacted a National Youth Service Program that, on the basis of freely selected work in public service, would entitle youth—all youth and not just special or disadvantaged youth—to various benefits." Among the benefits might be college scholarships, cash or a "myriad of other desirable rewards."

For social services, the Serious Habitual Offender Comprehensive Action Program (SHOCAP) suggests the following action steps in dealing with habitual offenders (Crowe, 1991, pp. 47–48):

Social Services . . . agencies will range from public to private, with sometimes erratic funding services. Occasionally, family and mental health services are combined with probation and parole agencies. Some actions are:

■ Identify or establish special service and placement opportunities for drug, alcohol, or behaviorally troubled habitual offenders;
■ Share case history or diagnostic information with appropriate officials and participate on case management teams formed to assist in the community control of habituals;
■ Request police patrol and crime analysis follow up on neglect, abuse, and other problem case areas;
■ Provide case support for obtaining civil commitments on troubled, problem, or delinquent youth who are designated as habituals.

THE ROLE OF THE SCHOOLS

Kirst (1991, p. 615) notes some of the risks facing children in schools in the 1990s:

Johnny can't read because he needs glasses and breakfast and encouragement from his absent father; Maria doesn't pay attention in class because she can't understand English very well and she's worried about her mother's drinking and she's tired from trying to sleep in the car.

Other students are worried about their physical safety. "You can't be concerned with the issues of learning if you have to worry about your hide." Everyday, 100,000 students go to school carrying a gun. On a given day 160,000 students will miss school not from sickness but because they fear bodily harm. Also during a single day 2,000 students will be attacked while attending school. Each hour of the average school day, 900 teachers will be threatened and 40 will actually be harmed (Draty and Elig, 1993, p. 11).

The traditional subjects taught in our schools have been expanded by including interpersonal skills in mediation and conflict resolution. Recall that this was one of the recommendations made by Attorney General Reno (Wilson, 1993, p. 3): "I support conflict resolution programs in our public schools to teach our children how to resolve conflicts peacefully."

Hamburger (1993, p. 11A) writes that Janet Reno received the heartiest applause at a day-long conference on violence as she called for controlling guns in the hands of our youth:

> We've got to let young people know that there is no excuse for putting a gun up beside somebody's head and hurting them—not poverty, not broken homes, not any of the circumstances that people sometimes ascribe as causes of these crimes. . . .
>
> There are 2 million guns out there now and they're going to be in the hands of children, and we've got to teach children right now that you don't solve problems with guns and fists and knives. And teachers are leading the way.

■ Important basic skills that schools are teaching in the 1990s are conflict resolution and mediation.

Smith (1990) describes a school-based program in a New Mexico training school that teaches youths to use mediation to settle their differences peacefully. The program seeks to break the cycle of violence and abuse by teaching anger and conflict management skills. In mediation, a neutral third-party listens objectively to both sides in a dispute, helps the disputants identify the issues, explore solutions and agree on a satisfactory compromise to settling the problem. It is a confidential, voluntary process that is meeting with much success, not only in this institution but in schools throughout the country.

Research supports the finding that students who have a positive school experience not only learn better but have higher self-esteem and are better socialized. They are much more likely to become contributing members of society. Because of this, in 1984 then President Ronald Reagan directed the Department of Justice and Education to form the National School Safety Center (NSSC). This center is structured in five specialized sections: law enforcement, education, legal, research and communications. Together, these five sections are to provide a comprehensive approach to school safety.

Another organization heavily involved in school safety is the National Crime Prevention Council. This organization, in conjunction with the National Institute for Citizen Education in the Law, has developed a program called Teens, Crime and the Community (TC&C), which combines education and student action to reduce crime and at the same time develop students' sense of mutual responsibility (Modglin, 1989, p. 9). Funded by the OJJDP, the TC&C curriculum includes information on how and why crimes occur, how community is defined and how individual and group action can help protect the community against crime. TC&C also includes information on 10 ways students can make their own schools safer (Modglin, 1989, p. 10):

1. School crime watches apply Neighborhood Watch concepts to the school.
2. Cross-age teaching provides a chance for middle and high school students to present prevention information to younger students.
3. Mediation programs, in which trained students act as a neutral third party, help resolve conflicts without violence.
4. Plays and prevention performances present information to the student body in appealing ways.
5. Student forums and discussions promote the use of research and resource persons to develop student insight into problems and possible solutions.
6. Surveys on crime and other issues collect facts, engage student interest and spread word of impending projects.
7. Crime prevention clubs teach students to watch out for and help overcome crime.
8. School crime prevention fairs or special observance days give students an opportunity to participate in workshops on prevention and safety.
9. Community service activities build students' self-esteem and school pride.
10. Student courts consider and dispose of student infractions.

The SHOCAP states the following regarding the role of the schools in dealing with habitual juvenile offenders (Crowe, 1991, p. 47):

. . . [S]chool districts must have a legally acceptable code of conduct and set of disciplinary procedures. Once these are established, the school district may:

■ Identify the school assignment of students who have been classified as habituals by local authorities;
■ Share disciplinary code violations and other pertinent data with the police, crime analysts, or other officials designated responsible for profiling habitual delinquents;
■ Separate designated habituals by school assignments;
■ Establish procedures for notification of principals and teachers regarding the presence and special needs of habituals (care must be taken to protect staff and students, while avoiding unfair discrimination against the habitual).

Gangs in the Schools

One important way that schools can be made safer is to address the problem of gangs in the school. This is the focus of a program called Gang Resistance Education and Training (GREAT). This program is patterned after the nationally used antidrug program DARE. As noted by Lesce (1993, p. 49): "The eight-week program teaches students how to set goals for themselves, how to resist pressure, and understanding how gangs impact the quality of their life." In the promotional material for this program, the success of the program is attributed to the mutual commitment of law enforcement and educational agencies to unite in a common goal to (1) provide children with accurate knowledge about gang involvement, (2) provide children with the skills necessary to combat the stresses that set the stage for gang involvement, (3) provide children with the skills to resist negative peer pressure and (4) to provide children alternatives to gang involvement.

Moriarty and Fleming (1990, pp. 15–16) offer the following 10-step plan for gang prevention in the schools:

1. Be honest. Admit to the potential for problems.
2. Get smart. Know the gang symbols and paraphernalia.
3. Identify your school's leaders and get them on your side.
4. Don't close the doors at 3:15. Keep students involved after school.
5. Work with the police.
6. Involve transfer students. Give new students activities and opportunities to fit in.
7. Educate the teaching staff.
8. Get parents on your side.
9. Find role models.
10. Provide career counseling for marginal students.

Daily preventive measures that can be taken in schools include being observant for signs of gang activity, allowing no unauthorized outsiders in the school, enforcing a policy of hall passes, practicing zero tolerance for infraction of school rules and enforcing such rules firmly, fairly and consistently.

THE ROLE OF VOLUNTEERS, COMMUNITY AGENCIES AND BUSINESSES

Oregon passed legislation to comply with the mandates of the Juvenile Justice and Delinquency Prevention (JJDP) Act, giving communities the chance to address their own youth problems in ways that suit their unique needs. Using the JJDP Act as a model, the Oregon Community Juvenile Services Act seeks to (1) establish statewide standards for juvenile services by creating a State Juvenile Services Commission; (2) provide appropriate preventive, diversionary and dispositional alternatives for young people; (3) encourage coordination of the various elements of the juvenile services system and (4) promote local involvement in developing improved services for youth (English, 1990, p. 8). Specific goals for the program include the following (p. 8):

■ The family unit shall be preserved;
■ Intervention shall be limited to those actions which are necessary and will utilize the least restrictive and most effective and appropriate resources;
■ The family shall be encouraged to participate actively in whatever treatment is afforded a child;
■ Treatment in the community, rather than commitment to a State juvenile training school, shall be provided whenever possible;
■ Communities shall be encouraged and assisted in the development of alternatives to secure temporary custody for children not eligible for secure detention.

Volunteer-based commissions work actively in each Oregon county to plan community-based programs targeted to their own high-risk youth.

SHOCAP, as might be expected, also stresses community involvement and coordination. As noted by Crowe (1991, p. 43): "Many of the agencies and officials have co-existed for years. Most are totally unaware of their ignorance of how other operations work, or of the problems and needs of other components of the system." SHOCAP has devised a community model for controlling habitual offenders as well a functional model for a community habitual offender program, as shown in Figures 12–1 and 12–2.

Successful efforts do not have to be so formalized. They can be as informal as the mayor of a city calling for the removal of graffiti as Minneapolis Mayor Sayles Belton did in her "Don't Deface My Space" campaign. Another practical, grass-roots approach is the "Neighborhood Tool Kit" series of stories about things citizens are doing and can do to make their neighborhoods "friendlier, safer, more vital, more attractive places to live" (Iggers, 1994, p. 1E). A lead-in to the column by Iggers quotes John McKnight, Center for Urban Affairs and Policy Research, of Northwestern University:

> There is a mistaken notion that our society has a problem in terms of effective human services. Our essential problem is weak communities. While we have reached the limits of institutional problem solving, we are only at the beginning of exploring the possibility of a new vision for community.

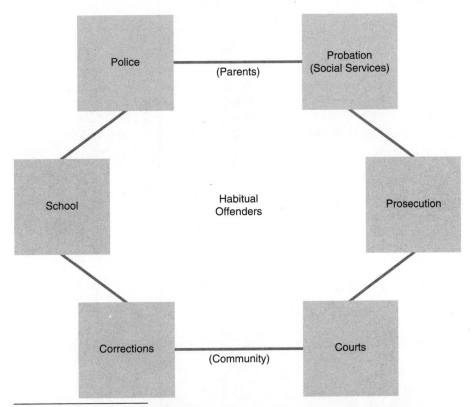

■ **FIGURE 12-1 A Community Model for Controlling Habitual Offenders**

SOURCE: Timothy D. Crowe, *Habitual Juvenile Offenders: Guidelines for Citizen Action and Public Responses,* Serious Habitual Offender Comprehensive Action Program (SHOCAP) (Washington, D.C.: Office of Juvenile Justice and Delinquency Prevention, October 1991), p. 44.

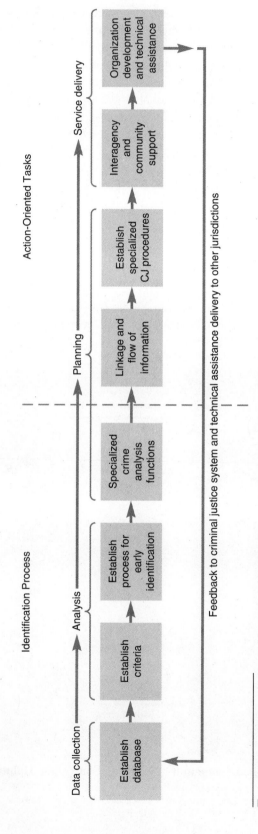

■ FIGURE 12-2 A Functional Model of a Community Habitual Offender Program
Model was developed by ICAP: SHO IMPLEMENTATION FUNCTIONAL MODEL

SOURCE: Timothy D. Crowe, *Habitual Juvenile Offenders: Guidelines for Citizen Action and Public Responses*, Serious Habitual Offenders Comprehensive Action Program (SHOCAP) (Washington, D.C.: Office of Juvenile Justice and Delinquency Prevention, October 1991), p. 45.

■ *The Green Chair Project in Minneapolis hires inner-city youth to build chairs that are sold to citizens for $50. In 1994 the project created jobs for 18 youth who built 200 chairs.*

This newspaper column focuses on removing eyesores, creating jobs, cleaning up alleys, combating crime, starting block clubs and the like.

COMMUNITY INVOLVEMENT AND VOLUNTEERS

Most community-based corrections programs' success is heightened by citizen involvement. Such community participation plays a crucial role in "normalizing" the environment and developing offenders' ties to the community, as well as in changing community attitudes toward offenders.

■ Community participation through volunteerism helps improve programs, breaks down isolation and helps youthful offenders explore possibilities for adjustment to the community.

Volunteers are encouraged to assess needs and review all activities, programs and facilities to ensure their suitability in light of community standards and offender needs. Volunteers are used in some institutions and as aides to adjunct institutional programs, such as work release, that are carried out within the community. In some jurisdictions volunteers serve as assistants in probation, parole and other community-based alternatives to incarceration.

Volunteers have been an integral part of justice for centuries. Traditionally, the function of volunteers in private endeavors has been to fill gaps between governmental social services and the actual need. In 1912, volunteers rallied for the child labor laws that were the result of the first White House Conference on Children in 1910. In the 1930s volunteers filled the gap in welfare and mental health programs until President Franklin Roosevelt made vast social changes.

The rehabilitative powers of the local community and its volunteers were popularized during the late 1960s and the 1970s. In the 1990s volunteerism continues to increase.

Some programs use senior-citizens as volunteers, working with high-risk juveniles. Briscoe (1990, p. 94) describes one such program in Jefferson County, Texas, which has a foster grandparent program in the county's juvenile detention center. She notes: "Even children who are sometimes hostile and aggressive work calmly and quietly in the presence of a foster grandparent."

Jobs and Restitution

Some community efforts focus on creating jobs for youth. As noted by Smith (1993, p. 14): "Work is important in defining who we are. It helps us measure our value both to ourselves and others."

Some dispositions of the juvenile court include restitution, either in the form of work or pay. Providing jobs for youth who are required to make restitution helps them to fulfill their obligation. As noted by Bazemore (1989): "Among some 400 juvenile restitution programs, 34 percent indicated in a recent national survey that they arranged paid job slots for referrals." Reasons given for investing time and effort to develop jobs for offenders include the following (Bazemore, p. 1):

▮ Increasing the possibility that poor or hard-to-employ offenders can make monetary restitution to victims.
▮ Avoiding lack of work as an excuse for nonpayment.
▮ Improving enforcement of restitution orders.
▮ Increasing the certainty and timeliness of payments to victims.
▮ Improving the program's efficiency in monitoring restitution.
▮ Permitting recommendation of realistic payment schedules to the court through program control over the source of earnings. (Program managers can be assured that restitution is not being paid by parents or through theft.)
▮ Allowing for larger restitution orders and greater return to victims.

Bazemore (p. 1) suggests that work is an important part of a balanced approach to juvenile justice: "From the accountability perspective, work can instill a sense of responsibility and an understanding of the value of goods and money. Work can be emphasized by those who argue that a major goal of juvenile justice should be to enhance offender competence, and advocates of

■ *As part of their penalty, youth caught marking up public buses in San Francisco must spend time removing graffiti from the buses.*

treatment emphasize the therapeutic effects of employment." She also notes: "Instilling positive work values and habits fits well with the accountability and responsibility ethic of restitution programs."

Successful job programs share the following common characteristics (Bazemore, p. 9):

- ■ "Sell" employers and the community on offender employment.
- ■ Build on existing community resources and support.
- ■ Develop a funding "package" adequate to provide ongoing support for the jobs component.
- ■ Select work placements and projects that have value to employers, offenders, and the community.

▌ Establish and maintain high standards of youth supervision and positive employer relations.

▌ Influence the priorities of the local juvenile justice system toward an emphasis on restitution and work.

Many of these programs have an advisory board to assist them. The Erie Earn-It Program in Texas, for example, has an advisory board consisting of a businessperson, a chamber of commerce member, a media representative, an attorney, a public accountant, a private citizen and a juvenile probation officer (Bazemore, p. 15).

▌ Jobs are important to youth not only for the money they can generate but for the feelings of self-worth that may accompany a job.

Two federal programs are important sources of jobs for young people. The first, the Job Corp, has 106 centers across the country with over 40,000 jobs filled at any given time. As noted by Conly (1993, p. 44): "About 30 percent of the residents complete vocational training; some complete their GEDs. . . . [Eighty-four] percent of its graduates are placed either in jobs (67 percent) or in school (17 percent).

The second program is Youth Opportunities Unlimited (YOU). This is a multimillion dollar demonstration project funded by the Department of Labor's Job Training Partnership. According to Conly (1993, p. 44): "The program is grounded in the assumption that many social problems—gangs, drug addiction, juvenile delinquency—have a common source: poverty and a lack of economic and educational opportunities." The YOU program attempts to address this problem by providing not only jobs but support programs in health care, housing, recreation and family services. The program is currently operating in seven communities of fewer than 25,000 people with poverty rates of 30 percent or higher. In San Diego, the YOU demonstration project is involved in the following efforts (Conly, 1993, pp. 44–45):

▌ An alternative school will serve 50 "at-risk" ninth and tenth graders.

▌ Local Boys' and Girls' Clubs will provide expanded sports and recreational activities, giving young people an alternative to gangs.

▌ An Hispanic organization will operate a family learning center.

▌ Local labor unions will sponsor a pre-apprenticeship program to help youth learn about possible careers.

▌ A teen parenting center is being established.

▌ Two social workers will provide case management to youths.

▌ Various community and city agencies will open offices at the YOU center to serve the needs of youths and families in the target area.

THE IMPORTANCE OF COORDINATION

The critical importance of coordinating efforts is clearly stated by Prothrow-Stith (1991, p. 139):

When a kid enters the emergency room with a gunshot wound to his thigh after having been shot in a dispute over a jacket, I want him to be as well treated for the "disease" of violence as he is for the traumatic injury he has sustained. When that young man is blanketed in therapeutic interventions that involve his parents, his pregnant girlfriend, the probation officer assigned to him on a previous case, the kid who shot him with whom perhaps he has had a long-standing feud, his school, which is about to expel him, and perhaps even his younger brother who has just started to act out violently—that's when we will start to make a difference.

Rosenfeld and Decker (1993, pp. 27–28) describe an Assault Crisis Team (ACT) that can provide such services. The team consists of medical, social service, educational and criminal justice professionals in addition to community residents with training in violence intervention. These teams operate in four settings: a hospital emergency room, a juvenile detention center, an adult jail and a high-risk neighborhood. According to Rosenfeld and Decker (1993, p. 28): "The function of ACT is three-fold: *Monitoring* levels and patterns of violence, *mentoring* youth at risk for violence, and *mediating* disputes with a high potential for violence."

Another example of cooperative efforts is the "Safe Policy" program in Sarpy County, Nebraska. "Safe Policy" is an acronym for "School Administrators for Effective Police, Prosecution Operations, Leading to Improved Children and Youth Services." An article in *Law Enforcement News* described the program as follows ("Network," 1994, p. 5):

Safe Policy is a countywide network involving officials from schools, law enforcement, juvenile justice, social service, business and private agencies, who meet monthly to share information and ideas to prevent juveniles from getting into trouble with the law and to help those who have already had brushes with the criminal justice system. . . .

The Safe Policy concept is an "open organizational theme" that urges agencies and institutions to overcome "organizational barriers" and identify the most pressing youth problems in the communities.

This is encouraging as the report of the American Psychological Association's Commission on Youth and Violence notes (n.d., p. 5):

The Commission's work overwhelmingly affirms a message of hope: Our society can intervene effectively in the lives of children and youth to reduce or prevent their involvement in violence. Violence involving youth is not random, uncontrollable, or inevitable.

The report warns, however, that intervention may be less than successful if society continues to accept violence and aggression in certain circumstances. Among the societal factors that may limit successful intervention are the following (pp. 61–62):

- ■ Corporal punishment of children, because harsh and continual punishment has been implicated as a contributor to child aggression;
- ■ Violence on television and in other media, which is known to affect children's attitudes and behaviors in relation to violence; and
- ■ Availability of firearms, especially to children and youth. Firearms are known to increase the lethality of violence and encourage its escalation.

The potential success of antiviolence interventions may be limited by the social and economic contexts in which some Americans spend their lives. These macrosocial considerations are beyond the scope of psychological interventions and require a society-wide effort to change. They include:

∎ Poverty, social and economic inequality, and the contextual factors that derive from these conditions (i.e., living in crowded housing and lack of opportunity to ameliorate one's life circumstances), which are significant risk factors for involvement in violence;

∎ Prejudice and racism, particularly because strongly prejudiced attitudes about particular social or cultural groups, or being a member of a group subjected to prejudice and discrimination, is a known risk factor for involvement in violence; and

∎ Misunderstanding of cultural differences, which must be addressed in intervention planning.

The Commission remains hopeful about the future because most of these factors are "within our power to change" (p. 5).

SUMMARY

The role of the broader community in assisting the juvenile justice system cannot be ignored. Community is not only the geographical area over which the justice system has jurisdiction, it is also a sense of integration, of shared values and a sense of "we-ness." Without such "we-ness" areas may experience the broken window phenomenon—if it appears no one cares, disorder and crime will thrive.

The importance of community is recognized in areas which have implemented community policing. Community policing embraces a proactive, problem-oriented approach to working with the community to make it safe.

Another important community resource is social services. Social workers have greatly influenced trends in juvenile justice policy in the areas of diversion, victim restitution, decriminalization of status offenders and deinstitutionalization. Social work functions in all aspects of the juvenile justice system, although in the first juvenile courts social workers were probation officers. The current emphasis in social services for youth is diversion to a wide range of community-based services and programs.

Other emphases include family therapy and learning conflict resolution and mediation skills. Studies suggest that family therapy is more effective in dealing with problems of youths than traditional juvenile justice intervention. Important basic skills schools are teaching in the 1990s are conflict resolution and mediation.

Community participation through volunteerism helps improve programs, breaks down isolation and helps youthful offenders explore possibilities for adjustment to the community. In addition, jobs are important to youth not only for the money they generate but for the feelings of self-worth that accompany a job.

■ Discussion Questions

1. Is there a sense of community where you live? Are there any instances of the broken window phenomenon?
2. What are the advantages and disadvantages of community policing? Is it used in your community?
3. Why is there a need for social workers? How extensively should social workers be involved in juvenile justice?
4. Should social workers handle youths directly from courts or probation officers? Why or why not?
5. Do social workers find the best approach to prevent recurrences of mischievous or antisocial juvenile behavior? What do they do?
6. Should social services provide education for disruptive youths who do not want to go to school? Why or why not?
7. A 15-year-old boy has been caught shoplifting food from a large supermarket. Security personnel call the police. While waiting for the police, the youth tells them that he has not eaten anything for a week. There is no food at his home. The police are advised of the youth's story. The police investigate, find the youth was telling the truth, and advise the supermarket. The supermarket manager does not want to make a formal complaint. Should this matter be handled by social services or the juvenile court? What would happen in your area?
8. What are the social service programs in your state? Do these programs serve the purpose they were designed for or do they add to the array of referral programs in existence?
9. Should all juvenile incidents be referred to the juvenile court, or is there justification for referral to other agencies as long as the offense is not serious? Which do you support? What criteria would you use?
10. Should schools be able to refer a disruptive juvenile to an agency that might help the juvenile rather than involve the police? Why or why not?

■ References

American Psychological Association. *Violence & Youth: Psychology's Response,* Vol. 1. *Summary Report of the American Psychological Association Commission on Violence and Youth.* n.d.

AuClaire, Philip, and Ira M. Schwartz. *An Evaluation of the Effectiveness of Intensive Home-Based Services as an Alternative to Placement for Adolescents and their Families.* Study conducted by the Hennepin County Community Services Department and the Hubert H. Humphrey Institute of Public Affairs, University of Minnesota. (paper) December 1986.

Bazemore, S. Gordon. *The Restitution Experience in Youth Employment.* Restitution Education, Specialized Training, and Technical Assistance Program (RESTTA), September 1989.

Briscoe, Judy Culpepper. "In Texas: Reaching Out to Help Troubled Youths." *Corrections Today,* October 1990, pp. 90–95.

Conly, Catherine H. *Street Gangs: Current Knowledge and Strategies.* Washington, D.C.: National Institute of Justice, August 1993.

Crowe, Timothy D. *Habitual Juvenile Offenders: Guidelines for Citizen Action and Public Responses.* Serious Habitual Offender Comprehensive Action Program. Washington, D.C.: Office of Juvenile Justice and Delinquency Prevention, October 1991.

Draty, David, and Gene Elig. "The High Cost of School Violence." *Security Concepts,* December 1993, pp. 11–21.

Drieland, Donald. "Social Work in Juvenile and Criminal Justice Settings—Review." *Social Work in Education,* 20. (Spring 1984) 2:87.

English, Tom. "Improving Juvenile Justice at the Local Level." *NIJ Reports,* March/April 1990, pp. 7–10.

Gershenson, Charles P. "The Twenty Year Trend of Federally Assisted Foster Care." *Child Welfare Research Notes #8.* Washington, D.C.: Administration for Children, Youth and Families, July 1984.

Gray, Ellen. *Child Abuse: Prelude to Delinquency?* National Committee for the Prevention of Child Abuse. Washington, D.C.: U.S. Government Printing Office, 1986.

Hamburger, Tom. "School Violence Common, Data Say." (Minneapolis/St. Paul) *Star Tribune,* 17 December 1993, pp. 1A, 11A.

Iggers, Jeremy. "The Solutions Have to Be on a Human Scale." (Minneapolis/St. Paul) *Star Tribune,* 23 May 1994, p. 1E.

Inkster, Norman D. "The Essence of Community Policing." *Police Chief,* March 1992, pp. 28–31.

Kirst, Michael W. "Improving Children's Services: Overcoming Barriers, Creating New Opportunities." *Phi Delta Kappan,* April 1991, pp. 615–618.

Klockars, Carl B. "The Rhetoric of Community Policing." In *Community Policing: Rhetoric or Reality,* edited by Jack R. Greene and Stephen D. Mastrofski. New York: Praeger, 1991, pp. 239–258.

Krisberg, Barry, and James F. Austin. *Reinventing Juvenile Justice.* Newbury Park, Calif.: Sage Publications, 1993.

Lesce, Tony. "Gang Resistance Education and Training (G.R.E.A.T.)." *Law and Order,* May 1993, pp. 47–50.

Manning, Peter K. "Community Policing as a Drama of Control." In *Community Policing: Rhetoric or Reality,* edited by Jack R. Greene and Stephen D. Mastrofski. New York: Praeger, 1991, pp. 27–45.

Mastrofski, Stephen D. "Community Policing as Reform: A Cautionary Tale." In *Community Policing: Rhetoric or Reality,* edited by Jack R. Greene and Stephen D. Mastrofski. New York: Praeger, 1991, pp. 48–67.

Miller, Alden, and Lloyd Ohlin. *Delinquency and Community.* Beverly Hills, Calif.: Sage Publications, 1985.

Miller, Linda S., and Kären M. Hess. *Community Policing: Theory and Practice.* St. Paul, Minn.: West Publishing, 1994.

Modglin, Terry. "School Crime: Up Close and Personal." *School Safety,* Spring 1989, pp. 9–11.

Monaghan, George. "Kids Crave Community, Fear Crime." (Minneapolis/St. Paul) *Star Tribune,* 4 January 1994, pp. 1E–3E.

Moriarty, Anthony, and Thomas W. Fleming. "Mean Suburban Streets: Youth Gangs Aren't Just a Big-City Problem Anymore." *American School Board Journal,* July 1990, pp. 13–16.

"Network Steers Youth Away from Trouble." *Law Enforcement News,* 14 February 1994, p. 5.

OJJDP Annual Report, 1990. Washington D.C.: Office of Juvenile Justice Delinquency and Prevention, 1990.

Prothrow-Stith, D. *Deadly Consequences.* New York: Harper-Collins, 1991.

Rosenfeld, Richard, and Scott Decker. "Where Public Health and Law Enforcement Meet: Monitoring and Preventing Youth Violence." *American Journal of Police,* 12 (1993), 3:11–57.

Smith, Melinda. "New Mexico Youths Use Mediation to Settle Their Problems Peacefully." *Corrections Today,* June 1990, pp. 112–114.

Smith, Robert L. "In the Service of Youth: A Common Denominator." *Juvenile Justice,* 1 (Fall/Winter) 2:1993, pp. 9–15.

Snow, Robert. "Agencies Turned Advocate." *Law and Order,* January 1992, pp. 285–287.

Stern, Harriet W. "Family Trouble Center." *Law and Order,* March 1991, pp. 72–75.

Treger, Harvey. "Social Work in the Justice System: An Overview." In *Social Work in Juvenile Justice Settings,* edited by A. Roberts. Springfield, Ill.: Charles C. Thomas, 1983, pp. 7–18.

Wilson, James Q., and George L. Kelling. "Broken Windows." *Atlantic Monthly,* March 1982, pp. 29–38.

Wilson, James Q., and George L. Kelling. "Making Neighborhoods Safe." *Atlantic Monthly,* February 1989, pp. 46–52.

Wilson, John J. "A National Agenda for Children: On the Front Lines with Attorney General Janet Reno." *Juvenile Justice,* 1 (Fall/Winter 1993) 2:2–8.

SECTION IV

Theory Into Practice in Juvenile Justice and a Look to the Future

As we enter the last decade of the twentieth century, the challenge of improving America's juvenile justice system to prevent and address delinquency more effectively continues to demand our best efforts. Our children and our Nation deserve no less.

OJJDP Annual Report, 1990

Section I provided the historical foundation of our juvenile justice system, how it evolved in the United States and its underlying philosophy and legal principles. Section II examined those served by the juvenile justice system—our youth, including how they typically grow and develop, the influence of family and school and then how they come into contact with the system, either as victims, as status offenders, as delinquents or as gang members. Section III detailed the contemporary juvenile justice system and the roles played by law enforcement, the juvenile/family court, corrections and the broader community.

This section takes a closer look at specific approaches to preventing abuse, delinquency and other problems associated with youth and describes some exemplary prevention programs (Chapter 13). This is followed by a review of specific approaches to treating youth who come under the jurisdiction of the system when preventive efforts fail and describes some exemplary treatment programs (Chapter 14). Although prevention and treatment are discussed in separate chapters, they are integrally related. When prevention efforts fail, if youths are found breaking the law, some intervention should be provided to prevent future offenses. Unfortunately, this is often a cycle of crime, with the treatment not preventing future offenses—or recidivism. This cycle is illustrated in Figure IV–1.

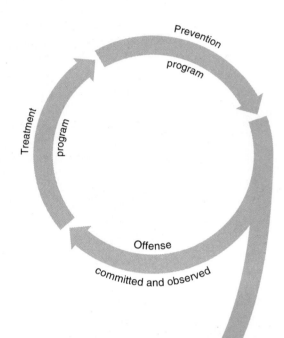

∎ **FIGURE IV–1   The Prevention/Treatment Cycle**

As noted by Crowe:*

∎ Nearly all children get into trouble during their upbringing without regard to social position.
∎ Nearly all children grow up to be law abiding and productive citizens, having developed positive behavior through the process of maturation.
∎ There are a very small number of children and adults who account for the majority of serious crime.

The question to the juvenile justice system is, Where should resources be focused? Some believe resources should be focused on first time offenders to make certain that the cycle of crime is broken for those most likely to be "rehabilitated." Others believe that youth who commit violent crimes and those who commit numerous crimes should be the top priority since most youth will "mature" out of unlawful behavior. This issue remains unresolved. The exemplary programs discussed in this section illustrate this issue as it affects programming and programming objectives.

The section and the book conclude with a brief overview of some promising juvenile programs being used in other parts of the world and a discussion of possible revisions in our current juvenile justice system.

*Timothy D. Crowe, *Habitual Juvenile Offenders: Guidelines for Citizen Action and Public Responses,* Serious Habitual Offender Comprehensive Action Program (SHOCAP) (Washington, D.C.: Office of Juvenile Justice and Delinquency Prevention, October 1991), p. 22.

CHAPTER

13

Approaches to Prevention: Theory Into Practice

The truism that an ounce of prevention is worth a pound of cure surely applies to delinquency. If we are to check the disturbing increase in violent crime by juveniles, we must go beyond treating symptoms, however, diligently, to examine causes. Nor must we be so preoccupied with what is wrong with a minority of our youth that our tunnel vision blinds us to what is right with the majority.

OJJDP Annual Report, 1990

▌ *Do You Know?*

What approach to the delinquency problem emerged in the late sixties?
What three approaches to prevention are?
What the three general levels of prevention are?
Whether "scaring the pants off" youths is an effective way to prevent delinquency?
How the numerator and denominator approaches to prevention differ?
What an effective prevention approach must address?
What kinds of programs are recommended by the Metropolitan Court Judges Committee to help prevent child abuse and neglect?
What the Committee recommends for disabled families?
What the Committee recommends for children-at-risk?
What the TARAD program does?
What antigang programs can be implemented?

▌ *Can You Define the Following Key Terms?*

denominator approach, numerator approach, primary prevention, secondary prevention, teritary prevention

INTRODUCTION

Common sense says that it is better to prevent a problem than to react to it once it arises. This is true for juvenile delinquency as well as for child neglect and abuse.

Traditionally our society's approach to youthful crime has been reactive. Juvenile courts and diversion programs have responded to crimes by juveniles with a wide range of services focused on punishment, control or rehabilitation.

In 1967, the President's Commission on Law Enforcement and Administration of Justice advocated *prevention* as the most promising and important method of dealing with crime: "In the last analysis, the most promising and so the most important method of dealing with crime is by preventing it—by ameliorating the conditions of life that drive people to commit crime and that undermine the restraining rules and institutions erected by society against anti-social conduct."

■ In the late 1960s a new approach for dealing with delinquency emerged—a focus on the prevention of crime.

Subsequently, this prevention emphasis was written into federal law in the Juvenile Delinquency Prevention Acts of 1972 and 1974, and the Juvenile Justice Amendments of 1977.

Each municipality, county and state is unique in its particular crime problems. Each is also unique in how it approaches crime and how it disposes of those who engage in crime. What constitutes delinquency is subject to varied interpretations across places, times and social groupings. A youth's behavior may be viewed as "delinquent" by police, as "acting out" by mental health professionals, as "sin" by a member of the clergy and as "just plain mischief" by someone who views some misbehavior as a normal part of growing up.

In Los Angeles in July of 1993, Attorney General Reno ("Reno Calls for Crime Prevention Programs," 1993) stated: "America would rather build prisons than invest in a child and we've got to change that. Unless we invest in children, we will never have enough dollars to build all the prisons necessary to house people 15 and 20 years from now."

This chapter begins with some theoretical considerations related to prevention, including prevention compared to control, the three levels of prevention, which youths should be targeted in prevention programs and prevention as an attack on causes. Next, the discussion focuses on specific approaches to preventing child abuse, drug and alcohol abuse, delinquency, violence and gangs. Exemplary programs in each area are described. The chapter concludes with a description of two comprehensive prevention programs achieving success in different parts of the country.

CLASSIFICATION OF PREVENTION APPROACHES
■■■■■■■■

Several approaches to classifying prevention efforts have been set forth. Following are two ways to look at and classify prevention efforts.

Prevention vs. Control

Technically, prevention is a measure taken *before* a delinquent act actually occurs to forestall the act; control is a measure taken *after* a criminal or delinquent act has been committed (Lejins, 1967). In this context, Lejins defines three kinds of prevention relevant for law enforcement.

■ Prevention can be corrective, punitive or mechanical.

- *Corrective prevention* focuses on eliminating conditions that lead to or cause criminal behavior.
- *Punitive prevention* relies on the threat of punishment to forestall criminal acts.
- *Mechanical prevention* is directed toward "target hardening" to make it difficult or impossible to commit particular offenses. Locks on doors, bars on windows, alarms, security guards and many other options are available to protect possible targets of criminal acts.

Another way to classify prevention efforts is by level. These levels encompass the three methods just discussed.

Three Levels of Delinquency Prevention

The National Coalition of State Juvenile Justice Advisory Groups (1993, p. 21) notes:

> **The first line of defense against all forms of juvenile crime is still prevention,** whether *primary,* directed at the population as a whole, or *secondary,* aimed at a specific at-risk population, or *tertiary,* targeted at an offending population in order to prevent repetition of the behaviors (bold and italic in original).

This is referred to as *treatment* in this text and is discussed in the next chapter.

■ Prevention may be primary, secondary or tertiary.

Primary Prevention

Primary prevention is directed at modifying and changing crime-causing conditions in the overall physical and social conditions that lead to crime.

∎ Primary prevention seeks to change conditions that cause crime.

Corrective and mechanical prevention fit into this level. An example of primary prevention is the community crime prevention program in Seattle, Washington. In this program prevention was directed toward residential burglaries. These were crimes of opportunity by juveniles who entered homes through unlocked doors and windows during the day when residents were away.

Prevention efforts were aimed at contributing environmental factors. Neighborhoods and types of housing were identified as being vulnerable to burglaries using demographics, criminal incidents and physical characteristics statistics. The community then gave citizens home security checklists. They encouraged citizens in target areas to protect their homes against relatively easy entry by burglars by using the home security checklists.

This program was directed at making crime more difficult, rather than at attacking individual motivations to commit crime. Such deterrent programs effectively increase the risks of and decrease the opportunities for burglary.

The National Coalition of State Juvenile Justice Advisory Groups (1993, p. 37) urges:

> We need a society that is committed to primary prevention, one that acknowledges that the variety and quality of support systems for families, particularly at the poverty level, are the best possible formula for preventing crime. Adequate health care, including the delivery of prenatal services to pregnant women, sufficient housing, strong Head Start and other preschool enrichment programs for all eligible children, an effective system of day care to allow parents to work while still providing for their children, safe neighborhoods, and quality educational opportunities all are necessary components of a society committed to its children.

As noted by the American Psychological Association (n.d., pp. 55–56) in its discussion of primary prevention programs: "Prevention programs directed early in life can reduce factors that increase risk for antisocial behavior and clinical dysfunction in childhood and adolescence." Among the most promising primary prevention programs are those including family counseling for pregnant women and for new mothers in the home, with continued visits during the first few years of the child's life. The American Psychological Association (p. 55) reports that in a 20-year follow-up of one "home visitor" program, positive effects were seen for both the at-risk child and the mother.

Preschools programs also hold promise if they include activities to develop intellectual, emotional and social skills and introduce children to responsible decision making. According to the APA (p. 56):

> Primary prevention programs of the type that promote social and cognitive skills seem to have the greatest impact on attitudes about violent behavior among children and youth. Skills that aid children in learning alternatives to violent behaviors include social perspective-taking, alternative solution generation, self-esteem enhancement, peer negotiation skills, problem-solving skills training, and anger management.

Secondary Prevention

Secondary prevention seeks early identification and intervention into the lives of individuals or groups that are found in crime-causing circumstances.

■ Secondary prevention focuses on changing the behavior of individuals likely to become delinquent.

Punitive prevention fits into this level. One highly publicized program of this type was undertaken in Rahway, New Jersey. Eighty boys and girls identified as being delinquency-prone were divided into experimental and control groups. The experimental group was taken to an adult prison in Rahway. According to Sprinthall and Collins (1984, pp. 340–341):

> [H]ard-core adult lifers verbally confronted them with the error of their ways. The adult criminals yelled at, bullied, and threatened the delinquents. They related the unvarnished truth about prison life, such as the brutality, the homosexual rapes, the degradation, and the lack of personal freedom.
>
> A film was made of the program for national television. The publicity became enormous, especially after preliminary findings revealed that from 80 to 90% of the treated teenagers had reversed their behavior. . . .
>
> When the follow-up results were carefully and objectively examined, however, the mighty promise of the project was undone. In fact, the findings . . . indicated that the program was worse than no treatment at all. The control groups had fewer subsequent arrests than the treatment group.

■ "Scaring the pants off" youths as a means to prevent juvenile delinquency does not appear to work.

The APA (p. 56) notes:

> Secondary prevention programs that focus on improving individual affective, cognitive, and behavioral skills or on modifying the learning conditions for aggression offer promise of interrupting the path toward violence for high-risk or predelinquent youth. . . .
>
> Programs that attempt to work with and modify the family system of a high-risk child have great potential to prevent development of aggressive and violent behavior.

Tertiary Prevention

Tertiary prevention, the third level, is aimed at preventing recidivism.

■ Tertiary prevention focuses on preventing further delinquent acts by youths already identified as delinquent.

Tertiary prevention, also called treatment or rehabilitation, is the focus of chapter 14.

WHICH YOUTH TO TARGET?

Recall that the public health model (chapter 7) called for focusing the scarce resources of the juvenile justice system on those identified at greatest risk— young black males living in areas of poverty, with high crime rates and drug dealing. Using a mathematical analogy, if we were to look at the number of at-risk youth compared to the total number of youth, the at-risk youth would be the *numerator* and the total number of youth would be the *denominator.* Smith (1993, pp. 10–11) suggests that we should be dealing with the denominator for best results:

> Delinquency programs that focus solely on juvenile offenders will not reduce the prevalence of youth crime any more than employment programs that focus exclusively on the unemployed will lower unemployment rates.
>
> The medical and scientific model demonstrates the effectiveness of the denominator approach. For example, numerator approaches in polio, tuberculosis, and other infectious diseases have made little impact on prevalence; but denominator approaches, such as vaccination, screening, and the like, have virtually eradicated a number of these diseases. The results have been dramatic and lasting. Denominator approaches work because they deal with the general public health as well as specific symptoms.

Smith suggests that one reason the denominator approach is ignored is because it tends to generate "turf fights" and to require innovative approaches to problems that we have almost come to accept. Further, says Smith (p. 11): "[T]he impulse [is] to do something now to relieve individual suffering rather than focus on a broader perspective that will prevent systemic suffering in the future."

▮ The **numerator approach** focuses on individuals (symptoms), whereas the **denominator approach** focuses on the entire group and causes.

PREVENTION AS AN ATTACK ON CAUSES

Of the three levels of prevention, primary and secondary prevention most closely approach the essence of the term *prevention,* in that they seek to preclude delinquent acts *before* such acts occur. Tertiary prevention is really remediation, aimed at forestalling future acts after an initial act has been committed and detected.

Primary and secondary prevention activities are not initiated as a result of apprehension by law enforcement personnel for a delinquent act. Primary and secondary prevention approaches can be effective only if they address the underlying causes of delinquency. To prevent a behavior from occurring, you must remove those factors that stimulate the behavior. Conditions that stimulate delinquent acts and a lack of constraints to inhibit those acts are both potential causes of delinquency; therefore, it is clear that effective prevention approaches must address both the conditions and lack of constraints.

■ **Effective prevention approaches must address the causes of delinquency.**

An editorial in the Minneapolis/St. Paul *Star Tribune* quotes former Minneapolis Chief of Police, Tony Bouza: "We have to stop swatting at the mosquitoes and start looking to the swamps that produce them" ("Fighting Crime," 1994, p. 10A). This editorial goes on to suggest:

> The best argument for betting on prevention is that nothing else seems to work. Punishment certainly doesn't. Since the mid-1970s sentences have gotten stiffer and the U.S. prison population has tripled—while the violent crime rate continues to inch upward. . . . A mountain of evidence links lawbreaking to poverty, abuse, school failure, joblessness and family chaos. . . .
>
> With crooks as with mosquitoes, it's far harder to get rid of this year's swarm than to prevent next year's from hatching. That takes foresight and forebearance— and an excruciating wait for the payoff. But the alternative to such patient, strategic crime-fighting is an onslaught that no amount of swatting will repel.

The National Center for the Assessment of Delinquent Behavior and Its Prevention (NCADBIP) has developed 12 strategies to distinguish among approaches to delinquency prevention. Each strategy addresses a distinct presumed cause of delinquency and an accompanying approach (Hawkins et al., 1980):

■ *Biological/Physiological* strategies assume that delinquent behavior derives from underlying physiological, biological, or biopsychiatric conditions. They seek to remove, diminish, or control these conditions.

■ *Psychological/Mental Health* strategies assume that delinquency originates in inherently maladaptive or pathological internal psychological states. They seek to directly alter such states and/or environmental conditions that generate them.

■ *Social Network Development* strategies assume that delinquency results from weak attachments between youths and conforming members of society. They seek to increase interaction, attachments, and/or involvement between youths and nondeviant others (peers, parents, and other adults). They also seek to increase the influence of nondeviant others on potentially delinquent youths.

■ *Criminal Influence Reduction* strategies assume that delinquency stems from the influence of others who directly or indirectly encourage youths to commit delinquent acts. They seek to reduce the influence on youths of norms toward delinquency and those who hold such norms.

■ *Power Enhancement* strategies assume that delinquency stems from a lack of control over impinging environmental factors. They seek to increase youths' ability or power to influence or control their environments either directly or indirectly (by increasing the power or influence of communities, institutions and groups in which youths participate).

■ *Role Development/Role Enhancement* strategies assume that delinquency stems from a lack of opportunity to be involved in legitimate roles or activities which youths see as personally gratifying. They attempt to create such opportunities. The roles developed or provided must be perceived by youths as worthwhile (i.e., sufficiently valuable or important to justify putting in time and effort). Furthermore, they must offer youths a chance to see themselves as: useful (they see their activities contributing to a legitimate social unit the youth values); successful (they see that they are achieving something desired, planned or attempted); or competent (they see that they are mastering a task).

▮ *Activities/Recreation* strategies assume that delinquency results when youths' time is not filled by legitimate activities. They seek to provide alternatives to delinquent activities. The condition they seek to achieve (i.e., filling youths' time with nondelinquent activities) is invariably met if the conditions of several other strategies are met. Thus, activities strategies are the lowest common denominator in a number of strategies.

▮ *Education/Skill Development* strategies assume that delinquency stems from a lack of knowledge or skills necessary to live in society without violating the laws. Education strategies provide youths with personal skills to prepare them to find patterns of behavior free from delinquent activities. They also provide skills or assistance to others so they can help youths develop needed skills.

▮ *Consistent Social Expectations* strategies assume that delinquency results from competing or conflicting demands and expectations placed on youths by organizations and institutions such as media, families, schools, communities, and peer groups. Inconsistent expectations or norms place youths in situations where conformity to a given set of norms results in an infraction of another set of norms. This situation results in confusion as to what conforming behavior is and cynicism toward legitimate expectations of any kind. These strategies seek to increase the consistency of the expectation from different institutions, organizations and groups that affect youths.

▮ *Economic Resource* strategies assume that delinquency results when people do not have adequate economic resources. They seek to provide basic resources to preclude the need for delinquency.

▮ *Deterrence* strategies assume that delinquency results because little risk or difficulty is associated with committing delinquent acts. They seek to increase the cost and decrease the benefit of criminal acts by restricting opportunities and minimizing incentives to engage in crime.

▮ *Abandonment of Legal Control/Social Tolerance* strategies assume that delinquency results from social responses that treat youths' behaviors as delinquent. Recall the previous discussion on the hazards of labeling. These responses may be viewed as contributing to delinquency almost by definition. The presence of social intolerance as expressed in the "black letter law," the actions of legal agents or the attitudes of community members may be viewed as creating opportunities for youthful behavior to be defined as delinquent. In addition, such responses may cause youths whose behaviors are so treated to perceive themselves as "outsiders." Consequently, they may engage in delinquent acts. These strategies seek to remove the label "delinquent" from certain behaviors. They take these behaviors as given and seek to alter social responses to them. Abandoning legal control removes these behaviors from the juvenile justice system, thus preventing them from being labeled or treated as delinquent. Increasing social tolerance for certain behaviors decreases the degree to which these behaviors are perceived, labeled and treated as delinquent.

These prevention strategies are summarized in Table 13–1.

TABLE 13-1 **Causes of Delinquency and Associated Strategies of Delinquency Prevention**

Presumed Cause	Strategy	Goal of Strategy
Physical abnormality/illness	Biological-physiological (health promotion, nutrition, neurological, genetic)	Remove, diminish, control underlying physiological, biological or biopsychiatric conditions
Psychological disturbance or disorder	Psychological/mental health (epidemiological/early intervention, psychotherapeutic, behavioral)	Alter internal psychological states or conditions generating them
Weak attachments to others	Social network development (linkage, influence)	Increase interaction/involvement between youths and nondeviant others; increase influence of nondeviant others on potentially delinquent youths
Criminal influence	Criminal influence reduction (disengagement from criminal influence, redirection away from criminal norms)	Reduce the influence of delinquent norms and persons who directly or indirectly encourage youths to commit delinquent acts
Powerlessness	Power-enhancement (informal influence formal power)	Increase ability or power of youths to influence or control their environments, directly or indirectly
Lack of useful, worthwhile roles	Role development/role enhancement (service roles, production roles, student roles)	Create opportunities for youths to be involved in legitimate roles or activities which they perceive as useful, successful, competent
Unoccupied time	Activities/recreation	Involve youths in nondelinquent activities
Inadequate skills	Education/skill development (cognitive, affective, moral, informational)	Provide individuals with personal skills which prepare them to find patterns of behavior free from delinquent activities
Conflicting environmental demands	Clear and consistent social expectations	Increase consistency of expectations/messages from institutions, organizations, groups which affect youths
Economic necessity	Economic resources (resource maintenance, resource attainment)	Provide basic resources to preclude the need for delinquency
Low degree of risk/difficulty	Deterrence (target hardening/removal, anticipatory intervention)	Increase cost and decrease benefits of criminal acts
Exclusionary social responses	Abandonment of legal control/social tolerance (explicit jurisdictional abandonment, implicit jurisdictional abandonment, covert jurisdictional abandonment, environmental tolerance)	Remove certain behaviors from control of the juvenile justice system; decrease the degree to which youths' behaviors are perceived, labeled, treated as delinquent

SOURCE: Hawkins et al. Reports of the National Juvenile Justice Assessment Center. *A Topology of Caused-Focused Strategies of Delinquency Prevention.* Washington, D.C.: National Institute for Juvenile Justice and Delinquency Prevention, U.S. Government Printing Office, 1980.

▮ *Activities such as participating on an athletic team can help prevent delinquency. Youths' time is spent constructively.*

PRESERVING FAMILIES TO PREVENT DELINQUENCY

The importance of families has been stressed throughout this text. As noted in the dedication to *Deprived Children: A Judicial Response* (Metropolitan Court Judges Committee, 1985, p. 2):

> The efforts of skilled and committed judges, legislators, law enforcement officers, health and child care workers, doctors, teachers, attorneys, volunteers and others involved in the lives of deprived children can do little without a rekindled national awareness that the family is the foundation of the protection, care and training of our children.

In keeping with the requirements of the JJDP Act, the Office of Juvenile Justice and Delinquency Prevention's *Annual Report* features " 'selected exemplary juvenile delinquency programs,' with emphasis on community-based programs 'that involve and assist families of juveniles' " (Sweet, 1992, p. 1). The 1990 report featured three such programs. One of the three, Court Appointed Special Advocates (CASA) was discussed in Chapter 10 under the discussion of guardians *ad litem*. Recall that these volunteers were to ensure that the courts are familiar with the needs of any neglected or abused child and that such children are most appropriately placed in the child's best interest.

The next program, Permanent Families for Abused and Neglected Children, is a training and technical assistance project of the National Council of Juvenile and Family Court Judges (NCJFCJ). During 1990 this program conducted nine training programs involving approximately 1,875 participants. A focus of the program is preservation of families suffering from drug abuse. When a drug-dependent infant is born and is placed outside its biological family, the court tries to learn if the mother is willing and able to undergo drug treatment with the goal being eventual reunification of the family.

The third program, Targeted Outreach, is a delinquency intervention program sponsored by the Boys and Girls Clubs of America (BGCA). According to Sweet (1992, p. 1): "Targeted Outreach is one of the latest developments in a series of progressive steps undertaken by Boys and Girls Clubs of America over the past 19 years to expand services to disadvantaged youth." Targeted Outreach provides positive alternatives for at-risk youth through a referral network that links the clubs with schools, courts, police and other community youth-service agencies. The core program activities are designed to promote a sense of belonging, competence, usefulness and power or influence (Sweet, 1992, p. 1).

These goals are very similar to the Boy Scouts of America who also have much to offer high-risk youth, as noted by Helgemoe (1992, p. 157): "To build a stronger America and to bring juveniles at risk into society's mainstream, we must instill or reaffirm ethical standards and moral values. The Boy Scouts of America offers an excellent method for accomplishing this goal."

Another program that emphasizes the family is Des Moines', Iowa, An In-Home Family Support Services, which views delinquency as resulting in some measure from an unstable home and family environment. In such situations, family members often are not supportive of each other, and adults are hindered from socializing children positively. The program seeks to improve family communication and stability, bolster self-esteem and develop more effective parenting skills.

PREVENTING CHILD NEGLECT AND ABUSE

Given that a disproportionate number of neglected and abused children become delinquents, preventing child neglect and abuse serves a dual function. According to the National Committee for the Prevention of Child Abuse (1986, p. 23):

> In general, it is agreed that the preventive strategies and programs aimed against child abuse would also prevent delinquency both indirectly, by preventing the abuse that leads to delinquency, and directly, by strengthening family and social supports for all individuals in the community.
>
> Preventive programs include: support programs for new parents; parent education; child care opportunities; treatment programs for abused children and young adults to prevent them from becoming abusing parents; life skills training for children and young adults; self-help groups and other neighborhood supports; and family support services.
>
> Generally, prevention should be offered early and without excessive intrusion. Prevention would most sensibly be aimed at reducing common causes or

correlates of child abuse and delinquency, such as poor parenting skills, isolation from positive community supports, and family stress.

Another influential group to consider the problems of children who have been abused, deprived or neglected is the Metropolitan Court Judges Committee, a committee of the National Council of Juvenile and Family Court Judges. The National Council was founded in 1937 to improve the nation's complex juvenile justice system. Located at the University of Nevada, Reno, its training division, the National College of Juvenile Justice, has reached more than 65,000 juvenile justice professionals, an influence unparalleled by any judicial training organization in the country.

The 1985–1986 Metropolitan Courts Judges Committee consisted of judges from our 40 largest states.

Recommendations of the Metropolitan Court Judges Committee

The Metropolitan Court Judges Committee also stresses the importance of preventive measures (1986, pp. 35–40): "The response of society to the tragedy of deprived children has been after-the-fact and ineffective. . . . Prevention of child abuse and neglect requires the awareness and involvement of the entire community. Deprived children are everyone's business. Their social and economic costs affect all Americans now and in the future." Among the Committee's recommendations are the following:

∎ *Priority for prevention.* Prevention and early intervention efforts must receive a high priority, with a greater emphasis placed on providing adequate services to prevent child abuse, neglect and family break-ups through adequate education, early identification of those at risk, and family-based counseling and home-maker services.

∎ *Parenting education.* Continuing education in parenting and in understanding the physical and emotional needs of children and families should be widely available in schools, health care systems, religious organizations, and community centers.

∎ *Teenage parents.* Communities must provide special parenting education and services for pregnant teenagers as well as teenage parents, including counseling on relinquishment and adoption.

∎ *Child care facilities.* Adequate child care facilities and services, with training, licensing, and monitoring of the providers, should be available to all parents needing such services.

∎ *Employee assistance programs.* Employer-sponsored assistance and counseling programs for family violence and child abuse or neglect, such as those used for alcoholism and drug abuse, should be established (italics in original).

∎ Early prevention programs should include making prevention a priority, and providing parenting education, programs for teenage parents, child care facilities and employee assistance programs.

∎ *Children's disabilities.* Identification and assessment of the physically, mentally, or emotionally disabled or learning disabled child must occur as early as possible.

■ *Help for disabled.* Services and education must be designed for and provided to mentally ill, emotionally disturbed, and physically or developmentally disabled children and parents.

■ Services and education must be provided for children with disabilities, e.g., learning disabled, emotionally disturbed, mentally ill or physically or developmentally disabled.

■ *Child support enforcement.* Judges must assure that child support orders are expedited and vigorously enforced and urge cooperation among all components of the child support enforcement process and all federal and state government agencies which may affect child support enforcement proceedings.

■ *Exploited children.* Persons convicted of exploiting children through pornography, prostitution, or drug use or trafficking must be severely punished. High priorities also must be given to national efforts to curtail the availability to children of pornography and excessively violent materials.

■ *Runaway and incorrigible children.* Courts and communities must provide services and courts must intervene, where necessary, to assist homeless, truant, runaway, and incorrigible children. Parents must be held personally and financially accountable for the conduct of their children.

■ *Truancy and school dropouts.* Courts should cooperate with schools and other agencies to substantially reduce truancy and dropouts by coordinating and providing services and assistance to the habitual truant.

■ *Security and custody.* The courts should have authority to detain, in a secure facility, for a limited period, a runaway, truant, or incorrigible child whose chronic behavior constitutes a clear and present danger to the child's own physical or emotional well-being, when the court determines there is no viable alternative.

■ All children at-risk, including runaways, habitual truants, the chronically incorrigible and those not receiving any or inadequate child support, must be considered when providing prevention services.

Appendix E contains a complete listing of the Metropolitan Court Judges Committee's recommendations.

OJJDP Exemplary Programs for Neglected and Abused Children

Most of the programs described in this chapter have been selected by the OJJDP as being exemplary. Three programs considered exemplary in their emphasis on community-based programs involving and assisting families of juveniles were discussed earlier in this chapter. Eleven programs described in this chapter have received the Gould-Wysinger Award, an award established in 1992 to give national recognition for local achievement in improving the juvenile justice system and helping our nation's youth. These programs' descriptions were written by Pam Allen (1993), director of special projects for the Coalition of Juvenile Justice and overseer of administration of the award solicitation process. These programs are designated GWA in the sections to come.

Kansas Children's Service League Juvenile Assessment and Intake Service

The Juvenile Assessment and Intake Service (JAIS), which serves Topeka and Shawnee Counties, protects children from unnecessary out-of-home placement and involvement with Social and Rehabilitation Services (SRS) and the juvenile court. The program advises SRS and the juvenile court about children who need special guidance, structure, or protection; reduces the number of children classified as Children-in-Need-of-Care who may be placed unnecessarily in locked detention; and assists law enforcement officers with decisions involving the placement of children.

Law enforcement officers, who provide all referrals to JAIS, increasingly use the service, and the number of contacts for information or referral has grown consistently. The rate of unnecessary placement of Children-in-Need-of-Services in locked detention has significantly decreased. In 1992 JAIS diverted 58 percent of youth for whom a diversion option was available from out-of-home placement. (GWA)

Home for the Prevention of Juvenile Delinquency, Puerto Rico

This program provides shelter and other support services to 28 girls, the majority of whom have been removed from their homes because of sexual abuse or abandonment. Most of the girls, who range in age from 4 to 18, have parents who are physically or mentally unable to care for them adequately. The program provides crisis intervention, counseling, tutoring, educational placement, community services, and recreational and social activities.

In the past year the program has acquired its own building, and the staff now includes a psychologist, a social worker, and four instructors. (GWA)

PROGRAMS IN THE SCHOOLS

Prevention programs in Rhode Island and Oregon schools use alternative education programs to reach at-risk youth. Such programs are based on the belief that failure in school increases the likelihood of youths committing delinquent acts. The school is considered an appropriate vehicle to help children meet their early developmental needs in six major roles in life: learner, individual, producer, citizen, consumer and family member. Helping children recognize and prepare for these roles should prevent problems, including delinquency, in later life.

Included in other prevention programs are:

▮ *Job/career programs* that help define a youth's career interests, provide vocational training and teach youths how to look for a job and other employment services.
▮ *Advocacy programs* in which youths, their families and school staff members monitor and pressure for needed changes in youth services.

OJJDP Exemplary Programs in the Schools

The following program descriptions are provided by Pam Allen (1993).

Anger Management Program, North Dakota

Located in Bismarck, the Anger Management Program works with youth and their parents to help them control outbursts of angry, aggressive behavior. The 10-week training program reduces the frequency of aggressive or violent incidents by developing awareness of anger patterns and teaching new skills for handling anger-provoking situations. The curriculum includes separate groups for parents, junior and high school students, and fifth and sixth graders.

The program completed its first year of operation in 1991 and has served more than 150 adolescents and 160 parents. Young people enrolled in the program have reduced their involvement in aggressive and violent incidents. The program draws on the resources of virtually every youth-serving agency, public and private, that maintains a local staff. The State training school and a private residential facility have requested training in anger management so that they can incorporate a similar component in their programs. (GWA)

Bright Future Project, Tennessee

This juvenile delinquency prevention project provides academic and social support to African-American youth age 5 to 15. Bright Future provides study resources to help youth complete their homework assignments. Reading and comprehension testing and prescribed tutoring are available for a limited number of youth. Decisionmaking rap sessions, discussions, and practice sessions are also provided. Supervised opportunities allow youth to contribute to their community by participating in neighborhood improvement projects.

The program serves some 30 children per day during the school year. About 330 young people have taken advantage of the afterschool tutoring and resource center, and 22 young people have participated in the special testing and remediating program. Teachers note that the quantity and quality of schoolwork of participants have improved.

The program has gained the respect of the community, and the Neighborhood Association has become the center of community life largely as a result of this project. (GWA)

McAlester Alternative School Project, Oklahoma

The McAlester Alternative School Project was developed to provide education services to at-risk students in the McAlester Public School District. The school allows students to learn at their own pace in a more relaxed setting. It provides onsite child care for teen parents and teaches fundamentals of child care. Class sizes are small, and a counselor is available throughout the day to provide personal, crisis, and career counseling. Attendance is voluntary.

In 3 years the program has served 174 students; 58 have graduated from high school, and 27 have entered vocational-technical training programs. Twenty-one students have been able to continue their education because of the onsite child care, and 9 parent/students have graduated. Increases in staff size have allowed the school to serve even more students, and initial enrollment has grown from 40 to 75. The school has helped meet the needs of a community experiencing serious socioeconomic problems. (GWA)

Griffin Alternative Learning Academy, Florida

Griffin Alternative Learning Academy (GALA) diverts students from failing in school, being suspended, needing court intervention, or dropping out of school. The program focuses on disruptive, unsuccessful, disinterested, and otherwise problematic students at Griffin Middle School in Leon County. The objective is to mainstream or promote 75 percent of the at-risk students back into regular classes by providing individualized academic assistance and business mentoring.

Started in 1989, during the 1991–92 school year GALA exceeded its expected 30-percent level of participation by minority youth and economically disadvantaged juveniles. A project evaluation confirmed overall improvement in participants' grade-point averages, a decrease in the number of absences and suspensions, and a reduction in delinquency referrals. All participants were promoted to the next grade. Because of the success of the program, the Governor's JJDP Advisory Committee funded replications of the project in two other schools during the 1992–93 school year. (GWA)

GENERAL DELINQUENCY PREVENTION PROGRAMS

Several programs are aimed at the general concept of delinquency prevention. Pam Allen (1993) describes five of the OJJDP exemplary projects that are general projects.

OJJDP Exemplary Programs

Project HELP, North Carolina

Project HELP (Helping Equip Little People) is an early intervention program that concentrates on delinquency prevention. The goals of the program are to promote wholesome values and moral living, impart work-readiness skills, develop social and cultural skills, give youth an opportunity to interact with positive adult role models, and involve parents in all phases of the program.

The program serves 20 youth age 6 to 10 who have exhibited behaviors that make them at-risk of entering the juvenile justice system. Volunteers, who are matched with an appropriate youth, work with program staff, parents, and youth to develop individual programs and create opportunities for leadership development.

To date, every parent of a child in the program has become involved, and three-quarters of the children have participated in the social and cultural enrichment programs. Everyone has participated in community service activities either through the schools, local civic groups, or the housing authority. Not one participant has become involved with the juvenile justice system. (GWA)

"Graffiti Street," Virgin Islands

"Graffiti Street" is a teen talk show designed to prevent juvenile delinquency by improving communication and developing understanding between youth and adults. The format uses a teen panel, guest speakers, and guest performers. Participants represent a cross-section of the population. The show is very popular with youth and adults and has received a national public broadcasting award. (GWA)

Hollandale Temporary Holding Facility, Mississippi

The Hollandale Temporary Holding Facility was established to provide a separate facility that meets all Federal and State standards for juveniles awaiting further action by a youth authority. Facility staff are on call 24 hours a day. Emergency care and crisis intervention include youth court counselors' services and referrals to a local community health service. The facility also provides supervised educational and recreational activities while youth are awaiting disposition or placement.

Between September 1991 and August 1992, the facility held 156 juveniles who would otherwise have been placed in an adult jail or lockup—decreasing by 90 percent the number of juveniles held in adult jails and lockups in the six counties served. (GWA)

Regional Juvenile Justice Program Development, Washington State

The Regional Juvenile Justice Program Development (RPD) program is an interagency approach to developing strategies for preventing and reducing juvenile delinquency in Snohomish County. The major goal of the program is to implement the Juvenile Justice and Delinquency Prevention Act. . . . Project staff develop and recommend procedures for coordination of local juvenile justice activities and work to ensure that duplication and conflict between agencies are minimized, service gaps are identified, and systemwide problems are addressed. The program serves as a resource for the State Advisory Group (SAG) in identifying technical assistance and training needs, providing information and assistance to local agencies to help them develop proposals responsive to SAG priorities, and reviewing and prioritizing proposals for SAG funding.

Other program activities include collecting data for a needs assessment to identify local juvenile justice needs. In addition, RPD was involved in developing a proposal to address the Target Site Program Area. One component, "Neutral Zone," a collaborative effort to provide recreational services for high-risk youth, many of whom are involved in gangs, has been implemented.

Rites of Passage, Iowa

Rites of Passage was developed to address minority overrepresentation by reducing the delinquency rate among middle school African-American males from high-risk situations. The project involves tutoring, mentoring, crisis intervention, individual and family counseling, and recreational activities. Development of participants' self-esteem and personal responsibility are emphasized. The project is so safe and supportive that participants come even when activities have not been scheduled. Since its inception in 1991, the project has built a community of trust among participants and their mentors. As a result, participants' family lives and academic performance have significantly improved. (GWA)

VIOLENCE PREVENTION

The OJJDP has released a report, "A Comprehensive Strategy for Serious, Violent, and Chronic Juvenile Offenders," that calls for increasingly intensive treatment. The report identifies six principles for preventing delinquent conduct and reducing serious, violent and chronic delinquency ("OJJDP Strategy," 1993, p. 3):

■ Strengthen families to instill moral values and provide guidance and support to children.

▮ Support core social institutions such as schools, religious institutions, and other community organizations to alleviate risk factors for youth.

▮ Promote delinquency prevention strategies that reduce the impact of risk factors and enhance the influence of protective factors for youth at the greatest risk of delinquency.

▮ Intervene immediately when delinquent behavior occurs.

▮ Institute a broad spectrum of graduated sanctions that provide accountability and a continuum of services to respond appropriately to the individual needs of an offender.

▮ Identify and control the small segment of serious, violent, and chronic juvenile offenders.

In written testimony at a hearing 23 October 1993, Wilson, acting director of OJJDP, wrote:

> Most delinquency prevention efforts have been unsuccessful because of their negative approach—attempting to keep juveniles from misbehaving. Our . . . strategy recommends instead positive approaches that emphasize opportunities for healthy social, physical and mental development ("OJJDP Strategy," 1993, p. 3).

The Center for Disease Control and Prevention has also established a set of strategies to prevent youth violence involving education, legal/regulatory change and environmental modification, as shown in Table 13–2.

DRUG PREVENTION PROGRAMS

Because of the known link between drug abuse and delinquency, many programs focus on drug prevention.

TABLE 13–2   Strategies to Prevent Youth Violence

Education	Legal/Regulatory Change	Environmental Modification
Adult mentoring	Regulate the use of and access to weapons:	Modify the social environment:
Conflict resolution	weapons:	Home visitation
Training in social skills	Weaponless schools	Preschool programs such as
Firearm safety	Control of concealed weapons	Head Start
Parenting centers	Restrictive licensing	Therapeutic activities
Peer education	Appropriate sale of guns	Recreational activities
Public information and	Regulate the use of and access	Work/academic experiences
education campaigns	to alcohol:	Modify the physical
	Appropriate sale of alcohol	environment:
	Prohibition or control of	Make risk areas visible
	alcohol sales at events	Increase use of an area
	Training of servers	Limit building entrances and
	Other types of regulations:	exits
	Appropriate punishment in	
	schools	
	Dress codes	

SOURCE: National Center for Injury Prevention and Control.

DARE

Probably the best known drug prevention program is the Drug Abuse Resistance Education (DARE) Program developed in 1983 by the Los Angeles Police Department and the Los Angeles Unified School District. As noted by the Bureau of Justice Assistance (1991, p. i), the DARE program has several noteworthy features, including the following:

- ■ DARE targets elementary school children.
- ■ DARE offers a highly structured, intensive fifth and sixth grade curriculum.
- ■ DARE uses uniformed law enforcement officers to conduct the class.
- ■ DARE represents a long-term solution to a problem that has developed over many years.

DARE's major goal is preventing substance abuse among school children (p. 3). To do so, it focuses on the following: (1) providing the skills for recognizing and resisting social pressures to experiment with tobacco, alcohol and drugs; (2) helping enhance self-esteem; (3) teaching positive alternatives to substance use; (4) developing skills in risk assessment and decision making and (5) building interpersonal and communications skills. Further, according to the Bureau of Justice Assistance (1993, p. 2), more than 14,100 officers have been trained to teach DARE and during the 1991–1992 school year more than 5 million students received DARE training.

The National DARE Parent Program

A new addition to the DARE program is the DARE Parent Program (DPP), created to stimulate interest in the community and motivate families to actively participate in preventing substance abuse. The program consists of a series of meetings at which parents learn about the DARE program their children are participating in, as well as how to recognize signs of drugs use, how to use local program resources and how to communicate effectively with their children.

DARE OFFICER JOHN ORTIZ

Ridgecrest has two full-time DARE Officers. Officer John Ortiz has been in DARE for two years. He works with grades K thru 7. DARE teaches our children to "Say No to Drugs." It is an exciting approach to preventing drug use among our school children. John was also Ridgecrest Police Officer of the year in 1990.

SAFETY TIP   3

Some people will tell you that alcohol or other drugs are harmless. Actually, both can ruin your health, your education, your future, and your life. Does that sound harmless? Don't take chances. Stay away from alcohol and other drugs. "D.A.R.E. To Say No!"

1991
This card comes to you as a gift from VFW of Ridgecrest Ship 4084 and Police Employees Association of Ridgecrest.
Ridgecrest Ship 4084   Produced by: McDag Productions, Inc.
P.O. Box 80826, Baton Rouge, LA 70898

■ *Some police departments print baseball-card-style DARE cards and other items to appeal to youth.*

The National Commission on Drug-Free Schools

The report of the National Commission on Drug-Free Schools (1990, p. iv) includes the following remark by then President George Bush in recognition of drug-free schools:

Ultimately the most important weapons in the war on drugs are the least tangible ones; self-discipline, courage, support from the family, and faith in one's self. The answer is traditional values. And if we want to stop our kids from putting drugs in their bodies, we must first ensure that they have good ideas in their heads and moral character in their hearts.

The report (pp. 35–36) suggests that a comprehensive drug education and prevention program should have eight key elements:

▮ Student survey, school needs assessment, and resource identification.
▮ Leadership training of key school officials and staff with authority to develop policies and programs.
▮ School policies that are clear, consistent, and fair, with responses to violations that include alternatives to suspension.
▮ Training for the entire staff on the following:
  — the school's alcohol and drug policies and policy implementation;
  — drug use, abuse, and dependency;
  — effects on family members and others; and
  — intervention and referral of students.
▮ Assistance programs/support for students from preschool through grade 12, including the following:
  — tutoring, mentoring, and other academic activities;
  — support groups (e.g., Alcoholics Anonymous and Children of Alcoholics);
  — peer counseling;
  — extracurricular activities (e.g., sports, drama, journalism);
  — vocational programs (e.g., work-study and apprenticeship);
  — social activities (including drug-free proms and graduation activities);
  — alternative programs (e.g., Upward Bound and Outward Bound); and
  — community service projects.
▮ Training for parents, including the following information:
  — the effects of drug use, abuse, and dependency on users, their families, and other people;
  — ways to identify drug problems and refer people for treatment;
  — available resources to diagnose and treat people with drug problems;
  — laws and school policies on drugs, including alcohol and tobacco;
  — the influence of parents' attitudes and behavior toward drugs including alcohol and tobacco, and of parents' expectations of graduation and academic performance of their children;
  — the importance of establishing appropriate family rules, monitoring behavior of children, imposing appropriate punishments, and reinforcing positive behavior;
  — ways to improve skills in communication and family and conflict management; and
  — the importance of networking with other parents and knowing their children's friends and their families.

▌ Curriculum for preschool through grade 12, including the following subjects:*
   — information about all types of drugs, including medicines;
   — the relationship of drugs to suicide, AIDS, drug-affected babies, pregnancy, violence, and other health and safety issues;
   — the social consequences of drug abuse;
   — respect for the laws and values of society, including discussions of right and wrong;
   — the importance of honesty, hard work, achievement, citizenship, compassion, patriotism, and other civic and personal values;
   — promotion of healthy, safe, and responsible attitudes and behavior;
   — ways to build resistance to influences that encourage drug use, such as peer pressure, advertising, and other media appeals (refusal skills);
   — ways to develop critical thinking, problem-solving, decision-making, persuasion, and interpersonal skills;
   — ways to develop active participation, cooperative learning, and consensus-building skills;
   — ways to increase self-control and self-esteem based on achievement and cope with stress, anger, and anxiety;
   — strategies to get parents, family members, and the community involved in preventing drug use;
   — information on contacting responsible adults when young people need help and on intervention and referral services;
   — sensitivity to cultural differences in the school and community and to local drug problems; and
   — information about how advertising works.
▌ Collaboration with community services to provide the following services:
   — student assistance programs;
   — employee assistance programs for school staff;
   — latch-key child care;
   — medical care, including treatment for alcohol and other drug abuse;
   — nutrition information and counseling;
   — mental health care;
   — social welfare services;
   — probation services;
   — continuing education for dropouts and pushouts;
   — in-service training for teachers and counselors in intervention techniques and procedures; and
   — programs for students at high-risk of drug use.

The report also includes a 24″ × 28″ chart detailing the roles and responsibilities for a drug-free school and community. Across the top are the specific groups involved: students, family, community organizations/parent groups, schools/colleges and universities, religious organizations, media, business/industry, health and social services, law enforcement/judicial and government. Down the left side are the functions to be undertaken: awareness/education, education/training, assessment, policy/legislation, prevention, intervention, treatment/aftercare, funding and research. Appendix F contains the content from this chart in list form.

---

*Curriculum must be developmentally oriented, age-appropriate, up-to-date and accurate. Individual components work best as part of a comprehensive curriculum program. Individually, components such as information about drugs can exacerbate the problem.

The National Crime Prevention Council's Programs

The National Crime Prevention Council has also focused efforts on drug abuse prevention. They identified three communities and highlighted their success in reducing drug abuse by using the talents of youth within the community. As noted in their "Foreword" (1992, p. i):

> Too many of us, when we look at young people, see problems or potential problems. What we could and should be seeing are enormous resources—talented, enthusiastic, able people who want to do good and want to be part of the community.
>
> Faced with a drug problem that (though modestly diminished) is still pernicious, we cavil against the shortage of resources but overlook millions of young people who can counsel, educate, organize, and otherwise prevent drug abuse and crime on behalf of their communities.
>
> NCPC believes strongly that young people can and want to be part of the solution to the drug problem. We believe that young people can design and carry out projects that will help reduce the demand for drugs in their communities, using modest fiscal resources combined with intelligence, dedication, and energy to effect remarkable changes. Moreover, youth working to prevent drug abuse deliver a far stronger and more effective message to peers than does adult carping and lecturing.

The NCPC lists the following reasons to use youth in the local drug wars (p. 1):

▮ The act of taking on responsibility, far from confounding adolescents, sustains them.

▮ Experience-based learning is a highly effective means of teaching a variety of skills and disciplines.

▮ Service to our communities is part of the dues all of us should expect to pay as members of a free, democratic society.

▮ Youth need to feel that they, as individuals, have a place and a stake in their communities, that they are needed and their contributions valued.

▮ Youth by working in partnership with adults gain important exposure to the adult world, exposure that is too often in short supply in modern communities.

▮ The value of reinforcing positive behaviors has long been known, but our social structures tend to concentrate on pathologies, on rehabilitating youth (which is appropriate in certain instances), rather than cherishing and rewarding that which is valuable, competent, and worthy.

Their program, called Teens as Resources Against Drugs (TARAD), is funded by the Bureau of Justice Statistics. TARAD was piloted at three sites: New York City (Teens Go After Worms in the Big Apple), Evansville, Indiana, (Drugs Are Out in Evansville) and communities in South Carolina (Kids in the Know Say No in South Carolina).

▮ The TARAD program of the National Crime Prevention Council uses youth to take on the community drug prevention challenge.

The concept is based on two premises: (1) teens are deeply concerned about the effects of drug abuse on their peers and on the community at large and (2) as young people go through adolescence they need to develop independence and a sense that their skills and accomplishments are needed and valued by their community.

Community support for TARAD is strong, and the types of projects developed are varied, as shown in Table 13–3. The NCPC reports the following "exciting and varied results" (p. 36):

■ For the communities: drug dealers moved out; communities more frequently turned to youth for assistance in policy making; a school changed its curriculum to acknowledge the value of community service, and annual abuse prevention activities are becoming part of local calendars.

■ For the youth: youth found a safer, drug-free environment; they had an opportunity to be themselves, "warts and all"; they came to believe they could make a difference; they got assistance with jobs and scholarships; and they learned new life skills.

COMPREHENSIVE PROGRAMS

Some programs offer a comprehensive range of prevention services. Among these are YouthCare and the CAR Program managed by CASA.

TABLE   TARAD Project Sponsors and Project Types
13–3

Project Sponsors	Project Types
High schools	Performance based
Middle schools	Cross-age teaching
Elementary schools	Peer helping
Special education	Mentoring
Alternative schools	Puppet troupes
Youth membership organizations	Awareness campaigns
Nonprofits	Awareness days
Community centers	Take back the park
Neighborhood organizations	Drug patrols
Neighborhood groups	Lock-ins
Churches	Establishing drug/alcohol-free organizations
Colleges	Drop-in or teen centers
Hospitals	Beautification of drug infested areas
City-wide	Murals
Group homes	Newspapers
Support groups	Contests with a message
Youth councils	Videos
Mental health centers	Products
Police athletic leagues	Conferences/events
	Health fairs

SOURCE: National Crime Prevention Council, *Given the Opportunity: How Three Communities Engaged Teens as Resources in Drug Abuse Prevention.* (Washington, D.C.: 1992), pp. 7, 9.

YouthCare

YouthCare is a private nonprofit agency in Washington State that provides services to young people in crisis. As noted in their annual report (1992, p. 30):

> To work through the challenges of adolescence and to successfully mature is not an easy task for any young person. For the children and young adults that YouthCare serves, it is often overwhelming. Many of them have encountered problems that would overwhelm most of us. They come from homes with severe difficulties; they have been abused; they have been abandoned in early childhood or later adolescence. In spite of these problems, they continue to grow and seek our help as they sort through the choices facing them. The ability to provide guidance and direction, while allowing youth to make their own choices, is a central theme of all our programming.

YouthCare collaborates with the public schools, the Catholic Community Services, the YMCA, the Seattle Mental Health Institute, the University of Washington, the Seattle Children's Home and several local health care facilities. They are supported by funding from businesses, churches, corporations, foundations and private groups. Their comprehensive programs are described below (1992, pp. 10–11).*

The Shelter

The Shelter is a short-term crisis facility for young people from 11 to 17 years of age. Both boys and girls who are runaway and homeless can be placed for a maximum of 14 days. The Shelter accepts youth from any referral source, including walk-ins. Services to youth in placement include: casework, counseling, academic evaluation and course work, drug-alcohol counseling, recreational activities and a 24 hour crisis line. The Shelter staff is committed to providing counseling and case management services to all clients in residence to assist them in creating and finding healthy, supportive environments in which to grow up.

Threshold

Threshold is a transitional living program designed to aid young women, 16 to 18 years old, in making the transition from a "street lifestyle" to a more productive way of living. The primary goal of the program is to provide a safe, home-like environment where residents receive intensive support and services to build a foundation for living within the community. Upon graduation from the Threshold house, individuals are placed in an independent living situation such as an apartment while YouthCare continues to provide counseling, casework and the support that they would normally receive from their families.

Straley House

Straley House is a 12 bed residential program that assists 18 to 21 year old young adults in their transition toward healthy independent living. The program is designed to serve a population of young people who are no longer eligible for youth programs, and who will be underserved in the adult system. Straley House works to address the needs youth have as they begin the path to adulthood. The

---

*Reprinted by permission of YouthCare, Seattle, Washington, from *YouthCare 1992 Annual Report* and additional material provided by YouthCare.

emphasis of the program is on building confidence and learning the independent living skills necessary to enter adult life. Straley House provides an environment balancing the needs of the individual and the community by emphasizing mutual respect, care and dignity.

Orion Multi-Service Center

The Orion Center programs serve young people between the ages of 11 and 20. Services are especially designed for homeless and high-risk youth. Youth served by the Orion Center include: adolescents who are homeless and on the street; youth with legal problems or histories of delinquency; youth with mental health problems; youth who are running away from home; gay and lesbian youth; youth who are abusing drugs or alcohol; youth involved in gang activity; adolescents who are struggling or failing in school; and young people who have been sexually abused.

Since its beginning, the Orion Center has worked in collaboration with many other community agencies and organizations to provide the most effective services possible. Other agencies at Orion include the Learning Center (through Seattle Public Schools), Catholic Community Services, the University of Washington Adolescent Clinic, Health Care for the Homeless, the YMCA, the YWCA, and Seattle Mental Health Institute.

Specifically, the Orion Center offers case management, drug and alcohol counseling, mental health services, individual, family and group counseling, a school program, recreational opportunities, meals program and referral to shelters. Through these services the staff of the Orion Center strive to assist youth to address the issues which have created the crisis they are experiencing.

Gang Prevention and Intervention

YouthCare plays an integral role in Seattle Team for Youth, a city-wide effort to provide gang prevention and intervention services. In partnership with the City of Seattle, the Police Department, Department of Social and Health Services and 11 other agencies, YouthCare works to offer positive alternatives to gang involvement to those youth who are at-risk.

Young people are referred to the Gang Prevention and Intervention Program by the Department of Youth Services, the Seattle Police Department, parents and schools. Upon referral, a number of services are offered. These services include drug and alcohol treatment, employment workshops, job placement, tutoring, mentoring, sports and recreation, leadership training, self-esteem building, and cultural activities. The Participant Service Fund, which provides food and clothing vouchers for the youth and their families, is a special financial assistance package within the program.

Family Reconciliation Services (FRS)

YouthCare maintains a goal of strengthening and reuniting families whenever possible. Through a contract with the Department of Social and Health Services, YouthCare works with families in crisis. The goal of the program is to provide counseling services to families who are in conflict. The program attempts to prevent the child from being placed out of the home, to reunite family if the youth has run away, to teach the family problem-solving skills, and to give the family the tools needed for dealing with conflict. Therapists have 15 hours to try and meet these goals with the family.

Outreach

The Outreach program of YouthCare comes to life through the outreach team, who maintains a presence on the streets in many areas of the city and county where youth gather. The team works to establish relationships with youth in order to provide services. Often, these youth have had no previous contact with any services or programs. Services provided include drug and alcohol education, AIDS prevention education, counseling, referral to shelter, food and medical care.

Case management is another aspect of the outreach efforts. Outreach workers, through established networks of providers, assist youth in returning to or remaining with their families and school, finding housing, medical care, drug and alcohol treatment, legal assistance or other services. This effort works closely with the Orion Center.

AIDS Education

There are estimated to be as many as 1,000 adolescents infected with HIV (the AIDS virus) in King County. The YouthCare education and prevention team provides both education to youth in high-risk situations and training individuals who work with these youth. The direct education takes place at the Department of Youth Services Juvenile Detention Facility, Echo Glen Children's Center, Ryther Adolescent Drug and Alcohol Treatment Program, The Shelter, Threshold and other sites where high-risk youth are found. The class focuses on changing the behavior that puts many of these youth at-risk for acquiring this life threatening illness.

YouthCare also provides HIV/AIDS prevention training and education for youth service providers. YouthCare has developed a training workshop called "Teen AIDS Prevention Education (TAPE)—a Practical Skills Training." The goal is to give the providers the "how to" skills to deliver appropriate AIDS prevention education to their clients.

Research and Evaluation

In an effort to provide the most effective services for its clients, YouthCare regularly conducts evaluation and research of its programs. This evaluation is accomplished by formal research endeavors, periodic testing of clients to determine changes, and regular program audits that contract with independent researchers to examine the efficiency of YouthCare's services.

Formal research projects currently include a three-year grant funded by the National Institute of Mental Health (NIMH). This effort examines the prevalence of mental health problems in the homeless youth population and measures the effectiveness of intensive case management services to this special youth population. Specialized case management is provided to a portion of YouthCare's client population. Research efforts measure change between youth from this group, young people receiving standard YouthCare services, and a population of youth receiving no services.

YouthCare is working collaboratively on this project with NIMH, the University of Washington, Seattle Mental Health Institute, Seattle Children's Homes, Washington State Division of Mental Health and King County Division of Mental Health.

YouthCare WestSound Serving Kitsap County

In late 1992, at the invitation of the Kitsap Commission on Children and Youth, YouthCare began YouthCare WestSound to serve Bremerton and Kitsap County and address the growing population of homeless and runaway youth in that region.

YouthCare WestSound works with a local Advisory Board and existing programs to increase awareness in the community of the issues of "street youth" and to develop a continuum of services for this population. These efforts will lay the foundation for expanding services to include shelter, a multi-service center modeled on the Orion Center, and transitional living programs.

Currently, YouthCare WestSound's Outreach program provides counseling, family reconciliation services, and referral services to youth who are runaways, homeless, or involved in or at-risk for criminal activity. Outreach workers maintain a presence on the streets to serve as role models for youth, to evaluate the needs of clients and to assist youth in accessing services. An education caseworker works with youth on the street and with youth at Magnuson Community School to identify special needs and help young people stay in or return to school. YouthCare WestSound also provides case management services.

YouthCare WestSound is funded by the Governor's Juvenile Justice Advisory Committee, the City of Bremerton, United Way of Kitsap County, individuals, groups, and private grants.

The CAR Program and CASA

The Children at Risk (CAR) program seeks to divert inner-city youth from getting involved with drugs, gangs and crime by providing an intensive program of activities, which include case management, after-school and summer programs, counseling (both individual and family), tutoring, mentoring, community policing and more. As noted by Hebert (1993, p. 6): "CAR is a unique public/private partnership between the Bureau of Justice Assistance (BJA), the Office of Juvenile Justice and Delinquency Prevention (OJJDP) and the National Institute of Justice (NIJ). The Center on Addiction and Substance Abuse (CASA) designed and manages the project." Says Hebert:

> The CAR program consists of a service intervention component that includes family intervention, tutoring, mentoring, and incentives for participation; and a criminal justice component that includes neighborhood-based activities designed to reduce the prevalence of drug dealing and drug use. In addition, schools, service providers, police, and other criminal justice agencies collaborate at both a policy and service delivery level to provide a coordinated array of services and support for at-risk youth.

CAR is currently being implemented in Austin, Texas; Bridgeport, Connecticut; Memphis, Tennessee; Newark, New Jersey; Savannah, Georgia; and Seattle, Washington. Participants must meet demographic requirements and at least one of the following high-risk eligibility criteria (Hebert, 1993, p. 8):

■ School-based factors
  Student is identified as at risk by the Austin Independent School District's guidelines.
  School behavior has resulted in disciplinary action.
■ Personal-based factors
  Experimentation with alcohol or drugs.
  Involvement in drug trafficking.
  Referred to juvenile court.

       Special education student.
       Pregnant, parent, or previous pregnancies.
       Abused child.
       Gang involvement.
▌ Family-based factors
       Family members involved in the criminal justice system.
       Family history of substance abuse.
       Family member is a known gang member.
       History of family violence.

Antigang Programs

The National School Safety Center (1988, p. 35) publication, *Gangs in Schools: Breaking Up is Hard to Do,* quotes Nester Bustamante, an assistant state attorney as noting: "We do a lot of work helping separate gang members from gangs. We want to give them a shot at making something of themselves. It's not easy." The Center suggests that "a positive, consistent approach to discipline and conflict prevention can achieve long-term and far-reaching results and improve the overall school climate" (p. 25). The Center suggests several prevention and intervention strategies.

Behavior codes should be established and enforced firmly and consistently. Such behavior codes may include a dress code, a ban on showing of gang colors and a ban on using gang hand signals. Friendliness and cooperation should be promoted and rewarded.

Graffiti removal should be done immediately. Graffiti is not only unattractive, it allows gangs to advertise their turf and their authority. A Los Angeles school administrator suggests that graffiti be photographed before removal so that the police can better investigate the vandalism. Evidence, such as paint cans and paint brushes, should be turned over to the police. In addition, students might design and paint their own murals in locations where graffiti is likely to appear.

Conflict prevention strategies can also be effective. Teachers should be trained to recognize gang members and to deal with them in a nonconfrontational way. All gang members should be made known to staff. Teachers should try to build self-esteem and promote academic success for all students, including gang members. School-based programs can combine gang and drug prevention efforts.

Crisis management should be an integral part of the administration's plan for dealing with any gang activity that might occur. A working relationship should be established with the police department, and a plan for managing a crisis should be developed. The plan should include procedures for communicating with the authorities, parents and the public. The National School Safety Center (1988, pp. 33–34) recommends the following action in a school crisis:

▌ Have a media policy worked out in advance. Spell out who will be the media spokesperson, and make it clear no one else should speak *officially* for the school or agency.

▌ Route all media inquiries to one person or, at least, to one office.

▌ Prepare an official statement responding to the particular crisis situation. Read from or distribute this statement when media inquiries are made. This will maintain consistency.

- ▌ Anticipate media questions and prepare and rehearse answers.
- ▌ Don't be afraid to say, "I don't know." This is better than lying or responding with the offensive phrase, "No comment." Volunteer to get the answer and follow up within a specified time.
- ▌ Start a rumor control center, if the situation warrants. Publish a number for media representatives to call if they hear a rumor or need information.
- ▌ Provide the news media with updates as events unfold, even after the initial crisis is handled.
- ▌ Keep calm and maintain a professional manner. Once calm has returned, it is imperative to begin work that will prevent a recurrence of the crisis.

Community involvement can also be extremely effective in reducing or even preventing gang activity. Parents and the general public can be made aware of gangs operating in the community, as well as of popular heavy metal and punk bands. They can be encouraged to apply pressure to radio and television stations and book stores to ban material that promotes use of alcohol, drugs, promiscuity or devil worship.

▌ Antigang programs include establishing behavior codes, removing graffiti, implementing conflict prevention strategies, developing a plan for crisis management and fostering community involvement.

Specific school and community programs that have been implemented to deal with gangs are outlined in Appendix G.

SUMMARY

In the late 1960s a new approach for dealing with delinquency emerged: the prevention of crime before youths engage in delinquent acts. Prevention can be corrective, punitive or mechanical. It can also be classified as primary, secondary or tertiary.

Primary prevention seeks to change conditions that cause crime. Secondary prevention focuses on changing the behavior of individuals likely to become delinquent. "Scaring the pants off" youths does not appear to be an effective secondary preventive approach. Tertiary prevention focuses on preventing further delinquent acts by youths already identified as delinquent, which is discussed in chapter 14.

Yet another way to look at prevention is the mathematical analogy of numerator/denominator. The numerator approach focuses on individuals (symptoms) whereas the denominator approach focuses on the entire group and causes.

Effective prevention approaches must address the causes of delinquency. Also critical are programs aimed at preventing child neglect and abuse. Such early prevention programs should include making prevention a priority, and providing parenting education, programs for teenage parents, child care facilities and employee assistance programs. Services and education also must be provided for children with disabilities, e.g., the learning disabled, emotionally disturbed, mentally ill or physically or developmentally disabled. All children at-risk, including runaways, habitual truants, the chronically incorrigible and those not receiving any or inadequate child support, must be considered when providing prevention services.

Other prevention programs are aimed at the drug problem and the gang problem. The TARAD program of the National Crime Prevention Council uses youth to take on the community drug prevention challenge.

Antigang programs include establishing behavior codes, removing graffiti, implementing conflict prevention strategies, developing a plan for crisis management and fostering community involvement.

■ Discussion Questions

1. Do you support the numerator or denominator approach to prevention? Be prepared to defend your choice.
2. Do delinquency prevention programs succeed? Do the programs deter delinquency?
3. What prevention programs are available in your area? Is there a specific target area?
4. Are all three levels of delinquency prevention applied in your area? Which one best suits your area? Why?
5. If social responses treat youths' behavior as delinquent in prevention strategies, does this cause a labeling effect? How would you handle a program so labeling was not a factor?
6. At what types of delinquency should programs be directed? Violent youth? Status offenders? Antisocial and criminal activity in general? Gang activity?
7. List assumptions you feel are basic to effective delinquency prevention programs. To what extent do you feel each assumption is justified?
8. What are some contemporary attempts to prevent delinquency? Why are they effective or ineffective?
9. What kinds of programs exist in your area to prevent child neglect and abuse?
10. What kinds of programs to prevent child neglect and abuse do you think have the most promise?

■ References

Allen, Pam. "The Gould-Wysinger Awards: A Tradition of Excellence." *Juvenile Justice,* 1 (Fall/Winter 1993) 2:23–28.

American Psychological Association. *Violence & Youth: Psychology's Response,* Vol. 1. *Summary Report of the American Psychological Association Commission on Violence and Youth.* n. d.

Bureau of Justice Assistance. *An Introduction to DARE: Drug Abuse Resistance Education,* 2nd ed. Washington, D.C., October 1991.

—— *An Introduction to the National DARE Parent Program.* Washington, D.C., June 1993.

"Fighting Crime: What Lawmakers Can Do in Safety's Name." (Minneapolis/St. Paul) *Star Tribune,* 7 February 1994, p. 10A.

Hawkins, J. David; Paul A. Pastor, Jr.; Michelle Bell; and Sheila Morrison. *Reports of the National Juvenile Justice Assessment Center: A Topology of Caused-Focused Strategies of Delinquency Prevention.* Washington, D.C.: National Institute for Juvenile Justice and Delinquency Prevention, U.S. Government Printing Office, 1980.

Hebert, Eugene E. "Doing Something About Children at Risk." *National Institute of Justice Journal,* November 1993, pp. 4–9.

Helgemoe, Ray. "Teaming Up with the Boy Scouts to Reach Our High-Risk Youths." *Corrections Today,* July 1992, pp. 156–157.

Lejins, P. "The Field of Prevention." In *Delinquency Prevention: Theory and Practice,* edited by Amos and Wellford. Englewood Cliffs, N.J.: Prentice Hall, 1967.

Metropolitan Court Judges Committee Report. *Deprived Children: A Judicial Response.* Washington, D.C.: U.S. Government Printing Office, 1986.

National Coalition of State Juvenile Justice Advisory Groups. *Myths and Realities: Meeting the Challenge of Serious, Violent, and Chronic Juvenile Offenders, 1992 Annual Report.* Washington, D.C.:1993.

National Commission on Drug-Free Schools. *Toward a Drug-Free Generation: A Nation's Responsibility.* Final Report, September 1990.

National Committee for the Prevention of Child Abuse. *Child Abuse: Prelude to Delinquency?* Washington, D.C.: U.S. Government Printing Office, 1986.

National Crime Prevention Council. *Given the Opportunity: How Three Communities Engaged Teens as Resources in Drug Abuse Prevention.* Washington, D.C.:1992.

National School Safety Center. *Gangs in Schools: Breaking Up is Hard to Do.* Malibu, Calif.: Pepperdine University Press, 1988.

"OJJDP Strategy for Juvenile Offenders Seeks Early Intervention." *NCJA Justice,* November 1993, pp. 3–5.

President's Commission on Law Enforcement and the Administration of Justice. *The Challenge of Crime in a Free Society.* Washington, D.C.: U.S. Government Printing Office, 1967.

"Reno calls for Crime Prevention Programs." *Los Angeles Times,* reported in (Minneapolis/St. Paul) *Star Tribune,* 11 July 1993, p. 1A.

Smith, Robert L. "In the Service of Youth: A Common Denominator." *Juvenile Justice,* 1 (Fall/Winter 1993) 2:9–15.

Sprinthall, Norman A., and W. Andrew Collins. *Adolescent Psychology: A Developmental View.* New York: Random House, 1984.

Sweet, Robert W. "Preserving Families to Prevent Delinquency." OJJDP Model Programs, Juvenile Justice Bulletin, April 1992.

YouthCare 1992 Annual Report. Seattle, Wash.

Approaches to Treatment: Theory Into Practice

In practice, treatment programs are still offered, but no one really believes that they will work, unless the young person wants to change. The truth is that no one really knows what works in treatment.

Timothy D. Crowe

▌ Do You Know?

What is one thing effective treatment programs often take advantage of?
What crisis intervention capitalizes on?
What recommendations for treating abused children have been made by the National Committee for Prevention of Child Abuse?
What treatment requirements are recommended by the Metropolitan Court Judges Committee?
What service requirements are recommended by this Committee?
What recommendations are made by the Committee for establishing permanency for the child?
What type of offender most boot camps target?

▌ Can You Define the Following Key Terms?

permanency, wizard

INTRODUCTION

The correctional portion of the juvenile justice system is most intimately concerned with treatment options, as discussed in chapter 11. Unfortunately, as noted in the opening quotation from Crowe, research is lacking or inconclusive in this area. As noted in their guidelines for citizen action (Crowe, 1991, p. 23): "The criminological literature has consistently reported on the failure of treatment programs for more than 40 years. The failures have consistently and uniformly been associated with what to do with serious or habitual delinquents once they are identified."

This chapter expands on the information from chapter 11, looking first at some theoretical concepts regarding treatment and some general characteristics of effective interventions. It then looks at treatment suggested for abused and neglected children. This is followed by descriptions of several alternative treatment programs being used around the country, including day treatment programs, "second chance" camps, boot camps and youth centers. The chapter concludes with descriptions of treatment programs or research projects identified by the OJJDP as exemplary and the potential role wizardry may play in treatment program success.

TREATMENT AS TERTIARY PREVENTION

Chapter 13 described three levels of prevention—primary, secondary and tertiary. The tertiary level focuses on preventing further delinquent acts by youths already identified as delinquents. That is the focus of this chapter and the challenge of the correctional portion of the juvenile justice system. However, as has been stressed throughout this text, no one segment of the system or the system itself can solve the problems associated with child abuse and neglect, delinquency, crime and violence. It takes a total community effort.

One example of this prevention process is the informal adjustment program authorized by the "Texas Family Code." The objectives of this program are:

- To meet the court's needs in fulfilling the intent of the family code as it relates to informal adjustment.
- To provide a coordinated, comprehensive service delivery system aimed at self-rehabilitation and short-term supervision, diversion and prevention from further involvement in the judicial system.
- To provide quality service to children under an informal adjustment contract.

The informal adjustment contract is a six-month informal probationary period, in which a child is supervised by a probation officer or counselor. Family and child must meet certain criteria, such as good school attendance, positive attitudes toward change, a demonstrated willingness to see and use resources that can help change behavior, good attitude toward authority figures and a willingness to cooperate with the juvenile probation department. Through this agreement, children are given a second chance.

Under this program, the probation officer, the parent and the child have clearly defined roles. The probation officer supervises and monitors the child's behavior during the six-month contract. Cooperation is essential for both parents and child. The parents provide emotional and financial support to the child, seek assistance from the probation officer as needed, advise the probation officer of any problems that arise, monitor activities of the child, report violations to the probation officer and provide supervision. The child must obey the rules set by the parents, attend school every day as required by law, keep parents informed of his or her whereabouts, have full-time employment if not in school and follow all rules agreed on in the contract.

The contract ends exactly six months after it is signed. The case is then closed and the file is returned to the probation department. A letter is sent to the parents advising them that the case has been closed and that they may request the court to seal the record.

A child can terminate the contract at any time. If this occurs, however, the probation officer returns the case for a court hearing. Should the child or parent decide not to enter into an informal adjustment contract, or should the child not meet the criteria established, the case is docketed for a court hearing.

Another example of tertiary prevention is a program in Lansing, Michigan, "The School Youth Advocacy Program." The program includes youths who have been institutionalized and then returned to school. It involves these youths in a structured peer support group to improve attitudes toward self and school and to improve academic achievement and, thereby, reduce chances of committing delinquent acts (Wall et al., 1981, p. 114).

Youths are recommended for program participation by faculty, administration, other youths and parents. They are selected among repeat offenders for leadership qualities, both negative and positive. Nine to 12 students participate in a group. The program has found that junior high youths are more comfortable talking about problems with peers of their own gender; thus groups are segregated by sex.

The group has decision-making capabilities regarding sanctions for any infractions of members. For example, if a student in the group is caught smoking marijuana, group members decide what measures should be taken and that decision is enforced. The groups do not get involved in the daily functions and decision-making powers of the school administration or in school government or policy formation.

A third tertiary prevention program is Denver's "Junior Partners with Senior Partners." This program links youths and adult community volunteers in a relationship that seeks mutual honesty, open communication and value sharing.

It targets youths 10 to 18 years of age who may or may not be in trouble but who have been in trouble in the past and who might get in trouble again without immediate intervention.

Yet another approach uses parental involvement in court, making parents responsible for their children's actions and, in some instances, fining parents for delinquent acts committed by their children. This approach is gaining momentum in some areas.

The American Psychological Association (n.d., p. 58) notes:

> Several promising techniques have been identified for treating children who already have adopted aggressive patterns of behavior. These include problem-solving skills training for the child, child management training for the parents (e.g., anger control, negotiation and positive reinforcement), family therapy and interventions at school or in the community.

Characteristics of Effective Intervention Programs

Two primary characteristics are associated with effective intervention programs (American Psychological Association, pp. 53–54): (1) they draw on the understanding of developmental and sociocultural risk factors leading to antisocial behavior and (2) they use theory-based intervention strategies known to change behavior, tested program designs and validated, objective measurement techniques to assess outcomes. Other key criteria identified by the American Psychological Association (pp. 54–55) include the following:

▌ They begin as early as possible to interrupt the "trajectory toward violence."
▌ They address aggression as part of a constellation of antisocial behaviors in the child or youth.
▌ They include multiple components that reinforce each other across the child's everyday social contexts: family, school, peer groups, media and community.
▌ They take advantage of developmental "windows of opportunity": points at which interventions are especially needed or especially likely to make a difference. Such windows of opportunity include transitions in children's lives: birth, entry into preschool, the beginning of elementary school and adolescence.

▌ Effective treatment programs often take advantage of windows of opportunity, times when treatment is especially needed (in crises) or likely to make a difference (during transition periods).

The Association (p. 54) suggests that adolescence is an important window of opportunity "because the limits-testing and other age-appropriate behaviors of adolescents tend to challenge even a functional family's well-developed patterns of interaction." In addition (pp. 54–55):

> [A]ntisocial behaviors tend to peak during adolescence, and many adolescents engage in sporadic aggression or antisocial behavior. Programs that prepare children to navigate the developmental crises of adolescence may help prevent violence by and toward the adolescent.

TREATMENT PROGRAMS FOR CHILDREN AND JUVENILES WHO HAVE BEEN ABUSED

A model of child abuse has been developed by Gomes-Schwartz and Horowitz (1988, p. 1), reproduced in Figure 14–1. Note that the child's development and the treatment provided are influenced by the family's and institution's reaction to the abuse.

The treatment in this case is the Family Crisis Program (FCP), Division of Child Psychiatry at the Tufts New England Medical Center in Boston. The treatment approach is based on "crisis theory," which begins with the assumption that at certain times in people's lives they are faced with insurmountable obstacles requiring more than the ordinary coping mechanisms.

■ Crisis intervention capitalizes on windows of opportunity when the individual may be especially receptive to treatment that establishes new approaches to problem-solving.

As noted by Gomes-Schwartz and Horowitz (1988, p. 11): "Thus, crisis intervention may not only relieve the distress of the individual, but it may also strengthen and modify the individual's capacity to withstand future stress."

FCP, drawing upon crisis theory, incorporates rapid intervention, outreach, focal treatment involving 12 intensive sessions and liaison with other agencies.

The Metropolitan Court Judges Committee (1986, p. 29) states in the introduction to the recommendations for treatment and planning for deprived children:

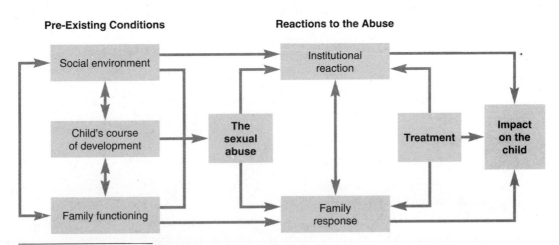

■ **FIGURE 14–1 A Model of Child Abuse**

SOURCE: Beverly Gomes-Schwartz and Jonathan Horowitz, *Child Sexual Abuse Victims and Their Treatment.* (Washington, D.C.: U.S. Department of Justice, National Institute for Juvenile Justice and Delinquency Prevention, July 1988), p. 1.

Although child victims frequently require help to alleviate the guilt they are experiencing about their family's problems, they are often placed into foster care without additional supports or necessary therapeutic intervention. The lack of immediate and effective treatment and coordinated planning and resources represents serious problems. Providing an adequate number of foster homes, trained foster parents, special homes for special needs children, emergency shelter care facilities and other alternatives prior to termination of parental rights are also critical. After termination, providing resources for the treatment and subsequent adoption of deprived children is the wisest investment society can make. An abused or neglected child, whether removed from the home or remaining in the home, needs assistance which is often not provided.

Although 80 percent of all substantiated cases of abuse or neglect receive "casework counseling," given the excessive caseloads, this response must be seen as more paperwork than counseling. (The ratio of cases to workers in some large jurisdictions has exceeded an unrealistic 150:1, allowing less than an hour per month for each deprived child.)

Treatment Recommendations of the Metropolitan Court Judges Committee

The following recommendations were made by the Committee (pp. 30–34):

▮ *Immediate treatment.* Treatment of abused and neglected children must be immediate, thorough, and coordinated among responsible agencies.

▮ *Family focus.* Treatment provided to children through court or agency intervention should involve the entire family or focus on family relationships and should stress the primary responsibility of the parents for their children's welfare and protection. Family involvement, where at all possible, should be stabilized rather than disrupted as a result of intervention and treatment.

▮ *Parental responsibility.* Child protection agencies and the courts should require parental responsibility for children's well-being.

▮ *Positive parental behavior.* Judges must have authority to order treatment for the parents, to require other positive conduct and to impose sanctions for willful failure or refusal to comply.

▮ *Substance abuse.* Substance abuse treatment, if appropriate, should be mandated for parents and their children.

▮ *Mandated treatment.* Judges must have the authority to order the treatment determined necessary and should regularly review the efficacy of such treatment.

▮ *Youthful sex offenders.* Judges must require appropriate treatment for youthful sexual offenders, many of whom have been victims of sexual abuse. The cycle of young victims of sexual abuse later becoming perpetrators of sexual abuse must be broken. Unless intensive intervention and effective treatment of such youthful sexual offenders is provided, the cycle will continue.

▮ Treatment requirements recommended by the Metropolitan Court Judges Committee include immediate treatment, family focus, parental responsibility, positive parental behavior, treatment for substance abuse, mandated treatment and treatment for youthful sexual offenders.

Service Recommendations

The Committee also made recommendations for the provision of services to juveniles (pp. 30–34):

■ *Qualified treatment personnel.* Child protection caseworkers must be screened, trained, and certified to improve child protection services and treatment. People who work with deprived children should undergo detailed background investigation.

■ *Volunteer assistance.* Screened, qualified, and trained volunteers should be used to enhance the quality of services.

■ *Foster homes.* A sufficient number of foster homes, adequately reimbursed and provided access to treatment and support services, should be established. Strict screening, improved recruiting, professional training, licensing requirements and adequate compensation will encourage quality foster care.

■ *Foster care drift.* Frequently moving children from foster home to foster home is detrimental to children's physical and emotional well-being and must be reduced.

■ *Children with special needs.* Specialized foster homes and foster parents should be available for children with special needs. Older, minority, disabled, or seriously abused children require particular care, with specialized foster homes, trained foster parents, and continuing agency assistance tailored to their needs.

■ *Homeless children.* Homeless and runaway children must be provided proper emergency shelter facilities as well as necessary services. Much of the problem of at-risk or exploited children could be alleviated by improved and expanded emergency shelter facilities, with necessary services and counseling. Children who are "broke and on the streets" are particularly vulnerable.

■ In providing services, the Committee recommended that treatment personnel be well qualified, that volunteer assistance be used, that quality foster homes be available, that foster care drift be reduced, that children with special needs be provided special foster homes and that shelters be established for homeless children.

Permanency Recommendations

The final set of recommendations made by the Committee dealt with planning for **permanency** for children, that is, assuring the most lasting placement or solution possible: "The Court must find a way to provide a permanent and loving home for the child" (pp. 33–34).

■ *Termination of parental rights.* When there is clear, convincing evidence that the parents' conduct would legally permit termination of parental rights, and it is in the child's best interests to do so, termination should proceed expeditiously. The immediate availability of adoptive parents should not be required to terminate parental rights.

■ *Alternative permanent plans.* When reunification is not possible or termination of parental rights is not in the child's best interests, courts should consider other permanent plans. In some cases, terminating a parent's rights is inappropriate and the court should examine such alternatives as:

—Long-term custody—in a homelike setting such as placement with relatives, substitute or extended families, and foster grandparents;

—Permanent or temporary guardianship—after a finding of dependency and removal; or

—Any other solution short of termination leading to permanency for the child.

∎ *Expedited adoption process.* When needed, adoption should proceed as quickly as possible. Foster parents should be able to adopt their foster child.

∎ *Subsidized adoptions.* Subsidized adoption programs should be more widely available and used for special needs and hard-to-place children.

∎ In planning for permanency, the Committee recommends that when necessary, parental rights may be terminated, that alternative plans should be made if parental rights are not terminated and that the adoption process be expedited, including providing subsidized adoption programs for hard-to-place children.

DIVERSION ALTERNATIVES—COMMUNITY-BASED TREATMENT PROGRAMS

Zachariah (1992, p. 202) stresses: "The ideal placement maintains a balance of community protection, juvenile accountability and juvenile development." He lists the following as options currently available in most jurisdictions:

∎ Intensive community supervision (at least twice a week).
∎ Tracking (hiring staff to exclusively monitor juveniles).
∎ Electronic monitoring.
∎ Report centers (set up in accessible locations).
∎ Home detention.
∎ Home tutoring.
∎ Mentor tutoring.
∎ Day treatment.
∎ Evening and weekend programs (providing tutoring, recreation, work and treatment services).
∎ Work and apprenticeship (to develop a work ethic, a sense of responsibility, and a feeling of accomplishment).
∎ Restitution (in services or in cash).
∎ Community service (cleaning up parks, working in nursing homes, etc.).
∎ Volunteers (to tutor youths and supervise work and recreational activities).

Indiana has developed a continuum of alternative programs designed to provide services for offenders ranging from shoplifters to murderers.* Payne and Lee (1990, pp. 103–104) outline these "alternatives that work:"

---

*Reprinted from the October 1990 issue of *Corrections Today,* with the permission of the American Correctional Association, Laurel, MD.

■ **Project Challenge:** Project Challenge is a six-week program aimed at breaking the behavior cycles that lead youths to trouble. It includes a three-week wilderness camp that encourages youths to trust themselves and their peers, and provides vocational, family and individual counseling.

■ **Ivy Tech:** Ivy Tech is part of the state's technical school system, and offers vocational education for troubled youths who are functionally illiterate or in need of remedial education or extra attention in the classroom. Students learn skills such as auto mechanics, welding or how to use computers. Many students then find jobs in the community.

■ **Electronic Surveillance:** For four years, electronic surveillance has allowed Marion County to make sure students are home when they are supposed to be. The devices allow them to assume responsibility while ensuring community safety. Costs are relatively low—about $4.70 a day for electronic surveillance versus $55 a day for detention.

■ **Run, Don't Run:** Run, Don't Run is aimed at youths who have literally run from encounters with law enforcement officers. Developed by the juvenile court with the Indianapolis Police Department and the Marion County Sheriff's Department, the program is intended to establish respect between young offenders and law enforcement officials. Youths learn from police officers and a judge or magistrate how fleeing, resisting and striking police officers influences the officers' actions.

■ **Visions:** Visions is designed for the serious first referral or repeat offender who comes into contact with the court system. Youths are admitted to the juvenile detention center for one night, followed by a morning lesson about the juvenile justice system. That afternoon juveniles tour the Indiana Boys/Girls School and the Marion County Jail.

■ **Operation Kids CAN (Care About Neighborhoods):** Operation Kids CAN began in the summer of 1987, when more than 200 youths on probation picked up 3.5 tons of neighborhood trash. The program has now joined forces with the Indianapolis Clean City Committee. Youths spend mornings learning about the juvenile justice system. Then, they work in structured community service projects such as cleaning vacant lots and picking up garbage. In 1989, this program received a United Way award for outstanding community service.

■ **Garden Project:** In the Garden Project, youths and their parents plant vegetables and flowers during the summer. The program shifts in winter to craft projects. A greenhouse is now under construction at the new court complex.

■ **National Corrective Training Institute (NCTI):** NCTI instructors have small group discussions with youths charged with misdemeanors. They talk with children about values, attitudes and behavior.

■ **Paint It Clean:** Paint It Clean requires youths associated with destructive gang activities to paint over gang graffiti in local neighborhoods, parks and buildings. Under the supervision of court staff, Paint It Clean helps eliminate gang claims to territory and allows communities to reclaim their neighborhoods.

■ **Summer Youth Program:** The Summer Youth Program gives youths the chance to go canoeing, horseback riding, camping, hiking, caving and on a field trip to the Indiana Amusement Park. Probation's Dispositional Alternatives Department also sponsors monthly field trips throughout the year.

■ **Basketball:** For 11 years, the court and the Twilight Optimist Club have sponsored a basketball league for youths. This collaboration gives juveniles the chance to participate in structured recreation with positive role models.

■ **Near Peer Tutoring:** The Near Peer Tutoring program targets junior high school probationers having trouble in at least one class. High school honor students and adult volunteers tutor youths weekly at neighborhood probation offices. The program won the Governor's Exemplary Project Award in 1987.

Project New Pride

A model of community-based services that mirrors the Youth Service Bureau concept is Project New Pride, started in Denver, Colorado, in 1973. This program is geared toward the violent and serious offender rather than the minor offender and nondelinquent. The specific goals of the program are to work hard-core delinquents back into the mainstream and to reduce the number of rearrests. The program focuses on getting the youths back in school and on getting them jobs. It is a holistic approach. As noted in a program description (*Project New Pride,* p. 7):

> All facets of the child's life must be examined and all treatment services must be coordinated to ensure the greatest benefit for the youth. Raising a youth's academic performance is not sufficient if the family income is so low that he or she is hungry; warning a girl of the penalty for prostitution is not sufficient if she has no job skills; getting a job for a youth is not sufficient if he or she doesn't know how to apply for another job later; enrolling a youth in the school is not sufficient if he or she needs professional help with a severe emotional disturbance. New Pride youths usually suffer from a combination of problems. It takes a combination of services to help them. New Pride achieves "one-step program-ming" through intensive supervision from the youth's intake through the end of his or her involvement with the program.

The staff philosophy of New Pride programs, expressed in the greeting to youths at the door, aptly describes the theory behind the unique operation of Project New Pride:

> If we fish for you,
> You will live for a day.
> If we teach you to fish,
> You will live for a lifetime.

Project New Pride uses a holistic (treating the whole person) approach to work with hard-core delinquents.

Foster Homes

Foster homes are an important diversion alternative for many youth, both those who are victims and those who have been victimizers. Berquist (1994, p. 8) describes one such home run by Dianne Jensen, which has had success with teenagers with emotional and behavioral difficulties. Jensen dislikes the term *foster home,* feeling she provides a true home to those who come to live with her. According to Jensen: "Love is the catalyst that can help juveniles develop trust and motivation for success." Love, plus strict rules, firmly enforced and efforts to enhance their self-image are key to Jensen's success.

Intensive Supervision/Parole/Probation/Aftercare

To help juveniles identified as high-risk recidivists, Altschuler and Armstrong (1990, p. 170) developed a framework for aftercare based on five principles:

- Preparing youths for gradually increased responsibility and freedom in the community.
- Helping youths become involved in the community and getting the community to interact with them.
- Working with youths and their families, peers, schools and employers to identify the qualities necessary for success.
- Developing new resources and supports where needed.
- Monitoring and testing youths and the community on their abilities to interact.

Altschuler and Armstrong (p. 170) caution that assessment is a critical first step in determining if intensive supervision is a viable alternative because "[A]mple evidence suggests that subjecting low- or moderate-risk offenders to intensive supervision may lead to increased technical violations and subsequent unnecessary incarceration."

Day Treatment Programs

Day treatment programs are becoming more numerous and more popular as a diversion alternative, as attested to by the first national conference on day treatment held in March of 1993. This conference was attended by almost 200 juvenile justice practitioners from 30 states. Day treatment programs are designed around school settings or evening and weekend reporting centers. They have been found to be a cost-effective alternative to more costly residential programs for status offenders.

Alternative Schools

The Robert F. Kennedy School is a secure treatment facility in Massachusetts for hard-core delinquents. Konitzer (1993, p. 213) says: "The school's primary mission is 'to effect optimal growth and development of each resident in order to guarantee successful reintegration into the community'." The school has an academic program and a treatment regime. The treatment regime uses the "milieu therapy" approach, meaning every interaction between juveniles and staff is considered therapeutic. The program also offers counseling to families of the juveniles in the program.

Giddings State Home and School, a "way station for young criminals," is described by MacCormack (1993). This school houses the "worst of juvenile offenders." More than 100 of the 320 offenders are in for capital murder, murder or voluntary manslaughter. Another 100 are in for attempted murder, and many of the rest for crimes against the person such as rape or kidnapping. Stan DeGerolami, the assistant superintendent, says: "We punish kids by confining them to this facility and making them answerable for what they do here and accountable for what they did to get here." The underlying belief is that these young offenders have been "socialized" into who they are and that the school can "resocialize" them to fit into society. As noted by MacCormack (1993, p. 1A): "All are here on the theory that youthful offenders, even the most coldly criminal, are susceptible to rehabilitation."

Youth assigned to Giddings eventually leave for either freedom or prison. DeGerolami further notes: "We don't want to release kids who are dangerous. I don't want a kid to leave here and rape my daughter or assault my mother, so we make our recommendations very carefully."

Youth Centers

A youth center in Beloit, Kansas, is the only facility in Kansas for female juvenile offenders. One of the major challenges it faces is that 55 to 60 percent of the offenders admit to having been sexually abused. As noted by Moore (1991, p. 42): "Sexual abuse itself does not lead to delinquency; it is more the way in which a youth deals with the sexual abuse." The Beloit youth center has identified several factors that appear to have a significant role in fostering delinquent behavior (Moore, p. 42): anger and aggression toward others; alienation, resulting in withdrawal from positive relationships; distrust of authority and adults; self-blame; substance abuse and running away.

The voluntary program at the Beloit Center is held in a small house with comfortable chairs and couches and a kitchen. What happens during the group meetings is kept confidential, and the staff is specially trained in working with sexually abused juveniles. The goals of the program include the following (Moore, 1991, p. 45):

∎ Restoring self-confidence and self-esteem.
∎ Instilling the attitude of being a survivor instead of a victim.
∎ Restoring a sense of control and power over their lives.
∎ Restoring a sense of control over their sexuality and developing healthy sexual attitudes.
∎ Developing an understanding of how sexual abuse has affected their lives and ways of using positive coping skills.

The Southwest Utah Youth Center is a 10-bed rural detention center that is one of 14 sites using a federal program, Law Related Education (LRE). The program brings in local police officers, attorneys, judges and legislators in an effort to make the law relevant to these juveniles. The objectives of the program include the following (Weaver, 1993, pp. 174, 176):

∎ Give students a practical understanding of one or more aspects of law and show them how the legal system is relevant to their lives.
∎ Allow students to interact positively with each other, staff and community members.
∎ Enable students to begin to understand the need to be an effective citizen.
∎ Reinforce other important life skills, such as critical thinking, decision making and problem solving.
∎ Reinforce students' understanding of the role that laws, lawyers, law enforcement officers and the legal system play in their community.

LRE uses small group discussion, role playing, case studies and other types of interactive learning to keep student interest. Although no statistics on recidivism are yet available, the program reports that incidents of aggressive acts and rule violations have been "reduced tremendously."

Pennsylvania has a youth center that crosses generational lines. According to Maniglia (1993, p. 146): "The center is a true multipurpose facility. It houses a secure detention facility where youths are held awaiting adjudication and disposition as well as a courtroom in which the juvenile court judge hears all cases involving children. Attached to the building, but separate from the detention center, is a shelter housing abused and neglected children . . . and status offenders. . . ."

Seniors volunteer as role models and mentors for youths housed in the secure detention center. Weisman (1994, p. 57) notes: "An institution provides some children with a first chance to be taken care of by adults who do not hit or even yell." In addition, through the Teens and Tots program, youths learn parenting skills firsthand by working with the young children from the shelter.

Texas has a similar program, which uses a foster grandparent program in the county's juvenile detention center. As noted by Briscoe (1990, p. 92): "Even children who are sometimes hostile and aggressive work calmly and quietly in the presence of a foster grandparent."

Since the 1950s, the emphasis in most residential facilities for juvenile delinquents has followed a custody/clinical model, treating delinquent youths as deviant or abnormal. This approach has met with limited success. Ferrainola and Grissom (1990) suggest that a different model, a sociological model—stressing a positive environment—might be more effective. They give as an example, Glen Mills, Delaware County, Pennsylvania (pp. 118, 120):

> Glen Mills is the nation's most thoroughly documented program based on a sociological model. Students there are immersed in the most positive, carefully monitored and highly structured environment they will ever experience. The group culture—which is based on values of respect, loyalty, persistence, involvement and pride—is what changes the students, not any particular therapies or set of activities.
>
> Glen Mills' experience since 1974 suggests that it is not large institutions, but the custody/clinical model, which should be abandoned. . . .

The feature of the daily experience at Glen Mills that clearly sets it apart is confrontation. Everyone in the school, administrators, staff, and students are responsible for confronting negative behavior—never the student. The purpose is to instill positive norms of behavior. Peer group status is earned through positive behavior, which is also amply recognized.

Students at Glen Mills are successful not only academically, with over 1,000 students earning GEDs in the past six years, but also in sports, having won local, state and national championships.

Paint Creek Youth Center is a private correctional program for juveniles in New York. This treatment program centers on the concept of positive peer community and helping youths get along with each other. As noted by Speirs (1988, p. 3): "The premise of the positive peer community is that youth need help, particularly from their peers, to learn acceptable behaviors and develop positive, supportive, caring relationships." The program also builds on the work of nationally recognized psychologists William Glasser and Stanton Samenow and their emphasis on personal responsibility.

The Paint Creek Youth Center uses a point-and-level system designed to provide immediate, clear, consistent feedback on behavior and its acceptability. Youths enter the program at the orientation level and work their way up to the top level. In addition to learning a vocation, physical fitness and recreational therapy programs are also important to the Center. In addition, it has a family therapy and support component as well as intensive supervision as the aftercare alternative for the first three or four weeks of release from the program. Speirs (1988, p. 6) concludes that the program:

> . . .[R]epresents a viable alternative to traditional forms of correctional services. It combines treatment, education, employment, life skills, and specialized counseling and support services into one coordinated approach and provides staff and residents with a secure setting through intensive staff and peer supervision and influence. The Paint Creek Youth Center offers a unique way to facilitate changes in behavior and attitudes in a segment of the juvenile population that has become both problematic and frustrating to communities across the Nation.

"Second Chance" Camps

The Eckerd Youth Challenge Program first opened in Indian Head, Maryland, in 1987 as a community-based alternative to placing delinquents in training schools. Among the principles and practices of this program are the following (Stepanik, 1991, pp. 48–50):

- Positive relationships.
- Family involvement. Youths earn home visits (furloughs) and family is encouraged to visit.
- Challenging activities.
- Structure and discipline.
- Clinical and educational services.
- Aftercare.

The program is geared to improve self-esteem and behavior by focusing on challenges specifically designed to improve interpersonal and living skills. This experiential, action-oriented program includes canoe trips, hikes, a ropes course and community service projects.

Thistledew Camp, located on Minnesota's Iron Range, is operated by the Minnesota Department of Corrections. Like any other camp, it offers fishing, swimming, trapping, rock climbing and the like, but it also involves hard work and education. The camp does not accept youths who are assaultive. Most youths have a 100-day "stay" at the camp. In the final three weeks they go through the "Challenge," which is three days spent camping alone in the woods. It is not survival training; the youths take food and water along. It does give them time to themselves to think and to just "be." Immediately after these "solos," the youths go on a week-long wilderness trek in groups of 10. As noted by one of the camp leaders: "A lot of them have never known what it's like to get through any type of problem. It's why the suicide rate among teens is so high. This teaches them that they can make it through something difficult" (Mugford, 1994, p. 4).

Florida is experimenting with Youth Environmental Service camps, better known in Florida as swamp camps. In "U.S. Tries Ecological Tack to Counter Juvenile Crimes," the *Los Angeles Times* (1994, p. 7A) notes:

> The camp, modeled on the Civilian Conservation Corps of the 1930s, is the first of what White House officials envision as "last chance" detention centers on federal lands where felons under the age of 18 will work on environment cleanup projects while providing low-cost labor to the National Park Service.

The Florida camp is based at an abandoned sawmill which serves as home for up to 20 young offenders convicted of violent crimes. Supervised by counselors rather than guards, they spend up to a year cleaning trails, getting rid of weeds and trees and building boardwalks. They also receive vocational training at the camp.

A program also focusing on giving serious, chronic offenders a last chance operates at the Fort Smallwood Marine Institute near Baltimore, Maryland, where juvenile offenders learn maritime skills. Mardon (1991, p. 33) notes: "The youths . . . are gradually given more responsibility at sea. While they learn, their confidence and self-esteem grow." The program uses a point system. Juveniles earn points for participating in discussion, attendance and leadership. They can use the points to "buy" trips and other privileges. Says Mardon (p. 34): "Underlying the program's point system is the juveniles' understanding that if they do not succeed, they are likely to wind up in prison or dead." Mardon (p. 36) shows the success of the program by noting that: "Since the program opened, about 225 youths have completed the program. Program officials say the recidivism rate is between 20 and 30 percent, far lower than the rate at most secure facilities."

PRISON ALTERNATIVE—BOOT CAMPS

Oklahoma's Regimented Inmate Discipline (RID) is one of the country's oldest boot camps, opening in 1984. As noted by Frank (1991, p. 102): "The intense, highly structured program is designed to get offenders to the point where they can meet the challenges of daily life in the community." The boot camp is organized into a three-platoon system, with inmates entering at the third platoon and working their way up to the first platoon. According to Frank (p. 105): "The RID program works because it combines programming and discipline. Each is vitally important to the preparing of better educated, more confident and disciplined young men who can succeed as law-abiding, productive members of their communities."

■ Most boot camps target first-time offenders convicted of nonviolent crimes.

Inmates who successfully complete boot camp in Willow River, Minnesota, can have as much as two years taken off their original sentence, but it is not an easy six months. As noted by deFiebre (1993, p. 1A), the khaki-uniformed inmates spend "16-hour days full of military-style discipline and drill, strenuous physical training, manual labor, education and drug treatment. . . ."

Inmates in Butler Shock, New York, are sentenced to six months in what Waldron (1990, p. 145) calls "part of the newest fad in corrections—boot camp-style prisons." The superintendent there asserts: "We do break them down and then build them back up. Everything we do is done for a purpose." If the inmates make it through, they win parole, no matter how long the judge sentences them to serve (Waldron, 1990). In a typical group, about half make it to graduation.

MacKenzie (1993, pp. 22–23) describes a typical day in boot camp:

Upon arrival at the boot camp prison, male inmates have their heads shaved (females may be permitted short haircuts) and are informed of the strict program rules. At all times they are required to address staff as "Sir" or "Ma'am," must request permission to speak, and must refer to themselves as "this inmate." Punishments for even minor rule violations are summary and certain, frequently involving physical exercise such as push-ups or running in place. A major rule violation can result in dismissal from the program.

In a typical boot camp program for adult offenders, the 10- to 16-hour day begins with pre-dawn reveille. Inmates dress quickly and march to an exercise yard where they participate in an hour or two of physical training and drill. Following this they march to breakfast in a dining hall where they must stand at attention while waiting in line and move in a military manner when the line advances. Inmates are required to stand behind their chairs until commanded to

▌ *Standing at attention in the Lakeview Shock Camp, Brocton, New York, inmates must eat quickly and are not permitted to talk.*

sit and must eat without conversation. After breakfast they march to work sites where they participate in hard physical labor that frequently involves community service such as picking up litter in State parks or along highways. When the 6- to 8-hour work day is over, offenders return to the compound where they participate in more exercise and drill. Dinner is followed by evening programs that include counseling, life skills training, academic education, or drug education and treatment.

As their performance and time in the program warrants, shock incarceration inmates gradually earn more privileges and responsibility. A special hat or uniform may be the outward display of their new status. Those who successfully finish the program usually attend an elaborate graduation ceremony with visitors and family invited to attend. Awards are often presented to acknowledge progress made during the program, and the inmates may perform the drill routines they have practiced throughout their time in the boot camp.

Taylor (1992) stresses that boot camps must be tailored to fit juveniles' needs. He lists the following recommendations of the American Correctional Association for successful boot camps for juveniles (p. 124):

- It is important to focus on concrete feelings and self-concept, since both are strongly related to delinquent behavior. The more negative feelings a youth has, the lower his or her self-esteem. Counseling in the experiential context is powerful because it deals with daily activities in a real rather than artificial environment.
- It is important to provide discipline through physical conditioning. Physical conditioning improves health and boosts self-esteem, which helps reduce aggressive misbehavior.
- Structure, as well as discipline, is important since these juveniles tend to be manipulative and defensive.
- It is important to help the juveniles feel they have a sense of control over their lives, and to identify their strengths and channel them in positive directions. The experiential learning aspects of the program should help develop this sense of control.
- Successful programming involves literacy, academic and vocational education; intensive value clarification; and resocialization that makes participants aware of the long-term effects of their behavior.
- It is necessary for the juveniles to actively participate in the program for some time before they can begin drawing their own conclusions rather than having others do it for them.

In Georgia, boot camps are known as Special Alternative Incarceration (SAI). As noted by Bowen (1991, p. 100), Georgia's boot camps are unique in their five-tier approach extending from least to most restrictive:

1. Probation detention centers (PDCs) to rehabilitate low-risk offenders. Beds turned over every 120 days.
2. Probation/SAI Boot Camps for offenders needing more severe attention. Beds rolled over every 90 days.
3. Inmate Boot Camps for potential parolees. Beds turned over every 90 days.
4. Intensive Discipline Program (IDP) units for severe offenders assigned to isolation because of misconduct. Beds turned over every 30 days.
5. Intensive follow-up. Following boot camp, those who are released into the community have intensive supervision for 90 days.

Boot camps should be thought of as a foundation rather than as a "cure" according to Hengesh (1991). He believes most offenders entering the boot camps lack basic life skills, are in poor physical condition, have quit school and have had frequent encounters with the justice system. Their self-esteem is low and they are viewed by others as losers.

Hengesh (p. 106) contends: "Young offenders have a false sense of pride and have built up resentment for authority. This must be stripped away before we can begin to make any change." This is one of the primary functions of the prison boot camp, just as it is in a military boot camp. They are intended to provide a "foundation of discipline, responsibility and self-esteem" to be built on. Hengesh (p. 108) stresses that: "The programming, physical conditioning and work programs must all be geared to showing offenders they can achieve, and that it feels good to achieve."

The Effectiveness of Boot Camp

A report by the U.S. General Accounting Office (GAO) states that boot camps are cheaper than prison but that the long-term impact on recidivism is uncertain. The report notes that boot camps are still too new to adequately assess their effectiveness, but they do appear to be a cost-effective way to reduce prison crowding.

MacKenzie and Souryal (1991, p. 96), in a report on a survey of boot camps, note that all the boot camps had some sort of drug treatment and education in their programs. They agree that many offenders clearly need such treatment and education, but "it is not clear whether these programs are the most effective way to provide it."

As noted by Hengesh (1991, p. 106):

Boot camps spark conflicting opinions in the corrections arena. The public views them as places where young offenders pay their debts to society by working hard under strict discipline. Legislators see them as less expensive alternatives to prison for non-violent offenders. Many academicians consider them throwbacks to outdated correctional methods. And some corrections professionals see them as a threat, because if they really work we may not need as many prisons.

Hengesh suggests that each group is partially right, but that most are missing the underlying purpose of boot camp, which he sees as building a foundation, as stated earlier.

Arguments Against Boot Camps

Not all practitioners favor boot camps. Maynard (1991, p. 6) notes: "There has been much debate on the value of using such programs in corrections, where young, non-violent offenders—often seen as impressionable and salvageable— have become a target population." Among the dissenters is Salerno (1991, p. 28) who believes: "Unfortunately, boot camp programs are being applauded prematurely." He also notes: "Corrections seems to be particularly susceptible to accepting a new program as a panacea without proper research or follow-up study." Salerno cites the following shortcomings of boot camps:

- The program is too short and ends with the offender returning to the same criminal environment.
- The emphasis on coercion is likely to result in "game-playing" and not the desired results.
- They are not as cost effective as claimed.

Salerno (p. 32) concludes: "Boot camps may possess some degree of glamour and attractiveness. They may also have a theoretical foundation. But there are too many practical problems and too few proven benefits."

EXEMPLARY PROGRAMS

The following treatment programs or research projects received the OJJDP's Gould-Wysinger Award (GWA), which was described in the preceding chapter. These program descriptions were written by Pam Allen (1993), director of special projects for the Coalition of Juvenile Justice and overseer of administration of the award solicitation process.

Juvenile Intervention Project, Colorado

The goals of the Juvenile Intervention Project are jail removal and deinstitutionalization of status offenders. A training program for sheriff's officers explains screening criteria and procedures. Officers who perform intake screening are trained to provide status offenders with appropriate services. The program contracts with a host home to ensure a bed is available for status offenders. Crisis intervention, temporary holding or attendant care, and volunteer tracking and mentoring are also provided.

The program resulted in an immediate decrease in juvenile arrests and detention, and new patrol officers now participate in a special 4-hour field training program. (GWA)

Juvenile Detention Center, Western Nebraska Juvenile Services

The Juvenile Detention Center was established to provide programming, intervention, and rehabilitation services for juveniles. A 20-bed facility serving Scotts Bluff County and the surrounding area, it is the only secure juvenile detention center in western Nebraska.

The Center has a transitional living program designed to provide juveniles with the knowledge, skill, and experience to live independently. A family preservation component encourages the family to cooperate in the reconciliation of the offender to the family unit. A substance abuse program provides intervention and treatment. An educational program offers four types of programs: class continuation, credit work, GED programs, and college. The Center also offers a 4-H program, a craft program, and instruction in creative writing. Opportunities to attend church services are available.

As a result of the Center's programs, recidivism has been reduced by 50 percent. Acceptance of the Center has grown as other communities and counties increase their use of the facility. (GWA)

Partnership for Learning, Inc., Maryland

Partnership for Learning (PFL) was established in 1991 to screen first-time juvenile offenders appearing before juvenile court in Baltimore City and to identify and assist offenders diagnosed as learning disabled. After first-time offenders have been identified, tested, and interviewed, the requirements for participating in PFL are presented. Once an agreement has been executed, the child's case is postponed, and the child is matched with a tutor trained in a special reading and spelling program. Of the children matched with tutors, over 80 percent have successfully completed or are actively involved in the program and have not reoffended.

PFL is a joint project of the Office of the State's Attorney for Baltimore City, the Office of the Public Defender, the Department of Juvenile Services, the Maryland State Department of Education, the Baltimore City Department of Education, and the Maryland Associates for Dyslexic Adults and Youth. It has gained national and international attention as a cost-effective program that reduces the rate of recidivism among youthful offenders. (GWA)

Fremont County Youth Services, Wyoming

Begun in 1983, this program received its first OJJDP funding in 1988. Its goals are to improve the efficiency and the effective use of the juvenile justice system and existing services in Fremont County, to develop programs to serve county youth, to assist the county in developing policies for secure detention of juveniles as well as for alternatives to detention in the county jail, and to reduce the liability of the board of commissioners and Sheriff regarding detention of juveniles prior to a court hearing. The program provides report/intake for law enforcement and the county attorney, a deferred prosecution program, a youth council coordinator, a work alternatives program, a sentencing alternatives program, presentence investigation for county courts, formal probation supervision, limited predispositional reports for juvenile court, home detention program supervision, 24-hour intake at county jails, youth advocacy, a cooperative agreement to provide staff-secure shelter care, and a jail removal transportation subsidy program.

Serving hundreds of children a year in a county of more than 9,000 square miles, the program has enabled the county to address the mandates of the Juvenile Justice and Delinquency Prevention Act. (GWA)

Earn-It Project, New Hampshire

Earn-It is a victim restitution program that serves as a sentencing alternative for juvenile court and the Juvenile Conference Committee. Juvenile offenders are referred to the program for monetary and community service work placements. Earn-It arranges the work placement in an area business, nonprofit agency, or municipality by matching the offender's strengths with the needs of the worksite and monitors the youth's performance.

Since 1988 Earn-It has worked with more than 400 juvenile offenders in 17 towns within the jurisdiction of the Keene District Court. Over 80 percent of the offenders have completed their court-ordered community service obligations and restitution to their victims. Participants have performed hundreds of hours of community service work and have given thousands of dollars to victims. The recidivism rate for youths completing the program is below 30 percent. (GWA)

Juvenile Work Restitution, Alabama

Located in Tuscaloosa, this program instills a sense of personal accountability, improves behavior, and reduces recidivism. Jobs are created in the public and private sectors, and juvenile offenders are matched to an appropriate job. Offenders work to reimburse victims and provide community service.

In operation since 1987, the program has helped reduce minority overrepresentation in the State school and develop greater confidence in the juvenile justice system. Recidivism has been reduced by 10 percent. (GWA)

Prosocial Gang, New York

This unique intervention program implements Aggression Replacement Training (ART) with gang members who are involved in delinquent behavior. The program is conducted at two Brooklyn sites—the Brownsville Community Neighborhood Action Center and Youth DARES. ART improves prosocial skills, moral reasoning, and anger control by channeling aggressive behavior into a positive force so gang members become a constructive influence in the community.

Four evaluations found that the ART program significantly improves the quality of the youths' interpersonal skills; enhances their ability to reduce and control anger; decreases the level of egocentricity and increases concern for the needs of others; substantially decreases antisocial behaviors; substantially increases prosocial behaviors; improves community functioning, especially with peers; and decreases criminal recidivism. (GWA)

Sex Offender Assessment, Ohio

The Sex Offender Assessment research project, which involves 76 youths and 45 parents, was created to improve the assessment and treatment of juvenile sex offenders and enhance understanding of the victimization process. The project evaluates how offenders attempt to gain a victim's trust; what types of nonsexual behaviors are engaged in prior to the abuse; and how enticements, bribes, threats, and coercion are used to obtain cooperation in sexual activity. The last part of the project is to disseminate the study findings to practitioners during a daylong, Statewide workshop.

Prior to the project, little research was available to guide the assessment and treatment of adolescent offenders. The results will provide professionals with critically needed information and will improve caretakers' ability to treat offenders and victims. (GWA)

Study of Serious Juvenile Offenders, Virginia

This comprehensive study of serious juvenile offenders defines the population of juveniles who have been convicted in circuit court by offense and service history, compares transferred and convicted juveniles to those retained in the juvenile justice system and committed to learning centers, identifies jurisdictional variation in the transfer option, evaluates which factors influence the decisionmaking process for transfer-eligible juveniles, and develops recommendations for policymakers. Study findings are available in a detailed report.

The project makes a substantial contribution toward developing an informational base from which legislators can draw in deciding juvenile justice issues. There is a commitment to continue this important research. (GWA)

SOMETIMES YOU NEED A WIZARD

Knowledge, experience and a true interest in youth are needed to make prevention and treatment programs successful. Sometimes more is needed—a **wizard** as noted by Beyer (1991, p. 166): "The best juvenile programs start with a visionary leader, a wizard." Beyer (p. 172) suggests:

> One of the strengths of the wizards who operate effective adolescent programs is that they acknowledge that the goal of treatment is to change values. Wizards take charge of the brainwashing involved in getting youths to accept values that are non-violent, non-delinquent, anti-drug, pro-learning, and pro-employment.
>
> Wizards also recognize their responsibility for helping young people cope with the conflict between their new values and what they have come from. . . .
>
> Changes in behavior and values are only possible if young people can integrate their pasts with their new selves. Wizards whose residential or day treatment programs achieve enduring change in participants train staff to invest a substantial amount of their time enabling people to accept new values without rejecting their origins. . . .
>
> Wizards are the ultimate motivators. They are not bound by training or habit to one approach. They do what works. Their programs are driven by the needs of the young people.
>
> The wizard is the heart and mind of an effective program.

SUMMARY

Effective treatment programs often take advantage of windows of opportunity, times when treatment is especially needed (in crises) or likely to make a difference (during transition periods). Crisis intervention capitalizes on windows of opportunity when the individual may be especially receptive to treatment which established new approaches to problem-solving.

Treatment requirements recommended by the Metropolitan Court Judges Committee include immediate treatment, family focus, parental responsibility, positive parental behavior, treatment for substance abuse, mandated treatment and treatment for youthful sexual offenders.

In providing services, the Committee recommended that treatment personnel be well qualified, that volunteer assistance be used, that quality foster homes be available, that foster care drift be reduced, that children with special needs be provided special foster homes and that shelters be established for homeless children.

In planning for permanency, the Committee recommended that when necessary, parental rights may be terminated, that alternative plans should be made if parental rights are not terminated and that the adoption process be expedited, including providing subsidized adoption programs for hard-to-place children.

Treatment programs are found within juvenile institutions and in diversionary programs. A recent emphasis has been the use of boot camps for juveniles. Most boot camps target first-time offenders convicted of nonviolent crimes.

■ Discussion Questions

1. Which of the recommendations of the Metropolitan Court Judges Committee do you feel are most important?
2. Do you disagree with any of the Committee's recommendations? If so, which ones and why?
3. What kind of training should foster care providers have?
4. What diversionary alternatives are available in your community?
5. Does your state have any "second chance" camps for juvenile offenders? If so, have you heard anything about them?
6. Does your state have a boot camp? If so, have you heard anything about it?
7. Do you feel boot camps are effective for nonviolent first-time offenders? Why not use them for repeat offenders? Violent offenders?
8. If you were a juvenile and were adjudicated delinquent because you stole a car, what type of treatment program do you think would be most effective?
9. Of all the treatment programs discussed in this chapter, which do you feel offer the best chance for success? The least chance for success?
10. Can you think of other treatment programs that might be tried?

■ References

Allen, Pam. "The Gould-Wysinger Awards: A Tradition of Excellence." *Juvenile Justice,* 1(Fall/Winter 1993)2: 23–28.

Altschuler, David M., and Troy L. Armstrong. "Designing an Intensive Aftercare Program for High-Risk Juveniles." *Corrections Today,* December 1990, pp. 170–171.

American Psychological Association. *Violence & Youth: Psychology's Response,* Vol. 1. *Summary Report of the American Psychological Association Commission on Violence and Youth,* vol. 1, n.d.

Berquist, Paul. "Foster Home Helping Prepare for Success." (Minneapolis/St. Paul) *Star Tribune,* 27 April 1994, p. 8.

Beyer, Marty. "First, You Find a Wizard." *Corrections Today,* April 1991, pp. 166, 172–174.

Bowen, Andy. "In Georgia: Making Boot Camps Bigger and Better." *Corrections Today,* October 1991, pp. 98–101.

Briscoe, Judy Culpepper. "In Texas: Reaching Out to Help Troubled Youths." *Corrections Today,* October 1990, pp. 90–95.

Crowe, Timothy D. *Habitual Juvenile Offenders: Guidelines for Citizen Action and Public Responses.* Serious Habitual Offender Comprehensive Action Program (SHOCAP). Washington, D.C.: Office of Juvenile Justice and Delinquency Prevention, October 1991.

deFiebre, Conrad. "Hard Times, Happy Endings: 'Boot Camp' Inmates Give Their Best for Early Release." (Minneapolis/St. Paul) *Star Tribune,* 26 April 1993, pp. 1A, 11A.

Ferrainola, Sam, and Grant Grissom. "Reforming Our Reform Schools." *Corrections Today,* December 1990, pp. 118–126.

Frank, Sue. "Oklahoma Camp Stresses Structure and Discipline." *Corrections Today,* October 1991, pp. 102–105.

General Accounting Office. "GAO: Boot Camps Cheaper, But Recidivism Impact Still Uncertain." *NCJA Justice Research,* May/June 1993, pp. 3, 5.

Gomes-Schwartz, Beverly, and Jonathan Horowitz, with Albert P. Cardarelli. *Child Sexual Abuse Victims and Their Treatment.* Washington D.C.: U.S. Department of Justice, Office of Juvenile Justice and Delinquency Prevention, July 1988.

Hengesh, Donald J. "Think of Boot Camps as a Foundation for Change, Not an Instant Cure." *Corrections Today,* October 1991, pp. 106–108.

Konitzer, Kimberly. "Youth Facility Offers Model for Treating Juvenile Offenders." *Corrections Today,* August 1993, p. 213.

MacCormack, John. "Way Station for Young Criminals: Worst of Juvenile Offenders Get Chance for Rehabilitation." *San Antonio Express News,* 26 September 1993, pp. 1A, 12A–13A.

MacKenzie, Doris Layton. "Boot Camp Prisons in 1993." *National Institute of Justice Journal,* November 1993, pp. 21–28.

MacKenzie, Doris Layton, and Claire C. Souryal. "Boot Camp Survey: Rehabilitation, Recidivism Reduction Outrank Punishment as Main Goals." *Corrections Today,* October 1991, pp. 90–96.

Maniglia, Rebecca. "Pennsylvania Youth Center Program Reaches Across Generational Lines." *Corrections Today,* August 1993, pp. 146–149.

Mardon, Steven. "On Board, Not Behind Bars." *Corrections Today,* February 1991, pp. 32–38.

Maynard, Gary D. "Boot Camps: The Ins and Outs of Imposed Discipline." *Corrections Today,* October 1991, p. 6.

Metropolitan Court Judges Committee Report. *Deprived Children: A Judicial Response.* Washington, D.C.: U.S. Government Printing Office, 1986.

Moore, James. "Addressing a Hidden Problem: Kansas Youth Center Treats Sexually Abused Female Offenders." *Corrections Today,* February 1991, pp. 40–46.

Mugford, John. "Thistledew Works to Build Up Self-Esteem." *Minnesota Sun Publications,* 27 April 1994, p. 4.

Payne, James W., and Joe E. Lee. "In Indiana: A System Designed to Accommodate Juveniles' Needs." *Corrections Today,* October 1990, pp. 100–106.

"Project New Pride." Office of Juvenile Justice and Delinquency Prevention. Washington, D.C.: U.S. Government Printing Office, 1985.

Salerno, Anthony W. "Let's Give Shock Incarceration the Boot." *Corrections Today,* October 1991, pp. 28–32.

Speirs, Verne L. "A Private-Sector Corrections Program for Juveniles: Paint Creek Youth Center." OJJDP, Update on Programs, June 1988.

Stepanik, Ron. "The Eckerd Youth Program: Challenging Juveniles to Change." *Corrections Today,* February 1991, pp. 48–50.

Taylor, William J. "Tailoring Boot Camps to Juveniles." *Corrections Today,* July 1992, pp. 122–124.

"U.S. Tries Ecological Tack to Counter Juvenile Crime." *Los Angeles Times.* Reported in (Minneapolis/St. Paul) *Star Tribune,* 19 February 1994, pp. 7A–8A.

Waldron, Thomas W. "Boot Camp Prison Offers Second Chance to Young Felons." *Corrections Today,* July 1990, pp. 144–169.

Wall, John S.; J. David Hawkins; Denise Lisiter; and Mark Fraser. "Reports of the National Juvenile Justice Assessment Centers." *Juvenile Delinquency Prevention: A Compendium of 36 Models.* Washington, D.C.: U.S. Government Printing Office, 1981.

Weaver, Ed Wynn S. "LRE Helps Youth Center Bring the Law to Life." *Corrections Today,* April 1993, pp. 174–176.

Weisman, Mary-Lou. "When Parents Are Not in the Best Interests of the Child." *The Atlantic Monthly,* July 1994, pp. 43–63.

Zachariah, John K. "Placement Key to Programs' Success." *Corrections Today,* April 1992, pp. 202–203.

Rethinking Juvenile Justice: A Global View

The historical development of the juvenile justice system has produced a magnificent monster. The time has come to face the issues and propose solutions within the framework of a total, integrated system.

Institute of Judicial Administration, American Bar Association, Juvenile Justice Standards

▋ *Do You Know?*

What areas the juvenile court has become involved in?
What a justice model is?
What competence refers to?
In what two areas our juvenile justice system might be restructured?
What country has a law against spanking children?
What countries use panels of lay people to deal with nonviolent offenders?
Who is responsible for the prevalence and severity of crime within a community?

▋ *Can You Define the Following Key Terms?*

competence, competent, coproducers of justice, John Wayne effect, paradigm, restorative justice

INTRODUCTION

The juvenile justice system, according to many, is in need of retooling, perhaps even of replacing. Critics question if the juvenile court can serve both welfare and justice. For decades reformers have promoted the Four D's of decriminalization, diversion, deinstitutionalization and due process. Critics note that reforms of the past decades have had little impact on violent crime or violent youth. In the 1990s pressure is being applied to "get tough" with juveniles, even first-time offenders, as seen in the last chapter with the rise of boot camps.

According to Breed (1990, p. 70): "We have without question reached a point where the conflict between old and new policy agendas represents a watershed in the history of juvenile justice." Breed also notes: "These ideological disputes are taking place in a political context, dominated by heightened public fear of crime, media sensationalism, tightening budgets and political rhetoric that emphasizes law and order."

Current dissatisfaction with the juvenile system is also described by Greenwood (n.d., p. 2):

> Conservative critics, focusing on public safety, fault the system for giving serious offenders too many chances on diversion or probation and for imposing terms of confinement that are too short. These critics often characterize juvenile facilities as country clubs and argue that some juveniles should be confined in more punitive settings.
>
> Liberal critics, concerned with the problems of juveniles and anxious to protect them from unwarranted State intrusions, fault the system for being too tough. Where conservative critics use the evidence of "no rehabilitative effect" to argue for more explicitly punitive sanctions, liberals use the same evidence to argue for less State involvement altogether. Liberals generally support the view that subjecting juveniles to confinement only further criminalizes them, no matter how benign the treatment.
>
> Another liberal group, heavily represented by defense attorneys and other youth advocates, deplores the lack of adequate procedural protections for juveniles. This group argues that many young people are "railroaded" through the system that offers no adequate protection of their rights.

This chapter presents some issues involving the juvenile justice system and some reforms that juvenile experts suggest might improve the system. As a means of broadening the perspective on juvenile justice, the chapter covers innovations in the juvenile justice systems of Sweden, England, Israel, Canada, New Zealand and Scotland. This is followed by a discussion of the Bureau of Justice Statistics-Princeton Project to "re-examine both the concepts and the methodologies involved in conceptualizing, measuring, and evaluating the performance of those agencies and actors comprising the American criminal justice system" (Dillingham, 1992, p. iii).

JUVENILE COURT INVOLVEMENT

Juvenile justice in the United States has become more concerned with the rules than with "the best interest of the child." The juvenile court has become deluged with both criminal and civil issues: child development, psychological concepts of understanding maturity and public policy for the good of the community.

It has become involved with:

■ Abortion (*Bellotti* v. *Baird,* 1979; *City of Akron* v. *Akron Center for Reproductive Health,* 1983; *H. L.* v. *Matheson,* 1981; *Thornburgh* v. *American College of Obstetricians and Gynecologists,* 1986).

■ School prayer (*Wallace* v. *Jaffree,* 1985).

■ Search and seizure issues in the school locker or classroom (*Dow* v. *Renfrow,* 1981; *New Jersey* v. *T. L. O.,* 1985).

■ Interracial custody and adoption (*In re R. M. G.,* 1982; *Palmore* v. *Sidoti,* 1984).

■ Adolescent judgment and maturity (*Planned Parenthood of Kansas City* v. *Ashcroft,* 1983).

■ Determination that minors are "persons" entitled to the protection under the Bill of Rights (*Parham* v. *J. R.,* 1979).

■ Legal issues in terminating parental rights (*Jewish Child Care Association* v. *Elaine S. Y.,* 1980; *Nebraska* v. *Wedige,* 1980).

The involvement of the juvenile court in these social and legal issues has subtracted, to a point, from its primary matters of delinquency adjudication and protection of the child.

■ Juvenile courts have been involved in such issues as abortion, school prayer, search and seizure, interracial custody and adoption, adolescent judgment and maturity and legal issues in terminating parental rights.

This wide range of issues illustrates the courts' involvement in nondelinquent matters and its tendency to take on matters that many believe should not be legislated, or at least should not be legislated for juveniles any differently than they are for adults, for example, abortion and search and seizure.

A JUVENILE JUSTICE MODEL

Juvenile justice is at a junction. Should it become a totally adversarial system like the adult system? Or should the system be reorganized to a new order that declares the primary objective is punishment of crime?

Charles E. Springer, Vice-Chief Justice of the Supreme Court of Nevada, is one strong advocate of reform in the juvenile justice system. A nationally

▮ *Justice Charles E. Springer*

recognized authority on juvenile justice, Springer received the Outstanding Service Award from the National Council of Juvenile and Family Court Judges in 1980. His publication *Justice for Juveniles,* published by the Office of Juvenile Justice and Delinquency Prevention, is cited extensively in this final chapter. Springer (1986, p. 4) says: "Society sets standards that determine criminal conduct. We must live up to these standards or violate them at our peril. In this case, the term 'we' includes young people, who should be held accountable for their actions and punished for their wrongs, subject to some degree of diminished responsibility." Springer (p. 2) contends that:

> The first step in doing justice for juveniles is to revise juvenile court acts throughout the country so that when juvenile courts deal with delinquent children, they operate under a justice model rather than under the present treatment of the child welfare model.

▮ A justice model is a judicial process wherein young people who come in conflict with the law are held responsible and accountable for their behavior.

This position is contrary to the social welfare philosophy of the traditional juvenile court. But, as Springer (pp. 4–5) continues:

> However, it is not necessarily contrary to the way that juvenile court judges have traditionally handled delinquent cases. Treating and caring for youthful criminals,

rather than punishing them, is simply too contrary to our experience and folk wisdom and too counterintuitive to be accepted by judges or the general public. A philosophy that denies moral guilt, abhors punishment in any form, and views criminals as innocent, hapless victims of bad social environments may be written into law, but this does not mean that it will be followed in practice.

Springer (p. 2) suggests that: "Except for certain mentally disabled and incompetent individuals, young law violators should not be considered by the juvenile courts as being 'sick' or as victims of their environments. Generally speaking, young criminals are more wrong than wronged, more the victimizers than the victims." Springer goes on to note (p. 29):

> Law violators, young and old, should be punished for their crimes. Even at a very early age, young people are not the guileless, plastic, and pliable people they are portrayed to be by those who would free them from all moral and legal responsibility. Children understand punishment and they understand fairness.

He suggests that we too often spend time trying to "diagnose the 'problem' of some young offender, when in most cases it is obvious that the criminal youth does not have a problem—he or she *is* the problem" (p. 33).

This hard-line, "get tough with juveniles" perspective has been supported by legislators and some state judges in the 1980s and 1990s. Often the issue is one of competence.

THE COMPETENCE ISSUE

The concept of **competence** greatly influences how the legal system deals with children. Adults are presumed **competent,** that is, fit or qualified to understand right from wrong. Children (i.e., minors) are presumed incompetent under the law in virtually all contexts. While children may be "heard" on behalf of themselves or may be treated as adults in a variety of circumstances, these situations are generally preceded by a qualifying process, incorporated in some specific statutory or common law exception. The statute may be specific as to whether a juvenile offender is to be tried as an adult.

■ Under law, a person's competence is conceptualized as a specific functional ability.

The word *competent* is usually followed by the phrase "to . . ." rather than presented as a general attribute of a person. An adult who is deemed incompetent to stand trial for a specific offense may still be presumed competent to function as a custodial parent or to manage financial affairs. For the adult, specific incompetence must be proven case by case.

Conversely, minor children are presumed incompetent for most purposes, without any concern for whether the children have the capacity to make required decisions in a practical sense. Children who are deemed legally competent for one purpose are often considered generally incompetent in other decision-making contexts. For example, a juvenile offender who has been found competent to waive rights, and who has even been bound over for trial as an adult, would still be considered generally incompetent to consent to medical treatment or make contracts.

At the heart of the competence issue with juveniles is the question of knowing when an act is "wrong" and how justice can best be served. For example, does the teenager who runs away from home to escape sexual abuse by a parent do "wrong"? Running away is a status offense, but is justice served by treating the youth as a delinquent? Conversely, does the teenager who kills his entire family with an ax do "wrong"? Is such a youth better served by counseling, punishment or a combination?

Critics of the present system suggest that too often the runaway and the ax murderer are dumped into the same "pot"—the juvenile justice system—and that justice is often not provided for either. Restructuring the juvenile court system might provide one solution to this problem.

RESTRUCTURING

In Gilbert and Sullivan's operetta, the Mikado of Japan sings, "My object all sublime I shall achieve in time—To let the punishment fit the crime—The punishment fit the crime." In other words, the wrong done should determine the response that is made. The English Children and Young Persons Act of 1969 states: "Every court, in dealing with a child or young person who is brought before it, either as an offender or otherwise, should have regard to the welfare of the child or young person." There is similar language in the Constitution of the United States. To accomplish this, many argue that the juvenile court needs restructuring in two areas.

The first change often advocated is to clearly separate criminal and noncriminal acts. Noncriminal acts would be treated as civil matters. Juvenile courts, acting under the principle of *parens patrae,* do have the responsibility to intercede for children who are neglected, deprived or abused, but might do so more effectively under a civil jurisdiction. Likewise, youths who commit status offenses, particularly if they are not under the control of their parents, should not have full rein. They might initially be under the court's civil jurisdiction, with the warning that if they do not comply with the court's orders they may be declared "delinquent" and placed under the court's criminal jurisdiction.

The second change often advocated is to consider age more specifically. Rather than having one specific age at which a person comes within the jurisdiction of the adult courts (usually age 18), a two- or three-level approach might be more effective. Springer (1986, p. 46) notes that: "For centuries, children were divided by the common law into three categories: children who are so young as to be generally thought of as being beyond the proper reach of criminal punishment, prepubescent children who are hard to classify in terms of criminal responsibility, and children over the age of puberty." He suggests that the same three-tiered approach should be used in our juvenile justice system (p. 47): "The answer is to set out some overlapping age brackets of diminished responsibility for all but the most vicious of youthful offenders. As has always been the case, three levels present themselves." Springer suggests that the first level might extend to approximately age nine, that the second level encompass juveniles between ages nine and 14 or 15, and that the third level would encompass juveniles 14 or 15 and older—depending on the individual and the crime committed.

■ The juvenile justice system could be restructured in two areas: (1) civil and criminal jurisdictions could be separated, and within civil jurisdiction poverty-stricken, neglected and abused children could be separated from status offenders and those who are not under the control of their parents; and (2) jurisdictional age could also be considered.

POLICY RECOMMENDATIONS FOR CONSIDERATION

Gibbons and Krohn (1986, p. 174) describe in detail the work of Richard Lundman, a researcher who conducted a thorough review of the literature on juvenile delinquency. Based on this review, Lundman set forth six specific recommendations:

1. Traditional delinquency prevention efforts should be abandoned.
2. Diversion should be the first response of the juvenile justice system to status and minor offenders.
3. Routine probation should be retained as the first and most frequent sentencing option of juvenile court judges.
4. Efforts to scare juveniles straight should be abandoned.
5. Community treatment programs should be expanded to accommodate nearly all chronic offenders.
6. Institutionalization should continue to be used as a last resort, reserved primarily for chronic offenders adjudicated delinquent for index crimes against persons.

THE FUTURE FOR NEGLECTED AND ABUSED CHILDREN

The National Council of Juvenile and Family Court Judges, through the Metropolitan Court Judges Committee, has provided a guideline for judicial response to deprived children who occupy much of the juvenile court's time. The Committee has directed 73 recommendations to be considered by judges, legislators, child protection agency officials and local civic leaders that will ameliorate the problems of deprived children who require public custody and protection. Several of these recommendations have been outlined in preceding chapters. The judges' concern is that there must be more than just talk about the needs of children. They believe that complex problems can be solved, but only through the commitment of government and the community, in partnership, to develop and rigorously apply all their resources and talents. As noted in the Introduction of their report (pp. 5–6):

> The judges know that too often the processes of the system can exacerbate the abuse by its delays, procedures and rules which are insensitive to the feelings, perceptions and fears of children. . . . They know that agencies may override the rights of children in their zeal to help them, taking them out of their homes on mere assertion, placing them in foster homes, sometimes of another culture or at a distance from family, school and friends. . . . The judges know also that their own authority is often limited.

The 73 recommendations cover the role of judges; court procedures; detecting, reporting and evaluating; out-of-home placement; treatment and planning and prevention issues—all areas in which changes and reform might be appropriate. Appendix E contains the specific recommendations of the Metropolitan Court Judges Committee.

TIME FOR A CHANGE

Sullivan and Victor (1988, p. 156), state:

> [T]he winds of change are blowing across the nation's juvenile justice system. Traditional reforms are being replaced with a new and more conservative agenda of juvenile justice. This new reform movement emphasizes the welfare of victims, a punitive approach toward serious juvenile offenders, and protection of children from physical and sexual exploitation. Policies which favor diversion and deinstitutionalization are less popular. After many years of attempting to remove status offenders from the juvenile justice system, there are increasing calls for returning truants, runaways, and other troubled youth to juvenile court jurisdiction. In spite of these developments, there are many juvenile justice reformers who remain dedicated to advancing due process rights for children and reducing reliance on incarceration.

Clearly, there is conflict and tension between the old and new juvenile justice reform agendas.

Change is usually difficult. Almost five hundred years ago Machiavelli (1469–1527), an Italian diplomat, wrote in his classic work, *The Prince* (1513):

> There is nothing more difficult to carry out, nor more doubtful of success, nor more dangerous to handle, than to initiate a new order of things. For the reformer has enemies in all those who profit by the old order, and only lukewarm defenders in all those who would profit by the new order, this lukewarmness arising partly from fear of their adversaries, who have the law in their favour; and partly from the incredulity of mankind, who do not truly believe in anything new until they have had actual experience of it.

The difficulty of change is also noted by Breed (1990, p. 72):

> Many of us bear the scars, if not the open wounds, of previous encounters with policy and philosophy changes. Unfortunately, it is easy to bow to the inevitability

of crime; to acknowledge the social injustice that causes most of it; to make claims that nothing works; to let the federal government mandate our directions and the courts to order them; and to bend to the pressures of public opinion.

It's much harder to take the initiative to stand up for what is right when it is not popular; to be creative and fight mediocrity; to sense the responsibility of our current roles; to feel the intolerability of present conditions; and to seek the strength to change them.

Individuals and groups willing to take the initiative and propose reforms for the juvenile justice system do exist. Among them are Thomas R. English, Barry Krisberg and James Austin. English, director of the Oregon Council on Crime and Delinquency and president of the American Restitution Association, calls for "rejuvenating" juvenile justice. Krisberg, president of the National Council on Crime and Delinquency (NCCD), and Austin, executive vice president of the NCCD, call for "reinventing" juvenile justice.

Rejuvenating Juvenile Justice

English (1993, p. 19), in his article calling for rejuvenating juvenile justice, notes several problems with our juvenile justice system:

> If we examine the public bureaucracies in which juvenile justice programs and services are delivered, we find that they mirror the outdated, top-down manage-ment protocols of mass-production industrial economies.
>
> This approach has led to a juvenile justice bureaucracy whose hallmarks include categorical funding; large caseloads; top-down management; limited professional training; and accountability based on eligibility, rule compliance, and contract monitoring. . . .

English suggests that juvenile justice combine ideas from the business world, including Total Quality Management (TQM) and reinvention, along with the work of the Balanced Approach/Restorative Justice (BA/RJ) group.

W. Edward Deming's Total Quality Management concept, introduced in the fifties, is perhaps best known for its zero-defect philosophy. What is of interest to juvenile justice is how Deming proposed that zero-defects could be accom-plished. Rather than operating from a top-down management process, where only some problems are solved, every employee, from the president to the custodian, is required to determine if what they do is helping to achieve the organization's mission. A TQM approach might make reforms in the juvenile justice system more effective. English (p. 19) notes:

> We have increased opportunities for preschool pupils but not for high school dropouts; we have established child abuse reporting but not parent training; we have implemented mastery teaching but not peer group empowerment.

In addition to using concepts from TQM, juvenile justice reformers might also borrow from the work of the Balanced Approach/Restorative Justice Project, which seeks to accomplish three objectives simultaneously: competency devel-opment and accountability for offenders and protection for the community. Community-based programs incorporating ideas from TQM and the Balanced Approach (BA) might be characterized as follows (English, pp. 17–18):

▌ Front-line workers are accorded wide discretion.

▌ A broad spectrum of responsive, convenient and timely services is provided.

▌ Collaboration across traditional and professional boundaries is encouraged.

▌ Children are viewed in the context of the family and the family in the context of neighborhoods and communities.

▌ Programs have deep roots in the community and are customized to meet cultural needs.

▌ Parental cooperation and participation are solicited.

▌ Establishing a relationship of trust with children and their extended families is a priority.

▌ A long-term prevention orientation predominates.

▌ The organizational milieu is based primarily on outcomes rather than on regulation.

According to English (p. 20): "We have been attempting to force the square peg of community-based programs into the round hole of professional bureaucracies." He suggests that one approach to rejuvenating juvenile justice might be to take a lead from the musical world, beginning with an orchestra. Here many different musicians and instruments combine talents to create the power of a symphony. They all play from the same musical score, but each has a specific and vital part. English takes the analogy further to include the jazz band, where individuals not only play together, but improvise, building on the original melody and creating new notes and themes. He suggests (pp. 20–21):

> We can learn from this jazz band approach as well. We must learn to work as an ensemble within each community; at the local, state, and federal levels; as public and private organizations; and as individuals and groups—each taking the lead at times and playing a supporting role at others. We must encourage innovative and reactive approaches to the problems posed by juvenile delinquency. The time has come to abandon the one-man-band approach in which juvenile justice is managed by a mega-agency and instead emulate the creative harmony and innovative improvisation of a jazz band.

Reinventing Juvenile Justice

Krisberg and Austin (1993) suggest that much more than rejuvenation is needed for the juvenile justice system. Their extensive discussion on the contemporary juvenile justice system ends with the following conclusions (pp. 109–110):

> Our analysis paints a discouraging picture. Juvenile laws are vaguely worded and inconsistently applied, permitting extensive abuses in the handling of children by social control agencies whose discretion is largely unchecked. Instead of protecting children from injustices and unwarranted state intervention, the opposite effect frequently occurs. The practices and procedures of juvenile justice agents mirror our society's class and racial prejudices and fall disproportionately on African-American, Latino, and poor people.
>
> These conclusions are not new. Many practitioners within the juvenile court share this critical perspective. The vital question is, "What is to be done?" Most critics of the juvenile court continue to offer narrow reform measures that do not confront the relationship between inequities in the juvenile justice system and inequities within society. . . .

The quest for juvenile justice is tied inextricably to the pursuit of social justice.

For a different perspective on juvenile justice, the following pages describe how juveniles are treated in some other countries.

A GLOBAL PERSPECTIVE

The United States is not alone in its efforts to control crime and violence and at the same time provide justice for its youth. This section begins by looking at the differences in how youth are treated in two countries representing the extremes.

Singapore and Sweden

As a starting point, consider the two extremes of Singapore and Sweden. Singapore uses caning as a punishment for those who break the law. When American Michael Fay received four lashes from a rattan cane, many Americans were outraged. Many others, however, were supportive.

Singapore's streets are safe and spotless. Nothing less is tolerated. When gum caused a subway door to malfunction, gum chewing was simply outlawed. Individual liberty in Singapore takes second place to social order.

Sweden, on the other hand, took the lead in forbidding corporal punishment of children. Sweden has outlawed force and violence against children, thereby strengthening children's legal position. In March 1979, Sweden passed an "antispanking" law.

■ According to Sweden's antispanking law, the parent or guardian should exercise the necessary supervision in accordance with the child's age and other circumstances. The child may not be subjected to corporal punishment or other injurious or humiliating treatment.

During the debate on the bill, one representative argued that "in a free democracy like our own we use words as arguments, not blows. . . . We talk to people, not beat them. If we cannot convince our children with words, we shall never convince them with a beating" (Salzer, 1979, p. 13).

Most countries are neither as extreme as Singapore in placing social order ahead of individual liberty or as extreme as Sweden in passing an antispanking law. The United Nations, however, leans very close to the position of Sweden. The U.N.'s "Declaration of the Rights of the Child," adopted in 1959, is the first formal recognition of the need to provide special protection for children. The right to be free from force and violence is implicit in Principle 2:

> The child shall enjoy special protection, and shall be given opportunities and facilities, by law and by other means, to enable him to develop physically, mentally, morally, spiritually and socially in a healthy and normal manner and in conditions of freedom and dignity.

Swedish juvenile justice has been influenced by social welfare authorities. Children and youth cannot be punished for crimes committed before the age of 15, the age of criminal responsibility. Instead, any such cases are referred to the social welfare authorities. Fifteen is not an absolute limit, however. In practice, the social welfare authorities usually assume responsibility for persons under the age of 18 who have committed serious offenses. Even in this age group, fines are the most common sanctions for minor offenses. Youth who are mentally ill or have a severe substance abuse problem may be referred to medical care or for treatment for alcoholism or drug abuse. There are two strong reasons for these exceptions. First, their criminality is associated with personal difficulties or handicaps that negate the basic assumption that people are responsible for their own actions. Second, the penal system lacks the resources required to deal with people having such problems.

The majority of offenders are relatively young. The largest group is the 15- to 19-year-old population. Most offenses involving youth are handled through the social welfare authorities. The police, for whatever reason, do not get involved in juvenile crime or matters of abuse, neglect and abandonment.

Article 37a in their law states: "No child shall be subjected to torture or other cruel, inhuman or degrading treatment or punishment" which is consistent with the safeguard in the antispanking law.

Canada

The Canadian juvenile justice system was revamped by passage of the Young Offenders Act (YOA) in 1984. This Act established a uniform age for legal status, defining the range of 12 to 17 years to be the mandate for the youth court. The system shifted to a highly structured adversarial system resembling the adult court rather than the informal system that preceded it. As noted by Wass and Marks (1992, p. 91): "In the early '70s, the feeling was that children involved in the system would have been criminalized by the proposed bill [a similar bill which was defeated in the 1970's]. Now, some 15 years later, public criticism focused on how young 'criminals' were being treated like 'children'." The Young Offenders Act has the following operating principles (Wass and Marks, 1992, pp. 91–92):

▐ Young people are responsible for their illegal behavior, but are not always accountable in the same manner as adults.
▐ Society has a right to be protected from illegal behavior and has a responsibility to prevent crime.
▐ Young people have special needs.
▐ Young people have well-defined rights and entitlements, including the least possible interference with their freedom.
▐ Parents are responsible for the care and supervision of their children, who should remain in the home whenever possible.

The wide range of dispositions available under the Act include community and personal service, restitution, probation, fines, open custody, secure custody and treatment orders.

New Zealand

The approach to juvenile justice in New Zealand has as a central component the Family Group Conference. This lay panel was established by legislation passed in 1989 and applies to offenses committed by individuals between the ages of 10 and 18. Moore (1993, p. 4) describes the Family Group Conference process:

> The basic design of the Family Group Conference is disarmingly simple. A young person who has committed an offense against an identifiable victim is brought face to face with that victim. (There may be more than one offender or more than one victim; a single conference deals with the effects of the offense.) Both offender(s) and victim(s) are accompanied by family members, guardians, peers, or other people with a significant relationship to the offender or the victim. These people are collectively referred to as "supporters;" they may contribute to the search for restitution and to negotiations for reparation of the damage caused by the original offense. It is this insistence on collective, community involvement in the search for reparation that sets the Family Group Conference model apart from reparations schemes run in Britain and the United States since the 1970s.

The Family Group Conference is called into session by an official of the justice system. The session itself often entails not only shame on the part of the offender, but forgiveness by the victim. As noted by Moore (1993, p. 15): "The appropriate use of shame in civil society will be far more effective as a means of moral education than will legal retribution within the criminal justice system."

Israel

In Israel the juvenile justice system is divided into two segments: criminal and civil. Matters are referred to the juvenile court by the police, who have absolute power in matters dealing with children. The police have a special unit classified as juvenile officers. The juvenile officer handles all referrals. The matters must be related to a crime or directly related to the health, welfare and safety of the child. All crimes go to criminal court (no distinction of a juvenile court). All other matters are handled in civil court. The civil court handles divorce and foster care. There are no status offenses in Israel.

In criminal matters the police investigate, interview and determine to refer. The police referral includes the crime and contact with the juvenile and parents. All matters are referred to the welfare administration for disposition.

Israel shows the British influence in its juvenile justice process. All criminal and civil matters are heard by a magistrate. The Ministry of Labour and Social Affairs receives all matters, and trials and disposition are directed to the juvenile probation section. The police are youth workers in uniform. Juveniles between ages 12 and 18 are subject to the police. The police direct most cases to social services, which also has community corrections, group homes and foster care. In most cases, juveniles are placed on probation. Only 2 percent of youth are placed in a secure facility. There are only two secure facilities in Israel. All citizens of Israel are subject to military law. Children who engage in armed conflict, such as stone throwers, are referred to the criminal court due to the gravity of the offense. The juvenile probation system used in Israel is illustrated in Figure 15–1.

England

In 1989 England reorganized the juvenile justice system to set up a youth court that took over matters classified as delinquency. The Children's Act of 1989 placed matters into the hands of the police for the first incident, for example, shoplifting, vandalism and similar charges. If a youth is brought to the police station, the parents are notified. If the parents cannot or will not come to the station, a social worker is called and represents the child. If detained, the child is detained in a small room with a window.

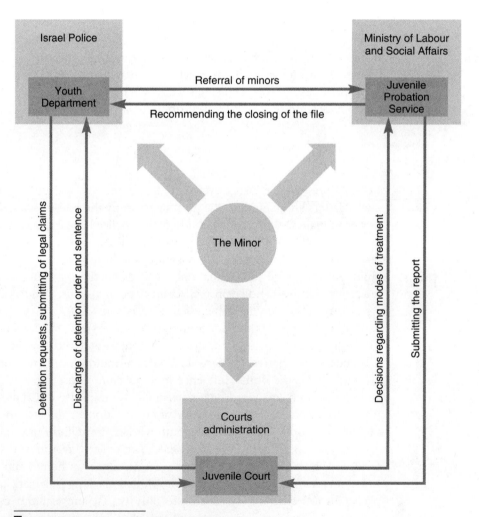

∎ **FIGURE 15–1 Juvenile Probation Service**

SOURCE: *Division for Youth Development and Correctional Services: An Overview.* Jerusalem: State of Israel, Ministry of Labour and Social Affairs, July 1993, p. 20. Reprinted with permission.

The police confront the parents of the offender and the offender in the police station where a caution against the wrongdoing is issued (a warning). The individual is released to the parents with a stipulation that the youth not commit the offense again. If the youth persists in getting into trouble by violating the law, the police may refer the matter to the youth court. Before the matter is provided to the court, it is reviewed by the Crown Prosecution Service to determine if there is sufficient evidence to proceed. If there is proof, the matter is referred to a Magistrate's Court consisting of three lay people who might not have any legal background and who can come from any social status or profession.

If a legal question arises, a magistrate's clerk interprets the law for them. In England, the age of reason is 10 years old, and the youth is subject to the Youth Court from the age of 10 to age 17. If a youthful offender receives several cautions, the police in charge send a form to the education department, social services and the probation office asking for comments and suggestions regarding the individual youth and the incident. The views, when received, are forwarded with the case file to the youth court to make a decision. The court makes a decision called a "conditional discharge" from the court, which is in effect for 12 months. All effort is made to avoid placing youths in detention or as it is referred to in England, "secure accommodations."

When a youth commits a felonious act that endangers the public such as robbery, murder, manslaughter and aggravated assault, the youth is taken to the Crown Court (adult court) without first being certified by the youth court. An example is the murder of a two-year-old by two 10-year-olds in Liverpool. The two-year-old was abducted from a shopping mall and taken to a railroad yard where he was tortured and murdered by the two male 10-year-olds. The event created national and international interest. The two offenders were tried in the Crown Court in the same process afforded to adults. They were provided a defense counsel, with trial by jury, and when convicted they were placed in prison, but in a facility suitable to their age. The matter is public record when a youth is convicted, and the youth's identity can be revealed.

If the youth is placed at risk, such as in abuse, neglect or abandonment cases, the matter is not referred to the youth court. Rather it is referred to a body called "Inter-Agency Unit." This unit consists of a panel of police, social workers and educators who make a decision of what is in the best interest of the child. This panel forwards its finding, if the child is a victim, to the Crown Prosecutor Service for further action, and the child is placed with social services until the matter is resolved.

Each district, such as Wales, West Yorkshire and the like, is mandated by the Children's Act of 1989. They all do not function in the same manner, however.

Scotland

The Scottish juvenile justice system is based on the concept of a "Children's Panel." The Children's Panel was developed under the Social Worker Act of 1968. This Act did away with the juvenile court and replaced it with a *lay tribunal*. The idea for the lay tribunal was the result of a report in 1964 from the

Kilbrandon Committee. This committee recommended that the juvenile court be replaced by a lay panel consisting of three people (with both men and women represented) drawn from a panel of people in the community who were aware of community affairs. The recommendation of the committee for the panel concept was based on the finding that children had special requirements over and above those of adults and that the law courts (even the juvenile courts) were primarily concerned with determining guilt and imposing punishment, not with the well-being and welfare of children appearing before them.

As noted in the resource manual for panel members (Peacock, n.d., p. 4): "The various parts of Scotland can be characterized by pronounced local differences, arising from geographic, social, economic, political and historical factors. These will influence the manner in which the local authority exercises its responsibility. . . ."

The committee felt that several factors contributed to children's problems: the attitudes and life styles of their parents, their schooling, housing conditions and physical health could influence the child's behavior. Consequently, the committee reasoned that the court when "sitting in judgment" on children's cases was faced with the difficulty of attempting to do two things at once: protecting society from criminal acts by imposing suitable punishment while at the same time trying to meet a responsibility for the child's welfare and acting in the best interest of the child. The committee believed it was unrealistic for a court that handled criminal law to be combined with a specialized welfare agency for children in trouble.

The Children's Panel deals with two important issues:

▮ Establishing guilt or innocence.
▮ Defining measures that would help each individual child.

The age of reason in Scotland is eight. Children are subject to the panel from age eight to age 17.

Serious juvenile offenses continue to be heard by a Sheriff's Court (a high court similar to a district or superior court in the United States). The Sheriff's Court could also be used for appeals. Only in exceptional circumstances would the court handle juvenile matters, however.

Along with the formation of the Children's Panel, the committee suggested that an independent official, a lay person, be responsible for initially assessing all children's cases. This official was designated as the "reporter."

The format of the Children's Panel is based on the social services concept. It is community-oriented social work, with the main objective being to serve the best interest of the child.

Since the panel came into existence in 1971, a child who is in trouble is referred to the reporter who reviews the referrals. If the matter is a serious offense, the reporter takes the case(s) to a procurator-fiscal (a county/district attorney) for evaluation as to whether the matter should go before the panel or to a court of law, as illustrated in Figure 15–2.

When the case is referred to the panel, the contacts may come from the police, school or social workers. When the police handle a youthful offender, they interview the individual about the offense. If the police, with parents, feel

Referral

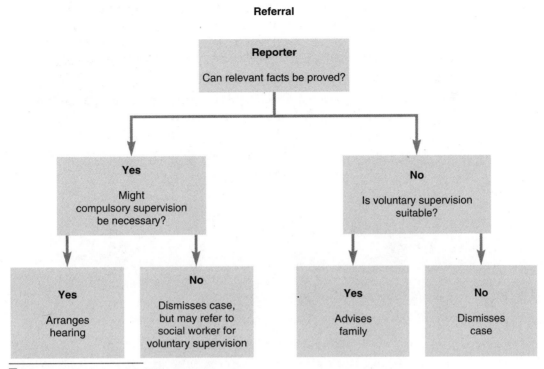

■ **FIGURE 15–2 The Reporter's Decision**

This flow-chart tries to clarify the general way in which the reporter would reach a decision. Note that it does not quite cover all the possibilities.

SOURCE: Geraldine Peacock, *The Children's Hearings System in Scotland. An Introduction for Panel Members* (Social Work Services Group, The Open University, n.d.), p. 25.

it is in the best interests of the child to be placed "under police supervision," the matter is handled by the police without any official referral for such police supervision. This happens only with matters brought to the attention of the police.

The schools also make referrals for those matters that are special to a school, for example, truancy. School matters are forwarded to the reporter for a hearing. For all panel hearings, the parents of the child are notified to appear with the child at a specific date and time. When they arrive, only the child sits before the panel. The parents sit behind the child. There is no legal counsel at the hearing. The child is asked to either affirm or deny the allegations presented. If he denies the allegations, the matter is automatically referred to the Sheriff's Court. If the child pleads guilty (affirms) to the matter, then the panel, in an atmosphere of a family discussion, asks the youth to explain (in their own words) about the circumstances surrounding the matter.

When the child explains, the panel asks specific questions aimed at having the child explain the reasons for the offending action. When the child has finished explaining, the panel asks the child what can be done to help keep it from happening again. After the matter is fully examined, a disposition is given immediately. There is no delay in the proceeding from start to finish. In most cases the matter is referred to the social worker to follow up. There is no probation. All probation officer positions were abolished and consolidated within social services. The social worker also handles matters related to the school. Figure 15–3 illustrates the process used in the Children's Panel.

> ▌ New Zealand, England and Scotland use panels of lay people to deal with nonserious, nonviolent youthful offenders.

This Children's Panel concept is being replicated in Anoka, Minnesota, beginning July, 1994, in the first program of its kind in the United States. The structure of Anoka's Special Advocate Children's Panel is illustrated in Figure 15–4.

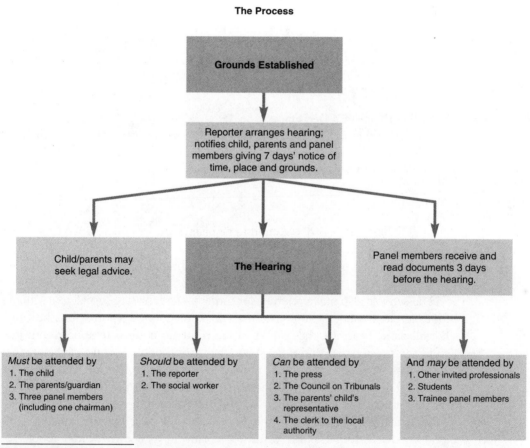

The Process

Grounds Established

Reporter arranges hearing; notifies child, parents and panel members giving 7 days' notice of time, place and grounds.

Child/parents may seek legal advice.

The Hearing

Panel members receive and read documents 3 days before the hearing.

Must be attended by
1. The child
2. The parents/guardian
3. Three panel members (including one chairman)

Should be attended by
1. The reporter
2. The social worker

Can be attended by
1. The press
2. The Council on Tribunals
3. The parents' child's representative
4. The clerk to the local authority

And *may* be attended by
1. Other invited professionals
2. Students
3. Trainee panel members

▌ **FIGURE 15–3 Children's Panel Flowchart: From Establishment of Grounds to the Hearing**

Note that the most usual composition of a hearing is the child, a parent, the reporter, two panel members, a panel chairman and a social worker. From June 1985, it is possible that a "safeguarder" may attend a hearing on behalf of a child. This is an important new development.

SOURCE: Geraldine Peacock, *The Children's Hearings System in Scotland. An Introduction for Panel Members* (Social Work Services Group, The Open University, n.d.), p. 33.

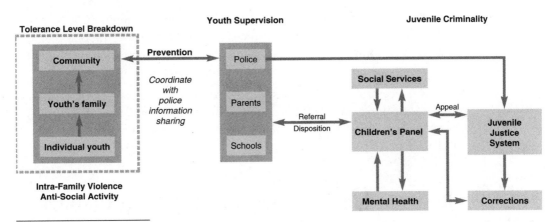

■ **FIGURE 15–4 Anoka's Special Advocate Children's Panel**

The United Nation's Position on Children

The Declaration on the Rights of the Child that was adopted by the General Assembly of the United Nations in November, 1989, states in the preamble: "The United Nations has proclaimed that childhood is entitled to special care and assistance" (Paragraph 4, p. 1). Article 3, Sub. L. states: "In all actions concerning children, whether undertaken by public or private social welfare institutions, courts of law, administrative authorities, or legislative bodies, the best interests of the child shall be a primary consideration" (p. 2).

After considering some international perspectives on juvenile justice, next consider some recommendations for "rethinking" the criminal justice system in the United States.

A CALL FOR RESTORATIVE JUSTICE

At the beginning of this chapter, advocates of "rejuvenating" or "reinventing" juvenile justice were cited. As a part of this rejuvenation or reinvention, some are calling for a new view of justice itself—restorative justice.

Van Ness (1990, p. 62) notes: "The Western view of crime and justice has become skewed. Rather than admitting that crimes injure victims, our laws define them as only offenses against government. Contemporary criminal justice is preoccupied with maintaining public order and punishing offenders. Victims are often ignored, and the government has taken over the community's role of maintaining the peace." Van Ness argues for a return to **restorative justice**, which returns to the ancient view that justice involves not two, but four parties: offender and victim, government and community—all are injured by crime. He notes that restorative justice has three underlying principles:

1. Crimes result in injuries to victims, communities, and offenders; therefore, the criminal justice process must repair those injuries.

2. Not only government, but victims, offenders and communities should be actively involved throughout the entire criminal justice process.
3. In promoting justice, the government should preserve order, and the peace should be maintained by the community.

This concept of restorative justice is expanded and refined by the Bureau of Justice Statistics–Princeton Project which is calling not only for a change in how justice is viewed but an entirely new paradigm for the criminal justice system itself.

THE BJS-PRINCETON PROJECT CALL FOR A NEW PARADIGM

The Bureau of Justice Statistics and Princeton University formed a study group, the BJS-Princeton University Study Group, to "re-examine both the concepts and the methodologies involved in conceptualizing, measuring, and evaluating the performance of those agencies and actors comprising the American criminal justice system" (Dillingham, 1992, p. iii). This group's first publication was *Rethinking the Criminal Justice System: Toward a New Paradigm*. A **paradigm** is a pattern, a way of looking at an entire field or concept. Scientific advances often come from the ability to view things in a new light or using a new paradigm. The move from reactive, incident-driven policing, to proactive, problem-oriented policing, involves a paradigm shift. Such shifts are difficult and require the ability to see beyond the status quo. As noted by English (1993, p. 16): "[I]nability to see beyond the status quo can lead to what may be called the John Wayne effect—'If it doesn't work, do more, and try harder, Pilgrim!' "

English notes three trends identified by the BA/RJ group that illustrate this **John Wayne effect:**

1. Increasing commitments to state institutions, especially for drug-involved youth.
2. Expanded out-of-home and quasi-residential placements.
3. Widespread transferring of juvenile offenders to adult court.

The call for a new paradigm for criminal justice by the BJS-Princeton Project is prefaced with a brief history illustrating the multiple, vague, contradictory purposes established for the criminal justice system—which can also be said of the juvenile justice system (DiIulio, 1992, p. 6):

The history of the American criminal justice system is a history of swings in public mood. Americans have long been ambivalent about the purposes of criminal justice. Among other things, they have wanted a criminal justice system that apprehends and visits harm upon the guilty (*punishment*); makes offenders more virtuous or at least more law-abiding (*rehabilitation*); dissuades would-be offenders from criminal pursuits (*deterrence*); protects innocent citizens from being victimized by convicted criminals (*incapacitation*); and enables most criminals to return as productive citizens to the bosom of the free community (*reintegration*). They have wanted the system to achieve these contradictory goals without violating the public conscience (*humane treatment*), jeopardizing the public law (*constitutional rights*), emptying the public purse (*cost containment*), or weakening the tradition of State and local public administration (*federalism*).

Because the competing public expectations cannot be easily met all at once, first one and then another dominate public attention (italics in original).

The BJS-Princeton Project has as its key concept the democratic vision of citizens as **coproducers of justice,** a phrase suggested by Harvard Professor Moore (1993, p. 9): "Citizens, not judges, prosecutors, law enforcement officers, or corrections officials, are primarily responsible for the quality of life in their communities, including the prevalence and severity of crime within them. . . . Citizens in a democracy must begin by holding themselves and their neighbors accountable for public affairs."

■ As coproducers of justice, citizens are responsible for the prevalence and severity of the crime within their communities.

To bring their democratic vision of citizens as coproducers of justice into reality, the group identified four civic ideals or purposes (DiIulio, p. 10):

■ Doing justice.
■ Promoting secure communities.
■ Restoring crime victims.
■ Promoting noncriminal options.

The group defined *justice* as "the quality of treating individuals according to their civic rights and in ways that they deserve to be treated by virtue of relevant conduct" (p. 10). *Doing justice* entails at least four things: (1) holding offenders fully accountable for their offenses, (2) protecting offenders' constitutional and legal rights, (3) treating like offenses alike and (4) taking into account relevant differences among offenders and offenses.

Promoting secure communities entails much more than simply lowering the crime rates (DiIulio, 1992, pp. 10–11):

> [I]t means providing the security to life, liberty, and property that is necessary for communities to flourish. It means enabling citizens to pursue their collective life as they see fit without undue fear of having that life disrupted or destroyed. It means securing communities against criminals who assault, rape, rob, defraud, deal drugs, burglarize, extort, and murder, but it also means securing them against the community-sapping disorders that are commonly associated with crime and the fear of crime—disorders such as petty crime, public drunkenness, aggressive panhandling, loitering, graffiti, abandoned cars, broken windows, and abandoned buildings.

Restoring victims refers to attending to victims' rights. It means to "honor the community's obligation to make victims of crime and disorder whole again" (p. 11). Crimes are *not* just against the state. They involve people: "Victims of crime have a special claim upon the criminal justice system's human and financial resources. Whatever else it may achieve, no system that dishonors that claim can be considered legitimate" (p. 11).

Finally, *promoting noncriminal options* suggests that punishment for crimes should "interfere as little as possible with the pursuit of noncriminal behavior. Even in prison, offenders need at least some opportunity to engage in meaningful, constructive, and legitimate activities" (p. 11).

The need for a new paradigm, a new way of thinking about the justice system, is also stressed by Crier (1993, p. 142), who notes: "We all know building more buildings and locking people away without providing alternative solutions simply won't work. We cannot keep this up. . . . We understand a new way of thinking is necessary." She recalls that Albert Einstein said we could not solve current problems with traditional thinking because it was that thinking that got us there in the first place. She concludes: "It's time to shake up the status quo. It's time to dream outrageous dreams and make them come to pass."

SUMMARY

Juvenile justice is far reaching. Juvenile courts have been involved in such issues as abortion, school prayer, search and seizure, interracial custody and adoption, adolescent judgment and maturity, and legal issues in terminating parental rights.

Critics suggest that the system should not be so heavily involved in such "social" matters and that a justice model would be more appropriate than a welfare model when dealing with juveniles. A justice model is a judicial process wherein young people who come in conflict with the law are held responsible and accountable for their behavior. Under law, a person's competence is conceptualized as a specific functional ability. To accomplish this, the juvenile justice system could be restructured in two areas:

1. Civil and criminal jurisdictions could be separated, and within civil jurisdiction poverty-stricken, neglected, and abused children might be separated from status offenders and those who are not under the control of their parents.
2. Jurisdictional age could also be considered.

Juvenile justice in other countries has many similarities to that in the United States, but also some striking differences. For example, according to Sweden's antispanking law the parent or guardian should exercise the necessary supervision in accordance with the child's age and other circumstances. The child may not be subjected to corporal punishment or other injurious or humiliating treatment.

New Zealand, England, and Scotland use panels of lay people to deal with nonviolent youthful offenders.

Another way that juvenile justice might be restructured to suit the needs of our society in the 1990s is to adopt the concept of restorative justice and to view citizens as co-producers of justice. As coproducers of justice, citizens are responsible for the prevalence and severity of the crime within their communities.

■ Discussion Questions

1. Should the juvenile justice system be reorganized to accommodate modern problems and concerns? How?
2. What would you change in the juvenile justice system in your state to be in tune with modern society?
3. Should the juvenile court be separated into different functions, criminal, civil and special needs? Why or why not?
4. Design a modern juvenile justice system for your state.
5. Design a juvenile justice act that all states could use.
6. Do you favor Sweden's antispanking law, Singapore's caning policy or a position somewhere in between? Why?
7. Which of the juvenile justice systems from other countries have elements that might be adopted in the United States?
8. Do you feel that restorative justice is a valid concept?
9. Do you believe a new paradigm for juvenile justice is needed? What types of thinking need to be modified?
10. Can you see other examples of the John Wayne effect in the juvenile justice system or in other areas of juveniles' lives?

■ References

Breed, Allen F. "America's Future: The Necessity of Investing in Children." *Corrections Today,* February 1990, pp. 68–72.

Crier, Catherine. "It's Time To Take Responsibility for Fixing Our Nation's Problems." *Corrections Today,* December 1993, pp. 142–143.

DiIulio, John J., Jr. *Rethinking the Criminal Justice System: Toward a New Paradigm.* Bureau of Justice Statistics-Princeton Project. Washington, D.C.: U.S. Department of Justice, December 1992.

Dillingham, Steven D. "Foreword." In *Rethinking the Criminal Justice System: Toward a New Paradigm,* by John J. DiIulio, Jr. Bureau of Justice Statistics-Princeton Project. Washington, D.C.: U.S. Department of Justice, December 1992, p. iii.

English, Thomas R. "TQM and All That Jazz: Rejuvenating Juvenile Justice." *Juvenile Justice,* 1 (Fall/Winter 1993) 2:16–21.

Gibbons, Don C., and M. D. Krohn. *Delinquency Behavior.* Englewood Cliffs, N.J.: Prentice Hall, 1986.

Greenwood, Peter. "Juvenile Offenders." National Institute of Justice, Crime File Study Guide, n.d.

Krisberg, Barry, and James F. Austin. *Reinventing Juvenile Justice.* Newbury Park, Calif.: Sage Publications, 1993.

Metropolitan Court Judges Committee Report. *Deprived Children: A Judicial Response.* Washington, D.C.: U.S. Government Printing Office, 1986.

Moore, David B. "Shame, Forgiveness, and Juvenile Justice." *Criminal Justice Ethics,* Winter/Spring 1993, pp. 3–25.

Peacock, Geraldine. *The Children's Hearings System in Scotland: An Introduction for Panel Members.* Social Work Services Group, The Open University, n.d.

Salzer, Mark. "To Combat Violence in the Child's World: Swedish Efforts to Strengthen the Child's Rights." *Social Change in Sweden,* 1979.

Springer, Charles E. *Justice for Juveniles.* Washington, D.C.: U.S. Department of Justice, Office of Juvenile Justice and Delinquency Prevention, 1986.

Sullivan, John J., and Joseph L. Victor, eds. *Criminal Justice 88/89*. Guilford, Conn.: Dushkin Publishing, 1988.

Van Ness, Daniel E. "Restoring the Balance: Tipping the Scales of Justice." *Corrections Today,* February 1990, pp. 62–66.

Wass, John, and Ron Marks. "Historical Overview: Young Offenders Act Revamps Juvenile Justice in Canada." *Corrections Today,* December 1992, pp. 88–93.

▮ Cases

Bellotti v. Baird, 443 U.S. 622, 99 S.Ct. 3035, 61 L.Ed.2d 797 (1979).

City of Akron v. Akron Center for Reproductive Health, 462 U.S. 416, 103 S.Ct. 2481, 76 L.Ed.2d 687 (1983).

Dow v. Renfrow, 475 F.Supp. 1012 (N.D. Ind. 1979), *aff'd in part, remanded in part,* 631 F. 2d 91 (7th Cir. 1980), *reh'g en banc denied,* 635 F. 2d 582 (7th Cir. 1980), *cert. denied,* 451 U.S. 1022, 101 S.Ct. 3015, 69 L.Ed.2d 395 (1981).

H. L. v. Matheson, 450 U.S. 398, 101 S.Ct. 1164, 67 L.Ed.2d 388 (1981).

Jewish Child Care Association v. Elaine S. Y., 73 A.D.2d 154, 425 N.Y.S.2d 336 (1980).

Nebraska v. Wedige, 205 Neb. 687, 289 N.W.2d 538 (1980).

New Jersey v. T. L. O., 469 U.S. 325, 105 S.Ct. 733, 83 L.Ed.2d 720 (1985).

Palmore v. Sidoti, 466 U.S. 429, 104 S.Ct. 1879, 80 L.Ed.2d 421 (1984).

Parham v. J. R., 442 U.S. 584, 99 S.Ct. 2493, 61 L.Ed.2d 101 (1979).

Planned Parenthood of Kansas City v. Ashcroft, 462 U.S. 476, 103 S.Ct. 2517, 76 L.Ed.2d 733 (1983).

In re R. M. G., 454 A.2d 776 (D.C.App. 1982).

Thornburgh v. American College of Obstetricians and Gynecologists, 476 U.S. 747, 106 S.Ct. 2169, 90 L.Ed.2d 779 (1986).

Wallace v. Jaffree, 472 U.S. 38, 105 S.Ct. 2479, 86 L.Ed.2d 29 (1985).

INFLUENCES ON DELINQUENCY

Appendix A summarizes the influences on delinquency discussed throughout the book. The first column lists the various philosophies and theories set forth to explain delinquency and crime in general. The second column summarizes the general explanation of causes underlying these theories. The next six columns show how each philosophy or theory perceives specific influences on the basic causes, that is how individual factors, the family, the community, the school, the social system and the criminal justice system are related to and influence delinquency.

Philosophical Influences on Delinquency

Perspective	Causes of Delinquency	Individual	Family	Community	School	Social System	Criminal Justice System
Classical school of criminality	People possess the ability to choose freely to do right or wrong—*free will.* They choose to do delinquent acts because the pleasure of the act outweighs the pain of punishment.	Free will is sole factor in considering delinquency and crime.	No influence	No influence	No influence	No influence	Purpose of punishment is *deterrence;* makes pain of punishment stronger than pleasure of act.
Positivist school of criminality	A variety of factors influence or *cause* one to be delinquent. Since these factors *cause* delinquency, there is no free will. In most cases, the person has little or no control over the influence of these factors.	Biological and some psychological theories view the individual as the focal point. Causes of delinquency are within the individual or the environment acting on the person.	Control and learning theories recognize the *positive* influence of family on definitions of delinquency.	Learning and cultural deviance theories include or focus on the community, neighborhood or gang. They define the *subculture.*	Bonding and other control theories view school as one of the elements binding the person to the *correct* value system.	Culture sets goals and means of attaining the goals. *Strain* occurs if the means are not available.	System represents outer control. System is at fault because it labels delinquent who lives up to the label.

Biological							
Early Theories	Criminals are *atavists* or biological throwbacks to a primitive state. Criminals are born, not developed.	Sole factor in causing delinquency is individual is *biologically defective*.	*Criminal families* are evidence of inherited criminal behavior.	No influence	No influence	No influence	Delinquents should be quarantined.
Inherited Crime	Children inherit a *predisposition* to violence or a central nervous system that predisposes the person to crime.	Genetic predisposition of individual causes delinquency.	Chromosomal complement is inherited.	No influence	No influence	No influence	
Psychological							
Psychoanalytical	Delinquents act out inner conflicts that result from pressure caused by failing to find appropriate releases. The psychic pressure is caused by poor or faulty child rearing.	Child did not develop properly through the infantile, latency and puberty periods.	Causes feelings of insecurity, rigidity, hostility or rebellion due to deficiencies in love, attention and child-rearing.	[Not considered]	Fails to recognize and deal with problems and to develop appropriate releases of pressure.	[Not considered]	[Not considered]

—continued

Philosophical Influences on Delinquency, *continued*

Perspective	Causes of Delinquency	Individual	Family	Community	School	Social System	Criminal Justice System
Frustration-Aggression	Certain stimuli—weapons, pain, noise, temperature, odors—may cause aggression.	Influenced or acted upon by outside forces.	Failed to establish tolerance or controls to counterbalance frustrations.	Stimuli may be a function of community—overcrowding.	[Not considered]	Economic status of child/family may require that they live in certain areas where stimuli are more plentiful.	[Not considered]
Learning Theory	Based on models for the youth's behavior, he learns "appropriate" ways of reacting to situations. Delinquents learn that aggressive, violent, hostile reactions are successful, therefore appropriate.	The person is a blank slate, then learns the means of dealing with difficult, hostile and frustrating situations.	Serves as a strong model for behavior—bad and good.	Serves as a stronger model for behavior during adolescence.	Provides environment for modeling and reinforcing of bad behavior.	[Not considered]	[Not considered]
Psychological/ Environmental Factors (similar to Frustration-Aggression)	Urban crowding and ambient temperature cause irritability, frustration and violence.	Individual is unwittingly acted upon by environmental factors.	[Not considered]	Population density is a function of community.	[Not considered]	Social class restricts one's ability to live in less populated, more comfortable environments.	[Not considered]

Learning Theories	Crime is learned in interaction with others.	A person is neither good nor bad but learns behavior that then directs him to certain acts or associates.	One of the primary social units where learning occurs.	Peers represent strong "significant others" from whom the person learns delinquency during adolescence and young adulthood.	Fails to reinforce definitions unfavorable to the violation of the law.	[Not considered]	[Not considered]
Differential Association	Criminal behavior is learned in interaction with those with whom delinquents associate and from whom they define law as favorable or unfavorable.	Learns behavior from others with whom he differentially associates.	One of the intimate personal groups in which delinquent definitions are formed.	Fails to counter the delinquent associations and definitions; also, peers represent community.	Fails to counter the definitions and associations.	Defines the needs and values that give rise to criminal (and) noncriminal behavior.	[Not considered]
Social Learning Theory	Deviant behavior is learned and reinforced through social and nonsocial reinforcers.	Influenced through operant conditioning.	Provides rewards and punishments for behavior; therefore may reinforce delinquency.	Provides rewards and punishments for behavior; therefore may reinforce delinquency.	Helps or fails to reinforce conventional behavior.	[Not considered]	[Not considered]

—continued

Philosophical Influences on **Delinquency,** *continued*

Perspective	Causes of Delinquency	Individual	Family	Community	School	Social System	Criminal Justice System
Labeling Theory	A youth is viewed as delinquent; therefore he sees himself as a delinquent and acts according to this social- and self-concept.	Unwittingly labeled and then perpetuates the label.	May influence the labeling process.	May influence the labeling process.	May influence the labeling process.	Acts toward the youth based on the label.	Justice system discriminates and labels underprivileged youth as *delinquent.*
Conflict Theory	Social conflict, based on authority, power and economy, results in the weak suffering at the hands of the justice system, while the rich and powerful can violate the law with impunity.	Everyone conforms and everyone deviates so it is unfair to categorize as good and bad. Categories based on status, not behavior.	No influence except as an example of the power/authority dynamic.	No influence	No influence	A classed society with the poor discriminated against in every way.	Pawns of the powerful and tools of the state.

SOURCE: William V. Pelphrey, *Explanations of Delinquency: Fact or Fiction?* Washington, D.C.: U.S. Dept. of Justice, Serious Habitual Offender Comprehensive Action Program (SHOCAP), n.d.

JOB DESCRIPTION: POLICE-SCHOOL LIAISON OFFICER

- Is directly responsible to the Flint Police Division, Juvenile Bureau. However, is readily available to school administrators in time of need or emergency school-police matters.
- Patrols school area when called upon or as deemed necessary by the Police-School Liaison Officer.
- Contributes helpful information to the Regional Counseling Team.
- Assists Community School Director to mitigate antisocial behavior by investigating delinquent or criminal acts that take place during the evening Community School Programs.
- Serves as a resource person or counselor for all youth, school administration and staff and members of the community with school-police related problems. Also is a resource person or counselor for those youth who have personal problems in their home.
- Acts as resource person and serves on committees that provide services for youth.
- Gives presentation on police-related subjects to students in the classroom and to business and community organizations.
- Serves as a resource person to the Police School Cadet Program when called upon.
- Supervises and prepares necessary records and reports as requested by the Flint Police Division and Flint Community Schools.
- Assists in crowd control at school athletic events.
- Serves as a resource person for other police personnel.
- Refers youths into Probate Court or District Court when necessary.
- Performs other related duties as assigned or as appropriate.
- Suppresses by enforcement of the law any and all illegal threats, such as drugs and acts of violence, that endanger the children's educational program, and improves community relations with police, schools and the general public.

SOURCE: Flint, Michigan, Police Department.

C.

JUVENILE COURT JURISDICTION: SELECTED STATE STATUTES

State	Type of Jurisdiction	Offenses Excluded	Jurisdictional Age	Waiver of Age
Alabama	Exclusive	None	18	14; waiver permitted only where child charged with felony or is already under commitment as a delinquent. Ala. Code § 12-15-34(a) (1986).
Alaska	Apparently exclusive	None given	18	None
Arizona	Apparently exclusive. *Eyman v. Superior Court,* 9 Ariz. App. 6, 448 P.2d 878 (1968).	None	18	None given
Arkansas	Concurrent. Ark. Stat. Ann. §§ 45-417, 45-418, 45-420 (Supp. 1981); *Monts v. State,* 233 Ark. 816, 349 S.W.2d 350 (1961).	None	18	None given
California	Exclusive	None	18	16
Colorado	Exclusive	Juvenile court does not have jurisdiction over: children 14 or older charged with crimes of violence classified as Class 1 felonies; children 16 or older who within the previous two years have been adjudicated delinquent for commission of a felony and are now charged with a Class 2 or Class 3 felony or any nonclassified felony punishable by death or life imprisonment (however, if felony charged is escape and the prior adjudication was for a Class 4 or 5 felony, case must originate in juvenile court); or children 14 or older charged with committing a felony subsequent to an earlier felony charge over which jurisdiction was waived. Colo. Rev. Stat. Ann. §§ 19-1-103(9)(b), 19-1-104(4) (1986).	18	14; waiver permitted only where child charged with felony. Colo. Rev. Stat. Ann. § 19-1-104(4)(a) (1986).

—continued

Connecticut	Exclusive	In effect, excludes certain cases from the juvenile court's jurisdiction where the child is 14 or older.	16 in case of child alleged to be delinquent or "defective"; 18 in case of child alleged to be abused, dependent, neglected, or "uncared for." Conn. Gen. Stat. Ann. § 46b-120 (1986).	14 where child is charged with Class A felony or serious juvenile offense designated a Class B or C felony and has previously been adjudicated delinquent for commission of a serious juvenile offense; waiver mandatory in case of child 14 or older charged with murder, child 14 or older charged with a Class A felony who has previously been adjudicated delinquent for commission of a Class A felony, or a child 14 or older charged with a Class B felony who has twice been adjudicated delinquent for commission of a Class A or B felony, provided the court finds probable cause to believe the child has committed such offense. Conn. Gen. Stat. Ann. §§ 46b-126, 46b-127 (1986).
Delaware	Exclusive	Excludes first degree murder, rape, and kidnapping, unless case is transferred to juvenile court from criminal court. Del. Code Ann. tit. 10, §§ 938 (a)(1), 939 (1974).	18	16; waiver also permitted where child is 14 or older and charged with commission of a felony. Del. Code Ann. tit. 10 §§ 937(c)(5), 938(c) (Supp. 1984).
District of Columbia	Concurrent; prosecutor has discretion to "charge" person 16 or older with murder, forcible rape, burglary in the first degree, robbery while armed, or assault with intent to commit any such offense, and thereby treat case as a criminal case. D.C. Code § 16-2301(3)(A) (1981).	None	18	15 where child is charged with felony; 16 where child is already under commitment as delinquent child, without regard to offense; and 18 where person is 18 or older and charged with any offense allegedly committed before reaching 18. D.C. Code § 16-2307(a) (1981).

State	Type of Jurisdiction	Offenses Excluded	Jurisdictional Age	Waiver of Age
Florida	Concurrent jurisdiction over children charged with offense punishable by death or life imprisonment; otherwise exclusive. Fla. Stat. Ann. § 39.02(5)(c) (Supp. 1984).	None	18	14; waiver mandatory upon demand of child and parent or guardian. Fla. Stat. Ann. § 39.02 (5)(a)–(b) (Supp. 1984).
Georgia	Concurrent jurisdiction over children charged with offense punishable by death or life imprisonment; otherwise exclusive. Ga. Code Ann. § 15-11-5(b) (1985).	In effect excludes certain burglary cases from the juvenile court's jurisdiction where child is 15 or older.	17 in case of delinquent or unruly child; 18 in case of deprived child. Ga. Code Ann. § 15-11-2(2)(A), (C) (1985).	15 generally; in case of a child charged with offense punishable by death or life imprisonment, waiver age is 13; waiver mandatory in case of child 15 or older charged with burglary if child has been adjudged to have committed burglary on three or more previous occasions and probable cause is established on the present charge. Ga. Code Ann. §§ 15-11-39(a)(4), 15-11-39.1 (1985).
Hawaii	Exclusive	In effect excludes Class A felonies in certain cases where child is 16 or older.	18	16 where child is alleged to have committed a felony; waiver mandatory in case of child 16 or older charged with a Class A felony who has previously been adjudged to have committed a Class A felony involving force or violence or the threat of force or violence, or to have committed two or more felonies within the previous two-year period. Hawaii Rev. Stat. § 571-22(a),(c) (Supp. 1984).

Idaho	Purports to be exclusive, Idaho Code § 16-1803 (Supp. 1986), *but see State v. Lindsey*, 78 Idaho 241, 300 P2d 491 (1956). Moreover, if a minor initially is brought before a criminal court, certain cases (a minor alleged to have committed an offense after becoming 14 and an adult alleged to have committed a felony before becoming 18) do not have to be transferred to juvenile court. Idaho Code § 16-1804 (Supp. 1986).	Excludes murder, attempted murder, robbery, rape (but not statutory rape), forcible sexual penetration with a foreign object, forcible or violent sodomy, mayhem, and assault or battery with intent to commit any of the foregoing offenses where child 14 or older is charged with any such offense. Idaho Code § 16-1806A(1) (Supp. 1986).	18	14; waiver also permitted where person 18 or older is charged with committing a felony prior to becoming 18 and where person 18 or older already under supervision of court is charged with committing any offense. Idaho Code § 16-1806(1) (Supp. 1986).
Illinois	Exclusive	Excludes murder, criminal sexual assault, armed robbery with a firearm, and possession of a deadly weapon in school committed by child 15 or older. Ill. Ann. Stat. ch. 37, § 702-7(6) (Supp. 1986).	13	17 in case of child alleged to be delinquent; 18 in case of child alleged to be minor requiring authoritative intervention, addicted minor, neglected or abused minor, or dependent minor. Ill. Ann. Stat. tit. 37, §§ 702-2 (1972), 702-3, 702-3.1, 702-4, 702-5 (Supp. 1986).

—continued

State	Type of Jurisdiction	Offenses Excluded	Jurisdictional Age	Waiver of Age
Indiana	Exclusive	Excludes murder, kidnapping, rape, robbery where committed while armed with a deadly weapon or where it results in bodily injury, dealing in a sawed-off shotgun, and any offense arising out of the same conduct joinable with any of the foregoing offenses, if child was 16 or older at time offense allegedly was committed. Ind. Code Ann. § 31-6-2-1(d) (Supp. 1986).	18	Waiver permitted where child is 14 or older and certain aggravating circumstances are present; in addition, unless specified mitigating circumstances are present, waiver is mandatory where child is 10 or older and charged with murder, or 16 or older and charged with a Class A or Class B felony, involuntary manslaughter as a Class C felony, or reckless homicide as a Class C felony, or where child of any age is charged with a felony and has been convicted previously of a felony or nontraffic misdemeanor. Ind. Code Ann. § 31-6-2-4(b)–(e) (Supp. 1986). 14
Iowa	Exclusive. *Mallory v. Paradise,* 173 N.W.2d 264 (Iowa 1969).	None	18	
Kansas	Exclusive	Excludes (1) any felony where child is 16 or older and has two prior felony adjudications, (2) any crime committed by a person described in category (1) who was prosecuted as an adult and convicted of the offense charged, and (3) the offense of running away from a juvenile institution and certain offenses committed against state property, juvenile institutions and employees of juvenile institutions where child is 16 or older. Kan. Stat. Ann. §§ 21-3611, 38-1602(b) (3)–(4), (6); 38-1604(a) (Supp. 1985).	18	16

Kentucky	Exclusive	None	18	14, in case of child charged with capital offense or Class A or B felony; 16, in case of child charged with Class C or D felony who has two prior delinquency adjudications for felonies; waiver also permitted in case of any child charged with felony who has a prior criminal conviction; provided, before certifying any child, court must find child has a delinquency adjudication for a felony within one year prior to commission of present charge and that child has failed to comply with terms of disposition following the prior adjudication. Ky. Rev. Stat. Ann. §§ 635.020(2)-(4), 640.010 (1986 Acts Issue).
Louisiana	Exclusive	Excludes first degree murder, second degree murder, manslaughter, and aggravated rape allegedly committed after child became 15, and armed robbery, aggravated burglary, and aggravated kidnapping allegedly committed after child became 16. La. Rev. Stat. Ann. § 13:1570(A)(5) (1983).	17 in case of child alleged to be delinquent; 18 in case of child alleged to be abused or neglected or in need of supervision. La. code Juv. Proc. Ann. art. 13(9) (1986).	Waiver allowed where child was 15 or older at time of alleged offense and court finds probable cause to believe child committed armed robbery, aggravated burglary, or aggravated kidnapping. La. Rev. Stat. Ann. § 13:1571.1 (A)(1),(4) (1983).
Maine	Exclusive	None	18	None given (waiver permitted where child is charged with murder or any Class A, B, or C offense; waiver mandatory where court finds probable cause to believe child committed any such offense and child is not amendable to juvenile treatment). Me. Rev. Stat. Ann. tit. 15, § 3101(4)(A), (E) (1980 & Supp. 1986).

—continued

State	Type of Jurisdiction	Offenses Excluded	Jurisdictional Age	Waiver of Age
Maryland	Exclusive	Excludes offenses punishable by death or life imprisonment committed by child 14 or older, and the offense of robbery with a dangerous or deadly weapon or attempted robbery with a dangerous or deadly weapon when committed by child 16 or older, unless the case has been transferred to juvenile court from criminal court; criminal court may not transfer case if child previously was waived to juvenile court and adjudicated delinquent, child was convicted in another unrelated case excluded from the juvenile court's jurisdiction, or child is charged with first degree murder and was 16 or older at time offense allegedly was committed. Md. Cts. & Jud. Proc. Code Ann. § 3-804(e)(1), (4) (Supp. 1986); Md. Code Ann. art. 27, § 594A (Supp. 1986).	18	15, except jurisdiction may be waived over any child charged with offense punishable by death or life imprisonment. Md. Cts. & Jud. Proc. Code Ann. § 3-817(a) (1984).
Massachusetts	Exclusive	None	17 in case of child alleged to be a delinquent, a runaway, or an incorrigible child; 16 in case of a child alleged to be truant or disobedient at school. Mass. Gen. Laws Ann. ch. 119, §§ 21 (Supp. 1985), 52 (1969).	Waiver permitted where child previously committed as a delinquent child is charged with felony allegedly committed after child reached 14; also permitted where child is charged with an offense involving infliction or threat of serious bodily harm allegedly committed after child reached 14. Mass. Gen. Laws Ann. ch. 119, § 61 (Supp. 1986).

State	Jurisdiction	Exceptions	Age	Waiver
Michigan	Exclusive; in addition, juvenile court has concurrent jurisdiction over persons between 17 and 18 charged with certain enumerated offenses or conduct. Mich. Compiled Laws Ann. § 712A.2(d) (Supp. 1986).	None	17	15 (waiver permitted only where child charged with felony). Mich. Compiled Laws Ann. § 712A.4(1) (Supp. 1986).
Minnesota	Exclusive	In effect, excludes offenses committed by children 14 or older who were previously certified for criminal prosecution and convicted of the offense or a lesser included offense.	18	14; waiver mandatory in case of child over whom jurisdiction was waived on a previous felony charge and who was convicted of such offense or a lesser included offense; prima facie case of nonamenability is deemed established if child is charged with one of certain enumerated offenses. Minn. Stat. Ann. § 260.125(1), (3) (3a) (1982 & Supp. 1987). [13]
Mississippi	Exclusive	Excludes offenses punishable by death or life imprisonment, unless case is transferred to juvenile court from criminal court. Miss. Code Ann. §§ 43-21-105(j), 43-21-159(3) (1981).	18	
Missouri	Exclusive	None	17	14; waiver permitted only where child charged with felony. Mo. Ann. Stat. § 211.071(1) (Supp. 1987).
Montana	Exclusive	None	18	16 in case of child charged with negligent homicide, arson, aggravated assault, robbery, burglary or aggravated burglary, sexual intercourse without consent, aggravated kidnapping, possession of explosives or criminal sale of dangerous drugs for profit; 12 in case of child charged with sexual intercourse without consent, deliberate homicide, mitigated deliberate homicide, or attempted deliberate homicide or attempted mitigated deliberate

—continued

State	Type of Jurisdiction	Offenses Excluded	Jurisdictional Age	Waiver of Age
				homicide. Mont. Code Ann. § 41-5-206(1)(a) (1985).
Nebraska	Concurrent jurisdiction with district court over child charged with felony or child 16 or older charged with any offense. Neb. Rev. Stat. § 43-247 (Supp. 1986). See also *State v. McCoy*, 145 Neb. 750, 18 N.W.2d 101 (1945).	None	18	No provision for waiver.
Nevada	Exclusive	Excludes murder and attempted murder. Nev. Rev. Stat. §§ 62.040(1)(b)(1), 62.050 (1985).	18	16 (waiver permitted only where child charged with felony). Nev. Rev. Stat. § 62.080 (1983).
New Hampshire	Concurrent jurisdiction over children charged with felonies who are beyond the jurisdiction of the state. N.H. Rev. Stat. Ann. § 169B-25 (Supp. 1986).	None	18	No age given (waiver permitted only where child charged with felony). N.H. Rev. Stat. Ann. § 169-B-24 (Supp. 1986).
New Jersey	Exclusive	None	18	14; waiver permitted only where child is charged with homicide, first degree robbery, aggravated sexual assault, sexual assault, second degree aggravated assault, kidnapping, or aggravated arson; or any crime following a delinquency adjudication for one of the preceding offenses; or any crime following a criminal conviction and confinement in an adult penal institution; or an offense committed in an aggressive, violent and willful manner or the unlawful possession of a firearm, destructive device or prohibited weapon, or arson; or certain drug-related offenses;

—continued

State					
		or crimes committed as part of a group; or an attempt or conspiracy to commit certain offenses; in addition, child 14 or older may elect to be transferred as may child under 14 charged with murder. N.J. Stat. Ann. §§ 2A:4A-26, 2A:4A-27 (Supp. 1986).	16 in case of child charged with felony or charged with assault with intent to commit a violent felony, or kidnapping, aggravated battery, dangerous use of explosives, rape, robbery, aggravated burglary, or aggravated arson; 15 in case of child charged with murder. N.M. Stat. Ann. §§ 32-1-29(A)(1), 32-1-30(A)(1) (1986).		No provisions for waiver.
New Mexico	Exclusive	None		18	
New York	Exclusive	Excludes children 13 or older charged with second degree murder and children 14 or older charged with second degree murder, felony murder, kidnapping in the first degree, arson in the first or second degree, assault in the first degree, manslaughter in the first degree, rape in the first degree, sodomy in the first degree, aggravated sexual abuse, burglary in the first or second degree, robbery in the first or second degree, attempted murder, or attempted kidnapping in the first degree, unless such case is transferred to the juvenile court from the criminal court. N.Y. Fam. Ct. Act § 301.2(1)(b) (McKinney 1983); N.Y. Penal Law §§ 10(18), 30(2) (McKinney Supp. 1987); N.Y. Crim. Proc. Law §§ 180.75, 190.71. 210.43, 220.10(5)(g) (McKinney 1982 & Supp. 1987).		16 in case of child charged with delinquent act; in case of child alleged to be a person in need of supervision, jurisdictional age is 16 for males and 18 for females. N.Y. Fam. Ct. Act §§ 301.2(1), 712(a) (McKinney 1983). The latter provision was held unconstitutional on equal protection grounds in *Patricia A. v. City of New York*, 31 N.Y.2d 83, 286 N.E.2d 432, 335 N.Y.S.2d 33 (1972).	

State	Type of Jurisdiction	Offenses Excluded	Jurisdictional Age	Waiver of Age
North Carolina	Exclusive	In effect, excludes capital offenses from juvenile court's jurisdiction where child is 14 or older. N.C. Gen. Stat. § 7A-608 (1986).	16 in case of child alleged to be delinquent or undisciplined; 18 in case of child alleged to be neglected, dependent, or abused. N.C. Gen. Stat. § 7A-517(1), (12), (13), (20), (21), (28) (1986).	14 (waiver permitted only where child charged with felony; however, waiver is mandatory if felony charged is a capital offense). N.C. Gen. Stat. § 7A-608 (1986).
North Dakota	Exclusive	None	18	14, except if child is 14 or 15, offense must involve infliction or threat of serious bodily harm; also, child 16 or older may request waiver and transfer. N.D. Cent. Code § 27-20-34(1) (Supp. 1985).
Ohio	Exclusive	In effect, excludes murder, aggravated murder, or any felony of the first or second degree, if the child previously had a case waived and was convicted. Ohio Rev. Code Ann. § 2151.26(G) (Supp. 1986).	18	15 (waiver permitted only where child charged with felony); waiver mandatory if child previously had a case waived and was convicted and is now charged with murder, aggravated murder, or any felony of the first or second degree. Ohio Rev. Code Ann. § 2151.26(A), (G) (Supp. 1986).
Oklahoma	Exclusive	Excludes child 16 or older charged with murder, kidnapping for purposes of extortion, robbery with a dangerous weapon, rape in the first degree, use of firearm or other offensive weapon while committing a felony, arson in the first degree, burglary with explosives, shooting with intent to kill, manslaughter in the first degree, or nonconsensual sodomy, unless such case is transferred to juvenile court from criminal court, Okla. Stat. Ann. tit. 10, § 1104.2 (Supp. 1987).	18	No age given (waiver permitted only where child charged with felony). Okla. Stat. Ann. tit. 10, § 1112(b) (Supp. 1986).

State				
Oregon	Exclusive	None	18	15, in case of child charged with murder, a Class A or B felony, or one of certain enumerated Class C felonies; however, 15-year-old shall not be certified unless charged with one of certain enumerated serious offenses. Or. Rev. Stat. § 419.533(1)(a)–(b), (3) (1985).
Pennsylvania	Exclusive	Excludes murder from jurisdiction of juvenile court, unless such case is transferred to juvenile court from criminal court. Pa. Stat. Ann. tit. 42, §§ 6302, 6322(a), 6355(e) (1982).	18	Waiver permitted where child is 14 and charged with felony; waiver mandatory in case of child charged with murder, unless case has been transferred to juvenile court from criminal court. Pa. Stat. Ann. tit. 42, § 6355(a) (1), (a)(4)(ii), (e) (1982).
Rhode Island	Exclusive	None; however, in case of child 16 or older who has been found delinquent for having committed two indictable offenses after reaching the age of 16, any subsequent offenses are prosecuted as in the case of an adult. R.I. Gen. Laws Ann. § 14-1-7.1 (Supp. 1986).	18	16 (waiver permitted only where child charged with indictable offense). R.I. Gen. Laws Ann. § 14-1-7 (1981).
South Carolina	Exclusive	None	17 in case of child alleged to be delinquent; 18 in case of child alleged to be dependent or neglected. S.C. Code § 20-7-390 (1985).	Waiver permitted where child of any age is charged with murder or sexual assault; waiver also permitted where child 16 or older is charged with misdemeanor or felony and where child 14 or 15 has two prior adjudications for assault, assault and battery with intent to kill, aggravated assault and battery, arson, housebreaking, burglary, kidnapping, attempted criminal sexual conduct, or robbery and is charged with a third or subsequent such offense. S.C. Code § 20-7-430(4)–(6) (1985).

—continued

State	Type of Jurisdiction	Offenses Excluded	Jurisdictional Age	Waiver of Age
South Dakota	Concurrent jurisdiction in felony cases. S.D. Compiled Laws § 26-11-3 (1984).	None	18	No age given
Tennessee	Exclusive	None	18	16 generally, except that jurisdiction may also be waived in any case in which the child was 14 or older at the time the offense allegedly occurred and the offense charged is murder, rape, aggravated rape, robbery with a deadly weapon, or kidnapping. Tenn. Code Ann. § 37-1-134(a)(1) (1984).
Texas	Exclusive	None	17	15 in case of child charged with felony; waiver also allowed where person is 18 or older and charged with committing a felony when 15 or older but before becoming 17. Tex. Fam. Code Ann. § 54.02(a)(1)-(2), (j) (1986).
Utah	Concurrent jurisdiction in case of child 16 or older charged with any class of criminal homicide or attempted criminal homicide, aggravated robbery, or forcible sodomy, aggravated arson, aggravated sexual abuse of a child, aggravated sexual assault, aggravated burglary, or aggravated kidnapping. Utah Code Ann. § 73-3a-25(6) (Supp. 1986).	None	18	14 (waiver permitted only where child charged with felony). Utah Code Ann. § 73-3a-25(1) (Supp. 1985).

State				
Vermont	Exclusive; however, criminal court has discretion to transfer to juvenile court a person who was over 16 but under 18 at time offense was allegedly committed. Vt. Stat. Ann. tit. 33, § 635(b) (1981).	Excludes cases involving child 14 or older but under 16 charged with arson causing death, assault and robbery with a dangerous weapon, assault and robbery causing bodily injury, aggravated assault, murder, manslaughter, kidnapping, maiming, sexual assault, aggravated sexual assault, or nighttime burglary of a dwelling unless case is transferred to juvenile court from criminal court. Vt. Stat. Ann. tit. 33, §§ 635(b), 644(c) (1981).	16 in case of delinquent child; 18 in case of child in need of care or supervision. Vt. Stat. Ann. tit. 33, § 632(a)(1) (1981).	10 but less than 14 (waiver permitted only where child charged with arson causing death, assault and robbery with a dangerous weapon, assault and robbery causing bodily injury, aggravated assault, murder, manslaughter, kidnapping, maiming, sexual assault, aggravated sexual assault, or nighttime burglary of a dwelling). Vt. Stat. Ann. tit. 33, § 635a(a) (1981).
Virginia	Exclusive	None	18	15 (waiver permitted only where child charged with felony). Va. Code Ann. § 16.1-269(A) (1982).
Washington	Exclusive	None	18	No age given; a waiver hearing is mandatory, however, if the child is 16 or older and charged with a Class A felony or an attempt to commit a Class A felony, or if the child is 17 and charged with assault in the second degree, extortion in the first degree, indecent liberties, kidnapping in the second degree, rape in the second degree, or robbery in the second degree. Wash. Rev. Code Ann. § 13.40.110(1) (Supp. 1987).

—continued

State	Type of Jurisdiction	Offenses Excluded	Jurisdictional Age	Waiver of Age
West Virginia	Exclusive	None	18	Waiver required where demanded by child 16 or older; waiver permitted where (1) child of any age is charged with treason, murder, armed robbery, kidnapping, first degree arson, or sexual assault in the first degree, (2) child of any age is charged with violent felony and has previously been adjudged delinquent for commission of a violent felony, (3) child of any age is charged with felony and has been twice previously adjudged delinquent for commission of a felony, (4) child 16 or older is charged with violent felony, or (5) child 16 or older is charged with felony and has previously been adjudged delinquent for commission of a felony. W. Va. Code Ann. § 49-5-10(c)–(d) (1980).
Wisconsin	Exclusive	None	18	16
Wyoming	Concurrent jurisdiction allowed in case of child 13 or older, although case must originate in juvenile court (such cases may originate in either court if the maximum penalty does not include imprisonment for more than six months); concurrent jurisdiction also allowed in case of child 17 or older charged with an offense, and case may originate in either court. Wyo. Stat. Ann. §§ 14-6-203(c)–(f), 14-6-211 (1986).	None	19	No age given

SOURCE: Clark Boardman Co. Ltd. Reprinted, with permission, from *Rights of Juveniles*, by Samuel M. Davis (Clark Boardman Co. Ltd.: 1989), Appendix B.

SOCIAL HISTORY INTERVIEW NOTES

DATE DUE _____

IDENTIFYING INFORMATION

Name _____   Race _____

Address _____   Sex _____

D.O.B. _____   Parents _____

PEOPLE CONTACTED (Full Names and Titles)

THE PETITION

Date Petition Signed _____

Name of Petitioner _____

Title _____

Name of Offense _____

Date of Court Order _____

Court Order _____

PREVIOUS DIFFICULTY

Legal Background

Date   Offense   Disposition

Other Agencies

Date   Offense   Disposition

Placements

Name   Date   Reason

PRESENT FAMILY SITUATION
Parents

Natural Mother	_____	*Natural Father*	_____
D.O.B.	_____	D.O.B.	_____
Employment	_____	Employment	_____
Previous Marriage	_____	Previous Marriage	_____
Other Info	_____	Other Info	_____

Step-Father	_____	*Step-Mother*	_____
D.O.B.	_____	D.O.B.	_____
Employment	_____	Employment	_____
Previous Marriage	_____	Previous Marriage	_____
Other Info	_____	Other Info	_____

Siblings

Name   D.O.B.   Residence

Client

Placement in Family	_____	Age	_____
School	_____	Grade	_____
Work	_____	Weight	_____
Height	_____	Eyes	_____
Hair	_____	Scars or Marks	_____
Complexion	_____	Health	_____
Aliases	_____		
Other Info	_____		

INTERVIEW WITH PARENTS
Version of Offense

Origin of Problem—Attempts to Solve

Description of Child

Description of Spouse

Description of Self

Family (problems, interactions, history)

Discipline (sexual and physical abuse)

Drugs

Child's School

Child's Employment

Recommendation

INTERVIEW WITH YOUTH
Version of Offense

Origin of Problem

Description of Parents

Description of Sibling Relationships

Description of Self

Family (problems, interactions, history)

Discipline (sexual and physical abuse)

School

Employment

Drugs

Friends, Interests and Hobbies

Recommendation

EDUCATION
School _____ Grade _____
Attendance Data

Grades

Testing Info

Exam   Date   Interpretation

Comments from AP or counselor:
Name _____

ADDITIONAL INFORMATION
Chemical Dependency Evaluation

Psychological

Restitution

PROBLEM ASSESSMENT

RECOMMENDATION

ALTERNATIVE RECOMMENDATIONS

METROPOLITAN COURT JUDGES COMMITTEE: 73 RECOMMENDATIONS

Role of Judges

1. Judges must provide leadership within the community in determining needs and obtaining and developing resources and services for deprived children and families.

2. Juvenile and family courts must have the clear authority, by statute or rule, to review, order and enforce the delivery of specific services and treatment for deprived children.

3. Judges must encourage cooperation and coordination among the courts and various public and private agencies with responsibilities for deprived children.

4. Judges and court personnel must make every effort to increase media and public awareness of the complex and sensitive issues related to deprived children.

5. Juvenile and family courts must maintain close liaison and encourage coordination of policies with school authorities.

6. Judges must exercise leadership in (a) analyzing the needs of deprived children and (b) encouraging the development of adequate resources to meet those needs.

7. Judges should take an active part in the formation of a community-wide, multi-disciplinary "Constituency for Children" to promote and unify private and public sector efforts to focus attention and resources on meeting the needs of deprived children who have no effective voice of their own.

Court Procedures

8. Juvenile and family courts, to be effective, must have the same stature as general jurisdiction courts. Judicial assignments should be based on expressed interest and competence and be for a substantial number of years.

9. All judges of all courts must ensure sensitivity in the courtroom and encourage sensitivity out of the courtroom to minimize trauma to the child victim.

10. Juvenile and family courts should have immediate and primary jurisdiction over children who have been allegedly abused to ensure protection and treatment for the child victim, notwithstanding pending criminal proceedings.

11. Adult prosecution arising out of an allegation of abuse should be coordinated with juvenile and family courts.

12. Priority must be given to abuse and neglect cases in the trial court as well as in the appellate process.

13. Juvenile and family courts must have funding to allow reasonable judicial caseloads and an adequate number of judicial officers to assure the necessary time for each case.

14. Court-appointed and public attorneys representing children in abuse and neglect cases, as well as judges, should be specially trained or experienced.

15. Court Appointed Special Advocates (CASAs) should be utilized by the court at the earliest stage of the court process, where necessary, to communicate the best interests of an abused or neglected child.

16. Juvenile and family courts should consider the use of judicially appointed citizen advisory boards to assist the court with independent screening, monitoring and review of individual placements, services, facilities and treatment.

17. A person supportive of the child witness should be permitted to be present in court and accessible to the child during the child's testimony without influencing that testimony.

18. Family members should be permitted to offer suggestions or testify in aid of the disposition of the case.

19. Evidentiary and procedural rules consistent with due process must be adopted to protect the child victim from further trauma.

20. All courts should be granted authority to issue protective or restraining orders to prevent further abuse. Such orders should be freely used and vigorously enforced.

Detecting, Reporting and Evaluating

21. All persons who work with children on a regular basis should be trained to recognize indicators of abuse, neglect or significant deprivation.

22. All persons working with children must promptly report known or reasonably suspected abuse and neglect. Communication and witness privileges must not impede the reporting, investigation and adjudication of alleged child abuse.

23. Appropriate governmental agencies, schools of medicine and social work, and the media should widely publicize in each community reliable indicators of vulnerable families, child physical and sexual abuse and child neglect.

24. Abusive or potentially abusive persons should be encouraged to acknowledge their problem, seek help and participate in voluntary treatment for themselves and their families.

25. Agencies must respond immediately to reports of child abuse and neglect and provide follow-up information to the reporter.

26. A central registry of complaints of alleged abuse and neglect must be developed and maintained in each state with mandatory reporting of data from child protection and health agencies, as well as law enforcement and school officials, with access on a demonstrated "need to know" basis.

27. A thorough assessment of a child's problems and family is needed at all public and private intake facilities.

28. Child protection services and facilities should be available 24 hours a day to assure that allegations of serious neglect or abuse can be assessed and protection provided.

29. Reports of abuse and neglect should be evaluated immediately and, where necessary, a coordinated plan of action should be developed by law enforcement, the child protection agencies and the prosecutor.

30. Emergency removal of the child from the home must be subject to prompt judicial review.

31. The alleged offender, rather than the child, should be removed from the home, whenever appropriate.

32. A suspected child victim of abuse and the non-offending family members should not be subjected to repetitious and unsystematic interviews.

Out-of-Home Placement

33. A child should not be removed from home until consideration is given as to whether the child can remain at home safely.

34. The number, duration and traumatic impact of out-of-home placements of deprived children must be reduced by "reasonable efforts" to seek alternatives consistent with the child's need for protection and treatment.

35. Judges should evaluate the criteria established by child protection agencies for initial removal and reunification decisions and determine the court's expectations of the agency as to what constitutes "reasonable efforts" to prevent removal or to hasten return of the child.

36. In placing children, courts and child protection agencies must give consideration to maintaining racial, cultural, ethnic and religious values.

37. Programs which promote family preservation and prevention of out-of-home placement by providing early intensive services for the at-risk child and family must be developed and utilized in all communities.

38. Agreements between parents and a child protection agency which voluntarily place a child out of the home should be in writing, filed with the court and reviewed by the court within 30 days.

39. As required by federal law, independent judicial review of all placements by the court or by a judicially appointed citizen review board must be conducted at least every six months. Eighteen months following placement, the court must conduct a full hearing to review the family service plan and the progress of the child for the purpose of establishing permanency planning for the child.

40. Provision must be made for minimum standards and frequent review and inspection of all out-of-home placement facilities, staff and treatment programs.

41. A child removed from home must be returned to the family as soon as conditions causing the removal have been substantially corrected and safeguards established.

Treatment and Planning

42. Treatment of an abused and neglected child must be immediate, thorough and coordinated among responsible agencies.

43. Treatment provided to the child through court or agency intervention should involve the entire family or focus on family relationships as they impact on the child, and should stress the primary responsibility of the parents for the child's welfare and protection.

44. Child protection agencies and the courts should require parental responsibility for a child's well-being.

45. Judges, as part of the disposition for the child, must have authority to order treatment for the parents, to require other positive conduct, and to impose sanctions for willful failure or refusal to comply.

46. Substance abuse treatment, where appropriate, should be mandated for the parents and the child.

47. Judges must have the authority to order the treatment determined to be necessary and should regularly review the efficacy of such treatment.

48. Judges must require appropriate treatment for youthful sexual offenders, most of whom have been victims of sexual abuse.

49. The court should require the offender to pay the costs of treating the child victim.

50. Child victims of abuse or neglect should be eligible for victims assistance and compensation programs.

51. In child support, custody and dependency hearings, if parents have or can obtain health care insurance, the court should order coverage.

52. Child protection caseworkers must be screened, trained and certified in order to improve child protection services and treatment.

53. Screened, qualified and trained volunteers should be used to enhance the quality of services to deprived children and families.

54. A sufficient number of foster homes, adequately reimbursed and provided with access to treatment and support services, should be established.

55. Frequent movement of children from foster home to foster home is detrimental to a child's physical and emotional well-being and must be reduced.

56. Specialized foster homes and foster parents should be established in each community for children with special needs.

57. Homeless and runaway children must be provided proper emergency shelter facilities as well as necessary services.

58. When there is clear and convincing evidence that the conduct of the parents would, under law, permit the termination of parental rights, and it is in the best interests of the child to do so, termination should proceed expeditiously.

59. When reunification is not possible or termination of parental rights is not in the best interests of the child, courts should consider other permanent plans.

60. When needed, adoption should proceed expeditiously. Foster parents should not be precluded from adopting their foster child.

61. Subsidized adoption programs should be more widely available and used for special needs and hard-to-place children.

Prevention Issues

62. Prevention and early intervention efforts must receive a high priority, with a greater emphasis placed on providing adequate services to prevent child abuse, neglect and family break-ups through adequate education, early identification of those at risk, and family-based counseling and homemaker services.

63. Continuing education in parenting and in understanding the physical and emotional needs of children and families should be widely available in schools, health care systems, religious organizations and community centers.

64. Communities must provide special parenting education and services for pregnant teenagers as well as teenage parents, including counseling on relinquishment and adoption.

65. Adequate child care facilities and services, with training, licensing and monitoring of the providers, should be available to all parents needing such services.

66. Employer-sponsored assistance and counseling programs for family violence and child abuse and neglect, such as those used for alcoholism and drug abuse, should be established.

67. Identification and assessment of the physically, mentally, emotionally or the learning disabled child must occur as early as possible.

68. Services and education must be designed for and provided to mentally ill, emotionally disturbed and developmentally disabled children and parents.

69. Judges must assure that child support orders are expedited and vigorously enforced and urge cooperation among all components of the child support enforcement process and all federal and state government agencies which may impact on child support enforcement proceedings.

70. Persons convicted of exploiting children by means of pornography, prostitution, drug use or trafficking must be severely punished. High priorities also must be given to national efforts to curtail the availability to children of pornography and excessively violent materials.

71. Courts and communities must provide services and courts must intervene, where necessary, to assist homeless, truant, runaway, and incorrigible children. Parents must be held personally and financially accountable for the conduct of their children.

72. Courts should cooperate with schools and other agencies to substantially reduce truancy and dropouts by coordinating and providing services and assistance to the habitual truant.

73. The courts should have authority to detain, in a secure facility for a limited period, a runaway, truant or incorrigible child whose chronic behavior constitutes a clear and present danger to the child's own physical or emotional well-being, when the court determines there is no viable alternative.

SOURCE: Metropolitan Court Judges Committee Reports, *Deprived Children: A Judicial Response* (Reno, Nev.: National Council of Juvenile and Family Court Judges, 1986).

ROLES AND RESPONSIBILITIES FOR A DRUG-FREE SCHOOL AND COMMUNITY

Students

Awareness/Education

Become aware of:

—the effects of drugs, including alcohol

—signs of chemical dependency

—resources available at school and in the community

—local laws and school policies on drugs, including alcohol

—friends' attitudes about drugs, including alcohol.

Education/Training

Set goals for graduation and education achievement.

Participate in school and community drug-free activities.

Participate in training that teaches refusal skills.

Learn communication and conflict management skills to better deal with family, teachers, peers, and others.

Assessment

Provide honest answers on school and community alcohol and other drug surveys.

Policy/Legislation

Participate in the development of school policies through student groups or student government.

Obey and show respect for school policies and local laws.

Prevention

Participate in drug-free activities with family and friends, at school and in the community.

Explore "discovery" activities, i.e., skiing, hiking, canoeing, dance, music, art, zoo, museum.

Avoid situations that make it hard to say no to drugs, including alcohol.

Develop friendships with people who are known for not using drugs, including alcohol.

Volunteer for community service projects.

Encourage other students to resist drugs, including alcohol.

Intervention

Know:

—warning signs of use

—what to say when

—when and how to refer someone to a professional

—where to get help at school and in the community.

Treatment/Aftercare

Provide a supportive environment and be a peer helper.

Encourage involvement in support groups.

Know treatment alternatives.

Funding

Support and conduct fundraising efforts for local drug education and prevention programs.

Research

Provide constructive feedback during evaluations of drug education and prevention programs.

Participate in research activities.

Family

Awareness/Education

Become aware of:

—the effects of drugs, including alcohol

—signs of chemical dependency

—resources available in the community for intervention, treatment, and aftercare

—history/characteristics of disease in the family

—child's friends and activities

—local laws and school policies on drugs, including alcohol.

Education/Training

Model healthy and expected behavior.

Support child's education:

—set expectations for graduation and academic achievement

—provide encouragement, support, and guidance

—model respect for education and school

—reinforce school-based programs through active participation.

Seek to develop for children and parents:

—communication skills

—decision making skills

—conflict management skills

—refusal skills

—ability to analyze media messages and other information

—self-responsibility.

Assessment

Examine family use of drugs, including alcohol.

Participate in school and community assessment process.

Policy/Legislation

Establish rules and guidelines for children about drugs, including alcohol, that are consistent with local laws.

Assist in the development and yearly review of school policies.

Obey and show respect for the law.

Work to reduce the effects of alcohol and tobacco advertising.

Prevention

Have specific family time (individual and group) with planned activities.

Plan "discovery" activities, i.e. skiing, hiking, canoeing, dance, music, art, zoo, museum.

Celebrate without alcohol.

Bring teen activities back into the home.

Promote drug/alcohol-free parties.

Participate in local parent groups.

Volunteer in a variety of community and school prevention activities.

Intervention

Intervene at the first signs of drug use.

Understand concept of "tough love."

Understand types and availability of services.

Seek outside help.

Treatment/Aftercare

Involve all family members.

Understand concept of codependency.

Provide a supportive environment.

Know treatment alternatives.

Encourage involvement in support groups.

Promote acceptance that aftercare is long term.

Take part in child's reentry into school.

Funding

Contribute to local drug education and prevention efforts.

Be aware of public funds allocated and spent for drug education.

Research

Support and, when appropriate, participate in research activities.

Community Organizations/Parent Groups

Awareness/Education

Develop ways to distribute information about drugs, including alcohol.

Review laws and ordinances related to the sale or use of drugs, including tobacco and alcohol, to determine how laws can better protect students.

Update local substance abuse materials.

Organize local speakers bureau.

Education/Training

Cosponsor ongoing educational programs.

Provide parenting classes and related activities.

Provide drug prevention training and technical assistance to educators and other adults who work with students.

Assist in providing training for peer helper programs.

Participate in the development and selection of drug education and prevention programs in the schools.

Assessment

Establish a drug prevention task force to analyze the nature and extent of drug problems, including alcohol, among youths living in the community.

Policy/Legislation

Actively participate in policy development and implementation at schools and places of business.

Support school policies and enforce all laws on the sale and distribution of alcohol and tobacco to minors.

Reinforce school policy in community-based youth organizations.

Promote adoption of substance abuse policies for all professional groups.

Prevention

Recognize student participation in drug-free activities.

Model appropriate use of leisure time by offering and cosponsoring alternative recreational activities for youth.

Provide and sponsor programs and activities in school facilities, to provide after-hours activities for youth.

Ensure that activities reach all segments of the community.

Volunteer in a variety of community and school prevention activities.

Intervention

Know resources for referral.

Train community volunteers and staff in intervention techniques.

Provide volunteer services to local programs and schools.

Treatment/Aftercare

Increase community awareness of treatment centers available in area.

Foster support groups (provide meeting place, etc.) and promote establishment if not available.

Promote programs that encourage active family participation.

Funding

Support and conduct fundraising efforts for local drug education and prevention programs.

Research

Conduct regular evaluations of all sponsored drug education and prevention programs and incorporate findings into program design.

Cooperate with research initiatives.

Publicize current findings for public awareness.

Schools/Colleges and Universities

Awareness/Education

Make available information on the physical and psychosocial consequences of using drugs.

Educate the public that alcohol use by underage students is as harmful to students as other forms of illegal drug use.

Conduct and distribute results of student incidence and prevalence surveys at regular intervals.

Have updated materials available in the media center.

Know and use Department of Education's Drug-Free Schools Program.

Reinforce principles of civic and individual values and responsibilities.

Education/Training

Provide administrator and employee in-service training on leadership, alcohol and other drug-related matters at least twice a year.

Develop and introduce multicomponent K-12 drug education and prevention programs based upon assessment of drug problems, including alcohol and tobacco, of students and staff.

Conduct mandatory drug education and prevention orientation sessions for all new students.

Teach students the basic concepts of marketing alcohol and tobacco products.

Provide peer helper training.

Raise academic standards for students and improve teaching techniques for staff.

Develop classes for parents that include information about drugs and techniques for improving communication skills and managing conflict.

Develop and implement programs to educate parents and alumni on drug issues, including alcohol, and to change attitudes about social and experimental use of drugs.

Assessment

Establish a task force to conduct yearly evaluations of all drug education and prevention programs and incorporate findings into prevention strategy and design.

Conduct school surveys every two to three years to assess drug of preference and patterns of use on campus.

Policy/Legislation

Develop a long-term drug education and prevention strategy.

Develop comprehensive policy on: the possession, use, promotion, distribution, and sale of drugs, including alcohol and tobacco. Policy should apply to students, staff, and anyone attending school functions.

Review policies annually with students, faculty, and parents.

School boards should reopen discussion on including values education in the school curriculum and programs.

Prohibit alcohol and tobacco use and advertising at all school-sponsored events.

Require all organized group residences to develop risk management plans.

Prevention

Develop comprehensive prevention and education programs.

Recognize prevention efforts of individuals and groups.

Promote drug-free events for students and staff.

Allow students ownership of events.

Develop linkages with community organizations involved in education, prevention, and treatment.

Volunteer in a variety of community and school prevention activities.

Develop mechanisms to keep the school open after hours as a community resource.

Ensure that college students who want to remain drug/alcohol-free are placed in dorms with others who share their perspective.

Intervention

Train entire staff and peer helper groups in early intervention techniques.

Identify high-risk students and provide both individual and group support.

Provide student assistance programs.

Provide employee assistance programs for staff.

Develop workable relationships with substance abuse treatment centers.

Assign school counselors where needed to maximize early intervention.

Treatment/Aftercare

Become knowledgeable about effective treatment programs and various types of treatment.

Maintain effective communication with treatment providers.

Provide instructional materials and/or teachers so that students can continue their education while in treatment.

Require debriefing/reentry conference with treatment provider when students return.

Assign staff to work with treatment provider on aftercare support.

Ensure that schools have adequate support programs for students and staff who need help with drinking problems.

Provide support groups in schools.

Involve peer helpers.

Funding

Maximize dollars available through coordination of school and community prevention efforts.

Commit funding for enough time to develop, implement, and assess multicomponent prevention programs.

Research

Use current research findings in developing or revising programs.

Ensure that packaged education prevention programs are based upon sound research and evaluation findings.

Conduct regular evaluations of all drug education and prevention programs and incorporate findings into program design.

Religious Organizations

Awareness/Education

Become aware of:

—the effects of drugs/alcohol

—signs of chemical dependency

—resources available in the community for intervention, treatment, and aftercare.

Speak out on drug issues, including alcohol, in sermons, youth groups, classes, etc.

Education/Training

Encourage mandatory training in substance abuse counseling during cleric education.

Offer clergy workshops that provide skills to identify and intervene with chemically dependent members and families.

Use substance abuse issues as speaking topics.

Develop substance abuse curriculum for adult and youth education classes.

Provide youth leadership training.

Offer parenting classes.

Instill values.

Assessment

Participate in community assessments.

Policy/Legislation

Develop position on substance abuse to include program development and advocacy.

Clarify position on use and non-use of alcohol on religious property.

Prevention

Provide activities for youth.

Provide positive leisure and family activities that are drug/alcohol free.

Encourage schools and communities to provide drug/alcohol-free activities through use of church-owned facilities.

Volunteer to help in a variety of community and school prevention activities.

Intervention

Provide counseling and referral when appropriate.

Serve as liaison to substance abuse programs.

Provide peer helper training.

Facilitate support groups, i.e., Children of Alcoholics.

Provide employee assistance programs for clergy, employees, and families.

Treatment/Aftercare

Know treatment modalities and available resources in the community.

Visit and support chemically dependent people.

Provide site for meetings of groups such as Alcoholics Anonymous and Narcotics Anonymous.

Funding

Support drug education activities as part of the budget.

Designate specific offerings for drug prevention causes.

Research

Support and participate in research activities.

Media

Awareness/Education

Be knowledgeable about drug-related issues.

Create local public service announcements.

Provide equal time for health-related information announcements.

Provide factual reporting that also portrays positive news.

Be aware of the influence of alcohol/tobacco advertising.

Education/Training

Provide regular news articles/TV and radio shows about drug issues, including alcohol.

Provide more comprehensive documentary features on special aspects of the drug problem.

Use the captive audience from prior recommendation to demonstrate "what works."

Assessment

Promote and publicize community and school assessment results.

Policy/Legislation

Have a clear policy that provides guidelines on the reporting of substance abuse issues to ensure that events, individuals, or groups do not glamorize drugs.

Develop strategy of long-term commitment to addressing drug issues, including alcohol.

Keep abreast of local school policies to ensure accuracy of reporting.

Establish and abide by policies regarding the promotion of alcohol and tobacco.

Prevention

Develop public service announcements in conjunction with communitywide prevention initiatives.

Publicize prevention activities.

Promote and sponsor drug-free events.

Volunteer in community and school prevention activities.

Intervention

Publicize:

—warning signs of use

—when and how to intervene

—where to get a professional assessment

—costs and sources of financial assistance.

Promote employee assistance programs.

Treatment/Aftercare

Publicize components of effective treatment.

Publicize locations of support groups for aftercare.

Funding

Conduct and support fundraising efforts of local programs.

Provide public service announcements for antidrug messages and prevention activities.

Research

Publicize current findings for general public awareness.

Business/Industry

Awareness/Education

Sponsor drug prevention awareness sessions for employees.

Distribute prevention information pamphlets and brochures to employees and to the public.

Education/Training

Provide employee assistance programs that include training in parenting.

Provide training and technical support for mentoring programs, job banks, career opportunity seminars, "executive loan," and "shadowing" programs for schools.

Train supervisors to identify and refer problem behavior.

Assessment

Help schools and communities conduct assessments and analyze results, including providing computer time to process data.

Policy/Legislation

Develop policies that address the consequences of use/possession/distribution, including disciplinary action.

Enforce school alcohol and tobacco policies on the job for students under 21.

Adopt voluntary alcohol and tobacco advertising and promotional standards that:

—do not use young models

—target *only* the population for which use is legal

—inform consumers that drinking and smoking are illegal for youth

—do not market/advertise in areas with a high proportion of young people.

Limit the amount of alcohol advertising during sporting activities.

Establish a smoke-free workplace.

Consider the use of urine testing for employees returning from treatment.

Prevention

Establish programs to reward drug-free youth through scholarships, jobs, shopping discounts, etc.

Participate in mentor programs, job banks, career opportunity seminars, "executive loan," and "shadowing" programs for students.

Provide employees with time off for involvement in community and school prevention activities. .

Intervention

Provide employee assistance programs.

Establish support groups for employees whose children are involved with drugs.

Treatment/Aftercare

Train supervisory personnel about relapse behaviors.

Promote acceptance of aftercare as an important part of the treatment process.

Provide support groups for parents of children involved in drug use.

Encourage the use of support programs for individuals and families.

Provide jobs for recovering addicts and alcoholics.

Funding

Support community/school prevention partnerships.

Assist in fundraising to support drug education programs.

Provide in-kind contributions.

Research

Publishers of textbooks and other program materials should apply the latest research in developing drug curriculums and programs.

Encourage and support research-based prevention.

Health and Social Services

Awareness/Education

Inform the community about the resources available for drug-alcohol treatment.

Target public housing tenants and low-income families for information and services.

Education/Training

Offer seminars and other education programs to the community and schools.

Provide teacher training on the nature and development of drug dependency.

Provide training on drug addition, including alcohol, to medical students and health-related professionals.

Provide additional training, technical assistance, and service delivery information where needed.

Assessment

Assist in the development and/or support mechanism to ensure accurate assessments.

Policy/Legislation

Become familiar with all school policies in referral region.

Provide input in development of school policies by serving on advisory committees or other special task forces.

Incorporate a personnel policy on drug and alcohol use.

Develop a mechanism for coordinating community services with school prevention efforts.

Prevention

Promote healthy life-style options via special seminars, conferences, and related activities.

Provide programs designed to build specific skills, encourage self-esteem, and promote personal growth to high-risk populations.

Provide drug-free activities for youth.

Volunteer in community and school prevention activities.

Intervention

Offer on-site community programs in high-risk communities.

Serve as a primary provider for services and support private initiatives.

Establish and encourage support groups.

Provide intervention services in schools.

Provide guidelines for employee assistance programs.

Treatment/Aftercare

Provide on-site outpatient centers in high-risk communities.

Increase availability of inpatient treatment beds for youth.

Promote helpful communication and cooperation among treatment providers.

Provide treatment and aftercare alternatives for public use.

Advocate school-based, for-credit support groups for recovering youth.

Funding

Through grants, contracts, foundations, fundraising efforts, and for-profit monies, support all local drug abuse and alcohol prevention, education, and treatment programs.

Research

Cooperate with research initiatives.

Distribute research findings to the general public in easy-to-understand language.

Law Enforcement/Judicial

Awareness/Education

Obtain current, accurate information on drugs, including alcohol.

Support and publicize community efforts to reduce demand, i.e., Neighborhood Watch, Officer Friendly, McGruff.

Education/Training

Assist in training of staff for community and school programs.

Provide accurate information through appropriate classroom activities.

Provide training on local demand reduction programs to all segments of the community.

Assessment

Determine the frequency of drug use and drug of choice in the community through arrest records, hospitalizations, and community surveys.

Policy/Legislation

Help develop schools' policies to ensure that school policies adhere to state and local laws.

Support local and state statutes targeting school-yard offenders.

Prevention

Help develop a comprehensive community strategy.

Implement antidrug activities in community groups, schools, workplaces, and churches.

Hold parents liable for their own illegal acts that may encourage their children to engage in illegal activities.

Enforce policies and statutes related to drug use, including alcohol, among youth.

Volunteer in community and school prevention activities.

Intervention

Help identify youth with potential problems.

Be prepared to direct youth to the appropriate service provider.

Treatment/Aftercare

Mandate treatment when appropriate during sentencing proceedings and enforce through probation and parole sanctions.

Provide treatment programs in jails and prisons.

Funding

Help sponsor local fundraisers for programs and activities to reduce the demand for drugs.

Research

Support and participate in research, particularly research dealing with the criminal justice system, its offenders, and how they affect society.

Government

Awareness/Education

States should collect and maintain data on alcohol-related violations of the law.

Be aware of the relationships between substance use, high school dropouts, and the economic effects on the community and state.

Provide accurate, current information on all drugs.

Develop/distribute a list of antidrug programs, concepts, and activities that have proven to be effective.

Launch statewide campaigns against drugs, smoking, and drinking.

Require counter alcohol and tobacco advertising.

Education/Training

Distribute newsletters containing information about drugs, including alcohol and tobacco.

Promote in-service training for all legislators and other government employees.

Develop training programs for use by school personnel.

States should develop technical assistance centers comparable to federal regional centers.

Develop a national training and technical assistance center for colleges.

Help small school districts enter into a consortium to make more efficient use of Drug-Free Schools funds.

Assessment

Develop and distribute assessment standards and model survey instruments to assist with assessment.

Require schools and colleges to conduct comprehensive, written surveys of students and staff every two years to determine their drug problems, including alcohol, and their prevention needs.

Review sanctions for violations of alcohol and tobacco laws.

Policy/Legislation

Require all schools, colleges, and universities to adopt and enforce strict alcohol and drug policies.

Restrict the availability of alcohol at off-campus, school-related functions.

Develop certification and recertification standards on health and social skills education, including drug prevention, for professionals who work with students.

Coordinate management of drug education and prevention funds through a central state office or organization.

Expand Drug-Free School Zones legislation to include colleges and universities.

Ensure that local laws on drugs, including alcohol and tobacco, are enforced fairly and consistently.

Enforce current regulations required for schools, colleges, and universities to receive federal funds.

Require all stores selling tobacco to be licensed.

Ban cigarette vending machines.

Restrict use of driver's license for drug offenders.

Adopt and reinforce antiparaphernalia laws.

Restrict display of alcoholic beverages, especially beer and wine coolers.

Prevention

Require evidence of sound research and demonstrated effectiveness to continue funding.

Promote drug-free activities.

Create drug-free recognition programs for schools, colleges and universities, associations, parent groups, etc.

Ensure that all recognition and awards programs take schools' drug policies and programs into account equally with other factors.

Provide administrative leave time for employees volunteering for prevention activities in the school or community.

Intervention

Provide employee assistance programs for legislators and other government employees.

Encourage a "parent component" in all publicly funded drug education, prevention, and treatment programs.

Treatment/Aftercare

Understand the different types of treatment (i.e., inpatient, outpatient) and various costs related to each.

Ensure access for indigent persons.

Require insurance companies to cover treatment for addicts and families.

Develop a mechanism to measure treatment effectiveness.

Funding

States should match a percentage of federal contributions for receipt of Drug-Free Schools and Communities Act funds.

Increase appropriations for prevention programs, especially at the college and university level.

Increase taxes on the sale of alcohol and tobacco products and return the additional revenue to prevention efforts.

Encourage state expenditure of asset forfeiture funds on a variety of antidrug efforts.

Establish a drug education and prevention fund by collecting fines from drug and alcohol offenses.

Research

Continue support for longitudinal research that provides data for prevention program development and evaluation.

Establish a national Drug Education and Prevention Research Center to collect, summarize, and distribute prevention research.

Give the U.S. Department of Education the authority and resources to conduct drug education and prevention research.

SOURCE: Portions of this list are excerpts from the *New Mexico Demand Reduction Prevention/Treatment Matrix* developed by the Office of Drug Control of the New Mexico Department of Public Safety. Adapted from National Commission on Drug-Free Schools, *Toward a Drug-Free Generation: A Nation's Responsibility,* Final Report, September 1990.

SCHOOL AND COMMUNITY PROGRAMS

The following programs were identified and described by the National School Safety Center in their publication *Gangs in Schools: Breaking Up Is Hard To Do,* copyright 1988, Pepperdine University Press. The Center has granted permission to reprint their descriptions of the programs.

Each program was contacted and requested to update the information on their specific effort. The descriptions which follow are a combination of the National School Safety Center's descriptions and the specific projects' updates. Addresses and telephone numbers are current as of the spring of 1993.

Andrew Glover Youth Program
100 Center St.
Manhattan Criminal Court, Room 1541
New York, NY 10013
212/349-6381

A privately funded organization, the Andrew Glover Youth Program works to protect neighborhoods in New York's Lower East Side from crime. Another objective of the Program is to steer youth away from negative and illegal activities. The Program serves a large number of black and Hispanic young people by working with police, courts, youth services, and social services to provide counseling, gang mediation, family counseling, and housing assistance.

Youth workers are in contact with kids where they spend most of their time: on the streets. The youth workers also live in the community and are available for assistance twenty-four hours a day. The program was named after a local police officer who cared about and tried to help youth and who was shot to death in the line of duty by teenagers.

B.U.I.L.D. (Broader Urban Involvement and Leadership Development)
1223 N. Milwaukee Ave.
Chicago, IL 60622
312/227-2880

Non-profit B.U.I.L.D. works with gang members on the streets, trying to involve them in athletic or social recreational events and to encourage them to participate in education and job training programs. Many of the streetworkers are "graduates" of street gangs who the organization assisted.

B.U.I.L.D. also runs a prevention program for twenty-eight junior high school students identified as at-risk for joining gangs by school and police authorities. The program includes a weekly class session and after-school activities to teach kids about the dangers of joining gangs and offers positive alternative activities. The project is supported by Chicago's social, civic and corporate sectors.

Center for Urban Expression (C.U.E.)

The Dorchester Youth Collaborative
1514A Dorchester Ave.
Dorchester, MA 02122
617/228-1748

The Center for Urban Expression steers youth into structured, goal-oriented activities with a special focus on community organizing. The Common Ground prevention club, sponsored by the Center, brings youths of diverse ethnic backgrounds together to work on a variety of projects and performances.

Community service teams may shovel snow or clean garages for community residents; others may become involved in youth leadership programs. Common Ground groups have given song/rap performances in six states and have become very visible locally through their anti-drug audio and video public service media announcements.

Chicago Intervention Network

Department of Human Services
Youth Delinquency Prevention Division
510 N. Peshtigo Court, Section 5B
Chicago, IL 60611-4375
312/744-0881 or 312/744-1820

The Chicago Intervention Network works with students of all ages and provides the schools with the following programs and services: (1) early intervention and prevention curriculum, including activities in anger management, impulse control, and empathy training; (2) twenty-week delinquency prevention sessions in eighty schools; (3) attitude development sessions covering self-esteem, resisting peer pressure, and understanding and managing conflict; (4) Safe School Zone Law presentations; (5) School Watch programs; Truancy follow-up; (6) assessments on gang problems in and around schools; (7) mediation and prevention of gang violence; (8) technical assistance and information for teachers and parents on how to identify gang activity through symbols, colors, and signs; (9) help in securing Safe School Zone signs for schools; and (10) individual and group counselling for challenged youth.

Gang Awareness Resource Program (GARP)

The California State Office of Criminal Justice Planning provided grant funds for the Gang Awareness Resource Program (GARP). The Program is now in its fourth year. It places an Operation Safe Streets gang investigator deputy on the Carson High School campus in a highly visible "resident" capacity. The investigator serves the high school, as well as feeder junior high and elementary schools, through the following services: training and instruction of faculty, administrators, school police, parks and recreation personnel, community groups, parents, and civic officials on gang awareness, and coordination of information between schools and between law enforcement and schools. The investigator also establishes a partnership with the business sector for their support in the effort to eliminate street gang violence.

The bridge which GARP has built between law enforcement and the schools (both faculty and students) has led to enhanced communications, reduced gang versus gang incidents, and resulted in diminished gang activity on or about the high school campus. The GARP staff has developed and published a gang awareness pamphlet for community distribution and a pocket gang directory for school administrators and police.

The GARP deputy is in daily contact with many gang members and, as a result, has arrested many for crimes committed not only on the campuses, but also in the community. He has identified hundreds of new gang members who have not, as yet, entered the criminal justice system. He has assisted in the solution of many other crimes based upon his day-to-day contacts with students throughout the Carson city schools. The GARP deputy has made hundreds of gang awareness presentations before school staff, student assemblies, and community groups. As a consequence, both school campuses and the community benefit from reduced gang violence.

Gang Crime Section

Chicago Police Department
1121 South State Street
Chicago, IL 60605
312/747-6328

The first formal gang unit in the Chicago Police Department was formed in 1967. Known by various names over the years (Gang Intelligence Unit, Gang Crimes Investigations Division, Narcotics and Gangs Unit, and Gang Crimes Enforcement Division), it became the Gang Crime Section in 1984 and has retained that name since.

The Gang Crime Section is composed of tactical (uniformed) police and detective level Gang Crime Specialists (plainclothes) police officers. Specialists conduct follow-up investigations on gang-related incidents while tactical personnel conduct directed patrol missions in areas of the city experiencing increased gang activity.

The activity of all active street gangs is monitored by gang specialists and reported on periodically. With each arrest the files of known gang members is updated. Computer analysis of reported gang incidents and statistical analysis of arrest activity and weapon seizures is prepared by administrative personnel. The results of this analysis are used to initiate directed-missions in the most active areas of the city.

House of Umoja (Unity)
1410 N. Frazier St.
Philadelphia, PA 19131
215/473-5893

Known as the first urban "Boys' Town," the house has taken in more than 2,500 youths since it began in 1968. At the time of the House of Umoja's inception, the deadliest phenomenon facing the youth of Philadelphia was gang warfare. The concern of Falaka and David Fattah over their own son's involvement led them to open their home in West Philadelphia to gang members. The House of Umoja quickly developed into a communal living facility, geared toward keeping young men off the streets and giving them the education and life skills necessary to enter into society and the work force. Realizing that for many of these youths, a street gang acts as a surrogate family, providing a sense of belonging and self-worth, the Fattahs created a family system of their own.

The House of Umoja Boystown has since become one of the most acclaimed and successful youth service programs in the country. Now occupying most of the original block of Frazier Street, the stated purpose of the house is to "provide a non-traditional, community-based experience which offers a positive learning environment for young men who lack a sufficient family support structure." Umoja provides not only the basic amenities of food and shelter, but also educational and emotional support often lacking even in the most "stable" of American families.

The house's outreach program has sponsored the Black Youth Olympics, cultural exchange programs with boys from Belfast, Ireland, and local cultural programs. In the wake of the first Rodney King verdict in Los Angeles, Umoja cooperated with the Quaker Friends Society to call for peaceful response. The House also speaks on behalf of the community at local meetings, city hearings, or any gathering where a concerned voice is required.

The Paramount Plan: Alternatives to Gang Membership
Human Services Department
City of Paramount
16400 Colorado Ave.
Paramount, CA 90723
213/531-3503

The highly regarded Paramount Plan stresses disapproval of gang membership while working to eliminate the future gang membership base and to diminish the influence of gangs. The program sponsors neighborhood meetings and provides anti-gang curricula and posters on request. Community meetings are led by bilingual leaders and are held in neighborhoods identified by the sheriff's office as "under gang influence." The community meetings are aimed at parents and preteens.

A fifth-grade anti-gang curriculum was introduced in the Paramount Unified School District in 1982 that emphasized constructive activities available in the neighborhood.

Say Yes, Incorporated
3840 Crenshaw Blvd., Suite 217
Los Angeles, CA 90008
213/295-5551

This program offers crisis intervention, field monitoring, and workshops for school staffs. The workshops teach staff about the gangs operating in the neighborhood and describe gang characteristics and problems.

Say Yes teams monitor selected athletic events to stop violence in its formative stages. These teams supplement regular school, security and law enforcement personnel. The staff also monitors elementary, junior and senior high schools, provides rap sessions, and sponsors Neighborhood Watch, athletic and summer job programs.

U.S. Department of Justice Community Relations Service
5550 Friendship Blvd., Suite 330
Chevy Chase, MD 20815
301/492-5929

This service specializes in conciliating and mediating race-related conflicts in any context—for example, on school campuses, between police and minority communities, and in housing developments. The Community Relations Service has been called in to ease tense transitions in school desegregations in Boston and New York and other related incidents. There are Community Relations Service regional offices in Boston, New York, Philadelphia, Atlanta, Chicago, Kansas City (Missouri), Denver, Dallas, Seattle, and San Francisco. There are also field offices in Detroit, Houston, and Miami. Telephone numbers of branch offices should be listed under the U.S. Department of Justice, Community Relations Service in local telephone directories.

The Community Relations Service has a hot line that can be used to report incidents of racial harassment and hate violence and to request conflict resolution assistance. The telephone number is 1-800-347-HATE.

Youth Development, Inc. Gang Intervention Program
6301 Central Ave. N.W.
Albuquerque, NM 87105
505/831-6038

Youth Development, Inc. (YDI) is a social services organization offering more than thirty different programs to assist children, youth, and families. The different components offer education, residential counseling, corrections, prevention, recreation, and employment assistance to at-risk youth and their families.

The YDI Gang Intervention Program works on three levels: prevention, diversion, and intervention. Puppetry, theater presentations and educational programs focus on preventing gang violence and activities. Diversion involves directing at-risk youth into positive activities and behaviors, while the intervention component works with gang members and court-ordered youth to stop self-destructive behavior.

A major project is a regular ten-week workshop for court-ordered gang members. Youths participate in community activities such as feeding the homeless, team building events such as a ropes course, and educational programs including visiting a medium security prison. Each youth also has a counselor who works intensively with him or her on a one-to-one basis during the ten-week program.

The Gang Intervention program is successful because it focuses on working with the youths as individuals, rather than as gang members. Also the YDI program is not against gangs per se, but against gang violence and illegal activities.

GLOSSARY

Number following definition refers to chapter in which term is defined.

Abuse *see* child abuse.

Acting out the free, deliberate, often malicious indulgence of impulse that frequently leads to aggression as well as other manifestations of delinquency, such as vandalism, cruelty to animals and sometimes even murder. 7

Adjudicate to judge. 10

Adjudicated having been the subject of completed criminal or juvenile proceedings and having been cleared or declared a delinquent, status offender or dependent. 10

Adjudication juvenile court decision ending a hearing, affirming that the juvenile is a delinquent, a status offender or a dependent, or that the allegations in a petition are not sustained. 10

Adjudicatory hearing the fact-finding process in the juvenile justice system, where the juvenile court determines if evidence is sufficient to sustain the allegations in a petition. 10

Admit a plea of guilty in a juvenile delinquency proceeding.

Adult supremacy subordinating children to the absolute and arbitrary authority of parents and, in many instances, teachers. 5

Adversary procedure a means to determine guilt or innocence that pits the defense against the prosecution in court proceedings with a judge acting as arbiter of the legal rules. Under the adversary system, the burden is on the state to prove the charges beyond a reasonable doubt. 10

Adversary process in adult court, pitting prosecution and defense attorneys against each other. The American tradition of justice regards this as the fairest means of determining guilt. Until recently juvenile court avoided this process since the determination of guilt was not considered its primary function; rather, its function was considered to be formulating a rehabilitation plan "in the best interests of the child." Demands for due process for children in the juvenile court, including introduction of defense counsel, developed as a result of the

Gault decision. "Adversary" versus "best interests" are shorthand ways of referring to these conflicting philosophies of the juvenile court. 10

Aftercare supervision given children for a limited time after they are released from confinement but are still under the control of the institution or of the juvenile court. 11

Antisocial personality disorder a disorder existing in individuals at least age 18 who show evidence of a conduct disorder before age 15 as well as a pattern of irresponsible and antisocial behavior since the age of 15. 7

Arrest taking individuals into custody to restrain them until they can be held accountable for an offense at a court proceeding. The legal requirement for an arrest is probable cause; *see also* take into custody.

Arrest warrant court order written by a judge or magistrate authorizing and directing that an individual be taken into custody to answer criminal charges.

Attention deficit hyperactivity disorder a common childhood disruptive behavior disorder characterized by heightened motor activity, short attention span, distractibility, impulsiveness and lack of self-control. 4

Beyond a reasonable doubt degree of proof required for guilt in a juvenile court proceeding. It is less than absolute certainty, but more than high probability. If there is doubt based on reason, the accused is entitled to the benefit of that doubt by acquittal.

Boot camp a correctional facility stressing military discipline, physical fitness, strict obedience to orders and education and vocational training; designed for young, nonviolent, first-time offenders; also called *shock incarceration.* 11

Bridewell first correctional institution, which confined both children and adults considered to be idle and disorderly. 1

Broken window phenomenon states that if it appears "no one cares," disorder and crime will thrive. 12

601

Burden of proof duty of proving disputed facts in the trial of a case. The duty commonly lies with the person who affirms an issue and is sometimes said to shift when sufficient evidence is furnished to raise a presumption that what is alleged is true.

Case law law derived from previous court decisions; opposed to statutory law, which is passed by a legislative process.

Certification a procedure whereby juvenile court waives jurisdiction and transfers the case to the adult criminal court; also called a *waiver.* 10

Child in most states, a person under 18 years of age. 3

Child abuse any physical, emotional or sexual trauma to a child for which no reasonable explanation, such as an accident, can be found. Child abuse includes neglecting to give proper care and attention to a young child. 6

Child savers groups who promoted the rights of minors at the turn of the century and helped create a separate juvenile court. Their motives have been questioned by modern writers who see their efforts as a form of social and class control. 1

Child welfare agency an agency licensed by the state to provide care and supervision for children. An agency that provides service to the juvenile court and who may accept legal custody. It may be licensed to accept guardianship, to accept children for adoption and to license foster homes.

Children in need of supervision (CHINS) an adjudicatory designation available to the juvenile court when children are status offenders or habitually act to endanger their own morals or those of others. The court may claim jurisdiction over such children, but dispositional alternatives are more limited than in the case of children adjudged delinquent. 2

Children's Aid Society early child-saving organization, which attempted to place homeless city youths with rural families. 1

Chronic juvenile offender a youth who has a record of five or more separate charges of delinquency, regardless of the gravity of the offenses. 7

Civil law all law that is not criminal, including torts (personal wrongs), contract law, property law, maritime law and commercial law. The juvenile court functions under a blend of civil and criminal law.

Classical view of criminality sees delinquents as responsible for their own behavior, as individuals with free will. 1, 3

Classical world view holds that humans have free will and are responsible for their own actions. 3

Coercive intervention out-of-home placement, detainment or mandated therapy or counseling. 10

Collective abuse attitudes held as a group in a society that impede the psychological and physical development of children. 6

Community refers to not only the geographic area over which the justice system has jurisdiction but also to a sense of integration, of shared values and a sense of "we-ness." 12

Community policing a philosophy embracing a proactive, problem-oriented approach to working with the community to make it safe. 12

Competence a specific, functional ability. 15

Competent properly qualified, adequate. 15

Conduct disorder a behavioral disorder characterized by prolonged antisocial behavior ranging from truancy to fistfights. 7

Contagion a way to explain the spread of violence, equating it with the spread of infectious diseases. 7

Coproducers of justice citizens are responsible for the prevalence and severity of the crime within their communities. 15

Corporal punishment inflicting bodily harm. 1

Corporate gang highly structured and disciplined with strong leader; main focus is participating in illegal money-making ventures; also called *organized gang.* 8

Corrections institution confinement facility with custodial authority over delinquents and status offenders committed to confinement after a dispositional hearing. 11

Corrective prevention focuses on eliminating conditions that lead to or cause criminal behavior; also called *primary prevention.* 13

Court, juvenile agency of the judicial branch of government established by statute and consisting of one or more judicial officers with the authority to decide on controversies in law and disputed matters concerned with intake, custody, confinement, supervision or treatment of alleged or adjudicated delinquents, status offenders and children in need of care. 1

Court report a document submitted by a person designated by the court before the disposition of cases. The report contains a social history of the child and a plan of rehabilitation or treatment and care.

Crack children children exposed to cocaine while in the womb; may exhibit social, emotional and cognitive problems. 4

Crew a group of taggers. 8

Crime offense against the state; behavior in violation of law for which a penalty is prescribed. 7

Cruel and unusual punishment physical punishment or punishment far in excess of that given to a person under similar circumstances and, therefore, banned by the Eighth Amendment.

Custodian a person other than a parent, guardian or agency to whom legal custody of a child has been transferred by a court, but not a person who has only physical custody. A person other than a parent or legal guardian who stands in *loco parentis* to the child or a person to whom legal custody of the child has been given by order of a court. 3

Custody a legal status created by court order that vests in a person the right to have physical custody of a child; the right to determine where and with whom the child will live; the right and duty to protect, train and discipline the child, to provide food, shelter, legal services, education, ordinary medical and dental care. Such rights are subject to the rights and duties, responsibilities and provisions of any court order. 9

Custody, discharge from legal release from custody. State statutes specify that a child shall be released to a parent, guardian or legal custodian unless it is impractical, undesirable or otherwise ordered by the court. The legal custodian serves as a guarantor that the child will appear in court and may be asked to sign a promise to that effect. This takes the place of bail in adult court.

Custody, taking into the term used rather than "arrest" when a child is taken by a law enforcement officer. State codes and laws prescribe that a child may be taken into custody only under the following conditions: (1) when ordered by the judge for failure to obey a summons (petition); (2) when a law enforcement officer observes or has reasonable grounds to believe the child has broken a federal, state or local law and deems it in the public interest; (3) when the officer removes the child from conditions that threaten his or her welfare; (4) when the child is believed to be a runaway from parents or legal custody and (5) when the child has violated the conditions of probation. 9

Decriminalization legislation to make status offenses noncriminal acts. 2

Deinstitutionalization providing programs in a community-based setting instead of in an institution. 2

Delinquency actions or conduct by a juvenile in violation of criminal law or constituting a status offense. An error or failure by a child or adolescent to conform to society's expectations of social order, either where the child resides or visits. 7

Delinquent a child adjudicated to violate a federal, state or local law; a minor who has done an illegal act or who has been proven in court to misbehave seriously. A child may be found delinquent for a variety of behaviors not criminal for adults (status offenses). 1, 7

Delinquent act act committed by a juvenile for which an adult could be prosecuted in a criminal court. 3

Denominator approach states that focus of efforts should be on the whole population of youth, not just on the delinquents. 13

Deny a plea of "not guilty" in juvenile proceedings.

Dependency legal status of children over whom a juvenile court has assumed jurisdiction because the court has found their care to fall short of legal standards of proper care by parents, guardians or custodians.

Dependent a child adjudged by the juvenile court to be without parent, guardian or custodian. The child needs special care and treatment because the parent, guardian or custodian is unable to provide for his or her physical or mental condition; or the parents, guardian or custodian, for good cause, desire to be relieved of legal custody; or the child is without necessary care or support through no fault of the parents, guardian or custodian.

Deprived child one who is without proper parental care or control, subsistence, education as required by law or other care or control necessary for his or her physical, mental or emotional health or morals, and the deprivation is not due primarily to the lack of financial means of the parents, guardians or other custodians. 3

Deserts views punishment as a kind of justified revenge; the offending individual gets what is coming. 2

Detention temporary care of a child alleged to be delinquent who is physically restricted pending court disposition, transfer to another jurisdiction or execution of a court order. 9, 11

Detention center a government facility that provides temporary care in a closed, locked facility for juveniles pending a court disposition. 11

Detention hearing a hearing in juvenile court to determine if a child held in custody shall remain in custody for the best interest of the child and in the public interest.

Determinism a philosophy that maintains human behavior is the product of a multitude of environmental and cultural influences. 1

Deterrence views punishment as a means to prevent future lawbreaking. 2

Deviance behavior that departs from the social norm. 4

Disposition a juvenile court decision that a juvenile be committed to a confinement facility, placed on probation or given treatment and care; meet certain standards of conduct or be released or a combination of court decrees. 3, 10

Dispositional hearing an adjudicated process by the juvenile court, either formal or informal, on the evidence submitted with a guarantee of due process of law for the child in a matter before the court, as specified in the Fifth, Sixth and Fourteenth Amendments of the Constitution (e.g., *In re Gault*). 10

Distributive justice provides an equal share of what is valued in a society to each member of that society. This includes power, prestige and possessions. 3

Diversion the official halting of formal juvenile proceedings against an alleged offender and the referral of the juvenile to a treatment or care program by a private or public service agency. 2

Double jeopardy being tried for the same offense twice. 2

Due process difficult to define term; due process clause of the United States Constitution requires that no person shall be deprived of life, liberty or property without due process of law. 2

Educare as defined by Attorney General Janet Reno: safe, constructive child care for all children. 5

Emancipation giving up the care, custody, welfare and financial support of a minor child by renouncing parental duties.

Ephebiphobia a fear and loathing of adolescents. 7

Expressive violence an acting out of extreme hostility, in contrast to instrumental violence. 8

Extrafamilial sexual abuse sexual abuse of a child by a friend or stranger, a nonfamily member. 6

Fact-finding hearing as applied in juvenile court, a hearing to determine if the allegations of the petition are supported; also referred to as an *adjudicatory hearing*.

Family court court with broad jurisdiction over family matters, such as neglect, delinquency, paternity, support and noncriminal matters and behavior.

Felony criminal offense punished by capital punishment or confinement for one year or more in a locked facility.

Fetal alcohol syndrome (FAS) children exposed to excessive amounts of alcohol while in the womb may exhibit impulsivity and poor communication skills, be unable to predict consequences or use appropriate judgment in daily life. Is the leading cause of mental retardation in the western world. 4

Foster group homes a blend of group home and foster home initiatives. It provides a "real family" concept and is run by a single family, not a professional staff. 11

Foster homes unlocked facilities, licensed by the state or local jurisdiction and operated by a person or couple, to provide care and maintenance for children, usually one to four such children; *see* group home. 11, 14

Funnel effect at each point in the juvenile justice system, fewer and fewer youths pass through. III

Gang a group who form an allegiance for a common purpose and engage in unlawful or criminal activity; any group gathered together on a continuing basis to commit antisocial behavior. 8

Graffiti wall writing, indoors or outdoors. Outdoors it is sometimes referred to as the "newspaper of the street." 8

Group homes nonconfining residential facilities for adjudicated juveniles intended to reproduce as closely as possible the circumstances of family life and at a minimum to provide access to community activities and resources. 11

Guardian *ad litem* an individual appointed by the court to protect the best interests of a child or an incompetent in the juvenile justice process. In some states this can only be an attorney. The appointed individual is a surrogate parent, guardian or custodian and can be replaced for the best interest of the child at any point in a juvenile proceeding. 10

Halfway house a nonconfining residential facility for adjudicated juveniles to provide an alternative to confinement; also used to house juveniles on probation or in need of a period of readjustment to the community after confinement.

Hearing presentation of evidence to a juvenile court judge for consideration and disposition. 3

Hedonistic gang focuses on having a good time, usually by smoking pot, drinking beer and sometimes engaging in minor property crimes. 8

In loco parentis in place of the parent. Gives certain social and legal institutions the authority to act as a parent might in situations requiring discipline or need. Schools have this authority. 5

Incarceration placing a person in a locked facility or a secure confinement for punishment, deterrence, rehabilitation or reintegration into the community. 11

Individual child abuse physical or emotional abuse by parents or others as individuals. 6

Institutional child abuse includes approved use of force and violence against children in the schools and in the denial of children's due process rights in institutions run by different levels of government. 6

Instrumental gang focuses on obtaining money, committing property crimes for economic reasons rather than for the "thrill." 8

Instrumental violence violence used for some type of gain, such as robbery; in contrast to expressive violence. 8

Intake the point in the juvenile justice process that reviews referrals to the juvenile court and decides the action to be taken, which is in the best interest of the child or of the public good. 9

Intake unit receives referrals to the juvenile court and screens them, either to divert them from the system to a social services agency or to file a petition. 9

Integrated community a geographic/political area where people feel ownership and take pride in what is right and responsibility for what is wrong. 12

Intensive supervision a highly structured form of observation provided by probation. 11

Intrafamilial sexual abuse sexual abuse of a child by a parent or other family member. 6

John Wayne effect inability to see beyond the status quo: "If it doesn't work, do more, and try harder, Pilgrim!" 15

Judge a judicial officer elected or appointed to preside over a court who hears and makes decisions on matters in the best interest of juveniles and the public safety.

Jurisdiction the authority of courts and judicial officers to decide a case. 10

just deserts *see* deserts. 2

Justice fairness in treatment by the law. 1

Justice model judicial process wherein young people who come in conflict with the law are held responsible and accountable for their behavior. 2

Juvenile a person not yet of legal age.

Juvenile court court having jurisdiction over individuals defined as juveniles and alleged to be delinquents, status offenders, dependents or in need of decisions by the court regarding their health, safety and welfare. 1

Juvenile justice a system that provides a legal setting in which youths can account for their wrongs or receive official protection. 1

Juvenile justice agency an agency that functions for the juvenile court in investigation, supervision, adjudication, care or confinement of juveniles whose conduct or condition has brought or could bring them within the juvenile court's jurisdiction.

Juvenile Justice and Delinquency Prevention Act of 1984 a federal law establishing an office of juvenile justice within the Law Enforcement Assistance Act to provide funds to control juvenile crime.

Juvenile justice process a justice proceeding for juveniles that differs from the adult criminal process. The philosophy and procedures are informal and nonadversarial, invoked in the best interest of the child rather than as punishment. A petition is filed rather than a complaint; the matter is not public and the purpose is rehabilitation rather than retribution.

Juvenile record a confidential document that is kept separate from adult records and is not open to public inspection. It contains an account of behavior and antisocial activity of youthful individuals who appeared before a juvenile court.

Labeling giving names to things; names may become self-fulfilling. 4

Labeling theory theory that views society as creating deviance through a system of social control agencies that designate certain individuals as deviants. This stigmatizes individuals; they are made to feel unwanted in the normal social order. Eventually the individuals begin to believe that the label is accurate and begin to act to fit the label. 4

Law method to resolve disputes. A rule of action to which people obligate themselves to conform. 1

Learning disability one or more significant deficits in the essential learning processes. 4

Least restrictive means phrase referring to the use of dispositional alternatives for children. 2

Lex talionis a legal principle establishing the concept of retaliation, that is, an eye for an eye. 1

Mechanical jurisprudence suggests that everything is known and that, therefore, laws can be made in advance to cover every situation. 10

Mechanical prevention directed toward "target hardening" to make it difficult or impossible to commit particular offenses. 13

Medical model viewing offenders as victims of their environment, curable. 1

Minor a person under the age of legal consent.

Misdemeanor an offense punishable by a fine and less than one year in jail. Varies from state to state.

National Council on Crime and Delinquency (NCCD) a private national agency promoting efforts at crime control through research, citizen involvement and public information efforts.

Neglected a child is adjudged neglected by the juvenile court if: abandoned, without proper care; without substance, education or health care because of neglect or refusal of a parent, guardian or custodian; in need of supervision as a result of the neglect. 6

Net widening more diversion to other programs and agencies rather than diversion *away* from the system. 2

Nonjudicial disposition a decision in a juvenile case by an authority other than a judge or court of law. This is usually an informal method that determines the most appropriate disposition in handling a juvenile.

Nonresidential program program allowing youths to remain in their homes or foster homes while receiving services. 11

Nonsecure facility a facility that emphasizes the care and treatment of youths without the need to place constraints or a concern about public protection. 11

Norman Rockwell family a working father, a housewife mother and two children of school age (6 percent of U.S. households in the 1990s). 5

Numerator approach states that focus of efforts should be on those youth who are at greatest risk. 13

Organized gang highly structured and disciplined with strong leader; main focus is participating in illegal money-making ventures; also called *corporate gang.* 8

Paradigm a pattern, a way of looking at an entire concept or field. 15

Parens patriae literally, "parent of the country." The legal provision through which the state may assume ultimate parental responsibility for the custody, care and protection of children within its jurisdiction. The right of the government to take care of minors and others who cannot legally take care of themselves. 1

Parole supervised early release from institutionalization. 11

Person in need of supervision (PINS) a youth usually characterized as ungovernable, incorrigible, truant or habitually disobedient. 2

Petition the formal process for bringing a matter before the juvenile court. A document alleging that a juvenile is a delinquent, status offender or dependent, and asking the court to assume jurisdiction. The petition in the juvenile process is the same as a formal complaint in the adult criminal process. 3

Petition not sustained judgment that a petition is insufficient; there is a lack of evidence to support any allegations submitted against the juvenile.

Police-school liaison program places law enforcement officers within schools to help prevent juvenile delinquency and to improve community relations. 9

Poor laws established the appointment of overseers to indenture poor and neglected children into servitude. 1

Positivist view of criminality sees delinquents as victims of society. 1, 3

Positivist world view holds that humans are shaped by their society and are the product of environmental and cultural influences. 3

Predatory gang commits more violent crimes against persons, including robberies and street muggings; likely to use harder drugs, which contributes to their volatile, aggressive behavior. 8

Preventive detention the confinement of youths who might pose a danger to themselves or to others or who might not appear at their trial. 2

Primary deviance the original act defined as deviant by others. 4

Primary prevention seeks to change conditions that cause crime; also called *corrective prevention*. 13

Probable cause grounds that a reasonable and prudent person would believe an offense was committed and that the accused committed the crime.

Probation sentence entailing the release of an individual into the community under the supervision of the court, subject to certain conditions for a specific time. Only the court can provide probation. 11

Probation officer a correctional officer under the principle direction of the court. In juvenile matters, handles intake and presentence investigations for dispositional hearings and assists the court in determining the proper treatment of and care for juveniles. 11

Proof beyond a reasonable doubt the standard of proof needed to convict in a criminal case. The amount of absolute certainty that the defendant committed the alleged offense (e.g., *In re Winship*).

Psychopath virtually lacking in conscience; does not know right from wrong. 7

Psychopathic behavior chronic asocial behavior rooted in severe deficiencies in the development of a conscience. Virtually lacking in conscience; unable to distinguish right from wrong. 7

Public defender a lawyer who works for the defense of indigent offenders and is reimbursed for services by a public agency.

Punitive prevention relies on the threat of punishment to forestall criminal acts. 13

Recidivism repetition of criminal behavior; habitual criminality. 2

Referee a lawyer who serves part-time or full-time to handle simple, routine juvenile cases. 3

Referral to intake a request by police, parents, schools or social service agencies to take appropriate action concerning a juvenile alleged to have committed a delinquent act, status offense or to be dependent. 9

Reform school a juvenile facility designed to improve the conduct of those forcibly detained within. 1

Rehabilitation restoring to a condition of constructive activity. 1

Release from detention the authorized release from detention of a person subject to juvenile justice proceedings. 9

Representing a manner of dressing that uses an imaginary line drawn vertically through the body and shows allegiance or opposition. 8

Residential childcare facility a dwelling other than a detention or shelter facility providing care, treatment and maintenance for children. Such facilities include foster family homes, group homes and halfway houses. 11

Restitution making right. Restoring property or a right to a person who has been unjustly deprived of it. 10

Restorative justice a return to the ancient view that justice involves not two, but four parties: offender and victim, government and community—all are injured by the crime. 15

Retributive justice justice that is served by some sort of punishment for wrongdoing (*lex talionis*); also called *social justice*. 3

Reverse certification when the criminal court has exclusive jurisdiction and it transfers the case to the juvenile court. 10

Runaway the status offense of leaving the custody and home of parents, guardians or custodians without permission and failing to return within a reasonable time. 6

Scavenger gang urban survivors who prey on the weak of the inner city; crimes are usually petty, senseless and spontaneous; has no particular goals, no purpose. 8

Secondary deviance an act that results because society has labeled an individual a deviant. 4

Secondary prevention focuses on changing the behavior of individuals likely to become delinquent. Includes punitive prevention. 13

Seesaw model a model to demonstrate the functional family where stresses and resources are balanced and the nonfunctional family where stresses are greater than the resources to cope with them, resulting in an unbalanced family. 6

Self-fulfilling prophecy occurs when people live up to the labels they are given. 4

Serious Habitual Offender Comprehensive Action Program (SHOCAP) federally funded program of the OJJDP intended to provide guidelines to various components of the juvenile justice system and the community in dealing with serious habitual offenders. 9

Serious juvenile offender a juvenile who has been convicted of a Part I offense as defined by the FBI Uniform Crime Reports, excluding auto theft or distribution of a controlled dangerous substance, and who was between 14 and 17 years of age at the time the offense was committed. 7

Shelters nonsecure or unlocked places of care and custody for children awaiting court appearances and those who have already been adjudicated and are awaiting disposition. 11

Shock incarceration correctional facility stressing military discipline, physical fitness, strict obedience to orders and education and vocational training; designed for young, nonviolent, first-time offenders; also called *boot camp*. 11

Social contract a philosophy where free, independent individuals agree to form a community and to give up a portion of their individual freedom to benefit the security of the group. 1

Social justice provides an equal share of what is valued in a society to each member of that society, including power, prestige and status; also called *retributive justice*. 3

Socialized delinquency youthful behavior that violates the expectations of society but conforms to the expectations of other youths. 8

Sociopathic behavior *see* psychopathic behavior. 7

Station adjustment handled by the police within the department and released. 9

Status offender a juvenile who has committed a status offense; usually not placed in a correctional institution. 7

Status offense an offense by a juvenile that would not be a crime if committed by an adult, e.g., truancy, running away, curfew violation, incorrigibility or endangering health and morals. 1, 7

Street gang a group of individuals who meet over time, have identifiable leadership, claim control over a specific territory in the community and who engage in criminal behavior. 8

Street justice when police decide to deal with a status offense in their own way—usually by ignoring it. 9

Summons a legal document ordering an individual to appear in court at a certain time on a certain date. 3

Tagging a new form of graffiti whose dominant visual impression includes words, though the graffiti leaves only a hint of words. Often added to existing graffiti. 8

Take into custody the physical apprehension by a police action of a child engaged in delinquency; *see also* arrest. 9

Termination of parental rights termination by the court, upon petition, of all rights to a minor by his or her parents. Parents may be judged incapable and their rights terminated because of the following: debauchery, use of drugs and alcohol, conviction of a felony, lewd or lascivious behavior or mental illness. 14

Territorial gang designates something, someplace or someone as belonging exclusively to the gang. 8

Tertiary prevention the third level of prevention. Aimed at preventing recidivism. Focuses on preventing further delinquent acts by youths already identified as delinquents. 12, 13

Therapeutic intervention recommendation of an appropriate treatment program. 10

Thrownaways children whose family has kicked them out. 6

Training school a correctional institution for juveniles adjudicated delinquent by a judicial officer. 11

Transfer hearing a hearing to determine whether a juvenile alleged to be delinquent will be tried in juvenile court or waived to adult criminal court. The juvenile must be 16 years or older to be considered for the waiver or transfer to adult court.

Turf area claimed by a gang. 8

Uniform Crime Reports (UCR) the FBI's Uniform Crime Reporting program. 7

Violent juvenile offender a youth who has been convicted of a violent Part I offense, one against a person rather than property and who has a prior adjudication of such an offense or a youth convicted of murder. 7

Waiver a procedure whereby juvenile court waives jurisdiction and transfers the case to the adult criminal court; also called *certification*. 10

Window of opportunity times when treatment is especially needed (in crimes) or likely to make a difference (during transition periods). 14

Wizard a visionary leader of programs or projects. 14

Youth gang self-formed association of youths distinguished from other types of youth groups by their routine participation in illegal activities. 8

Youth Service Bureau a neighborhood youth service agency that coordinates all community services for young people, especially designed for the pre-delinquent or early delinquent. 2

Youthful offender a person adjudicated in a criminal court who may be above the statutory age limit for juveniles but below a specified upper age limit for special correctional commitment.

AUTHOR INDEX

SUBJECT INDEX

PHOTO CREDITS

P. 2, The Granger Collection, New York; p. 9, © 1995 Stock Montage; P. 19, © 1995 Stock Montage; p. 22, The Granger Collection, New York; p. 23, The Bostonian Society/Old State House; p. 25, Kansas State Historical Society; p. 26, © 1995 Stock Montage; p. 29, The Bettmann Archive; p. 36, The Granger Collection, New York; p. 40, Courtesy, Colorado Historical Society; p. 47, The Bettmann Archive; p. 64, Cleo Photography/PhotoEdit; p. 78, The Bettmann Archive; p. 89, PhotoEdit; p. 100, Bob Daemmrich/Stock, Boston; p. 108, Tony Freeman/PhotoEdit; p. 134, Myrleen Ferguson Cate/PhotoEdit; p. 138, Rick Reinhard, Impact Visuals; p. 147, Andrew Lichtenstein, Impact Visuals; p. 155, © 1994 STAR TRIBUNE/Minneapolis-St. Paul; p. 162, David Young-Wolff/PhotoEdit; p. 166, Tony Freeman/PhotoEdit; p. 170, © 1994 STAR TRIBUNE/Minneapolis-St. Paul; p. 147, Thor Swift, Impact Visuals; p. 175, Teun Voeten, Impact Visuals; p. 183, © The Stock Market/Mug Shots 1989; p. 197, ©The Stock Market/David Woods 1990; p. 208, Ted Soqui, Impact Visuals; p. 215, David Young-Wolff/PhotoEdit; p. 229, Donna DeCesare, Impact Visuals; p. 240, Andrew Lichtenstein, Impact Visuals; p. 262, Ted Soqui, Impact Visuals; p. 263, Katherine McGlynn, Impact Visuals; p. 266, Allain McLaughlin, Impact Visuals; p. 286 © 1987 Brodin Studios, Inc. All rights reserved.; p. 291, Stephen McBrady/PhotoEdit; p. 295, Donna Binder, Impact Visuals; p. 323, Mary Kate Denny/PhotoEdit; p. 327, David Eyestone/Minnesota Sun Publications; p. 334, James L. Shaffer/PhotoEdit; p. 347, Robert Drowns; p. 374, James L. Shaffer/PhotoEdit; p. 394, Frost Publishing Group, Ltd.; p. 397, John Annerino/Liaison; p. 410, © 1994 STAR TRIBUNE/Minneapolis-St. Paul; p. 411, © 1994 STAR TRIBUNE/Minneapolis-St. Paul; p. 413, Linda Rosier, Impact Visuals; p. 414, Mary Kate Denny/PhotoEdit; p. 432, Cleo Photography/PhotoEdit; p. 436, Jim West, Impact Visuals; p. 449, © 1994 STAR TRIBUNE/Minneapolis-St. Paul; p. 451, Rick Gerharter, Impact Visuals; p. 462, © Kolvoord/TexaStock; p. 481, Courtesy Ridgecrest, CA, Police Dept.; p. 494, Andrew Lichtenstein, Impact Visuals; p. 510, Andrew Lichtenstein, Impact Visuals; p. 520, Archive Photos/Lambert; p. 524, Courtesy Justice Charles E. Springer.